Dictionary of the Ponca People

Dictionary of the Ponca People

LOUIS HEADMAN

with Sean O'Neill

With the Ponca Council of Elders:
Vincent Warrior, Hazel D. Headman,
Louise Roy, and Lillian Pappan Eagle

UNIVERSITY OF NEBRASKA PRESS | LINCOLN

This book is published as part of the Recovering Languages and Literacies of the Americas initiative. Recovering Languages and Literacies is generously supported by the Andrew W. Mellon Foundation.

♾

Library of Congress Cataloging-in-Publication Data
Names: Headman, Louis author. |
O'Neill, Sean, 1969– author.
Title: Dictionary of the Ponca people / Louis Headman; with Sean O'Neill; with the Ponca Council of Elders: Vincent Warrior, Hazel D. Headman, Louise Roy, and Lillian Pappan Eagle.
Description: Lincoln: University of Nebraska Press, 2019.
Identifiers: LCCN 2017045889
ISBN 9781496204356 (cloth: alk. paper)
ISBN 9781496204424 (pbk.: alk. paper)
ISBN 9781496205742 (epub)
ISBN 9781496205759 (mobi)
ISBN 9781496205766 (pdf)
Subjects: LCSH: Ponca dialect—Dictionaries—English. |
English language—Dictionaries—Ponca.
Classification: LCC PM2071.Z9 P665 2019 |
DDC 497/.52539—dc23 LC record available at
https://lccn.loc.gov/2017045889

Set in Merope Basic by Tseng Information Systems, Inc.

CONTENTS

Preface vii

Acknowledgments xi

Introduction: Notes on Ponca Pronunciation and Grammar 1

PART ONE. PONCA TO ENGLISH 41

PART TWO. ENGLISH TO PONCA 213

Bibliography 389

PREFACE

At the beginning of the twentieth century, the English language was spoken by few Ponca. Once the processes of adopting the cultural traits, social patterns, and language of the European peoples were underway, the Ponca began to lose their own language. It seems that the Ponca people never conceived the necessity of writing the language, and there has been no extensive written work done on the vocabulary by the Ponca people. The first written pages of the Ponca language were composed by the Reverend James O. Dorsey, a Protestant minister. The stories and cultural accounts Dorsey gathered were written while he was living among the Ponca ca. 1871–73. Although these materials were accessible through institutions of higher education, Ponca tribesmen seldom had knowledge of these writings. Only scholars interested in languages knew about language materials relating to the Ponca. In modern times some linguists and anthropologists provided materials to some interested tribal persons.

The content of this work is the language that the parents and grandparents of the Council of Elders heard and spoke. The senior researcher, Louis Headman, had accumulated over twenty-five hundred words before this project was initiated. Those words needed verification of definitions and parts of speech. For our purposes the approximately five thousand words now listed and defined in this volume encompass the main artery of the language. This expanded set of words includes some that deal with modern devices used in today's world. The dictionary also contains some complex Ponca word forms that are best translated as phrases in English, since a single Ponca word is often composed of many grammatical elements. Since this collection of words is not intended to recover or regain a cultural period or practice, it should be viewed and read only as a reference to the spoken language of the people. The dictionary contains words coming from the language spoken by a generation of Ponca who were relocated to Indian Territory in about 1878, living in what eventually became the state of Oklahoma. Additional words were researched in other documents cited below.

In this first edition of a Ponca dictionary, completed in 2016, the terms are arranged alphabetically and each entry gives the part of speech: noun, pronoun, verb, adverb, adjective, preposition, conjunction, or interjection. Illustrative quotations in English and Ponca clarify some definitions. Some old words rarely or no longer used are termed "archaic," and approximate years when these rare words were in use are included for those who are seeking information regarding their earliest usage. The introduction includes general information on word composition, especially how the words or entries are formulated. The diacritics for writing Ponca words include ogoneks, hačeks, acute and grave accents, apostrophes, and elevated periods marking long vowels. Other helpful explanations included in the dictionary are pronunciations, syllable structures, abbreviations, and nomenclature for various plants and animals.

Among the many tribes in North America, there was always a person or a group of people who assisted in the preservation of the languages, often working in collaboration with tribal members to document the language of the community. Dorsey's detailed handwritten description of the Ponca language in *Grammar of the Ponca Language* and *Ponca and Omaha Letters* remains an important resource for research. Dorsey's record contains the language that the elders understand and know, the language that was spoken by their parents. Franz Boas also wrote a paper on the dialects of the Teton and Santee Sioux with remarks on Ponca. Although Boas's work appears to be more of a comparative notation of these languages, it was helpful in preparing this volume.

Apparently no one has consulted with the Ponca elders since the time of Dorsey, Boas, and a few others. In modern times several attempts were made by visiting individuals to provide a writing system for the Ponca language, but these fell short of what most tribal leaders and scholars wanted. In 1966, when many tribesmen were singing tribal hymns, a writing system was initiated. The words of nearly one hundred traditional and translated hymns were recorded. These hymns were sung with no musical notation. These hymns are still being sung. In 1965, in *The Ponca Tribe*, Dr. James H. Howard used what he called the "Michigan" system for writing Ponca words (Pike 1947:5, 7). The work was readable by the elders of the tribe. That system is the most viable solution for writing Ponca words and preserving stories. The Ponca Tribe's Council of Elders chose to utilize this system in 1980. Before the adoption of the system for writing, it was used primarily for teaching.

In the early years in Indian Territory, under the tutelage of government teachers and employees, the Ponca learned their second language, English. In this process, there was a loss of words relating to their ancient culture and other social practices. The language that related to a generation of people who came to Oklahoma from their ancient homelands and to their social world seemed to have no relevance to the next generation of people. The social implications of Western thought and philosophy overshadowed the meaningful world structure of past generations. It is understood by the elders of the people that the loss of the language was largely due to the desire to succeed in the modern world, where the demand to speak the dominant language was essential for survival. Practically every family on the Ponca reservation spoke the language fluently until the 1940s, when English began to replace the Ponca language. The loss of the language became apparent when children entered government boarding schools in or out of state. However, the children who remained at home, attending schools in Kay and Noble Counties, spoke the language. In later years, it became amusing to others to hear a child speak. Some of these children felt they were being taunted for speaking the language and discontinued using it. This also downgraded the use of the language and contributed to its loss.

On a historical note, the earliest account of the Ðégihà people, the ancestors of the modern Ponca, suggests they are of the woodland culture of Native Americans from the eastern parts of this continent. The Ponca story of their history in the east is accounted for by names for landmarks. The Smoky Mountains, for example, are P'ahéušúde. Niagara Falls is Ní'uxp'áde, the Atlantic Ocean is Ní' t'ága, the land in the state of Ohio is Ohá'ì, the Kahokian Mounds are P'ahé'žíde, and so on. The story of the separation of the Ðégihà people has varied accounts of where they eventually settled and what territory they claimed as hunting grounds or shared hunting grounds. The commonality of the language, however, began to change over a long span of time. Pronunciations of words, although different in some instances, could still be understood by various speakers of the language.

The Ponca Tribe of Oklahoma and the Ponca Tribe of Nebraska share a common historical background in the states of Nebraska and South Dakota. Prior to the trial of Chief Standing Bear in 1879, all Ponca people spoke the language. During that landmark civil rights case the chief said, "Nабé agút'aitè, xįháte ʃawak'igabažì. Ðažá, akížahè tedì aníet'amikè . . . díšti, dakížahè tedì daníet'anikè, wamí xt'até ʃawak'igat'aitè. Wak'áda enáwitená wáda wáxaì. Niášiga bдì hà!" Any Ponca who understands the language can interpret these words: "The color of our hands is not the same complexion. But if I pierce my hand I will feel pain . . . and if you pierce your hand you too will feel pain, the blood that flows will be the same. The same God made us both. I am a man!" It was noted that Standing Bear and other Ponca chiefs spoke only the Ponca language during their lifetimes. This means that the primary language spoken well into the twentieth century was Ponca. In 1994 Louis Headman visited with Carolyn Knudsen in Niobrara, Nebraska. At the time Carolyn was one of the last remaining Northern Ponca who understood and spoke the language. She had requested a visit because she said she had not heard the language for many years. Many Ponca are expressing this sentiment today.

The Ponca Tribe is one of several tribes or nations who speak a similar language. There are tribes or bands of other nations in North America well into Canada who speak a language similar to the Ðégihà language, but in recent years the Ðégihà language designation has been narrowed to five tribes who have a cultural affinity. The term *Ðégihà* means "people on our side" and is used to describe the languages of the Ponca, Omaha, Osage, Kaw, and Quapaw people. The closest language in similarity to Ponca is that of the Omaha Tribe of Nebraska, followed by those of the Osages, Kaws, and Quapaws. The neo-Indian movement in the twentieth century has brought many tribes together. In this, we hear songs with words of the people being sung at many social gatherings. Native American hobbyists in major cities across the country, too, sing Ponca songs at their "white" powwows. Under the tutelage of earlier Ponca elders, these professional men chose to learn Ponca songs because of the Ponca history told in the songs. They learned the drumming, tunes, and words of the songs. And the songs have a good rhythm to dance to. Organized hobbyists were assisted by the late Sylvester Warrior, Lamont Brown, Joe Rush, Harry Buffalohead, Albert Waters, and Jim Waters to establish the Ponca Hedúškà in their communities.

The preservation of the language in some degree is ensured in the songs of the people. However, a multiplicity of factors interplay with the diffusion of tribal identity. It is possible that each tribe may infuse their words into other tribal melodies. And it is not unusual for various tribes to make claim to the same tunes and songs. The same melody often appears across linguistic and social boundaries with different meanings and lyrics attached. Cultural diversity and dissimilarity are now characteristic of each tribe, with each tribe claiming to be significant to themselves. However, the cultural practices that we now know have created a common ground for the first inhabitants of this continent by bringing them together in what has been termed pan-Indianism. It can be said unbiasedly that songs with words known by the singers preserve and perpetuate the language.

Finally, the Ponca Tribe of Oklahoma still conducts language classes for children and adults. This is done periodically through the year.

ACKNOWLEDGMENTS

Our deepest thanks go to the generations of Ponca who lived and passed on to each succeeding generation the language that we know today as the Ponca language. The demise of practically all Ponca speakers in the late twentieth century left a void in the near loss of a once-great language. Today the language is spoken by a few living Ponca. Members of the Council of Elders confess that they cannot speak the language but they understand every spoken word. Their knowledge, of course, is credited to their families, relatives, and tribal members. That earlier generation had limited use and knowledge of the English language. They encouraged their children to get an education because they lived in a country that spoke English. For them, to communicate, one had to learn the dominant language. The contents in this work are born out of the Ponca language that was spoken by the elders' parents.

For reasons beyond our thinking, the Ponca people have always had a group of elders who were considered knowledgeable of the tribe's history and culture. They were not elected or appointed by the tribe but simply tribal members who enjoyed speaking of their "Indian ways." It was stated by past generations that this was so because the elders always passed on historical information by word of mouth and song. It was said that the culture of the people is embedded in the language. From them we learned the value of the language.

At the beginning of this personal project to preserve words, the words were handwritten on notepads and legal tablets; later they were entered into a computer. Linguist's Software of Edmonds, Washington, manufactured the Ponca font in 1993. Lexical and grammatical information was limited primarily because the words were written by those with no formal training in linguistics. At the beginning, there was no analysis of or descriptive structure for the language. Dr. Sean O'Neill, a linguist and anthropologist at the University of Oklahoma, wrote the introduction. He provides a clear explanation of the formulation of words. To him we give our acknowledgments and special thanks for his expertise and friendship.

We thank the Ponca Tribal Council of Oklahoma for providing office space, meeting room, utilities, and other amenities for this work. Chairman Earl Howe III graciously supported this effort through his personal interest in the preservation of the Ponca language. We also thank the current staff members of the tribal administration, who also created a friendly atmosphere at the workstation, for their support. We also thank various members of the staff at the Dana Knight Building for their contributions of English phrases that are applicable or equivalent to grammatically complex Ponca words. Although it may have seemed minimal to them, it was beneficial in the research process.

The Indian Center, Inc., of Lincoln, Nebraska, was founded in 1969 and has provided services to the Native people and the community for many years. Their mission is to "provide value to the Native American community by creating and obtaining programs that empower self-sufficiency and positive quality of life standards in individuals and families." The center's purpose includes providing human services, education, housing, health care, business development, youth and senior services, employment and training, food and nutrition information, and Native language and Native culture teachings. For their outreach to help others and their help with the greater completion of this work, we acknowledge the Indian Center, Inc., for the ANA Grant #90NL0595 "Community-Based Ponca Language Dictionary" and the Endangered Language Fund for support of the Ponca Council of Elders. We also thank Mr. Clyde Tyndall, director of the Indian Center, Inc., for his interest in Native languages and for providing the gateway for the grants and the equipment for the composition of the dictionary. We further thank Ms. Amy Kuchara, journalist and administrator for the ANA project, for providing office supplies in a timely manner.

We are deeply indebted to Mary Katherine Nagle, LLD, and Randy Ross for offering their talents and expertise in advisement and encouragement in completing this work. We also thank Dr. Matthew Bokovoy, PhD, for his interest in the publication of the Ponca dictionary. Randy has been an unending resource to keep us updated on the status of funding and meetings. These people who have explicitly shown special interest in the Ponca people and the preservation of the language are known only by their friendship and by freely giving their time to this project.

It is our pleasure to thank Dr. Dennis Hastings, PhD, of the Omaha Tribe in Nebraska for sharing a disc copy of their dictionary, *Umoⁿhoⁿ iye te ede' noⁿ' ya?* We also acknowledge the Kaw Tribe for allowing us to view their dictionary, *Kaáⁿze Íe Wayáje.* Also Louis Headman respectfully acknowledges with thanks the gift presented to him by the late Dr. Mark Swetland. Dr. Swetland's compilation of phrases from James O. Dorsey's work on the Ponca language was helpful. These dictionaries served as excellent resources for comparison of words with our own work on the Ponca language.

As is the custom of the people, this part acknowledges the Ponca Council of Elders for their very important role in making this dictionary possible. Their critique of each word in pronunciation, spelling, and definition was invaluable. The first phase in the project included an explanation of the usage of the Ponca alphabet. The learning of diacritics was a first-time experience for two of the elders. Once the alphabet and diacritics were learned, 150 Ponca words were presented at each session. The senior researcher (Louis Headman) had accumulated and prerecorded at least twenty-five hundred words that needed to be read, verified as correct with a simple but accurate definition, and matched with their part of speech. There may be other words and one-word phrases in private collections of the people. This work, then, is the result of the efforts of those elders who see this as a final act to pass on what they learned from their parents and grandparents. The Ponca words compiled are the result of years of special interest.

When the concept of a "community-based" dictionary was suggested, it became necessary to find members of the Ponca Tribe of Oklahoma who understood the language. Only two women were fluent Ponca speakers. One was Ms. Fanny Little Cook Deere, who lives away from the Ponca reservation, and the other was Ms. Geraldine Primeaux, who is a resident in a nursing home. These two women, whose ages prevented them from attending meetings, are honored for their retention of the Ponca language. It was difficult to find additional persons with an acceptable knowledge of the language.

The five members who constituted the Ponca Council of Elders are knowledgeable and are semifluent in the language. Their interest in the project is evident in their faithful attendance and discussion of Ponca words at each session. There was no assignment for them to find words. The unadulterated pronunciations, synonyms, translations, and parts of speech they provided for terms in the Ponca language were vital in the formulation of the dictionary.

At the time of this dictionary's creation, the Ponca Council of Elders was composed of two men and three women. All understood and used the language from childhood. Vincent Warrior, age seventy-nine, Hazel D. Headman, age eighty, Louise Roy, age eighty-three, and Louis V. Headman, age eighty-four, compose the council. Lillian Pappan Eagle has since passed

Vincent Warrior: Vincent is a retired serviceman who served in the U.S. Marine Corps and the U.S. Air Force for twenty-seven years. After the passing of his mother, as a child he lived with his father, Sylvester Warrior, a man known for his knowledge of all Ponca ceremonial songs and who spoke the Ponca language with his contemporaries, as well as in the home. Vincent's aunt Florence Warrior also contributed to his knowledge of the language. Later he lived with his grandfather Norman "Willie" Cry (Cries for War), who seldom spoke English and was a leader in the Native American Church. He spent much of his childhood with his great-grandmother Suzanna Primeaux, who did not speak English. He heard and spoke the Ponca language in all his growing years. Being an affluent member of the Ponca tribe, his grandfather often invited other menfolk to come and eat with his family. Here, Vincent heard stories and experiences told in the Ponca language. He said that as a child, when following his grandmother, who spoke only Ponca, they often conversed about the weather, community, and family. Vincent contributed much to identifying the grammatical parts of speech for the Ponca language. He is a graduate of Arizona State University and now resides in Ponca City, Oklahoma.

Hazel D. Headman: Hazel is a retired counselor in alcohol and drug addiction. Although she has never taken a drink of alcohol or used drugs, she has worked with women addicts for over eighteen years. She previously worked with Native preschool children in the Ponca City Public Schools for over ten years. The Ponca language was spoken in her household as the main language. She reminisces often about how the generation of people before her visited, laughed, and told family experiences of shopping, congregating, and traveling. She said no one ever spoke the English language during those sessions. She and her sisters learned the Ponca language from childhood. They were taught stories and the history of the tribe. They learned and practiced every ethical teaching that young Ponca women were taught. Although Hazel and her sisters spoke English among themselves, English was the secondary language in their home. Her father, Albert Makescrye Sr., a Ponca orator, spoke in the Ponca language in public gatherings. He was also a composer and singer of traditional Christian hymns. Like her father, her mother, Beatrice, composed many tribal Christian hymns. She was practically raised in the church and learned of her Christian faith in the Ponca language. Hazel's exposure to the Ponca language, then, made her a valuable asset to the formulation of definitions of Ponca words. While working for the Ponca Tribe she was brought into contact with many elders of the tribe who spoke only the Ponca language. While formulating the dictionary, she gave a strong critique of the work. As one who understood the language, her contribution to the dictionary was invaluable. Majoring in elementary education, she received her bachelor of science degree and graduated from Oklahoma State University in Stillwater.

Louise Roy: Louise and her sister, as children, were cared for by their grandfather Logan Cerre while their mother worked to support the household. Her grandfather Logan was one of the last Ponca men to practice traditional medicine. As a staunch member of the Native American Church and a leader, he was often called upon to aid tribal members confronted with illnesses. During her growing years Louise's grandfather told old stories of the Ponca people and legends of the tribe. She recalls staying with her paternal grandparents, Ed and Beulah Roy, who were also elders in the tribe. Her grandmother's sister, Martha Running Over Water, also lived at the same residence. She learned from her mother's and grandmother's teachings concerning ethics of life and living. She recalls during those years that all she heard was the Ponca language. She learned the language through this exposure of listening and practicing. Like most of her peers, she understood but seldom spoke the language. Her knowledge of Ponca lore substantiated all that was included in some definitions in the dictionary. She is a graduate of Northern Oklahoma College at Tonkawa.

Lillian Pappan Eagle: Lillian, along with her brothers and sister, was raised in a home where the Ponca language was spoken. Her heritage included parents who strongly supported the preservation of their language simply by speaking it to their children. Of special influence in her life was her grandmother Grace Standing Buffalo, daughter of Chief Standing Buffalo, who told her stories in the Ponca language. While staying with her grandmother, she learned tribal manners and other behavior expectations of young women. Bedtime stories were part of her growing years. She, like other children, learned her family relationships and Ponca history. Lillian was raised up attending church when the people still spoke the Ponca language. She listened and heard stories, tribal hymns, and testimonies given in the Ponca language. She and her brothers and sister learned to speak the language. As with most families, the primary language in the home was Ponca. She attended church as she grew up and is still an active member. In her growing years she learned terms relating to the faith of her parents as they spoke of the church beliefs in the Ponca language.

Louis Headman: As the senior researcher, Louis was responsible for initiating the Ponca dictionary. From early childhood he spoke the Ponca language. Like all Ponca children of his generation, he learned the stories and history of the tribe. On one occasion, at the age of fifteen or sixteen, his father and tribal historian Peter LeClair of the Northern Ponca people took him to several ancient village sites of the Ponca people in Nebraska and South Dakota. This dictionary is mostly composed of words he compiled during the later years of his father's and mother's lives. They both spoke only the Ponca language in the home. His father repeated stories of the past about adventurous Ponca men who accomplished great deeds for the tribe. He recalls his grandmother, who never spoke the English language, telling him many bedtime stories. His grandmother Virginia Big Soldier Headman could not speak English and did not wish to learn. Born in 1854, she succumbed in 1957 at 103 years of age. True Ponca stories had no logical conclusions. The hearer had to decipher and learn from these stories, as they had abrupt endings. Many of Louis's contemporaries learned the same stories with minor differences that existed from house to house. His brothers and sisters also spoke the language in the home but ultimately spoke only the English language. As a young man, he attended the Native American Church with his father, where he heard and learned prayers and prayer songs to the Creator. In later years, with his father's approval, he accepted and joined the Christian church. He attended and graduated from the C. H. Cook Bible School, which was under the auspices of the United Presbyterian Church. Following his graduation from the Pastor's School at Perkins School of Theology, he was ordained an elder with the United Methodist Church, which he served for fifteen years. He has since served in the Church of the Nazarene for the past thirty-eight years. Being bivocational, he received his secondary education teaching certificate from Oklahoma State University. It was during this time that he became concerned about the Ponca language being lost. He has taught the Ponca language since 1975 with limited teaching materials. During his years of research he made informal visits to tribal members in which he wrote tribal stories and recorded conversations. Foremost in providing information were his parents, Kenneth and Katherine Cries for War Headman, who conversed only in the Ponca language. Other relatives and friends also contributed to his knowledge of the language and history. Outstanding Ponca speakers included Albert Makescrye Sr., Norman "Willie" Cry (Cries for War), Napoleon "Bird" Buffalohead, James Poor, David Buffalohead, William Cries for War, Robert and Helen Washington Little Dance, Adam and Bessie LeClair, Stanford White Star, Nancy Maker, Molly Roy, Carrie Little Voice Tyndall, and Albert Makescrye Jr. These were the last fluent Ponca speakers who aided him, and they provided a great contribution of words in the Ponca language. He is indebted to them and thanks them for voluntarily offering their knowledge of the language and Ponca history.

As early as 1939 tribal members, without skills in writing, a writing system, or an alphabet, made individual efforts to preserve stories and songs. We are grateful to the elders of that time who phonetically wrote some of our traditional and translated hymns. We humbly acknowledge the late Albert and Beatrice Pappan Makes Cry, Robert and Helen Washington Little Dance, Suzette DeLodge Buffalohead, and Prudence Primeaux Rush for the preservation of these nearly one hundred traditional and translated hymns. The retention of the language is exhibited and retained in these hymns. We also thank the families in the Ponca Tribe who retained myths and historical accounts of the tribe. Without their foresight, much of our history and language would be lost.

In the complexity of language, we do not simply learn a system of communication but we also gain knowledge of our expectations in life. From those of the past, we learn terms of the earth and its influences upon the people. We learn months (or moons) of the year and its four seasons. We learn terms of compassion for mankind in ethical teachings combined with the knowledge of the Creator, Wak'ą́da. We learn terms for unacceptable behavior and solutions for mending problems for mankind. Included with the physical parts of the human body, we learn of various sicknesses that might affect the tribe. From them came the ways of ritualism, ceremonialism, and healing. Through the songs of the Ponca, we learn our history, the history of great men, and about the respect and dignity given to persons of valor and of good rapport.

It is hoped by the Council of Elders that this work of Ponca words and definitions will be beneficial to coming generations of Ponca and those interested in Native languages.

Introduction

Notes on Ponca Pronunciation and Grammar

The Ponca language has never had an established orthography or a generally accepted approach to writing within the community. Until relatively recent times the language had always been passed down strictly by word of mouth—as part of an "oral tradition" where children learned the language in the home by listening to their elders throughout childhood. With the exception of the monumental writings of James O. Dorsey (1848–95) in the late nineteenth century, very little has been done to develop a regular system for writing the language or a standardized system for teaching the grammar. While Dorsey's system remains intelligible among fluent speakers to this day, his method of writing has not been widely adopted—or accepted—within the community. Instead many competing systems have circulated within the Ponca community, including the practical system proposed herein. In many ways the language has hardly changed over the course of the past century—a broad statement of fact that includes everything from the grammatical structures to the pronunciation of words and phrases. This is evident in reading Dorsey's *Omaha and Ponca Letters* (1891). The stories and letters preserved therein are still readable and understandable by any Ponca-speaking person to this day. In this section we hope to present the Ponca language in a fashion that will be intelligible to the "layman," without drawing unnecessarily on specialized terminology.

PRONUNCIATION GUIDE

This section is intended to help the reader pronounce the words correctly—that is, in a way that could be easily understood by a fluent speaker of the Ponca language. Speaking, of course, begins and ends with proper pronunciation; whatever the language, one must be understood from the perspectives of both the listener, who must understand what is being said, and the speaker, who wants to be understood. With this in mind, we explain the use of the many diacritic marks found throughout this work, which go beyond the familiar marks found in standard contemporary English. The intention of this section is to make the written language readable and understandable both to fluent speakers and to active learners of the language. Future generations will also want to know how to speak the language appropriately.

The orthography in this dictionary loosely follows the "Michigan" system (see Pike 1947:5–7), which has more broadly come to be known as the "American-ist system" among scholars who work with the many thousands of indige-nous languages throughout the Americas. Furthermore, to present this work in a reasonably modern fashion, it has been necessary to utilize current writ-ing methods and explanations used in English. We chose to compile words and definitions by those standards, including the use of a pronunciation guide that assumes a working knowledge of English sounds. Most readers will be familiar with English even if they are keenly interested in learning Ponca, which they may not know as well at the beginning.

Among the special marks used throughout this work are the **acute** [á] and **grave** [à] **accents** for **vowels**, which indicate the **relative stress** placed on adjacent syllables; acute accents indicate primary stress, while grave accents indicate secondary stress. Without an accent marking, a vowel occupies a contrastive middle position between these two extremes. The **ogonek**—or **forward hook** [ą]—is another common modifier on vowels, indicating **nasalization**, or the free movement of air through the nasal passages. When it comes to **conso-nants**, another common modifier is the hacek [š], which generally indicates a movement of the tongue toward the roof of the mouth, a process that is known as *palatalization* since it involves the palate. The reader will need to become ac-quainted with these symbols.

Before reading the dictionary, one must first understand the alphabet (or or-thography) used in this book. All of the words in this dictionary are first spelled out in the Ponca alphabet, followed by detailed explanations of words broken down by separation of each syllable with *hyphens. Apostrophes* and *superscript let-ters* indicate other features of pronunciation, as described below. These notes on pronunciation are given between slashes, like this //. Consider the following example, which should be easy to pronounce—using both the Ponca alphabet and the phonetic key—after reviewing this pronunciation guide:

Šą́ge t'anąhà   /shon'-gā t'ä-non-hä'/ *n.*, wild horse, mustang

Continuing with the alphabet, the **basic vowels** in the Ponca orthography are as follows: the letters between brackets represent the standard values of the International Phonetic Alphabet, a system used by linguists around the world.

A/a	/ä/ as in the *a* in "father"	[ɑ]
E/e	/ā/ as in the *a* in "ate"	[e]
I/i	/ē/ as in the *e* in "me"	[i]
ʃ	/ʃ/ as in the *i* in "tip"	[ɪ]
O/o	/ō/ as in the *o* in "go"	[o]
U/u	/ü/ as in the *u* in "flu"	[u]
ə	/ə/ schwa as in the initial and final sounds in "America"	[ə]

Nasalized vowels are indicated by the diacritic **ogonek** [̨]. Standard English vowels are pronounced with the velum (or soft palate) blocking the nasal passage such that air passes only through the mouth. The nasalized vowels in Ponca are pronounced in the same way as their counterparts above except that the velum is lowered and air passes through both the mouth *and* the nose:

Ą/ą	/oⁿ/ as in the vowel of "father" and "on," but pronounced with air passing through both the mouth and nose	[ɑ̃]
Ę/ę	/āⁿ/ as in the vowel of "ate" and "main," but pronounced with air passing through both the mouth and nose	[ẽ]
Į/į	/ēⁿ/ as in the vowel of "me" and "mean," but pronounced with air passing through both the mouth and nose	[ĩ]
ʃ̨	/ʃⁿ/ as in the vowel of "tip" and "in," but pronounced with air passing through both the mouth and nose	[ɪ̃]
Ǫ/ǫ	/ōⁿ/ as in the vowel of "go" and "own," but pronounced with air passing through both the mouth and nose	[õ]
Ų/ų	/üⁿ/ as in the vowel of "flu" and "moon," but pronounced with air passing through both the mouth and nose	[ũ]

The **stress** placed on a vowel is a significant factor when speaking Ponca (or any language) with a natural-sounding accent. Therefore, throughout this work, vowels in Ponca words are consistently marked for stress, sometimes in conjunction with **nasalization**. Primary stress is indicated with an **acute accent** [́], while secondary stress is marked with a **grave accent** [̀]—meaning that adjacent syllables are generally pronounced at different timing and volume, creating a **melodic** effect. The **mid-stress** remains unmarked. For some speakers pitch plays a role in the articulation of these sounds, with the tonal qualities rising and falling in proportion to the relative stress—that is, the higher the stress, the higher the pitch assigned to the vowel. For this reason outside scholars, going back to the time of Dorsey, have sometimes described Ponca as a **tone language**. Yet most speakers today experience these sounds mostly as "stress," with emphasis on the relative timing and duration of the vowel (and the adjacent syllable). Illustrative examples are given below for the letter **A/a**, though the same principles apply to **all of the vowels**.

Á/á	primary stress
Ą́/ą́	primary stress with nasalization
A/a	mid-stress (no stress in relation to other syllables)
Ą/ą	mid-stress (no stress in relation to other syllables) with nasalization
À/à	secondary stress
Ą̀/ą̀	secondary stress with nasalization

The diacritic **hacek** (ˇ) is used to modify the letters *s*, *z*, and *c* as shown below:

S/s	/s/ as in the *s* in "see"	[s]
Z/z	/z/ as in the *z* in "zest"	[z]
Š/š	/sh/ as in the *sh* in "show"	[ʃ]
Ž/ž	/zh/ as in the *s* in "leisure"	[ʒ]
Č/č	/ch/ as in the *ch* in "church"	[tʃ]

Several other letters in the Ponca alphabet require special explanation for the English speaker, since these sounds do not occur normally in English speech.

Đ/đ	/th/ as in the *th* in "them" (in the past it may have been pronounced laterally with air also passing over the sides of the tongue)	[ð]
X/x	/x/ as in the *ch* of German "Bach"	[x]

The **apostrophe** (') indicates a glottalized release (or "ejective") when it follows the consonants *p*, *t*, or *k* (and sometimes *x*). These glottalized sounds do not occur in standard English and are best illustrated by listening to recordings or mimicking fluent speakers. Physically they are produced by releasing a short puff of air that has been built up in the mouth by briefly closing off the vocal cords. While the vocal cords are closed, air from the lungs presses up on them. This pressure of air is suddenly released from the point of closure in the mouth, such as the tip of the tongue, when making the glottalized **t'**. When making the sound properly you can feel the "voice box" (larynx) rise quickly and then fall like a plunger.

P'/p'	/p'/ as in the Ponca word **P'áxe** 'I made'	[p']
T'/t'	/t'/ as in the Ponca word **T'á** 'dehydrated meat'	[t']

K'/k'   /k'/ as in the Ponca word **K'ą́de'** 'plums'   [k']

Following all other letters, the **apostrophe** indicates a glottal stop, which is a brief closure of the vocal cords, as in the English expression *uh-oh* [ʌʔoʊ].

'   as in the Ponca expression **hąį'**   [ʔ]

Note: this a male expression of surprise, as when something slips from the hand

This Ponca alphabet may impose a steep learning curve on some readers. Thus, for ease of access we have further clarified all of the pronunciations with symbols that will be easily mastered by English speakers — considering that English is now the first language for many members of the Ponca community and thus a critical point of entry for learning this heritage language. Each entry is therefore followed with symbols that are meant to be self-explanatory, though for ease of use they are summarized below:

/ä/   as in the *a* in "father"
/oⁿ/   as in the *a* in "father," but nasalized
/ā/   as in the *a* in "ate"
/āⁿ/   as in the *a* in "ate," but nasalized
/b/   as in the *b* in "book"
/ch/   as in the *ch* in "church"
/d/   as in the *d* in "dog"
/ē/   as in the *e* in "me"
/ēⁿ/   as in as in the *e* in "me," but nasalized
/g/   as in the *g* in "go"
/h/   as in the *h* in "hat"
/ʃ/   as in the *i* in "tip"
/ʃ̨/   as in the *i* in "tip," but nasalized
/j/   as in the *j* in "judge"
/k'/   as in the Ponca word **K'ą́de'** 'plums' (/k/ with glottalized release)
/k/   as in the *k* in "kin"
/m/   as in the *m* in "milk"
/n/   as in the *n* in "no"
/ⁿ/   pronounce the preceding vowel with nasalization, as in the pronunciation guide for /oⁿ/
/ō/   as in the *o* in "go"
/ōⁿ/   as in as in the *o* in "go," but nasalized
/p'/   as in the Ponca word **P'áxe** 'I made' (/p/ with glottalized release)
/p/   as in the *p* in "put"

/s/	as in the *s* in "see"
/sh/	as in the *sh* in "she"
/t'/	as in the Ponca word **T'á'** 'dehydrated meat' (/t/ with glottalized release)
/t/	as in the *t* in "tall"
/th/	similar to the *th* in "them"
/ü/	as in the *u* in "flu"
/ü^n/	as in the *u* in "flu," but nasalized
/ə/	schwa as in the initial and final sounds in "America"
/w/	as in the *w* in "walk"
/x/	as in the *ch* in German "Bach"
/y/	as in the *y* in "yes"
/z/	as in the *z* in "zest"
/zh/	as in the *s* in "leisure"
/-/	boundary between syllables
/'/	When following a vowel or nasalized vowel in the pronunciation guides, the apostrophe marks stress or accent, and you should pronounce the preceding syllable with greater volume than neighboring syllables and for a slightly greater duration. When following a *p, t,* or *k* in the pronunciation guides, an apostrophe still indicates an ejective sound.
/·/	pronounce and hold the preceding vowel for a slightly longer duration

For ease of pronunciation, primary stress is marked with an apostrophe ['] in the pronunciation guides (as opposed to the system of acute and grave accents in the Ponca words themselves); these syllables are drawn out a little more perceptually, meaning they may be articulated with slightly greater volume and for a slightly greater moment of time.

Now, take a moment to return to the following example:

Šáge t'anḥà   /sho^n'-gā t'ä-no^n-hä'/ *n.*, wild horse, mustang

This entry should now be easy to pronounce—using both the Ponca alphabet and the phonetic key.

Before leaving this section, it is important to note that certain families still have a quite distinct pronunciation of many words, which may be surprising to some given that the Ponca people have been reduced to a small tribe. Yet significant variation can exist even in a relatively small speech community. It should also be noted that these differences are not particularly great—nor are these variations significant enough to create even minor social boundaries within the speech community. Thus the samples of Ponca vocabulary given here are understandable and do meet the criteria for a **standardized form** of written language, with the implicit assumption of variation among speakers. Those who read this dictionary will identify the words through definitions and explanations, even if there are minor differences of pronunciation and meaning among the many families. Within the Ponca speech community, there are no particularly insurmountable barriers in how the language is spoken. And there is not a geographical separation so large that the form of language would drastically change, either in written representation or in oral understanding.

PARTS OF SPEECH

Every entry in the Ponca to English section of this dictionary begins with at least one sample Ponca word, along with an English translation and an indication of the **part of speech** in Ponca. Parts of speech and other structural details are given as abbreviations in the entries; thus the reader may wish to consult the table below. Note that the verb is at the heart of the language and many other parts of speech derive from verbs, including many nouns and adjectives.

adj.	adjective
adj. phr.	adjective phrase
adv.	adverb
adv. phr.	adverbial phrase
archaic	archaic
art.	article
aux. v.	auxiliary verb
conj.	conjunction
fem.	feminine
1st pers., 2nd pers., 3rd pers.	first, second, third person
interj.	interjection
masc.	masculine
n.	noun
n. phr.	noun phrase
past part.	past participle
past t.	past tense

pers. pron.	personal pronoun
pl.	plural
poss. pron.	possessive pronoun
prep.	preposition
prep. phr.	prepositional phrase
pres. t.	present tense
pron.	pronoun
pron. phr.	pronoun phrase
sing.	singular
slang	slang
v.i.	intransitive verb
v. phr.	verb phrase
v.t.	transitive verb
abbr.	abbreviated
e.g.	for example
esp.	especially
lit.	literally
orig.	originally
usu.	usually

THE PONCA VERB

The Ponca verb cannot stand alone without a great deal of supporting grammatical material that very clearly spells out what is happening in any given scene. To carry meaning, a verb must be combined with a series of prefixes and suffixes according to regular grammatical rules. On the other hand, a bare verb stem—without these many prefixes and suffixes—is in fact meaningless to most fluent Ponca speakers. Therefore, to understand even a simple utterance in the Ponca language, one must first gain a sense of the many **conjugations** associated with the verb system. In this way, the verbs of the Ponca language are particularly expressive, often containing a long string of prefixes and suffixes that carry a great deal of information about the scene being described—as much as an entire phrase or sentence in many other languages, such as English.

Most verbs in this dictionary are listed in a fairly **basic form**, with some of the required prefixes and suffixes, though without the context-specific information about the "personnel" who are associated with the **action** or **state** that the verb describes. These special prefixes and suffixes are commonly known as "**person markers**," since they often identify the specific people who stand in the grammatical roles of **subject** or **object**—that is, "actor" or "acted upon." It is customary, in this sense, to identify the speaker as the "first person," since that is where the words begin—with the person who is speaking. Continuing in this way, the person listening is often called the "second person," since this is the next person in the act of speaking. Anyone else, beyond the immediate context, is called the "third person." When more than one person is involved, the person marker moves from **singular** to **plural**. Thus, when one person is speaking, as in the case of English "I," the subject is "first person singular"; when speaking for many people, as in the case of English "we," the subject becomes "first person plural." Likewise for the other person markers. Thus, in English, second person singular is "you," while second person plural is "you all." Third person singular is "he," "she," or "it," while third person plural is "they." The reader will need to become familiar with these concepts to read the charts in this section, though English translations (such as "I" or "we") are provided throughout. Note also that some entries go beyond the person markers and provide examples in sentences or short phrases, with a simple tilde (~) standing in place of the main entry.

Consider the **person markers** that can be linked with the relatively straightforward verb **í'bahą**, which refers to the state of "knowing" in the Ponca language. Such a verb is said to be **conjugated** when the appropriate person markers are assigned during the act of speaking. A full set of conjugations, listing all of the possible personnel, is called a **paradigm**, as illustrated in the examples below. The dictionary entry is as follows:

í'bahą   /ḗ'-bä-hoⁿ'/ *v.*, to know, *idáp'ahą*, I know; *í'šp'ahą*, you know; *í'bahąi*, they know; *í'bahąi*, he/she/it knows

With this basic information in hand, including several **conjugations**, a fluent speaker could infer an entire **paradigm**, since the rules of the grammar are fairly regular. Note below that the **past** and **present** paradigms are identical; one must infer from context whether the speaker is referring to the past or present in any given moment, though it is usually fairly obvious during the act of communication. Either the speaker is referring to events in the moment or to some distant scene in the past.

í'bahạ̀	to know	
Sing. **Idáp'ahạ̀**		I know/knew
í'šp'ahạ̀	You know/knew	
í'bahạ̀ì	He/she/it knows/knew	
Pl. **Ạdạ́'bahạ̀ì**		We know/knew
í'šb'ahạ̀ì	You all know/knew	
í'b'ahạ̀ì	They know/knew	

Now consider the parallel paradigm for the act of *writing* in Ponca:

Wabáxu	to write	
Sing. **Wap'áxu**		I write/wrote
Wašp'áxu	You write/wrote	
Wabáxuì	He/she/it writes/wrote	
Pl. **Ạwạ́baxùi**		We write/wrote
Wašp'áxuì	You all write/wrote	
Wabáxuì	They write/wrote	

For further contrast, consider the full paradigm associated with the act of *walking* in Ponca:

Mạdí	to walk	
Sing. **Mạbdị́**		I walk/walked
Mạnị́'	You walk/walked	
Mạdị́'	He/she/it walks/walked	
Pl. **Ạmạ́dị**		We walk/walked
Mạnị́'ị	You all walk/walked	
Mmạdị́'ị	They walk/walked	

VERB CLASSES

The person markers of the Ponca language shift—or take different forms—based on the **type of verb** that is being conjugated. This can be clearly seen by studying the examples above, where the second person is sometimes marked with an **š-** and sometimes with an **n-** (or nasal element). In this section we provide a guide to the many **different paradigms**, known as **verb classes**, which eventually become as predictable as clockwork to fluent speakers as they become familiar with the grammatical rules. Most of the entries in this dictionary give enough information about the conjugations for the reader to gain a sense of the class that the verb belongs to.

The reader should note that the third person forms, which translate as "he," "she," "it," or "them" in English, generally remain unmarked in most of these Ponca paradigms. These **unmarked** forms are notated throughout this general introduction with the symbol **Ø-**. To illustrate the concept with a familiar example from English, consider the first person construction "I walk," where the English verb *walk* carries no actual suffix. Now compare this to the third person construction "He walk**s**," where the third person is marked with the suffix **-s**, signaling both the third person and the present tense. Using special notation, this distinction could be represented as "I walk-**Ø**" versus "He walk-**s**" in English. In Ponca, on the other hand, it is the third person that often remains unmarked, which is notated below with the symbol **Ø-**. This means there is no actual third person prefix in Ponca, and the verb just stays in the basic form — generally one that is close to the primary dictionary entry.

BASIC VERB PARADIGMS IN PONCA

Many verbs in the Ponca language follow a **basic paradigm** that looks roughly like the chart below, in the abstract. Verbs in this general class feature the first person singular **A-** 'I' and the second person marker **Ða-** 'you'. The reader should pay close attention to this pattern when reviewing the sample verb forms given throughout this dictionary, as even just one or two examples will suggest the full paradigm — for this verb class — as given here:

Second person **Ða-** 'you' with first person **A-** 'I'

	SINGULAR	PLURAL
1ST PERSON	**A-** I	**Ą-** we
2ND PERSON	**Ðá-** you	**Ðá-**…**-ì** you all
3RD PERSON	**Ø-** he/she/it [**E'-**]	**Ø-**…**-ì** they [**Ei'-**]

Note that while the third person verb forms often remain unmarked, sometimes — for emphasis — these verbs take a special emphatic prefix, appearing as **E'-** in the singular and **Ei'-** in the plural.

To begin with a straightforward case, consider the Ponca verb for *running*, as given below:

T'ą́di 'to run'

At'ą́bdi	**At'ą́di**
I run	We run
Đat'ąni	**Đat'ąnii**
You run	You all run
T'ą́di	**T'ą́di**
He/she/it runs	They run
[**E'**t'ą́di]	[**Ei'**t'ą́di]

Moving on to a slightly more complex case, the Ponca verb for *stabbing* follows almost exactly the same pattern:

Žáhai 'to stab, to prick, to stick'

Žá'ahè	**Žáąhài**
I stab it	We stab it
Žá'dahè	**Žá'daheì**
You stab it	You all stab it
Žáhaì	**Žáhaì**
He/she/it stabs it	They stab it
[**E'**žáhaì]	[**Ei'**žáhaì]

The only complication here is that the person markers follow the initial **ža-** of the verb stem. This case illustrates the fact that the reader should pay close attention to where the person markers appear within the structure of the verb, as illustrated in the examples given in the dictionary.

A special note is warranted for verbs that start with *g*. This verb-initial **g sound** is sometimes **lost** in the **second person**, as well as the **first person singular**, in abbreviated forms. Here the Ponca verb for *chopping wood* illustrates the optional contraction:

Gasé 'to chop or cut wood'

	SINGULAR	PLURAL
1ST PERSON	**Agáse** **á'se** (abbrev. form) I chop wood	**Ą́gásaì** We chop wood
2ND PERSON	**Đagáse** **Đáse** (abbrev. form) You chop wood	**Đáse'ì** You all chop wood
3RD PERSON	**Gasái** He/she/it chops wood	**Gasái** They chop wood

VERBS WITH FIRST PERSON Ą- 'I' AND SECOND PERSON Đɪ-'YOU'

In contrast to the paradigms given above, the reader should be on the lookout for verbs that feature **Ą-** (as opposed to **A-**) in the first person singular when reviewing the entries in this dictionary; verbs in this class also generally appear with the second person **Đi-** 'you'. *Verbs in this class generally refer to states that a person **experiences**, rather than **actions** that a person carries out.* (Note that these verbs are conjugated very differently from those in the previous section; the reader may wish to consult the tables below for the full paradigm.) Verbs in this class generally take the prefix **Wá-** in first person plural forms that translate as "we" in English, as noted in the entries throughout this dictionary. (In a more abstract way, the prefix **Wá-** is associated with forms that include *two or more entities*, such as the speaker ["I"] and other parties ["we"], as seen in the example below. We will call it a DUAL marker for now, since it includes at least two entities.) These verbs fall into a class that is marked as follows, when the full paradigm is taken into consideration:

Verbs with first person plural **Wá-**

	SINGULAR	PLURAL
1ST PERSON	**Ą-** I	**Wá-** dual
2ND PERSON	**Đi-** you	**Đi-…-ì** you all
3RD PERSON	**Ø-** (can be Ei-) he/she/it [**E'-**]	**Ø-…-ì** they [**Ei'-**]

Starting with a straightforward example, consider the Ponca verb for being sick, as illustrated in the paradigm given below:

Wakégaì 'to be sick, to be ill'

Ą̇wą́kegà	**Wawákegaì**
I am sick	We are sick
Wadíkegà	**Wadíkegaì**
You are sick	You all are sick
Wakégaì	**Wakégaì**
He/she/it is sick	They are sick

Again, special rules apply to verbs that begin with *g*. This verb-initial *g* **sound** is generally **lost** in the **first person singular ("I")**, as well as the **first person plural ("we")**. At the same time, person markers take on the character of one of the vowels in the verb stem, going from **ą-** to **į-** in the singular (under the influence of the **í** in **Gíde**) and from **wá-** to **wé-** in the plural (under the influence of the **e** in **Gíde**), as given below. Here the Ponca verb for *being happy* illustrates the general pattern:

Gíde 'to be happy'

Į́·de	**Wéde**
I am happy	We are happy

As we shall see in the section on Ponca verb prefixes, this paradigm contains the marker **(G)i-**, referring to action that is performed on behalf of someone. One is a recipient of happiness in this sense. We'll have more to say about this later.

VERBS WITH SECOND PERSON Š- 'YOU'

Many other verbs follow separate paradigms, taking a different series of conjugations when assigning personnel to the scene that the verb portrays. One class in particular stands out for its use of the second person **š-**, as first seen in the verb for *to know*, given above; we will return to this case in a moment, after reviewing the general paradigm.

Verbs with second person š-

	SINGULAR	PLURAL
1ST PERSON	(P')a- I	A̧- we
2ND PERSON	Š- you	Š-...-ì you all
3RD PERSON	Ø- he/she/it	Ø-...-ì they

To start with a simple case, consider the verb for *sweeping*:

Bábexį̀ 'to sweep'

P'ábexį̀ I sweep it	**A̧bábexį̀** We sweep it
Šp'ábexį̀ You sweep it	**Šp'ábexį̀į̀** You all sweep it
Bábexį̀ He/she/it sweeps it	**Babéxį̀į̀** They sweep it

Note that the **b sound** in the verb stem becomes **p'** in the first and second person forms, in a completely predictable fashion. Other verbs follow this pattern as well.

Moving on to a slightly more complicated case, consider the verb **Wabáxu** 'to write' (above), which belongs to this class, with some minor variations. Here the only departure from the model is in the third person plural form, where the suffix **-mà** is used in addition to **-i** at the end of the paradigm.

Wabáxu 'to write'

Wa̧p'áxu I write	**A̧wá̧baxùi** We write
Wašp'áxu You write	**Wašp'áxuì** You write
Wabáxuì He/she/it writes	**Wabáxuimà** They write

Moving on to a still more complicated case, consider the verb for *making* (**Gáxe**), which also belongs to this general verb class in the Ponca language, as illustrated below:

Gáxe 'to make'

P'áxe	**Ągáxaì**
I make	We make
Škáxe	**Škáxaì**
You make	You all make
Gáxaì	**Gáxaì**
He/she/it makes	They make

Several notes on the grammar are warranted here. Note that the initial *g* of **(g)áxe** is transformed into a *k* sound in the second person. The sounds for *g* and *k* are articulated in the same place and manner in the mouth. The only difference between the two is their "voicing"—whether or not the vocal cords vibrate while pronouncing the sound. *G* is voiced (the vocal cords vibrate) and *k* is voiceless (the vocal cords do not vibrate). In essence the shift from a *g* sound to a *k* sound amounts to silencing the *g* sound a little bit, making it into a *k* sound. This silencing accommodates the neighboring sound *š*, which is also quiet by comparison (voiceless). This process is known as **assimilation**, since the voiceless sound of the *š* spreads to the neighboring *g*, which becomes *k*.

We can now return to the verb **Í'bahą̀** 'to know', which mostly follows the general rules established here, apart from the unexpected **da-** in the first person. Verbs in all languages are **irregular** in this way, which is something the speaker must note as he or she learns the language. The reader should take comfort in the fact that **inconsistencies** like this are noted throughout this dictionary, with examples of such **irregular forms** supplied with the main entry (as illustrated below), wherever they occur:

Í'bahą̀	to know	
Sing. **Idáp'ahą̀**	I know/knew	
Íšb'ahą̀	You know/knew	
Íb'ahąì	He/she/it knows/knew	
Pl. **Ądą́bahąì**	We know/knew	
Íšb'ahąì	You all know/knew	
Íb'ahąì	They know/knew	
Í'bahą̀	/ē'-bä-hoⁿ/ *v.*, to know, *idáp'ahą̀*, I know; *íšp'ahą̀*, you know; *i'bahąì*, they know; *i'bahąì*, he/she/it knows	

VERBS WITH FIRST PERSON B- AND SECOND PERSON NA-

In contrast to the paradigms considered above, a handful of verbs stand out for their use of **b-** in the first person singular ("I") and **na-** in the second person ("you"). Readers should pay close attention to this pattern when reviewing the examples given in the dictionary entries, as these subtle clues will provide a guide to proper conjugation. Generally verbs that feature the letter **đ** in the **stem** follow this pattern, as illustrated in all the examples given in this section.

Verbs with first person **B-** and second person **Na-**

	SINGULAR	PLURAL
1ST PERSON	**B-**	**Ą-**
	I	we
2ND PERSON	**N(a)-**	**Na-…-ì**
	you	you all
3RD PERSON	**Ø-**	**Ø-…-ì**
	he/she/it	they

This general pattern can be clearly illustrated in the following paradigm for the Ponca verb for *eating*, which actually **starts** with the **letter đ**, as given below:

Đate 'to eat something'

Bđáte	**Ąđátaì**
I eat it	We eat it
Náte	**Nátaì**
You eat it	You all eat it
Đatái	**Đatái**
He/she/it eats it	They eat it

Please also note that the **đ-** sound in the verb stem is generally **lost** in the second person; this rule can be further illustrated with the verb **Đixą́**, which also belongs to this general class:

Đixą́ 'to break'

Bđíxą	**Ąđíxą̀i**
I break it	We break it

Níxá	**Níxàì**
You break it	You all break it
Ðixái	**Ðixái**
He/she/it breaks it	They break it

Taking a slightly more complicated case, the Ponca verb for *eating something* also belongs to this class of verbs. This verb, as illustrated below, clearly follows a similar paradigm, taking a parallel form that is less specific about what the subject is eating, with the prefix **Wa-** for *something*. Here the stem **Ðate** 'eat' still drops its initial **d**-sound in the second person, though it is preceded by the prefix **Wa-** in basic form. The person markers, on the other hand, occur immediately before the stem **Ðate**, triggering exactly the same effects, with the loss of the **d** in the second person.

Waðate 'to eat something'

Wabðáte	**Awádataì**
I eat	We eat
Wanáte	**Wanátaì**
You eat	You all eat
Waðátaì	**Waðátaì**
He/she/it eats	They eat

Taking still another complex case, the Ponca verb for *walking* also belongs to this general class, as illustrated in the paradigm below:

Mądí	to walk
Sing. **Mąbðí**	I walk/walked
Mąní'	You walk/walked
Mądí'	He/she/it walks/walked
Pl. **Amádi**	We walk/walked
Mąní'i	You all walk/walked
Mądí'imà	They walk/walked

Note, however, that the verb for *walking* takes a different third person plural form, with the addition of the suffix **-mà** instead of only the more common **-i** at the end of the paradigm. Grammar is full of exceptions; the speaker is obligated to master these idiosyncrasies as part of the generally accepted "code" when learning to speak a new language.

VERBS WITH BOTH SUBJECT AND OBJECT MARKERS

In most of the previous examples, only the **subject** appears on the surface, as a prefix that appears directly with the verb, modifying its basic form. Moving from these relatively simple cases to those with grammatical markers for *both* the **subject** and the **object**, consider the conjugations surrounding the Ponca verb **Ðihą́** 'to lift'. Clearly, when it comes to the act of lifting, the speaker must consider both the subject (or **agent**) who *performs* the act as well as an object (or **patient**) that is somehow transformed by the activity in question.

Starting with a paradigm where the speaker initiates the event, consider the following verb paradigm; this is called a **first person object** paradigm, with a range of different subjects performing the act:

Ðihą́	'to lift'
Akígðihà	**I** lift myself
Ą́nihà	**You** lift me
Ádihà	**He/she/it** lifts me
Ą́ðihąì	**They** lift us

Throughout this particular paradigm, the Ponca object marker holds roughly constant, appearing mostly as the letter **Ą́**, which is a *nasalized* **a** that also bears *stress* (**ą́**). More abstractly, we might represent the first person object/patient as **ą́-**, recognizing that this character may also be capitalized as **Ą́-**, as it appears in the examples above. In these examples the hook below the letter **a** (which represents the *nasal* element) is lost *only in the first person*, where it appears before the **reflexive** element **kig-**, which signals that the subject (or agent) acts upon itself (as object). Therefore it is not surprising that the first person marker changes here, when one considers the fact that the speaker occupies the roles of *both* subject *and* object. Thus the first person reflexive takes the special form **Akig-** 'I act upon myself', specifically lacking the nasalization associated with the other first person object forms in the paradigm (taking the form **Akig-** 'I act upon myself'). This particular form is **reflexive**, meaning that the actor acts upon itself, blurring the ordinary boundary between subject and object.

Consider what happens, on the other hand, as we move to a paradigm that reflects the shapes the Ponca verb takes when the speaker occupies the role of subject—that is, when the speaker is the one who *initiates* the act and *carries* it out. This series of verb forms is known as a **first person subject paradigm**:

Ðihą́	'to lift'
Akígðihà	I lift **myself**

Wíbɖihą̀	I lift **you**
Bɖíhą	I lift **he/she/it**
Ąwą́ɖiʼihą	We lift **you all**
Ąwą́ɖiʼihą	We lift **them**

Here we see a recurrence of the first person reflexive form **akig-** 'I act upon myself', which is expected at this point. The remainder of the forms also take the anticipated **b-**, which is associated with a first person subject before a verb stem that begins in **ɖ**, as discussed in previous sections. Additionally, the second person singular (**Wíbɖihą̀-**) features the prefix **Wí-**, which signals a circumstance where 'I act upon you'. Moving to cases where the object of the activity is plural (here the active "lifting"), the verb itself changes shape, taking the **intensive plural infix -ʼi-**, which signals a plurality of both subjects *and* objects, as illustrated with contrasting second person plural form **Ąwą́ɖiʼihą** 'we lift you all'. This infix, which is positioned *within* the stem (rather than *before* or *after* it) changes the shape of the verb; the basic verb goes from the basic stem **Ɖihą́** 'to lift (one thing)' to the modified form **Ɖiʼihą** 'to lift *multiply*' (that is, more than one subject and object).

Taking a closer look at the **first person subject paradigm**, where the speaker instigates the act, we may now extend our consideration of the grammar as follows:

First person singular subject ("I") — **Ɖihą́** 'to lift'

Akígɖihą̀	**Akíg-** 'I (act upon) myself' + **ɖihą́** 'to lift'
I lift (myself)	= **A-** 'I' + **kíg-** 'subject acts on self'
Wíbɖihą̀	**Wíb-** 'I (act upon) you' + **ɖihą́** 'to lift'
I lift you	= **Wí-** 'I act on you' + **b-** 'I'
Bɖíhą	**B-** + **ɖihą́** 'to lift'
I lift him/her/it	= **B-** 'I' + **Ø-** 'he/she/it'
Wíbɖiʼihą	**Wib-** + **ɖiʼihą́** 'to lift (*many*)'
I lift you	**Wi-** 'I act upon you' + **b-** 'I'
Wábɖiʼihą	**Wáb** + **ɖiʼihą́** 'to lift (*many*)'
I lift them	**Wa-** 'dual' + **b-** 'I'

As an aside, it is worth noting that **Wi-** 'I act upon you' (in verbs) is also a first person possessive prefix meaning 'my' when it occurs with a **noun**, as in **Wiẑį́ge** 'my son'. See the section below on possessive prefixes on nouns.

Moving on to the **second person subject paradigm**, where it is the addressee ("you") rather than the speaker ("I") who instigates the act, we may now consider what happens when another series of grammatical markers enter into combination with one another:

Second person singular subject ("I") — **Ðihą́** 'to lift'

Ą́nihą̀ You lift me	**Ą́n-** + **(n)ihą́** 'to lift' = **Ą-** 'me (obj.)' + **n-** 'you (subj.)'
Ðak'ígdihą You lift yourself	**Ðak'íg-** + **dihą́** 'to lift' = **Ða-** 'you' + **k'íg-** 'act upon self'
Wánihą̀ You lift him/her/it	**Wán-** + **(d)ihą́** 'to lift' = **Wá-** 'dual' + **n-** 'you' + **Ø-** 'him/her/it'
Wáni'ihą You lift us	**Wán-** + **(n)i'ihą́** 'to lift (*many*)' = **Wá-** 'dual' + **n-** 'you'
Ðák'igdi'ihą You lift you all	**Ðak'íg-** + **di'ihą́** 'to lift (*many*)' = **Ða-** 'you' + **k'íg-** 'act upon self' …
Wáni'ihą You lift them	**Wán-** + **(n)i'ihą́** 'to lift (*many*)' = **Wá-** 'dual' + **n-** 'you' + **Ø-** 'him/her/it'

Several forms here require explanation. In this paradigm the second person subject form shifts from **da-** to **n-** when it occurs immediately before a verb stem beginning with **d**, as established in previous sections. Thus, with a second person singular subject, the verb takes the shape **Ą́nihą̀** 'you lift me', while the second person **Ða-** reappears in the form **Ðak'ígdihą** 'you lift yourself', and the reflexive prefix **k'ig-** appears immediately before the stem (**dihą**). Otherwise, most of the remaining forms feature the **dual prefix Wá-**, given that two or more entities are involved in the scenes, however ambiguous the reference to the actual personnel. The only exception is the reflexive form **Ðák'igdi'ihą** 'you lift us all', where the reflexive prefix **k'ig-** specifies that the second person agents (**n-**) act upon themselves, as specified by the plural form of the stem (**di'ihą́**).

The underlying structure of the Ponca verb becomes even clearer when considering the **third person subject paradigm**, given the fact that the third person ("he/she/it") often goes unmarked in the Ponca language, without an explicit prefix or suffix that appears on the surface:

Third person subject ("he/she/it") paradigm — **Ðihą́** 'to lift'

Ádihą̀ He/she/it lifts me	**Á-dihą́** 'to lift' = **A-** 'me' + **Ø-** 'he she it'

Đídihạ̀ He/she/it lifts you	**Đí-dihạ́** 'to lift' = **Đi-** 'you (obj.)' + **Ø-** 'he she it'
Đihạ́i He/she/it lifts him/her/it	**Đihạ́** 'to lift' + **-i** = **Ø-** 'he she it' . . . + **-i** 'plural'
Wádi'ihạ He/she/it lifts us	**Wá-di'ihạ́** = **Wá-** 'dual' [= *us*] + **Ø-** 'he she it'
Đídi'ihạ He/she/it lifts you all	**Đi-di'ihạ́** = **Đi-** 'you (obj.)' + **Ø-** 'he she it'
Wádi'ihạ He/she/it lifts them	**Wá-di'ihạ́** = **Wá-** 'dual' [= *them*] + **Ø-** 'he she it'

Most of these verbs now take the expected shape, starting with the third person form **Đihạ́i**, which is almost identical to the bare stem **Đihạ́** 'to lift'. The only exception is the addition of the suffix **-i**, which indicates the presence of two or more entities in the scene—here the combination of the third person subject ("he/she/it") and the third person object ("him/her/it"). Otherwise the objects take their expected forms in the first and second persons, as indicated by the grammatical prefixes **A-** 'me' and **Đi-** 'you'. The **dual** marker **Wá-** also makes an appearance in the form **Wádi'ihạ'**, which signals both the first and third person objects, translating both as "he/she/it lifted us" and as "he/she/it lifted them." The two forms are identical, with plural objects in both cases, translating either as "us" (I *plus* you) or "them" (again, *two or more* people), depending on context.

Moving now to cases with **plural subjects**, consider what happens when the speaker acts in tandem with another person, creating a *compound subject* that is translated as "we" in English. We now consider the **first person plural subject**, as given in the paradigm below:

First person plural paradigm—**Đihạ́** 'to lift'

Ạdídihạ̀i We lift you	**Ạdí-dihạ́-i** = **Ạ-** 'I/(we)' + **dí-** 'you (obj.)' . . . + **-i** 'plural'
Ạwạ́dihạ̀i We lift him/her/it	**Ạwạ́-dihạ́-i** = **Ạ-** 'I/(we)' + **w(ạ́)-** 'dual' + **Ø-** 'he she it' . . . + **-i** 'plural'
Ạk'ígdi'ihạ̀i We lift ourselves	**Ạk'ig-di'ihạ́-i** = **Ạ** 'I/we' + **k'ig-** 'act upon self' . . . + **-i** 'plural'

Ą́dídi'ihą̀i We lift you all	**Ą́dí-di-ihą́-i** = **Ą-** 'I/(we)' + **dí** 'you (obj.)' + **-i** 'plural'
Ąwą́di'ihą̀i We lift them	**Ąwą́-di-ihą́-i** = **Ą-** 'I/(we)' + **w(ą́)-** 'dual' ... + **-i** 'plural'

The plural scenario introduces several changes to the system. Throughout the paradigm the **first person subject** prefix **Ą-** translates not simply as "I," where the reference is to the speaker, but as "we," where the reference is to the *speaker plus another actor*, who also participates in the event as a coinstigator of the act. Thus, in this set of examples, the prefix **Ą-** is glossed (or translated) as both 'I' and 'we', since it can carry both meanings in different settings; it is the addition of the plural suffix **-i** that signals the shift to the plural subject here. The second person object continues to take the form **Đí-**, appearing in conjunction with the **intensive stem infix -i-** only in the second person plural, where there are several addressees ("you **all**"). It is also worth noting that the **dual prefix Wá-** 'two or more' becomes *nasalized* (taking the shape **Wą́-**) when it follows the nasal element in the **person subject** prefix **Ą-**. Here again we witness a **spreading of sound qualities,** with nasalization passing from one prefix to another.

These expected patterns continue in the **second person plural paradigm,** where two or more people *act together* in the role of the **addressee** ("you all") — or the *group of people* that the speaker is talking with:

Second person plural subject paradigm ("you all") — **Đihą́** 'to lift'

Ą́nihą̀i You all lift me	**Ą́ni-đihą́-i** 'to lift' = **Ą-** 'me' + **n-** 'you (subj.)' ... + **-i** 'plural'
Đak'ígđihą̀i You all lift you	**Đak'íg-đihą́-ì** = **Đa-** 'you' + **k'ig-** 'act on self' + **-i** 'plural'
Wánihą̀i You all lift him/her/it	**Wán-(đ)ihą̀i** = **Wá-** 'dual' + **n-** 'you (subj.)' ... + **-i** 'plural'
Wáni'ihą̀i You all lift us	**Wán-+ (đ)i'ihą́** = **Wá-** 'dual' [= *us*] + **n-** 'you (subj.)' ... + **-i** 'plural'
Đak'igđi'ihą̀i You all lift yourselves	**Đak'ig-đi'ihą́-i** = **Đ(a)-** 'you' + **k'ig-** 'act on self' ... + **-i** 'plural'
Wáni'ihą̀i You all lift them	**Wá-(n)i'ihą̀-ì** = **Wá-** 'dual' + **n-** 'you (subj.)' ... + **-i** 'plural'

Again in this paradigm, the **second person plural** forms behave exactly as expected, given the examples we reviewed in previous sections. The subject takes the form **Đa-** when it is separated from the basic verb stem, with another prefix occurring before it. Thus the verb **Đak'ígđihạì** 'you all lift you' features the expected subject **Đa-** when it occurs specifically before the reflexive prefix **kig-**, which separates it from the stem itself. (The same is true of the plural form **Đak'igđi'ihạì** 'you all lift yourselves', which differs only in the use of the intensive stem **đi'ihạ́** 'to lift [many]', as modified by the intensive infix -**'i-**.) On the other hand, the remaining forms feature the second person subject prefix **n-**, which occurs before verb stems that begin with the letter **đ**, such as **Đihạ́** 'to lift', as illustrated in this paradigm.

Moving on to the **third person plural paradigm**, all of the forms uniformly take the expected plural suffix -**i**, clearly indicating that there are **multiple subjects** instigating the act. Otherwise the **third person** is indicated only by the absence of a prefix (**Ø-**), taking on plural connotations with the addition of the plural subject suffix -**i**. The full paradigm is given below:

Third person plural subject paradigm — **Đihạ́** 'to lift'

Ą́dihạì
They lift me

= **Ą́-** 'me' + **Ø-** 'he/she/it' … + -**i** 'plural (subj.)'

Đídihạì
They lift you

= **Đí-** 'you (obj.)' + **Ø-** 'he/she/it' … + -**i** 'plural (subj.)'

Đihạ́i
They lift him/her/it

= **Ø-** 'he/she/it' + … -**i** 'plural (subj.)'

Wádi'ihạì
They lift him/her/it

= **Wá-** 'dual' [= *us*] + **Ø-** 'he/she/it' … + -**i** 'plural (subj.)'

Đídi'ihạì
They lift you all

= **Đí-** 'you (obj.)' + **Ø-** 'he she it' … + -**i** 'plural (subj.)'

Wádi'ihạì
They lift them

= **Wá-** 'dual' [= *them*] + **Ø-** 'he/she/it' … + -**i** 'plural (subj.)'

Here the **second person object** appears as the expected form **Đí-** 'you', appearing with the intensive verb stem **đi'ihạ́** only where multiple subjects are present ("you all"). As is often the case in Ponca, there is some **ambiguity** between the third person forms as we move from singular to plural subjects, which both take the shape **Wádi'ihạì**, translating both as 'he/she/it lifts them' and as 'they lift them', depending on context. The two forms are **identical**, though in context the separate meanings are usually clear, as the speaker is usually pointing out either a singular object or a series of objects.

The basic **system** of conjugation is now apparent. The user may find it useful to consult the following chart summarizing the full system of **conjugations** for the verb **Ðihą́** 'to lift', which follows the familiar paradigm for verbs that begin with the letter **ð**; note, in this sense, the appearance of the first person **b-** immediately before the stem, which is expected here.

	I	YOU	HE/SHE/IT	WE	YOU	THEY
ME	Akígdihą̀	Ą́nihą̀	Ádihą̀	—	Ą́nihąì	Ádihąì
YOU	Wíbdihą̀	Ðak'ígdihą	Ðídihą̀	Ądídihąì	Ðak'ígdihąì	Ðídihąì
HIM/HER/IT	Bdíhą	Wánihą̀	Ðihą́i	Awą́dihąì	Wánihąì	Ðihą́i
US	—	Wáni'ihą	Wádi'ihą	Ak'ígdi'ihąì	Wáni'ihąì	Wádi'ihąì
YOU	Wíbdi'ihą	Ðák'igdi'ihą	Ðídi'ihą	Ądídi'ihąì	Ðak'igdi'ihąì	Ðídi'ihąì
THEM	Wábdi'ihą	Wáni'ihą	Wádi'ihą	Awą́di'ihąì	Wáni'ihąì	Wádi'ihąì

Other verbs follow a similar pattern, though the paradigms shift slightly depending on the **initial sound** of the stem. Without the complications introduced by the stem initial **ð** sound, the paradigm takes a simpler shape, as illustrated below with the verb **-ną́ą** 'to hear (something)'. Starting with the first person subject ("I"), which is marked with the usual prefix **A-**, we also see the expected shift to the **Wi-** when the object is in the second person ("I act upon you").

Winą́ą	I heard you	**Wi-** 'I act upon you'
Aną́ą	I heard him	**A-** 'I' + **Ø-** 'her/him/it'
Awáną́ą	I heard them	**A-** 'I' + **-wa-** 'dual'

Moving to the second person subject forms, the expected prefix **Ðá-** 'you (subj.)' appears in each of the conjugations, along with the usual object markers.

Ądáną́ą'	You heard me	**Ą-** 'me' + **-ðá-** 'you (subj.)'
Ðaną́ą	You heard him	**Ðá-** 'you (subj.)' + **Ø-** 'him/her/it'
Wadáną́ą̀	You heard us or them	**Wa-** 'dual' + **ðá-** 'you'

Third person forms, again, occur without a prefix (**Ø-**) on the surface, appearing only with the object markers in terms of how the conjugations operate.

Ąną́'ąì	He heard me	**Ą-** 'me' + **Ø-** 'he/she/it'
Ðiną́'ąì	He heard you	**Ði-** 'you' + **Ø-** 'he/she/it'
Waną́'ąì	He heard us or them	**Wa-** 'dual' + **Ø-** 'he/she/it'

Finally, the first person plural forms take the expected prefix **Ą-** 'I/we', along with the basic object prefixes, as given below:

Ądína'ąì	We heard you	**Ą-** 'I/we' + **di-** 'you'
Aną'ąì	We heard him	**Ą-** 'I/we' + **Ø-** 'he she it'
Awáną'ąì	We heard them	**Ą-** 'I/we' + **w(ą́)-** 'dual'

VERB PREFIXES

As the reader can now see, Ponca verbs generally begin with a long series—or "string"—of prefixes, which are the first things that the listener hears. It is understood that each **prefix** in a language is interpretable according to surrounding linguistic processes, which provide a context for establishing the ultimate meaning, including the broader social context of the utterance. For an initial glimpse into this process, consider how a **basic verb**, such as **Sé-** 'cut', can be modified with a number of **instrumental prefixes** to create the following verb bases, which provide information about how an act is carried out:

Verb forms with instrumental prefixes — **Sé** 'to cut'

Basé	to cut with **sharp instrument** (with **Ba-** 'using the body or hands, with sharp thing')
Bisé	to cut with **pressure** (with **Bi-** 'pressing down or weighing by hand')
Đisé	to cut with **hands** (with **Đi-** 'by hand')
Gasé	to cut with **instrument by force** (with **Ga-** 'with hitting motion')
Ną̀sé	to cut by **stepping on** or **running a vehicle** with wheels over (with **Ną-** 'by foot')

Many **transitive verb stems** with a *subject that acts upon an object* can be modified with these instrumental prefixes (like **Se** 'to cut', above); the following chart summarizes the meaning of some of these **instrumental prefixes**:

Ba-	Bi-	Đi-	Đa-	Ga-	Ki-	Mu-	Ma-	Na-	Ną-
action by pushing	*action by pressing*	*action by hands*	*action by mouth*	*action by force*	*action by self*	*action from inside*	*action by cutting*	*action by heat*	*action by feet or machine*

The reader should pay close attention to the appearance of these prefixes when reviewing this dictionary, as can be further illustrated in the following entries based the stem **Xíáda** 'to fall':

Baxíáda	/bä-xē'ä'-thä/ *v.*, fall; go down; fall down; fall over by pushing
Bixíáda	/bē-xē'ä'-thä/ *v.*, fall; go down; fall down; push over by the use of hands
Đixíáda	/thē-xē'ä'-thä/ *v.*, fall; go down; fall down; fall over by being pulled with the hands
Gaxíáda	/gä-xē'ä'-thä/ *v.*, fall; go down; fall down; fall over by force, chopping, or kicking with feet
Nąxíáda	/noⁿ-xē'ä'-thä/ *v.*, fall; go down; fall down; fall over by being driven over or stepped or stood on

Moving on to another set of grammatical markers, several prefixes play an **adverbial role** in the Ponca language, suggesting a **source** or **path** for the motion portrayed by the verb. Consider the adverbial prefix **Á'-**, which suggests the state of being on, atop, above, or over something:

Á /ä'/ *prefix*	atop of, on top, above
Á'nądà	cover; spread over (clouds)
Á'hè	walk on, crawl on, climb on
Á'kà	lean on
À'gđi	sit on a chair
Á'žą́	lie on a bed
Á'gahà	be atop of (as a sheet of paper atop other sheets)
Á'tą̀	step on
Á'nąžì	stand on
Á'di'è	sprinkle on (as salt)
Á'bišnidè	spread on (as peanut butter)
Á'gđą̀	place on top (as putting object on top of table)

In contrast the adverbial prefix **Í'-** suggests the presence of an **instrument** that stands at the source of the activity in question, as illustrated in the examples below:

Í'bikà	wipe with
Í'idižà	wash with
Í'bašnidè	make greasy, buttery by means of
Í'mądąt'ą̀	hang on to by means of

Í'diže	use to pick up, get, take by means of
Í'bixą̀	inflate with
Í'gaxè	make or create with
Í'dihidè	handle, manipulate, or manage with
Í'dat'ą̀	drink with
Í'datè	eat with
Í'sabè	self-suffering, enduring by means of
Í't'é'	death by means of
Í'nidè	getting cured by means of

The adverbial prefix **Ú'-**, on the other hand, suggests an ongoing state or **condition** that a person occupies, loosely translating as "in (a state)" in English:

Ú'gidè	being in a state of happiness
Ú'wakegà	condition of sickness
Ú'gisidè	a thing that causes a remembrance (e.g., a gift or special day)
Ú't'exì	in the condition of difficulty
Ú'p'ežì	in the condition of domestic or social difficulty

Finally, the prefix **Gi-** occurs with some forms, signaling that the activity in question is performed on someone's behalf; in the first person, the form becomes **Į́-** 'on my behalf', as illustrated below:

Gíde 'to be happy'

Į́·de	**Wé·de**
I am happy	We are happy
Đį́de	**Đídaii**
You are happy	You all are happy
Gį̀de	**Gidemà**
He/she/it is happy	They are happy

VERBAL SUFFIXES

Just as the prefix is the first thing the listener hears, suffixes complete the act of uttering a verb. Many suffixes in the Ponca language play an adverbial role, modifying the basic meaning established by the verb and its many prefixes by providing supplementary—and often contextual—information about the scene. Consider the particle **čábe** or **áčą**, which intensifies the meaning of the verb, as illustrated below:

čábe 'very, extremely'

U'sní čábe	It's very cold
Nákade čábe	It's very hot
Ní'ke škube čábe *or* **Ní'ke škúbe áčą**	The water is very deep

Others provide further background about the spatial or temporal dynamics of the scene, such as the suffix **-tigdè**, which suggests action at a considerable distance or, at the opposite end of the spectrum, a scene that unfolds in the immediate future:

Bą'tigdè	calling from afar (distant action)
Xdážetigdè	screaming from afar (distant action)
Íyetigdè	speaking from afar (distant action)
Nąžítigdè	suddenly raining (temporal proximity)

Other verb-final grammatical markers suggest abstract qualities, such as CAUSE or NEGATION:

-áde	CAUSE
-ažÍ	NOT
-badą	FOR WANT OF, WANTING TO
-ští'	TOO, ALSO **Ągúšti** 'us too'; **Duámaštì** 'these too'

A handful of these suffixes are sensitive to **gender dynamics**, such as the particle **há'**, which male speakers use to suggest urgency with their assertions. For example, they might say **Mągdíga há!**, 'Go home now!' rather than simply saying **Mągdíga**, which means 'Go home'. The contrasting feminine expression is **Mągdíá hé·!**, also meaning 'Go home now!', though taking the contrasting feminine form **hé·**. Finally, consider the usage of **gá** and **á** as verbal particles, appearing after the main verb that is conjugated. As illustrated below, the particle **gá** is prototypically masculine, while **á** is feminine:

Mądí ga	You go! (male speaker)
Mądí á	You go! (female speaker)
Gdį́ ga	You sit! (male speaker)
Gdį́ á	You sit! (female speaker)

TENSE MARKING IN THE PONCA LANGUAGE: PAST, PRESENT, AND FUTURE

So far we have been working with examples of verbs that are not specifically marked for **tense**, referring only to *general states of affairs* that could exist in either the **past** or **present**, or even in the **imaginary flow** of some storyline. However, Ponca verbs can also be marked for tense, with a series of special **verb-final markers** that place the scene either in the past or future, with an added distinction between events that have or have not reached **completion**. To illustrate the general process of Ponca **tense marking**, let us start by reviewing the basic conjugations for the verb **Wadáte** 'to eat (something)', though *without* tense marking. Again, these **unmarked forms** simply refer to a *single instance of the event* in question (here 'eating') from a perspective where the action is *ongoing* at the time it is being witnessed (in speech):

Unmarked verb paradigm, without explicit tense — **Wadate** 'to eat something'

Wabadate	**Ą́wądataì**
I eat/ate	we eat/ate
Wanáte	**Wanátaì**
you eat/ate	you all eat/ate
Wadátaì	**Wadátaì**
he/she/it eats/ate	they eat/ate

Moving now to the past, the Ponca language allows the speaker to reference an event that was specifically **completed in the past**, suggesting that the audience view the scene in question from a perspective where the action has already reached its **conclusion**. Consider the following paradigm, also based on the verb **Wadate** 'to eat something', here in the **past perfect**:

Past perfect forms in Ponca — **Wadate** 'to eat something'

Wabdáte mikè	I have eaten (1st person singular) (with verb-final **mikè**)

Wanáte nikè	you have eaten (2nd person singular) (with verb-final **nikè**)
Wanátema	he/she/it has eaten (3rd person animate singular) (with verb-final **-ma**)
Ą́wądate mąká	we have eaten (1st person plural) (with verb final **mąká**)
Wanáte nąka	you have eaten (2nd person plural) (with verb-final **nąka**)
Wadáte dąka	they have eaten (3rd person plural) (with verb-final **dąka**)

In each case, the **past perfect** marker takes a *slightly different form*, though it always follows the verb in question, appearing as a **verb-final modifier**. As is often the case with language, this particular paradigm is irregular in the third person singular, featuring with verb-final **-ma**. For the sake of comparison, consider another paradigm, which is more regular in the third person:

Past perfect forms in Ponca—**Đizé** 'to get (something)'

Bđíze mikè	I got it (with verb-final **mikè**)
Níze nikè	you got it (with verb-final **nikè**)
Đizé đikè	he/she/it got it (with verb-final **đikè**)
Ą́dízeą mąkà	we got it (with verb-final **mąkà**)
Nnízeì nąkà	you all got it (with verb-final **nąkà**)
Đízei dąkà	they got it (with verb-final **dąkà**)

This paradigm features most of the same tense markers, though with the expected verb-final marker **mąkà** in the third person singular. Now it is clear that all of the **past perfect** markers appear with the core element **-kè** with singular subjects, switching to **-kà** with plural subjects. Furthermore, the first person forms always start with **m-**, the second person with **n-**, and the third person with **đ-**, each of them followed by the vowel **-i-** in the singular and **-ą-** in the plural. The following chart summarizes the regular shapes of the past perfect tense markers:

Basic past perfect markers in Ponca (verb-final)

	SINGULAR	PLURAL
1ST PERSON	**mikè** (mi-kè)	**mąkà** (mą-kà)
2ND PERSON	**nikè** (ni-kè')	**nąka** (ną-kà)
3RD PERSON	**dikè** (di-kè) [sometimes **-ma**]	**dąkà** (dą-kà)

Ponca verbs take a similar shape when conjugated in the future tense, specifically when considered from a perspective where the action in the future has already been completed; here the **future perfect paradigm** is illustrated for the verb **Wadate** 'to eat something':

Future perfect paradigm for **Wadate** 'to eat something'

Wabadate tamikè	I will have eaten (with verb-final **tamikè**)
Wanáte tanikè	you will have eaten (with verb-final **tanikè**)
Wanáte tamà	he/she/it will have eaten (with verb-final **tamà**)
Áwądate t'ągatą̀	we will have eaten (with verb-final **t'ągatą̀**)
Wanáte tamašè	you all will have eaten (with verb-final **tamašè**)
Wadáte tamà	they will have eaten (with verb-final **tamà**)

Generally, the future perfect forms resemble the past perfect forms, though with the addition of the prefix **ta-**, as illustrated with the distinction between **Wabdáte mikè** 'I have eaten' (PAST PERFECT) and **Wabadate tamikè** 'I will have eaten' (FUTURE PERFECT). This parallel continues in the second and third person singular forms, where it is only the prefix **ta-** 'future' that distinguishes the past and future perfect conjugations. However, the plural subject forms begin to depart from this pattern, becoming **t'ągatą̀** in the first person plural ("we"), **tamašè** in the second person plural ("you all"), and **tamà** in the third person plural ("they"). Again, the verb **Wadate** is irregular in some cases, especially in the third person (as seen above with the irregular past perfect **-ma**.) Returning to the verb **Đizé** 'to get (something)', the structure of the future perfect becomes even clearer:

Future perfect paradigm for **Đizé** 'to get (something)'

Bdíze t'amikè I will have gotten it	**Ądíze t'ągatą̀** we will have gotten it
Níze t'anikè you will have gotten it	**Nízeì t'amašè** you all will have gotten it
Đizé t'akà he/she/it will have gotten it	**Đíze t'amà** they will have gotten it

These basic shapes of the future perfect paradigm are given below, though the forms do change slightly based on the verb, as seen throughout this section:

Future perfect markers in Ponca (verb-final)

	SINGULAR	PLURAL
1ST PERSON	**tamikè**	**t'ągatą̀**
2ND PERSON	**tanikè**	**tamašè**
3RD PERSON	**t(')aká** [sometimes **tamà**]	**tamà**

We conclude this overview of Ponca tense marking with the **general future paradigm**, which is slightly simpler, taking the following form, illustrated again with the verb **Đizé** 'to get (something)':

General perfect paradigm for **Đizé** 'to get (something)'

Bdíze tįkè I will get it	**Ądíze t'aitè** we will get it
Níze t'atè you will get it	**Nízeì t'atè** you all will get it
Đizé t'akà he/she/it will get it	**Đíze t'amà** they will get it

While the first and second person forms are significantly shorter in the **general future**, when compared with their counterparts in the **future perfect** paradigm, the third person forms are otherwise identical to those of the future perfect paradigm. These basic contours of the Ponca general future paradigm are given below, though as noted above, the forms do change slightly based on the verb:

General future markers in Ponca (verb-final)

	SINGULAR	PLURAL
1ST PERSON	t'į̀kè	t'aitè
2ND PERSON	t'atè	t'atè
3RD PERSON	t(')aká	t'amà

VERB INTERNAL MODIFIERS

A handful of verbs in the Ponca language can be modified with markers placed within the verb stem, changing the meaning by introducing an additional element of motion, beyond the basic activity suggested by the verb. To begin, consider the verb stem **Agiđe**, which suggests the act of going to retrieve something:

Basic paradigm for **Agiđe** 'to get something'

Ap'í'bđè	**Ągágiądaì**
I go to get	We go to get
Aškí'ne	**Aškíneì**
You go to get	You all go to get
Agíde	**Agídemà**
He/she/it goes to get	They go to get

Like many verbs in its class, the verb-initial *g* sound is lost in the second person, as well as the first person singular, while the verb follows the **second person š-conjugation** pattern.

With the addition of the stem-internal modifier **-mą-**, the verb itself can be modified to suggest the **manner of motion**, suggesting the act of "walking to get something" in this case:

Basic paradigm for **Agimąđe** 'to walk get something'

Ap'ímąbđì	**Ągágiąmą́di**
I walk to get it	We walk to get it

Aškí'mąnì	**Aškímąní'i**
You walk to get it	You walk to get it
Agímądì	**Agímądíma**
He/she/it walks to get it	They walk to get it

PONCA ARTICLES AND CLASSES OF OBJECTS

Nouns in the Ponca language are often preceded by a **definite article** that draws attention to one possibility among many when the speaker wishes to refer to a specific person, thing, or entity, either in the immediate environment or in the established flow of the conversation. Functionally, these are somewhat like *the* or *a* in the English language, though **Ponca articles** are far more specific about the **class of objects** that the speaker wishes to reference. As the reader will soon see in the examples below, the English article *the* is very general in meaning when compared with its Ponca counterparts.

Ponca articles

Áka	Originally used with singular **animate** subjects, now used with **inanimate** subjects
Áma	Used with **animate** subjects, either **singular** or **plural**, showing **action** or **movement**; however, in certain usage the subject may show no action or movement
Amé	Used with **the one**, as in "he's the one"
Đą́	Used with nouns that describe parts of the **human body**; it is also used with **circular** objects, either singular or plural
Đą́kà	Used with **animate plural subjects**; like the article *Đíkè*, it is a descriptive word that is used in connection with the position a person or object is in, that is, at rest, reclining, or sitting, and connotes a place such as home, an office, or a familiar place
Đíke	Designates a **specific animate subject**; also used in connection with the position of a person or object, that is, at rest, reclining, or sitting, and connotes a place such as home, an office, or a familiar place
Gé	Designates things that are in **groups** or a **collection** of things, or things that are naturally scattered
Ké	Used with words that describe an **inanimate thing** or **idea** (*Mą́ze wédixđì ~ údą̀* '~ computer is good')

Má	Designates **animate subjects**; it can be confused with *Áma*, which can be used with either plural or singular (*Šą́t'ągà ~ wat'é'dè dip'i* '~ wolves know how to kill')
Tą́'	**Singular** article, designates singular standing animate subject (*Núžįgà ~ snędé t'ągà* '~ boy is tall')
Té	**Plural article**, used with words that describe an inanimate thing or idea (*T'í' ~ é'gazizì'xtì gáxà bíkè* 'They have built ~ houses in a row)
Wí'	Designates **indefinite singular animate or inanimate objects**; it is similar to the English *a* and *an*

DEMONSTRATIVE PRONOUNS

These are similar to the English demonstratives *this, that, these, those,* and *them* in that reference can be made to **animate** or **inanimate** things that are **single** or **plural**. Additionally, many of these prefixes make reference to **relative distance** from the speaker. The following examples show the usage for **inanimate things**:

Duá/Duáke	this one (refers to a thing **close at hand** or **in the hand**)
Đé/Đéke	this one (refers to a thing **near** or **next to the speaker**)
Šé/Šéke	that one (refers to a thing **away from the speaker**, perhaps across the room)
Gá/Gáke	this or that thing or situation (refers to a thing **out of sight**, or an idea or plan in the speaker's mind)

INTERJECTIONS

In the Ponca language a cry or an utterance is usually a word or sound added to convey an idea or emotion. Consider, for example, the expression **T'énahà!** or **T'éna!**, which signals a mood of indignation on the part of the speaker. By contrast, the use of **Hįdakè!** (between sentences) conveys a general sense of "okay, let's see" or "all right" to the audience. In stories many sentences begin with the Ponca word **Gą́'ki**, which loosely translates as 'and then'. Some of these interjections are differentiated by gender, with typically masculine and feminine forms used according to the gender of the speaker. Consider the male expression **Wə'!**, which indicates surprise, occurring alongside **Hąí'!**, meaning '(one) dropped something from hands'. Compare these with the feminine forms **Xé·** or **Xéna**, meaning 'Oops! My mistake!' Here the contrasting masculine counterpart is **Xénahà!** 'Oops! My mistake!'

POSSESSIVE PREFIXES

When indicating ownership, relationships, or possessions, Ponca nouns can be modified with the following prefixes, as illustrated with the word **Ižíge** 'son'.

Wižíge	**Wi'žíge (áma)**
My son/sons	Our son/sons
	or **Ižíge ągút'a**
Đi'žíge	**Đi'žígeàma**
Your (sg.) son/sons	Your (pl.) son/sons
I'žíge	**I'žígemà**
His/her son/sons	Their son/sons

1ST PERSON	**Wi-**	**Wi-**
	my	our
2ND PERSON	**Đi'-**	**Đi-…-mà**
	your (sg.)	your (pl.)
3RD PERSON	**I'-**	**I'-…-mà**
	his/her	their

Note that the first person form **Wi'žíge** applies to both singular and plural possession, translating both as 'my son' or 'our son', depending on context. To stress the plurality of the possession in the first person, the speaker could say **I'žíge ągút'a** 'our son'.

RELATIONSHIPS BETWEEN OMAHA AND PONCA

A short note is warranted on the relationship between Omaha and Ponca, which are sometimes approached as mere "dialects" of a common language, based on the considerable degree of mutual intelligibility between the two speech communities. Socially speaking the two groups have had little regular contact since the late nineteenth century, when the southern Ponca were forcibly removed from the northern plains to their current location in north central Oklahoma, in the vicinities of White Eagle and Ponca City. Yet according to oral history, these groups separated several centuries before that and were only briefly reunited several times in the aftermath. As a result of this long-standing geographical and political separation, the Omaha and Ponca speech communities have drifted apart, leading to a number of fundamental differences in vocabulary, pronunciation, and meaning, as briefly reviewed below:

ENGLISH	PONCA	OMAHA	NATURE OF DIFFERENCE
auto	**K'ipínągè**	**K'inánáge**	vowel quality, nasalization, accent
forearm	**Á'hidè**	**Áusnì**	contraction, vowel quality
frost	**Xéwągé**	**Áxewà**	contraction, loss of nasal
jail	**Ugánąhąpazè t'i'**	**T'ibút'a**	different neologisms
North Star	**Miká'e škáažì**	**Mikáe mądíážidà**	different neologisms
school	**Wagáze**	**T'ápuskà**	different neologisms
Thanksgiving Day	**Zizík'a wadatè**	**Ába wék'išnà**	different neologisms
wagon	**Žáínągè**	**Žąnáge**	different stress and vowel quality
very good	**Údą áča**	**Udáč'**	contraction, stress
Where are you going?	**Áwaket'a néa**	**Ákt'a néa**	contraction (with conservatism in Ponca)
pelican	**Hudáte**	**Bdéxe**	semantic shift: a small crane is **Bdéxe** in Ponca

PONCA NUMERICAL SYSTEM

PONCA WORD	ARABIC NUMERAL
Wí'	1
Nąbá	2
Đábdì	3
Dúba	4
Sát'ą	5
Šáp'è	6
P'énąbà	7
P'edábdì	8
Šą́k'a	9

PONCA WORD	ARABIC NUMERAL
Gdébą	10
Agdíwį	11
Agdínąbá	12
Agdídábdì	13
Agdídúba	14
Agdísát'ą	15
Agdíšáp'è	16
Agdíp'énąbà	17
Agdíp'edábdì	18
Agdíšąk'a	19
Gdébąnąbá	20
Gdébąnąbá kí wí'	21
Gdébąnąbá kí nąbá	22
Gdébąnąbá kí dábdì	23
Gdébąnąbá kí dúba	24
Gdébąnąbá kí sát'ą	25
Gdébąnąbá kí šáp'è	26
Gdébąnąbá kí p'énąbà	27
Gdébąnąbá kí p'edábdì	28
Gdébąnąbá kí šąk'a	29
Gdébądábdì	30
Gdébądábdì kí wí'	31
Gdébądábdì kí nąbá, etc.	32
Gdébądúba	40
Gdébądúba kí wí', etc.	41
Gdébąsét'ą	50
Gdébąšáp'è	60
Gdébąp'énąbà	70
Gdébąp'édábdì	80

PONCA WORD	ARABIC NUMERAL
Gdébąšą́k'à	90
Gdébąhiwí'	100
Gdébąhiwí' kí wí'	101
Gdébąhiwí' kí nąbá, etc.	102
Gdébąhiwí'nąbá	200
Gdébąhiwí'nąbá kí wí'	201
Gdébąhiwí'nąbá kí nąbá, etc.	202
Gdébąhiwí'dábdì	300
Gdébąhiwí'dúba	400
Gdébąhiwí'sát'ą	500
Gdébąhiwí'šáp'è	600
Gdébąhiwí'p'énąbà	700
Gdébąhiwí'p'edábì	800
Gdébąhiwí'šą́k'a	900
K'úgewì	1,000
K'úgenąbà	2,000
Kúge gdébą hí wí	100,000
Kúge gdébą hí wí šą́ka kí k'uge gdébą šą́ka kí kúge šą́ka kí gdébąhí wí šą́ka kí gdébą šą́ka kí šą́ka	999,999

1

Ponca to English

A

a /ä/ first vowel in the Ponca alphabet

Á /ä'/ *prefix*, atop of, on top, above

Á· /ä'·/ *interj.*, yes, affirmative, yeah, uh-huh

ą /oⁿ/ first nasalized vowel in the Ponca alphabet

Á' /ä'/ *n.*, arm

Ą́' /oⁿ/ *prefix*, me, us, we

Á'ą'dè /ä'-oⁿ-thä'/ *n./v.*, interest, be of interest, take interest to help with somebody's dilemma or situation; *á'ądext'ì*, having deep concern or interest in somebody's dilemma or situation

Á'ą'sì /ä'-oⁿ-sē'/ *v.*, to jump on, to leap upon

Á'ą'wà /ä'-oⁿ-wä'/ *n.*, information, 1. a phrase used to acquire information about the identity or nature of somebody or about the purpose of something 2. also an inquiry concerning consequence, outcome, or end result, as in "what happened to . . ."

Á'ąà? /ä'-oⁿ-ä'/ *adj.*, what, a word used in direct or indirect questions concerning the outcome of a situation; a related term is *eą́'a?*, what do you think?

Á'ąbażì /ä'-oⁿ-bä-zhē'/ *adj.*, denied, an indication of a negative response to a request made about something or somebody

Á'ądà /ä'-oⁿ-thä'/ *v.*, infect, lit., to pass something on to somebody, to contaminate, refers, e.g., to passing a common cold to somebody else

Á'ądè /ä'-oⁿ-thä'/ *v.*, care, to be concerned; to become involved or do something to keep something or somebody safe

Á'ąhè /ä'-oⁿ-hä'/ *v.*, place, to place upon

Á'ba'è' /ä'-bä-ä'/ *v.*, to decorate lavishly, e.g., *hįbé'á'baè*, moccasins that are entirely beaded

Á'batè /ä'-bä-tä'/ *v. phr.*, sew on, to ~ something, as in a patch on a child's blue jeans or a ribbon on a shawl

Á'bazù /ä'-bä-zü'/ *v.t.*, point, to point at a particular animate or inanimate thing

Á'bit'à /ä'-bē-t'ä'/ *v.*, touch, 1. pressing with fingers, as in pressing a lever on a water fountain 2. *2nd pers. sing.*, you touch

Á'bitądè /ä'-bē-toⁿ-thä'/ *adj.*, having traits in common, bearing resemblance, as in a person having the traits and mannerisms of another by virtue of their behavior

Á'bizè /ä'-bē-zä'/ *v.*, to dry up, usu. refers to an animate or inanimate object that is set out in the sun without moisture and so eventually dries up

Á'dà /ä'-doⁿ/ *adv.*, therefore, so, and so, for that reason

Á'dadè /ä'-thä-dä'/ *v.*, to read, recite, interpret some written material

Ą́'dàwądišp'egà /oⁿ-thoⁿ'-woⁿ-thē-shp'ä-gä'/ *adj.*, undemonstrative, in control of yourself, calm, as in, "I am kept back or restrained on account of it"

Á'dazabażì /ä'-thä-zä-bä-zhē'/ *v.*, emphasize, to state or stress, to give special wording to something the speaker wishes to convey

Á'di'ą /ä'-thē-oⁿ/ *v.*, sprinkle, to sprinkle something upon something, e.g., salt on food

Á'gabdįdà /ä'-gä-bthēⁿ-thä'/ *v.*, twisted, something causing a thing to become twisted or uneven

Á'gażì /ä'-gä-zhē'/ *v.*, prompt, to prompt someone to say or do something

Á'gda /ä'-gthä/ *v.*, to accuse, to put blame on

A'gdá'i /ä-gthä'-ē/ *v.*, *3rd pers. sing.*, leaving, he/she/it is leaving

A'gdá'ka'mągè /ä-gthoⁿ'-kä-moⁿ'-gä/ *n.*, raspberry, a perennial plant of the genus *Rubus*

Á'gdadè /ä'-gthä-thä'/ *n.*, havoc, a condition of havoc or chaos caused by somebody or something, usu. said to have happened to a person

A'gdé' /ä-gthā'/ *v., 1st pers. sing.,* going back, "I'm leaving and returning to a certain place"

Á'gdį̀ /ä-gthēⁿ'/ *n.,* chair, seat, stool

Á'gdį́' /ä-gthēⁿ'/ *v., 1st pers. sing.,* sit, I sit; *ágdį̀,* to sit on something

Á'gdì'snedè /ä-gthē'-snä-dā'/ *n.,* couch, divan, sofa, settee, bench

Á'gidè /ä'-gē-thā'/ *v.,* to be happy, to be happy over somebody or something

Á'gidè /ä'-gē-thā'/ *v.,* rejoice, to be glad or to take delight in

Á'he /ä-hā/ *v.,* walk upon, 1. walking on steps going up 2. climbing

Á'hidè' /ä'-hē-dā'/ *n.,* lower arm, forearm, that part of the arm where the ulna and radius are located

Á'idą̀ /ä'-ē-thoⁿ'/ *v.,* alight, to descend from the air and come to rest, as a bird comes to rest on a limb of a tree

Ą́'k'ažì /oⁿ'-k'ä-zhē'/ *n.,* no, never, refusal, no way; *ą́k'ažit'ią̀, ~,* not at all, by ~ means

Á'k'iá'stà /ä-k'ēä'-stä'/ *v.,* to stack, making a large pile of things heaped up high or piled up

Á'k'inè /ä-k'ē-nä'/ *n.,* embracing, hugging each other affectionately

Á'k'išugà /ä-k'ē-shü-gä'/ *adj.,* dense, 1. intense, as in a downpour of rain 2. refers to people crowded close together

Á'ką̀ /ä'-koⁿ'/ *v.,* lean, to lean on

Á'ki'é /ä-kē-ā'/ *n.,* crowd, usu. used in connection with a throng of people present at a gathering

Á'ki'hą̀ /ä-kē-hoⁿ'/ *adj.,* 1. more, additional 2. further, go farther on

Á'ki'hidažì /ä-kē-hē-dä-zhē'/ *v.,* neglect, to be inattentive, to disregard

Á'ki'hidè' /ä-kē-hē-dā'/ *v.,* tend, watch over, look after, to take care of

Á'ma'è /ä-mä-ā'/ *v.,* slice, as in slicing potatoes

Á'madè /ä-mä-thā'/ *v.,* snow on, usu. refers to being snowed on while doing something

Á'mustà /ä-mü-stä'/ *prep.,* above, over; *á'mustà'ta, prep.,* from above

Á'múšudè /ä-mü-shü-dä'/ *v.,* to be dusty, making dust come over them or us

Á'ną'ą̀ /ä-noⁿ-oⁿ'/ *v.,* listen, to listen or hear, being attentive and mindful when another offers advice; paying serious attention to another

Á'ną'sè /ä-noⁿ-sä'/ *n.,* a barrier to prevent something or someone from passing through, a shutter

Ą́'ną̀nà /oⁿ'-noⁿ-noⁿ'/ *interj.,* ouch, an expression of pain or injury; *ádədù,* expression of pain

Á'ną̀xiádaidą̀ /ä-noⁿ-xē-ä'-thä-ē-thoⁿ'/ *v.,* tackle, as in the game of football, to chase and bring down an opponent

Á'nazeatą̀ /ä-nä-zā-ä-toⁿ'/ *prep. phr.,* from behind, something coming from behind

Á'nè /ä'-nä'/ *v.,* hug, to hug, to ~ somebody affectionately or to put your arms around something

Á'nudą̀ /ä-nü-doⁿ'/ *v.,* war upon, to go and make war upon someone

Ą̀'pą̀ /oⁿ'-poⁿ'/ *n.,* elk, a large North American deer (*Cervus canadensis*) that lives in herds

Ą́'sagì /oⁿ'-sä-gē'/ *adj.,* fast runner, quick and speedy on the feet

Á'šiáda /ä'-shēä'-thä/ *adj.,* decisive, as in making a definite choice quickly without consideration for the outcome of the situation

Á'snuè /ä'-snü-ā'/ *n./v.,* ooze, to flow or leak slowly, usu. refers to a liquid substance

Á'snusnu'ì /ä'-snü-snü-ē'/ *adj.,* syrupy, slithery and gooey

Á't'à /ä'-t'ä'/ *adj.,* excellent, first rate, superior, high quality, etc.

Á'tą̀ /ä'-toⁿ/ *n.* step, stair, rung, staircase, stairway, flight of steps

Á't'ašą̀ /ä'-t'ä-shoⁿ/ *adj.*, extravagant, exaggerated or beyond something that is within reason

-á't'ašą̀ /ä'-t'ä-shoⁿ/ *v.*, suffix, exaggerate, exceed, overdo it, too much

Á'ubísną /ä'-ü-bē'-snoⁿ/ *n.*, an armband or wrist ornament of the Heḍúškà dance paraphernalia

Á'ukíte /ä'-ü-kē'-tā/ *n.*, elbow joint, a hinge joint between the humerus in the upper arm and radius and ulna in the forearm

A'ut'ą́ga /ä'-ü-toⁿ'-gä/ *n.*, upper arm, humerus, the armbone that extends from the shoulder to the elbow

Áwa /ä'-wä/ *prefix.*, where; *áwat'aneà*, where are you going?

Á'wą /ä'-woⁿ/ *adj.*, used, worn out, usu. refers to old clothing; *áwą̀žixt'ì*, not too worn or old

Ą'wą́'gí't'exì /oⁿ-woⁿ'-gē'-t'ä-xē'/ *v.*, to be disheartening, *1st pers. sing.*, I am grieved, disturbed, troubled, disconcerted over something that has happened

Ą'wą́'šką'ì /oⁿ-woⁿ'-shkoⁿ-ē'/ *v.*, *1st pers. pl.*, struggle, we tried hard

Ą'wą́dataì /oⁿ-woⁿ'-thä-tä-ē'/ *v.*, *1st pers. pl.*, *past t.*, ate, we ate

Á'xt'ą̀ /ä'-xt'oⁿ'/ *adj.*, not likely, not viable, out of the question

Á'žawà /ä'-zhä-wä'/ *v.*, to be entertaining, exciting, and enjoyable and done through actions taken upon others, as in horse stealing from another tribe of Indians in the past

Ą́'zè /oⁿ'-zā'/ *n.*, shade, the blocking of sunlight by an object

À'zegaxè /oⁿ'-zā-gä-xā'/ *n.*, umbrella, a handheld, collapsible canopy to provide shade from the sun or protection from rain

Á'žì /ä'-zhē'/ *adj.*, different, not the same kind

Á'žiḍąḍà /ä'-zhē-thoⁿ-thoⁿ'/ *n.*, assortment, lit., different things, a variety of things, hodgepodge

Ą́'žįgà /oⁿ'-zhēⁿ-gä/ *n.*, hazelnuts, *Corylus avellana*

Ą́'žįgà /oⁿ'zhēⁿ-gä'/ *n.*, peanut, also called the groundnut, *Arachis hypogaea*

Ą́ba /oⁿ'-bä/ *n.*, day, daytime, daylight; *e'siḍádi*, the day before a certain day; *e'gasąḍì*, on the morrow after a certain day; *e'hąádi*, on the night before; *e'siḍádi guádìšą̀*, two days before or on the second day before

Ą́ba'gdè /oⁿm'-bä-gthä'/ *n.*, corn dumpling, a Ponca food made from corn

Ą́ba'idàugdè /oⁿm'-bä-ē-thä'-ü-gthä'/ *prep. phr.*, all day, refers to doing something throughout the day, as in walking throughout the day on a journey

Ą́ba'waxúbe /oⁿm'-bä-wä-xü'-bā/ *n.*, Sunday, the day set aside for worship

Àba'waxúbe't'ą̀ga /oⁿm'-bä-wä-xü'-bā t'oⁿgä'/ *n.*, Christmas Day

Ą́ba'waxúbe ḍišt'ą́ki /oⁿm'-bä-wä-xü'-bā thē-sht'oⁿ'-kē/ *n.*, Monday, the second day of the week, the day after holy day, Sunday

Ą́ba'wé'dabdì /oⁿm'-bä-wä'-thä-bthēⁿ'/ *n.*, Wednesday, lit., day number three

Ą́ba'wé'sat'ą̀ /oⁿm'-bä-wä'-sä-t'oⁿ'/ *n.*, Friday, lit., day number five

Ą́ba aḍáikedì /oⁿm'-bä ä-thä'ē-kä-dē'/ *adj.*, coming days, the days that follow today or the future that follows from now on

Àba aḍáikedì /oⁿ'-bä ä-thä'-ē-kä-dē'/ *adv.*, today, on this day as they go forth in their lives

Ábaáxe /ä'-bä-ä'-xä/ *v.*, scrape, to remove by scraping a hard substance against another thing

Ábačižè /ä'-bä-chē-zhä'/ *adj.*, impetuous, hasty, rash, characterized by doing something without thinking

Ábadą /oⁿ'-bä-doⁿ/ *n.*, daytime, during the day

Ábadè /oⁿ'-bä-thä'/ *adv.*, today, in the present day

Ábaè /ä'-bä-ä'/ *v.*, waiting, waiting on prey or the enemy to come by

Ábaè /ä'-bä-ä'/ *v.*, hunt, to hunt, stalk, or to seek out prey

Ábaè /ä'-bä-ä'/ *n.*, hunters (~ *mà ágdì*, the ~ have returned)

-abaè' /ä-bä-ä'/ *n.*, *suffix*, covering, 1. something laid or covered over a thing, esp. embellished decorations on Ponca ceremonial garb, e.g., moccasins covered with beads, as in *hįbé* ~ 2. a breakout of the skin, caused by a sickness, such as measles, chicken pox, etc. (his arm has a ~ of red bumps)

Ába édąbè /oⁿ'-bä ä'-thoⁿ-bä'/ *n.*, daybreak, sunrise, sunup

Ába ék'iną /oⁿ'-bä ä'-k'ē-noⁿ/ *n./adv.*, every day, day after day, daily, usu. refers to a certain number of days or a period of time

Ába et'ądeát'a /oⁿ'-bä ā-t'oⁿ-thä-ä'-t'ä/ *n.*, future, lit., the days yet to come

Ába et'ádišą /oⁿm'-bä ā-t'ä-thē-shoⁿ'/ *n.*, dawn, toward the morning; dawn of the day

Ábagdà /ä'-bä-gthä/ *v.*, to be hesitant, feeling uncertain or being unsure about something

Ábagdè /oⁿ'-bä-gthä/ *n.*, pudding, sweetened ground corn cooked in water

Àba ída /oⁿ'-bä ē'-dä/ *n.*, birthday, a day celebrating the anniversary of one's date of birth

Ába ídawà /oⁿ'-bä ē'-thä-wä/ *adv./adj.*, daily, every day; something done every day

Ába ídawà /oⁿ'-bä-ē'-thä-wä/ *n./adv.*, all day, all the day long

Ábak'à /oⁿ'-bä-k'ä'/ *v.*, provoked, being provoked to do something in retaliation

Ábak'ù /ä'-bä-k'ü/ *n.*, scapula, shoulder blades, the two flat bones at the upper part of the back

Ábanà /ä'-bä-noⁿ/ *v.*, *sing.*, to look at or gaze at an individual person or thing

Ába p'íáži /oⁿ'-bä p'ē'-ä'-zhē/ *n.*, storm, lit., bad weather, rainstorm, snowstorm, thunderstorm

Ába udúhe /oⁿ'-bä ü-thü'-hä/ *n.*, *archaic*, day after, the day after today

Ába wé'šap'è /oⁿm'-bä wä-shä-p'ä'/ *n.*, Saturday, lit., day number six

Ábašibè /ä'-bä-shē-bä'/ *v.*, pass the buck, avoid responsibility by passing it on to someone else

Ábaškì /ä'-bä-shkē'/ *v.*, scrub, to scrub, to rub hard to make something clean, such as clothing

Ábaskíde /ä'-bä-skē'-thä/ *adj./v.*, furious, to be furious or incensed

Ábaskidè /oⁿ'-bä-skē-thä'/ *v.*, *1st pers. sing.*, exasperated, irritated, "I am ~"

Ábastà /ä'-bä-stä/ *v.*, patch, to patch a piece of cloth or material to another to repair or cover a tear or worn area

Ábašudè /ä'-bä-shü-dä'/ *v.*, sweep, to sweep dust upon somebody or something

Ábatąštì /oⁿ'-bä-toⁿ-shtē'/ *adv.*, someday, one of these days

Ábat'ù /ä'-bä-t'ü'/ *v.*, brace, to hold or prop something up

Ábatè /oⁿ'-bä-tä'/ *n.*, weather, usu. this weather, as in the current conditions of the weather (*ábätè eá'a?*, how's the weather?)

Ábaxą /ä'-bä-xoⁿ/ *v.*, attach, pin, as in sticking something into the hair, such as an ornament or a hair clasp

Ábaxą /ä'-bä-xoⁿ/ *v.*, stick, to stick something in the hair, clothing, anything

Ábaxù /ä'-bä-xü/ *v.*, mark, in the sense of marking upon something, such as paper or any other surface

Ábaxù /ä'-bä-xü/ *v.*, write on, to write on the surface of something, such as paper or

stone; to write over something or to copy
something

Ábdagè /ä'-bthä-gā/ *v.*, sheltered, usu. on the
side sheltered from the wind

Ábdagè /ä'-bthä-gā/ *n.*, calm, on the sheltered side of a windbreak, usu. refers to a
place where people are standing or sitting
at an outdoor event or activity

Ábe /ä'-bā/ *n.*, leaf or leaves

Ábixà /ä'-bē-xoⁿ/ *v.*, boil, simmer, bubble,
e.g., water changing from a liquid to a vapor
with the addition of heat

Ábizè /ä'-bē-zā/ *n.*, something dried, as in
dried up in the sun

Ą́da /oⁿ'-thä/ *v.*, discard, dispose of, throw
away, get rid of

Adá'ži /ä-thä'-zhē/ *v.*, stayed, to stay or remain in place

Adį́'ayáda /ä-thēⁿ'-ä-yä'-thä/ *v.t.*, abduct,
make off with, to snatch, usu. refers to
taking somebody away

Ą́dadéde /oⁿ'-thä-thā'-thā/ *v.*, throw, toss or
throw something, such as a ball, a discus,
or a frisbee in games

Ádahà /ä-thä-hä'/ *n.*, smear, a dirty spot
made by touching or rubbing something
on something else

Ádahà /ä-thä-hä'/ *v.*, wear, 1. putting on a
piece of clothing 2. to smear something on
the surface of something, as in smearing
food on one's clothing

Ádasądè /ä'-thä-soⁿ-dä/ *adj.*, tight fitting, as
in tight-fitting clothes or a tight-fitting cover

Ádaskabè /ä'-thä-skä-bä/ *v.*, stick, adhere,
to stick on the surface of something

Ą́dą́wądišp'egà /oⁿ-thoⁿ'-wä-thē-shp'ä-
gä/ *n.*, state of being restrained, lit., "as I
am kept back or ~ from speaking or doing
something on account of it," an expression
of being kept back or restrained on account
of something

Adį́ /ä-thēⁿ/ *v.*, have, to have; *abdí*, 1st pers.
sing., I have; *aní'*, 2nd pers. sing., you have;
adí', 3rd pers. sing., he/she/it has; *ągádį*, 1st
pers. pl., we have; *aní'i*, 2nd pers. pl., you
have; *adí'i*, 3rd pers. pl., they have

Adį́' /ä-thēⁿ/ *v.*, keep, reserved for future use;
agdádį, has or keeps in reserve; *akígdadì*,
keeping something always

Adí' /ä-thē'/ *v.*, possess, to own, to own something, as in property, money

Adį́'ágadà /ä-thēⁿ-ä'-gä-thä'/ *v.*, carry, to
carry away something openly; *áigadà*, to
carry something openly

Ádi'stà /ä'-thē-stä/ *v.*, bandage, as in bandaging a wound

Adį́ágadì /ä-thēⁿ-oⁿ'-gä-thēⁿ/ *v.*, *pl.*, bringing, bringing a specific thing (*uxp'éte ~*, we
are ~ the dishes)

Adiáhi /ä-thēä'-hē/ *v.*, deliver, to take or carry
something to a person or place

Adiáti /ä-thēä'-tē/ *v.*, *past t.*, brought here,
to have brought a specific thing to this place

Adį́ áti /ä-thēⁿ-ä'-tē/ *v. past t.*, *past part.* of
"to bring"

Adį́ gdè /ä-thēⁿ' gthä'/ *v.*, take home, a gift or
earnings being taken home

Adį́già(gá) /ä-thēⁿ'-gē-ä'(gä')/ *v.*, bring, a
command *to bring*; *adíáhi*, brought something to that place

Ádikà /ä'-thē-koⁿ/ *adj.*, lopsided, uneven,
unbalanced

Ádikà /ä'-thē-koⁿ/ *v.*, to be slanted, imbalanced, something that is not level or even

Ą́dinǫ̀ /oⁿ'-thē-noⁿ/ *adj./interj.*, ridiculous, an
expression that connotes something done
ridiculously or even in a silly manner; *archaic*, nearly acted, nearly said something,
nearly did something that did not end appropriately

Ą́dinǫ̀ /oⁿ'-thē-noⁿ/ *adv.*, approximately, just
about, nearly, not quite, came near

Ą́dìnạ̀ /oⁿ-thē-noⁿ/ *adv.*, almost, nearly, just about, not quite

Ą́·dìnạ̀ /oⁿ-·-thē-noⁿ/ *adj.*, ludicrous, absurd, ridiculous, nonsensical, laughable, as in something obviously absurd

Ą́dísídè /oⁿ-thē̌-sē-thä̌/ *v.*, *1st pers. pl.*, remember, to remember some people; *wegísídè*, *1st pers. sing.*, I ~ you

Ádiškabè /ä-thē-shkä-bä̌/ *v.*, climb, to climb using hands and feet

Ádit'à /ä-thē-t'ä̌/ *adv.*, across (*úwe kè ~ adái*, he is going ~ the field)

Ádiudạ̀ /ä̌-thē-ü-doⁿ/ *adv.*, left behind, as in being present when all have left a place that was once crowded and is now empty of people, but clean and clear of debris

Ádiudè /ä̌-thē-ü-dä̌/ *v.t.*, *past t.*, abandoned, left somebody behind

Ą́dixčìègạ̀ /oⁿ-thē-xchē̌-ā-goⁿ/ *adv.*, easily, without difficulty, without problems, simply, effortlessly

Ádixudè /ä̌-thē-xü-dä̌/ *n.*, blur, something that is unclear or fuzzy

Adúha /ä-thǚ-hä/ *adj.*, first, to be the first to act, to initiate something before others do

Adúha /ä-thǚ-hä/ *v.*, lead, to go first; to do something first or to lead in a task to be done; *adúhagà*, you go first

Adúhagà /ä-thǚ-hä-gä̌/ *v. phr.*, go first, usu. a command to proceed ahead of others; to act before others on specific things

Adúhagè /ä-thǚ-hä-gä̌/ *adj.*, last, the last of some people or animals coming

Ádut'ạ̀ /ä̌-thü-t'oⁿ/ *adj.*, on target, on course, doing or saying something just right

Ága /ä̌-gä/ *v.*, say, utter, state, verbalize, say this

Ą́gabagdaì /oⁿ-gä-bä-gthä-ē̌/ *v.*, *3rd pers. pl.*, to be hesitant, we hesitate; being uncertain, diffident (as in "we do not like to ask for a favor"); to feel uncertain or being not sure about something

Ágabdà /ä̌-gä-bthä̌/ *v.*, spread out, an opening up caused by something, such as wind

Ágabdị̀ /ä̌-gä-bthē̌ⁿ/ *v./n.*, blow on, something blown upon

Ągádè't'è /oⁿ-gä-thä̌-t'ä̌/ *v.t.*, *1st pers. pl.*, depart, let us depart, let us go; *agádaì*, we are departing or going

Ągádịt'ạgatạ̀ /oⁿ-gä-thē̌ⁿ-t'oⁿ-gä-toⁿ/ *v.*, *1st pers. pl.*, *future perfect tense*, we will have had

Ágahà /ä̌-gä-hä̌/ *prep.*, upon, on the surface

Ágahadì /ä̌-gä-hä-dē̌/ *adv.*, afterward, later on or subsequently, usu. refers to something being done after something has started

Ágahanạp'áze /ä̌-gä-hä-noⁿ-p'ä̌-zä/ *v.*, overshadow, to cast a shadow over something, as in heavy clouds casting a shadow over the land

Ágahạnạp'azè /ä̌-gä-hoⁿ-noⁿ-p'ä-zä/ *n.*, darkness, state of dimness or darkness caused by covering or turning off lights in a room

Ágahat'à /ä̌-gä-hä-t'ä̌/ *n.*, outside, exterior, the outer surface, such as walls

Ágamù /ä̌-gä-mǚ/ *adj.*, dripping wet, wet from rain, sopping wet, or sodden from some source

Ágamuxt'ạ̀ /ä̌-gä-mü-xt'oⁿ/ *v.*, drip upon, causing water to drip upon or be sprayed upon them or us or on something

Áganaxè /ä̌-gä-nä-xä̌/ *v.*, to be sprayed or sprinkled upon with water, usu. refers to walking in rainy conditions or under a watering device in a park

Ágaškè /ä̌-gä-shkä̌/ *v.*, fasten, to attach, clasp, secure something from opening

Ágasp'è /ä̌-gä-sp'ä̌/ *v.*, cover, 1. hide from view, put out of sight, connotes something that either has been hidden deliberately or was found under something 2. in a ritual Ponca giveaway, used to indicate that an individual was honored with much material goods, usu. the placing of many Pendleton blankets or shawls upon or covering the person in the ritual dance

Ágaxadè /ä'-gä-xä-dä'/ *v.*, cover, to cover up something (to use a lid to ~ the food); *idági-gdaxadè*, covered his own

Ágaxdè /ä'-gä-xthä'/ *adj.*, moving, something or somebody moving with the current of the water or wind

Ágaxdè /ä'-gä-xthä'/ *n. phr.*, current, the flow of the wind or current of the wind (the flaps at the top of a tepee serve as a damper for the inner ~ of air)

Ágaxù /ä'-gä-xü'/ *v./n.*, bloodletting, a medical procedure for drawing blood for relief, bleed or to draw blood

Ágažadè /ä'-gä-zhä-dä'/ *adv.*, astride, straddling, as in horseback riding with legs on both sides of the horse

Ágažì /ä'-gä-zhē'/ *v.*, command, to command or to order somebody to do something; *áwi-gažì*, I ordered or commanded you; *wá'agažì*, I ordered or commanded them; *áwadagažì*, you ordered or commanded me; *wádagažì*, you ordered or commanded them; *ádigažì*, he ordered or commanded you; *wáa̧ga'gažì*, we ordered or commanded them

Ágda /ä'-gthä/ *v.*, blame, hold responsible

Ágda̧' /ä'-gtho{}^{n}/ *v.*, set, to set something upon something

Ágda'adì /ä'-gthä-ä-thē{}^{n}'/ *v.*, mistreat, abuse somebody, treat badly; *ágdawádì*, 1. treated them badly, as in prisoners 2. to be beating the other team or winning by a large score in sports

Agdábdì /ä-gthä'-bthē{}^{n}/ *v.*, I have my own, in possession of one's own; *agdádi*, he has his or he possesses his own

Ágdabè /ä'-gthä-bä'/ *adj.*, calm, tranquil, peaceful, serene, usu. in regard to people's conditions of life and living

Ágdadè /ä'-gthä-thä'/ *v.*, 1. causing someone to have a hard or difficult time 2. something that causes somebody to have or to meet up with something hard or difficult to handle

Ágdadè /ä'-gthä-thä'/ *adj.*, adverse, unfavorable, undesirable, or harmful

Ágdadè /ä'-gthä-thä'/ *n.*, detriment, something causing detriment, disadvantage, harm or loss

Agdádi /ä-gthä'-thē{}^{n}/ *v., 1st pers. sing.*, has, he/she has his/her own or possesses his/her own

Agdádi'akì /ä-gthä'-thē{}^{n}-ä-kē'/ *v.*, returned with, brought back his own

Agdádi atì /ä-gthä'-the{}^{n} ä-tē'/ *v. phr.*, bring, to ~ his own

Agdákahà /ä-gtho{}^{n}'-kä-hä'/ *n.*, sides, both the left and right side of an object

Agdákahà /ä-gtho{}^{n}'-kä-ho{}^{n}'/ *adv.*, on both sides, on each side of something

Ágdawadè /ä'-gthä-wä-thä'/ *n.*, the act of bringing calamity or misfortune to somebody

Agdí' /ä-gthē'/ *v.*, come back, he/she/it/they come back, returning to a previously occupied place or station, 1. came home, refers to a person who had been away and has now come home 2. refers to the seasons and animals, as in the winter has returned or the geese have returned

Ágdi baiázazà /ä'-gthē{}^{n} bä-ē-ä'-zä-zä'/ *v.*, rocking chair, a chair mounted on two curved pieces of wood made for rocking oneself to and fro

Agdídabdì /ä-gthē'-thä-bthē{}^{n}/ *n.*, thirteen, the number thirteen (13); something consisting of ~ units; *agdídabdìhà*, a group of ~; *agdídabdìà*, ~ times; *agdídabdìažà*, ~ times again, or always; *agdídabdìxčì*, only ~; *agdídabdìegà*, just about ~; *agdídabdìda*, the ~th one; *agdídabdìdadà*, ~ apiece or ~ each

Agdíṣ̣akà /ä-gthē{}^{n}'-sho{}^{n}-kä'/ *n.*, nineteen

Agdít'amà /ä-gthē'-t'ä-mä/ *v. phr.*, coming back, he/she/it/they "will come back" (*míxa amà* ~, the ducks are ~)

Agí /ä-gē'/ *v.*, returning, to come back to a place after leaving it, usu. refers to someone who went away and is returning

Agí'de /ä-gē'-thä/ *v. phr.*, get, to go and get a specific thing

Agí'ki /ä-gē'-kē/ *v. phr.*, come after, one coming to get something that belongs to him/her

Agí'kigdè /ä-gē'-kē-gthä/ *v. phr.*, retrieve, to go get his own (something)

Agímądía(gá) /ä-gē'-moⁿ-thēⁿ'-ä(gä')/ *v.*, bring, fetch, go and get (*mąkásabè dúba* ~, ~ some coffee)

Agít'ąbè /ä-gē'-t'oⁿ-bä/ *v. phr.*, I got to see my own relative, usu. used when a person has not seen his close relative, such as a son or daughter who has been away, for a long period of time

Ągú' /oⁿ-gü/ *pron.*, we, refers to the self and one or more persons (~ *edí ągáhi*, us, we went there)

Ąguágadį /oⁿ-güoⁿ'-gä-thēⁿ/ *pron.*, we, used more as a reference to ~ as a group who planned, accomplished, etc.

Ąguágadį /oⁿ-gü'-ä'-gä-thēⁿ/ *pron.*, us, a group that includes me; *ągù ~ ągúádi*, it is or was ~; *ągúáwawà*, it was caused by ~; *ągúášt'ì* ~ too; *ągúágądit'adišą*, toward ~

Águdì'štì'dądą /ä'-gü-dē'-shtē'-thoⁿ'-thoⁿ'/ *adv.*, everywhere, here and there

Águdištiwą /ä'-gü-dē-shtē-woⁿ'/ *n.*, wherever, anyplace, no matter where

Águdišt'iwążì /ä'-gü-dē-sht'ē-woⁿ-zhē/ *adv.*, nowhere, at no place; a place that doesn't exist

Ągúšt'ì /oⁿ-gü'-sht'ē'/ *pron. phr.*, we too, us too

Ągút'a /oⁿ-gü'-t'ä/ *pron.*, ours, our, something belonging to us

Ąguw'ʃte /oⁿ-güw-ʃⁿ-tä/ *interj.*, and do you know, an expression used by women

Ągúwąì /oⁿ-gü'-woⁿ-ē'/ *v., 1st pers. pl.*, we burned it

Ą́he /oⁿ'-hä/ *v.*, flee, get away from, usu. from coming disaster (~ from the tornado); *gí'ąhè*, to flee from somebody

Ą́hį /ä'-hēⁿ/ *n.*, wing, the wings of birds

Ahí' /ä-hē'/ *v., 3rd pers. pl., past part.*, arrived, they ~ there

Ahí' /ä-hē'/ *v.*, came, came there, came to that place; *atí'*, came here; *šuhí'*, they came there; *šiáhi*, they came there again; *šup'í'*, I came there

Ahíbažì /ä-hē'-bä-zhē/ *adj.*, absent, not present, not present at a certain place

Ahíbažì /ä-hē'-bä-zhē/ *v., sing./pl.*, did not come here, did not come there; *hiáži*, abbr., he did not come here; *tíbaži*, abbr., they did not come here; *kiáži*, abbr. form, he/she/it did not come here

Áhigè /ä'-hē-gä'/ *adj.*, many, lot of, plentiful

Áhigè /ä'-hē-gä'/ *adv.*, plenty, lots, much

Áhigedè /ä'-hē-gä-thä'/ *v.*, accumulate, accrue, amass, to gather or collect

Áhigidè /ä'-hē-gē-thä'/ *adj.*, more, somebody adding or saving an additional amount of something

Ahó' /ä-hō'/ *interj.*, hello, male greeting, Ponca greeting or salutation between men (In archaic usage, *ahó'* was interjected by a man relating a story, as in "okay . . ." or "all right . . ." in the middle of a sentence. In modern times, the term is often used at many different tribal gatherings, esp. at intertribal dances to denote "thank you," a usage that is said to be of Kiowa origin.)

Áhušigè /ä'-hü-shē-gä'/ *v.*, demand, insist, ask for something forcefully

A·í' /ä·ē'/ *v.*, approach, coming toward where

I am or where we are, to draw closer to us; *aíbadǫ̀*, they are approaching us

Aí badǫ̀ /ä-ē' bä-doⁿ/ *v. phr.*, coming, "they are or somebody is ~ because" of wanting something or wanting to do something

Áigadà /ä'-ē-gä-thä'/ *v. phr.*, carry in the open, carry openly, to lay aside openly

Aít'amà /ä-ē'-t'ä-mä'/ *v.*, coming, "they are coming" as we anticipate their arrival

Ak'íwahà /ä-k'ē'-wä-hä'/ *v.*, divide, share, usu. refers to an activity between two individuals or to dividing up between two groups or persons

Ák'í'p'azǫ̀ /ä'-k'ē'-p'ä-zoⁿ/ *prep.*, across, facing something or somebody across an intervening space

Ák'ibanǫ̀ /ä'-k'ē-bä-noⁿ/ *v.*, to come toward and meet somebody or come toward a place

Ak'ídahà /ä-k'ē'-thä-hä'/ *adv.*, separately, refers to two, both (*mázeskàte ~ awá'i*, I gave money ~ to both of them); *ak'íwahà*, refers to more than two, all (*wǫ́gidèxtì*, ~ *waį́ xdíxdí waí*, everyone present was given a Pendleton blanket)

Ák'inǫ̀zì /ä'-k'ē-noⁿ-zhē'/ *v.*, depend upon, to rely or place trust in another for one's well-being (Although used more for family members and friends, it was historically part of the Ponca Heɖúškà fraternal organization of men who defended the camp and did good deeds.)

Ák'ip'à /ä'-k'ē-p'ä'/ *v.*, meet, encounter, meet up with; *á'ak'ip'à*, *1st pers. sing., past part.*, I met

Ák'ip'anǫ̀ /ä'-k'ē-p'ä-noⁿ/ *v.*, meet, coming toward each other on the path or roadway

Ak'íwahǫ̀ /ä-k'ē'-wä-hoⁿ/ *v.*, *1st pers. sing.*, to pray for oneself

Ǫk'íwahǫ̀i /oⁿ-k'ē'-wä-hoⁿ'-ē'/ *v.*, thank, to thank others for oneself and others; *ák'iwahǫ̀i*, to thank others for oneself

Ák'usǫdè /ä'-k'ü-soⁿ-dä'/ *prep.*, past, went past, went beyond, further than

Áka /ä'-kä/ *adj.*, the, definite article (originally used with singular animate subjects, now used with inanimate subjects)

-aké' /ä-kä'/ *n.*, suffix, one, denotes a particular person or thing, as in "that's the one"; *ɖéke*, this one closest to me; *duáke*, this one; *gáke*, speaking of a particular thing; *še'akè*, that one; *ámǫkè*, the other one

Aké' /ä-kä'/ *v.*, prefix, is, *3rd pers. sing.* of *be*

Aki' /ä-kē/ *v.*, *3rd pers. sing.*, returned, he/she/it returned

Áki'kihidè /ä'-kē-kē-hē-dä'/ *v.*, take care or precautions for yourself

Akíbaźì /ä-kē'-bä-zhē'/ *v.*, *sing./pl.*, did not return, did not come home; *kiáži* /kē'-ä'-zhē/ usu. used in singular form

Ákibe's'į̀ /ä'-kē-bä-s-ēⁿ/ *v.*, to turn over and over, usu. refers to a car wreck

Ákidà /ä'-k'ē-dä'/ *n.*, sentry, sentinel, guard, 1. a person who is on duty to provide security for an establishment or prison 2. caretaker or caregiver, somebody who looks after somebody, or somebody physically ill or emotionally disabled

Ákidà /ä'-kē-thä'/ *v.*, challenge, contest, match, as in fighting

Akídé /ä-kē'-thä'/ *v.*, let, consent to (*Heɖúškà wačígaxè*, I ~ him Heɖúškà dance)

Akidé /ä-kē-thä'/ *v.*, to cause one to do something

Ákidit'à /ä'-kē-thē-t'ä'/ *v.*, cross, traverse, to pass through or go across, as in crossing a field

Ákigdahà /ä'-kē-gthä-hä'/ *n.*, layers, to put additional coverings on something or to put on additional clothing, such as a sweater or coat

Ákigdašǫ̀ /ä'-kē-gthä-shoⁿ/ *n./v.*, to be upside down, anything that normally is upright that is upside down (the car was ~)

Ákigđašą̀ /ä'-kē-gthä-shoⁿ/ *adj. phr.*, upside down, as in the position of an automobile that overturns in an accident

Ákigđašą̀ /ä'-kē-gthä-shoⁿ/ *v.*, overturn, tip over, capsize

Ákigđaskabè /ä'-kē-gthä-skä-bā'/ *v.*, to stick, two things sticking or glued together

Ákihą̀ /ä-kē-hoⁿ/ *adv.*, beyond, further than, past where you are; *uwák'ihą̀, n.*, often refers to generations, as in designating a relationship of parents to future generations

Ákihą̀ /ä-kē-hoⁿ/ *adv.*, farther, 1. in travel, to go farther, refers to going past a place or going beyond the destination 2. in buying, to get more

Ákihidè /ä'-kē-hē-dä'/ *v.*, oversee, 1. to take care of someone or something 2. to oversee and protect someone or something

Ákikidà /ä'-kē-kē-thä'/ *v.*, compete, struggle to win, as in in sports such as football, basketball, baseball, boxing; *ákiđà*, to compete with one opponent

Ákinągè /ä'-kē-noⁿ-gä'/ *n./v.*, collision, crash into, as in two automobiles colliding

Akínąxđè /ä-kē'-noⁿ-xthä'/ *v.*, hiding, someone or a group in hiding

Ákinè /ä'-kē-nä'/ *v.*, cuddle, two persons holding each other affectionately, to hug tenderly

Ákip'azą̀ /ä'-kē-p'ä-zoⁿ/ *v.*, disunite, to disunite or make a boundary (This can be an unwanted thing. Sometimes a person in a tribal gathering would separate himself or herself from other family members in a "give-away" and do his or her own thing.)

Ákišugà /ä'-kē-shü-gä'/ *adj.*, thick, dense, 1. usu. refers to crowded things, people close together 2. may refer to torrential rain (*nąží ~*, torrential rain)

Akíwahà /ä-kē'-wä-hä'/ *v.*, to give or divide something up equally between two persons or things

Áma /ä'-mä/ *adj.*, the, definite article (with animate subjects can be either singular or plural, showing action or movement; however, in certain usage the term may show no action or movement)

Ą́mą̀ /oⁿ-moⁿ/ *adj.*, other, another, another one (~ *kè ą'íđagà*, hand me the ~ one)

Ámąđì /ä'-moⁿ-thē'/ *v.*, walk upon, to walk upon (*žį̀gá đį̀kè, iđádi mí'xe kè', ~kiđaì*, they caused the child to ~ the grave of his father)

Ámąk'ažì /ä'-moⁿ-k'ä-zhē'/ *adj./v.*, to be tired of, to grow disgusted with something or somebody, to be sick of it or him, annoy, to irritate, aggravate, or get on one's nerves; *ámąk'ažiwađè*, something that a person can get tired of

Ámašp'è /ä'-mä-shp'ä'/ *v.*, to cut off a piece of something; *ímašpè*, cut off a piece for me; *đimašpè*, cut off a piece for you; *wémašpè*, cut off a piece for them, as with food

Ą́mąt'adišą̀ /oⁿ-moⁿ-t'ä-thē-shoⁿ/ *adv.*, happening on the other side, toward the other side; suggests something occurring on the other side of a structure, place, or things animate or inanimate

Ą́mąt'adišą̀ /oⁿ-moⁿ-t'ä-thē-shoⁿ/ *adv.*, opposite, on the other side or ~ side of something

Ą́mąt'adišą̀ /oⁿ-moⁿ-t'ä-thē-soⁿ/ *adj.*, other side, flip side, backside, reverse side

Ámątì /ä'-moⁿ-tēⁿ/ *v.*, bump, to bump into something; *ákimątè*, to bump into each other

Ámątį̀tì /ä'-moⁿ-tēⁿ-tēⁿ/ *adj.*, bumpy, e.g., refers to something that bumps and jolts along a roadway while riding in some kind of vehicle

Ámątį̀tì /ä'-moⁿ-tēⁿ-tēⁿ/ *v.*, bumping, e.g., when a shutter continuously bumps against the wall or window

Ámąxp'ì /ä'-moⁿx-p'ē'/ *adj.*, cloudy, referring to scattered clouds of any type

Amé /ä-mä'/ *n.*, the one, as in "he's the one"

Ą́nạ /ä'-noⁿ/ *n.*, population, lit., how many, refers to the number of things or people

Ána'ù /ä'-nä-ü'/ *v.*, *past t.*, passed by, went close by it or somebody

Ánábdì /ä-noⁿ'-bthē'/ *v.*, *1st pers. sing.*, mistaken, I am (was) mistaken

Ánągè /ä'-noⁿ-gä'/ *v.*, run over, squash, flatten out (she ~ the bicycle)

Ánạsạdè /ä'-noⁿ-soⁿ-dä'/ *v.*, block, block a door with one's body by leaning against it or placing a foot at the bottom of the door to keep it from opening

Ánạsạdè /ä'-noⁿ-soⁿ-dä'/ *v.*, pressed down, holding down with feet or stepping on to hold something still (he ~ on the animal); *ábisạdè*, holding down by pressing down with the body

Ánạsạdè /ä'-noⁿ-soⁿ-dä'/ *v.*, hold down, squeezing, to hold in place with the feet; *ábasạdè*, hold in place by using one's own body; *ábisạdè*, hold in place by pressing down

Ánạsạdè /ä'-noⁿ-soⁿ-dä'/ *v.*, squeeze, usu. done with the feet; to be pressed down by a person or thing

Ánạsè /ä'-noⁿ-sä'/ *n./v.*, close, to close or fasten shut, block, to block, barrier, blockade, barricade

Ánạsè /ä'-noⁿ-sä'/ *v.*, lock, to prevent use by unauthorized persons; to stop something from passing through, as in turning the water off

Ánạsè /ä'-noⁿ-sä'/ *v.*, shut off, turn off, switch off something, as in turning the water off

Ánạskà /ä'-noⁿ-skä'/ *n.*, size, dimension, sizing to fit (~ *à*?, what ~?)

Ánạxdè /ä'-noⁿ-xthä'/ *v.*, conceal, to hide a person or something, to hide feelings or facts

Ánaxihidè /ä'-nä-xē-hē-thä'/ *v.*, absorb, taking in or taking up the rays of sunshine, as in basking in the sun

Ánạxt'ì /ä'-noⁿ-xt'ē'/ *adj.*, some, a suggestion of more in number rather than fewer

Ánạxt'iegà /ä'-noⁿ-xt'ē-ä-goⁿ'/ *adj.*, several, more than a few but not too many of something

Ánazatạ /ä'-nä-zä-t'oⁿ'/ *adv.*, behind, "from behind"

Ánáži̧ /ä-noⁿ'-zhēⁿ/ *v.*, *1st pers. sing.*, stand, I stand; *á'nạži̧*, *n.*, the act of standing upon something

Ánạži̧ /ä'-noⁿ-zhēⁿ/ *v.*, rain on, to get rained on

Áne /ä'-nä/ *v.*, embrace, to give a hospitable or loving embrace, hug, cuddle

Ápạ hútạ mí' /oⁿ'-poⁿ hü'-toⁿ mē'/ *n.*, September, lit., moon when the elk bellow, the ninth month in the year

Asáži̧gà /ä-sä'-zhēⁿ-gä'/ *n.*, fourth born, usu. a name given to a fourth-born female child

Áši'ạdà /ä'-shē'-oⁿ-thä'/ *v.*, throw out, evict, force a person out of, 1. dismissing or ousting somebody from an office or a place 2. banish from an organization or tribe

Áši̧áda /ä'-shē-ä-thä/ *n./prep. phr.*, without concern, a wrongful act of saying or doing something without concern for others; the act of taking something from a friend or some aquaintance in their presence without asking

Ášiadì /ä'-shē-ä-dē'/ *adv.*, happening outside, 1. an indication of something outside at a certain place 2. somebody outside of a group or crowd of people

Ášiat'à /ä'-shē-ä-t'ä'/ *adv.*, happening or located outside, exterior, usu. refers to something outside of a building, dwelling, or house

Ą́ska /oⁿ'-skä/ *n.*, thing, an unspecified item, whachacallit

Áškà /ä'-shkä'/ *adv.*, 1. refers to stopping at or

near the completion of doing something
2. to come near or close to someplace

Áskù' /ä-skü'/ *n.*, braid, a singular braid worn by the Đíxidą̀ and Níkapášną̀ clansmen (The braid was part of the "mohawk" hairstyle, where the short hair was cut to the crown of the head and the rest of the hair grew long and was braided into a single braid by the Đíxidą̀; the Níkapášną̀ did not have the braid but tied eagle feathers where the hair grew long below the crown of the head.)

Ásku snedè /ä-skü snä-dā'/ *n.*, a Chinese person, lit., a long single braid, a native of China

Ásnì /ä'-snē'/ *v.*, cool; *ásnidè*, cooling

Ásnidè /ä'-snē-thä'/ *adj.*, cool down, to make cool as with food, a room, and other conditions or things that retain heat

Ásnik'idè /ä'-snē-k'ē-thä'/ *v. phr.*, cool oneself off, stand outside of the dwelling in a breeze

Ásnu'è /ä'-snü-ā'/ *v.*, streaming, issuing or flowing, as in tears (*įdédą įštabdì ~ gdí'akà*, she was sitting with tears ~ down her face)

Ast'úhi /ä-stü'-hē/ *n.*, elbow, the elbow joint between the upper and lower arm

Ášudè /ä'-shü-dā'/ *v.*, to fan smoke upon (The smoke or incense from cedar leaves is used in prayers and for healing.)

Ášudè /ä'-shü-dā'/ *n./v.*, smoke ritual, usu. refers to ritual use of smoke from the needle-like leaves of the cedar tree; *ášudekidè*, to fan oneself with the cedar smoke (The Hísadà clan of the Ponca people was designated as the clan to handle the cedar-burning ritual that is considered a sacred rite of the people.)

Ášudè /ä'-shü-dā'/ *v./n.*, fan, to ceremonially fan using an eagle tail to ~ the smoke of cedar upon a person or persons

Ášudek'idè /ä'-shü-dä-k'ē-thä'/ *v.*, smoke self, refers to ritual use of smoke from the needle-like leaves of the cedar tree as directed by the one conducting the rite

-át'adišą̀ /ä'-t'ä-thē-sho^n/ *adv.*, *suffix*, pertaining to a direction or toward something

Át'ąk'idądà /ä'-t'o^n-k'ē-tho^n-tho^n/ *adv.*, alternating, interchanging, to repeatedly interchange

At'ą́štì /ä-to^n-shtē'/ *adv.*, occasional

Ąt'íbadì /o^n-t'ē'-bä-dē'/ *n.*, *slang*, wife, "the one who lives in my house"

-ata /ä-tä/ *prep.*, *suffix*, at, as in *gáat'à*, ~ that place over there; *usniát'a*, ~ the place where it is cold

Atą́'šti'dądà /ä-to^n-shtē-tho^n-tho^n/ *adv.*, occasionally, on different occasions, from time to time, now and then, every so often, etc.

Atą́'xt'iadì /ä-to^n-xt'ē-ä-dē'/ *adv.*, previously, when something occurred in the past

Atą́dià /ä-to^n-dē-ä'/ *adv.*, when, introduces a question regarding at what time a thing happened; *atą́xtiádi*, in the remote past

Atą́diádi /ä-to^n-dē-ä'-dē/ *conj.*, when, question that asks what time something happened

Atą́diaditą̀ /ä-to^n-dē-ä'-dē-to^n/ *conj.*, when from the past, reiteration of something of the past

Átą dimą́ši /ä'-to^n thē-mo^n'-shē/ *n.*, escalator, lit., steps that lift

Atą́ditą̀ /ä-to^n'-dē-to^n/ *adv.*, ever since, ever since when, from then to now

Atą́ditą̀ /ä-to^n'-dē-to^n/ *conj.*, since, since that time

Atą́ną /ä-to^n'-no^n/ *adv.*, a question about how much time or how long

Atą́nądì /ä-to^n'-no^n-dē'/ *adv.*, a question about what time a thing happens, when

Atą́šti /ä-to^n'-shtē/ *adv.*, sometimes, at times, now and then

Atą́štidą̀dą̀ /ă-ton'-shtē-thon'-thon'/ *adv.*, periodically, from time to time, once in a while

Atą́štiwą̀ /ă-ton'-shtē-won'/ *pron.*, anytime, whenever, at any time

Atí' /ă-tē'/ *v.*, *3rd pers.*, to arrive, he/she/it/ they ~ here

Atídą̀dą̀ /ă-tē'-thon-thon'/ *v.*, refers to people who come to this place little by little

Aú' /ă-ü'/ *v.* to win, "I won!"; *ú'i*, he/she won (In Ponca hand games, including cards, dice, or Indian dice, the term is applied as if saying "Checkmate!")

Aú'k'ą̀t'ą̀ /äü'-k'on-t'on'/ *n.*, biceps, muscle in the upper arm

Áwa /ă'-wä/ *adv.*, where (Prefix *áwa* is also where; however, singular usage of the word is rare; used to ask about the whereabouts of somebody or something.) (*áwadià?*, ~ is he, she, it?; *áwakeà?*, ~ is it?)

Áwa /ă'-wä/ *pron.*, which, a thing out of a group (*Áwa* can serve as a prefix in words asking a question.)

Ąwą́dą̀i /on-won'-thon-ē'/ *v.*, they caught me, to apprehend, to get caught doing something; *udídą̀i*, they caught you; *uwádą̀i*, they caught us

Áwadià /ă'-wä-thē-ä'/ *adv.*, where (~ is he/ she/it?)

Áwadikešt'iwą̀ /ă'-wä-thē-kä-shtē-won'/ *n.*, either, word that connects two situations, one of which may be eliminated or may be included

Áwadi'štì /ă'-wä-dē-shtē'/ *adv.*, somewhere, wherever

Ąwą́'i' /on-won'-ē/ *adj.*, gift, a gift to me

Áwake /ă'-wä-kā/ *adv.*, which, asking which one of several items or things; *áwatè*, group or selected items from many things

Áwakedìštewą̀ /ă-wä-kā-dē-shtē-won'/ *adv.*, elsewhere, in another or different place

Áwaket'à /ă'-wä-kā-t'ä'/ *adv.*, where, used

to ask about a direction that somebody or something is coming from or going to

Áwaket'adišą̀ /ă'-wä-kā-t'ä-thē-shon'/ *adv. phr.*, which direction, a question asking for a direction

Ąwą́ną̀dì /on-won'-non-thē'/ *v.*, *1st pers. pl.*, mistaken, we are (were) mistaken

Áwat'adišą̀ /ă'-wä-t'ä-thē-shon'/ *adv.*, which side, question asking which side of something

Áwategą̀ /ă'-wä-tā-gon'/ *adv.*, how, introduces a question about how something is done or happened

Áwategą̀'á /ă'-wä-tā-gon-ä'/ *interj.*, questioning expression of "what now?"

Áwategą̀štì /ă'-wä-tā-gon-shtē'/ *adv.*, somehow, by some means or way, in one way or another

Áwawą̀t'à /ă'-wä-won-t'ä'/ *adv.*, which way, refers to a question asking in which direction a thing or a person is located

Ąwą́zą̀dè /on-won'-zon-dä'/ *n.*, a feeling of suspicion or dread that encompasses a person, one's feelings reacting to that suspicion

Áwązì /ă'-won'-zhē'/ *adj.*, nearly new, refers to clothing that has hardly been worn

Ąwą́žiazì /on-won'-zhēä-zhē'/ *v. phr.*, lit., it is not in me, usu. refers to somebody who is part of a group but cannot get excited or have a deep interest in what is happening or being planned

Awíʃwadą̀ /ă-wē'-ʃ'-wä-thon'/ *pron.*, which, a question asking which particular one, in regard to things; *awíʃwaą̀*, which one of them (persons)

Awíp'i /ă-wē'-p'ē/ *v.*, come or came to get you

Áxa /ă'-xä/ *v.*, cry, to cry for, as in a child crying for something

Axíbe /ä-xē'-bä/ *n.*, bracelet

Áxt'ą̀ /ä'x-t'on'/ *adj.*, unlikely, not likely to happen, improbable

Áxt'idè /oⁿ-xt'ē-thä'/ *n./v.*, honor, respect, mark of respect, reverence, esteem, hold in highest regard; *áxt'idè* is used in "respect to" one person; *áxt'iwadè*, respect to more than one person; *áxt'ikidè*, self admiration or personal pride; *áxt'iwidè*, I respect and hold you in high regard, usu. refers to God, Wak'áda

Ayádaì /ä-yä'-thä-ē'/ *v., 3rd pers. sing./pl.*, left, to go away from one place to another

Áẓą /ä'-zhoⁿ/ *v.*, lie on, to lie upon something, such as a bed, a bench, or grass

Azá'ẓì /ä-zä'-zhē'/ *adj.*, tasteless, not tasty, not delicious, not yummy, bland

Áząt'asì /ä'-zoⁿ-t'ä-sē'/ *n.*, kidneys, the organs of humans and other vertebrate animals that process waste matter

Azé /ä-zä'/ *n.*, something that is flavorful, food that has a very pleasing taste, delectable, usu. refers to certain meat dishes

Azé' /ä-zä'/ *adj.*, savory, tasty, palatable, usu. refers to baked or fried meats

Ázegidaì /oⁿ-zä-gē-thäē'/ *v., 3rd pers. pl.*, they relaxed

Ázegidè /oⁿ-zä-gē-thä'/ *v.*, rest, relax, take a break, recess

Ážiámà /ä-zhē-ä'-mä/ *pron.*, somebody else, somebody not from here

Ážiamà /ä'-zhē-ä-mä/ *adj.*, other, as in another person or persons

Ážidą /ä'-zhē-doⁿ/ *v. phr.*, bedew, becoming wet from dew overnight

B

b /bē/ first consonant in the Ponca alphabet

B'ą' /b-oⁿ/ *v.*, holler, to call out to somebody

B'ą́bą' /b-oⁿ-boⁿ/ *v.*, hollering, to continuously holler

B'aí /b-ä-ē'/ *adj.*, sharp, razor sharp; *dib'ái*, sharpen

B'aí /b-ä-ē'/ *n.*, quills, lit., sharp, refers to the quills of a porcupine

B'aí /b-ä-ē'/ *n.*, porcupine, a large rodent with quills, of the order Rodentia, family Erethizontidae

B'áxet'à /b-ä'-xä-t'ä/ *n.*, diarrhea, complications causing frequent bowel movements

B'ézi /b-ä'-zē/ *n.*, gooseberry, a small, round fruit of the family Grossulariaceae, genus *Ribes*

B'igúdidądà /b-ē-gü'-dē-thoⁿ-thoⁿ/ *adv.*, moreover, furthermore, what is more, additionally

B'úšį /b-üⁿ-shēⁿ/ *adj.*, plump, 1. chubby, fleshy, or fat 2. refers to something more round or spherical

Bá /bä'/ *prefix*, action by pushing

Ba'dią́'ąbà /bä-thē-oⁿ-oⁿ-bä'/ *v.*, polish, buff, shine and sparkle

Ba'dią́'babà /bä-thē-oⁿ-bä-bä'/ *v.*, polish, buff, to make something shine and sparkle

Bą́'tigdè /boⁿ-tē-gthä'/ *v.*, to hear someone holler in the distance

Babáxu' /bä-bä'-xü/ *v.*, to make a ripple in water, as in a fish swimming upstream

Babdáze /bä-bthä'-zä/ *v.*, rend, tear, shred

Babé'xì /bä-bä'-xēⁿ/ *v.*, sweep, to sweep, to make a sweeping motion by pushing with an instrument such as a wide broom or an automated sweeper of some sort

Babú't'à /bä-bü'-t'ä/ *v.*, rounded, to make round by force or pushing

-badą́ /bä-doⁿ/ *v., suffix*, for want of or wanting to, showing reason why something will be or was done; implies a reason for such action

Badą́ /bä-doⁿ/ *v.*, push, shove, move forward

Bagíze /bä-gē'-zä/ *v.*, squeak, to make a sharp, high-pitched sound usu. caused by two things rubbing against each other; *bagígíze*, squeaky (the prefix *ba* indicates the pushing of something against something else repeatedly, as in using a bow and violin to make high- and low-pitched sounds); *bigíze*, squeak by pressing down; *bigígíze*, squeaking continuously; *nągíze*, squeaky (the prefix *ną* indicates the use of the feet to make a squeaking sound, e.g., squeaky shoes or a squeaky floor); *nągígíze*, the making of a continuous squeaking, as in walking on a squeaky floor

Bahá /bä-hä'/ *v.*, to show, illustrate, present, display; *n.*, *wábahà*, showing, a presentation or performance, the act of showing or displaying something

Bahášiat'à /bä-hä'-shē-ä-t'ä'/ *adv.*, above, indicates something that is on top of or overhead

Bahé /bä-hä'/ *v.*, shove, push, shoving or pushing something or someone away from oneself; *bahé dédé*, pushing something or somebody completely away

Bahí /bä-hē'/ *v.*, pick, to harvest, as in to pick pecans, to pick up items dropped on the floor

Bahí /bä-hē'/ *v.*, select, to choose from or decide on which one of a group

Baí'áži /bä-ē'-ä'-zhē/ *adj.*, dull, not sharp, not finely honed

Baiáxa /bäē-ä'-xä/ *v./adj.*, open, as in a door left open intentionally or unintentionally (*t'ižébe ké ~ itédaì*, he left the door ~)

Bajáška /bä-jä'-shkä/ *adj.*, stuffed, overstuffed, overfed (*níxa etáikè ~*, his stomach was overstuffed)

Bak'ú /bä-k'ü'/ *v.*, to lie with covers over the head

Bamámąxè /bä-moⁿ-moⁿ-xä'/ *v.*, to continuously walk forward and downward while bending the knees and bending part of the body, as in sneaking up on somebody or something

Bamáši /bä-moⁿ-shē/ *v.*, push up, as in pushing a thing above the head to a shelf

Bamáxe /bä-moⁿ-xä/ *v.*, stoop, bend forward, to bend over with head down, stoop down

Banáge /bä-noⁿ-gä/ *v.*, push, to push something on wheels, such as a wagon or wheelbarrow

Banáge /bä-noⁿ-gä/ *v.*, roll, to roll something on wheels or to roll a ball

Bánahò(-hù) /bä'-nä-hō' (hü')/ *n.*, owl

Bánikì /bä'-nē-kē'/ *n.*, Bannock Tribe of Native Americans

Bap'áde /bä-p'oⁿ-dä/ *v.*, rock, to move back and forth or cause something to move back and forth

Bap'áp'áde /bä-p'oⁿ-p'oⁿ-dä/ *v.*, rock, to continuously move back and forth, as with a table or chair with uneven legs

Bas'į' /bä-s-ēⁿ'/ *adv.*, head first, usu. refers to falling forward with the head down

Bašáda /bä-shoⁿ-thä/ *v.*, to empty, to pour out any substance, liquid or solid, from a container

Basása /bä-sä'-sä/ *n.*, something that is cut up, 1. segmented, something that has been divided up in pieces, as with a log 2. partition, usu. refers to real estate, namely, inherited fractionalized land (*mążá basása*, lands held in trust by the federal government and inherited by succeeding generations of the original allottee's family)

Bašášádà /bä-shoⁿ-shoⁿ-thä'/ *v.*, to spill out continuously, to empty something continuously from a container

Basé /bä-sä'/ *n./v.*, partition, divider, something that separates two or more things; *mążá bašè*, partition of acreage of land

Bašédą /bä-shä'-thoⁿ/ *v.*, pay for, pay for something

Baší /bä-shē'/ *v.*, to drive, steer, chauffeur, etc.

Bašíʼšíbe /bä-shē'-shē'-bā/ *adj./v.*, to open continuously by pushing (*tʼižébe té ~ dédaì*, he continuously ~ the doors)

Bašíbe /bä-shē'-bā/ *adj./v.*, to open by pushing, usu. used when something, such as a door, could not be normally opened (*tʼižébe ké ~ dédaì*, he ~ the door)

Bašíbe /bä-shē'-bā/ *v.*, push open, as in to ~ a door with the weight of the body

Basį́mągdè /bäs-ēⁿ'-moⁿ-gthā'/ *n.*, somersault , a movement usu. done by children in which the body is rolled over forward, head on the ground, before returning to an upright position

Bašíšižè /bä-shē'-shē-zhā'/ *v.*, to crack, crumble, or crush a solid substance continuously

Bašíže /bä-shē'-zhā/ *v.*, to crack, crumble, or crush with the use of the hands by pressing

Baskíde /bä-skē'-thā/ *adj.*, incensed, being incensed or infuriated, being aroused with anger within although not expressed openly (A person in such a state may suddenly act upon his/her emotions.)

Baskíde /bä-skē'-thā/ *adj.*, aggravated, irritated, provoked

Baskíde /bä-skē'-thā/ *v.*, anger, being incensed or infuriated

Baskíde /bä-skē'-thā/ *v.*, exasperate, upset, to be beside yourself, irritate

Basnáde /bä-snä'-dā/ *adj.*, high, elevated, far above ground, usu. refers to somebody or something standing high above

Basnú /bä-snü'/ *v.*, push, pushing and sliding something on a flat surface

Bašnúʼde /bä-shnü'-dā/ *v.*, remove, to remove by prying, as in removing a sealed lid; *bašnúʼšnudè*, to take off hurriedly by prying, piece by piece

Bašnúde /bä-shnü'-dā/ *v.*, take off, as in taking a nail from a board by the action of pushing with the hands and the use of a tool (e.g., a claw hammer or crowbar); *bašnúšnúde*, take off continuously, as in taking a nail from a board by the action of pushing with the hands and the use of a tool (e.g., a claw hammer or crowbar)

Basták'ì /bä-stä-k'ē'/ *v.*, glance, to glance off of the body of somebody or of an animal; *bisták'ì*, to glance off after pressing down on an object; *disták'ì*, to glance off of something by use of the hands; *gasták'ì*, to glance off of something by force; *nąsták'ì*, to glance off of the feet or a wheel

Bat'ą́t'ądì /bä-t'oⁿ-t'oⁿ-thēⁿ'/ *v.*, push, connotes causing a person to walk fast, as in a stumbling fashion, repeatedly holding and pushing (*udą́i kí, waną́še amà ~ adí adái*, when arresting him, the police, ~ing him, took him)

Bat'é /bä-t'ā'/ *n./v.*, cluster, a group of things or people that are tightly connected (*niášigà ma ~ gdiáma*, the people ~ together)

Bat'é /bä-t'ā'/ *n.*, clump, as in a thicket or a clump of grass

Bat'é /bä-t'ā'/ *v.*, pile, to pile something or lay something one upon another, as with a pile of clothing or papers

Bat'é' /bä-t'ā'/ *n.*, heap, pile, things that are thrown atop one another in no order

Bat'éte /bä-t'ā'-tā/ *n.*, clumps, as in clumps of bushes and trees growing scattered out in the prairie; *baną́ną*, clumps

Bat'úidáda /bä-t'ü'-ē-thä'-thä/ *v.*, gallop at the gait of a horse

Bawé'gdìʼsagì /bä-wā'-gthē'-sä-gē'/ *n.*, cheese, solid food made from milk from mammals

Bawégdì /bä-wā'-gthē'/ *n.*, butter, lit., churning to butter, a soft, creamy spread

Bawíwíze /bä-wē'-wē'-zā/ *adj.*, winding, zigzagging, as of a roadway that has lots of curves

Baxá' /bä-xoⁿ'/ *v.*, thrust, to stab or ~ a knife into a wild animal or a person

Baxáp'i /bä-xä'-p'ē/ *v.*, to stick a knife or something like a knife into a tree, a wall, a log, or a board

Baxdíxdi /bä-xthē'-xthē/ *v.*, mash, usu. refers to food, as in potato salad or a purée

Baxdú'xdu'dè /bä-xthü'-xthü-dä'/ *v.*, peel, to continuously peel by pushing apart

Baxdúde /bä-xthü'-dä/ *v.*, pry, to pull apart or open with a tool such as a lever or crowbar

Baxdúde /bä-xthü'-dä/ *v.*, push apart, an action of pushing with an instrument to remove a covering from something (he used a tool to ~ the bark from the trees to make teepee poles)

Baxdúde /bä-xthü'-dä/ *v.*, peel, to peel by pushing apart

Baxiáda /bä-xēä'-thä/ *v.*, pushed down, to push down something, usu. refers to an upright structure (he ~ a rotten tree)

Baxíáda /bä-xē'-ä'-thä/ *v.*, fell, push down by force or the body or machinery

Baxíxe /bä-xē'-xä/ *v.*, crack, to crack by applying pressure

Baxt'é /bäx-t'ä'/ *n.*, strawberry, a small, edible sweet red berry, *Fragaria ananassa*

Baxú /bä-xü/ *n.*, ridge, a long, narrow, elevated piece of land that runs continuously over a distance

Baxú /bä-xü/ *v.*, mark, to ~ a line or make a visible impression on the surface of something

Baxú /bä-xü/ *v.*, write, to write, as in writing a letter

Bažą́žą /bä-zhoⁿ'-zhoⁿ/ *adj.*, crooked, anything that appears to be or is ~ or uneven, as in a ~ board, land that has many knolls, a bumpy road

Bazí'zi /bä-zē'-zē/ *n.*, elasticity, flexibility

Bažį́de /bä-zheⁿ'-dä/ *v.*, 1. to stick one's hands

into a crevice or hole, as in reaching into a hollow log to catch a rabbit 2. put one's hands into one's pants pockets

Bažį́de /bä-zhēⁿ'-dä/ *v.*, prod, to poke, thrust

Bažúžu /bä-zhü'-zhü/ *adj.*, lumpy, like something having lumps, not smooth or even

Bdą́' /bthoⁿ'/ *adj.*, odoriferous, giving off an odor, sometimes morally offensive, sometimes a pleasant smell

Bdą́' /bthoⁿ'/ *v./n.*, smell, an odor or smell that can be either agreeable or disagreeable ("the perfume ~ good"; "the garbage can has a bad ~")

Bdá'adihà /bthä-ä-thē-hä'/ *v./n.*, spread, the range over which things extend (when a group of things are arranged some distance apart)

Bdą́'ze /bthoⁿ'-zä/ *adj.*, narrow, thin, slender

Bdáda /bthä'-thä/ *adj.*, level, being horizontal, something that is even with the ground—the Niobrara River in Nebraska, e.g., is called Níúbdadà because of its flat or level appearance in the landscape

Bdą́ p'iáži /bthoⁿ' p'ēä'-zhē/ *adj.*, putrid, as in something that smells rotten, decaying, rank, decomposing

Bdáska /bthä'-skä/ *adj.*, flat, plane

Bdáškadadà /bthä'-shkä-thä-thä'/ *v.*, speaking to stir them up in their minds

Bdáwagazù /bthä'-wä-gä-zü'/ *v.*, I told it clearly, to voice something to a group with absolute clarity

Bdą́xt'i /bthoⁿ'-xt'ē/ *n.*, scent, an odor in the air that is left by a person or animal and can be traced

Bdazáde /bthä-zä'-thä/ *v.*, tear, slit, rip, rend; *bdábdázadè*, continuous tearing, ripping

Bdazáde /bthä-zä'-thä/ *v.*, tore, *past. part.* of tear, slit, rip, rend

Bdą́ze /bthoⁿ'-zä/ *adj.*, slender, having small proportions in width and height, long and thin

Bdé /bthã'/ *v., 1st pers. sing.,* going, I'm going (over there or someplace)

Bdé'k'ažįgà /bthã'-kä-zhēⁿ-gä/ *n.,* nickel, 1. five-cent piece 2. proper female name in the Đíxidą clan of the Ponca people

Bdé'ka /bthã'-kä/ *adj.,* thin, sheer

Bdé'xe /bthã'-xä/ *n.,* small crane, one of many species of cranes

-bdį' /bthēⁿ/ *pron./suffix,* me, commonly used with *wíʃbdį,* it's ~, or *é·bdį̀,* it's ~

Bdí'bexį /bthē'-bä-xēⁿ/ *v.,* swept, *past t. sing.* of sweep—I swept

Bdí'wagazù /bthē'-wä-gä-zü/ *v.,* to personally examine something closely

Bdibdída /bthē-bthēⁿ-thä/ *adj.,* warped, something that is misshapen, bent, twisted; something that is out of shape from a straight form

Bdípe /bthē'-pä/ *n.,* something that is powdery, chalky, a fine grind, reduced to powder or dust

Bdípe /bthē'-pä/ *n.,* talcum powder, derived from a clay mineral, hydrated magnesium silicate (The products of talcum include fragrant cosmetic powder that women use for keeping skin dry and that is used on babies to prevent rashes.)

Bdúga /bthü'-gä/ *pron.,* all, the whole of, entirety

Betą' /bä-toⁿ/ *v.,* fold, to bend a piece of paper, cloth, a flag, clothing, etc. over itself

Bə /bə/ *interj.,* expression, an expression that connotes the element of surprise over some action or statement made by another; also the element of surprise in seeing something unusual or different

Bí /bē'/ *prefix,* usu. used with verbs, action done by pressing

Bi'bį'bįžè /bē-bēⁿ'-bēⁿ-zhä'/ *v.,* whimpering, continuously whimpering, weeping, sniveling

Bį'bį'že /bēⁿ'-bēⁿ'-zä/ *v.,* whimper, weep, snivel

Bí'ze /bē'-zä/ *adj.,* used to describe dry substances, including land that has very little water; *bi'bí'ze, v.,* dry, to make dry by pressing down and wringing out with the hands; *bízedè, v.,* dry, to let dry, or to dry by a mechanical device; *gabíze, v.,* to dry by flapping in the wind, e.g., clothes on the clothesline; *nąbíze, v.,* dry, 1. to dry by using a modern dryer 2. to dry caused by driving an auto over a wet, muddy road

Bí'zedè /bē'-zä-thä'/ *v.,* dehydrate, dry, to remove water from to make dry

Biákigdašą /bē-ä'-kē-gthä-shoⁿ'/ *v.,* turn over, refers to a vehicle turning over

Biáza /bē-ä'-zä/ *v.,* rock, to rock something like a baby's cradle

Biázazà /bē-ä'-zä-zä'/ *v.,* rocking, to sway to and fro, backward and forward, or from side to side, usu. caused by pushing with the feet (she sat ~ the chair)

Bibdá'skà /bē-bthä'-skä'/ *v.,* flatten, to cause something to become flat by pressing down with the hands

Bibdí'bdi'dà /bē-bthē'-bthē-thä'/ *v.,* to continuously bend, turn, or twist a thing by use of a tool

Bibdí'dà /bē-bthēⁿ'-thä'/ *v.,* to bend, turn, twist by use of a tool

Bibdúbdúga /bē-bthü'-bthü'-gä/ *n.,* cornball dumpling, finely ground corn cooked with beans

Bibút'a /bē-bü'-t'ä/ *v.,* round, to make something round

Bidíąba /bē-thē'-oⁿ'-bä/ *v.,* shine, to polish, to restore a luster on something that was dull

Bidúže /bē-dü'-zhä/ *v.,* to burst something open with an instrument, as in breaking open a yolk in an egg cooked over easy

Bidúže /bē-dü'-zhä/ *v.,* squash, to squash by

pressing down on; *badúže*, squash by using force; *didúže*, squash with the use of the hands; *gadúže*, squash by hitting; *nạdúže*, crush or mash with the feet

Bihégažì /bē-hā'-gä-zhē'/ *v.*, to make a loud sound by pressure, e.g., to press down on a balloon until it pops

Bihúhut'ạ̀ /bē-hü'-hü-t'oⁿ'/ *v.*, to continuously blow a horn or whistle

Bihút'ạ̀ /bē-hü'-t'oⁿ'/ *v.*, 1. to blow a horn or whistle; *bihúhut'ạ̀*, to continuously blow a horn or whistle 2. pressing down on the horn in an automobile

Biká /bē-kä'/ *v.*, wipe, to wipe up, to clean; *biká, 2nd pers. sing.*, you wipe or clean it

Biná'gdè /bē-nä'-gthä'/ *v.*, to bother and annoy another person or an animal

Biná'ži /bē-nä'-zhē/ *v.*, extinguish, to put out, quench, douse a fire by pressing down on it with something in the hands, as in using a wet cloth to put out a small fire; *dináži*, to turn off a light switch; *ganáži*, wind (~ a kerosene lamp, ~ a grass fire with a wet gunnysack)

Bináka /bē-nä'-koⁿ/ *n.*, flashlight, 1. a hand-held device with batteries and bulb to make light 2. *v.*, to cause a light to come on

Bináka tigdè /bē-nä'-koⁿ tē-gthä'/ *v.*, flash, to give off light suddenly from some source

Bináxdi̜ /bē-nä'-xthēⁿ/ *v.*, to start a fire by blowing on embers

Bip'ámạxè /bē-p'ä'-moⁿ-xä'/ *v.*, bow, making somebody bow by pressing down on their head

Bisá'du /bē-sä'-thü/ *v.*, rattling, to make a rattling noise by pressing down on something

Bisá'sa /bē-sä'-sä/ *v.*, to cut to pieces by pressing a sharp instrument onto a thing; *nạsása*, to cut to shreds by stepping on continuously or driving over continuously

Bisá'sadù /bē-sä'-sä-thü'/ *v.*, rattling, to make

a continuous rattling noise by pressing down on something

Bisábe /bē-sä'bä/ *v.*, blacken, to make something black by pressing down on

Bisáda /bē-sä'-dä/ *v.*, pressed, to remove unwanted creases from a piece of cloth using a hot iron

Biskábe /bē-skä'-bä/ *v.*, 1. to paste something onto some surface 2. refers to smearing or spreading a greasy, wet substance on or over something

Bišná'hà /bē-snä'-hä'/ *v.*, smooth, to smooth a surface, polishing, applying furniture polish to treat wood

Bisp'ą́ /bē-sp'oⁿ'/ *v.*, nudge, 1. to press on or poke somebody gently 2. *disp'ą́*, to nudge somebody gently with the hands; *basp'ą́*, to nudge somebody with the arm, elbow, or knee

Bisp'áspà /bē-sp'ä'-spä/ *v.*, creep, to move along with the body bent and close to the ground

Bisp'é /bē-sp'ä'/ *n.*, crouch, act of bending low close to the ground

Bispé /bē-sp'ä'/ *v.*, hunker, to sit on one's heels, squat down; *bispáspa*, to continually crouch, walking close to the ground

Bistá /bē-stä'/ *v.*, press, press down, bear down on

Bit'éga /bē-t'ä'-gä/ *adj.*, polish, lit., to cause to be new, refers to putting a new gloss, luster, or smoothness on an old surface

Bit'éga /bē-t'ä'-gä/ *v.*, refinish, as in to sand and polish old furniture

Bit'ú'tubè /bē-t'ü'-t'ü-bä/ *v.*, ground, to grind or crumble continuously

Bit'úbe /bē-t'ü'-bä/ *v.*, ground, to grind or to crumble

Bixá· /bē-xoⁿ'·/ *v.*, 1. to inflate by blowing, to blow up a balloon, to air up a tire 2. to blow on embers to start a fire

Bixą́’ /bē-xoⁿ/ *v.*, break, to cause something to come to pieces; *bixą́’xą̀*, pressing down on something, breaking it into pieces by use of the hands; *baxą́’*, to break something by pushing down; *baxą́xą*, to continue to break something to pieces by pushing down; *dixą́’*, to break something with the hands; *dixą́’xą̀*, break, continue to break something to pieces with the hands; *gaxą́’*, to break something to pieces by force; *gaxą́’xą*, break, to continue breaking something to pieces by force; *nąxą́’*, to break something to pieces by running over it or by stepping on it; *nąxą́’xą*, to continue to break something to pieces by running over or stepping on it

Bixá’xabè /bē-xä’-xä-bā/ *v.*, scrape, to take off continuously or repeatedly

Bixábe /bē-xä’-bā/ *v.*, scrape, scrape the skin, to take off, as in husks from corn or hulls from nuts

Bixą́í’ /bē-xoⁿ-ē/ *v.*, *past t.*, to be broken, fractured, cracked, caused something to separate into pieces

Bixt’ą́ /bē-xt’oⁿ/ *v.*, to pour, to cause to flow, to cause to drain out of something

Bixt’ą́’xt’ą /bē-xt’oⁿ-xt’oⁿ/ *v.*, to pour, to cause to continuously flow, to cause to continuously drain out of something

Biza’e /bē-zä-ā/ *n.*, noise, a loud rattling, smacking noise; *bizá’za’è*, *v.*, to continuously make a loud rattling, smacking noise

Bízext’iáži /bē’-zā-xt’ē-ä’-zhē/ *adj.*, damp, slightly wet, said of something that still has some moisture in it

Bižú’ /bē-zhü/ *v.*, rub, 1. to remove grain by rubbing 2. to rub parts of the body, as in a massage

Bižú’žu /bē-zhü’-zhü/ *v.*, rub, 1. to continuously remove grain by rubbing 2. to con-

tinuously rub parts of the body, as in a massage

Búbut’ą̀ /bü’-bü-t’oⁿ/ *adj.*, rounded, refers to a number of things that are rounded; usu. refers to things that are made, such as balls of various sizes, certain foods being prepared to be cooked

Búšna /bü’-shnä/ *adj.*, dull, something that is rounded, blunted, such as a knife or spear point

Bút’a /bü’-t’ä/ *adj.*, circular, round, spherical, rotund, ring-shaped

Bút’a udíšą /bü’-t’ä ü-thē’-shoⁿ/ *v.*, circle, go around

Bút’audíšą /bü’-t’ä-ü-thē’-shoⁿ/ *adv.*, around (he circled ~ the building)

C

This letter is not included in the Ponca alphabet.

Č

č /ch/ second consonant in the Ponca alphabet

Č’éškà /ch-ā’-shkä/ *adj.*, short, not long

Č’ú’ /ch-ü’/ *n.*, green, the color green (*péžit’ù* is an Omaha reference to the color green, from a blue-tinted plant)

Č’ú’ /ch-ü’/ *n.*, spittle, saliva, or something ejected from the mouth

-čábe /chä’-bā/ *adv. suffix*, very, exceedingly, intensely, as in *usníčábe*, very cold (The suffix *-čábe* is a derivative of the word *át’ašą̀*, which means very, exceedingly, and intensely.)

-čábe /chä’-bā/ *adj.*, *suffix*, much; *usníčabè*, much cold, very cold

Čák’ì /chä’-k’ē/ *v.*, slouch, 1. to walk or sit lazily or in a lazy way; an extremely casual way of walking 2. a lazy way of keeping house

Čáza /chä'-zä/ *adj.*, messy, untidy, cluttered, in disarray

Čú' /chü'/ *v.*, spit, to spit out or expel saliva from the mouth

D

d /də/ third consonant in the Ponca alphabet

đ /th/ fourth consonant in the Ponca alphabet

Đá /thä'/ *prefix*, action done by mouth or by biting

Đą́ /tho^n'/ *adj.*, the (used with nouns that describe parts of the human body; also used with circular objects; can be either singular or plural)

Dá' /dä'/ *v.*, freeze, ice up, usu. refers to anything that becomes frozen by extreme cold temperature

Dą́'be /do^n'-bā/ *v.*, see, visualize, view, behold, to see or observe

Dą́'bedįgè /do^n'-bā-the^n-gā'/ *adj.*, neglected, lacking care, usu. refers to someone who is homebound without care or is disabled and not visited

Dą́'dè /do^n'-thä/ *v.*, love, expression of extreme love or liking for a man or woman or between a boy and girl; a love or liking of a person that interferes with other matters in life

Dá'dį /dä'-the^n/ *adj./v.*, intoxicated, drunk, drunken

Đa'é'tewadè /thä-ä'-tā-wä-thä'/ *adj.*, pathetic, pitable

Đa'í'í'da /thä-ē'-ē'-thä/ *n.*, itch, prickling, tingling, itchiness

Đá't'a /thä'-t'ä/ *adj.*, left handed, the dominant use of the left hand, anything done with the left hand

Đá't'àt'adišą̀ /thä'-t'ä'-t'ä-thē-sho^n'/ *adj.*, left side, toward the left of a person

Đaá' /thä-ä'/ *adj./v.*, unconsumed, uneaten, could not consume all the food, usu. refers to food that is left in the dish

Đaá't'ašą̀ /thä-ä'-t'ä-sho^n'/ *v.*, exaggerated, overstated, refers to bragging about the performance of a person's accomplishments; *điá't'ašą̀*, performing or doing something over and beyond what is necessary

Đábdì /thä'-bthē/ *n.*, three, the number three (3)

Đábdį'ą̀ /thä'-bthe^n-o^n'/ *n.*, thrice, three times

Đábdį'dą̀dà /thä'-bthe^n-tho^n-tho^n'/ *n.*, threes, by threes, as in they came in three at a time

Dábewadè /do^n'-bā-wä-thä'/ *n.*, something to behold, a thing to see or view, as in seeing the Grand Canyon

Đadą́ /thä-do^n'/ *v.*, draw in air, to draw air into the lungs

Đadą́bažì /thä-tho^n'-bä-zhē'/ *v.*, derogate, put down, to make a remark to or about another person in an insulting or critical manner

Dádąbè /do^n'-do^n-bä'/ *adj.*, watchful, observant, vigilant

Đadé /thä-dä'/ *v.*, tell of, telling the name of a person or thing

Đadéxt'ì /thä-dä'-xt'ē'/ *v.*, emphasize, lit., say again (strongly), to stress or put emphasis on something to somebody

Dádiamà /dä'-thē-ä-mä'/ *n.*, drunkard, those who habitually drink alcoholic beverages; *xúbe* (The term *xubé* originally was used in relation to those who possessed medicines that were considered sacred as well as relics that were also kept sacred by the people. In the early twentieth century the term was applied to those who imbibed too often. A man was said to have sat by the trail that led into a city, waiting for a free ride on a wagon. After he sat for a very long time, a man saw him lift his arms up, probably stretching, and said of him jokingly, "Xúbe k'igáxaìte . . . " [He is making himself use mysterious powers to catch a ride.] Being overheard, the term *xubé* became commonly used for those who drink much.)

Đadídį /thä-dēⁿ-dēⁿ/ *v.*, voice loudly, make an extreme pronouncement with the vocal cords

Đadíge /thä-thēⁿ-gā/ *v.*, exhaust, to make an exceptional verbal display of words to keep somebody from saying more, usu. making another person's words seem less than important

-dadíše /thä-thēⁿ-shä/ *pron./v.*, *suffix*, you are, you have (The suffix usu. refers to Wak'ą́da or somebody who outstandingly has special abilities or talent, as in *Wak'ą́da bǘga íšp'ahą ~*, God ~ knowledgeable of all things.)

Đaédąbè /thä-ä'-thoⁿ-bä'/ *v.*, to cause someone to show up after speaking of them (It was believed that to speak of someone excessively would cause that person to come by or show up.)

Đaéde /thä-ä'-thä/ *n.*, love, 1. agape love (God love) 2. philia love (love for family, friends, etc.)

Đaéde /thä-ä'-thä/ *v.*, pity, to have sympathy for or feel sorry for, to have compassion for someone who is suffering or unhappy

Đaéga /thä-ä'-gä/ 1. *adj.*, haggard, worn down, gaunt 2. *n.*, someone who has an exhausted appearance

Đaégą /thä-ä'-goⁿ/ *adj./n.*, ugly, unattractive, a person or thing that is not good to look at

Đaégą /thä-ä'-goⁿ/ *adj.*, wretched, pitiable, dejected, deplorably bad in body, dismal, awful

Đaék'idè /thä-ä'-k'ē-thä/ *adj.*, unhappy or remorseful

Đaétewadè /thä-ä'-tä-wä-thä/ *v.*, to be pitiful, pitiable, unfortunate, sad, poor

Đagdégdešnà /thä-gthä'-gthä-shnä'/ *v.*, muddled, messed up, mixed up, refers to mixing the nature of stories or songs confusedly

Đagdúze /thä-gthü'-zä/ *v.*, speaking to, asking of, requesting information causing confusion to the person spoken to, as in a cross-examination or interrogation of a witness in court

Đahą́ /thä-hoⁿ/ *v.*, to praise, 1. to glorify, make expressions of worshipping God 2. *n.*, giving honor to somebody who did something praiseworthy

Đahą́wadè /thä-hoⁿ'-wä-thä/ *adj.*, praiseworthy, laudable, usu. refers to Wak'ą́da (God) or Wak'ą́da Ižíge (Son of God)

Đahé /thä-hä'/ *v.*, grasp with mouth, hold onto with mouth, hold with mouth, as a dog may carry a stick in its mouth

Đahé'gažì /thä-hä'-gä-zhē'/ *adv.*, loudly, to voice words loudly or deafeningly in order to be heard above other sounds

Đahí'de /thä-hē'-dä/ *v.*, tease, to taunt or kid somebody

Đahíde /thä-hēⁿ'-dä/ *v.*, to be able to speak or sing (~ *akégą*, so he/she thinks he/she can speak or sing) (The term usu. is used negatively, as in questioning a person's ability.)

Đahúni /thä-hü'-nē/ *v.*, inhale, to breathe in air

Đahúni /thä-hü'-nē/ *v.*, swallow, gulp down, to cause food to pass through the mouth and throat into the stomach without much chewing (A colloquial expression or slang suggesting taking food into one's system without chewing.)

Đaį' /thä-ēⁿ'/ *adj.*, unchewable, 1. meat that

is sinewy, stringy, fibrous, or just tough to chew 2. *v.*, to spit up, vomit

Đákà /thoⁿ-kä/ *adj.*, the, definite article (describes animate subjects and is in the plural form; like the article *díkè*, it is a descriptive word that is used in connection with the position a person or object is in, i.e., at rest, reclining, or sitting—connotes a place such as home, office, or a familiar place)

Đanánì /thä-noⁿ-nē/ *v.*, mistaken, *2nd pers. sing.*, mistaken, you are (were) mistaken

Đanánì /thä-noⁿ-nē-ēⁿ/ *v.*, *2nd pers. pl.*, mistaken, you all are (were) mistaken

Đašádu /thä-shä'-thü/ *adj.*, guttural, gruff sounding, a deep, raspy sound

Đasági /thä-sä'-gē/ *adv.*, loudly, usu. refers to words that are strong enough to make an impression on another or a group (The term also describes scolding children.)

Đási /thä'-sē/ *n.*, James O. Dorsey, Ponca corruption of the name *Dorsey* (James Owen Dorsey, October 31, 1848–February 4, 1895, was an Episcopalian missionary and linguist who recorded the Ponca language ca. 1870–71 while working with the Ponca near current Niobrara, Nebraska.)

Đašíge /thä-shē'-gä/ *v.*, decry, to say something in response to what someone says about a report or tale that is unbelievable

Đašíže /thä-shē'-zhä/ *v.*, crack, to ~ with the teeth

Đáškadadà /thä'-shkä-thä-thä/ *v.*, contemplate, cause to contemplate or "stir up in their minds"

Đaškí' /thä-shk'ē/ *v.*, chew, to chew, gnaw on food with teeth

Đašná /thä-shnoⁿ/ *n.*, error, the act of not speaking or singing correctly, an unintentional mistake

Đasní /thä-snē/ *v.*, devour, eating something up, nothing left

Đasní'bè /thä-snē'-bä/ *v.*, lick, to lick

Đašnúde /thä-shnü-dä/ *v.*, cough, to extract phlegm from the chest or cough up phlegm

Đašp'é /thä-shp'ä/ *n.*, bite off, biting off a piece of food, such as a cookie

Đastásták'i /thä-st'ä'-st'ä-k'ē/ *v.*, lit., to throw around (speak) words (Among the Ponca in the early years of acculturation, the term usu. referred to a person who, supposedly, knew how to speak the English language expertly, as in *wáxe i'yaì kí, ~ íye nái*, when she speaks she can just throw white man words around.)

Đašúde /thä-shü-dä/ *v.*, blow smoke, as in smoking a pipe, cigarette, etc.

Đašúde /thä-shü-dä/ *n.*, smoking, exhaling smoke (The term apparently became used after cigarettes and cigars were introduced.)

Đat'á' /thä-t'oⁿ/ *v.*, drink, to drink any liquid beverage; *i'đat'à*, something to drink from—dipper, cup, hands

Đat'á'xì /thä-t'ä'-xē/ *v.*, to make a loud cracking sound with the teeth while eating nuts

Đat'éxt'ì /thä-t'äⁿ-xt'ē/ *v.*, to speak of something as being very difficult to accomplish

Đat'íze /thä-t'ēⁿ'-zä/ *n.*, nazalize, talk through the nose

Đaté' /thä-tä/ *v.*, eat, to eat, to consume food

Đatí' /thä-tē/ *v.*, *2nd pers. sing.*, arrive, you ~ here

Đaúja /thä-ü'-joⁿ/ *v.*, make one wish for something that somebody is eating—fruit, candy (derivative of *đaúđa*, to make something sound good or to eat something that appears to be good)

Đawá /thä-wä/ *v.*, count, to engage in the act of counting (*~ ukíhi*, he can ~)

Đawágazù /thä-wä'-gä-zü/ *adj.*, correct, to tell something or say something correctly, as in *~ uwíđagà*, Tell it ~ly to him

Đáxe /thä'-xā/ *n.*, lungs, the two organs that breath is taken into; *t'é'đáxè*, bison or bovine lungs

Đáxe /thä'-xā/ *n.*, melon, the edible, fleshy part of the melon, of the family Cucurbitaceae

Đaxp'ą́' /thä-xp'oⁿ/ *n.*, mudhen, the American coot

Đáxt'à /thä'x-t'ä/ *v.*, to bite (*šánudà áka, niášigà đįkè ~ì*, the dog ~ the man); *đaxà*, to break something by biting; *gđáxt'à*, to bite himself as in biting his lip or tongue

Đaxt'áži /thä-xt'ä'-zhē/ *adj.*, uninteresting, boring, someone who says that something was uninteresting

Đaxt'áži /thä-xt'ä'-zhē/ *v.*, belittle, degrade, put down, usu. refers to something done, performed

Đą́xt'ì /thoⁿ-xt'ē/ *adj.*, content, being happy, satisfied, comfortable

Đą́xt'i /thoⁿ-xt'ē/ *v.*, established, settled, settled down or became peaceful

Dą́xt'ì /doⁿ-xt'ē/ *adv.*, even more so, to a greater extent of something that has already been said or accomplished

Đaxú /thä-xü/ *v.*, suck, to draw liquid out of something, 1. with the mouth, as in using a straw in a soft drink 2. with machinery, as in a dairy's automized milking machines

Đaxúbe /thä-xü'-bā/ *v.*, to be remarkable, recognizing a person who does something extraordinary or significantly noteworthy

Đaxúbe /thä-xü'-bā/ *v.*, slurp, to drink something noisily; to sip, gulp, swig

Đąžą́ /thoⁿ-zhoⁿ/ *adv.*, however, though, nevertheless

Đąžą́ /thoⁿ-zhoⁿ/ *conj.*, although, used to show that something does not happen without something else happening

Đažáwa /thä-zhä'wä/ *v.*, brag, to brag or boast about somebody's accomplishments;

wáđažawà, to brag or boast about a group; *k'igđížawà*, to brag or boast about oneself

Đažáwa /thä-ä'-wä/ *v.*, to make a statement about something that happened that brought great pleasure and delight

Đažáwa /thä-zhä'-wä/ *v.*, to speak of something that was or is impressive or fantastic from one point of view, i.e., the one speaking (*núžįgà đįké, ~ íye nąží te*, he spoke of the boy as being outstanding)

Đažúbažì /thä-zhü'-bä-zhē/ *v.*, disparage, ridicule, criticize, put somebody down

Đé /thä/ *adj./pron.*, this, indicates somebody or something distinct from somebody else or another thing

Đé' /thä/ *v.*, go, to go; *ađái*, went, *past t.* of *go*

Đé'gedì /thä'-gā-dē/ *adv.*, here, refers to something a short distance from where you stand

Đé aną́žįtè /thä' ä-noⁿ'-zhēⁿ-tä/ *n.*, locus, lit., "here I stand" (In ancient Ponca philosophy, an individual sees his/her position at the center of all things created, so his/her position in the universe is at the center, below the zenith and above the nadir. However, he/she oftens says in communications with the Creator, *Ebé bđį́ mą́ži*, I am nothing/nobody.)

Đébahì /thä'-bä-hē/ *n.*, jaw, that part of the facial structure where teeth are set, either the mandible or the maxilla

Đébahì t'ą́gà /thä'-bä-hē' t'oⁿ-gä/ *adj.*, verbose, refers to somebody who uses an excessive number of words and keeps talking

Đédaì /thä'-thäē/ *v.*, *past part.*, sent, 1. to have ~ something (or mailed something) away 2. to cause somebody to be moved from one place to another (refers to a person imprisoned or institutionalized)

Đédąkà /thä'-thoⁿ-kä/ *pron.*, these, refers to people or animals (the plural of *déke*, this)

Đéde /thã'-thã/ *v.t.*, send, to make something move from one place to another (he will ~ a letter to his friend); *gdéde*, to send back

Đédehà wadą́be /thã'-dä-hä' wä-doⁿ'-bä/ *v.*, watch, looking—using the eyes to search without moving the head, to watch somebody or something with peripheral vision

Đédehà wadą́be /thã'-dä-hä' wä-doⁿ'-bä/ *adj. phr.*, side glance, looking to the side without turning the head

Đédewakidè /thã'-thä-wä-kē-thã'/ *n.*, banishment, expulsion (Among the Ponca, banishing from the reservation a person who violates tribal moral codes too often, including those who commit murder. They are not welcomed back.)

Đédįkè /thã'-thēⁿ-kä'/ *adv./n.*, this one, refers to somebody standing close by or somebody spoken of; *déke*, this one, refers to something close by

Đédu /thã'-thü/ *adv.*, here, refers to something in this place, namely, a house, building, land, country, and sometimes our walk of life, as in *dédu ąmádi kedì*, where we live our lives

Đéduadì /thã'-thü-ä-dē'/ *adv.*, here, refers to something in or at this place near where the speaker stands

Đédudítą' /thã'-thü-dē'-toⁿ/ *prep. phr.*, from here (~ this time or place); *edítą*, from there

Đégą /thã'-goⁿ/ *adv.*, this way, like this, like so, instructions on how to do something (~ *gáxagà*, do it ~)

Đegą́ádi /thã-goⁿ'-ä'-dē/ *adv.*, immediately, at once, without delay

Đegą́di /thã-goⁿ'-dē/ *adv.*, now, at the present time or moment (go there ~)

Đégąnądì /thã'-goⁿ-noⁿ-dē'/ *adv. phr.*, when it happens in that manner

Đégihà /thã'-gē-hä'/ *n.*, on our side, 1. used when a Ponca addresses members of the Ponca Tribe 2. refers to the five tribes, namely, the Kaw, Omaha, Osage, Ponca, and Quapaw, who speak the same language

Đéke /thã'-kä/ *adj./pron.*, this, some person or something that is close by the speaker

Đéną /thã'-noⁿ/ *adv.*, this much (measurement), as in showing with hands; *dénądądà*, giving of some things to each of a group of people (~ *waí' dédaì*, he gave away ~) or the accounting for something that remains (~ *ušté*, ~ is left)

Đénǫ́' /thã-noⁿ/ *adv.*, again, "do it again," connotes an action taken one more time

Đénąskà /thã'-noⁿ-skä'/ *adv./adj.*, this size, the accounting of things of the same size; *dénąskaskà*, these sizes

Đéška ídidą̀ /thã'-shkä ē'-thē-doⁿ'/ *n.*, hame, one of two curved pieces placed on the collar of an animal harness to which the traces are attached

Đéškaxdú'a /thã'-shkä-xthü'-ä/ *n.*, esophagus, a muscular tube through which food passes from the pharynx to the stomach

Đét'a /thã'-t'ä/ *n.*, navel, umbilicus, or belly button, a small depression in the center of a person's belly where the umbilical cord detached after birth

Đét'adišą̀ /thã'-t'ä-thē-shoⁿ'/ *adv.*, on this side, toward this side (suggests something close by)

Đét'adišą̀ /thã'-t'ä-thē-shoⁿ'/ *n.*, an object over that way, usu. referring to a direction, a point of reference away from the speaker

Đétą /thã'-toⁿ/ *adv.*, this far, 1. in measurement, in length 2. in making or doing something, as in completing a task in part 3. in time as it relates to the time of day

Đétą́ /thã-toⁿ'/ *n.*, length, extent of distance from here to there; an estimated ~, as in "this long"

Ðétạdạhì /thä'-toⁿ-doⁿ-hē'/ *adv.*, by now, something that happened or was required to happen at or before a particular time

Ðétạha /thä'-toⁿ-hä/ *n.*, height, stature, "this tall"

Ðéxạdè /thä'-xoⁿ-dä/ *n.*, cheek, the part of the face that is soft below the eyes; *déxạdè wahí*, cheekbone

Ðéze /thä'-zä/ *n.*, tongue, the organ inside the mouth of humans and most animals that is used for tasting, swallowing, licking, and in humans, speech; *déze p'asì*, tip of the tongue

Ði /thē'/ *prefix*, action done by use of the hands

Ðí' /thē'/ *pron.*, you; *dìə'ni*, you're the one; *dínạnì*, you only; *dínạket'adišà*, toward you

Dí'xe /dē'-xä/ *v.*, chap, to become sore and cracked by exposure to wind or cold

Dí'xe /dē'-xä/ *n.*, smallpox, an infectious disease caused by two virus variants, variola major and variola minor; orignally known as the pox in England

Ði'zwé žạ́ /thē-zwä' zhoⁿ'/ *v.*, lie, to stay at rest in a horizontal position, to put oneself in a prostrate position on the ground or on a bed

Ðiá' /thē-ä'/ *v.*, can't, contraction of *cannot*; *bдí'a*, I can't; *ní'a*, you can't; *diá'i*, he/she/it/they can't

Ðiá't'ašạ̀ /thē-ä'-t'ä-shoⁿ/ *v.*, embellish, lit., more than, blown up, adding to something—native dance clothing, dancing, or any personal act of speaking or singing

Ðiá'wadè /thē-ä'-wä-thä/ *adj./n.*, unable, a task or situation that is not possible to do or overcome

Ðiạ́ba /thē-oⁿm'-bä/ *n.*, lightning, a flash of light in the sky when there is a thunderstorm

Ðiạ́babà /thē'-oⁿ-bä-bä/ *v.*, scintillate, to emit sparks, sparkling

Ðiạ́babà /thē-oⁿ-bä-bä/ *adj.*, sparkling, dazzling, shining

Díáda /dē'-ä'-thä/ *adj.*, threadbare, said of a piece of old cloth that tears easily

Diáda /dēä'-thä/ *v.*, to be worn, a fabric that is old and easily torn

Ðiákiwahà /thē-ä'-kē-wä-hä'/ *v.*, revert, to change back, as in going back to the original pattern or style

Ðiát'ašạ̀ /thē-ä'-t'ä-shoⁿ'/ *adj./v.*, extreme, doing or making something immoderate

Ðiáxa /thē-ä'-xä/ *v./adj.*, open, an open door or a door left open

Ðiáži /thē-ä'-zhē/ *v.*, change, alter, modify

Ðibдá /thē-bthä/ *v.*, spread out, as in to spread a quilt out, to open a package and spread out the contents

Ðibдá' /thē-bthä/ *v.*, unfold, unfolding, unfurling, spreading out something with the hands; *gabдá*, unfold, unfolding or unfurling by force of wind

Ðibдá'bдazè /thē-bthä'-bthä-zä'/ *v.*, shred, to shred to pieces, to tear to pieces

Ðibдá'skà /thē-bthä'-skä/ *v.*, flatten, to flatten out by the use of the hands only

Ðibдáze /thē-bthä'-zä/ *v.*, tear, to tear, as in tearing a piece of cloth by use of the hands; *dibдábдazè*, to continuously tear to pieces, as by use of the hands; *bibдáze*, tearing a piece of cloth by pressing down; *gabдáze*, tearing a piece of cloth by use of force, such as by the wind

Ðibдí /thē-bthē'/ *v.*, plow, to till the ground or plow up, as in plowing up a field to sow grain

Ðibдí'dà /thē-bthē'-thä'/ *v.*, to bend, as in bending a wire or turning a handle of a door by use of the hands

Ðibдípe /thē-bthē'-pä/ *v.*, sift, to separate particles, as in sifting flour; *ịde'bдìpe, 2nd pers.*, you sifted it for me

Ɖibébetà /thē-bā'-bā-toⁿ/ *v.*, wrap, wrapping something carelessly around a thing

Ɖibéni /thē-bā'-nē/ *v.*, turn, to turn any vehicle by use of the hands, e.g., a horse-drawn wagon, an automobile with a steering device; *nabéni*, to turn a vehicle (horse-drawn wagon, automobile, train) with a steering mechanism that turns at some point, whether on a track or a road; *dibébéni*, turning, making more turns as one travels

Ɖibés'į /thē-bā's-ēⁿ/ *v.*, twist, to twist up; *bibés'į*, twist by pressing down on; *gabés'į*, twist by force; *nabés'į*, twist by stepping on or driving over

Ɖibéxį /thē-bā'-xēⁿ/ *v.*, sweep, to sweep with a common broom by use of the hands

Ɖidą́ /thē-doⁿ/ *v.*, pull, tow, to draw or pull along behind

Ɖidą́'agì /thē-doⁿ-ä-gē'/ *v./n.*, to jerk, 1. something jerked or yanked away from some source 2. refers to something that is moving and jerking, such as an auto that misfires

Ɖidą́'agìgi /thē-doⁿ-ä-gē'-gē/ *v.*, jerking, refers to something that is moving, an auto that misfires

Ɖidáze /thē-dä'-zā/ *n.*, spark, flash; *didádazè*, sparkle

Ɖídį /dēⁿ-dēⁿ/ *adj.*, rigid, something that is stiff or inflexible

Ɖidíge /thē-theⁿ'-gā/ *v.*, exhaust, deplete, use up, as in there isn't anything left; *gadíge*, use up by hitting, as in hitting limbs of a tree to remove nuts; *nadíge*, use up, as in running out of gasoline; *wénadįgè*, to use theirs up

Ɖidít'a /thē-thē'-t'ä/ *pl. pron.*, yours, refers to things that belong to you

Ɖidít'aì /thē-thē'-t'äē'/ *pl. pron.*, yours, refers to something that belongs to a group of people being spoken to

Ɖiésa /thē-ā'-sä/ *adj.*, unremitting, becoming constant in effort, as in working seriously at a task; may also be applied to some situation or condition

Ɖiéžubà /thē-ā'-zhü-bä/ *n.*, person who is sincere, truthful, honest, straight, and frank

Ɖigdá' /thē-gthä'/ *v.*, unwrap, undo, open something up that was tied together, such as a bundle

Ɖigdą́'p'à /thē-gthoⁿ'-p'ä/ *v.*, to be unadorned, plain, bare, bald, as with hair

Ɖigdé'gdéžè /thē-gthä'-gthä-zhä'/ *v.*, smeared, applied unevenly

Ɖigdégdezè /thē-gthä'-gthä-zhä'/ *v.*, to continuously make something messy

Ɖigdéže /thē-gthä'-zhä/ *v.*, to make something messy

Ɖigdíze /thē-gthē'-zä/ *n.*, electricity, a phenomenal form of energy that is descriptive in electric charge, current, field, electromagnetic wave, chemistry, circuits, power, electronics, etc.

Ɖįgé' /thēⁿ-gä/ *adj.*, gone, 1. used up, consumed, spent; *gadíge*, used up by means of striking or being windblown, usu. refers to pecan and other nut trees; *nadíge*, used up, usu. refers to running out of gas 2. refers to the deceased

Ɖigeátiagdè /thēⁿ-gä-ä'-tē-ä-gthä'/ *v.*, disappear, to go away suddenly

Ɖįgé gáxe /thēⁿ-gä' gä-xä/ *v.*, erase, lit., cause to be gone, to remove, to wipe away

Ɖigétigdè /thēⁿ-gä'-tē-gthä'/ *v.*, vanish, to disappear suddenly, to be here and then gone (The usage entails ancient stories of men possessing powers to disappear from the presence of others only to appear elsewhere. The term is also used in modern times for people who clear a building or any gathering immediately after an event.)

Đigí'gdizè /thē-gē'-gthē-zā'/ *n.*, electrical storm, usu. refers to extreme continuous lightning

Đigúgúže /thē-gü'-gü'-zhā/ *n.*, zigzag, a series of short turns and angles

Đigúže /thē-gü'-zhā/ *adj.*, bent, curved, crooked, not straight—recently applied to people who are dishonest or are involved in criminal activity; *đigúgúže*, zigzag, more than one curve or bend in a thing

Đihą́ /thē-hoⁿ'/ *v.*, to lift, elevate, lift up, hoist

Đihébe /thē-hā'-bā/ *v.*, to lessen, to decrease or minimize

Đihébeàdì /thē-hā'-bā-ä'-dē'/ *v.*, 1. do a little less (Ponca crafts, namely, dance paraphernalia, were not gaudy but very conservative. Elders said *simplicity* was the keyword for creating one's dance or ceremonial clothing.) 2. in construction, to shorten the material being used, e.g., a board or a pole

Đihí·de /thē-hē'--dā/ *v.*, lower, let down, refers to lowering a thing or dimming the light, as in *nákąkè đihídagà*, turn the light down

Đihįde /thē-hēⁿ'-dā/ *n.*, ability, capacity or ability to do something with the hands, such as repairing or making something

Đihút'ą /thē-hü'-t'oⁿ/ *v.*, to cause a loud sound, as in honking a car horn with the hands

Điją́' /thē-joⁿ'/ *n.*, oodles, plenty, lots of, loads (usu. used in jest, referring to one getting money, but can be used for other things received in excess)

Đik'ú' /thē-k'ü'/ *n.*, cramps, an involuntary, painful muscle contraction

Đikápi /thē-kä'-pē/ *v.*, snatch, to grasp hastily, to grab suddenly

Đįke /thēⁿ'-kā/ *adj.*, the, definite article (designates a particular or specific animate subject; this article has also been described as

a word that is used in connection with the position a person or object is in, i.e., at rest, reclining, or sitting, and connotes a place such as a home, office, or familiar place)

Đikúde /thē-kü'-thā/ *v./n.*, hurry, rush, usu. the urgency to get something done

Đimą́gde /thē-moⁿ'-gthā/ *v.*, to stand something upright, usu. by use of the hands

Đimą́ši /thē-moⁿ'-shē/ *v.*, elevate, to raise, to lift up with the use of the hands or with machinery, to lift something upward from a lower level to a higher level

Điná'ži /thē-nä'-zhē/ *n./v.*, snuff out, to turn off a household oil lamp, to ~ a fire (now, to turn off electric lights)

Đinágdè /thē-nä'-gthā'/ *n.*, abuse, lit., handle as a captive, ill treatment, but not violent

Điną́ge /thē-noⁿ'-gā/ *v.*, operate, 1. to make something function (~ an automobile) 2. to operate a mechanical device with the hands

Đip'á'zè /thē-p'ä'-zā/ *v.*, pull hair, refers to hair pulling between women fighting

Đip'ą́de /thē-p'oⁿ'-dā/ *v.*, shake, rock, or sway by use of the hands, as in leaning on a table; *đip'ąp'ądè*, shaking, continuously rocking, or swaying movement caused by the use of the hands

Đip'áze /thē-p'ä'-zā/ *v.*, pulling hair, tousled, usu. refers to women fighting and pulling each other's hair, causing their hair to be disheveled

Đip'í· /thē-p'ē'·/ *v.*, fix, repair, mend, put right, put back into working order

Đip'iát'ašą̀ /thē-p'ēä'-t'ä-shoⁿ/ *adj.*, 1. skilled, accomplished 2. *n.*, expert, a skilled person in some field, a specialist

Đip'iáži /thē-p'ē'-ä'-zhē/ *v.t.*, ruin, to ruin or spoil a thing with the hands; *nąp'iáži*, to ruin or spoil a thing such as machinery, an auto, a lawn mower; *gap'iáži*, to ruin a thing by force, wind; *bip'iáži*, to ruin by pressing

Đip'íbažì /thē-p'ē'-bä-zhē/ *n.*, faux pas, blunder, a social blunder, as in arriving too early at a formal gathering

Đip'íp'iažì /thē-p'ē'-p'ē-ä-zhē/ *adv.*, haphazardly, chaotically, not uniformly, done without concern for neatness or correctness

Đip'įze /thē-p'ēⁿ-zā/ *v.*, blink, blink the eyes; *įšt'á đip'įze*, blink the eyes

Điš'í'agì /thē-sh-ē'-ä-gē/ *v.*, jerk, to move involuntarily, usu. refers to jerking related to some cause, such as Parkinson's disease or other neurological conditions

Điš'í'ágigì /thē-sh-ē'-ä-gē-gē/ *v.*, jerking continuously, moving involuntarily, usu. refers to jerking continuously related to some cause, such as Parkinson's disease and other neurological conditions

Đis'ú /thēs-ü/ *v.*, scrape, as in "to scrape the wood clean" with the hands

Đisá'đu /thē-sä'-thü/ *v.*, rattle, to rattle an instrument or an object with the hands

Đišá'ge /thē-shä'-gā/ *v.*, curl, to make a curved shape or wave, as with hair

Đisá'sađù /thē-sä'-sä-thü/ *v.*, rattle, to continuously rattle an instrument or an object with the hands

Đišą́da /thē-shoⁿ-thä/ *v.*, spill, to spill; *đišą́'sądà*, spill or sprinkle out continuously any substance, liquid or solid, from a container

Đisé /thē-sā/ *v.*, clip, to cut or trim something, as in trimming the hair with shears

Đišédą /thē-shä'-thoⁿ/ *v.t.*, disassemble, the process of taking something apart; dismantle, to take apart or take to pieces

Đišédą /thē-shä'-thoⁿ/ *v.*, demolish, to break or tear down by hand, machinery, or other forces

Đišíbe /thē-shē'-bā/ *v./adj.*, open, to unlock a door or gate with a key, or to ~ some device with the hands

Đisíhi /thē-sē'-hē/ *v.*, clean, to clean something with the hands

Đisíʃ' žą́ /thē-sēʃ' zhoⁿ/ *v. phr.*, to lie on one's side

Điškέ /thē-shkā/ *adj.*, untied, unhooked, undone

Điskébe /thē-skā'-bā/ *v.*, having a limited idea or clue about a particular subject matter or thing

Điskébe í'bahąžì /thē-skā'-bā ē'-bä-hoⁿ-zhē/ *v.*, doesn't know even in part, 1. doesn't have an inkling (*įdádą gáxaìke ~*, he doesn't have ~ of how to do that) 2. has no knowledge of the subject matter, not even partial knowledge

Điškí /thē-shkē/ *v.*, wring, wringing out; *uđí-škì*, the process of twisting and squeezing out water from washed clothing; *uđíškiškì*, to continuously wring

Điskí' /thē-skē/ *v.*, to be tight, taut, to fix something that is unyielding

Đišną́ /thē-shnoⁿ/ *v.*, drop or dropped, to fumble, something slipping from the hands

Đisną́ /thē-shnoⁿ/ *v.*, rip, to tear apart, to open a piece of cloth by the seams

Đišnáha / thē-shnä'-hä/ *v.*, smooth out, to smooth out something that is rough and bumpy by use of the hands and hand tools

Đišnáp'a /thē-shnä'-p'ä/ *adj.*, clear, rid of any or all physical material—clearing debris, grass, or weeds from the ground; after hair cutting, leaving one nearly bald

Đisné /thē-snä/ *n.*, cut, a minor cut made on the skin by an animal, a scratch made by coming into contact with a sharp object

Đisnéde /thē-snä'-dä/ *v.*, extend, to lengthen, to make longer

Đisnù /thē-snü/ *v.*, pull, to pull with use of the hands or a mechanical device, usu. sliding on the floor or ground

Đisnú' /thē-snü'/ *v.*, to drag, pulling by sliding or dragging an object on the ground, floor, or any flat surface

Đišnúde /thē-shnü'-dā/ *v.*, take off, as in taking a screw off a device or removing one's coat by use of the hands; remove, to remove by use of hands and hand tools; *đišnú'šnudè*, take off continuously, as in taking bolts off some machinery or removing one's clothing

Đišpé /thē-shpā/ *v.*, tear off, to tear off a piece of something by the use of the hands

Đišt'ą́ /thē-sht'oⁿ/ *v.*, stopped, finished, wrapped up, that's the end of it

Đišt'ą́ /thē-sht'oⁿ/ *adj./v.*, free, let go, release, liberate, unleash

Đišt'à /thē-sht'oⁿ/ *v.*, finish, quit, end, bring to an end or close

Đišt'ą́tedì /thē-shtoⁿ-tā-dē/ *adv.*, afterward, subsequent to, or something that will happen after something has been completed

Đištą́ déde /thē-shtoⁿ thā'-thā/ *v.*, release, to set free from confinement or bondage

Đištą́ga /thē-shtoⁿ-gä/ *v.*, *archaic*, soften, to make softer or to become softer by use of the hands and hand tools (Deerskin was drawn over a blunt pole continuously until it became soft and supple; the term applies to modern uses of chemicals to soften skins.)

Đistúbe /thē-stü'-bā/ *n.*, thankfulness, a hand gesture of thankfulness, gratitude, appreciation, etc. to somebody for something (Draw down the right arm and raise the open hand toward an individual as a signal of respect and acknowledgement. It is also a gesture of thanking a person or persons.)

Đišúp'a /thē-shü'-p'ä/ *v.*, tidy up, to put things in order, to neaten or clean up

Điʃ' /thē-ʃ/ *n.*, torso, upper body, chest

Điʃ'idádisądè /thē'-ʃ-ē-thä'-thē-soⁿ-dä'/ *n.*, vest, a man's garment for the upper body

Điʃ' mątè /thēʃ moⁿ-tā/ *n.*, the thoracic cavity

Điʃ'xdú'a /thē-ʃⁿ-xthü'-ä/ *n.*, diaphragm or chest cavity

Điʃmątè /thē'-ʃ-moⁿ-tā/ *n.*, brassiere, bra, a woman's undergarment that covers and supports the breasts

Điʃmątè /thēʃ-moⁿ-tā/ *n.*, internal, in anatomy, refers to that area inside the human form that houses the organs from the heart to the stomach area

Điʃwadák'i'ą̀ /thē'-ʃ'-wä-thä'-k'ē-oⁿ/ *v.*, you brought it upon yourself, refers to someone who did a deed of any sort that caused him/her disappointment, pain, or injury, usu. caused by his/her own intellectual or physical weaknesses

Điʃwawikè /thē-ʃ'-wä-wē-kä'/ *v.*, lit., I mean you; *điʃwadikè*, lit. he/she/it/they mean you

Đit'ą́ /thē-t'oⁿ/ *v.*, feel, to feel or touch with the hands

Đit'à /thē'-t'ä/ *adj.*, your, refers to something that belongs or relates to you (*wadáge ~ ké údą*, ~ hat is a good one)

Đit'ą́ga /thē-t'oⁿ-gä/ *v.*, enlarge, to make bigger or increase size with the hands

Đit'a t'ągà /thē'-t'ä t'oⁿ-gä'/ *n.*, pigeon, of the family Columbidae (There are two birds: pigeons, the larger bird, and doves, the smaller bird. They feed on fruits, seeds, and plants.)

Đit'ì' /thē'-t'ē'/ *n.*, ribs, in human anatomy, the ribs, costae, are long, curved bones that form the rib cage

Đit'i't'ągà /thē'-t'ē-t'oⁿ-gä'/ *n.*, turtledove, refers to the mourning dove, *Zanaida macroura*

Đit'úbè /thē-t'ü'-bā/ *v.*, 1. pinch, tweak, nip, squeeze 2. to break off a piece with the hands

Đi·ú' /thē·-ü'/ *v.*, scratch (an itch); *điú'u'*, 1. to scratch itches continually 2. to scratch around on the ground to find something, as in finding nuts fallen from a tree

Điúdą /thē-ü'-doⁿ/ *v.*, left, to leave a place or site in a clean condition

Điwádíšna /thē-wä'-thē'-shnä/ *v.*, revealed, exposed, something laid open to view; *gí-wadišnà*, to reveal something specifically to somebody

Điwágazù /thē-wä'-gä-zü'/ *v.*, to personally examine something; *ądí'wagazù*, we, as a group of two or more, examined something

Điwágazù /thē-wä'-gä-zü'/ *v.*, examine, scrutinize, scan, inspect

Điwágazubažì /thē-wä'-gä-zü-bä-zhē'/ *v.*, overlook, to miss seeing or determining something, usu. through inspection

Điwásek'ą /thē-wä'-sä-koⁿ'/ *v.*, cause something to go faster by use of the hands, usu. refers to any type of machinery requiring use of the hands

Điwásekà /thē'-wä'-sä-koⁿ'/ *v.*, to go faster, to make something go faster

Điwí' /thē-wēⁿ'/ *v.*, buy, pay money for, purchase; *bđíwį*, I buy or bought; *níwį*, you buy or bought; *ądíwì*, we bought; *ądíwìt'ągatà*, we will have bought

Đixábe /thē-xä'-bā/ *v.*, peel, to remove with the hands, as in peeling a banana

Đixábe /thē-xä'-bā/ *v.*, shuck, to skin, as to remove the husk or pod from something with tools or the hands; *dixá'xabè*, to continuously skin, to continuously shuck in order to remove the husk or pod from something with the hands

Đixábe /thē-xä'-bā/ *v.*, skin, to skin, to scrape one's knee, elbow, etc.

Đixádą /thē-xä'-doⁿ/ *v.*, open the eyes a little, usu. as seen by somebody when an individual is awakening

Đixáxábe /thē-xä'-xä-bā/ *v.*, peel, to continuouly peel with hands, as in peeling a banana

Đixdá /thē-xthoⁿ'/ *v.*, to grasp or clutch some things out of any container (When some things are made available, someone may grab or seize some without considering what and how many.)

Đixdíge /thē-xthē'-gä/ *v.*, to be worn out, something that is old, shabby, dilapidated

Đixé' /thē-xā'/ *v.*, chase, to pursue, to follow something or somebody in order to capture or overtake

Đi·xí /thē·-xē'/ *v.*, awaken, to awaken somebody from sleep, to rouse somebody from sleep

Đixíáda /thē-xē'-ä'-thä/ *v.*, fell, pushed down by force, by use of the hands

Đixídą /thē'-xē-doⁿ/ *n.*, the Đíxidą clan of the Ponca people (Đíxidą men were considered "shock troops," along with the Níkapášnà clan. The Đíxidą men wore a hairstyle with a single braid at the back of the head and were also referred to as *síde adį*, those who have tails.)

Đixt'ą /thē-xt'oⁿ'/ *v.*, drain, to draw off (drain) water from the sink

Đixt'áži /thē-xt'ä'-zhē/ *n./v.*, to see something as unimportant, something that is of no consequence (Note the pronounciation and spelling with *díxt'ažì*, *v.*, *2nd pers. sing.*, you don't like.)

Đixú /thē-xü'/ *n.*, a drawing, a sketch, a picture made with the use of a pencil or pen

Đíxu'sagì'hì /thē'-xü-sä-gē'-hē'/ *n.*, willow tree, a tall willow used for tipi poles

Đíxu'šp'ą̀ hì /thē'-xü-shp'oⁿ' hē'/ *n.*, willow tree, one of the three willows known and used by the Ponca in northern Nebraska and Oklahoma

Đíxutibđábđaxèhì /thē'-xü-tē-bthoⁿ'-bthoⁿ-xä'-hē'/ *n.*, diamond willow tree, a willow known by the Ponca in Nebraska that grows in the north country (The wood is deformed into diamond-shaped segments with alternating colors of red and white when debarked.)

Đixúxu /thē-xü'-xü/ *v.*, look cross, to make an unpleasant face

Đižá' /thē-zhä'/ *v.*, wash, cleanse, rinse; *wadíža*, wash, the act of washing clothes, linens; *k'igdíža*, to wash up

Đižábe /thē-zhä'-bā/ *v.*, to scrape off, to remove a thin layer of a substance from the main body, such as the skin off a potato, the scab off a healing wound

Đizą́de /thē-zoⁿ'-dā/ *adj.*, sitting, ~ motionless or unmoving; *diządext'ì*, sitting pompously

Đizą́de /thē-zoⁿ'-dā/ *adj.*, obstinate, sitting obstinately proud

Đizái /thē-zä'ē/ *v.*, *3rd pers.*, *past part.*, to get, got, he/she/it/they got

Đižážą /thē-zhoⁿ'-zhoⁿ/ *v.*, shaking, shaking something with hands; *gažážą*, shaking by use of wind or other forceful means; *bážážą*, shake by pushing with the body; *bižážą*, shake by pressing down, *nążážą*, shake with the feet

Đizé /thē-zä'/ *v.*, get, obtain, acquire

Đizé /thē-zä'/ *v.*, receive, to receive or to own for oneself something that was offered or given

Đizí' /thē-zē'/ *v.*, stretch, to stretch something out, such as a rubber band

Đizí'zi /thē-zē'-zē/ *v.*, stretch, to stretch something over and over again

Đižį́de /thē-zhēⁿ'-dā/ *v.*, to reach inside, to reach inside some item or structure with the hands

Đižį́de /thē-zhēⁿ'-dā/ *v.*, reach in, reaching in one's pockets

Đižį́ga /thē-zhēⁿ'-gä/ *v.*, make small, downsize, lessen

Đižį́ga /thē-zhēⁿ'-gä/ *adj.*, smaller, lesser, making something smaller; *đižį́ga*, you are young, usu. refers to an elder addressing a young man concerning history or some matter that he may think the younger man doesn't know; *di·žį́ga*, you are younger, refers to age

Đižuáži /thē-zhüä'-zhē/ *v.*, demean, put down, to debase somebody

Đižúážigà /thē-zhü-ä'-zhē-goⁿ'/ *v.*, belittle, put down, discredit, or disgrace, lit., he/she belittled you

Đizúbe /thē-zü'-bä/ *v.*, to make pointed, as in shaping a projectile point or arrowhead

Dú'ba /dü'-bä/ *n.*, four, the number four (4)

Dúádądì /dü-ä'-thoⁿ-dē'/ *adv.*, here, stating something about this place closer to where one is or close at hand

Duádąkà /dü-ä'-thoⁿ-kä'/ *pl. pron.*, these, refers to people or animals here

Đuádįkè /thüä-thēⁿ-kä'/ *adj./pron.*, this, this person or animal standing, sitting, or lying close to the speaker

Duádišà /düä-thē-shoⁿ'/ *prep.*, on this side, around on this side

Duáhidądi /dü-ä'-hē-thoⁿ-dē'/ *adv.*, nearby, something being closer to the speaker

Duáke /düä'-kä/ *adj./pron.*, this, a thing that is in hand or closer to the speaker

Duát'adišà /düä-t'ä-thē-shoⁿ'/ *adv.*, this way, toward this way from another direction (suggests something closer at hand, next to or in the hand)

Duáte /düä'-tä/ *pl. pron.* these, refers to things (plural of *duáke*, this)

Duátet'atà /dü-ä'-tä-t'ä-toⁿ'/ *prep.*, from over there, referring to something that came from a place away from the speaker, usu. pointing to a place or in a certain direction

Dúba /dü'-bä/ *adj.*, some, a few, several, as in number of people or things

Dúda /dü-dä/ *v.*, come here, expression made
to somebody by the one who is speaking,
usu. made to a child

Dúdahà /dü-dä-hä'/ *adj.*, closer, to come
closer or bring the self and/or something
closer

Dúdihà /dü-dē-hä'/ *adv.*, this way, come
closer, or draw near

Đút'ą /thü'-t'oⁿ/ *adj.*, straight, without an
angle, bend, or curve, be exactly vertical or
horizontal; *biđú't̨ą*, to straighten by pressing down on with or without tools; *điđú't'ą*,
to straighten out by use of the hands;
gađú't'ą, to straighten by force with a tool

Dúədišą̀ /dü-ə-thē-shoⁿ'/ *prep.*, this side,
around ~

E

e /ā/ second vowel in the Ponca alphabet

ę /āⁿ/ second nasalized vowel in the Ponca
alphabet

E' /ā/ *v.*, dig, excavate

É' /ā'/ *v.*, say, to express oneself with words;
edé'a?, what was said?, *e'akà*, somebody said;
ábi, he said; *ái*, was said; *áme*, they said; *ehé*,
I said

É'ądigè /ā'-oⁿ-thē-gä'/ *v.*, to assert that something does not matter or is unimportant

É'akà /ā'-ä-kä'/ *interj.*, that's it, that was it,
that was them, that was him/her

E'ą́št'iwì dizá(ga) /ā-oⁿ'-sht'ē-wē' thē-
zä'(gä)/ *v.*, choose, select, or decide to get
from several things

E'bé' /ā-bä'/ *n.*, somebody, a person of significance or a person of position in the community (*niášigà ~ te éí· akè*, that person is ~)

E'bé' /ā-bä'/ *n.*, somebody, an unspecified
person; *ebéšt'iwą̀*, anybody

É'dąbà /ā'-thoⁿ-bä'/ *pron.*, both, as in both
were present

É'dądąbè /ā'-thoⁿ-thoⁿ-bā'/ *v.*, 1. to come
into view in small numbers, usu. refers to
people and animals 2. *adj.*, refers to plants
that sprout thinly, not thick or dense

É'de /ā'-dā/ *adv.*, so, consequently, hence

E'dí· /ā-dē'·/ *n.*, present, here, in attendance,
at hand, etc.

É'gà̀xt'ì /ā'-goⁿ'-xt'ē'/ *adv.*, same, exactly the
same, refers to something that was duplicated, made, or done in the same manner

É'gidą̀ /ā'-gē-doⁿ'/ *n.*, suitable, something
that a person is especially suited for, as in
a place, employment, or their condition,
situation, and/or state of affairs (The Ponca
would include clothing, family composition, and property, including things that are
just right for him/her/them.)

É'gidè /ā'-gē-thä'/ *conj.*, and there was, as it
was, and you know, an introductory statement to something that happened

É'gihà /ā'-gē-hä'/ *v.*, enter, to go into a house or
building as some animals go into burrows

É'kidè /ā'-kē-thä'/ *adj.*, usu., 1. persons related by blood 2. things that have a common origin

É'kidè /ā'-kē-thä'/ *n.*, kin, kindred, relatives,
family members

É'kigà̀ /ā'-kē-goⁿ'/ *adj.*, same, refers to two or
more things that are identical, matching, or
alike; *égąxt'iáži*, not quite the same

É'ną /ā'-noⁿ/ *pron.*, all, the total amount,
everything, the entire (~ *ušté*, that's ~ that's
left)

É'ną̀skà /ā'-noⁿ-skä'/ *adj.*, right fit, as in
clothing

É'sa'xt'ì /ā'-sä-xt'ē'/ *adv.*, purposely, with
intent, calculatingly

É'saxt'ì /ā'-sä-xt'ē'/ *n./prep.*, feeling of, an
emotional sensation not connected to
sight, hearing, taste, or smell, but thoughts
of want or desire

É'saxt'ì /ā'-sä-xt'ē'/ *interj.*, crave, thirst after, be consumed with desire, as in "Boy! I'd like to have soda right now!"

É'skąną̀ /ā'-skoⁿ-noⁿ'/ *v.*, yearn, having a strong desire for something that is possible to receive or reach

É'skąną̀ /ā'-skoⁿ-noⁿ'/ *v.*, it is hoped, long for, longed, wished, a desire or wish for something to become a reality

É'št'eą̀ą̀ /ā'-sht'ā-oⁿ'-oⁿ'/ *n.*, moodiness, inconstancy, instability

É'št'ínikè /ā'-sht'ē'-nē-kā'/ *n.*, monkey, refers to some primates that have tails or are tailless (It is thought that the original Ponca term referred to the North American river otter, *Lontra canadensis*, because of its playful behavior. Hence the term *é'št'ínikè*, so, that's the way you are.)

É'šte'ą́'ą́' /ā'-shtā-oⁿ'-oⁿ'/ *adj.*, ambivalent, unsure, mixed feelings, conflicting feelings about something

É't'ą̀dì /ā'-t'oⁿ-thē'/ *prep.*, ahead of, earlier than or sooner than others

E't'ą́dià̀t'a /ā-t'oⁿ-thē'-ä'-t'ä'/ *adv.*, before, earlier than, usu. refers to a task or duty to be there or do something before it is due

E't'ą́dišą̀ /ā-t'ä'-thē-shoⁿ'/ *n.*, direction, in the direction of something

E't'ą́ai /ā-t'ä'-ē/ *poss. pron.*, his/hers/its/theirs, something belonging or attributed to him/her/it

E'wáš'nągè /ā-wä-sh-noⁿ-gä'/ *n.*, train, locomotive; *e'wáš'nągè niášigà wé'ì*, passenger train; *e'wáš'nągè wat'úgdà*, freight train

E'wáš'nągè uhè /ā-wä-sh-noⁿ-gä' ü-hä'/ *n.*, railroad track

E'wáš'nągè uną́št'ą̀ /ā-wä-sh-noⁿ-gä' ü-noⁿ'-sht'oⁿ'/ *n.*, train depot, a station where people embark on or disembark from a passenger train

E'wáš'nągè užą́ /ā-wä-sh-noⁿ-gä' ü-zhoⁿ'/

n., berth, usu. refers to a sleeping bed on a train

É'žą́'skà /ā'-zhoⁿ'-skä'/ *n.*, white elm tree

É'žą́'žíde /ā'-zhoⁿ'-zhē'-dä/ *n.*, red elm tree

É'žą̀hì /ā'-zhoⁿ'-hē'/ *n.*, elm tree (Three varieties are located on the Ponca reservation in Oklahoma: the red elm, *é'žą̀ žíde* or *žą́šídehì*, the white elm, *é'žą̀ skà*, and the Chinese elm, no Ponca name, of the genus *Ulmus*

Eą́a /ā-oⁿ'-ä/ *n.*, the condition, quality, or degree of something in question

Eát'ą /ā-ä'-t'oⁿ/ *adv.*, why, for what purpose, cause, or reason (~ *né'a?*, ~ are you going?)

Ebábišt'iwąžì /ā-bä-bē-sht'ē-woⁿ-zhē'/ *n.*, nobody, finding there really wasn't anyone there after thinking there was a person present

Ebé' /ā-bä'/ *pron.*, who, introduces a question about a person or persons; *ebéwadakè*, who are you speaking of?

Ebé'et'a /ā-bā'-ä-t'ä/ *poss. pron.*, whose, something that belongs to somebody

Ebé'št'ì /ā-bā'-sht'ē'/ *pron.*, whoever

Ebé'št'ìšt'è /ā-bā'-sht'ē'-sht'ä'/ *pron.*, whosoever

Ebé'št'ìšt'ewą̀ /ā-bā'-sht'ē'-sht'ä-woⁿ'/ *pron.*, whomsoever

Ebé'št'iwą̀ /ā-bā'-sht'ē-woⁿ'/ *pron.*, whomever

Ebé'štiwą̀ /ā-bā'-shtē-woⁿ'/ *pron.*, anyone, any one person

Ebébišt'iwąžì /ā-bä'-bē-sht'ē-woⁿ-zhē'/ *n.*, nobody, refers to a person who is a nobody

Ebédįkeštiwą̀ /ā-bā'-thēⁿ-kā-shtē-woⁿ'/ *pron.*, anybody, anybody who is somebody (of importance or fame) or an average person

Ebéšt'i /ā-bā'-sht'ē/ *pron.*, someone, a person not named who has to or is called upon to do something

Ebéšt'iwąžì /ā-bā'-sht'ē-woⁿ-zhē'/ *n./pron.*, nobody, not anyone, refers to nobody being there

Edábe /ā-dä'-bā/ *adv.*, also, in addition, included, usu. refers to adding another one of something

Edábe /ā-dä'-bā/ *v.*, include, being included (*ugášą ąđái kí ~ ąđí ąđái*, he was ~ in the trip)

Édąbè /ā'-thoⁿ-bā/ *v.*, appear, come into sight, become visible

Édąskadè /ā'-thoⁿ-skä-thä/ *v.*, try on, as in trying on clothing

Edážegą̀ /ā-thä'-zhā-go̱ⁿ/ *adj.*, safe, secure, in safe hands, safe and sound, free of hardships

Éde /ā'-dā/ *conj.*, but, excepting that, since

Éde /ā'-thä/ *n.*, relations, family, kin; *é'kiđè*, refers to people who are related

Edé'gą /ā-dā'-go̱ⁿ/ *aux. v.*, should have, refers to something that somebody ~ done because it was the correct or right thing to do when it availed itself

Edégą /ā-thä'-go̱ⁿ/ *v.*, imagine, think of, bring to mind, forming a mental image of something

Edégą /ā-thä'-go̱ⁿ/ *n.*, thought, contemplation, ideas, or plans that come from thinking

Edégą /ā-thä'-go̱ⁿ/ *v.*, to think, imagine reflect, reason; *ebđégą*, I think; *enégą*, you think; *edégąi*, he/she/it/they think

Edégąwadažì /ā-thä'-go̱ⁿ-wä-thä-zhē/ *adj.*, unthinking, not reasoning, did not take any consideration of the situation at hand but acted upon it

Edégąwadè /ā-thä'-go̱ⁿ-wä-thä/ *adj.*, conceivable, something that is possible or plausible

Edégaxt'ì /ā-thä'-gä-xt'ē/ *v.*, wonder, to think curiously about something

Edége udį́šį̀ /ā-dä'-gä ü-thē̱ⁿ'-shē̱ⁿ/ *adj.*, stubborn, a person or animal that is inflexible or pigheaded

Edéšt'ašt'à /ā-dä'-sht'ä-sht'ä/ *n.*, things, objects, bits and pieces of things, lots of different things

Edéšt'e'à /ā-dä'-sht'ā-ä/ *v.*, whine, bellyache, to continue to complain in an annoying way; *n.*, someone who grumbles and complains, usu. because of discontent

Edí /ā-dē/ *adv.*, here, a response to a question about where a person or thing is (*núžįgà tą̀ ~ à?*, is the boy ~?; answer: *núžįgà tą̀ ~*, the boy is ~)

Edí /ā-thē/ *n.*, there, refers to a location or place (*núžįgà tą ~ akà*, the boy was ~)

Edí'ą́đì /ā-dē'-o̱ⁿ-thē/ *v.*, 1st pers. pl., past t., we were there, usu. refers to a specific or a particular location where something occurred

Edí'bđì /ā-dē'-bthē/ *v.*, 1st pers. sing., past t. I was there

Edí'ni /ā-dē'-nē/ *v.*, 2nd pers. sing., past t., you were there

Edí'tedą̀dì /ā-dē'-tä-tho̱ⁿ-dē/ *adv.*, then, at that time, at that point in time

Edí'úk'íhibažì /ā-dē'-ü-k'ē'-hē-bä-zhē/ *adj.*, untalented, inept, incompetent, unskilled

Edídą̀dą̀ /ā-dē'-tho̱ⁿ-tho̱ⁿ/ *adj.*, closer, coming closer little by little or bit by bit

Edíǝk'íhiažì /ā-dē'-ǝ-k'ē'-hē-ä-zhē/ *adj.*, inept, lacking ability, ineffectual

Edíhi /ā-dē'-hē/ *adv.*, then, reaching that point and time

Edíʃ'sà /ā-dē'-ʃ-sä/ *v.*, persist in, continue, carry on, go on, persevere with

Edítą /ā-dē'-to̱ⁿ/ *prep.*, from, starting; the source from which something comes or from where a race begins

Edítą /ā-dē'-to̱ⁿ/ *v. phr.*, past time, since then or of a ~

Edítedą̀dì /ā-dē'-tä-tho̱ⁿ-dē/ *adv.*, meanwhile, at that time, during that period

Edítedą̀dì /ā-dē'-tä-tho̱ⁿ-dē/ *adv.*, when, what point something happened at the time something else happened

Edí udátą /ā-dē ü-thä'-to̱ⁿ/ *adv.*, subsequently, next, the next one

Égą /ā'-goⁿ/ *v.*, to be correct, right, exact

-égą /ā'-goⁿ/ *suffix*, denotes something that has a general likeness or resemblance, as in *žíde~*, reddish, *hú'te é'xt'i~*, his voice is really similar to ——

Égà'ebdégà /ā'-goⁿ-ā-bthā'-goⁿ/ *v.*, guess, suppose, or suppose something; conjecture

Égą'gà /ā'-goⁿ-gä'/ *v.*, proceed, go ahead or begin what you intend to do

Égą'idák'uhe /ā'-goⁿ-ē-thä'-k'ü-hā/ *n.*, dreading, feeling anxiety over something that happened or could happen

Égą ahí /ā'-goⁿ ä-hē'/ *v.*, become, to come to be; *égą ahít'įkè*, I will come to be; *égą šít'anikè*, you will come to be; *égą ahít'akà*, he/she/it will come to be; *égą ągáhit'aitè*, we will come to be; *égą sít'amašè*, you (all) will come to be; *égą ahít'amà*, they will come to be

Égą àži /ā'-goⁿ ä'-zhē/ *adj.*, different, differing in form or quality

Égądążà /ā'-goⁿ-thoⁿ-zhoⁿ/ *conj.*, but, lit., that may be, ~ or except that

Ę́gądążà /āⁿ'-goⁿ-thoⁿ-zhoⁿ/ *prep.*, except, but, as in "that's the way it was ~"

Égą ebdégą /ā'-goⁿ ä-bthā'-goⁿ/ *v.*, guess, conjecture, supposing something to be

Égąigà /ā'-goⁿ-ē-goⁿ/ *adj.*, similar, comparable; generally, a likeness or resemblance

Égąįgà /ā'-goⁿ-ēⁿ-goⁿ/ *n.*, semblance, something that is similar, likeness of another thing

Égąįgà /ā'-goⁿ-ēⁿ-goⁿ/ *v.*, resemble, to have a likeness to another thing

Égasądì /ā'-gä-soⁿ-thē'/ *n.*, the day after of any other day, a past or future day

Égasàdi gúədišà /ā'-gä-soⁿ'-thē gü'-ə-thē-shoⁿ/ *adv.*, the next morning after a certain day

Égą šášą /ā'-goⁿ' shoⁿ'-shoⁿ/ *adj.*, constant, continuous, likely to continue on and on, refers to a situation or condition that will always be the same

Égą šášą /ā'-goⁿ shoⁿ'-shoⁿ/ *adv.*, invariably, something that is consistent, continually, always the same

Égą šášą /ā'-goⁿ-shoⁿ'-shoⁿ/ *adj.*, permanent, usu. refers to a situation or condition that will always be the same

Égaxè /ā'-gä-xā'/ *v.*, surround, encircle, to enclose on all sides, besiege

Égàxt'ì /ā'-goⁿ-xt'ē'/ *adj.*, verifiable, factual, not questionable

Égaxt'iáži /ā'-goⁿ-xt'ē-ä'-zhē/ *adj.*, dissimilar, unlike, not really comparable

Égaxt'i wé'ą /ā'-goⁿ-xt'ē wā'-oⁿ/ *n.*, vengeance, to punish another or another group in retaliation for injury

Égazezè /ā'-gä-zā-zā'/ *adv.*, in a row, consecutively, one after the other

Égąžì /ā'-goⁿ-zhē'/ *adj.*, false, incorrect, not in line with the facts, erroneous, untrue, inaccurate, flawed

Égąžì /ā'-goⁿ-zhē'/ *adj.*, untrue, false, not factual

Égąžiáčą' /ā'-goⁿ-zhē-ä'-choⁿ/ *adj.*, absurd or absurdity, something that is unreasonable or even foolish

É'gdągè /ā'-gthoⁿ-gä'/ *n.*, husband, the male partner in the marriage of a man and woman

Égià /ā'-gē-oⁿ'/ *v.*, shut, close, close it, as in closing a door (*t'ižébe kè ~gà*, ~ the door)

Égidà /ā'-gē-dä'/ *v.*, match, match with something or somebody, combine well with something; *égijà*, matching with something or somebody cute

Égidą /ā'-gē-doⁿ'/ *adj.*, just right, 1. usu. refers to the size of a thing that fits appropriately, as in clothing 2. something that is appropriate for a person (*nikášigà dįkè, údit'ą te ~*, the job is ~ for that person); *égijà*, just right, usu. refers to the fit of girls', women's, babies' clothing

Égihà /ā'-gē-hä'/ *prep.*, under, something or somebody goes ~ a thing, entering willingly or unwillingly, as in slipping into a pool of water; *v.*, refers to entering or going into something

Égijà /ā'-gē-joⁿ/ *adj.*, just right, usu. refers to the size of a cute thing for children that fits appropriately, as in clothing

Égipįà' /ā'-gē-pēoⁿ/ *v.t.*, accustom, adjust to, adapt to, to get used to or become familiar with something or to people, to become accustomed to any condition

Éi' /ā'/ *n.*, he, 1. he/she/it 2. he's/she's/it's the one 3. that's it

Ei'ná /ā-nä'/ *interj.*, expression, a woman's expression of strong feelings denoting dislike for another's behavior in speech or action, usu. directed to the individual

Ék'itąhà /ā'-k'ē-toⁿ-hä'/ *adj.*, simultaneous, concurrent, at the same time

Ékigà gáxe /ā'-kē-goⁿ gä-xā/ *n.*, a duplicate, copy, replica, reproduction

Ékinąskà /ā'-kē-noⁿ-skä'/ *adj.*, 1. something or persons of equal size 2. clothing that fits perfectly or is just the right size 3. *n. phr.*, persons of the same height and age 4. *pron.*, none, no more of something, as in "that's all" or "not any"

Ékitąhà /ā'-kē-toⁿ-hä'/ *adj./n.*, 1. same height, of equal height 2. same time (~ *ahí*, they arrived at the ~)

Eną /ā-noⁿ/ *pron.*, none, no more of something, as in "that's all" or "not any"

Énąskà /ā'-noⁿ-skä'/ *v.*, to fit, to be the proper size or shape of clothing for somebody

Énąskadè /ā'-noⁿ-skä-thä'/ *v.*, try on, fit, to try on clothing

Enáúdą /ā-noⁿ'-ü'-doⁿ/ *adj.*, best, usu. refers to something that is higher or to one who is utmost in perfection

Enáxčì /ā-noⁿ'-xchē'/ *pron.*, alone, something or somebody being by itself or themselves

Enáxčì /ā-noⁿ'-xchē'/ *adj.*, one only, refers to a solitary person, a single play in sports, or a thing (~ *uštè*, ~ person was left)

Ešą' /ā-shoⁿ'/ *adj./adv.*, near, close at hand, very close, adjacent

Ešądi /ā-shoⁿ'-dē/ *prep.*, by, something or somebody is close to something or somebody

Ešáxt'ì /ā-shä'-xt'ē'/ *adj.*, closest, very close by

Éskąnà /ā'-skoⁿ-noⁿ'/ *v.*, long for, longed, wished

Ešną /ā-shnoⁿ'/ *adj.*, alone, refers to a person (or group) who did or wanted to do something alone

Ešną'ahà /ā-shnoⁿ'-ä-hä'/ *adj.*, close, refers to being close to a particular thing or group; *ešą'ahàbažì*, did not come around or close to a thing or group, as in tribal gatherings

Ešną'ahàhà /ā-shnoⁿ'-ä-hä'-hä'/ *adj.*, close, always being close by or near

Ešnąadi/ ā-shnoⁿ'-ä-dē/ *adj.*, close, close by, nearby

Ést'eą'ą' /ā'-st'ā-oⁿ-oⁿ/ *adj.*, erratic, 1. usu. refers to things going wrong, lack of consistency or uniformity 2. modern usage may refer to how an automobile performs

Éšte'ą'ą /ā'-shtā-oⁿ-oⁿ/ *adj.*, unsettled, a person lacking in stability, order, and certainty

Et'á /ā-t'ä'/ *n.*, refers to a place mentioned at an earlier time (~ *ągáhì umądįkà ámątedądì*, we went ~ last year)

Et'á /ā-t'ä'/ *prep.*, at, denotes a presence or occurrence on or near something

Et'ádįgè /ā-t'ä'-thēⁿ-gä'/ *adj.*, illegitimate, lit., belonging to none, a child born to a woman not married

Et'ą́dikidè /ā-t'oⁿ'-thē-kē-thā/ *v.*, prepare, to put things in order, to devise a plan to be ready for something that may happen

Et'ádišą̀ /ā-t'ä'-thē-shoⁿ/ *prep.*, toward, in the direction of something

Et'áha /ā-t'ä'-hä/ *adv.*, farther, farther than

Et'áha /ā-t'ä'-hä/ *adv.*, move over, a function word that indicates position and distance, as in telling someone to move a little farther over or away (~ *gdíga*, ~ that way)

Et'áhažì /ā-t'ä'-hä-zhē/ *adj.*, antisocial, unwilling to associate in a normal or friendly way with other people, responds disruptively to the established social order, has bad ways; refers to somebody who has poor social skills (A person, whether educated or uneducated, can offend others by his/her actions or speech.)

Ét'ą̀ /ā'-t'oⁿ-ē/ *adv.*, before, usu. used to begin an activity in advance of others (*ukíte amà ~ wak'idà*, start in this battle ~ the enemy acts)

Et'ái /ā-t'ä'-ē/ *adj.*, their, something belonging to them, as in "that is ~ father"

Etái /ā-tä'-ē/ *v.t./adj.*, *3rd pers.*, he/she/it/they own/s, possess, belonging to them, as in property

Éwą /ā'-woⁿ/ *n.*, the cause or source of something that happens

Éwakią̀' /ā'-wä-kē-oⁿ/ *n.*, fault, an unfortunate situation or something that a person brought upon themselves, being responsible for one's own failure, one's own fault; *ɖíʃwadakią̀*, you brought it upon yourself

Éwawà /ā'-wä-woⁿ/ *n.*, caused by, attributable to something or somebody

É·xt'iáži /ā'--xt'ēä'-zhē/ *adj.*, queer, different in some way, not quite the same thing, questionable

Éya snedè /ā'-yä snā-dā/ *adj.*, long-winded, overtalkative, verbose

F

This letter is not included in the Ponca alphabet.

G

g /gə/ fifth consonant in the Ponca alphabet

G'é' /g-ā/ *n.*, turtle, any of various types of reptiles of the order Testudines or Chelonia

G'é'gdé'ze /g-ā'-gthā'-zā/ *n.*, box turtle, terrapin, family Emydidae, a land turtle that has a moveable hinge on the lower shell that allows it to retract in the shell and close up

G'é' t'ą̀gà /g-ā' t'oⁿ-gä/ *n.*, snapping turtle, a turtle with a smooth, hard shell with a ridge from front to rear; *g'é' t'at'axì*, a large turtle with large projections or bumps on its hard shell

G'éda /g-ā'-thä/ *n.*, clear sky, a sky with no clouds, usu. said following cloudy skies

G'ehábedą̀ /g-ā-hä'-bä-doⁿ/ *n.*, soft-shelled turtle, genus *Apalone*, family Trionychidae, the species known by the Ponca were referred to as sand turtles

G'énąxdè /g-ā'-noⁿ-xthā/ *n.*, shadow, a dark area between something and rays of light

G'i'é' /g-ē-ā/ *v.*, scratch, to scratch oneself

G'igdíp'úp'u /g-ē-gthē'-p'ü'-p'ü/ *v.*, nestle, to settle snugly or to lie in a sheltered way, wrapping up in a blanket to keep warm and comfy

G'igdístubè /g-ē-gthē'-stü-bä/ *v.*, groom, to spruce up, trim, usu. refers to animals that clean their feathers with the beak or clean their fur with the tongue

G'íšą̀žì /g-ē-shoⁿ-zhē'/ *adj.*, dissatisfied with some plan, decision, activity, etc.

Gá /gä/ *prefix*, action of human force by striking or force from such things as wind, water, etc.

Gá' /gä/ *adv.*, here, refers to somebody giving or showing somebody something, offering something to someone

Gą́' /gonⁿ/ *n.*, manner, a way of doing something, a method or style; *égą*, in that manner

Gá' /gä/ *v.*, hand over, to give something to somebody

Ga'áxe /gä-ä'-xä/ *v.*, to make a scraping sound against metal

Ga'ázazà /gä-ä'-zä-zä/ *n.*, swinging motion, as a door left partially left open, moving to and fro, or a children's playground swing moving by the force of the wind

Gą́'da áčą /gonⁿ-thä ä'-chonⁿ/ *v.*, crave, *3rd pers. pl.*, yearn for, desire, long for, hunger after

Gá'dądì /gä-thonⁿ-dē/ *adv.*, here, at this place, may refer to a place out of sight of where you speak

Ga'íye /gä-ē'-yä/ *n.*, discussion, consideration given by argument, comment, etc., not restricted to but usu. a term used in reference to a committee meeting, esp. one concerning matters to look for or to find or explore solutions

Gą́'ki /gonⁿ-kē/ *conj.*, and (*t'áwągdąta ahí ~ t'í ke t'á agdài*, they went to the city ~ went home)

Gá't'adišà /gä-t'ä-thē-shä/ *adv.*, that way, toward no particular place or direction ("stand over ~")

Gabdá /gä-bthä/ *v.*, bloom, to come into flower, refers to flowers opening

Gabdá'skà /gä-bthä'-skä/ *v.*, flatten, to flatten out or smash by striking with an object

Gabdáze /gä-bthä'-zä/ *v.*, burst, to break open, to rupture something

Gabdíže /gä-bthē'-zhä/ *v.*, knock down, to knock down with force, usu. refers to somebody being pushed or knocked down by somebody or something

Gabįxe /gä-bēⁿ'-xä/ *v.*, splash, to cause liquid to splash or small solid substances to blow into the air; *ágabixà*, to be splashed upon, as when a pot boils over

Gabíže /gä-bē'-zhä/ *v.*, wag, to move something to and fro, such as a dog wagging its tail; *gabíbíže*, wagging

Gačáki /gä-chä-kē/ *v.*, slap, usu. to strike with the flat of the hand

Gą́čegà /gonⁿ-chä-gonⁿ/ *adj./adv.*, later, refers to doing something later on or afterward

Gačíže /gä-chē'-zhä/ *v.*, crash, a loud sound made by something banging or striking against something else, such as a falling tree hitting the ground; *ígačiže*, something that falls against something with a loud crashing sound

Gą́da /gonⁿ-thä/ *v.*, want, wanting some material needs, such as food, clothing, an automobile, or enough money to take a trip; *ągádaì*, we want; *gą́daì*, they want; *ągádagatà*, we, who were wanting

Gadą́ /gä-donⁿ/ *v.*, bat, to hit something away, as in striking a baseball away

Gadą́ /gä-donⁿ/ *v.*, hit, to hit or strike something with the hands or with something in the hand, e.g., using a baseball bat

Gądádįšè /gonⁿ-thä'-thēⁿ-shä/ *v.*, you will come to be 1. refers to somebody who will eventually come to be in a state or condition of good health, prosperity, long life 2. of somebody who will eventually come to a bad end

Gą́dawadè /gonⁿ-thä-wä-thä/ *n.*, desirable, something attractive, worthy of desire

Gą́daxtì /gonⁿ-thä-xtē/ *v.*, desire, yearning, longing

Gą́daz̧ì /gonⁿ-thä-zhē/ *v.*, reject, decline, to refuse to accept something; *gą́da'baz̧ì*, refers to somebody who doesn't want something when offered, something that is turned down

Gǫ́dažiwadè /goⁿ-thä-zhē-wä-dä/ *adj.*, undesirable, somebody or something that is not wanted

Gadé /gä-thä/ *n.*, giveaway, refers to the act of giving something away

Gádįkè /gä-thēⁿ-kä/ *adj./pron.*, this, someone or something away from the speaker that is out of sight; someone or something kept in mind

Gadúxe /gä-dü'-xä/ *v.*, crack, to crack something open, such as an egg

Gaé' /gä-ä/ *adj.*, public, something open to view; *gaé' itéde*, *v.*, to place something out in the open or make it accessible

Gaégą /gä-ä'-goⁿ/ *adv. phr.*, in that manner, a way something is done

Gaé mążą̀ /gä-ä' moⁿ-zhoⁿ/ *n.*, unallotted lands, public lands on the Ponca reservation (Under the Dawes Act of 1887, these lands were part of the trust lands on the reservation but still held in trust for the tribe. They are restricted by the U.S. government.)

Gagégą /gä-gä'-goⁿ/ *n. phr.*, like these things, like those or them

Gahá' /gä-hä'/ *prep.*, on, suggests something atop or positioned at the top

Gahé /gä-hä'/ *v.*, to comb, the act of combing hair

Gahį́da /gä-hēⁿ'-thä/ *v.*, to blow away, as in anything not secured on a windy day

Gahí'e /gä-hē'-ä/ *n.*, meeting, talks, consultation; a committee coming together to discuss some topic or topics, usu. in a formal setting (The word probably is a derivative of *gaíye*.)

Gahí'e /gä-hē'-ä/ *n.*, council, usu. refers to the tribal council of the Ponca people

Gahí'e niášigà /gä-hē'-ä nē-ä'-shē-gä/ *n.*, councilman, 1. a person who is a member of the tribal council 2. a politician in any government

Gahí'e út'i /gä-hē'-ä ü'-t'ē/ *n.*, (new word, ca. 2005) Ponca Tribal Affairs Building, a building in White Eagle Community where some tribal offices are located

Gáhidè /gä'-hē-thä/ *prep./adv.*, over there, in that direction that is out of sight from the speaker

Gáhideamà /gä'-hē-thä-ä-mä/ *pron.*, those over there, refers to any group of people within a short distance from the speaker or those who are not in sight

Gáhidéát'a /gä'-hē-thä'-ä'-t'ä/ *adv.*, there, "over there" (The speaker is giving the general direction of a place, including the distance from where he/she stands.)

Gáhimà /gä'-hē-mä/ *pron.*, those over there, refers to a *specific* person or people who are not in sight or people being spoken of

Gaiáxe /gä-ēä'-xä/ *v.*, scrape, scraping the bottom of a pail with a dipper for water (*néxe ké ~aì*, he ~d the pail)

Gaiyázazà /gä-ē-yä'-zä-zä/ *v.*, swinging, to swing between two points as an open door swings to and fro by the force of the wind

Gak'ák'ámà /gä-k'ä'-k'ä'-moⁿ/ *v./n.*, clanging, to make a clanging sound repeatedly

Gak'úge /gä-k'ü'-gä/ *v.*, drum, to beat and hear the sound of a drum with a drumstick; *kúge utį̀*, one striking or hitting a drum, as a member of a singing group at a tribal dance

Gáke /gä'-kä/ *adj./pron.*, this, something that is away from the speaker, something that is out of sight, or something that is kept in mind or is part of a plan

Gáket'adišà /gä'-kä-t'ä-thē-shoⁿ/ *n.*, direction, the direction of something spoken of

Gakúge /gä-kü'-gä/ *v.*, knock, to strike something, as a door; *gakúkugè*, to continually knock or strike, as in knocking on a door

Gamą́gde /gä-moⁿ'gthä/ *v.*, to cause something to come upright

Gamą́ši /gä-moⁿ'-shē/ *v.*, rising, a cause that forces a thing to rise into the air or ascend upward; *đimą́ši*, to lift something upward; *bamą́ši*, to use the body to push something upward; *bimą́ši*, to press something upward

Gamą́xp'i /gä-moⁿ'-xp'ē/ *adj./n.*, cloudy, clouds forming or wind blowing up clouds

Gamú' /gä-mü'/ *v.*, pour, 1. to pour the contents of something into a container at once 2. rain coming down in a downpour, as in *Nąží akà ~ tigđài*, The rain came down in a down ~

Gamú'i /gä-mü'-ē/ *n.*, outgushing, pouring out in profusion

Gamúe /gä-mü'-ā/ *v.*, pour out, 1. refers to any kind of liquid being poured out suddenly 2. refers to any solid substance being poured out, e.g., gravel from a dump truck

Ganą́gè /gä-noⁿ'-gā'/ *v.*, spin, the revolving motion of something caused by some force, such as wind, water, or mechanical means; *ganą́nągè*, spin, the continuous revolving motion of something; *điną́ge*, spin, the revolving motion of something caused by use of the hands; *điną́nągè*, spin, the continuous revolving motion of something caused by use of the hands

Ganáxe /gä-nä'-xā/ *v.* sprinkled on, usu. refers more to being sprinkled upon in the rain or by a water hose; *ugánaxèxt'ì, past t.*, to have been sprinkled on resulting in being drenched

Ganí' /gä-nē'/ *v.*, to fan, to use an eagle-feathered fan to fan a person ceremonially, usu. done in the home but often done in the Native American Church; *wegáni*, to fan more than one person

Gap'ą́de /gä-p'oⁿ'-dā/ *v./n.*, to jar, a physical jolt, to give a violent jerk or bump; *gap'ą́p'ą́de*, to continuously violently jerk or bump

Gap'ą́dedà̀ /gä-p'oⁿ'-dā-thoⁿ'/ *v.*, jar, something that is put down or falls down with a violent jerk or bump; a person who sits down ungracefully with a jerk or bump

Gap'ái /gä-p'ä'-ē/ *adj.*, sharpen, to make sharp with an instrument, such as a revolving sharpening stone; *đip'ái*, sharpening with the hands using a whetstone

Gap'i /gä-p'ē/ *adv.*, accurately (Suggests something that is done exactly the right way. The prefix *ga* usu. indicates something done by force, as in striking or by wind. ~, then, may refer to someone hitting a baseball at a precise place on the bat, causing the ball to travel a great distance.)

Gap'í /gä-p'ē'/ *v.*, hit, hitting something at the right place, as in to ~ a baseball far away

Gap'í' /gä-p'ē'/ *adj./v.*, perfect hit, to hit, strike, punch, smack something or somebody perfectly

Gap'íáži /gä-p'ē'-ä'-zhē/ *v.*, an uncontrolled fall, usu. caused by tripping

Gap'íp'iažì /gä-p'ē'-p'ē-ä-zhē'/ *adj.*, a hard or rough fall or ride, 1. usu. refers to somebody or something falling by being pushed or struck by something 2. refers to riding some sort of a vehicle on a rough road, causing the occupants to bounce around

Gapúki /gä-pü'-kē/ *v.*, dull sound, 1. to strike something, making a dull sound 2. something falling, making a dull sound

Gasá'đu /gä-sä'-thü/ *v.*, rattle, to rattle an instrument or object, e.g., shaking a gourd using force to cause it to rattle

Gasá'p'ì /gä-sä'-p'ē/ *v.*, smacking sound, to strike something with a strap, making a smacking sound, as with a bullwhip; *đisáp'i*, make a snapping sound with the use of something in the hands, such as a rubber band stretched to snap; *nąsáp'i*, make a snapping sound by stepping on or rolling something over something

Gasá'sadù /gä-sä'-sä-thü'/ *v.*, rattle, to continuously rattle an instrument or object, e.g., using force to cause a gourd to rattle

Gasą́de /gä-sonⁿ-dä/ *n.*, braid, three separate strands of human hair in an intertwined arrangement (This was a Ponca hair fashion worn by men and women as well as children. Men and boys wore the braids over the front of the shoulders while women and young girls wore theirs over the back.)

Gasą́di /gä-sonⁿ-thē/ *n.*, tomorrow, the day after today

Gasą́di gúədišą̀ /gä-sonⁿ-thē gü'-ə-thē-shonⁿ/ *adv./n.*, the day after tomorrow

Gasági /gä-sä'-gē/ *v.*, harden, usu. refers to a heavy wind blowing upon something

Gasáp'i /gä-sä'-p'ē/ *n./v.*, whip, to make a whip (bullwhip) snap or to make a cracking sound; to use any flexible material, such as a piece of leather, to hit any surface, making a snapping sound

Gasáp'i /gä-sä'-p'ē/ *v.*, lash, to whip with a stinging blow

Gasása /gä-sä'-sä/ *v.*, chopping, chopping continuously by using a tool such as an ax

Gasásap'ì /gä-sä-sä-p'ē'/ *adj.*, flapping sound, something blowing and flapping in the wind, such as cloth

Gasé /gä-sä'/ *v.*, chop, chop by using a tool such as an ax

Gašíbe /gä-shē'-bä/ *v.*, emerge, to come out of or come forth into view

Gašíbeahí /gä-shē'-bä-ä-hē'/ *adv.*, out of, not in, implies getting oneself out of something

Gašíbeàt'a /gä-shē'-bä-ä'-t'ä/ *adv.*, outside of, being ~ something that one was involved in or locked up in

Gašíbəát'a /gä-shē'-bəä'-t'ä/ *adj.*, separate, outside of or separated from an inner group, tribe, or organization; *gašíbe k'igáíze*, to get oneself out of an organization, group, etc.

Gasíhi /gä-sē'-hē/ *v.*, clear up, clearing up (the sky ~ after a storm)

Gašíšižè /gä-shē'-shē-zhä'/ *v.*, to crack something with an instrument by hitting or striking continuously

Gašížè /gä-shē'-zhä'/ *v.*, to crack something with an instrument by hitting or striking

Gask'í' /gä-sk'ē'/ *v.*, exhausted, tired out, all-in, tiredness after running a long distance or from doing heavy labor; being completely out of breath

Gašką́ /gä-shkonⁿ/ *v.*, shake, to be shaken by the wind or other forceful medium

Gaskábe /gä-skä'-bä/ *v.*, drive into the mud, usu. refers to a vehicle getting stuck in the mud on a dirt road

Gaškáp'ì /gä-shkä'-p'ē/ *v.*, to fall or something that fell with a wet, flat slapping sound (he ~ right in the water puddle)

Gaškáp'i /gä-shkä'-p'ē/ *v.*, plop, somebody or something falling down heavily on the ground or floor

Gaskí /gä-skē'/ *adj.*, breathless, out of breath, gasping, winded, fighting for breath

Gašną́ /gä-shnonⁿ/ *v.*, miss, failing to hit something with something in the hands or with the hand, as when using a bat to try to hit a ball

Gasné'snè /gä-snä'-snä'/ *n.*, fringes, tassel

Gasnú /gä-snü'/ *v.*, slide, to slide by force, usu. on the snow or ice; to slide on a smooth surface; *basnú*, slide by pushing; *đisnú*, slide by pulling with hands; *bisnú*, slide by pressing on with use of the hands on an instrument; *nąsnú*, slide by using feet

Gasnú'gidè /gä-snü'-gē-thä'/ *v./n.*, sledding, child play involving sliding downhill on a sled or sliding on ice

Gašnúde /gä-shnü'-dä/ *v.*, to knock off, as in removing a bolt from something by striking it; *gašnúšnúde*, to knock off continuously, as in removing a bolt from something by striking it

Gašp'é /gä-shp'ä'/ *v.*, chip, as in cutting off, chipping, a piece of wood from a log; *đišp'é*, to tear off a piece using the hands; *đašp'é*, to bite off a piece of food; *nǫšp'é*, to chip off by stepping on or driving over

Gasp'é /gä-sp'ä'/ *v.*, recede, 1. to become less or ebb, as after the flooding of a river 2. clearing of any liquid (e.g., water) when debris goes to the bottom of a container

Gašt'ą́k'a /gä-sht'on-k'ä/ *v.*, appease, pacifying somebody to get something from them; bribe, to get something from or to make a person do something by offering something desirable to them

Gastá' /gä-stä'/ *v.*, flatten, to flatten by striking or stepping on, usu. refers to weeds or grass

Gasúse /gä-sü'-sä/ *v.*, flow swiftly, usu. a small stream of fast-flowing water

Gát'a /gä'-t'ä/ *adv.*, yonder, something not within sight and a longer distance away

Gat'á'xì /gä-t'ä'-xē/ *v.*, to make a knocking sound by striking, falling, spinning, etc.

Gát'adišą̀ /gä-t'ä-thē-shon/ *adv.*, over there, 1. to indicate a place out of sight, toward a position away from the speaker 2. that way, toward no particular place or direction (stand over ~) 3. to indicate that a statement close to an idea or plan could have or should have been included in one's speech or presentation

Gát'adišą̀ /gä-t'ä-thē-shon/ *n.*, direction, generally toward an unspecified direction

Gat'ámą /gä-t'ä'-mon/ *v.*, hollow echo (A modern term, ca. 1800s, refers to sound coming from a metal barrel.)

Gat'ę́ /gä-t'än/ *v.*, killed, got killed (*k'ip'ínągè kedí ~ biámà*, he was ~ in a car accident)

Gat'ú'be /gä-t'ü'-bä/ *v.*, to grind or break up by striking with an instrument

Gat'ú'šì /gä-t'ü'-shē/ *v.*, to make a popping or cracking sound using some instrument of force

Gátą'hì' /gä-ton-hē/ *adv.*, this far, refers to something that was done or a period of time being passed when another thing was finally begun, as in dinner served an hour late

Gatą́ádi /gä-ton-ä'-dē/ *adv.*, by this time, as a result, if after an incident occurred prior to the main event then something else could have happened

Gátedì /gä'-tä-dē/ *adv.*, then, at that time

Gatégą /gä-tä-gon/ *adj./interj.*, "that's the way it is"

Gátešt'ì /gä-tä-sht'ē/ *adj.*, this or that one, refers to something that may be present or close by or could be out of sight, esp. something that is distinct from others

Gaúdį̀ /gä-ü'-thēn/ *v.*, whirl, twirl, spin

Gaúdibdì /gä-ü'-thē-bthēn/ *v.*, blowing wind, something or somebody causing things or debris to blow upon something or on people

Gáwadì /gä'-wä-dē/ *adv.*, there, refers, 1. to a specific physical place away from the speaker or out of sight of the speaker and hearer 2. a specific word or statement where an interjected idea should have or could have been said

Gáwakè /gä'-wä-kä/ *pron.*, that or this particular one, thing, situation, statement, or condition

Gawásek'ą̀ /gä-wä'-sä-k'on/ *v.*, cause something to go faster by force, usu. something spinning

Gawį́xe /gä-wēn-xä/ *v.*, descend, glide, lit., to fly close by, usu. refers to birds flying low above housetops; refers also to low-flying aircraft

Gaxá' /gä-xä'/ *v.*, pass, get ahead of another traveler

Gaxábe /gä-xä'-bä/ *v.*, peel, as in removing or taking off the bark of a tree by striking it with an instrument

Gaxát'a /gä-xä'-t'ä/ *adv.*, away from a particular thing or place; *prefix* for a proper male name in the Wašábe clan of the Ponca people (The name Gaxát'a nąží' implies a bison standing apart from the herd.)

Gaxát'a /gä-xä'-t'ä/ *adv.*, separate, separated or apart from others

Gaxát'à wadábe /gä-xä-t'ä' wä-doⁿ'-bä/ *n.*, drone, unmanned aerial vehicle (UAV) (A drone is a controlled device, situated apart from a main body, with the capability of monitoring varied conditions in the community and providing security surveillance for home and country. Other uses include film making, filming sports, monitoring livestock, conducting rescue missions, etc.)

Gaxáudíšį /gä-xä'-ü-thēⁿ'-shēⁿ/ *adj.*, unsurpassable, cannot be exceeded, incomparable

Gaxdá /gä-xthoⁿ'/ *n.*, tribal bison hunt, when a group of hunters with their families and belongings pursued the bison herd until they were successful in making the kill

Gaxdà /gä-xthoⁿ'/ *adv.*, archaic, together, something done jointly by a group of people, such as a bison hunt (The families of hunters were part of the entourage.)

Gaxdá /gä-xthoⁿ'/ *n.*, archaic, hunting party, a large hunting party, usu. including families

Gaxdí /gä-xthē'/ *v.*, whip, flog, to beat someone up

Gaxdí' /gä-xthē'/ *v.*, slay, 1. usu. refers to slaughter of animals 2. to beat up or whip a person

Gaxdíážì /gä-xthē'-ä'-zhē'/ *n.*, quietude, the state of quiet, usu. refers to stillness or calmness after a storm

Gáxe /gä'-xä/ *v.*, make, to make, create; *p'áxe*, I made; *škáxe*, you made; *gáxaì*, he made

Gáxe /gä'-xä/ *v.*, do, did, done

Gaxíáda /gä-xē'ä'-thä/ *v.*, knock down, to cause to fall by striking with an instrument; knock down in boxing

Gaxíáda /gä-xē'-ä'-thä/ *v.*, fell, as in cutting down a tree (connotes use of an instrument to fell a tree or high winds felling a structure)

Gaxíxe /gä-xē'-xä/ *v.*, crack or break, usu. refers to glass or ceramics cracking; *gaxíxixè*, to continuously crack

Gayázazà /gä-yä'-zä-zä'/ *n.*, motion, something moving to and fro from the wind; *k'igdíyazazà*, causing oneself to rock or move steadily, as in a rocking chair

Gazą /gä-zoⁿ'/ *prep.*, amid, mid, middle

Gazádį /gä-zoⁿ'-dēⁿ/ *prep.*, among, amid, "right there" in the middle

Gaząįhéde /gä-zoⁿ-ēⁿ'-hä'-thä/ *v.*, to knock out, to make unconscious (~ in the manly art of self-defense, i.e., boxing)

Gazáát'a /gä-zoⁿ'-ä'-t'ä/ *adv.*, amid, "way out there" in the middle

Gązé'dįgè /goⁿ-zä'-thēⁿ-gä'/ *adj.*, untaught, more directed toward children and teenagers who behave badly (The period for usage of the term preceded the concept of the influence of peer pressure notwithstanding parental teachings.)

Gázįgà /goⁿ'-zhēⁿ-gä/ *adj.*, unskilled, inexpert, doesn't know how

Gdadá /gthä-thä/ *v.*, unravel, come unbraided, when a thing that has been woven comes apart

Gdáde /gthä'-dä/ *v.*, sneak, sneak up on, to approach stealthily, usu. upon large animals or men; *gdáje*, sneak, sneak up on with delight (~ up on small game)

Gdádį /gthoⁿ'-thēⁿ/ *n.*, psychiatric disorder, the emotionally disabled, those who do not show good sense or behavior

Gdádi /gthoⁿ'-thē/ *adj.*, zany, crazy, wacky

Gdadį́' /gthä-dēⁿ/ *adv.*, across, refers to something lying across one's pathway, roadway, or, e.g., laying an object horizontally on something vertical, forming a ninety-degree angle

Gdą́gdą /gthoⁿ'-gthoⁿ/ *n.*, name calling, the use of offensive words toward another, usu. occuring in an argument

Gdą́ge /gthoⁿ'-gā/ *v.*, dive, plunge into the water headfirst with arms and hands extended forward

Gdą́p'a /gthoⁿ'-p'ä/ *adj.*, short, something that has been made short or worn away

Gdą́xe /gthoⁿ'-xä/ *adj.*, rancid, smelling of decomposing fats and oils, usu. in meats

Gdą́xe /gthoⁿ'-xä/ *v.*, bewitch, to affect somebody with a spell causing sickness (The Ponca people used medicines to cure people of sickness. This term may have been adapted from white people who practiced witchcraft. The Ponca word means rotten or rancid.)

Gdą́xe /gthoⁿ'-xä/ *n.*, sorcery, the practice of someone who is supposedly able to cast some evil upon another

Gdé' / gthä'/ *v.*, go back, went back or returned to where one came from

Gdé' /gthä'/ *v.*, homeward, to go back; *agdé*, I'm going homeward or back; *agdái*, he/she/it/they went homeward or went back; *ągágdaì*, we are going homeward or back

Gdé'be /gthä'-bä/ *n./v.*, vomit, heave, throw up; *i'gdebè*, vomitus, usu. refers to something specifically expelled from the stomach or ejected beyond the mouth from the stomach

Gde'dą́ áhįšut'à /gthä-doⁿ' ä'-hēⁿ-shü-t'ä/ *n.*, goshawk, a large hawk, the North American goshawk

Gdébą /gthä'-boⁿ/ *n.*, ten, the number ten (10)

Gdébą'hiwì' /gthä'-boⁿ-hē-wē'/ *n.*, one hundred; Roman numeral C; Latin term *centum*

Gdébą hiwì ídawà /gthä-boⁿ hē-wē' ē'-thä-wä'/ *n.*, one-hundred-dollar bill, U.S. currency

Gdébą'í'dawà /gthä-boⁿ-ē'-thä-wä'/ *n.*, ten-dollar bill, U.S. currency

Gdébą'nąbà'ídawà /gthä-boⁿ-noⁿ-bä-ē'-thä-wä'/ *n.*, twenty-dollar bill, U.S. currency

Gdébą'sat'ą'ídawà /gthä-boⁿ-sä-t'oⁿ-ē'-thä-wä'/ *n.*, fifty-dollar bill, U.S. currency

Gdébąšąkà /gthä-boⁿ-shoⁿ-kä'/ *n.*, ninety

Gdébąšąkà k'í šáka /gthä-boⁿ-shoⁿ-kä' k'ē' shoⁿ-kä/ *n.*, ninety-nine

Gdedą́ /gthä-doⁿ'/ *n.*, swift hawk, probably pigeon hawk, *Falco columbarius*

Gdedą́' /gthä-doⁿ'/ *n.*, hawk, any hawk of the genus *Accipiter*

Gdezá'zà /gthä-zä'-zä'/ *adj.*, striped, something painted or made in stripes, refers to something having bands or lines of varied colors

Gdedą́ xidáégą /gthä-doⁿ' xē-thä'-ä'-goⁿ/ *n.*, white-tailed hawk, the rough-legged hawk (*Buteo lagopus*, a hawk that flaps its wings and glides in upwinds, sometimes appearing stationary in the air.)

Gdežé /gthä-zhä'/ *adj.*, spotted, marked with spots; more than spots, a mottled, blotchy, messy pattern of color; *gdéška*, spotted, refers to a specific thing that is spotted

Gdežé /gthä-zhä'/ *v.*, speckle, to spot with a mottled, blotchy, messy pattern of color

Gdežé' /gthä-zhä'/ *adj.*, dappled, spotted, speckled (*šáge ~ wì àgdì*, he rode a ~ horse)

Gdį́' /gthēⁿ'/ *v.*, sit, to sit; *gdí'idą*, to sit down at once

Gdí'ha /gthē'-hä/ *v.*, *masc.*, returned, connotes somebody has ~ suddenly

Gdíze /gthē'-zä/ *v.*, *pres./past t.*, recover, get

back, to get something back that had been taken

Gdúba /gthü'-bä/ *n.*, group, a splinter group, unit, a specific small part of a larger party, usu. people or things

Gdúba /gthü'-bä/ *pron.*, all, refers to a specific group of people or things

Gé /gā'/ *art.*, the, plural article (designates things that are in groups, a collection of things, or things that are naturally scattered)

Gédišą̀ /gā'-thē-shoⁿ'/ *prep.*, other way, around the ~

Gé't'atą̀ /gā'-t'ä-toⁿ'/ *prep.*, from over there, from somewhere over there

Gí' /gē'/ *v.*, come, get nearer, approach

Gí'dikądè /gē'-thē-koⁿ-thä'/ *v.*, reserved, making a place or opening for somebody in a situation where others may be seated, speaking, standing, applying for, etc.

Gí'masè /gē'-mä-sä'/ *v.*, cut off, 1. to cut something off someone, as in *mą́de k'ą́ kè*, ~(aì), he ~ his bow string 2. a surgical procedure to remove a limb of the human body or to have a person's limb cut off in battle

Gí't'exì /gē'-t'ä-xē'/ *v.*, troubled, 1. being emotionally disturbed, as in ~ over something that has happened 2. suggests being troubled over some physical problem, as in having a stomachache, headache or any physical illness

Gí'žuažì /gē'-zhü-ä-zhē'/ *adj.*, unlucky, unsuccessful, ill omened

Gią́' /gē-oⁿ'/ *v./adj.*, fly, flying

Gíbą /gē'-boⁿ/ *v.*, call, summon, or yell to someone to come

Gídažì /gē'-thä-zhē'/ *adj.*, unhappy, lit., not happy

Gíde /gē'-thä/ *n.*, happiness, cheerfulness, gladness, bliss, etc.

Gídi /gē'-thē/ *adj.*, cheerful, jolly, joyful, merry, in good spirits

Gídik'ą̀ /gē'-thē-k'oⁿ'/ *v.*, allow, making or granting a way clear for somebody, may be a social issue or passageway

Gídik'ą̀ /gē'-thē-k'oⁿ'/ *v.*, relieve, to free or aid somebody from an unpleasant or painful situation

Gíga /gē'-gä/ *v.*, *2nd pers. sing.* (fem., *giá*), come back, come back to here, move back to here, get back to here; *gí'iga*, pl. (fem., *gí'iá*), come back, come back to here, move back to here, get back to here

Gigdé't'ą /gē-gthä'-t'oⁿ/ *adj.*, hereditary, refers to having characteristic traits of a parent or other relatives and ancestors

Gihá /gē-hä'/ *adv.*, beneath; *gigdát'a*, indicates that something is below or beneath another thing

Gík'ą /gē'-k'oⁿ/ *v.*, mourn, to express sadness over somebody's death by weeping openly

Gík'à /gē'-k'ä'/ *v.*, assist, help, to ask for help or support

Giná' /gē-nä'/ *v.*, to ask for something back

Giną́'ą /gē-noⁿ'-oⁿ/ *v.*, 1. to hear something back about oneself, usu. some gossip 2. refers to hearing from or about a close relative, such as a son, daughter, granddaughter who was far away

Gíną̌šè /gē'-noⁿ-shä'/ *v.*, take away, as in to take away from him/her/it, carry away from them/him/her/it

Gíną̌šè /gē'-noⁿ-shä'/ *v.*, seize, take away from, take control of

Gini /gē-nē'/ *v.*, *past t.*, recovered, got well

Gini /gē-nē'/ *v.*, heal, restore to health, get well from sickness

Gíšą̌ /gē'-shoⁿ'/ *adj.*, satisfied, content, pleased, made happy and contented; *dišą*, you are ~; *gíšą*, he/she/it/they are ~; *wéšą*, we are ~

Gišą́·bažì /gē-shoⁿ'-bä-zhē'/ *adj.*, unagreeable, not coming to an agreeable end with another person or persons; dissatisfied, not pleased or happy with something

Gíšą́xt'ì /gē'-shoⁿ-xt'ē'/ *v.*, fulfilled, overly satisfied

Gisí' /gē-sē'/ *v.*, save, saving something for oneself

Giší' /gē-shē'/ *v.*, bet, betting something in a Ponca gambling game (Historically, tribal members bet a variety of personal items in a gambling game, such as a necklace, ear-rings, moccasins, and now, money.)

Gisíde /gē-sē'-thā/ *v.*, remember, to remember something

Gisídeážì /gē-sē'-thā-ä'-zhē'/ *v.t./v.i.*, forget, cannot remember an idea or a thing

Gisídeəbažì /gē-sē'-thā-ə-bä-zhē'/ *v.t./v.i.*, forgot, *past t.* of *gisídeáží*, forget

Gisídewaɖažixt'ì /gē-sē'-thā-wä-thä-zhē-xt'ē'/ *adv.*, unforgettable, memorable, trea-sured or cherished, something that stays in one's mind

Gišką́ /gē-shkoⁿ/ *adj.*, speeding, causing any vehicle to move fast or to speed

Gišką́át'ašą /gē-shkoⁿ'-ä'-t'ä-shoⁿ'/ *adv.*, rapidly, to go rapidly, swiftly, briskly

Gisná /gē-snä'/ *n.*, leech, a bloodsucking aquatic worm that lives in the water, from the class Hirudinea, used by some tribes as medicine

Gisná /gē-snä'/ *n.*, a mythological creature, said to have lived in a lake that never froze during the coldest months of the year and described as looking like a leech or blood-sucker

Gít'exì /gē'-t'ā-xē'/ *adj.*, distressed, usu. asso-ciated with suffering by being distraught, worried, bothered

Gít'exì /gē'-t'ā-xē'/ *adj.*, miserable, an un-easy feeling that precedes becoming ill; *ąɖágít'exì*, personally feeling bad, as in after eating something disagreeable; *í'git'exì*, as in, he's not feeling well after he ate that food

Gíuɖą̀ /gē'-ü-doⁿ'/ *v.*, satisfied 1. being satis-fied or contented after a period of sickness 2. to be ~ with something one ate or drank 3. to receive physical pleasure; *įuɖą̀*, I am satisfied; *ɖiuɖą̀*, you are satisfied; *gíuɖą̀*, he/she/it is satisfied; *wéuɖą̀i*, we are satisfied

Giwádišnà /gē-wä'-thē-shnä'/ *v.*, reveal, to reveal something to a person in a culturally spiritual manner

Giwádišnà /gē-wä'-thē-shnä'/ *n.*, something that shows itself or is made clear by some spiritual entity

Gíwahą̀ì /gē-wä-hoⁿ'-ē'/ *v.t.*, thank, to thank others for someone

Gíwašt'ažì /gē'-wä-sht'ä-zhē'/ *adj.*, parsimo-nious, not willing to part with resources, frugal, thrifty

Gíwikè /gē'-wē-kā'/ *adj.*, truthful, truthful to him/her, being honest or straightforward; *wéwikè*, I am truthful to you/them; *wéwikài*, he/she/they was/were truthful to us

Gíwikè /gē'-wē-kā'/ *adj.*, faithful, loyal, de-voted, committed

Gíxek'à /gē'-xā-k'ä'/ *adj.*, unconfident, self doubting, not being sure something can be done

Gíxek'à àčą /gē'-xā-k'ä' ächoⁿ/ *adj.*, uncer-tainty with fear

Gíxek'à bažì /gē'-xā-k'ä' bä-zhē'/ *adj.*, con-fident, not apprehensive, not anxious, not fearful

Gíža /gē'-zhä/ *v.*, doubt, to doubt him/her, have reservations, disbelief, or simply not believing him/her; *wéža*, doesn't be-lieve him/her/it; *wažá*, doesn't believe or doubts what he/she hears; *į·ža*, doesn't be-lieve or doubts me; *ɖíža*, doesn't believe or doubts you

Gíža /gē'-zhä/ *v./n.*, question, having reserva-tions about a thing or a situation

Gizé' /gē-zä'/ *v.*, creak, something that makes

a grating or squeaking sound; *gígíze,* to continuously make a creaking sound; *bigíze,* make a creaking sound by pressing down

Gížu /gē'-zhü/ *adj.,* fortunate, lucky, chance happening, good fortune, windfall

Guáhidat'à /gü-ä'-hē-thä-t'ä/ *adv.,* yonder, something not within sight over there, to that place over there a shorter distance away

Gúáhidat'a /gü-ä'-hē-thoⁿ-t'ä/ *adv./pron.,* over there, something nearby, something away from the speaker, usu. indicated by pointing toward an area a short distance away

Guáhidị̀ /gü-ä'-hē-theⁿ/ *n.,* that one farther away from me

Gubé'hì /gü-bä'-hē'/ *n.,* hackberry tree, of the genus *Celtis*

Gúədišạ̀ /gü-ə-thē-shoⁿ/ *prep.,* on that side, around on that side

H

h /hə/ sixth consonant in the Ponca alphabet

H'ạ́i! /hoⁿ'-ē!/ *interj.,* oops!, a male expression of one's own clumsiness, mistake, or blunder; used more often when something is accidentally dropped

Há' /hä'/ *n.,* hide, rawhide, the untanned hide of an animal

Há' /hä'/ *n.,* leather, the skin of any animal, usu. softened or dressed for use

Hạ́' /hoⁿ'/ *n.,* night; darkness; *hạ́'ádi,* last night; *hạ́'di,* tonight; *hạ́'ádi guádišạ̀,* the night before last; *hạ́'ámạt'à,* the other night; *e'hạ́adi guádišạ̀,* on the second night before

Há' /hä'/ *interj.,* an appendage to an exclamatory statement, usage is a masculine assertion (used to make strong emphasis, *mạ-gdííga hà'!,* go home now!)

Há' /hä'/ *adj./pron., fem.,* what?

Há'baxdúde /hä'-bä-xthü-dä/ *v.,* shed,
1. refers to a snake shedding its skin
2. proper male name in the Wažážè clan of the Ponca people

Hạ́'dạ /hoⁿ'-doⁿ/ *n.,* nighttime, at night, nocturnal

Hạ́'egạčè /hoⁿ'-ā-goⁿ-chä/ *n., adj.,* morning, daybreak, sunup

Hạ́'idàugdè /hoⁿ'-ē-thä-ü-gthä/ *prep. phr.,* throughout the night

Há'k'ugdè/ hä'-k'ü-gthä/ *n.,* whip-poor-will, of the family Caprimulgidae, *Astrostomus vociferus*

Há'nit'à /hä'-nē-t'ä/ *n.,* sleeve, that part of clothing that covers the arms

Hạ́'uskạ́ska /hoⁿ'-ü-skoⁿ'-skä/ *n.,* midnight, twelve o'clock at night

Há'utạ̀ /hä'-ü-toⁿ/ *n.,* leggings, men's leather leggings, usu. made from the skin of a deer; two pieces of clothing that covered the legs of men like the legs of trousers

Há'utạ̀(tạ̀) /hä'-ü-toⁿ'(toⁿ')/ *n.,* buckskin leggings, leggings, lit., leggings made from deerskin

Há'xdú'à /hä'-xthü-ä'/ *n.,* unintelligent, a person who lacks the mental capacity to solve problems and is regarded as one lacking in intelligence

Ha'xúde hị̀ /hä'-xü-dä heⁿ'/ *n.,* wool, the fibers or fleece taken from sheep and other animals to make textiles

Hạ́dạt'adišạ̀ /hoⁿ'-doⁿ'-t'ä-thē-shoⁿ'/ *prep.,* toward the night

Hạ́dạ ahítedì /hoⁿ'-doⁿ ä-hē'-tä-dē/ *n.,* nightfall, lit., when it comes to night, at the close of the day

Háde / hä'-thä/ *n.,* clothing, refers to a covering of garments for people; clothes

Hạ́de /hoⁿ'-thä/ *n.,* dream, images that come to mind while sleeping; sometimes real and imaginary places, people, and events are seen

Háde /hoⁿ-thā/ *n.*, tonight, this present night

Háde disíhi t'ì /hä'-thä thē-sē'-hē t'ē'/ *n.*, dry cleaners, establishment for professional cleaning of various types of garments

Hádewadạbè /hä'-dā-wä-doⁿ-bā'/ *n.*, horned toad, an insect-eating lizard with spikes on its head, of the genus *Phrynosoma*; — Ponca name derived from the placement of the eyes, which are located on the side of the skull, giving the ability to see in varied directions

Hạ́di /hoⁿ-dē/ *adv/n.*, last night

Hạ́di'tạ̀ /hoⁿ-dē-toⁿ/ *conj.*, since darkness, or since night

Hạ́di gúəđišạ̀ /hoⁿ-dē gü'-ə-thē-shoⁿ/ *adv/n.*, night before last

Hádizàha /hä'-thē-zä'-hä/ *n.*, narrow escape, just barely got away from danger or trouble

Hạ́ga /hoⁿ'-gä/ *n.*, leader, usu. refers to a male person up front, at the head of, the one up front

Háhadè /hä'-hä-dā'/ *adj.*, light, refers to weight—buoyant, feathery

Háhe /hä'-hā/ *interj.*, eh?, an expression of confirmation or agreement for something said

Hạ́nạdì /hoⁿ'-noⁿ-dē'/ *adv./n.*, on the night

Hánit'à č'éškà /hä'-nē-t'ä' ch-ā'-shkä'/ *n.*, short-sleeved, refers to any garment with short sleeves

Hánugahì /hä'-nü-gä-hē'/ *n.*, smartweed, genus *Polygonum* of the Polygonaceae family, causes skin to itch on contact

Háši /hä'-shē/ *adj.*, last, end, after everything else

Haská /hä-skä'/ *n.*, flag, lit., white hide or soft deerskin (orig. carried by the Ponca and members of other tribes as a symbol of peace), a rectangular piece of cloth with

symbols that designate the identity of a nation

Haská ímuzà /hä-skä' ē'-mü-zä'/ *n.*, flagpole, a pole on which a flag is hoisted

Hạ́sni /hoⁿ-snē/ *v.*, the coldness in the dwelling during the night, also refers to the coldness left over in the dwelling overnight

Hạ́t'egà /hoⁿ'-t'ä-gä/ *n.*, housefly, an insect of the family Muscidae, a fly that lives around human beings and is capable of spreading disease

Hạ́t'ẹgà ígaxđì /hoⁿ'-t'äⁿ-gä' ē'-gä-xthē'/ *n.*, flyswatter, a fly-killing instrument also used for controlling other flying insects

Háwadahà /hä'-wä-thä-hä'/ *n.*, buckskin clothes or deerskin clothing, lit., clothing made from animal skins

Háwatè /hä'-wä-tā'/ *n.*, deerskin dress, lit., dress made from animal skins, 1. buckskin or leather dress, a woman's garment 2. a proper name of a female member of the Hísadà clan of the Ponca people

Haxúde /hä-xü'-dā/ *n.*, sheep, livestock known and raised throughout the world, of the family Bovidae, *Ovis aries*

Haxúde'hé't'ạgà /hä-xü'-dā-hä'-t'oⁿ-gä'/ *n.*, bighorn sheep

Haxúde'hé't'ạgà mạ́de /hä-xü'-dā-hä'-t'oⁿ-gä' moⁿ'-dä/ *n.*, strong bow, lit., bighorn sheep bow (The elders tell a story of a strong bow made of the horns of the bighorn sheep and wood.)

Haxúde wákidà /hä-xü'-dā wä'-kē-dä'/ *n.*, shepherd, a person or persons who tends to and guards a flock of sheep

Házi /hä'-zē/ *adj.*, purple, the color purple, also lavender, violet (*T'ú'žíde*, reddish blue, is also used to describe the color purple.)

Házi /hä'-zē/ *n.*, grape, an edible fruit that grows in clusters on woody vines, the species of the *Vitis* genus known and eaten by the Ponca; term now applies to any species of grape

Házi bdáze /hä'-zē bthonⁿ-zā/ *n.*, possum grapes, a woody vine with very small grapes, *Ampelopsis cordata*

Házi bdáze /hä'-zē bthonⁿ-zā/ *n.*, raisin, a dried grape, said to have health benefits

Hážigà /hä'-zhēⁿ-gä'/ *n.*, rope, cord, twine

Házi ní' /hä'-zē nē'/ *n.*, wine, the fermented juice of grapes

Hazízigè /hä-zē'-zē-gä'/ *n.*, rubber, lit., stretchy hide, a stretchy and flexible material that is waterproof, derived from the *Hevea* tree from South America (prehistoric [ca. 1600 BC] use by the Mayans)

Hé' /hä'/ *n.*, head louse (*Pediculus humanus capitis*) that causes infestation (These parasites spend their entire life on the human scalp, feeding on human blood.)

Hé' /hä'/ *n.*, horn, a pointed projection made of hardened protein over bone on the head of some animals, such as cattle, deer, sheep

Hé·' /hä·'/ *interj.*, an appendage to an exclamatory statement, usage is a feminine assertion (used to make strong emphasis, *mągdíiá he·'!*, go home now!)

Hé'ga /hä'-gä/ *adj.*, little, a small amount, usu. refers to a small amount of things

He'gá'bažì /hä-gä-bä-zhē'/ *adj.*, much, lit., not a small amount or not a little

Hé'šádagè /hä'-shä'-thä-gä'/ *n.*, 1. branching horn of the bull elk 2. proper male name among the Ponca people

He'sak'í'bà /hä'-sä-k'ē'-bä'/ *n.*, goat, lit., between two horns, an animal with backward-curved horns, straight hair, and a short tail; *he'sak'í'ba nugà*, billy goat, a male goat; *he'sak'í'ba migà*, nanny goat, a female goat; *he'sak'í'ba žigà*, kid goat

Hé'úbažà /hä'-ü'-bä-zhonⁿ/ *n.*, brow, lit., where

the horns are — above right and left of the brow or forehead, the area at the hairline

He'xága /hä-xä'-gä/ *n.*, elk, lit., rough horn, a large deer (*Cervus canadensis*) native to western North America

Hé'xdì /hä'-xthē'/ *n.*, ground squirrel, a little squirrel that lives underground

Hebádi /hä-bä'-dē/ *n.*, part of the way, stopping after reaching or partially completing a task

Hebádi /hä-bä'-dē/ *adj.*, part of, part of the way, refers to something that was incomplete (*~xčí ahí*, he went only ~ the way)

Hébe /hä'-bä/ *n.*, piece, part of, fraction, a piece or bit of something

Héčį /hä-chēⁿ/ *v.*, sneeze, an involuntary expulsion of air through the nose and mouth caused by some irritation in the nasal passage

Hedú'bažà /hä-thü'-bä-zhonⁿ/ *n.*, swing, a child's swing

Hedúškà /hä-thü'-shkä'/ *n.*, *archaic*, a fraternal organization of the Ponca people consisting of good, upright men who offered ethical teachings to boys (six or seven years old and up), went on hunting expeditions to provide food for widows and the aged, and defended the village in warfare; the term is Hedóška when pronounced in song (The Hedúškà organizations, ca. 1900, among the Southern Ponca included Hedúškà wanáxe, Hedúškà wahádįgè, Hedúškà wasísíge, and Hedúškà gdádi.)

Hedúska'wačí'gaxè /hä-thü'-shkä-wä-chē'-gä-xä'/ *n.*, a dance commonly called the "war dance," a man's dance held in conjunction with the Hedúškà organization

Hedúškà wádahà /hä-thü'-shkä' wä-thä-hä'/ *n.*, the dance paraphernalia of the Hedúškà dancer

Héga /hä'-gä/ *n.*, buzzard, 1. a North American vulture 2. a proper name in the Wažážè clan among the Ponca people

Hegá /hā-gä/ *pron.*, little bit, a small amount of something

Hesą́' /hā-soⁿ/ *n.*, nit, the egg of a parasitic insect, the egg of a louse

Héə'bažą̀ /hā'-ə-bä-zhoⁿ/ *n.*, above the brow, lit., where the horns stick out (The expression designates an area of the face analogous to where the horns of the American bison are, slightly above a man's or woman's brow)

Hí /hē'/ *n.*, teeth (The purpose of teeth is to cut or break down food or crush it to small pieces in the digestive system.)

Hį· /heⁿ'·/ *interj.*, expression made by women when something goes wrong

Hí' /hē'/ *n.* stem, how woody and herbaceous plants can be identified by; *éžąhì'*, elm tree; *wamą́skihì'*, wheat plant

Hį́' /hēⁿ/ *n.*, hair, body hair, hair that develops on the human body other than the hair on the head

Hí'ídižà /hē'-ē'-thē-zhä/ *n.*, toothbrush, a device that consists of bristles on a handle used to clean the teeth and gums

Hí'ídižà /hē'-ē'-thē-zhä/ *n.*, mouthwash or mouth rinse, usu. a flavored antiseptic solution for cleansing the mouth and freshening the breath

Hí'mągdè /hē'-moⁿ-gthä/ *n.*, crutch, cane, a support to help the lame in walking—one end fits under the armpit, with a crosspiece and a handle at mid length that can be held by the hands

Hí'ni'é /hē'-nē-ä'/ *n.*, toothache, a sharp, throbbing pain around a tooth that is caused by dental problems such as a cavity, a cracked tooth, an abscessed tooth, or gum disease

Hí'nušiáha /hē'-nü-shē-ä'-hä/ *n.*, short dog, smaller than a Ponca aborginal dog, called *įšt'á dubà*, four eyes

Hį́'škúbe /hēⁿ-shkü-bä/ *adj.*, hairy, furry, covered with hair

Hí'u'špedì /hē'-ü-shpä-dē/ *n.*, incisors, the sharp-edged front teeth used for cutting food

Hí'úkitè /hē'-ü-kē-tä/ *n.*, joints or bone joints, a place where bones of humans and other vertebrate animals are connected

Hí'usági /hē'-ü-sä'-gē/ *n.*, back of the shin, the calf, the back part of the leg below the knee

Hí'ut'ą́ga /hē'-ü-t'oⁿ-gä/ *n.*, molars, twelve large back teeth used for chewing and grinding food

Hi'wádit'ą̀ /hē-wä'-thē-t'oⁿ/ *n.*, dentist, a person who is a trained practioner in the branch of medicine that deals with treatment of the teeth and related conditions

Híážitedì /hē'-ä'-zhē-tä-dē/ *adv.*, beforehand, making arrangements for something or somebody before a designated time

Hibdį́gè /hē-bthēⁿ'-gä/ *n.*, beans, any type of bean

Hįbdį́ge /hēⁿ-bthēⁿ'-gä/ *n.*, wild sweet peas, *Lathyrus japonicus*

Hibdį́gè bút'ą̀ /hē-bthēⁿ-gä' bü-t'ä/ *n.*, peas, a seed that grows in a pod and is edible, a fruit of the plant *Pisum sativum*

Hibdį́si /hē-bthēⁿ-sē/ *n.*, bean seeds, usu. saved for planting

Hįbé /hēⁿ-bä/ *n.*, shoes, foot covering, usu. made of leather, now made of many synthetic materials

Hįbé'ukédį /hēⁿ-bä-ü-kä-thēⁿ/ *n.*, moccasins, Native American "shoe" made of deerskin or other soft leather from moose and elk; the soles were made from the tough hide of the bison

Hįbégawįxe /hēⁿ-bä-gä-wēⁿ-xä/ *n.*, stockings, hose, nylons, socks, a soft knitted covering worn on the feet

Hįbéką /hēⁿ-bā'-koⁿ/ *n.*, shoelaces, shoe-strings

Hįbé uwákihą̀ /hēⁿ-bā ü-wä'-kē-hoⁿ'/ *n.*, overshoes, galoshes, a large kind of rubber shoe or boot that fits over shoes for protection from water, mud, or snow

Hįdá /heⁿ-thä'/ *interj.*, a female expression indicating something is not or was not done right

Hidá /hē-thä'/ *v.*, swim, go swimming

Hidá' /hē-thä'/ *v.*, bathe, 1. to bathe, wash, cleanse, clean, etc. 2. to swim

Hįdakè /hēⁿ-dä-kä'/ *adj.*, okay, all right, also said as *Hįdá* ("~, let's look into this situation")

Hįdawì /hēⁿ'-thä-wē'/ *n.*, garter, an elastic band to hold socks or stockings in place

Híde /hē'-dä/ *adv.*, below; *hideát'a*, at a certain place below

Hidéá't'adiš'ą̀ /hē-dä'-ä'-t'-ä-thē-shoⁿ'/ *adj.*, southeasterly, in a southeasterly direction

Hídeát'a /hē'-dä-ä'-t'ä/ *n.*, bottom, at the lowest place or bottommost part of something; *hiḋéát'à't'adiżą̀*, toward the bottom of something

Hidéát'a /hē-dä'-ä'-t'ä/ *n.*, southeast, lit., at the bottom, one of the forty-five-degree nautical points on the compass

Hídedéde /hē'-dä-thä'-thä/ *v.*, lower, lowering something with some sort of device

Hidék'idè /hē-thä'-k'ē-thä'/ *v./n.*, hurry, usu. refers to rushing to get ready to go someplace

Hidəát'à /hē-də-ä'-t'ä'/ *n.*, Haskell, Haskell Indian School, Lawrence, Kansas, now Haskell University

Hįdiʃwadaì /hēⁿ-thēʃ'-wä-thäē'/ *v.*, he/she/they hurried us, them

Híga /hē'-gä/ *n.*, story, legend, fable, saga, a true historical or mythological narrative, usu. children's stories of anthropomorphized animals that have a moral

Hígabù /hē'-gä-bü'/ *n.*, the Kickapoo Tribe of Native Americans

Hímągdè /hē'-moⁿ-gthä'/ *n.*, cane, a walking cane, usu. made of wood, now aluminum

Hísadà /hē'-sä-dä'/ *n.*, the Hísadà clan of the Ponca people, lit., straight legs (Alice Fletcher and Francis LeFlesche said the term meant "stretched, referring to the stretch of the legs in running" [(1911)1972: 41–42]. J. O. Dorsey called them "thunder people" [1891:331–32]. They are known by the Ponca as "rain makers.")

Hįská /hēⁿ-skä'/ *n.*, bead, a very small to large rounded piece of glass, wood, or plastic that is pierced for stringing to make a necklace or other kinds of jewelry

Hiúbagudè /hēü'-bä-gü-dä'/ *n.*, toothpick, lit., dig into the teeth; a small stick made of wood or plastic and used to remove food particles from the teeth after a meal

Hiúgašadè /hēü'-gä-shä-dä'/ *n.*, between the teeth

Hiúgašáde íbagudè /hēü'-gä-shä'-dä ē'-bä-gü-dä'/ *n.*, toothpick, lit., something to use to dig between the teeth; a small stick made of wood or plastic and used to remove food particles from the teeth after a meal

Hiúk'itè /hēü'-k'ē-tä'/ *n.*, joint, a place in the skeletal structure where bones meet and are connected

Híxp'e /hēⁿ'-p'ä/ *n.*, cotton, a fluffy fiber from the cotton plant of the genus *Gossypium*, family Malvaceae

Hįxpé' /hēⁿ-xpä'/ *n.*, plume, the fluffy under-tail feathers of an eagle (The Ponca attached this plume of the eagle, considered to be sacred, to the hair for those who were set aside in the Wáwaą̀ ceremony to serve the people. This item has now become an ornamental part of modern Native American women's dance paraphernalia.)

Hižú′ /hē-zhü′/ *n.*, gums, the flesh that surrounds the roots of the teeth

Hižú′niè /hē-zhü′-nē-ä̀/ *n.*, gum disease, gingivitis and periodontitis—affects the tissue housing of the roots of the teeth

Hú /hü′/ *n.*, voice, sounds made by a human with the mouth in talking, laughing, singing, crying; *húsagì*, strong or loud voice; *hú′údą*, good voice; *hú žį́ga*, little voice (personal Wažážè clan name); *hú ḁit′į́ze*, speaking through the noise

Hú· /hü′·/ *v.*, howl, to cry out (*šą́nudà áka ~ gḁì*, the dog ~ed)

Hu′ḁáte /hü-thä′-tä/ *n.*, pelican, a web-footed bird of the family Pelecanidae that has an expanding beak used to catch and store fish

Hú′ḁugà /hü′-thü-gä/ *n.*, Newkirk, Oklahoma

Hú′į̀be /hü′-ē̄ⁿ-bä/ *n.*, fin (of a fish)

Hu′p′á′si′snedè /hü-p′ä′-sē-snä-dä̀/ *n.*, gar, 1. a freshwater fish with a long head and teeth (family Lepisosteidae) 2. sturgeon (family Acipenseridae)

Hú′t′ą̀ /hü′-t′oⁿ/ *v.*, 1. to cry out, as a trapped animal crying out 2. Waḁáhut′ą̀, proper male name in the Wažážè clan of the Ponca people

Hubḁą́ /hü-bthoⁿ′/ *n.*, Fish Smell Village lit., the smell of fish, the name of an ancient Ponca tribal village in Nebraska (This village site was one of the last three Ponca villages near the confluence of the Niobrara and Missouri Rivers before the Ponca's forced removal to Indian Territory)

Hubḁá′ska /hü-bthä′-skä/ *n.*, carp (*Cyprinus carpio*), a freshwater fish with scales

Hubḁáska /hü-bthä′-skä/ *n.*, drum fish, also called freshwater drum, *Aplodinotus grunniens*

Hubḁáska žį̀gà /hü-bthä′-skä zhē̄ⁿ-gä′/ *n.*, sun perch, genus *Perca* of the family Percidae

Húḁugà /hü′-thü-gä/ *n.*, camp circle, orig. referred to the circle of dwellings, usu. tipis (Ca. 1850s, photos show the Ponca encampment scattered with *mą̀it′i* and *t′í ukéḁi*, earthen lodges and tipis.)

Hugáse /hü-gä′-sä/ *v.*, fish, to go fishing

Huhú′ /hü-hü′/ *n.*, fish, generic term, a vertebrate that lives in water and has fins, scales, and gills

Huhú ít′ą̀gà /hü-hü′ ē̄′-t′oⁿ-gä′/ *n.*, bass, largemouth bass, *Micropterus salmoides*

Huhúsįse /hü-hü′-sē̄ⁿ-sä/ *n.*, fish scales (Some fish, such as salmon and carp, are covered with cycloid scales, while perch have ctenoid scales and sturgeon and gars have ganoid scales.)

Hút′ą /hü′-t′oⁿ/ *v.*, bellow, usu. refers to the bellow of a large animal; *nisúde ḁihút′ą*, to cause sound to come from an instrument or whistle, a horn, the whistle of a train

Hútą̀gà /hü′-toⁿ-gä′/ *n.*, the Winnebago Tribe of Native Americans

Huwégasì /hü-wä′-gä-sē̄′/ *n./v.*, fishing tackle, any sort of device used to catch fish, fishing equipment such as lures, baits, hooks, lines, sinkers

Húx′p′è /hü′x-p′ä/ *v.*, cough, a release of air through the windpipe and mouth, often expelling an obstruction, namely, phlegm

Húx′p′è gaštą́žì /hü′x-p′ä′ gä-shtoⁿ′-zhē̄′/ *v.*, hacking cough

Húxp′è /hü′-xp′ä′/ *n.*, common cold, a viral infection that causes coughing, sneezing, fever, etc.

Hužíde /hü-zhē̄′-dä/ *n.*, buffalo carp from the family Catostomidae of the genus *Ictiobus*

Hužíde /hü-zhē'-dä/ *n.*, salmon, one of the species of fish in the family Salmonidae known by the Ponca

I

i /ē/ third vowel in the Ponca alphabet

ị /ēⁿ/ third nasalized vowel in the Ponca alphabet

í' /ē'/ *n.*, mouth, the oral cavity in which humans and animals take food

í' /ē'/ *v.*, to give, offer, present, bestow, grant; *a·í'*, I give/gave; *đi·í'*, he/she/it gives/gave to you; *ạ·í'*, he/she/it, gives/gave to me; *ú'i*, they give/gave to them

ị' /ēⁿ'/ *v.*, carry, to hold while moving, as in ~ a box up the stairs

í'ákigđà /ē'-ä'-kē-gthä'/ *v.*, to kiss, to caress with the lips

í'b'ahạì /ē'-b-ä-hoⁿ-ē'/ *v.*, *3rd pers. sing.*, knew, *past and pres. t. of to know*

í'ba /ē'-bä/ *adj.*, swell, a temporary increase in size of an area of the body due to an injury or illness

í'bahạ̀ /ē'-bä-hoⁿ/ *v.*, to know, *iđáp'ahạ̀*, I know; *íšp'ahạ̀*, you know; knowing; *i'bahạ'ì*, they know; *í'bahạì*, he/she/it knows; *ạđá'bahạ'ì't'ạgatạ̀*, we will have known

í'betạ̀ /ē'-bä-toⁿ/ *v.*, go around, circle, circumnavigate, to walk close by in such a way as to avoid meeting something or someone, or to drive an automobile in such a way as to avoid another automobile or any structure

í'biskì /ē'-bē-skē'/ *v.*, close, usu. refers to somebody being or sitting very close to somebody

ị'čạxt'ì /ēⁿ'-choⁿ-xt'ē'/ *adj.*, recent, just a while ago, a short time ago

ị'čạxt'iàdi /ēⁿ'-choⁿ-xt'ē-ä'-dē/ *adv.*, recently, something that occurred recently at a certain day or time

í'čegạdà /ē'-chä-goⁿ-thä'/ *adj.*, tender, physically painful when touched or slightly bumped

í'da /ē'-dä/ *v.*, *past t.*, birthed, gave birth

Ị'dádạwagidè /ēⁿ-dä'-doⁿ-wä-gē-thä'/ *n.*, relatives, addressing a crowd of people with whom the speaker may be a kinsman

Ị'dadì /ēⁿ'-dä-thē'/ *v.*, to be intoxicated, to get intoxicated by some alcoholic beverage

í'dašudè /ē'-thä-shü-dä'/ *v.*, puff, using the peace pipe to draw and blow smoke

í'dawà /ē'-thä-wä'/ *v.*, cost, charge, rate, the value of something in terms of currency

í'de /ē'-thä/ *v.*, find, to locate something that was lost; *iđáde*, I found it; *íđadè*, you found it; *íđaì*, he/she/it found it

Ị'déugdạ̀ /ēⁿ-dä'-ü-gthoⁿ/ *n.*, Halloween, lit., put mask on, a festive time when Ponca children and adults put on masks and celebrate (Considered to be "all saints day" or "all saints eve" by the Europeans, when children played pranks on others. Joining in, the Ponca people usu. have parties at home and at church for a fun time. Other activities include Native American dances and contests for most comically dressed persons.)

í'didạ̀dạ̀ /ē'-thē-doⁿ'-doⁿ/ *v.*, tug, to tug or jerk and yank repeatedly

í'digdạ̀' /ē'-thē-gthoⁿ/ *v.*, control, manage, regulate, direct

í'dihidè /ē'-thē-hē-dä'/ *v.*, utilize, to make use of something such as a tool

í'dišedà /ē'-thē-shä-thä'/ *n.*, ending, at the conclusion, usu. something that happens or is a part of the ceremonial dances or gatherings that precede the closing

í'dist'à /ē'-thē-st'ä'/ *adj.*, an abundance, 1. refers to fruits on trees, such as wild plums, nuts 2. refers, e.g., to excessive use of decorations on native dance apparel

Į'e á'idą̀dì /ēⁿ-ā ä'-ē-thoⁿ-dē'/ *n.*, "where he came to rest on a stone" (Refers to a historic site where a man was said to have flown as a bird across the Missouri River and left his footprints on a stone.)

Į'e ák'iną̀'ą̀ /ē'-yā ä'-k'ē-noⁿ-oⁿ'/ *v.*, listen, when two or more persons or entities listen to each other in seriousness

Į'e átą /ēⁿ'-ā ä'-toⁿ/ *n.*, sidewalk, a concrete walkway along the side of a street

Į'e gadadą̀ /ē'-ā gä-dä-thoⁿ'/ *n.*, prison, lit., breaking rocks, penitentiary, penal complex

Į'e gajabè /ēⁿ'-ā gä-jä-bā'/ *n.*, marble, a small glass ball used in a game of marbles

Į'ę ná'židè /ēⁿ'-āⁿ nä'-zhē-dä'/ *n.*, stone brick, used for construction of houses and buildings

Í'e nážidedè /ē'-ā nä-zhē-dä-thä'/ *n.*, brick, a made or baked block of clay or other material that is used to build buildings

Į'e žįgà /ēⁿ'-ā zhēⁿ-gä'/ *n.*, pebble, small rock (The Ponca also referred to the *wéši* in the handgame as a "little rock.")

Į'ę' /ēⁿ'-āⁿ/ *n.*, rock, stone, solid mineral aggregate

Í'e'dašádu /ē'-ā-thä-shä'-thü/ *n.*, German people, lit., speaks with guttural sounds, a native or inhabitant of Germany

Í'gadì /ē'-gä-dē'/ *n.*, toilet paper

Í'gadužè /ē'-gä-thü'-zhä'/ *v.*, stir, to stir with a ladle something cooking in a pot

Í'gasè /ē'-gä-sā'/ *v.*, cut with, the instrument used to ~, as in *Mąhí et'áike ~*, He used his knife to ~

Í'gą̀zè /ē'-goⁿ-zā'/ *v.*, mock, ridicule or make fun of

Í'gdebè /ē'-gthä-bā'/ *v.*, regurgitate, vomit, to expel partly digested food from the stomach back to the mouth and out

Í'giudą̀ /ē'-gē-ü-doⁿ'/ *prep. phr.*, lit., to get better from something, benefit from, suggests getting better through some sort of aid in times of sickness or other hardship

Í'giúdą̀žì /ē'-gēü'-doⁿ-zhē'/ *adj.*, ineffective, futile, usu. refers to medicines taken

Í'giúdą̀žì /ē'-gē-ü'-doⁿ-zhē'/ *v. phr.*, did not make him feel well, taking a medicine that was ineffectual on his health

Í'įgè /ēⁿ'-ēⁿ-gā'/ *adj.*, unwanted, not needed, something left over that was not wanted

Í'įgè /ēⁿ'-ēⁿ-gā'/ *v.*, reject, not wanting a thing or things that are unappealing

Í'íge /ēⁿ'-ēⁿ'-gā/ *v.*, beg off, reject, doesn't want something viewed or offered

Í'ji'jì! /ē'-jē-jē'!/ *interj.*, exclamation, an exclamation upon touching something hot

Í'k'ib'ahą̀žì /ē'-k'ē-b-ä-hoⁿ-zhē'/ *adj.*, comatose, being in a state of coma, being unconscious

Í'k'idì /ēⁿ'-k'ē-thē'/ *v.*, tangle, knot, snarl, kink, something that is tangled and twisted, such as hair

Í'k'idibdą̀ /ē'-k'ē-thē-bthoⁿ'/ *v.*, mix, to make a mixture or to combine things into one mass or collection of things

Í'kidibdą̀ /ē'-kē-thē-bthoⁿ'/ *v.*, blend, to mix together, mixture

Í'k'igdaè /ē'-k'ē-gthä-ā'/ *v.*, *pres./past t.*, shared, giving each person in the group the same amount (*mázeskàte ~*, they ~ the money among themselves)

Í'k'ištè /ē'-k'ē-shtä'/ *adj.*, ashamed of something done personally, 1. shame, guilt, embarrassment for personally doing something unbecoming of oneself 2. shamed by owning or having made something on display that is/was inferior to others

Í'kidè /ē'-kē-thä'/ *v.*, awake, conscious, up

Í'kip'ahą̀ /ē'-kē-p'ä-hoⁿ'/ *v.*, awaken, waking up following a period of being comatose or unconscious

Íʼkisǫdà /ē'-kē-soⁿ-thä'/ *v.t.*, to pass from view ("he went over the hill," "he went behind the building out of sight")

Íʼkižù /ē'-kē-zhü'/ *adj.*, proud, pleased and satisfied, usu. about some new possession, such as clothing or jewelry

Íʼmǫdà /ē'-moⁿ-thä'/ *n.*, revenge, seeking to administer punishment in return for something that was done in the past

Íʼmǫdà /ē'-moⁿ-thä'/ *adj.*, vengeful, retaliatory, somebody who wants revenge, ready to take counteraction

Íʼmǫgdè /ē'-moⁿ-gthä'/ *n.*, staff, walking stick

Íʼnǫbdǫ'k'idè /ē'-noⁿ-bthoⁿ'-k'ē-thä'/ *n.*, perfume, Native American man's perfume, derived from the plant *Thalictrum purpurascens*

Íʼnǫgè /ē'-noⁿ-gä'/ *n.*, fare, cost of ticket, money for gasoline and food

Íʼnǫsnùsnu /ē'-noⁿ-snü'-snü/ *v.*, shuffle, to walk without lifting the feet, dragging the feet or taking sliding steps

Íʼnidè /ē'-nē-thä'/ *v.*, to get cured by or with medicine or something else (The Ponca believed that some physical activity, such as dancing, could make a person well.)

Íʼniedè /ē'-nē-ä-thä'/ *n.*, pain, something that causes pain, as in brushing a hand against a sharp object

Íʼnitè /ē'-nē-tä'/ *v.*, admonish, reprimand, and caution somebody concerning something; *wénitè*, to admonish or reprimand two or more

Íʼpʼidagè /ē'-p'ē-thä-gä'/ *n.*, belt, usu. refers to a strip of leather worn around the waist to hold the trousers up; refers to any material around the waist such as a cummerbund or sash

Íʼpʼidagè idágaškè /ē'-p'ē-thä-gä' ē-thä'-gä-shkä'/ *n.*, belt buckle

Íʼšnuga'tʼadišǫ /ē'-shnü-gä-t'ä'-thē-shoⁿ'/ *adj.*, southwesterly, in a southwesterly direction

Íʼšnugat'à /ē'-shnü-gä-t'ä'/ *n.*, southwest, one of the forty-five-degree nautical points on the compass

Íʼšpʼahǫ /ē'-shp'ä-hoⁿ'/ *v.*, *2nd pers. sing.*, you know

Íʼšpʼahǫ'ì /ē'-shp'ä-hoⁿ-ē'/ *v.*, *2nd pers. pl.*, you all know

Íʼštʼè /ē'-sht'ä'/ *adj.*, ashamed, ashamed of, feeling shame, guilt, or disgrace because of some foolish act or statement made; *idák'iaštè*, *1st pers.*, ashamed of something; *ík'ištaì*, *3rd pers.*, ashamed of something

** Įʼštá dipį́že** /ēⁿ-shtä' thē-pēⁿ'-zhä/ *adj.*, closed eyes

Įʼštá ígabižè /ēⁿ-shtä' ē'-gä-bē-zhä/ *n.*, wink, a way of communicating by closing or blinking one eye; flirting by blinking one eye at the opposite sex

Įʼštè /ēⁿ'-shtä'/ *v.*, seem, kind of an impression that something is a certain way, or appears to be

Įʼštegà /ēⁿ'-shtä-goⁿ'/ *adv.*, seemingly, apparent to the senses but not necessarily real

Įʼštegǫ̀žì /ēⁿ'-shtä-goⁿ-zhē'/ *adv.*, seriously, not a triviality, significantly, of value

Íʼštewadè /ē'-shtä-wä-thä'/ *adj.*, ashamed of, the feeling of shame, guilt, embarrassment for unbecoming behavior

Íʼtʼa /ē'-t'ä'/ *v.*, touch, usu. reaching with the tips of the fingers to touch something, as in the act of touching ceremonial sacred items

Íʼtʼadè /ē'-t'ä-thä'/ *n.*, dislike, objectionable, being erroneous in some unwanted act or behavior (*~wadéxt'ì p'áxe*, I did an unlikeable or objectional thing) where the act is not purposeful; *wawéatʼade*, disliking a person for what he/she accomplished (the term is closely related to envy)

Į́'t'ade'áčąì /ē'-t'ä-thā-ä-choⁿ-ē'/ *v.t.*, despise, to look at with contempt or scorn

Į́'t'adè'wadè /ē'-t'ä-thā-wä-thā'/ *v.*, to be unlikeable, to make or do something undesirable; *n.*, something unlikeable

Į́'t'adè át'ašą̀ /ē'-t'ä-thā' ä-t'ä-shoⁿ'/ *v.*, hate, abhor, detest

Į́'t'at'à /ē'-t'ä-t'ä'/ *n.*, northeast, lit., touching here or there, one of the nautical points on the compass

Į́'t'at'à't'adišą̀ /ē'-t'ä-t'ä'-t'ä-thē-shoⁿ'/ *n./adj.*, northeasterly, in a northeasterly direction

I't'áxeá't'adišą̀ /ē-t'ä-xā-ä'-t'ä-thē-shoⁿ'/ *n./adj.*, northwesterly, in a northwesterly direction

I't'áxeát'a /ē-t'ä-xā-ä'-t'ä/ *n.*, northwest, one of the nautical points on the compass

I't'ígądà žįgà /ē-t'ē'-goⁿ-thä' zhēⁿ-gä'/ *n.*, Indian commissioner, referring to the U.S. commissioner of Indian affairs

I't'í'gąde'àt'à wabáxu ité'daikè t'í /ē-t'ē'-goⁿ-thā-ä'-t'ä' wä-bä'-xü ē-tā'-thä-ē-kā' t'ē'/ *n.*, the Library of Congress in Washington DC

I't'í'gąde'àt'à wabáxu ité'daikè ut'í' /ē-t'ē'-goⁿ-thā-ä'-t'ä' wä-bä'-xü ē-tā'-thä-ē-kā' ü-t'ē'/ *n.*, the National Archives in Washington DC

I't'ígąde /ē-t'ē'-goⁿ-thā'/ *n.*, the president of the United States of America

I't'ígąde'át'à /ē-t'ē'-goⁿ-thā-ä'-t'ä/ *n.*, Washington DC, lit., where the president of the United States of America is

Į́'t'ígąde žįgà /ē-t'ē'-goⁿ-thä' zhēⁿ-gä'/ *n.*, vice president, namely, the vice president of the United States of America

Į́'tą /ēⁿ'-toⁿ/ *adv.*, now, at the moment, at this time, at this instant, etc. (~ you can hear it); *į́'čą*, now

Į́'tą'wą̀ /ēⁿ'-toⁿ-woⁿ'/ *adv./interj.*, now what?, an expression used as a remark about a state-ment made or an action taken, usu. said in questioning one's honesty or directness

Į́'ugítį /ē'-ü-gē'-tēⁿ/ *n.*, lit., hit one's own mouth (In ancient times, at the return of a warrior or warriors who had fallen following a war experience, Ponca women hit their lips lightly to emit a staccato cry.)

Į́'u'si'št'à /ē'-ü-sē-sht'oⁿ'/ *v.*, lie, to fabricate, to say an untruth, to deceive, to make a false statement

Į́'ųtį /ēⁿ'-üⁿ-tēⁿ'/ *n.*, handgame (A Plains Indian social guessing game where two persons each hide an object in either of their hands and a person attempts to guess which hands the objects are in. Two opposing teams participate, along with scorekeepers.)

Į́'wadanąžì /ē'-wä-thä-noⁿ-zhē'/ *adv.*, straightaway, immediately, without delay

Į́'wanąžì̀xt'i /ē'-wä-noⁿ-zhēⁿ'-xt'ē/ *conj.*, suddenly, without hesitation, responding to something said or done

Į́'wetį /ēⁿ'-wä-tēⁿ'/ *n.*, hammer, 1. a tool, usu. used for driving nails into wood surfaces 2. a tool used to deliver an impact to flatten or shape an object or to break up objects

Į́'winibdà /ē'-wē-nē-bthä'/ *v.*, I come to you, usu. connotes one petitioning (term now used in prayers)

Į́'xa /ē'-xä/ *v.*, to laugh

Į́'xa'xà /ē'-xä-xä'/ *v.*, laugh at, laugh to scorn, sneer at, make fun of, mock, jeer

Į́'xetewadè /ē'-xā-tā-wä-thä'/ *adj.*, comical, lit., someone or something that makes one laugh, is comical, funny, humorous

Į́'xt'à /ē'-xt'ä'/ *n.*, hex, a spell, a curse; *v.t.*, hexed (*núžįgà akà ~ akà*, the boy was ~)

Į́'xt'amąžì /ēⁿ'-xt'ä-moⁿ-zhē'/ *pron./v.*, dislike, *1st pers. sing., pres. t.*, I don't like it, to dislike an inanimate thing or activity, not caring for the activity, object, or thing, such as a car, a hunting experience, or watching a sporting event

Í'yè' /ē'-yā'/ *v.*, speak, to speak, to talk, to verbalize

Í'yèk'idè /ē'-yā'-k'ē-thā'/ *adj.*, opinionated, lit., cause himself to speak, speaking to a gathering from his/her point of view

Į'žą /ēⁿ'-zhoⁿ/ *v.*, cover with, something used to sleep under, such as a blanket used to cover or sleep under

I'žáge /ē-zhoⁿ'-gā/ *n.*, daughter, lit., his/her daughter, relationship of female child to parent

Íbahą'wanádehidè /ē'-bä-hoⁿ'-wä-noⁿ'-dā-hē-dāⁿ'/ *n.*, philosophy, love of wisdom

Íbahąnąwakidè /ē'-bä-hoⁿ-noⁿ-wä-kē-thā'/ *v. phr.*, let them or cause them to know

Íbahąži /ē'-bä-hoⁿ-zhē'/ *n./adj.*, ignorant, lit., does not know, a person untaught, uneducated, illiterate

Įbe /ēⁿ'-bā/ *n.*, tail feathers, ~ of any bird

Įbe'žąk'à /ēⁿ'-bā-zhoⁿ-k'ä'/ *n.*, scissortail, 1. flycatcher, a bird with long forked tail feathers 2. personal male name in the Đíxidą clan of the Ponca people

Įbehį /ēⁿ'-bā-hēⁿ'/ *n.*, pillow, head support, a bag filled with feathers or other soft material used to cushion the head during sleep or for sitting upon

Įbehį št'ągá /ēⁿ'-bā-hēⁿ' sht'oⁿ-gä'/ *n.*, cushion, a soft pad or pillow used for sitting, kneeling, or lying down

Įbehį udį́šį /ēⁿ'-bā-hēⁿ' ü-thēⁿ'-shēⁿ'/ *n.*, pillowcase, a sacklike, removable cotton covering for a pillow

Íbetą /ē'-bā-toⁿ'/ *v.*, circumnavigate, circle, go around something or somebody to get to the other side of them

Íbist'à /ē'-bē-st'ä'/ *v.*, touch, touching with tips of fingers, as in touching a sacred relic

Ičą́ga /ē-choⁿ'-gä/ *n.*, general term for mice and rats

Ičą́gaskà /ē-choⁿ'-gä-skä'/ *n.*, ermine, 1. the common name for a white northern weasel that has a small, long body with short legs and tail (*Mustela erminea*) 2. white weasel, a male Ponca name

Įčą́gažįgà /ēⁿ-choⁿ'-gä-zhēⁿ-gä'/ *n.*, mouse, a small rodent

Įčą́t'ągà /ēⁿ-choⁿ'-t'oⁿ-gä'/ *n.*, rat, a large, long-tailed rodent of the Muridae family

Ídą /ē'-thoⁿ'/ *v.*, alight, to land, to descend from the air onto the ground or water (a duck can ~ on the water)

Idá'dą'wagądà /ē-dä'-doⁿ-wä-goⁿ-thä'/ *n./v.*, want, usu. refers to a person who yearns for, wishes for, desires material goods; a greedy person

Idá'dè /ē-thä'-thä'/ *v.*, *1st pers. sing.*, I found

Įdá'di'žįgà /ēⁿ-dä'-dē-zhēⁿ-gä'/ *n.*, little father (man or woman saying, my ~) (In the patrilineal kinship system of the Ponca, one designates one's father's younger brother as "little father.")

Įdá'dįgè /ēⁿ-dä'-thēⁿ-gä'/ *n.*, no father, lit., no father, a mythological character described as a large, hairy being, sometimes called Bigfoot or Sasquatch (Searches for such a being have been inconclusive in modern times.)

Idá't'abdè /ē-thä'-t'ä-bthä'/ *pron./v.*, dislike, *1st pers. sing., pres. t.*, lit., I don't like, to dislike an animate thing—humans or lower animals

Idá'ugdè /ē-thä'-ü-gthä'/ *adv.*, always, often, frequently, time and again, regularly

Idábaè /ē-thä'-bä-ä'/ *n.*, quarry, an animal or human being hunted, pursued—usu. refers to waiting for the enemy to come by after carrying out the chase (~ *gdį̨įte*, he waited for the enemy)

Idábašnà /ē-thä'-bä-shnä/ *n.*, scissors, a cutting instrument for cloth, hair, etc.

Idábat'ù /ē-thä'-bä-t'ü/ *adj.*, bracing, holding, or propping something up

Ídąbè /ē'-doⁿ-bä'/ *n.*, center, usu. relates to something that is seen in the middle of a group of things or people

Ídąbeádi /ē'-doⁿ-bä-ä'-dē/ *prep.*, between, flanked by, in the middle where something or somebody can be seen

Įdádą /ēⁿ-dä'-doⁿ/ *pron.*, something, more of an inquiry, as in "What is it?"

Įdáda'ą̀ /ēⁿ-dä-dä-oⁿ/ *pron.*, what, connotes a thing or something (*šé'te ~à ?*, ~ is that?)

Įdádą adį̀ /ēⁿ-dä-doⁿ ä-theⁿ/ *n.*, property, possessions, belongings, stuff

Įdádą bdúga /ēⁿ-dä-doⁿ bthü'-gä/ *pron.*, everything, the whole lot, entirety

Įdádąšt'ewą̀ /ēⁿ-dä-doⁿ-sht'ä-woⁿ/ *pron.*, whatever, whatever one or whatever situation

Įdádąšt'ì /ēⁿ-dä-doⁿ-sht'ē/ *pron.*, whatever, something, an unspecified thing (~ *égidą̀ gą́dái k'i égidą nąi*, he says ~ he likes to say)

Įdádąšt'iáži /ēⁿ-dä-doⁿ-sht'ē-ä'-zhē/ *pron.*, nothing, "it's nothing at all"

Įdádąšt'ìšt'ì /ēⁿ-dä-doⁿ-sht'ē'-sht'ē/ *pron.*, whatsoever

Įdádąštiwą̀ /ēⁿ-dä-doⁿ-shtē-woⁿ/ *pron.*, anything, any kind of thing, whatever

Įdádąšt'iwą̀ /ēⁿ-dä-doⁿ-sht'ē-woⁿ/ *pron.*, something, a suggestion for getting or selecting any of several things

Idádáte /ē-thä'-thä'-tä/ *n.*, tableware, refers to items used to set a table for eating, such as bowls, dishes, plates, knives, forks, and spoons

Įdádąwagidè /ēⁿ-dä-doⁿ-wä-gē-thä'/ *n.*, kinsmen, a term for addressing a group of kinsmen of varied relations, as in, "Kinsmen!/Relatives!, I would speak to you."

Įdádąž̀i /ēⁿ-dä-doⁿ-zhē/ *adj.*, inconsequential, of no concern or nothing to worry about

Įdádi /ēⁿ-dä'-dē/ *n.*, father, *masc./fem.* male parent (my ~ works every day); *idádi*, his father; *įdádi*, my father; * điá'di*, your father

Idádidaì /ē-thä'-dē-thä-ē'/ *n.*, agent, refers to U.S. government agents on Indian reservations

Idádidaì /ē-thä'-dē-thä-ē'/ *n.*, father, 1. refers to someone saying "his father," as related in the Ponca kinship system 2. refers to the government agent at the reservation-level office

Idádidaì /ē-thä'-dē-thäē'/ *n.*, Indian agent, a person who was authorized by the federal government to interact with Native Americans and to approve or disapprove their land leases and land sales; *idádiđait'à*, agency, the office of the agent

Idádisądè /ē-thä'-thē-soⁿ-dä'/ *v.*, tie, wrapping something around a thing to stabilize or secure it

Ídaedè /ē'-thä-ä-thä'/ *n.*, an understanding, having knowledge and interpretation of something, where modern science is unable to explain certain phenomena; phenomena, that process of human experiences that may or may not be observable, sometimes seem physically impossible, and may be termed paranormal in the modern world

Idágaspè /ē-thä'-gä-spä'/ *v.*, collapse, to cause something to sink in or to be weighed down by excess covering

Idágaxadè /ē-thä'-gä-xä-dä'/ *n.*, covering, something used to cover something of any size

Idáhąbdè /ē-thä'-hoⁿ-bthä'/ *v.*, *past. t.*, dreamed, lit., I dreamed; *iđahąbè*, you dreamed; *íhąbđaì*, he/she/they dreamed

Idáhidè /ē-thä'-hē-dā'/ *v.*, interest, to come into interest through a noticeable situation, or to be called to attention or awareness of a situation

Idáhusà /ē-thä'-hü-sä'/ *v., 1st pers. sing.,* scold, lit., I scold

Idák'uhè /ē-thä'-k'ü-hā'/ *adj.,* apprehensive, for fear that, uneasy about something

Idákuhè /ē-thä'-kü-hā'/ *v.,* dread, to be anxious about, worried about disappointment

Ídap'idį /ē'-thä-p'ē-thēⁿ'/ *adj.,* slow, something that is sluggish or dawdling, usu. refers to speed, as in walking or the movement of an automobile

Ídap'idįxt'ì /ē'-thä-p'ē-thēⁿ'-xt'ē'/ *adv.,* very slowly, gradually, bit by bit or little by little

Idáúgdè /ē-thä'-ü-gthā'/ *adv.,* frequently, often, recurrently, habitually

Idáugdè /ē-thä'-ü-gthā'/ *prep.,* throughout, through the whole of something or all parts of; *hą́'dą̀'idáugdè,* throughout the night, right through the night, during all the night; *ą́ba'idáugdè,* throughout the day

Ídaúsi'št'ą̀ /ē'-thä-ü'-sē-sht'oⁿ'/ *v., 2nd pers. sing., pres. t.,* you fabricated a story, you lied

Íde /ē'-thā/ *v.,* speak of, to speak of a person, place, or thing; *íwidè,* 1st pers. sing./pl. pres./past t., speak of, I speak/spoke of you; *í'dadè,* 2nd pers. sing./pl. pres./past t., speak of, you speak/spoke of it/these/those/them/this; *ídaì',* 3rd pers. sing./pl. pres./past t., speak of, he/she/it speaks/spoke of it/these/those/them/this

Í·de /ēⁿ'·-thā/ *v., 1st pers. sing.,* happy, I'm happy, I'm joyful

Įdé' /ēⁿ-dā/ *n.,* face, the front part of the head from the top of the forehead to the base of the chin

Idé' /ē-thä'/ *v., past t.* of *go,* went

Įdé'udíšą /ēⁿ-dā-ü-thē'-shoⁿ/ *n.,* halter, unlike a bridle, a type of a headgear used to lead horses and other animals

Įdé'wabaxù'šką /ēⁿ-dā'-wä-bä-xü'-shkoⁿ'/ *n.,* movies, lit., moving pictures

Įdéáganì /ēⁿ-dā-ä'-gä-nē'/ *n.,* fan, 1. a handheld device for producing a flow of air to one's face 2. the feathers of various fowl that form a feathered fan, esp. eagle tail feathers

Ídedè /ē'-thā-dā'/ *n.,* corner of the mouth

Įdé hį́ škúbe /ēⁿ-dā' hēⁿ' shkü'-bā/ *n.,* beard, lit., thick hair on the face

Įdé sábe'ág'idè /ēⁿ-dā' sä-bä-ä'-g-ē-thä'/ *v. phr.,* I blackened my face, refers to Ponca warriors who painted their faces black before they went to war, meaning they were prepared to die if necessary

Įdé skámà /ēⁿ-dā' skä-mä'/ *n.,* white faces, refers to warrior enemies of the Ponca people

Įdéugdą̀ /ēⁿ-dā'-ü-gthoⁿ'/ *n.,* mask, usu. refers to using a mask at a masquerade

Įdé wábaxù /ēⁿ-dā' wä-bä-xü'/ *n.,* picture, photograph, portrait; an image made by painting, by drawing, with a camera

Įdéwabaxù ídizè /ēⁿ-dā'-wä-bä-xü' ē'-thē-zā'/ *n.,* camera, a device for taking photographs

Ídewadažì /ē'-thā-wä-thä-zhē'/ *adj.,* unspeakable, not to speak of extremely bad things, things that are foul or revolting

Í'didądą̀ / ē'-thē-doⁿ'-doⁿ'/ *v.,* tugging, to tug or jerk and yank repeatedly

Í·digdą̀ /ē'·-thē-gthoⁿ'/ *adv.,* gently, quietly, lightly, smoothly, soothingly, tenderly

Ídisą́de /ē'-thē-soⁿ'-thā/ *v.,* turn over, turn something over, food being cooked; *ídisą́da,* fem., command to turn something over; *ídisą̀dagà,* masc., command to turn something over

Ídišį̀ /ē'-thē-shēⁿ'/ *v.,* feed, usu. refers to providing a meal for somebody but is also used to refer to feeding an animal; *íwadíšį*, to feed them

Ídižǎ /ē'-thē-zhä'/ *v.*, to wash with, as in using an additive in laundering clothes

Idúagdè /ē-thü'-ä-gthä'/ *adj.*, continuous, endless, perpetual

Ígadizè /ē'-gä-dē-zä'/ *v.*, pass by, refers to passing through or by the village dwellings in a ritualistic manner during the Ponca Sun dance ceremony (*Ígadizè waą́*, songs, were sung during the ritual of riders on horseback dragging the sacred pole through the village before the Sun dance commenced. These songs were slow, mournful supplications of a prayerful nature that called for the crowd to be quiet.)

Ígadužà /ē'-gä-thü-zhä'/ *v.*, rinse, lit., to stir, as in swirling clothing around in water to remove the detergent

Ígaskądè /ē'-gä-skoⁿ-thä'/ *v.*, try, attempt, sample, 1. to try or attempt to do something or accomplish something 2. to test the effect of something, as in tasting food or drink

Ígaskądè /ē'-gä-skoⁿ-thä'/ *v.*, taste, to test or discern the flavor of something (To ~ something to determine if the food is too sweet, bitter, bland, sour, tart, etc.)

Ígat'ą̀ /ē'-gä-t'oⁿ'/ *v.*, moan in pain because of some illness or injury

Ịgdą́' /ēⁿ-gthoⁿ'/ *n.*, a mythological creature that dwells in clouded, stormy skies (The word for the sound of thunder comes from the name of this astronomical creature.)

Ịgdą́'hút'ą̀ /ēⁿ-gthoⁿ'-hü-t'oⁿ'/ *n.*, thunder, the sound of the mythological creature called Ịgdą̀

Ịgdą́'si'snedè /ēⁿ-gthoⁿ'-sē-snä-dä'/ *n.*, mountain lion, cougar, puma

Ịgdą́ga /ēⁿ-gthoⁿ'-gä/ *n.*, cat, any domes-

ticated cat (The Ponca Boarding School, where Ponca children learned to speak English, was established ca. 1884. The children were not allowed to speak Ponca. Employees of the school used the term *pussy*. The children used a corruption of the English version, saying *b'ú'sį*. The term became standard use even when speaking Ponca.)

Ịgdą́ga /ēⁿ-gthoⁿ'-gä/ *n.*, black panther, the panther, cougar, or mountain lion (This variety of large cat roamed along the rivers in Oklahoma and has been seen by tribal members many times along the banks of the Arkansas River, running along the east boundary of the Ponca reservation.)

Ịgdą́ga'mą́t'anąhà /ēⁿ-gthoⁿ'-gä-moⁿ'-t'ä-noⁿ'-hä/ *n.*, bobcat, *Lynx rufus* of the cat family Felidae 2. tiger, following the introduction of exotic animals to America

Ịgdé' /ēⁿ-gthä'/ *n.*, feces, solid waste from the body

Ịgdé'babút'à /ēⁿ-gthä'-bä-bü'-t'ä/ *n.*, dung beetle, from the insect order Coleoptera

Ịgdéze /ēⁿ-gthä'-zä/ *n.*, cacophony, a meaningless mixture of sounds, as in cackles, wails

Ịgdéze /ēⁿ-gthä'-zä/ *n.*, speaking voices, esp. the sound of many people speaking at once

Íginąhì /ē'-gē-noⁿ-hē'/ *v.*, permit, let him/her/it do something, permit somebody to do something

Íha /ē'-hä/ *n.*, lips (The upper and lower lips are referred to as labium superius oris and labium inferius oris, respectively.)

Íhą́ dįgè /ē'-hoⁿ' thēⁿ-gä/ *adj.*, motherless, having no living mother or having no known mother

Íha ížidedè /ē'-hä ē'-zhē-dä-thä'/ *n.*, lipstick, a cosmetic product of varied colors applied to the lips

Íhasè' /ē'-hä-sä'/ *n.*, cleft palate, a defect in

newborn babies where the tissues of the lip or palate do not fuse normally

Ịhát'ạgà /ēⁿ-hoⁿ-t'oⁿ-gä/ *adj./n.*, mama's boy, a little boy or teenage boy who clings to his mother (The term does not relate to the Freudian oedipus complex. A boy may also cling to his father in the same manner.)

Ịhát'ạgà /ēⁿ-hoⁿ-t'oⁿ-gä/ *adj./n.*, mama's girl, a little girl or teenaged girl who clings to her mother (The term does not relate to the Freudian electra complex. A girl may also cling to her father in the same manner.)

Ihátạwị /ē-hoⁿ-toⁿ-wēⁿ/ *n.*, the Yankton Tribe of Native Americans

Íha uxága /ē'-hä ü-xä'-gä/ *v.*, chapped lips, lips that become dry and sometimes cracked because of a lack of moisture; also referred to as cheilitis simplex or common cheilitis

Íhe /ē'-hä/ *prep.*, through, by way of, 1. a person performed an action through something 2. a person traveled by a particular route

Íhe /ē'-hä/ *v.*, pass through, go through, lead through, cross through

Ihéde /ē-hä'-thä/ *v.*, lay aside, put aside, set down, put down, to put something down horizontally; *itéde*, *v.*, *pl.*, lay aside, to put things down horizontally

Íhị /ē'-hēⁿ/ *n.*, mustache, the hair growth on a man's upper lip, usu. grown long to drape down on each side of the lips—now such hair is grown to trim and style

Íhudà /ē'-hü-thä/ *n.*, protocol, process, taking steps through something or some person or entity in order to reach or speak to someone

Íhusà /ē'-hü-sä/ *v.*, scold, to scold him/her/it

Ik'á /ē-k'oⁿ/ *n.*, *masc./fem.*, grandmother, his/her grandmother

Ik'á'gi't'è' /ē-k'oⁿ-gē-t'ä/ *n./v.*, toad, lit., death of his/her/its grandmother; a small amphibian similar to a frog

Ịk'ihị /ēⁿ'-k'ē-hēⁿ/ *n.*, whiskers, beard, the hair on a man's chin, cheeks, and above the upper lip

Ík'ik'awadè /ē'-k'ē-k'ä-wä-thä/ *v.*, exchange, 1. to part with in order to receive something of the same value 2. trade, to give something and receive something of the same value

Ík'ik'à /ē'-k'ē-k'oⁿ/ *v. phr.*, gamble with, traditionally the Ponca gamble material goods in their gambling games

Ík'ip'ahà /ē'-k'ē-p'ä-hoⁿ/ *n.*, consciousness, to come back from a period of unconsciousness

Ík'itè /ē'-k'ē-tä/ *v.* cheat, to cheat him/her

Íkạdè /ē'-koⁿ-thä/ *n.*, handle, 1. grip, knob, a device used to hold on to something by hand 2. a device used to attach something to something else

Ikágè /ē-kä'-gä/ *n.*, friend, buddy, pal

Ikágek'idè /ē-kä'-gä-k'ē-thä/ *n.*, friendship, companionship, a special relationship between two or more people; an interpersonal bond

Ịkì /ēⁿ'-kē/ *n.*, chin, in human anatomy, that part of the face protruding under the lips

Íkididà /ē'-kē-thē-doⁿ/ *n.*, rein, a strap or straps attached to the bit of a bridle by which a rider controls the horse

Íkigdaskạdè /ē'-kē-gthä-skoⁿ-thä/ *v.*, rehearse, practice, to do over and over before presentation

Ịkihị /ēⁿ'-kē-hēⁿ/ *n.*, goatee, lit., hair on chin, a style of hair growth on the chin (Historically, Ponca men grew a long goatee and a mustache that hung downward.)

Ịkihị ígaskébe /ēⁿ'-kē-hēⁿ ē'-gä-skä'-bä/ *v.*, shave, to remove hair from the chin with a sharp instrument

Ímądà /ē'-moⁿ-thä'/ *v.*, ill-willed, to have or harbor enmity or hostile feelings against somebody; *wémądà*, having or harboring enmity or hostile feelings against more than one person

Ímąxè /ē'-moⁿ-xä'/ *v.*, ask, asking an individual about a person, place, or thing; *wémąxè*, asking a group of people about a person, place, or thing; *ądámąxaì*, asking me personally about something

Íną'ù' /ē'-noⁿ-ü'/ *v. phr.*, walk close by, to walk or go close by something; *ądáną'ù*, *v.*, *past t.*, passed by me, went close by me

Inądaì /ē-noⁿ-thäē'/ *v.*, *past t.*, placed, to put, place, stand, or lie something specifically somewhere

Inąde /ē-noⁿ-thä'/ *v.*, store, to put a thing away in a particular place

Ínahà /ē'-nä-hä'/ *n.*, *masc./fem.*, mother (my ~ is a caring person)

Ínahà'žįgà /ē'-nä-hä'-zhēⁿ-gä'/ *n.*, little mother (a man or woman saying, my ~) (In the patrilineal kinship system of the Ponca, one designates one's mother's younger sister or one's mother's brother's daughter as "little mother.")

Ínąhì /ē'-noⁿ-hē'/ *v.*, approve, somebody approves; *idánąhì*, *1st pers.*, I approved of; *idanąhì*, *2nd pers.*, you approved something; agree to, to consent, acquiesce

Ínąhį /ē'-noⁿ-hēⁿ'/ *v.*, agree, agree to, to consent, acquiesce

Įnąšè /ēⁿ'-noⁿ-shä'/ *v.*, take away, as in to take away from me, carry away from me

Ínedè /ē'-nä-thä'/ *n.*, kindling, material to start a fire, usu. small sticks and wood chips

Íp'ašedą̀ /ē'-p'ä-sha-thoⁿ'/ *v.*, return quickly, usu. refers to somebody going to a specific destination to conduct business and returning immediately

Íp'idagè á'ba'è /ē'-p'ē-thä-gä' ä'-bä-ä'/ *n.*, beaded belt, *íp'idagè hįská á'ba'è*, belt covered with beads; *hįbé á'ba'è*, moccasins covered with beads

Iš'áge/ /ēsh-ä'-gä/ *n.*, elder or aged man, an old man; *waú'žįgà*, lit., little woman, elder or aged woman, an old woman

Iš'áge /ēsh-ä'-gä/ *n.*, old man, a term of respect; venerable

Isá·ąt'ì /ē-soⁿ'·-oⁿ-t'ē'/ *n.*, the Santee Tribe of Native Americans

Ísabè /ē'-sä-bä'/ *adj.*, grave, refers to a person who is in serious to critical condition due to sickness or injury

Ísabè /ē'-sä-bä'/ *v.*, being distressed, concerned, or worried about a person who has a medical condition and to whom one provides care— *Niášigà dįkè, ~xt'ì ákihidè adį̀*, With distress and concern, he takes care of the person

Ísabè /ē'-sä-bä'/ *v.*, suffer, to suffer, 1. being ill, having a medical condition, affliction 2. distress or concern, worry

Íše /ē'-shä/ *adj.*, abundant, usu. refers to some things that are available in abundance

Íše /ē'-shä/ *adj.*, much, usu. a large amount of something desirable to possess

Íše /ē'-shä/ *adj.*, plenty, usu. refers to particular things, specific things

Iškáážiwadè /ē-shkoⁿ'-ä'-zhē-wä-thä'/ *adj.*, immovable, incapable of being moved

Íškadè gáxe /ē'-shkä-dä' gä'-xä/ *n.*, play, lit., make play activities, e.g., rides in a carnival; refers to other fun activities, as in a circus or at dances, pow-wows, or rodeos

Íškade'gàxe /ē'-shkä-dä-gä-xä/ *n.*, festivities, a place where play activities are happening, carnival

Įšt'á'dú'ba /ēⁿ-sht'ä'-dü'-bä/ *n.*, Four Eyes, lit., an aboriginal short dog with long hair and small spots above the eyes (now extinct), hence "four eyes" (Four Eyes is one of the oldest Ponca family names.)

Įšt'á' gdák'ą /ēⁿ-sht'ä' gthä'-k'oⁿ/ *adj./n.*, cross-eyed, strabismus, a condition that prevents a person from directing both eyes at the same time toward the same point, resulting in double vision

Įšt'á'snì /ēⁿ-sht'ä'-snē/ *n.*, sore eyes, usu. referring to a stye

Įšt'á ádixudè /ēⁿ-sht'ä' ä'-thē-xü-dä'/ *n.*, blur, visual problems causing things to be seen as obscure or indistinct

Įšt'ábdì /ēⁿ-sht'ä'-bthē/ *n.*, a tear, clear saline fluid secreted by the lacrimal gland

Įšt'ádedè /ēⁿ-sht'ä'-thä-dä'/ *n.*, corner of the eye

Įšt'ákiadà /ē-sht'ä'-kē-ä-dä'/ *n.*, snow blindness, inflammation of the eyes caused by exposure to rays reflected from snow or ice

Įšt'áska /ēⁿ-sht'ä'-skä/ *n.*, good vision, lit., white eyes, a person with exceptional vision

Įšt'áxdį /ēⁿ-sht'ä'-xthēⁿ/ *n.*, eye mucus, a slimy substance that lubricates and protects the mucous membranes, associated with the eyes when awakening in the morning

Įšt'į'p'à /ēⁿ-sht'ēⁿ-p'ä/ *n.*, opossum, a marsupial commonly seen in the Western Hemisphere

Įšt'ínikè t'ągá /ē-sht'ē'-nē-kä' t'oⁿ-gä'/ *n.*, ape, refers to any of the large primates; does not include humans

Įštá' /ēⁿ-shtä/ *n.*, eye or eyes, the organ of vision

Įštá'mu'sna'dè /ēⁿ-shtä-mü-snä-dä'/ *n.*, Japanese people, lit., slanted eyes, a person of Japanese descent, a native of Japan

Įštá'úgdè /ēⁿ-shtä-ü'-gthä'/ *n.*, eyeball socket, that cavity in the skull where the eye is situated

Įštá'ušábedą /ēⁿ-shtä'-ü-shä'-bä-thoⁿ/ *n.*, pupil, lit., the dark circular opening in the center of the eye, pupil of the eye

Įštáhà /ēⁿ-shtä'-hä/ *n.*, eyelid, that thin fold of skin that covers and protects the eye

Įštáhį /ēⁿ-shtä-hēⁿ/ *n.*, eyelashes

Įšte /ē'-shtä/ *v.*, shame, as in embarrassment about something personal, to be made uncomfortable

Įštewadè /ē'-shtä-wä-thä/ *adj.*, shameful, disgraceful, as in an act that brings embarrassment or dishonor to oneself or others

Įštúgaxt'ą /ēⁿ-shtü'-gäx-t'oⁿ/ *n.*, eye drops, a solution of liquid drops for eyes, such as lubricants, eyewashes

Įštúskà /ēⁿ-shtü'-skä/ *n.*, sclera, the white part of the eye

It'ą́diàdi /ē-t'oⁿ'-thē-ä'-dē/ *n.*, old, something that has been used for a long time, usu. showing wear and tear

It'ígą /ē-t'ē'-goⁿ/ *n., masc./fem.*, grandfather, his/her grandfather

It'ígądài t'í et'áidà /ē-t'ē'-goⁿ-thä'ē t'ē' ä-t'ä'ē-thoⁿ/ *n.*, White House, ca. 1870, the house of the president of the United States

It'ígądè waną́p'į /ē-t'ē'-goⁿ-thä' wä-noⁿ'-p'ēⁿ/ *n.*, presidential medals (These medals were presented to Native American leaders who went the U.S. capital for tribal matters.)

It'úš'p'à /ē-t'ü'-sh-p'ä/ *n., 3rd pers. sing./pl.*, grandchild (a man or woman saying, his/her ~); *t'ú'šp'à hó*, *1st pers. sing.*, male using abbreviated form addressing ~; *t'ú'šp'à hà*, *1st pers. sing.*, female using abbreviated form addressing ~

Įtąwà· /ēⁿ'-toⁿ-woⁿ'·/ *interj.*, an exclamation expressing an emotion of surprise, as in "what now?"

Itéde /ē-tä-thä/ *v.*, store, putting away some things; *itąáde*, I put some things away; *itédadè*, you put some things away; *itédaì*, he/she/they put some things away; *ihéde*, to put something away; *ihąádè*, I put it away; *ihédadè*, you put it away; *ihédaì*, he/she/they put it away

Įtédi /ēⁿ-tä'-dē/ *v.*, compel, to cause somebody to do something that they should have done after they disregarded the matter

Iúgdą̀ /ēü'-gthoⁿ/ *v.*, put in the mouth, the act of putting food or an object in the mouth

Íwakegà /ē'-wä-kä-gä'/ *v.*, sicken, usu. refers to becoming sickened by something consumed; to become sickened by exposure to extreme cold weather conditions

Íxačačà /ē'-xä-chä-chä'/ *v.*, giggle, chuckle, laugh nervously

Íxa dašt'ą́ži /ē'-xä thä-sht'oⁿ'-zhē/ *n.*, hysterics, condition of laughing or crying

Íxagaskí t'ę̀ /ē'-xä-gä-skē' t'äⁿ/ *adj.*, hysterical, a fit of uncontrolled laughter or crying

Íxt'à /ē'-xt'ä'/ *v.*, bewitched, somebody determined to be ~

Íye /ē'-yä/ *v.*, talk, speak

Íye'mąsà /ē'-yä-moⁿ-sä'/ *v.*, speak conceitedly, 1. to speak boastfully 2. to speak with high and lofty words as though one is better or smarter than others

Íye'nążį̀' /ē'-yä-noⁿ-zhēⁿ/ *v.*, orate, to lecture; to give a speech, oration

Íye'udà /ē'-yä-ü-thä'/ *n./v.*, storyteller, 1. to tell a story 2. a proper male name among the Ponca people

Íye'udàdà /ē'-yä-ü-thä'-thä'/ *n.*, gossip, to gossip; to spread a rumor

Íye'wadéga /ē'-yä-wä-dä'-gä/ *adj./v.*, mouthy, refers to a person who speaks as though he/she knows everything yet speaks with shallow words

Íye ákikì /ē'-yä ä'-kē-kē'/ *v.*, argue over, to argue over some specific thing

Íye ákikidà /ē'-yä ä'-kē-kē-thä'/ *n.*, quarrel, a verbal dispute or conflict between two entities

Íye ákikída /ē'-yä ä'-kē-kē'-thä'/ *n.*, debate, usu. refers to a contentious viewpoint of some concern; a formal argument in public

Íye ákikidà /ē'-yä ä'-kē-kē-thä'/ *v.*, dispute, to question or disagree about something, leading to argument

Iyé bahá /ē-yä' bä-hä'/ *n.*, *archaic*, town crier or herald, a person in the Ponca Nation designated as one who makes public announcements in the camp and proclamations during ceremonies

Íyečačà /ē'-yä-chä-chä'/ *v.*, talking, making "small talk" about no particular subject

Íyegàxe /ē'-yä-gä-xä/ *n.*, speech, lit., making talk, a verbal communication to an audience

Íyeskà /ē'-yä-skä'/ *n.*, interpreter, 1. one who translates a language unknown to others 2. proper feminine name in the Hísadà clan of the Ponca people

Íye tigdè /ē'-yä tē-gthä'/ *n.*, murmur, something said quietly, as somebody speaking in a low, indistinct voice; more than a whisper

Íyeudà /ē'-yä-ü-thä'/ *n.*, rumor, 1. story, buzz, chitchat, something people are repeating without confirming its truth 2. storytelling. See *Híga*, story.

Íye úgdà /ē'-yä ü'-gthä'/ *v.*, to tell a story

Íye wáną̀ą̀ /ē'-yä wä'-noⁿ-oⁿ/ *adj.*, obedient, lit., "one who listens," refers to a young person who practices good social behavior

Íye wáną̀ą̀žì /ē'-yä wä'-noⁿ-oⁿ-zhē'/ *adj.*, disobedient, lit., one who does not listen, rebellious, defiant, behaving badly

Íye wáną̀ą̀'žì /ē'-yä wä'-noⁿ-oⁿ-zhē'/ *adj.*, rebellious, unruly, defiant, deliberately will not listen to someone in authority

Ižą́de /ē-zhoⁿ'-thä/ *n.*, elder sister, lit., the eldest of two or more sisters, usu. refers to the one who is older

Ižáže /ē-zhä'-zhä/ *n.*, name, a person's name, identity, as in a brand; *ižáže dadè*, to call the name of somebody at a gathering for some purpose; *ižáže'í*, to name somebody or something

Ižáže wádadè /ē-zhä'-zhā wä'-thä-dā/ *n.*, roll call, refers to calling out a list of names to determine who is present

Ĺže /ēⁿ'-zhā/ *n.*, vagina, the female organ for copulation; part of the birth canal that leads from the uterus to the external orifice

Ižíge /ē-zheⁿ'-gā/ *n.*, son, lit., his/her son; in the Ponca kinship system, the relationship of child to parent

∫

∫ /∫/ fourth vowel in the Ponca alphabet

∫ /∫/ fourth nasalized vowel in the Ponca alphabet

ɉ

ɉ /jə/ seventh consonant in the Ponca alphabet

Jísasà /jē'-sä-sä/ *n.*, Jesus, the Son of God, Jesus of Nazareth, the second person in the trinity, the Messiah (The one who came into the world offering immortality to all who believe that he was resurrected and is the Son of God.)

Júba /jü'-bä/ *adj.*, some, a few, several, as in number of people or things, sometimes used to characterize less than few or several; *n.*, a thing left in small amounts

Júba /jü'-bä/ *n.*, small amount, a little bit

K

-'k'ite' /k'ē-tā/ *n. suffix*, a place in the skeletal structure where bones meet and are connected; *á' ~*, arm ~; *astúhi ~*, elbow ~; *šinádeu ~*, knee ~

k /kə/ eighth consonant in the Ponca alphabet

K'ą̇́' /k'oⁿ/ *n.*, blood vessel, artery, the vessel that carries blood throughout the body, coming from the heart

K'á'xe hà ínap'į̀ /k'ä'-xā hä' ē'-noⁿ-p'ēⁿ/ *n.*, crow feathers, the entire skin and feathers, including the head, of the crow (This ancient symbolic piece of Ponca Heɖúškà paraphernalia was worn over the left shoulder.)

K'á'xemįgɖà /k'ä'-xā-mēⁿ-gthoⁿ/ *n.*, the crowbelt; a part of a Ponca Heɖúškà member's dance paraphernalia consisting of the feathers of four predatory birds: eagle, hawk, owl, and crow

K'á'xe ník'ašìgà /k'ä'-xā nē'-k'ä-shē-gä/ *n.*, the Crow Tribe of Native Americans (The tribe is also referred to as Húp'a't'i)

K'aɖą́ /k'ä-thoⁿ/ *n.*, noise, a noise caused by metal hitting or being hit by some other object; *k'ak'áɖą*, a continuous noise made by metal hitting or being hit by some other object

K'ą̇́de' /k'oⁿ-dā/ *n.*, plum, a small, round, edible fruit; *k'ą̇́de'hì*, plum tree and plum bush, genus *Prunus*

K'ą̇́de hį́škubè /k'oⁿ-dā hēⁿ-shkü-bä/ *n.*, apricot, a small, round, fuzzy fruit from the genus *Prunus*

K'ą̇́de x'áde /k'oⁿ-dā x'ä'-thā/ *n.*, fall plum, lit., sour plum, a plum tree that bears fruit in the late summer and early fall (*k'ą̇́de x'áde hì*, fall plum tree)

K'ą̇́ge /k'oⁿ-gä/ *adv.*, near, usu. refers to the time of day—close to noon, almost night, near morning; approaching destination, as in ~ly there

-k'ą̇ha /k'oⁿ-hä/ *n. suffix*, side, alongside, as in *xɖabék'ą̇hà*, alongside the timber; *ník'ą̇hà*, alongside the river; *užą́gek'ą̇hà*, side of the road or roadside

K'áiwà /k'ä'-ē-wä/ *n.*, the Kiowa Tribe of Native Americans

K'amą́ /k'ä-moⁿ/ *v./n.*, clang, to make a ringing sound when two pieces of metal hit each other (hear the bells ~)

K'áši /k'ä'-shē/ *n.*, period, time, long time, long period of time (~ *wit'ába mąžì*, I haven't seen you for a ~ of time)

K'ąsi /k'oⁿ-sē/ *n.*, dice, lit., plum seed, orig. used in a Ponca family game called Indian dice, now refers to dice, two small cubes with one to six spots marked on the sides, used in a gambling game

K'áši /k'ä'-shē/ *n.*, long time, a lengthy period of time, ages, for years and years

K'ąt'ą /k'oⁿ-t'oⁿ/ *v.*, tie, to bind, secure, to tie or tether an animal up so that it cannot get away; *ak'ąt'ą*, 1st pers. sing., I tied; *idágik'ąt'ą*, 3rd pers., he tied his own; *idák'ąt'ą*, 1st pers., I tied with (something)

K'áxe /k'ä'-xā/ *n.*, raven, a large crow with glossy black feathers, *Corvus corax*

K'áxe wádihì /k'ä'-xā wä'-thē-hē'/ *n.*, scarecrow, a figure of a man made of straw to scare crows and other birds away from crops

K'i'ą /k'ē-oⁿ'/ *v.*, paint, to put paint on the face, usu. among those who would be going into battle with the enemy

K'í'ška'dè /k'ē'-shkä-dä/ *n.*, joking, to do or say something causing laughter and amusement, 1. to joke with 2. to do something with intention

K'i'u /k'ē'-ü/ *v.*, wounded (in war)

K'ią /k'ē-oⁿ/ *v.t.*, apply, refers to the Ponca practice of putting on or applying ocher or charcoal on the face in preparation for battle (*idé'sabèàde*, I make my face black)

K'iáda /k'ē-oⁿ'-thä/ *n.*, divorce, separation, dissolving or legally ending a marriage

K'íbaxdà /k'ē'-bä-xthä/ *v.*, face, to stand facing toward somebody or something

K'íbaxdą /k'ē'-bä-xthoⁿ/ *adj.*, opposite,

facing another person located directly across from one

-k'idè /k'ē-thä/ *v.*, *suffix*, caused to, an action made by oneself, as in *íyek'idè*, to talk or speak; *xúbek'idè*, to prepare oneself to use one's own spiritual powers; *k'iák'ik'íde*, to prepare oneself for war by putting on war paint, usu. black paint

K'ídikąži'udíšį /k'ē'-thē-koⁿ-zhē-ü-thē'-shēⁿ/ *v.*, refuse, will not accept help or aid; *k'ídikąžiwadè*, would not be able to help or aid following a refusal of offered help

K'ídišibè /k'ē'-thē-shē-bä'/ *v.*, to unlock oneself after being locked up

K'ídixè /k'ē'-thē-xä'/ *n.*, breed, breeding partners in animals

K'ídixè /k'ē'-thē-xä'/ *v.*, mating, in the case of horses, when a mare is sexually receptive toward a stallion and physically prepared for conception

K'igdá't'à /k'ē-gthä'-t'ä'/ *prep.*, underneath, under something (*wádatè kedì ~ itédagà*, place it ~ the table)

K'igdáde /k'ē-gthä'-thä/ *v.*, volunteer, to offer oneself for service without receiving anything in return; *gigdáde*, to offer or present a very personal gift to somebody

K'igdáhidè /k'ē-gthä'-hē-dä/ *v.*, tease, two persons who habitually tease each other

K'igdáxe /k'ē-gthoⁿ'-xä/ *n.*, 1. wasp, a stinging insect with a slender body 2. bee, wasp, yellow jacket

K'igdáxe /k'ē-gthoⁿ'-xä/ *n.*, honeybee, a bee of the the genus *Apis* that gathers nectar from wildflowers and produces sweet food called honey

K'igdáxe /k'ē-gthoⁿ'-xä/ *n.*, honey, a syrupy sweet food made by bees of the genus *Apis*

K'igdáxet'ągà /k'ē-gthoⁿ'-xä-t'oⁿ-gä'/ *n.*,

bumblebee, a large black and yellow bee of the genus *Bombus*, in the family Apidae

K'igdázu /k'ē-gthä'-zü/ *v.*, recover, that point of recovering from a state of sickness — something like awakening from being comatose, the start of recovery

K'igdét'ą /k'ē-gthä'-t'oⁿ/ *n.*, relatives, refers to a person who has one or more relatives whom he/she favors in personal behavior and looks

K'igdéže /k'ē-gthä'-zhä/ *v.*, fall from or become less, as in lowering of self-esteem after doing or accomplishing something of worth

K'igdí'ežubà /k'ē-gthē-ā-zhü-bä/ *n.*, dignity, to dignify self, the state of being worthy of respect or holding a position of respect

K'igdí'wagazù /k'ē-gthē'-wä-gä-zü'/ *v.*, to take a self inventory of one's way of life or dress and appearance

K'igdíbut'à /k'ē-gthē'-bü-t'ä'/ *n.*, 1. coiled snake, usu. refers to a snake that is ready to strike 2. proper male name in the Wažážè clan of the Ponca people

K'igdíežubà /k'ē-gthē'-ā-zhü-bä/ *n.*, self-respect, self-esteem, pride, dignity

K'igdíp'ì /k'ē-gthē'-p'ē'/ *v.*, redeem, to extricate oneself from something detrimental

K'igdíp'up'ù /k'ē-gthē'-p'ü-p'ü'/ *v.*, bundle up, usu. refers to wrapping oneself up with blankets or, as in times past, robes

K'igdísiduà' /k'ē-gthē'-sē-dü-ä'/ *n.*, a person who is undressed, nude; has sexual implications

K'igdíšk'ášk'ą /k'ē-gthē'-shk'oⁿ-shk'oⁿ'/ *v.*, shake, to shake oneself, as when a dog exits from the river and shakes the water off

K'igdíškąškà /k'ē-gthē'-shkoⁿ-shkoⁿ'/ *v.*, wiggle, to move with quick, jerky motions

K'igdíštą /k'ē-gthē'-shtoⁿ'/ *n.*, finish, a single person or a group completing a task

K'igdíšup'à /k'ē-gthē'-shü-p'ä'/ *v.*, clean up, clean one's dwelling or rooms up

K'ik'ák'áda /k'ē-k'oⁿ'-k'oⁿ'-thä/ *adj./v.*, 1. brushing or shaking something off oneself 2. *n.*, an act of readjusting one's lifestyle to something better

K'ík'ína /k'ē'-k'ē'-nä/ *v.*, fighting, engaging in a physical fight between two people or in combat

K'imúgdą̀ /k'ē-mü-gthoⁿ'/ *v.*, run away, break out, or run off, as when a student leaves boarding school without permission

K'ína /k'ē'-nä/ *v.*, fight, to engage in a fight

K'inák'uwįxè /k'ē-noⁿ'-k'ü-wēⁿ-xä'/ *v.*, wander, to go and do something in a haphazard manner; *ak'inąk'uwįxè*, I wandered around in a haphazard manner

K'inąsa /k'ē-noⁿ'-sä/ *v.*, stumble, trip, trip up, lose footing

K'inąse /k'ē-noⁿ'-sä/ *v.*, trip, to fall down by slipping or by one's feet catching something; *ak'inąsè*, I tripped; *đak'inąsè*, you tripped; *k'inąsaì*, he/she/they tripped; *ąk'inąsaì*, we tripped

K'inąšibè /k'ē-noⁿ'-shē-bä/ *v.*, 1. break out, usu. refers to animals, such as horses or cattle 2. take flight from, as a person may escape from confinement

K'ip'áda (ja) /k'ē-p'ä'-dä (jä)/ *n.*, chick, a baby chicken, hatchling

K'ip'áhahà /k'ē-p'ä'-hä-hä'/ *v.*, flaunt, show off, show off shamelessly, try to make an impression; *n.* show-off, one who always stands out in front of others to be seen

K'ip'ínągè /k'ē-p'ē'-noⁿ-gä'/ *n.*, automobile, auto, car

K'ip'ínągè t'ągà /k'ē-p'ē'-noⁿ-gä' t'oⁿ-gä'/ *n.*, bus, a long motor vehicle with many seats, usu. for fare-paying passengers

K'ip'ínągè t'ągà uná'št'ą /k'ē-p'ē'-noⁿ-gä' t'oⁿ-gä' ü-noⁿ'-sht'oⁿ'/ *n.*, bus depot

K'ip'ínągè unáštą /k'ē-p'ē'-noⁿ-gä' ü-noⁿ'-

shtoⁿ/ *n.*, parking lot, a parking lot for automobiles

K'ip'ínągè wat'ú'gdą /k'ē-p'ē'-noⁿ-gā' wä-t'ü'-gthoⁿ/ *n.*, pickup truck

K'ip'ínągè wat'ú'gdą t'ągà /k'ē-p'ē'-noⁿ-gā' wä-t'ü'-gthoⁿ t'oⁿ-gā'/ *n.*, semitruck, eighteen-wheeler

K'ip'ínągè wat'úgdą /k'ē-p'ē'-noⁿ-gā' wä-t'ü'-gthoⁿ/ *n.*, truck, refers to light, medium, or heavy trucks that carry vending foods, pickup trucks, fire trucks, dump trucks, etc., but not semitrucks

K'iwáhąì /k'ē-wä'-hoⁿ-ē'/ *v.*, express gratitude, to thank others

K'iwášką /k'ē-wä'-shkoⁿ/ *v.*, strive, making a personal, exceptional effort, trying hard

K'ixída /k'ē-xē'-thä/ *adj.*, uncertain, unsure, doubtful, that which causes doubt about accomplishing a task

K'ixídabažì /k'ē-xē'-thä-bä-zhē'/ *adj.*, has no uncertainty, 1. is not doubtful, not afraid to try anything 2. proper male name in the Đíxidą clan of the Ponca people

K'íza /k'ē'-zä/ *adj.*, open, open or clear of people and things, a sense of emptiness due to a lack of people and things

K'íza /k'ē'-zä/ *n.*, an open area, clear of any obstruction

K'u'é /k'ü-ā'/ *v.*, sudden move, usu. a vehicle unexpectly moving rapidly toward or away from a person or place

K'ú'gdì /k'ü'-gthē'/ *adj.*, clear, crystal clear, translucent (The Arkansas River was said to be crystal clear when the Ponca first came to this land in Indian Territory in 1878.)

K'ú'gè /k'ü'-gā'/ *n.*, box, trunk, chest, case, crate

K'ú'ge'hįwį'ídawà /k'ü'-gā-hēⁿ-wēⁿ-ē'-thä-wä'/ *n.*, thousand-dollar bill, U.S. currency

K'ú'gewì /k'ü'-gā-wē'/ *n.*, one thousand, the highest number in Ponca (The number one thousand was called *gdébą'hiwì' t'ągà*, big one hundred. According to some historians, the U.S. government issued one thousand dollars in cash to the Ponca in the early 1800s in exchange for passage through their territory and use of the Missouri River. The money was delivered in a case, *k'úge*. Thereafter the Ponca used the term to mean one thousand.)

K'ú'he /k'ü'-hā/ *v.*, scared, to be emotionally fearful, usu. refers to being scared of ghosts

K'ú'he'wadè /k'ü'-hā-wä-thā'/ *n.*, scary, 1. a place that is scary; something that makes a place scary 2. one of the three ancient Ponca village sites near the confluence of the Niobrara and Missouri Rivers

K'ú'wixè /k'ü'-wē-xā'/ *v.*, roam, ramble, wander, etc.

K'ué' /k'ü-ā'/ *n.*, *adj.*, speeding, moving quickly toward, refers to a person in a vehicle that comes quickly toward a person or thing

K'úge /k'ü'-gā/ *n.*, ca. twentieth century, drum, a percussion instrument made of a hollow cylinder with the hide of a bovine or bison stretched over both sides; *k'úge t'ągà*, ceremonial drum, usu. used for various dances and other activities; *mąk'ádatè k'úge*, Native American Church drum

K'úge hà /k'ü'-gā hä'/ *n.*, drum hide (The original hides for making drums were bison hides. The hide used for drums was considered a revered and sacred item in the Ponca Heđúškà organization.)

K'úhe /k'ü'-hā/ *v.*, fearful, fearful of ghosts

K'úhewadè /k'ü'-hā-wä-thā'/ *v./n.*, to haunt, a place that a spirit or ghost makes scary

K'uk'úmi /k'ü-k'ü'-mē/ *n.*, cucumber, 1. a long green vegetable with white inner flesh, usu. eaten in salads 2. pickle, a

cucumber that is flavored with dill and preserved with vinegar and other preservatives

K'úk'úsi' unáži /k'ü'-k'ü'-sē ü-noⁿ-zhē/ *n.*,
pigsty, lit., where the pigs stand, pigpen

K'úkusì /k'ü'-kü-sē'/ *n.*, pig, hog, swine

K'úwįxè /k'ü'-wēⁿ-xā/ *v.*, wander, to go or
travel from place to place without a plan or
itinerary

Kąbdáde /koⁿ-bthä'-dā/ *n.*, palate, the roof of
the mouth

Kąze /koⁿ'-zā/ *n.*, the Kaw Tribe of Native
Americans

Ké /kā'/ *art.*, the, singular article (used with
words that describe an inanimate thing or
idea) (*máze wédixdì ~ údą̀*, ~ computer is
good)

Kí' /kē'/ *conj.*, and, in addition to (*gdébą nąbá
~ wí'*, twenty ~ one)

Kí' /kē'/ *n.*, if, stipulation, usu. used after a
verb (*ítą adái kí', nąp'í' ahí t'akà*, if he goes
now, he'll get there right on time)

Kí'de /kē'-dā/ *v.*, shoot, to discharge a projectile at a target by bow or firearm; *k'ídagà*,
shoot it; *đákíkíde*, you shot yourself (The
term was derived from a scalp dance song
speaking of an enemy warrior.)

Ki'kíbaną̀ /kē-kē'-bä-noⁿ'/ *v.*, race, compete,
competition, usu. in running on foot or on
horseback, but the term is also appropriate
for any type of race on wheels; *kíbaną̀*, race
between two people

Kigdái /kē-gthä'-ē/ *v., 3rd pers. pl.*, departed,
people have left an area to go to their own
home or village

Kigdáni /kē-gthä'-nē/ *v.*, fan, to cool oneself
by using a fan

Kigdáwa /kē-gthä'-wä/ *v.*, count, to count his
own

Kigdáxe įgdè /kē-gthoⁿ'-xä ēⁿ-gthä'/ *n.*, beeswax, wax made by honeybees of the genus *Apis*

Kú'zi /kü'-zē/ *adj*, pallid, having a pale complexion

Kúda wičáša /kü-dä wē-chä'-shä/ *n.*, Lower
Brule Band of the Dakota Nation

L

This letter is not included in the Ponca
alphabet.

M

m /mə/ ninth consonant in the Ponca
alphabet

Má /mä'/ *art.*, the, plural article (designates
animate subjects; can be confused with
áma, which can be either plural or singular)
(*šą́t'ągà ~ wat'é'đè đip'i·*, ~ wolves know how
to kill)

Má /mä'/ *prefix*, action done by cutting with a
knife or other sharp instrument

Má' /mä'/ *n.*, snow, precipitation consisting of
snowflakes that fall from the clouds during
the winter

Mą́' /moⁿ'/ *n.*, a projectile point such as an
arrowhead or spearhead

Má'a' /mä-ä/ *n.*, cottonwood, refers to the
cottonwood tree, genus *Populus*

Má'ahì /mä'-ä-hē/ *n.*, cottonwood tree, genus
Populus, found on the Ponca reservation in
Oklahoma

Má'de /mä'-thä/ *n.*, winter, lit., snowing, one
of the four seasons in the year; *mádeádi*, in
the past winter; *mádedą̀*, in the wintertime

Má'dè /mä'-thä/ *v.*, snowing, precipitation
falling from the clouds as snow

Mą́'de /moⁿ'-dä/ *n.*, bow, a weapon for shooting arrows, usu. made of wood from the
Osage orange tree

Má'dè'uskądskà /mä'-thä'-ü-skoⁿ'-skä/ *n.*,

midwinter, winter solstice, usu. refers to the shortest day of the year

Má'dè gašúde /mä-thä' gä-shü'-dä/ *v.*, snowstorm, refers to a cold blast of air driving snow over the land, blizzard conditions

Mǫ'dehì /moⁿ'-dä'-hē'/ *n.*, arrow shaft, usually made of lightweight wood (One end of the arrowhead is attached and the other end is feathered and nocked, accommodating the bowstring of the bow.)

Mǫ'dèhì /moⁿ'-dä'-hē'/ *n.*, lance, a spear or lance, a weapon made of wood sharpened at one end or with an attached flint projectile point (The lance was primarily used by Comanche warriors in the old days. A one-time battle with the Ponca resulted in a trade of Ponca bows and arrows for Comanche horses in a peace agreement.)

Mǫ'ga /moⁿ'-gä/ *n.*, skunk, a mammal of the order Carnivora, family Mephitidae

Mǫ'gdǫgè /moⁿ'-gthoⁿ-gä/ *n.*, corn hill, the ancient ground preparation for planting corn, building a small hill with a depression where the seed corn was placed and covered

Mǫ'sa' /moⁿ'-sä/ *adj.*, arrogant, conceited, pompous, egotistical

Má'zi bdáska /mä'-zē bthä'-skä/ *n.*, arborvitae, a flat-leaf evergreen of the genus *Thuja*

Má'zihì /mä'-zē-hē'/ *n.*, any cedar or coniferous tree

Mǫá' /moⁿ-ä'/ *n.*, cliff, precipice, crag (A Ponca Heɖúškà song refers to *mǫá zì*, which refers to the yellow cliffs along the north bank of the Missouri River in South Dakota.)

Mǫázi' /moⁿ-ä'-zē/ *n.*, Yellow Cliffs, famous battle site of the Ponca on the north side of the Missouri River where they fought off the enemy

Mǫbíze /moⁿ-bē'-zā/ *adj.*, arid, very dry, bone dry, usu. referring to parts of the country that have very little water or rainfall

Mǫčú /moⁿ-chü'/ *n.*, pear, orig. European, an edible fruit of the genus *Pyrus* (The Ponca, during the first white contact, heard the English word for pear and mistakenly thought it to be *bear*. They applied the Native word for bear to the fruit, hence *mǫčú*, pear.)

Mǫčú' /moⁿ-chü'/ *n.*, bear, a large, omnivorous animal, usu. referring to the grizzly bear, *Ursus arctos horribilis*

Mǫčú Iš'áge /moⁿ-chü' ēsh-ä'-gä/ *n.*, Old Man Bear, the name of a legendary dog who fought the enemy with the Ponca

Mǫčú Nǫžì /moⁿ-chü' noⁿ-zhē''/ *n.*, Standing Bear, a chief of the Ponca people (The chief filed a writ of habeus corpus against the U.S. government in 1879, resulting in the landmark declaration that Indians are persons and entitled to all rights under the Constitution of the United States of America.)

Mǫčúšagè /moⁿ-chü'-shä-gä/ *n.*, bearclaw necklace (The Ponca made these necklaces from the claws of the grizzly bear.)

Máda /mä'-thä/ *v. phr.*, to lie back or to lie down on the back

Mǫdá /moⁿ-dä'/ *adj.*, frozen, icy, ice covered, usu. refers to the ground

Mǫdá xdí't'ù /moⁿ-thoⁿ' xthē'-t'ü/ *adj.*, mean, to be malicious underhandedly, secretly, and sneakily

Mǫdá xdít'ù /moⁿ-thoⁿ' xthē'-t'ü/ *adj.*, unkind, being underhandedly offensive, sneaky, mean

Mǫdé' /moⁿ-dä'/ *n.*, canoe, boat, ship

Mǫdé'giá' /moⁿ-dä'-gē-oⁿ/ *n.*, aircraft, lit., flying canoe, airplane, or jet-propelled aircraft

Mądé'gią' unąšt'ą /moⁿ-dā'-gē-oⁿ' ü-noⁿ'-sht'oⁿ'/ *n.*, airport, a facility where flights take off and land that includes a control tower for incoming and outgoing aircraft

Máde gašúde /mä'-thā gä-shü'-dā/ *n.*, blizzard, a strong, cold wind driving snow, a snowstorm

Mądégią waséką /moⁿ-dā'-gē-oⁿ' wä-sā'-koⁿ/ *n.*, jet aircraft, an aircraft powered with jet engines or jet propulsion

Máde oskąska /mä'-thā ō-skoⁿ'-skä/ *n.*, December, lit., middle of the time when it snows, the twelfth month of the year

Mądé unąšt'ą /moⁿ-dā' ü-noⁿ'-sht'oⁿ/ *n.*, harbor, a place where boats dock

Máde wažį́'gà /mä'-thā wä-zhēⁿ'-gä'/ *n.*, snowbird, generic term for birds that come during snowy winters

Mądí' /moⁿ-thē'/ *v.*, walk, 1. to walk, stride, move on foot 2. "in the walk of life," as in *Údą ~ tenà údą*, To ~ a good life is good

Mądį́'ga(à) /moⁿ-thēⁿ'-gä(ä')/ *v.*, *masc./fem.*, go, a command to go

Mądí'k'a'šižè /moⁿ-thē'-k'ä-shē-zhä'/ *n.*, fox, a general term used for various breeds of small omnivorous animals of the Canidae family

Mądí'xdi'bè /moⁿ-thē'-xthē-bä'/ *n.*, mud, mud on shoes and clothing from walking on muddy paths

Mądiáži /moⁿ-thēä'-zhē/ *n.*, paraplegic, lit., cannot walk, somebody incapacitated by some kind of sickness or injury, somebody who has lost the use of his/her legs, somebody who is bedfast, an invalid

Mądį́ga /moⁿ-thēⁿ'-gä/ *n.*, mole, a small burrowing animal that lives underground, digging tunnels in search of food

Mądík'a xudè /moⁿ-thē'-k'ä xü-dä'/ *n.*, prairie dog, a burrowing rodent that has light brown fur

Mądíka šíbe /moⁿ-thē'-kä shē'-bä/ *n.*, worm, lit., earth intestines, an elongated, soft-bodied nonvertebrate, usu. called fishing worms

Mąé' /moⁿ-ā'/ *v.*, dig, lit., dig ground, dig the ground, as with hands or tools

Mągášudè /moⁿ-gä-shü-dä/ *adj.*, dust storm, consisting of hard-blowing dust from the ground, rising and then settling in or on the ground, people, or things

Mą́gdè /moⁿ-gthä'/ *adj.*, upright, something or somebody that is standing upright, vertical; *dimą́gdè*, to erect something

Mą́ge /moⁿ'-gä/ *n.*, chest, thorax, breast or chest of the upper front part of the human body, the ventral region, that part of the human body between the throat and abdomen

Mą́ge'ni'é /moⁿ'-gä-nē-ā'/ *n.*, tuberculosis, also called TB (A disease of the lungs, TB may spread to any part of the body, such as the brain, kidney, or spine. It is caused by a bacterium called *Mycobacterium tuberculosis*.)

Mą́ge'wahì /moⁿ'-gä-wä-hē'/ *n.*, collarbone, in human anatomy the clavicle, the bone over the top of the chest

Mą́ge'židè /moⁿ'-gä-zhē-dä/ *n.*, robin, lit., robin redbreast, 1. American robin 2. a migratory bird of the thrush family named for its red breast

Mągí'xt'à /moⁿ-gē'-xt'ä/ *n.*, 1. oriole, a small black bird, probably Bullock's oriole (The bird known by the Ponca is probably of the species *icterus*, family Icteridae. The males are black and orange, while females are plain.) 2. any black birds, e.g., common grackle

Mągí'xt'à't'ągà /moⁿ-gē'-xt'ä-t'oⁿ-gä'/ *n.*, magpie, a bird of the genus *Pica*; ~ *áhįšut'à* or *įbe snedè*, magpie (A bird of the crow family with black and white feathers and a long, wedge-shaped tail.)

Máhį /moⁿ’-hēⁿ/ *n.*, knife, 1. blade, table knife, carving knife, cook's knife, dagger, stiletto, etc. 2. proper name of a nonclan member of the Ponca people

Máhí’ /moⁿ-hē’/ *n.*, tallgrass, prairie grasses such as indiangrass (*Sorghastrum nutans*), big bluestem (*Andropogon gerardii*), and little bluestem (*Schizachyrium scoparium*) (The Ponca lands in Nebraska included these tall grasses. In modern times any tall grass is referred to as *mahí’*.)

Mąhí’ /moⁿ-hēⁿ/ *adj.*, weedy, a piece of land full of or consisting of weeds

Mąhí ínąsède /moⁿ-hēⁿ ē’-noⁿ-sā-thā/ *n.*, mower, a push mower or a gas-powered lawn mower

Mąhí škúbe /moⁿ-hēⁿ shkü’-bā/ *n.*, deep weeds, land that is full of deep, thick weeds

Máhi t’ągà /moⁿ’-hē t’oⁿ-gä’/ *n.*, American, lit., big knife (circa 1800s)

Máhi t’ągà /moⁿ’-hē t’oⁿ-gä’/ *n.*, sword, lit., big knife, a weapon with a long steel blade

Máhi t’ú /moⁿ’-hē t’ü’/ *n.*, blue knife (Mentioned by elders of the tribe, a blue flint was quarried to make knives and other usable implements.)

Máhi žįgà /moⁿ’-hē zhēⁿ-gä’/ *n.*, pocketknife, penknife, switchblade

Mąiti /moⁿ-ē’-tē/ *n.*, earthen lodge, mound dwelling, a circular dwelling composed of wooden poles and a thatched roof covered with dirt

Mąk’ą́ /moⁿ-k’oⁿ’/ *n.*, medicine, drug, tablet, pill, medication

Mąk’ą́ /moⁿ-k’oⁿ’/ *n.*, peyote, *Lophophora williamsi*

Mąk’ą́ /moⁿ-k’oⁿ’/ *n.*, the Mąk’ą́ clan of the Ponca people, lit., medicine clan

Mąk’ą́p’ežì /moⁿ-k’oⁿ’-p’ā-zhē’/ *n.*, intoxi-

cant, intoxicating beverages; new, mind-altering drugs

Mąk’ą́datè k’úge /moⁿ-k’oⁿ’-thä-tā’ k’ü’-gā/ *n.*, peyote drum (The drum is composed of an iron kettle measuring usu. 9½ inches at the top and about 8 inches deep. A fitted wet deerskin placed over the top is tied tightly with a cotton rope. Water is also put into the kettle.)

Mąk’ą́ ínąbdą̀ k’idè /moⁿ-k’oⁿ’ ē’-noⁿ-bthoⁿ k’ē-thā’/ *n.*, perfume, columbine, a Native American man's perfume, lit., black medicine perfume, *Aquilegia canadensis* L. (see Howard 1965:69)

Mąką́ bút’a /moⁿ-koⁿ’ bü’-t’ä/ *n.*, aspirin, a medicine that relieves pain and is known as acetylsalicylic acid

Mąką́datè /moⁿkoⁿ’-thä-tā’/ *n.*, lit., eats medicine, Native American Church

Mąką́ sábe /moⁿ-koⁿ’ sä’-bā/ *n.*, coffee, lit., black medicine, the ground seeds from the coffee tree used to make a stimulating drink, drunk with or without sugar and cream

Mąką́ sábe ínąt’ubè /moⁿ-koⁿ’ sä’-bā ē’-noⁿ-t’ü-bā’/ *n.*, *archaic*, coffee grinder, nineteenth- and early twentieth-century product used by the Ponca

Mąką́ sábe nąxdé /moⁿ-koⁿ’ sä’-bā noⁿ-xthā’/ *n.*, coffee grounds

Mąką́ sábe udúhą /moⁿ-koⁿ’ sä’-bā ü-thü’-hoⁿ/ *n.*, coffeepot, a pot to brew coffee in

Mąką́ údiwįt’ì /moⁿ-koⁿ’ ü’-thē-wēⁿ-t’ē’/ *n.*, drugstore, a store that has a pharmarcy and sells miscellaneous medical products and a variety of household and personal items

Mąną́dihà /moⁿ-noⁿ’-thē-hä’/ *v.*, roam, to roam about aimlessly

Mąną́dì /moⁿ-noⁿ’-thē’/ *adj.*, unintentional, accidental, inadvertent, not on purpose

Mąnądį /moⁿ-noⁿ'-thēⁿ/ *v.*, mistake, 1. wrongly understood, wrong or incorrect in understanding, perception, or opinion of a thing or idea 2. to do something unintentionally 3. wander away

Mąnądihahà /moⁿ-noⁿ'-thē-hä-hä'/ *v.*, wander, to drift, to stray from the pathway by mistake or error—suggests searching

Mąnądiwadè /moⁿ-noⁿ'-thē-wä-thä'/ *n.*, a mythological creature, lit., leads astray, a creature that has the appearance of a dwarf or midget who moves about during the early morning, at sundown, and on foggy days, and who has powers to lead a person away

Mąnąni /moⁿ-noⁿ'-nē/ *v., 2nd pers. sing.*, you made a mistake; *mąnąbdì, 1st pers. sing.*, I made a mistake

Mąníni /moⁿ-nē'-nē/ *n.*, quicksand, a mixture of water and sand

Mąnąniáčą /moⁿ-noⁿ'-nē-ä'-choⁿ'/ *v.*, mistaken, "you are badly ~"

Mą́šą /moⁿ'-shoⁿ/ *n.*, feather, plumage on birds; *įbe*, tail feathers of birds; *xidá mą́šą*, eagle feathers; *xidá íbe*, tail feathers of an eagle; *xidá hįxp'é*, eagle plume; *xidá áhį*, eagle wings

Mąsą́'dihà /moⁿ-soⁿ'-thē-hä'/ *n.*, fifty-cent piece, half dollar—(A U.S. coin no longer in circulation.)

Mą́šą'hągà /moⁿ'-shoⁿ-hoⁿ-gä'/ *n.*, center tail feather of the eagle

Mą́šą'p'agdą̀ /moⁿ'-shoⁿ-p'ä-gthoⁿ'/ *n.*, feathered headdress, eagle-feathered headdress, sometimes referred to as warbonnets (*Warbonnet* is a misnomer. The headdress was worn by leaders of men in most tribes at important meetings and other special occasions.)

Mą́šą'šabè /moⁿ'-shoⁿ-shä-bä'/ *n.*, black eagle feather, orig. worn in the hair by new young members of the Hedúškà organization

Mása'xt'i'hì' /moⁿ'-sä-xt'ē-hē'/ *n.*, dogwood tree, lit., the tree that became proud, the dogwood tree, genus *Cornus*

Mąšą́de /moⁿ-shoⁿ'-dä/ *n.*, cave, 1. a hollow place in the ground big enough for a man to enter 2. a small hollow tunnel made by small burrowing animals

Mąšą́de /moⁿ-shoⁿ'-dä/ *n.*, hole, den, burrow, lair (*mądíxudè dįké ~ ke égihà adái*, the prairie dog went into a ~)

Mąsą́di /moⁿ-soⁿ'-thē/ *adj.*, other side, something usu. described as being over or across a thing, such as a river, lake, or ocean (*ní't'ągà ~ at'à adái*, he went to the ~ of the ocean)

Másasà /mä'-sä-sä'/ *v.*, cutting, to cut into strips or pieces with a knife

Mąščį́'gè /moⁿsh-chēⁿ'-gä'/ *n.*, rabbit, cottontail

Mąščį́'ge'sí'snedè /moⁿsh-chē-gä-sē'-snä-dä'/ *n.*, snowshoe hare, *Lepus americanus*, so named because of its large hind legs and feet; also called snowshoe rabbit; its fur turns white during the winter and brown during the summer

Mąščį́'skà /moⁿsh-chēⁿ'-skä'/ *n.*, jackrabbit, *Lepus californicus* (A jackrabbit is a hare, not a rabbit.)

Mąščį́ge wadatè /moⁿ-shchēⁿ'-gä wä-thä-tä'/ *n.*, carrot, an orange, tubular, edible root vegetable (a ~ is considered rabbit food)

Mąščį́ge wadatè /moⁿsh-chēⁿ'-gä wä-thä-tä'/ *n.*, lettuce, an edible broadleaf vegetable (~ is considered rabbit food)

Mási /mä'-sē/ *n.*, hail, frozen rain, small pellets of ice

Mási'žįgà /mä'-sē-zhēⁿ-gä'/ *n.*, sleet, 1. small ice pellets formed by freezing raindrops 2. a proper male name in the Hísadà clan among the Ponca people

Mąšíádì /moⁿ-shē'-ä'-dē'/ *adj.*, high, a place

that is towering, such as a high mountain

Mǫšíáhà /moⁿ-shē'-ä'-hä/ *adj.*, high, anything that relates to height (*t'inǫ́k'a ké* ~, the roof is high)

Mǫšiát'a mǫdì waú /moⁿ-shēä'-t'ä moⁿ-thē' wä-ü'/ *n.*, queen, lit., woman who walks above, refers to women monarchs of foreign countries

Mǫ́škà /moⁿ'-shkä/ *n.*, crawdad, same as crayfish, freshwater crustacean with large claws like a lobster

Mǫska'ska'be /moⁿ-skä'-skä-bä/ *n.*, mud, muddy, sludge, mire

Mǫšt'é /moⁿ-sht'ä'/ *n.*, sunny day, a beautiful sunshiny day

Mǫštéá't'adišǫ̀ /moⁿ-shtä-ä'-t'ä-thē-shoⁿ'/ *adj.*, southerly, in a southerly direction

Mǫštéát'a /moⁿ-shtä'-ä'-t'ä/ *n.*, south, compass point

Mǫšté p'ahǫ́ga /moⁿ-shtä' p'ä-hoⁿ'-gä/ *n.*, June, lit., beginning of sunny days, the sixth month in the year

Mǫt'ánǫhà /moⁿ-t'ä'-noⁿ-hä/ *adj.*, wild, usu. refers to certain nondomesticated animals, such as horses or cats

Mǫtáta /moⁿ-tä'-tä/ *adv.*, inward, on the inside

Mǫ́te /moⁿ'-tä/ *prep.*, in, usu. refers to somebody or something inside a particular place

Mǫ́teádi /moⁿ'-tä-ä'-dē/ *n.*, inside (*t'í'te* ~ *adaì*, he went ~ the house)

Mǫteádi /moⁿ-tä-ä'-dē/ *adv.*, inwardly, innermost self, privately

Mǫ́teát'a /moⁿ'-tä-ä'-t'ä/ *adj.*, inner, inside (*híská te*, ~ *itédaì*, she put the beads in the ~ part of the box); *mǫteát'a*, *n.*, inner recesses, as in a hollow place like a wall, niche, or inner place

Mǫ́ ugánaxdì /moⁿ' ü-gä'-nä-xthēⁿ'/ *n.*, rocket, sky rocket, space rocket

Mawádanì /mä-wä'-dä-nē'/ *n.*, the Mandan Tribe of Native Americans

Mǫ́xe'át'a mǫdé'gi'ǫ̀ /moⁿ'-xä-ä'-t'ä moⁿ-dä'-gē-oⁿ'/ *n.*, spaceship, space shuttle

Mǫ́xe'át'atǫ wadǫ́be /moⁿ'-xä-ä'-t'ä-toⁿ' wä-doⁿ'-bä/ *n.*, satellite, a man-made object circling the earth or other celestial body for purposes of gathering data or providing services for TV, radio, GPS, personal locators, and other devices

Mǫ́xeà't'adišǫ̀ /moⁿ'-xä-ä'-t'ä-thē-shoⁿ'/ *adv.*, upward, in the direction of the sky; *máxeá't'a*, up

Mǫ́xeàt'a /moⁿ'-xä-ä'-t'ä/ *n.*, sky, the sky, heavens, everything above the earth

Mǫxp'í' /moⁿx-p'ē'/ *n.*, cloud, clouds, general term for clouds

Mǫxp'í' bat'á't'à /moⁿx-p'ē' bä-t'ä'-t'ä/ *n.*, cumulus clouds

Mǫxpíat'ǫ̀ /moⁿ-xpē'-ä-t'oⁿ'/ *n.*, the Arapaho Tribe of Native Americans, "Stands on the clouds" (A variant meaning or pronunciation among the Ponca is *mǫxpíat'ù*, blue cloud)

Máxu /mä'-xü/ *n.*, notch, score with a tool, cut into wood to make a mark (a ~ is made at the end of an arrow)

Máxu /mä'-xü/ *v.*, carve, artistic carving into wood by cutting and shaping something; engraving

Mǫxúde /moⁿ-xü'-dä/ *n.*, ashes, residue, cinders

Mǫxúde /moⁿ-xü'-dä/ *n.*, gunpowder, a chemical substance that explodes on impact

Máxudè /mä'-xü-dä/ *n.*, Iowa, the Iowa Tribe of Native Americans

Máxudè waáidǫdì /mä'-xü-dä' wä-ä'-ē-thoⁿ-dē'/ *n.*, lit., where the Iowa Tribe of Native Americans began to cultivate the ground (The village site was Ponca. The custom for the Ponca was to live in one village site for two years, move to another to allow the land to replenish itself, and then move back. It was during the Ponca's absence that the Iowas had come, thinking that no one occupied the land. They were asked to leave.)

Mąžą́ /mo^n-zho^n'/ *n.*, country, a section or region in the world that has its own government, geographic boundaries, and citizens

Mąžą́ /mo^n-zho^n'/ *n.*, land, ground, terra firma

Mąžą́ /mo^n-zho^n'/ *n.*, earth, land

Mąžą́baxù /mo^n-zho^n'-bä-xü'/ *n.*, map, lit., land drawing; mapping

Mąžą́ baxú /mo^n-zho^n' bä-xü'/ *n.*, landmark (To the Ponca, this refers to unique features of the landscape, including rivers and other land features, such as Niagara Falls, Kahokian Mounds, the Mississippi River, Pike's Peak, and mountain ranges and great rivers that were recognizable, especially ones that enabled them to identify their location.)

Mąžą́ha /mo^n-zho^n'-hä/ *n.*, red fox

Mąžą́ iš'áge /mä-zho^n' ēsh-ä'-gä/ *n.*, homelands, refers to original lands of the Ponca that covered hundreds of thousands of acres of land west of the Missouri to western parts of the current state of Nebraska (Information about village sites of the Ponca may be read in Howard 1970.)

Mąžą́ snąsną́ /mo^n-zho^n' sno^n'-sno^n'/ *n.*, flatlands, composed of lands that are nearly level (In the early years in Indian Territory, certain families were allotted good farmlands, *mąžą́ snąsną́*. The elders said that these lands were given to the "half breeds." The real Ponca got rough lands.)

Mąžą́ unà /mo^n-zho^n' ü-nä'/ *n.*, farmer, lit., land borrower, leaser of land, commonly used for the person who leases land, namely, a farmer

Mąžą́ uná /mo^n-zho^n' ü-nä'/ *n.*, lease, 1. usu. refers to a lease of land, the authorized signing of a lease agreement between the Bureau of Indian Affairs and an Indian landowner 2. refers to one (a farmer) who wants to lease land

Mąžą́xe /mo^n-zho^n'-xä/ *n.*, onion, a round, pungent, edible bulb that can be eaten raw or cooked

Mąžą́xe /mo^n-zho^n'-xä/ *n.*, wild onion, genus *Allium*

Mą́ze /mo^n'-zä/ *n.*, metal, iron

Mązé /mo^n-zä'/ *n.*, breast, the upper front part of the female human body, the ventral region

Mązé'dahè /mo^n'-zä-thä-hä'/ *n.*, bridle, a harness for a horse's head

Mązé'į' /mo^n'-zä'-ē^n/ *v.*, breastfeed, to feed an infant with breast milk from female breasts

Máze'í'udà /mo^n'-zä-ē'-ü-thä'/ *n.*, telephone, a telecommunications device that permits two or more persons to speak to one another when they are far apart

Máze'í'udà žįgà /mo^n'-zä-ē'-ü-thä' zhe^n-gä'/ *n.*, cell phone, cellular phone

Máze'ídisè /mo^n'-zä-ē'-thē-sä'/ *n.*, pliers, a hand tool with hinged arms and a jaw to grip something or remove something, such as a bolt

Mązé'k'amạ̀ /mo^n'-zä-k'ä-mo^n'/ *n.*, bells, lit., clanging metal, sleighbells

Mązé'ni /mo^n'-zä-nē/ *n.*, milk

Mązé'p'à /mo^n-zä'-p'ä'/ *n.*, nipple, tip of the mammary gland

Máze'p'è /mo^n'-zä-p'ä'/ *n.*, lit., metal adz, ax

Máze'skà /mo^n'-zä-skä'/ *n.*, money, lit., white metal, currency

Máze baídadà /mo^n'-zä bä-ē'-thä-thä'/ *n.*, barbed wire, usu. two twisted fencing wires with sharp points set at varied intervals used to fence farmland and other types of property to keep something in or out

Máze bdáskà waą /moⁿ'-zā bthä'-skä' wä-oⁿ'/ *n.*, compact disc (CD), a disc used to store digital data, such as recorded music

Mázebdązè /moⁿ'-zā-bthoⁿ-zā'/ *n.*, baling wire (This type of wire was used for agricultural and industrial purposes.)

Mázedahè /moⁿ'-zā-thä-hā'/ *n.*, bit, the metal part of a bridle that goes into the horse's mouth to control the animal

Máze dibébés'į /moⁿ'-zā thē-bā'-bā'-s-ēⁿ/ *n.*, corrugated tin, tin roofing

Máze įdé'wábaxù'škąšką /moⁿ'-zā ēⁿ-dā'-wä'-bä-xü-shkoⁿ'-shkoⁿ/ *n.*, television

Máze ídišnudè /moⁿ'-zā ē'-thē-shnü-dä'/ *n.*, crowbar, a tool made of steel, usually flattened on both ends, with one end bent to be used as a lever to remove nails or other materials affixed to a structure

Máze įšt'á'ugdą /moⁿ'-zā ēⁿ-sht'ä'-ü-gthoⁿ'/ *n.*, eyeglasses, lit., metal on the eye, eyeglasses, spectacles, glasses, etc.

Máze íudà /moⁿ-zā ē'-ü-thä'/ *n.*, radio, an early electronic device that receives news and music from a transmitter or radio station, now may receive a broadcast from a satellite

Mázemà /moⁿ'-zā-moⁿ'/ *n.*, bullet, lit., metal projectile point, shell, ammunition

Mázepè žįgà /moⁿ'-zā-pā' zhēⁿ-gä'/ *n.*, hatchet, a small, short ax that has the head of a hammer opposite the blade

Máze siúgadą /moⁿ'-zā sē-ü'-gä-doⁿ'/ *n.*, horseshoe, a U-shaped piece of metal nailed to the hooves of horses

Mázeskà t'ą' /moⁿ'-zā-skä' t'oⁿ'/ *adj.*, wealthy, rich, very prosperous

Mázeska uží' /moⁿ'-zā-skä ü-zhē'/ *n.*, purse, a handbag women carry filled with many things; billfold, a man's small folded flat case for carrying a couple of dollars

Mázeskà užì /moⁿ'-zā-skä' ü-zhē'/ *n.*, wallet, a small folded leather case for money

Mázeskà wadíšnà /moⁿ'-zā-skä' wä-thē'-shnä/ *n.*, cash, the actual physical form of money, dollars and cents

Máze údiwįt'ì /moⁿ'-zā ü'-thē-wēⁿ-t'ē'/ *n.*, hardware store, a store that sells tools, utensils, locks, hinges, wire

Máze udúgaškè /moⁿ'-zā ü-thü'-gä-shkä'/ *n.*, bolt, a round metal bar with threads of various lengths used with a nut to fasten two or more pieces of solid material together

Máze uk'íądè /moⁿ'-zā ü-k'ē'-oⁿ-thä'/ *n.*, trap, a metal device to catch animals

Máze unéde /moⁿ'-zā ü-nä'-thä/ *n.*, *archaic*, cookstove, lit., metal fireplace, refers to a wood-burning range; *weúhą unéde*, cooking stove or gas or electric range

Máze wa'ą /moⁿ'-zā wä-oⁿ'/ *n.*, radio, lit., metal that sings, refers to a radio or any modern device that provides music

Máze weánąsądè /moⁿ'-zā wää'-noⁿ-soⁿ-dä'/ *n.*, clamp, vise, a device used to hold or fasten two things together

Máze wébatè /moⁿ'-zā wä'-bä-tä'/ *n.*, sewing machine, a machine used to sew various materials together with thread

Máze wédąbè /moⁿ'-zā wä'-doⁿ-bä'/ *n.*, binoculars, also called field glasses, used to magnify objects in the distance

Mázè wédixdì /moⁿ'-zā' wä-thē-xthē'/ *n.*, computer, lit., metal brain, processor, PC

Máze xáxadè /moⁿ'-zā xä'-xä-dä'/ *n.*, screen, a frame with a fine wire mesh designed to prevent entry of insects, usu. on doors and windows

Máze'udúgadą /moⁿ'-zā-ü-thü'-gä-doⁿ'/ *n.*, nails

Máze'udúgaškè /moⁿ'-zā-ü-thü'-gä-shkä'/ *n.*, nuts and bolts, metal fasteners such as nuts, bolts, and screws

Máze'ugásni gáxè /moⁿ'-zā-ü-gä'-snē gä'-xä'/

n., air conditioner, ca. mid-twentieth century, lit., metal that makes cool

Máze utį /moⁿ'-zā ü-tēⁿ/ *n.*, *archaic*, telegraph, lit., hit the metal (The telegraph was the first electric device used to send messages through wire using the invention by Samuel Morse called Morse code. Messages were coded by using dots and dashes embossed on a strip of paper.)

Mázi /mä'-zē/ *n.*, needles of the cedar tree used in tribal rituals and ceremonies

Mázi'žù /mä'-zē-zhü'/ *n.*, mulberry, a small, edible, sweet fruit

Mázi'žùhì /mä'-zē-zhü-hē'/ *n.*, mulberry tree, genus *Morus* in the family Moraceae

Mážihà /moⁿ'-zhē-hä'/ *n.*, quiver, arrow quiver, a case made from the hide of a bison to hold arrows

Mé' /mä'/ *n.*, spring, the season that precedes summertime; *me'ádi*, last spring; *mé'dą*, in the spring

Mé' oskáska /mä' ō-skoⁿ'-skä/ *n.*, July, lit., middle of the summer, the seventh month in the year

Mé' p'ahága /mä' p'ä-hoⁿ'-gä/ *n.*, May, lit., the beginning of summer, the fifth month in the year

Mé máde /mä' mä'-thā/ *v.*, *archaic*, spring snow (The term probably has its origins in the North Country, as it rarely snows in the spring in Oklahoma; however, when it does snow, the term applies.)

Mí' /mē'/ *n.*, month, 1. the period between new moons 2. a month as calculated according to the Gregorian calendar

Mí' /mē'/ *n.*, sun, in our solar system, a star that is a hot ball of fire

Mí'bidehì /mē'-bē-dä-hē'/ *n.*, sumac, one of the shrubs or trees belonging to the genus *Rhus*

Mí'dą máši /mē'-thoⁿ moⁿ'-shē/ *n.*, noon, lit., when the sun is high, noon hour

Mí'dą máši ákihà /mē'-thoⁿ moⁿ'-shē ä'-kē-hoⁿ'/ *n.*, afternoon, the time between noon and evening

Mí'édąbè't'adišą /mē'-ä'-thoⁿ-bä-'t'ä-thē-shoⁿ'/ *adj./adv.*, in an easterly direction, toward the east

Mí'édąbèt'à /mē'-ä'-thoⁿ-bä-'t'ä/ *n.*, east, lit., where the sun comes and shows itself, one of the cardinal points on the compass

Mí'gdą /mē'-gthoⁿ'/ *v.*, married—used in regard to men

Mí'ídąbè /mē'-ē-doⁿ-bä/ *n.*, clock, lit., a sun-seeing device, a device used to measure time, may refer to a sundial, wrist watch, or other device

Mí'idáp'e /mē'-ē-thä'-p'ä/ *v.*, court, adulate, to flatter and adore, seeking the love or affection of a girl

Mí'ídawà /mē'-ē'-thä-wä/ *n.*, calendar, lit., month counter, 1. a system of keeping track of the time in a year (The Ponca counted twelve moons in a year and recognized each moon by natural occurrences.) 2. monthly, referring to something happening every month (~ *a'tí nái*, he comes here ~)

Mí'idé /mē'-ē-thä/ *n.*, sundown

Mí'idé't'à /mē'-ē-thä'-t'ä/ *n.*, west, lit., where the sun goes away, one of the cardinal points on the compass

Mí'idé't'adišą /mē'-ē-thä'-t'ä-thē-shoⁿ'/ *adj./adv.*, in a westerly direction, toward the west

Mí' núxe dátedè /mē' nü-xä dä'-tä-thā'/ *n.*, January, lit., moon when ice begins to form, the first month of the year (The elders also used the following for January: *má'spà*, snow melts, *t'áxt'i má' anągè*, when deer paw the snow, i.e., in search for food.)

Mí'udúnąžiwadažì /mē'-ü-thü'-noⁿ-zhē-wä-thä-zhē'/ *n.*, February, lit., undependable moon, the second month of the year (The elders also used *míxa agdáike*, when the ducks go back [north])

Mi'wá'da /mē-wä'-dä/ *adj.*, jealous, refers to a man who is jealous

Mí'wadixè /mē'-wä-thē-xä'/ *n.*, daughter-in-law (a man or woman may say, "my ~")

Midá'dà /mē-dä'-dä'/ *v.*, crawl away, to move quickly along on hands and knees, as if fleeing

Mída máši wadáte /mē'-thoⁿ moⁿ-shē wä-thä'-tā/ *n.*, dinner, the most important or main meal of the day, which can be served at noon or in the evening

Midé' /mē-dā'/ *v.*, crawl, to crawl (*šéžįgà dįkè ~ ukíhi*, the baby can ~)

Midígdą /mē-thē'-gthoⁿ/ *v.*, flirt, usu. a male's playful act to show that he is attracted to a female

Mí' édąbè /mē' ä'-thoⁿ-bä/ *n.*, sunup, sunrise, daybreak, break of day

Migá' /mē-gä'/ *n.*, female of any adult breed of mammals or fowl, including cattle, seals, moose, chickens, etc.

Mik'áhe /mē-k'ä'-hä/ *n.*, comb, an instrument to run through and untangle hair

Mík'asì /mē'-k'ä-sē'/ *n.*, coyote (*Canis latrans*), a carnivorous canine related to the wolf

Miká' /mē-kä'/ *n.*, raccoon, a nocturnal animal of the genus *Prolcyon*

Miká'e /mē-kä'-ā/ *n.*, star, a luminous sphere of plasma (The nearest star to the earth is the sun.)

Miká'e škáažì /mē-kä'-ā shkoⁿ'-ä-zhē'/ *n.*, North Star, lit., the star that does not move, also called the polestar

Miká'e t'ągà /mē-kä'-ā t'oⁿ-gä'/ *n.*, Venus (The planet, seen sometimes in the evening and other times in the morning, appears large because of its luminosity.)

Miká'e uxp'áde /mē-kä'-ā üx-p'ä'-thā/ *n.*, meteorite, 1. a meteorite on the ground

2. a meteorite falling (The one significant meteorite known to the Ponca was located in the area of Keyapaha, South Dakota. It was call *í'ę dihádądì*, which was also the name of a temporary village site for games. The location was called *í'ę dihádądì*. The term means "where they lifted the rock.")

Miká'e uxp'áde /mē-kä'-ā üx-p'ä'-thā/ *n.*, falling star, a name for a meteorite entering the earth's atmosphere, becoming visible to the human eye

Miká'ídawà /mē-kä'-ē'-thä-wä/ *n.*, quarter, lit., the price of a racoon, a quarter of a dollar

Mikáe uxp'ádetedądì /mē-kä'-ā üx-p'ä'-thā-tä-thoⁿ-dē'/ *n.*, meteor shower (Refers to the great meteor shower that occured ca. 1833. That date was often used as a mark of time for various events, such as birth dates that occurred before or after the meteor shower. The Ponca named a village site for that celestial event.)

Mikáexdì /mē-kä'-ä-xthē'/ *n.*, morel, genus *Morchella*, a pitted, cone-shaped edible fungi (*morel* comes from *L. maurus*, meaning brown), usu. found in the early spring (Resembling the lining of the stomach, ~ is also called *t'eníxa ugdéže*. This term is believed to be of Omaha origin. The term *t'eníxa ugdéže*, in Ponca, refers to part of the stomach of the American bison.)

Míxa /mē'-xä/ *n.*, duck, the common name for a large number of species in the Anatidae family of swimming birds

Míxa agdáikedì /mē'-xä ä-gthä'-ē-kä-dē'/ *n.*, March, lit., when the waterfowl returns home, the third month in the year (The elders also used *įštá ukiadà*, sore eyes [caused by snow glare].)

Míxa gdáxe /mē'-xä gthoⁿ'-xä/ *n.*, black duck, refers to a little black duck that elders say is "not good to eat"

Míxa p'áhį t'ú' /mē'-xä p'ä-hēⁿ t'ü'/ *n.*, mallard, a wild male duck that has a dark green head with a white ring around its neck

Míxasì t'ągà /mē'-xä-sē' t'oⁿ-gä/ *n.*, Big Dipper (Ursa Major), lit., big duck's feet, seven stars resembling a duck's feet

Míxa sì žįgà /mē'-xä sē' zhēⁿ-gä/ *n.*, Little Dipper (Ursa Minor), lit., little duck's feet, seven stars resembling a duck's feet

Míxa skà /mē'-xä skä/ *n.*, white swan, 1. a large waterfowl of the family Anatidae, genus *Cygnus* 2. a proper male name for nonclansmen among the Ponca people

Míxat'ągà /mē'-xä-t'oⁿ-gä/ *n.*, goose, lit., big duck, any of various domesticated or wild geese, such as the Canada goose

Míxe /mē'-xä/ *n.*, cemetery, a place where dead people are buried, a graveyard, a burial ground

Míxe /mē'-xä/ *n.*, grave, a burial site

Míxe Bdáze /mē'-xä bthoⁿ-zä/ *n.*, Narrow Grave, an ancient village site near Ponca, Nebraska, where the Ponca people once lived

Mixúga /mē-xü'-gä/ *n.*, homosexual, gay, usu. refers to a male person feeling sexual attraction toward another male; a person who is sexually attracted to a person of the same sex

Mixúga waù /mē-xü'-gä wä-ü'/ *n.*, lesbian, a female homosexual; homosexual, refers to a female who feels sexually attracted to another female

Mížįgà /mē'-zhēⁿ-gä/ *n.*, girl, a young female, an adolescent female

Mǫmána /mōⁿ-mä'-nä/ *n.*, Morman, a member of a religious sect saved by the Ponca (According to the elders, this group of people were starving and in "pitiful condition" when they came to the Ponca asking for help. The Ponca allowed them to stay on Ponca property for about two or three years, and then they went on their way.)

Mú /mü'/ *prefix*, action done with a force from within

Mú' /mü'/ *n.*, *prefix*, force, indicates force from within

Mú'bixà /mü'-bē-xoⁿ'/ *v.*, spray, water spraying from a sprinkler

Mú'dįgè /mü'-thēⁿ-gä/ *v.*, disintegrate, fall to pieces or apart and be gone by implosion

Mú'gdądì /mü'-gthoⁿ-thē/ *v.*, *slang*, refers to a person who, at one time, "runs wild," has a fling, is unrestrained, sows his "wild oats"

Mú'gidè /mü'-gē-thä/ *n.*, *slang*, the early stages of intoxication, drunk from alcohol consumption

Mú'šedą /mü'-shä-thoⁿ'/ *v.*, destroy, blow to pieces, obliterate, demolish

Mú'xt'ą /mü'-xt'oⁿ'/ *v.*, gush, to gush out by force, refers to liquid flowing out, pouring out

Múbdazè /mü'-bthä-zä/ *n.*, explosion, blast, detonation

Múbixą /mü'-bē-xoⁿ'/ *v.*, inflate, to inflate a balloon, pump up a tire

Múdadà /mü'-dä-dä/ *adj.*, throbbing, usu. associated with pain, hurting, agonizing, aching

Músisi' /mü'-sē-sē/ *n.*, spasm, usu. refers to an involuntary contraction somewhere in the body

Múšną /mü'-shnoⁿ/ *v.*, miss, to fail to hit a target with a gun, bow and arrow, or stone; *muášną*, *pers. pron.*, I missed the target

Mút'úši /mü'-t'ü'-shē/ *v.*, discharge, go off, as in the use of a gun; *t'uší'*, the popping or cracking sound of a cartridge being fired

Mút'ušì /mü'-t'ü-shē/ *v.*, explode, self-explosion, e.g., when a gun with a "hair-trigger" expends a cartridge with a slight touch

Mút'ušì /mü'-t'ü-shē'/ *v.*, implode, an explosion from forces within

Múxa /mü'-xä/ *adj.*, spread out, unfold or open out, as when flowering or blooming

Múxt'ạ žại /mü-xt'oⁿ' zhoⁿ'-ē/ *v.*, flow, stream, run, water or some liquid moving in a stream

N

n /nə/ tenth consonant in the Ponca alphabet

Ná /nä'/ *prefix*, action done by heat or burning

Ná /nä'/ *v.*, ask for, to ask for something from somebody, such as a favor or material goods; *giná*, to ask for something back

Nǫ́ /noⁿ'/ *adj.*, old or older, refers to the age of a person (*núžįgà aka, eí ~i*, the boy is ~)

Nǫ́ /noⁿ'/ *prefix*, action done by use of the feet or a mechanical device

Nạ'ạ́ /noⁿ-oⁿ'/ *v.*, hear, having the sense of hearing

Ná'bdạ /nä'-bthoⁿ'/ *v.*, smell, usu. 1. a good smell that is derived from something delightfully cooked 2. a bad smell that comes from anything that is burnt

Nǫ́'be /noⁿ'-bä/ *adj.*, umami, Japanese origin, describes tastes in cheeses, vegetables, soy sauce

Nǫ́'de /noⁿ'-dä/ *n.*, heart, in anatomy, the organ that pumps blood through blood vessels in humans and animals

Ná'dįgè /nä'-thēⁿ-gä'/ *v.*, burn up, something consumed by fire

Ná'gdè /nä'-gthä'/ *n.*, prisoner, namely, a war prisoner

Ná'šabedè /nä'-shä-bä-thä'/ *v.*, darken, usu. refers to making deerskin darker in color

Ná'sagì /nä'-sä-gē'/ *adj.*, 1. crispy, usu. refers to something that is ~, such as crackers 2. refers to something that has been overcooked or burned to a crisp

Ná'šti'dè /nä'-shtē-dä'/ *v.*, warming, to increase the temperature to a desirable level, as in a dwelling (house) or water being warmed over the fire

Nǫ́t'i't'à /noⁿ'-t'ē-t'ä'/ *n.*, pods, e.g., pods that hold black seeds from a thorn tree

Nǫ́t'i't'ahì /noⁿ'-t'ē-t'ä-hē'/ *n.*, thorn tree, one of the species known to the Ponca in Oklahoma that has long pods with large black seeds

Ná't'u'bè /nä'-t'ü-bä'/ *v.*, boiled, cooked to pieces, usu. something boiled, e.g., meat, potatoes

Ná't'u'šì /nä'-t'ü-shē'/ *v.*, pop, popping sound made by heat, e.g., popcorn, fireworks

Ná'xdį /nä'-xthēⁿ'/ *adj.*, ablaze, aflame, usu. refers to wood burning in the fireplace or the wick on an oil lamp

Ná'xdį /nä'-xthēⁿ'/ *n.*, a proper male name among nonclan members of the Ponca people

Ná'xdį /nä'-xthēⁿ'/ *n.*, flame, from something burning

Nǫ́'xe /noⁿ'-xä/ *n.* glass, any kind of glass, a drinking glass, tumbler, glass jar

Nǫ́'xe /noⁿ'-xä/ *n.*, spirit, 1. phantom, apparition 2. transparent

Ná'zi /nä'-zē/ *v.*, tan, burn to yellow, e.g., toasted bread

Ná'ži /nä'-zhē/ *adv.*, out, something no longer burning or lit, 1. fire is no long burning 2. light bulb has gone out (Most homes until ca. 1950 had oil lamps. The lamp was put out [*bináži*] by blowing on it.)

Ná'zudè /nä'-zü-thä'/ *v.*, singe, char (The process of cooking certain animals included singeing the hair off the animal)

Nạ́ạba /noⁿ-oⁿ'-bä/ *v.*, walk throughout the night until daylight

Nǫ́ áma /noⁿ' ä'-mä/ *n.*, elderly, the elderly; *íš'áge*, elderly (The term originally referred to both men and women. The generations of the early twentieth century began to apply the term to men only.)

Nǫbá /noⁿ-bä'/ *n.*, two, the number two (2)

Nǫbá'ą̀ /noⁿ-bä'-oⁿ/ *adv.*, twice, two times

Nǫbá' ída /noⁿ-bä' ē'-dä/ *n.*, twins, two children conceived in the same pregnancy (Twins may be monozygotic [identical], looking alike, or dizygotic [fraternal], not looking alike.)

Nǫbdá'skà /noⁿ-bthä'-skä/ *v.*, flatten, to flatten something that contains air, usu. a tire on an automobile

Nǫbádądà /noⁿ-bä'-thoⁿ-thoⁿ/ *n.*, twos, "by twos," as in they came in by twos or two at a time; *dábdįdądà*, by threes; *dúbadądà*, by fours, etc.

Nǫbáha /noⁿ-bä'-hä/ *n.*, pair, duo, two of a kind, two things that are identical or similar

Nǫbáha /noⁿ-bä'-hä/ *adv.*, double, two together

Nǫbé /noⁿ-bä'/ *n.*, hand, in human anatomy, that part of the body that has a palm, fingers, and thumb and is located at the end of the arm

Nǫbé' /noⁿ-bä'/ *n.*, fingers, in anatomy, the five digits of the hand

Nǫbé'ibík'à /noⁿ-bä-ē-bē'-k'ä/ *n.*, towel, hand towel; *idéibik'à*, face towel (Both terms refer to an absorbent cloth used to dry hands, face, and body.)

Nǫbé'p'asì /noⁿ-bä-p'ä-sē/ *n.*, fingertips

Nǫbé' šágè /noⁿ-bä' shä'-gä/ *n.*, fingernails, that part of the human anatomy that covers the tips of the fingers, composed of keratin

Nǫbé'šáge'wahì /noⁿ-bä'-shä-gä-wä-hē/ *n.*, fingernail bone, that part of the human anatomy under the fingernails called the phalanx bone

Nǫbé'šą́k'à /noⁿ-bä'-shoⁿ'-k'ä/ *n.*, fist, the fingers tightly curled into the hand

Nǫbé'uɖí'šį̀ /noⁿ-bä'-ü-thē'-shēⁿ/ *n.*, gloves, a protective covering for the hands

Nǫbé'ušą́šą /noⁿ-bä-ü-shoⁿ'-shoⁿ/ *n.*, wrist

Nǫbé'wé'bazù /noⁿ-bä'-wä'-bä-zü/ *n.*, pointing finger, refers to the index finger, trigger finger, forefinger

Nǫbé'wé'dabɖì /noⁿ-bä'-wä'-thä-bthē/ *n.*, middle finger, third finger

Nǫbé'wé'dubà /noⁿ-bä'-wä'-dü-bä/ *n.*, ring finger

Nabé bahá /nä-bä' bä-hä/ *v.*, lit., show of hands, surrender, a hand gesture to declare one is defeated (The word originated during World Wars I and II, when enemy soldiers were captured. In ancient times, the Ponca took no captives except women and children.)

Nǫbé bazú /noⁿ-bä' bä-zü/ *v.*, greeting, the Plains Native American sign language greeting of rubbing hands together upon seeing a friend or relative after a long period of time, indicating delight and happiness over meeting again

Nǫbé gačáčakì /noⁿ-bä' gä-chä'-chä-kē/ *n./v.*, applaud, an expression of approval made by clapping the hands

Nǫbéhi ut'ą́ga /noⁿ-bä'-hē ü-t'oⁿ'-gä/ (*masc./fem.*) (**Nǫbóho t'ągà** /noⁿ-bō'-hō t'oⁿ-gä/ [*masc.*]) *n.*, thumb

Nǫbéhi užį́ga /noⁿ-bä'-hē ü-zhēⁿ'-gä/ (*masc./fem.*) (**Nǫbúhu žį́gà** /noⁿ-bü'-hü zhēⁿ'-gä/ [*masc.*]) *n.*, little finger

Nǫbé í'snaɖè /noⁿ-bä' ē'-snä-thä/ *n.*, hand lotion, a commercial product to help keep skin soft and smooth, usu. used by women (The term applies to all body creams and lotions.)

Nǫbép'asì /noⁿ-bä-p'ä-sē/ *n.*, tip of fingers

Nǫbéúɖą /noⁿ-bä'-ü-thoⁿ/ *n.*, handshake, a greeting by two people grasping right hand to right hand and pumping with an up-and-down movement

Nǫ̨beúdixdà /noⁿ-bāü'-thē-xthä'/ *n.*, ring,
a circular piece of jewelry worn around a
finger, usu. made of some precious metal,
such as silver or gold

Nǫ̨béudíźa /noⁿ-bā'-ü-thē'-zhä/ *n.*, washbasin, 1. a bowl-shaped plumbing fixture
used to wash one's hands 2. a sink (*įdéuɖíźa*,
to wash one's face in)

Nǫ̨béudúdǫ̨ /noⁿ-bā'-ü-thü'-doⁿ/ *n.*, palm,
the surface of the open hand

Nǫ̨bé ukíte /noⁿ-bā' ü-kē'-tā/ *n.*, knuckles, the
joints in the fingers

Nǫ̨ɖádehà /noⁿ-thä'-dā-hä'/ *n.*, temple, the
side of the head between the eyes and ears

Nǫ̨ɖádehà hị /noⁿ-thä'-dā-hä' hēⁿ/ *n.*, sideburns, hair in front of the ears

Nǫ̨ɖáha /noⁿ-dä'-hä/ *v.*, live on, live on well, a
spiritual word that connotes hope for indi-
vidual(s) to carry on their lives with good
health, emotional stability, and prosperity

Nǫ̨ɖáha /noⁿ-dä'-hä/ *adj.*, ongoing, long-
lasting, enduring, usu. refers to continuing life in good health, happiness, contentment, etc.

Nǫ̨ɖáha /noⁿ-dä'-hä/ *adv.*, walk further, refers
to a person's condition in life, to live long in
continuing good health

Nǫ́de /noⁿ-dā/ *n.*, floor, that part of a building or house that is walked or stood on

Nǫ́de /noⁿ-thā/ *adj.*, erroneous, thoughts or
ideas that contain error, incorrect or wrong
answers

Nǫ́·de /noⁿ'-dā/ *n.*, rear, in the back part, at
the rear of something, the part that is farthest from the front

Nǫ́dè'ǫ̨wǫ́gdegà /noⁿ-dā'-oⁿ-woⁿ'-gthä-goⁿ'/
v., believe, lit., because it is in my heart
(The Ponca understanding or truth of a
thing was based upon the premises of investigation, practice, and tradition. The
truth of God was having confidence in

something unseen but experienced in the
real world they lived in, so they maintained
that proposition or premise that, in turn,
solidified their religious belief.)

Nǫ́dè'gídaźì /noⁿ-dā'-gē'-thä-zhē'/ *v.*, saddened; feeling emotionally sorrowful, unhappy, sad, etc.

Nǫ́de' gíudǫ̨ /noⁿ-dā gē'-ü-doⁿ/ *n.*, happiness, includes fulfillment (I feel good
about this)

Nǫ́dè'įsadįgè /noⁿ-dā-ēⁿ-sä-thēⁿ-gä/ *adj.*,
discontented, being in the state of discon-
tentment, being miserable and gloomy

Nǫ́de'ísawadèxt'ì /noⁿ-dā-ē-sä-wä-thä'-
xt'ē'/ *n.*, a place of contentment one pleasing or to one's liking (*mǫ̨źá ke, ~ ǫ̨gɖí*, we live
in the land that is a place of great ~)

Nǫ́de ǫ̨pí'mǫ̨żị̀ /noⁿ-dā oⁿ-pē'-moⁿ-zhēⁿ/
aux. v., 1st pers. sing., distressed, 1. emotional distress 2. supressed anger, disturbed
feelings over an incident or action by another that may lead to a confrontation

Nǫ́de ǫ̨pí'mǫ̨żị̀ /noⁿ-dā oⁿ-pē'-moⁿ-zhēⁿ/
adj./n., troubled, lit., heart, love, distressed,
1. emotional distress 2. suppressed anger,
disturbed feelings over an incident or
action by another that may lead to a confrontation

Nǫ́de ǫ̨p'ímǫ̨żị̀ /noⁿ-dā oⁿ-p'ē'-moⁿ-zhēⁿ/
aux. v., 1st pers. sing., worried, I am worried

Nǫ́degdà /noⁿ'-dā-gthä'/ *v.*, repulse, disgust,
revolt, nauseate

Nǫ́degda'wadè /noⁿ-dā-gthä-wä-thä'/ *adj.*,
unsightly, unpleasant, unlikeable, repulsive, disgusting, nauseating, gross, abhorrent

Nǫ́de gídaźì /noⁿ-dā gē'-thä-zhē'/ *adj.*, sorrowful, heartbroken, an expression of sadness, as when hearing of the death of a
friend

Nǫ́de ísawadàżì /noⁿ'-dā ē'-sä-wä-thä'-zhē'/

n., discontent, dissatisfied, not to one's liking

Nǫ́de ísawaḏè /noⁿ'-dā ē'-sä-wä-thä'/ *n.*, contentment, content, pleasantness, usu. refers to a physical location of a place, home, or land and its topography (*mǫzǫ́ ke ~*, the land is a place of ~)

Nǫ́de ísaẓì /noⁿ'-dā ē'-sä-zhē'/ *adj.*, downhearted, unhappy or in low spirits

Nǫ́dewádaskabè /noⁿ'-dä-wä'-thä-skä-bä'/ *n.*, *archaic*, digestive problems, usu. refers to a long-term illness (This word may have referred to acid reflux/heartburn.)

Nǫ́dewakéga /noⁿ'-dä-wä-kä'-gä/ *n.*, heart disease, refers to any heart ailment, cardiac problems

Nǫ́de waxp'ádi /noⁿ'-dä wä-xp'ä'-thē/ *n.*, dispiritedness, lit., heart made poor, the state of being discouraged or disheartened by someone

Nǫ́dèwaxp'ádi /noⁿ'-dä'-wäx-p'ä'-thē/ *n.*, anguished, emotional distress because of something that has happened

Nǫ́dį /noⁿ'-thēⁿ/ *v.*, *3rd pers. sing./pl.*, mistaken, he/she/it/they was/were mistaken

Nǫ́dibaẓì /noⁿ'-thē-bä-zhē'/ *adj.*, unerring, faultless, no mistakes (The term more often is used sarcastically toward one who has a "know it all" attitude.)

Nǫdíge /noⁿ-thē'-gä/ *v.*, deplete, to decrease or use up the supply of things or a thing that causes the loss of something

Nǫdíge /noⁿ-theⁿ'-gä/ *v.*, run out, to exhaust supplies, as in "~ of gas"

Nǫdút'ą /noⁿ-thü'-t'oⁿ/ *v.*, walk straight, usu. referring to a person who is en route to a specific destination without making any detours (*~ mǫdíga*, walk or go straight to your destination)

Nágdè /nä'-gthä'/ *n.*, captive, one held as a prisoner or kept within bounds

Nagé /nä-gä'/ *n.*, warfare, armed conflict between nations; fight

Nǫ́ge /noⁿ'-gä/ *v.*, 1. revolve, as in an automobile motor running 2. a wheel spinning 3. *archaic*, a galloping horse

Nǫ́ge /noⁿ'-gä/ *v.*, run, something that is running, such as machinery, horses

Nǫ́gedè /noⁿ'-gä-thä'/ *v.*, run, 1. to operate, to run or control some sort of machinery 2. to control religious or secular meetings

Nǫ́gedè /noⁿ'-gä-thä'/ *v.*, manage, oversee, 1. to manage a business 2. to direct a religious ceremony or service

Nǫgdíze /noⁿ-gthē'-zä/ *n.*, battery, a device that has electrochemical cells and makes electrical energy

Nǫʃ'sa /noⁿ-ʃ'-sä/ *v. phr.*, begin walking seriously, usu. after sauntering along, something about one's destination makes one begin to walk faster

Náhǫgè /nä'-hoⁿ-gä'/ (**Ðáhǫgè** /thä'-hoⁿ-gä'/) *n.*, mosquito, a small flying insect that feeds on blood (The pronounciation of words such as this could vary from village to village. *Ðáhǫgè* is now used at the discretion of the speaker.)

Náhǫgè uk'íǫdè /nä'-hoⁿ-gä' ü-k'ē'-oⁿ-thä'/ *n.*, mosquito net, a thin netting used to cover a bed or window for protection against mosquitoes (alternative pronounciation, *ḏáhǫgè uk'íǫdè* /thä'-hoⁿ-gä' ü-k'ē'-oⁿ-thä'/)

Náhǫgeẓĭgà /nä'-hoⁿ-gä-zhēⁿ-gä'/ (**Ðáhǫgeẓĭgà** /thä'-hoⁿ-gä-zhēⁿ-gä'/) *n.*, gnat, a small, annoying biting fly of the dipterid suborder Nematocera (The prefix of this word, *ná/ḏá*, is differently pronounced by tribal members. No information is available as to why this is done.)

Nǫhé'be /noⁿ-hä'-bä/ *v./n.*, wait, pause, hang on or hold on, usu. refers to somebody who is anxiously ready to leave while the job or conditions are not complete

Ną̄hégażì /noⁿ-hā'-gä-zhē'/ *v.*, run fast on feet, faster than a trot, running at top speed

-nái /nä'-ē/ *v.*, *suffix*, always (*akì ną́di, wadáte~*, he ~ eats when he gets home)

Ną́jegda'wadè /noⁿ'-jā-gthä-wä-thā'/ *adj.*, cute; adorable (This term is a derivative of the word *ną́degdàwadè*, unsightly, unpleasant, unlikeable. But it is assigned to cuteness in babies, puppies, and other small animals or things.)

Nák'adè /nä'-k'ä-dā'/ *adj.*, hot, may refer to a hot day, hot water

Ną́ką /nä'-koⁿ/ *n.*, light, bright, radiated light from a source such as a lightbulb

Ną́ka /noⁿ'-kä/ *n.*, the back area of a vertebrate animal's body

Ną́ka /noⁿ'-kä/ *v.*, injure, hurt; *íną̄k'à*, to be hurt by; *ną́k'ak'idè*, to hurt oneself; *ną́k'awadài*, to hurt them

Ną́kądè /nä'-koⁿ-thā'/ *v.*, light, to light a lamp, to turn the lights on

Ną́ką ímuzà /nä'-koⁿ ē'-mü-zä/ *n.*, light post, usu. refers to streetlights, yard lights

Ną́ką nážutąwadè /nä'-koⁿ nä'-zhü-toⁿ-wä-thā'/ *n.*, incubator, an apparatus to hatch eggs artificially

Ną́kawahì /noⁿ'-kä-wä-hē'/ *n.*, vertebrae, also pronounced *ną́xahì*, the vertebrate spine or spinal column; *ną́ka uk'íte*, the joints of the vertebrae

-ną̄mą́ /noⁿ-moⁿ'/ *adj.*, *suffix*, used to, something that was done before, as in *Égą̀ páxe ~*, I ~ do that

Ną̄mą́mą̀dà /noⁿ-moⁿ'-moⁿ-thä'/ *v.*, walking, 1. refers to the way a person or animal walks, usu. with a upper-body swaying motion 2. *n.*, a name for nonclan members among the Ponca people

Ną̄ną́ge /noⁿ-noⁿ'-gä/ *n.*, wheel, 1. tire 2. bicycle (Probably a description of the early bicycle with one large front wheel and one small rear wheel, now refers to all types of bicycles.)

Ną̄ną́ge bdáska /noⁿ-noⁿ'-gä bthä'-skä/ *n.*, flat tire, when a tire on a vehicle goes flat or is deflated

Ną̄ną́ge gazáza /noⁿ-noⁿ'-gä gä-zä'-zä/ *n.*, *archaic*, the spokes on a wagon wheel, the supporting wooden shafts attached to the wooden rim of the metal wheel

Ną́p'a /noⁿ'-p'ä/ *n.*, chokecherry, an edible berry that grows in clusters on a large shrub, usu. the Ponca people found them in Nebraska and South and North Dakota, *Prunus virginiana*, var. *demissa*, western chokecherry

Ną̄p'éhi /noⁿ-p'ā'-hē/ *adj.*, hungry, ravenous, famished

Ną̄p'éhi t'è̄ /noⁿ-p'ā'-hē t'āⁿ'/ *v.*, starve, go hungry, to not have anything to eat

Ną́p'ewadè /noⁿ'-p'ā-wä-thā'/ *adj.*, fearsome, formidable, causing intense or extreme fear

Ną́p'ewadè /noⁿ'-p'ā-wä-thā'/ *n.*, proper male name in the Osage Tribe of Native Americans

Ną́p'ewadè /noⁿ'-p'ā-wä-thā'/ *adj.*, ferocious, brutal, extremely fierce

Ną́p'į /noⁿ'-p'ēⁿ'/ *v.*, wear, displaying or showing something on clothing (This may include rings, bracelets, necklaces, brooches, pins, etc.)

Ną̄p'í /noⁿ-p'ē'/ *adv.*, correctly, doing something ~ or something running ~

Ną̄p'í' /noⁿ-p'ē'/ *v.*, to be synchronized or work together in unison, usu. refers to foot movement in dancing

Ną̄péza /noⁿ-pā'-zä/ *v.*, plod, tread wearily, to walk heavily and laboriously

Ną̄sá'du /noⁿ-sä'-thü/ *v.*, rattle, to rattle

something with the foot or legs, e.g., a Hedúškà dancer rattling the deer hooves that are wrapped around his lower legs or a Creek women's stomp dancer shaking shells wrapped around her lower legs

Nǫsá'sadù /noⁿ-sä'-sä-thü'/ *v.*, rattle, to continuously rattle something with the foot or legs, e.g., a Hedúškà dancer rattling the deer hooves wrapped around his lower legs or a Creek stomp dancer shaking shells

Nášabè /nä'-shä-bä'/ *v., past t.*, tanned, refers to making hides of animals' skins, producing varied tanned colors

Násabède /nä'-sä-bä'-thä'/ *v.*, blacken, 1. to make something black, either by burning or by painting 2. *ịdé sabedè*, to blacken the face, refers to the apperance of Ponca warriors on a war journey

Nǫsáda /noⁿ-sä'-dä/ *v.*, stretch, extending one's limbs or body out full length; *k'inǫsadà*, stretch self by walking; *ak'inǫsadà*, I stretched or stretched by walking; *dak'inǫsadà*, you stretched or stretched by walking; *ǫk'inǫsadài*, we stretched or stretched by walking

Násadedè /nä'-sä-dä-thä'/ *v.*, iron, to flatten or press something flat with heat

Nǫsági /noⁿ-sä'-gē/ *v.*, harden, harden by stepping on something; *unǫsagì*, harden by continuously stepping on or driving over

Nǫ́šǫmà /noⁿ'-shoⁿ-moⁿ'/ *n.*, blackhaw fruit, a small, flat seed covered with a sweet-tasting hull (*nǫ́šǫmàhì*, blackhaw tree, *Viburnum rufidulum*, is a flowering shrub that grows on the Ponca reservation along the Arkansas River in northern Oklahoma.)

Nǫsásǫdè(jè) /noⁿ-soⁿ'-soⁿ-dä'(jä')/ *v.*, flounce, to move about or walk about in a jerky or bouncy motion in addition to jerking the shoulders, usu. applied to women

Nǫsi /noⁿ'-sē/ *n.*, hickory nuts, genus *Carya* of

the Juglandaceae family, that grow within an outer husk

Nǫsi'hì /noⁿ'-sē-hē'/ *n.*, hickory tree, of the genus *Carya*

Nǫšk'í /noⁿ-shk'ē'/ *n.*, head, that part of the body that has a face—eyes, nose, ears, etc.—and has a cavity for the brain

Náskà /nä'-skoⁿ'/ *v.*, melt, usu. refers to something unfreezing, as in ice changing to water; to change from a solid to a liquid state, esp. by heating

Náskǫdè /nä'-skoⁿ-thä'/ *v.*, defrost, thaw out, unfreeze

Nǫškí'ni'é /noⁿ-shkē'-nē-ä'/ *n.*, headache, a pain in the head or neck (This includes any type of headache, such as migraines.)

Nǫškì'wahì /noⁿ-shkē'-wä-hē'/ *n.*, cranium, skull, the part of the skeleton that encloses the brain

Nǫškí šnahá /noⁿ-shkē'-shnä-hä'/ *adj.*, bald, bald headed, somebody who has no hair on his/her scalp; *t'axp'í šnà*, being bald at the crown of the head

Nǫšnǫ́ /noⁿ-shnoⁿ'/ *v.*, miss, usu. 1. refers to missing the correct passageway or roadway 2. misalignment of two or more boards or poles when building a structure

Nǫšnáha /noⁿ-shnä'-hä/ *v.*, slip, to lose footing, as in slipping on ice

Nǫst'á /noⁿ-st'ä'/ *v.*, flatten, to flatten something with the feet or wheels, as with grass flattened by walking over it or driving over it repeatedly

Nǫst'áp'i wačígaxè /noⁿ-st'ä'-p'ē wä-chē'-gä-xä'/ *n.*, a tiptoeing dance, a man's dance, a ceremonial dance similar to the trot dance, a part of the Hedúškà *wačígaxè*

Nǫstá /noⁿ-stä'/ *v.*, press, being pressed down while being walked on repeatedly, usu. refers to grass

Nášta /nä'-shtä/ *adj.*, warm or lukewarm,

tepid, usu. refers to water or a drink, heated water, hot water cooled down to warm water

Nąštą' /noⁿ-shtoⁿ'/ *v.*, stop, end, discontinue, bring to a standstill

Nąstáp'i /noⁿ-stä'-p'ē/ *n.*, 1. tiptoe song 2. dance step made quietly on the toes

Nąstáp'i /noⁿ-stä'-p'ē/ *v.*, prance, strut, as in the horse began to ~

Nąšúde /noⁿ-shü'-dā/ *adj.*, dusty, making dust by driving over a dirt or gravel road

Nąsúi /noⁿ-sü'-ē/ *adj.*, smooth running, like a quiet, smooth-running automobile, bus, or train

Nąt'it'ahì /noⁿ'-t'ē-t'ä-hē'/ *n.*, coffee bean tree, *Gymnocladus dioicus*, a tree in the sub-family Caesalpinioideae of the pea family Fabaceae; a thorny tree with pods

Nąt'ú'be /noⁿ-t'ü'-bā/ *v.*, ground, to grind by use of the feet or machinery

Nąt'úbe /noⁿ-t'ü'-bā/ *v.t.*, pulverize, to make something small by crushing or beating by mechanical means or by stepping on

Nąté /noⁿ-tā'/ *v.*, kick, 1. boot, punt 2. dance

Nąúdą /noⁿ-ü'-doⁿ/ *adj.*, operative, lit., runs good, run, refers to machinery, as in an automobile engine

Nąwásek'ą /noⁿ-wä'-sā-k'oⁿ'/ *v.*, cause something to go faster by use of feet or wheels, usu. referring to any type of vehicle

Nąwáseką /noⁿ-wä'-sā-koⁿ'/ *adj.*, run fast, making machinery run fast, pedalling fast on a bicycle, or engaging the accelerator in an automobile or other conveyance by use of the feet

Nąwáseką /noⁿ-wä'-sā-koⁿ'/ *v.*, speed up, to speed up by depressing the accelerator in an automobile or other conveyance with the feet

Nąwązì /noⁿ'-woⁿ-zē'/ *adj.*, jealous, refers to a woman who is jealous

Nąxahì t'úxà /noⁿ'-xä-hē' t'ü'-xä/ *n.*, hump-back, a crooked back caused by injury or kyphosis

Nąxdę́ /noⁿ-xthāⁿ'/ *n.*, ashes, the residue of something after burning

Nąxdé /noⁿ-xthā'/ *n.*, charcoal, a black form of carbon produced by heating or burning wood until it is black

Nąxdé /noⁿ-xthā'/ *n.*, coals, the black residue on burnt wood (Ponca men used this residue to blacken their faces when they went to meet the enemy in battle. The color was symbolic of death.)

Nąxe /noⁿ'-xä/ *n.*, soul, spirit of man, the essence of man

Nąxe'diwágazù /noⁿ'-xä-thē-wä'-gä-zü'/ *n.*, psychological examination or evaluation

Nąxe g'ip'áxudądì /noⁿ'-xä g-ē-p'ä'-xü-thoⁿ-dē'/ *n.*, a historic Ponca site on the Missouri River where men marked their height on the walls of a cave

Nąxe k'ip'áxu /noⁿ'-xä k'ē-p'ä'-xü/ *v.*, to mark the height of oneself upon a wall; now, measuring the height of an individual

Nąxe p'éži /noⁿ'-xä p'ä'-zhē/ *n.*, devil, Satan (In the Judeo-Christian faith Satan is a fallen angel who opposes all that is good, often referred to as the adversary.)

Nąxeskàži' /noⁿ'-xä-skä'-zhē/ *n.*, dizziness, a condition caused by something being wrong with one's spatial perception

Nąxe xubè /noⁿ'-xä xü-bā'/ *n.*, Holy Spirit, the third person of the holy trinity in Christianity (The Holy Spirit is also referred to as the Comforter, Healer, Friend, Advocate, Teacher, etc.)

Nąxəáda /noⁿ-xə-ä'-thä/ *v.*, fall, push down by force, by use of the feet or machinery

Nąxíáda /noⁿ-xē-ä'-thä/ *v.*, fell, push down by force, by use of the feet or machinery

Nąxíde /noⁿ-xē'-dā/ *n.*, ear, the inner ear,

labyrinth, a part that also senses the state of one's equilibrium

Nąxíde'ni'é /noⁿ-xē̄-dā-nē-ā'/ *n.*, earache, a sometimes sharp to dull pain that can last for a short span of time or be a long-term condition, referred to as otalgia, and not always associated with inner ear diseases, may be caused by other conditions

Nąxíde ḑįgè /noⁿ-xē̄-dā thēⁿ-gā'-/ *adj.*, mischievous, lit., has no ear, behaves badly, does not listen to good advice

Nąxídehidè /noⁿ-xē̄-dā-hē-dā'/ *n.*, earlobe, the fleshy lower part of the external ear

Náxp'ehì /noⁿ'-xp'ā-hē'/ *n.*, shin, the front part of the two bones (the tibia and fibula) in the leg below the knee

Náxudè /nǟ-xü-dā'/ *v.*, burnt, scorched, usu. refers to cooked food

Náxudè /nǟ-xü-dā'/ *v.*, char, 1. to darken something, e.g., wood, by burning 2. to scorch food

Náxudè /nǟ-xü-thā'/ *v.*, brand, to burn a mark or symbol on cattle

Nąza /noⁿ'-zä/ *n.*, fence, 1. barrier, railing, enclosure 2. a fortified enclosure (The Ponca people, descendents of the eastern culture, namely, the Middle Mississippian culture, built fortified villages. The last such fort was built in current Knox County, Nebraska. The fort was called Nąza by historians.)

Nąza /noⁿ'-zä/ *n.*, Ponca Fort (The Ponca Fort site is the location of a once-fortified earthlodge village in Knox County, Nebraska, approximately eight miles west of Niobrara. It was a post palisade fort. The area covered approximately three acres of land. "The fort was well situated from a defensive point of view, being located on a prominence, one of the bluffs of the Missouri, some 50 or 60 feet above the floor of the valley of Ponca Creek" [Howard 1965].)

Názahà /nǟ'-zä-hä'/ *v.*, back up, to go backward or move something backward

Názat'à /nǟ'-zä-t'ä'/ *n.*, back side, the part that is farthest from the front, at the rear of something (~ of a teepee or a building)

Názat'adišà /nǟ'-zä-t'ä-thē-shoⁿ'/ *adv.*, toward the back of something, toward the back of a person, group, or structure

Nąžáwa /noⁿ-zhǟ'-wä/ *n.*, dance with exuberance, dancing with energy, liveliness, high spirits, or enthusiasm

Náži /nǟ'-zhē/ *v.*, *past t.*, stopped burning, went out (*p'éde ké* ~, the fire ~)

Nązí /noⁿ-zēⁿ'/ *v.*, stand, to stand

Nąží /noⁿ-zhē'/ *v./n.*, rain, water that is formed in the clouds and falls to earth

Nąží'á /noⁿ-zhēⁿ'-ä'/ *v.*, *fem.*, command to arise, stand up

Nąží'gà /noⁿ-zhēⁿ'-gä'/ *v.*, *masc.*, command to arise, stand up

Nąží' ákišugà /noⁿ-zhēⁿ' ä'-kē-shü-gä'/ *n.*, rainstorm, deluge, cloudburst

Nąží'štà /noⁿ-zhēⁿ'-shtoⁿ'/ *n.*, April, lit., constant or recurring rain, the fourth month in the year

Nąží ák'išugà /noⁿ-zhēⁿ' ä'-k'ē-shü-gä'/ *n.*, cloudburst, usu. rain with hail and thunder

Nąžįáži /noⁿ-zhēⁿ-ä'-zhē/ *n.*, drought, when it does not rain in various places on earth for an extended period of time

Nąžíha /noⁿ-zhē̄'-hä/ *n.*, hair, hair on the head, tresses, locks

Nąžíha' idádisądè /noⁿ-zhē̄'-hä ē-thǟ'-thē-soⁿ-dā'/ *n.*, barrette, a clip or clasp to hold hair in place

Nąžíha ábaxà /noⁿ-zhē̄'-hä ä'-bä-xoⁿ'/ *n.*, hairpin, a piece of wire or some such used to hold a person's hair in place, usu. used by women to fasten up the hair or hold something on the hair

Nąžíha ábaxdadè /noⁿ-zhē̄'-hä ä'-bä-xthä-dā'/ *n.*, hair clasp, a device to hold a girl's or woman's hair in place, such as a barrette

Nąžíha disé /noⁿ-zhē'-hä thē-sä'/ *n.*, haircut, the act of trimming or styling the hair; *nąžíha wádisè*, barber

Nąžíha disè' /noⁿ-zhē'-hä thē-sä'/ *n.*, barber, lit., hair cutter, a person who cuts and styles boys' and men's hair

Nąžíha ídižà /noⁿ-zhē'-hä ē'-thē-zhä'/ *n.*, shampoo, a product to wash hair

Nąžíha ík'ąt'ą̀ /noⁿ-zhēⁿ'-hä ē'-k'oⁿ-t'oⁿ'/ *n.*, hair ties, usu. hair beads, jewelry, especially stringed beads attached to the braids of girls and women

Nąžíha wébagahè /noⁿ-zhēⁿ'-hä wä'-bä-gä-hä'/ *n.*, hairbrush (Orig. brushes were made from needlegrass awns [probably *Hesperostipa curtiseta*, a Canadian needlegrass] tied in bundles.)

Nąžíha zì /noⁿ-zhē'-hä zē'/ *adj.*, blond, blond hair; *n.*, refers to a person who is blond as "that blond"

Nąžíha žíde /noⁿ-zhē'-hä zhē'-dā/ *adj.*, red haired; *n.*, refers to a person with red hair

Nąžį́ną̀štó̞žį̀ /noⁿ-zhēⁿ'-noⁿ-shto̞ⁿ-zhēⁿ/ *v.*, rain consistently, refers to rainy days during spring

Nąžiškexč'ì /noⁿ'-zhē-shkäx-ch-ē'/ *adv.*, barely, not quite (~ *akí*, he ~ got home)

Nąžíšt'ą̀ /noⁿ-zhē'-sht'oⁿ'/ *adj.*, rainy, rain that comes often

Nąžíúbixà /noⁿ-zhē'-ü'-bē-xoⁿ'/ *n.*, sprinkling, sprinkling rain, drizzle

Nąžį̀xčì /noⁿ'-zhēⁿ-xchē'/ *adv.*, barely, just about, by very little or to a very small extent

Nąžìžà /noⁿ'-zhē-zhoⁿ'/ *adj.*, prayer and fasting (~ *adá biáma*, he went to pray and fast) (The Ponca people who studied the art of healing and solving social and psychological problems went into the wilderness to search in nature for the answers.)

Nážuè /nä'-zhü-ä'/ *adj.*, sizzle, sizzling, the sound of food frying in a pan, namely, bacon, meats, potatoes

Nážutądè /nä'-zhü-toⁿ-thä'/ *v.*, incubate, fowl hatching eggs by keeping them warm by sitting on them or carefully maintaining controlled heat

Né' /nä'/ *n.*, pond, pool

Né'de /nä'-thä/ *v.*, to build a fire

Né'št'à /nä'-sht'ä'/ *n.*, the now extinct Nésta clan of the Ponca people, lit., places of water

Né·dažibè /nä'--thä-zhē-bä'/ *n.*, screech owl, of the genus *Megascops*

Néde /nä'-thä/ *v.*, start a fire, start a fire with kindling

Negí /nä-gē'/ *pers. pron.*, *masc./fem.* uncle, my mother's brother, also my mother's brother's son; *dinégi*, your uncle; *inégi*, his/her uncle, *winégi*, my uncle

Né t'ąà /nä' t'oⁿ-gä'/ *n.*, lake, a large body of fresh water that is surrounded by land

Néxe /nä'-xä/ *n.*, *archaic*, drum, may be called a "percussion instrument"

Néxe /nä'-xä/ *n.*, pail, bucket

Néxe'gak'ú' /nä'-xä-gä-k'ü'/ *v.*, *archaic*, drumming, to drum, to beat upon a drum

Néže /nä'-zhä/ *n.*, urine, a liquid secreted by the kidneys and expelled from the body through a process called urination

Ní' /nē'/ *n.*, water, a colorless liquid on which all living things depend for survival, composed of oxide of hydrogen, H_2O

Ní'ága'šnahà /nē'-ä'-gä-shnä-hä'/ *n.*, oilcloth tablecloth, a tablecloth with vinyl covering; *archaic*, a close-woven cotton fabric coated with boiled linseed oil to make it waterproof

Ní'ágaxt'ądè /nē'-ä'-gä-xt'oⁿ-thä'/ *n.*, baptism, Christian baptism, refers to sprinkling or pouring water upon the individual being baptised

Ní'ágdè /nē-ä'-gthä'/ *n.*, *archaic*, water stand, a framework or structure that was designed to hold a washpan and a pail of water

Ní'ámuxt'à̧ /nē'-ä'-mü-xt'oⁿ/ *v.*, irrigate, cause water to cover an area, to flood an area with water

Ní' bdáska /nē'-bthä'-skä/ *n.*, Nebraska, the state of Nebraska (The name probably originated from the Ponca's name for the Platte River, Ní' bdáska, "flat river," because the river was very often level with the topography in many places.)

Ní'dè /nē'-dä'/ *n.*, light bread, wheat bread, dinner rolls, or any other commercially prepared bread

Ní'dè /nē'-dä'/ *v.*, 1. burn, usu. a person getting burned 2. used when food is ready, is cooked

Ní'de /nē'-dä/ *adj.*, ripe, mature, ready to eat, usu. refers to fruits on plants; *nážidè*, sun ripened

Ní'dè'dè /nē'-dä-thä'/ *n.*, cooked food that has been prepared to consume

Ni'é /nē-ä'/ *n*, pain, 1. physical pain 2. emotional pain

Ni'é /nē-ä'/ *n.*, sore, blister, boil, carbuncle, or any skin complaint

Ní'íbizè /nē'-ē'-bē-zä'/ *adj.*, thirsty, lit., dry from lack of water, the want of drink; *a̧dá̧bizè*, desirous of doing something

Ní'idá'umúbixà̧ /nē'-ē-thä'-ü-mü'-bē-xoⁿ/ *n.*, garden hose, sprinkler

Ní'idagè /nē'-ē-thä-gä/ *n.*, *archaic*, pail to carry water with

Ní'idát'à̧ /nē'-ē-thä'-t'oⁿ/ *n.*, dipper, a dipper for drinking water

Ní' ínašt'adè /nē' ē'-näsh-t'ä-thä/ *n.*, hot-water tank, a device that heats water

Ní'skà /nē'-skä/ *n.*, Arkansas River, lit., crystal-clear water (The Ponca who came to Indian Territory in the nineteenth century said the river was "crystal clear." It later became polluted following oil exploration, due to discharge from a refinery and raw sewage.)

Ní'škà̧áž̧ì /nē'-shkoⁿ-ä'-zhē/ *n.*, Stillwater, Oklahoma

Ní'snì /nē'-snē'/ *n.*, water well, where cool water comes from, a water pump

Ní't'à̧gà /nē'-t'oⁿ-gä/ *n.*, ocean, sea

Ní't'à̧gà ma̧sá̧dihà /nē'-t'oⁿ-gä moⁿ-soⁿ'-thē-hä/ *n.*, overseas, refers to countries beyond the Atlantic and Pacific Oceans

Ní't'à̧gà t'adésagì t'à̧gà /nē'-t'oⁿ-gä' t'ä-dä'-sä-gē' t'oⁿ-gä/ *n.*, hurricane, lit., big wind of the ocean, a powerful, destructive wind in the Western Hemisphere that usu. occurs along the eastern coast of the United States and the Gulf of Mexico

Ní' ubít'à̧ /nē' ü-bē'-t'oⁿ/ *v.*, immerse, dip, dunk (to ~ something or somebody completely in water)

Ní' ubíxt'à̧ /nē' ü-bē'-xt'oⁿ/ *v.*, pump, to pump water

Ní' udát'à̧ /nē' ü-thä'-t'oⁿ/ *n.*, water trough, a trough for animals to drink from

Ní'udít'ȩ̀ wačíškà /nē'-ü-thē'-t'ä̧ⁿ wä-chē'-shkä'/ *n.*, Ponca Creek, lit. the water to kill in creek, Knox County, Nebraska

Ni'ugabí'xà̧ uhída /nē-ü-gä-bē'-xoⁿ ü-hē'-thä/ *n.*, shower, in a bath or bath stall; a shower house

Ní'ut'ási /nē'-ü-t'ä'-sē/ *n.*, Missouria, the Missouria Tribe of Native Americans

Ní'uxp'áde /nē'-üx-p'ä'-thä/ *n.*, Niagara Falls, a natural wonder in North America (The Ponca people, before their migration to the north central plains, considered the falls a landmark.)

Ní'uxp'áde /nē'-üx-p'ä'-thä/ *n.*, waterfall, the falling of water from a stream at a higher level

Ni'ží'dè /nē-zhē'-dä/ *n.*, Salt Fork River, Oklahoma, lit., river that is red

Nią́ba /nē-oⁿ'-bä/ *n.*, moon, the natural satellite of earth

Nią́ba /nē-oⁿ'-bä/ *n.*, moonlight, light from the sun that strikes the surface of the moon and is reflected to earth

Nią́ba wédixdì /nē-oⁿ'-bä wā'-thē-xthē'/ *n.*, Moonhead, spiritual leader of the Caddo Tribe of Native Americans, known primarily by the Osage Tribe of Native Americans

Niáda /nē-ä'-thä/ *v.*, wander, not knowing exactly which way to go to find or return to a familiar place, to wander aimlessly

Niášiga íye wadéga /nē-ä'-shē-gä' ē'-yä wä-dä'-gä/ *n.*, bigheaded, an arrogant person who speaks as though he/she knows everything; a "know it all"

Niášiga mąščį́'žįgè /nē-ä'-shē-gä' moⁿ-shchēⁿ'-zhēⁿ-gä'/ *adj.*, a pretentious person who acts as though he/she knows something that no one else knows

Niášiga nušiáha /nē-ä'-shē-gä' nü-shēä'-hä/ *n.*, short people, lit., short people, Native Americans who live in the Southwest

Niášigà ukédį Wak'ą́da wádahą̀ waą́ /nē-ä'-shē-gä' ü-kä'-thēⁿ wä-k'oⁿ'-dä wä'-thä-hoⁿ' wä-oⁿ'/ *n.*, Native American traditional Christian hymns, Native hymns composed by early Ponca Christians using ancient tunes applied to Christian principles

Niášigà waníte /nē-ä'-shē-gä' wä-nē'-tä/ *n.*, miser, somebody who is stingy, not generous, tight

Niášigà wašádįgè /nē-ä'-shē-gä' wä-shä'-thēⁿ-gä'/ *n.*, *archaic*, ca. 1800s, weak man

Niášigà wasé'žįgà /nē-ä'-shē-gä' wä-sä'-zhēⁿ-gä'/ *adj./n.*, tactless, a person without tact and inconsiderate of others

Niášigà wési'ažì /nē-ä'-shē-gä' wä-sē-ä-zhē'/ *n.*, a person who speaks with no respect to others

Niáwagidadè /nē-ä'-wä-gē-thä-thä'/ *v.*, healed us, 1. somebody using medicines cured us 2. refers to Wak'ą́da healing the physical body and spirit or soul of man

Níbdá'ska /nē'-bthä'-skä/ *n.*, Platte River, lit., flat water, the Platte River in the present-day state of Nebraska

Nidá /nē-doⁿ'/ *n.*, flood, the rising and overflow of water from a river or stream onto dry land

Nidą́'gaxá' /nē-doⁿ'-gä-xä'/ *n.*, driftage, usu. in reference to driftwood and other debris that piles up by the force of a flood

Nidá'xup'à /nē-thä'-xü-p'ä'/ *n.*, water moccasin, cottonmouth water moccasin, *Agkistrodon piscivorus*, a venomous snake

Nidą́bewačì /nē-doⁿ'-bä-wä-chē'/ *n.*, Sun dance, the Ponca Sun dance ceremony

Nídažì /nē'-dä-zhē'/ *adj.*, half cooked, any food that is poorly prepared or not cooked to proper, healthy standards, such as meats that are rare, vegetables still hard, so-called half-boiled eggs

Nídažì /nē'-dä-zhē'/ *adj.*, raw, usu. refers to uncooked food

Níde /nē'-dä/ *n.*, 1. buttocks 2. rump

Níde /nē'-thä/ *v.*, to cure, make well, restore to health

Níde'udíši /nē'-dä-ü-thē'-shē/ *n.*, 1. trousers, pants, slacks 2. panty

Nídeágdè /nē'-dä-ä'-gthä'/ *n.*, diapers, a square piece of cloth or absorbent material worn by babies as underwear

Nídeát'a gdadį̀ /nē'-dä-ä'-t'ä gthä-dēⁿ'/ *n.*, *archaic*, the doubletree on a draft-horse wagon

Nįde ská /nēⁿ'-dä skä'/ *n.*, Appaloosa, a breed of horse with a spotted coat, striped hooves, and other identifying features

(These horses were supposedly developed by the Shoshone people.)

Nídeudíši mate /nē'-dā-ü-thē'-shēⁿ moⁿ-tā/ *n.*, panty, panties, a type of undergarment designed for women and girls; may also refer to men's undergarments

Nídeudíši mate /nē'-dā-ü-thēⁿ-shēⁿ moⁿ-tā/ *n.*, underwear, men's undershorts, boxer shorts or briefs

Níde wahi /nē'-dā wä-hē'/ *n.*, coccyx, referred to as the tailbone, the final segment of the vertebral column, composed of three to five separate or fused vertebrae below the sacrum

Nié'ísnadè /nē-ā'-ē'-snä-thā'/ *n.*, salve, a medicinal ointment to soothe and help heal sores or wounds

Nié dige /nē-ā' thēⁿ-gā'/ *n.*, wellness, refers to good physical health and well-being, esp. through proper diet and excercise

Niégáxe /nē-ā'-gä'-xā/ *v.*, hurt, harmed, injured by something

Nigá't'uši /nē-gä'-t'ü-shē'/ *n.*, soda, lit., water that pops, a sweet soft drink also called pop, coke, any carbonated beverage; *gá't'uši*, abbr. form

Nigduze /nē-gthü'-zā/ *adj.*, watered down, weak, watery, usu. refers to drinks such as coffee, tea, juices

Ník'aha /nē'-k'oⁿ-hä/ *n.*, shore, bank, land along the edge of a river, lake, sea, or ocean

Níka /nē'-kä/ *n.*, human being, person, being, mankind

Níka'diha /nē'-kä-thē-hoⁿ'/ *n.*, elevator, lit., lift people, a lifting device that transports people up and down to various floors in tall buildings

Níka'gahi /nē'-kä-gä-hē'/ *n.*, chieftain, lit., person who is above all, tribal chief, chief, group leader, etc.

Níka naxè /nē'-kä noⁿ-xā'/ *n.*, aurora borealis, lit., the spirit of man, northern lights

Níkapášna /nē'-kä-pä'-shnoⁿ/ *n.*, the Níkapášna clan of the Ponca people, lit., man with a bald head (The warriors of this clan shaved their hair, wearing a "Mohawk"-style haircut. They tied a symbolic feather at the tail or back of the head. They, along with the Đíxida clansmen, were considered "shock troops.")

Níkašigà /nē'-kä-shē-gä'/ *n.*, person; *niášigà* (alternate pronunciation), person

Níkašigà'ukè'di /nē'-kä-shē-gä'-ü-kā'-thē'/ *n./adj.*, Native American, lit. common people, the indigenous people of North America (The term *Native American* has existed for many years, e.g., for the Native American Church, and is now commonly used in some public places and in modern writings beginning ca. 1970s. The term *Indian* is the original name Europeans gave to the inhabitants of North America; they used *Plains Indians* for those who lived on the Great Plains of America. *Indian* is still widely used by Native peoples.)

Níkašigà mása /nē'-kä-shē-gä' moⁿ'-sä/ *n.*, uppity person, a person who puts on airs of superiority or arrogance

Níkašigà mása /nē'-kä-shē-gä' moⁿ'-sä/ *n.*, Bristish people, lit., uppity person

Níkašigè wasésa /nē'-kä-shē-gā' wä-sā'-soⁿ/ *n.*, statue, e.g., a figure of a man, large or small

Níkawasà /nē'-kä-wä-sä/ *n.*, God, *archaic* ca. 1800s, a deity of God, a spiritual presence of the essence of God in ritual healing

Níkidè /nē'-kē-dā/ *n.*, pink conch shell, a marine shell made round and polished for use in the Hedúškà dance paraphernalia

Níkidè /nē'-kē-dā/ *n.*, seashell, the shell or outer layer made by snails and other crustaceans

Niní /nē-nē'/ *n.*, cigarette, or any kind of product that uses tobacco leaves

Niní' /nē-nē'/ *n.*, tobacco, orig. a mixture of certain plant leaves (of unknown species) used for smoking in tribal ceremonials and rituals (Now a word for present-day tobacco products, esp. those tobacco plants grown in the Southeast in the genus *Nicotiana* of the Solanaceae family.)

Niní'ba /nē-nē'-bä/ *n.*, calumet, a ceremonial pipe

Niní'ba waxúbe /nē-nē'-bä wä-xü'-bā/ *n.*, Sacred Pipe, the Sacred Pipe of the Ponca people

Niní'ba žą̀ /nē-nē'-bä zhoⁿ'/ *n.*, pipe stem, the stem of a tobacco pipe

Niní'į' /nē-nē'-ēⁿ/ *n.*, smoking, the inhaling of tobacco smoke or fumes into the lungs

Niníbažą̀ /nē-nē'-bä-zhoⁿ'/ *n.*, ceremonial staffs carried by two Wáwą (Pipe Dance) dancers (At one end of one of the two staffs ten white bald eagle feathers were attached. The other staff had twelve black golden eagle feathers attached. The staffs were about four feet in length.)

Niníú'žihà /nē-nē'-ü'-zhē-hä'/ *n.*, tobacco pouch, a decorated, fringed tobacco pouch

Níp'à /nē'-p'ä'/ *n.*, Bois D'Arc Creek, in Kay County, Oklahoma, a small tributary entering the Salt Fork River — referred to in Ponca as "bitter water"

Nipúki /nē-pü'-kē/ *n.*, Norfolk, Nebraska

Niskí'de /nē-skē'-thā/ *n.*, salt, table salt, sodium chloride

Niskí'de t'ą̀wą̀gđą̀ /nē-skē'-thā t'oⁿ-woⁿ-gthoⁿ'/ *n.*, Lincoln, Nebraska, lit., salt city (The city was so named because of the salt plains found nearby.)

Niskí'deuží' /nē-skē'-thā-ü-zhē'/ *n.*, salt-shaker, a condiment holder for salt

Niškú'škù /nē-shkü'-shkü'/ *n.*, barn swallow, of the species *Hirundo rustica*

Nisní /nē-snē'/ *n.*, water pump, lit., cold water, a pump to draw water for drinking (also *ní' íbixt'ą̀*, to cause water to come out)

Nisní'sabè /nē-snē'-sä-bā'/ *n.*, Blackwell, Oklahoma

Ništ'ášt'à /nē-sht'ä'-sht'ä'/ *n.*, wetlands, an area of land that characteristically has a high moisture content, such as bogs or swamps

Níst'ù /nē'-t'ü'/ *v.*, back up, to move oneself backward, usu. done when exiting a place that is considered holy or of a religious nature

Nisúde /nē-sü'-dā/ *n.*, flute, lit., whistle, understood in the context of a statement (*núžigà áka, ~ kè, mížigà đįké giá ahì*, the boy went to play his ~ for the girl)

Nisúde /nē-sü'-dā/ *n.*, whistle, flute, any wind instrument

Nít'a /nē-t'ä/ *adj.*, alive, a living thing; *aní't'à*, 1st pers. sing., I am alive; *đanít'à*, you are alive; *nít'aì*, he/she/they are alive; *ąnít'a*, we are alive

Nit'á' /nē-t'ä/ *n.*, outer ear, that part of the ear that extends on the side of the head, consisting of the pinna or auricle

Nit'á't'ągà /nē-t'ä'-t'oⁿ-gä/ *n.*, mule, the offspring of a horse and donkey that is sterile and has long ears and a short mane

Nít'a'uháge đįgè /nē-t'ä-ü-hä'-gä theⁿ-gä/ *n.*, eternity, infinity, lit., life without end

Nit'át'ągà núšiáha /nē-t'ä-t'oⁿ-gä' nü'-shē'-ä'-hä/ *n.*, burro, a small donkey found in Latin America

Niú' /nē-ü'/ *v.*, breathe, to inhale and exhale

Níúbdadà /nē-ü'-bthä-thä'/ *n.*, Niobrara River, Nebraska, lit., flat, wide, or broad water

Níú'k'igđas'į /nē-ü'-k'ē-gthä-s-ēⁿ'/ *n.*, mirror, lit., look into the water at self, reflect

Niú't'adì /nēü'-t'ä-thē'/ *v.*, suffocate, to have no respiration or to be deprived of oxygen, then die

Niúdạt'à /nē-ü'-thoⁿ-t'ä'/ *n.*, island, isle, atoll

Niúdizè /nē-ü'-thē-zā'/ *v.*, breathing, inhalation, gulp of air

Niúga'é'é /nē-ü'-gä-ä'-ä'/ *v.*, drip, liquid falling in drops

Niúgaskạdè /nēü'-gä-skoⁿ-thā'/ *adj.*, dissolve, to soften and liquefy in water

Niúgašpạ /nēü'-gä-shpoⁿ'/ *v.*, soak, absorbed with water

Niúgašúp'a /nē-ü'-gä-shü-p'ä/ *n.*, backwater, refers to water backed up from a main river that stands apart after a flood

Niúgdazù /nēü'-gthä-zü/ *v.*, take in an irregular or sporadic breath, usu. done by a child following his/her weeping

Niút'ę /nē-ü'-t'āⁿ/ *v.*, drown, lit., die in the water

Niúwagduzè /nēü'-wä-gthü-zā'/ *v.*, sob, sobbed, sobbing, to catch the breath spasmodically, caused by contractions in the throat that follow weeping or crying

Niúži /nēü'-zhē/ *n.*, puddle, water puddle

Niúžiwadè /nē-ü'-zhē-wä-thā'/ *n.*, blister beetle, any of the beetles (Coleoptera) that bite or secrete a blistering agent, causing redness and blisters on the skin

Níxa /nē'-xä/ *n.*, stomach (The stomach's function is to digest food.)

Níxa'ni'é /nē'-xä-nē-ā'/ *n.*, stomachache

Nú' /nü'/ *n.*, 1. man 2. potato, a root vegetable; *nú' skíde*, sweet potato

Nú' /nü'/ *n.*, potato, *Solanum tuberosum*

Nú'de /nü'-dā/ *n.*, throat, the digestive and breathing passage in the neck

Nú'de t'á'ši /nü'-dā t'ä'-shē/ *n.*, laryngeal prominence (Adam's apple), a large bump on the neck, formed by the angle of the thyroid cartilage, that is most noticeable on adult men

Nubdá' /nü-bthoⁿ'/ *n.*, perfume, lit., the smell of man, namely, in the use of "Indian" perfume

Nudá /nü-doⁿ'/ *v.*, warring, the act of going to battle with another nation

Nudá adái /nü-doⁿ ä-thä'-ē/ *n.*, warpath, *archaic*, a war expedition

Nudá ahạ́'ma /nü-doⁿ ä-hạ'-mä/ *n.*, veteran, those who were engaged in warfare for their country

Nudá ahạ́'ma waá' /nü-doⁿ ä-hạ'-mä wäoⁿ'/ *n.*, veteran's songs, songs that were specifically composed for returning veterans of war

Nudáhạgà /nü-doⁿ'-hoⁿ-gä/ *n.*, war leader, lit., war leader, 1. now, one in charge, boss, the headman, etc. 2. male name in the Ðíxidạ clan of the Ponca people

Nudá mạdì /nü-doⁿ moⁿ-thēⁿ'/ *n.*, warrior, 1. one or more persons going to battle with another person or nation 2. proper name in the Ðíxidạ clan of the Ponca people

Nudá wačígaxè /nü-doⁿ wä-chē'-gä-xä'/ *n.*, scalp dance, a woman's victory dance for men returning from battle

Nudá waú' /nü-doⁿ wä-ü'/ *n.*, a women's scalp dance society called "warrior women" (Organized in Indian Territory, the group is considered to be the elite scalp dance group and is composed of chiefs' wives, sisters, daughters, and granddaughters.)

Núde'ni'é /nü'-dä-nē-ā'/ *n.*, sore throat, a pain or irritation in the throat often caused by acute pharyngitis, an inflammation of the throat

Núde dit'á /nü'-dä thē-t'oⁿ'/ *v.*, choke, to block breathing, to obstruct breathing by hindering the air passageway to the lungs (The elders said this was not the proper way of taking the life of the enemy. The Ponca were known as or called P'á máse, "decapitators," in hand-to-hand combat. Otherwise, they used the bow and arrow.)

Núde íba /nü'-dā ē'-bä/ *n.*, mumps, also known as epidemic parotitis, noted by the swelling of the parotid glands

Núde wéį /nü'-dā wā'-ēⁿ/ *n.*, horse collar, lit., neck harness, part of the harness that fits around the horse's neck and shoulders, allowing it to pull a wagon and other loads

Nudíge /nü-thēⁿ'-gā/ *n.*, widow, 1. a woman who has lost her husband by death and who has not remarried 2. bachelorette, an unmarried woman

Nugá /nü-gā'/ *adj.*, 1. male, relates to the sex that produces sperm to fertilize female eggs 2. proper male name in the Mąk'ą clan of the Ponca people

Nugá' /nü-gā'/ *n.*, bull, any adult breed of mammals and fowl, including domestic cattle, seals, chickens, etc.

Núgdè /nü'-gthā'/ *n.*, turnip, a hard, round root that can be eaten raw or cooked, genus *Brassica*

Núgdè /nü'-gthā'/ *n.*, wild turnip, *Psoralea esculenta*

Nugé /nü-gā'/ *n.*, summer, that period of the year that encompasses the months of May, June, July, and August; *nugeádi*, last summer; *nugeádą*, in the summer

Nugé'úská'skà /nü-gā-ü'-skoⁿ'-skä'/ *n.*, midsummer, summer solstice, usu. refers to the longest day of the year

Nugéádi /nü-gā'-ä'-dē/ *n. phr.*, last summer

Nugédą /nü-gā'-doⁿ/ *prep. phr.*, in the summer

Núka /nü'-kä/ *adj.*, wet, damp, soaked, moist, watery

Nusí' /nü-sē'/ *n.*, armpit, the axilla or oxter

Nusí'axdadè /nü-sē'-ä-xthä-dā'/ *n.*, bandolier, orig. a leather strap worn over the shoulders and across the chest to support a pouch or some type of article, 1. a belt with small pockets for storing cartridges that was worn over the shoulders and across the chest 2. in the early twentieth century, a representation of the cartridge belt worn by dancers in the Ponca Hedúškà organization, consisting of hairpipe and metal and glass beads

Nušíáha /nü-shē'-ä'-hä/ *pron.*, short, lit., small or short person, usu. relates to stature, i.e., size

Núskidè /nü'-skē-thā'/ *n.*, sweet potato, an edible, orange-colored root

Nušną' /nü-shnoⁿ'/ *n.*, otter, a fish-eating water animal, subfamily Lutrinae

Nušną'ha /nü-shnoⁿ'-hä/ *n.*, otter skin (The skin has many uses, such as medicine bags, dance paraphernalia of the Hedúškà, caps. In the past, it was worn only by men who had knowledge of medicines and healing.)

Nušną́ha wadagè /nü-shnoⁿ'-ha wä-thä-gā'/ *n.*, otter-skin cap, a man's cap, a style now worn at Hedúškà dances

Núxe /nü'-xā/ *n.*, ice, 1. frozen water 2. male name in the Núxe clan of the Ponca people

Núxe /nü'-xā/ *n.*, the Núxe clan of the Ponca people, lit., ice

Núxe bawégdi /nü'-xā bä-wā'-gthē/ *n.*, ice cream, a dessert made milk and cream, along with other ingredients and various flavorings

Núxe ígašižè /nü'-xā ē'-gä-shē-zhā'/ *n.*, ice pick, an awl-like tool to crack or chip ice

Núxe snì /nü'-xā snē'/ *n.*, popsicle, lit., cold ice, also snow cone

Núxe t'ì /nü'-xā t'ē'/ *n.*, lit., ice house (like the Inuit word *igloo*, meaning snow house, hut, or any building)

Núze /nü'-zā/ *n.*, water turkey; the anhinga (*Anhinga anhinga*), snake bird, darter, American darter (some cultural practices refer to it as "water bird")

Núžįgà /nü'-zhēⁿ-gä/ *n.*, boy, young male, a youngster

O

o /ō/ fifth vowel in the Ponca alphabet

ǫ /ōⁿ/ fifth nasalized vowel in the Ponca alphabet

Osní' əhágе /ō-snē' ə-hoⁿ-gā/ *n.*, November, lit., the beginning of cold (weather), the eleventh month of the year

P

p /pə/ twelth consonant in the Ponca alphabet

P'á' /p'ä/ *adj.*, bitter, pungent

P'á' /p'ä/ *n.*, head, 1. head, the top part of the body of humans and other animals 2. nose, in anatomy, that part of the head that projects out in front of the face and is used to smell and to breathe in and exhale air in conjunction with the mouth

P'á' /p'ä/ *n.*, nose, in anatomy, the organ of smell that projects out in front of the face

P'a'dáge /p'ä-thä'-gä/ *n.*, bluff, a particular, known place in Nebraska where individual battles were fought

P'á' dát'ą /p'ä-thä'-t'oⁿ/ *n.*, drinks bitter, a women's victory dance society commonly called the "scalp dance society" (Organized in Indian Territory, the group served coffee, *p'á'*, as a featured drink, hence the name *p'á dat'ą́*.)

P'á' dįgé /p'ä' theⁿ-gā/ *n.*, drinks no bitter, a women's victory dance society commonly called the "scalp dance society" (Organized in Indian Territory, the group did not serve coffee, *p'á'*, as a featured drink, hence the name *p'á' dįgé*.)

P'á' gás'į̀' /p'ä' gä's-ēⁿ/ *v.*, peeking or looking, a toddler bending over, placing head on floor, and looking back between his/her legs

P'á'hiugdè /p'ä-hē-ü-gthä/ *n.*, nape, back of the neck, the indented center in the back of the neck

P'ą́'k'a /p'oⁿ-k'ä/ *n.*, the Ponca Tribe of Native Americans

P'a'máse' /p'ä-mä-sä/ *n.*, Ponca, *archaic*, lit., those who cut off the heads of enemies, usu. refers to warriors of the Ponca people

P'á'mą́xe /p'ä'-moⁿ-xā/ *v.*, bow, 1. to bow the head as in reverence during a prayer 2. to sit with a bowed head when in a state of emotional distress over something

P'a'mú' /p'ä-mü/ *adv.*, downhill, downward

P'á'są̀' /p'ä-soⁿ/ *n.*, bald eagle, a bird of prey in North America, *Haliaeetus leucocephalus*

P'á'šį̀ /p'ä-shēⁿ/ *n.*, flat nose (Authorities say this condition may come from a long range of causes, including skeletal abnormalities. Individuals born with this condition are rare among the Native American people.)

P'a'siát'adišà /p'ä-sēä-t'ä-thē-shoⁿ/ *adv.*, top side, toward the top side of a structure, such as a building or tree

P'á'šižé /p'ä-shē-zhä/ *n.*, tip of the nose

P'a'snut'à /p'ä-snü-t'ä/ *n.*, human like, lit., long, curved head, a real or mythological group of human-like creatures who lived in the North Country in ancient times and were said to have elongated heads

P'á'šudáde /p'ä-shü-dä-thā/ *n.*, nosebleed, epistaxis, an occurrence of bleeding from the nose

P'a'ú'de /p'ä-ü'-dä/ *n.*, the Caddo Tribe of Native Americans, lit., nose pierced

P'á'uskída /p'ä-ü-skē'-dä/ *n.*, eyebrows, that opening between the eyebrows

P'á'uskídà /p'ä-ü-skē'-dä/ *n.*, nose bridge, the upper bony part of the nose

P'á'xdugè /p'ä'-xthü-gä'/ *n.*, nasal passage, the interior parts of the nasal cavity

P'ádak'à /p'ä'-dä-k'ä'/ *n.*, the Comanche Tribe of Native Americans

P'ádį /p'ä'-theⁿ/ *n.*, the Pawnee Tribe of Native Americans

P'ádį pizà /p'ä'-thēⁿ pē-zä'/ *n.*, the Arikara Tribe of Native Americans, lit., sand Pawnee

P'adį́šį /p'ä-thēⁿ'-shēⁿ/ *v.*, to make or distort one's face in an expression to ridicule someone

P'adį́šį /p'ä-thēⁿ'-shēⁿ/ *v.*, make faces, lit., to crimp up the nose, to twist or contort the face to take on an unnatural or grotesque shape

P'agás'į /p'ä-gäs-ēⁿ/ *v./n.*, nod, 1. *v.*, concur or agree 2. *n.*, the okay or go-ahead sign 3. *v.*, a baby's nod to parents

P'á gašą̀ /p'ä' gä-shoⁿ/ *v.*, shaking the head as to signal no

P'á' gažį́' /p'ä' gä-zhēⁿ/ *v.*, to blow one's nose, to expel mucus from the nose

P'áhą /p'ä'-hoⁿ/ *v.*, arise, usu. refers to telling someone to get up out of bed

P'ahą́' /p'ä'-hoⁿ/ *n.*, knoll, hill, mound

P'ahą́'ga /p'ä'-hoⁿ'-gä/ *n./adj.*, first, at first, beginning, primary, earliest, usu. refers to beginning something

P'ahą́'gà /p'ä-hoⁿ'-gä/ *adj.*, before, first, primary, earliest, standing in front of

P'ahą́'gadì /p'ä-hoⁿ'-gä-dē'/ *n.*, long ago, at the beginning, start, first

P'ahą́gadì /p'ä-hoⁿ'-gä-dē/ *n. phr.*, in the beginning

P'ahą́gadì išáge /p'ä-hoⁿ'-gä-dē' ēsh-ä'-gä/ *n.*, reincarnation, lit., old man who lived before, philosophy or religious belief that some children had lived a previous life because of their talk of things past

P'ahą́gadìtą /p'ä-hoⁿ'-gä-dē'-toⁿ/ *adj.*, an-

cient, lit., something from the beginning, antiquated

P'ahą́ga gáxekè /p'ä-hoⁿ'-gä gä'-xä-kä'/ *n.*, original, the first of something that was made

P'ahą́ga uwída /p'ä-hoⁿ'-gä ü-wē'-thä/ *v.*, warn, tell something to somebody in advance

P'ahą́hą /p'ä-hoⁿ'-hoⁿ/ *adj.*, hilly, rolling hills (*mąžą́ ké ~*, the land is ~)

P'ahą́hą /p'ä-hoⁿ'-hoⁿ/ *n.*, knoll, being hilly, usu. refers to small hills

P'ahášiát'à /p'ä-hä'-shē-ä'-t'ä'/ *prep. phr.*, at the top, on the top (the papers are ~ shelf) (The term can be used, for instance, in regard to a two-story house, as in *t'í'p'ahášiát'à*, upstairs.)

P'ahé' /p'ä-hä'/ *n.*, hill, knoll, mound, butte

P'ahé't'ągà /p'ä-hä'-t'oⁿ-gä/ *n.*, mountain, 1. the surface of the earth higher in elevation than a hill 2. proper male name in the Đíxidą clan of the Ponca people

P'ahé'žé'egà /p'ä-hä'-zhä'-ä-goⁿ/ *n., archaic*, ca. 1600s, lit., the likeness of the phallus, a place near Colorado Spings, Colorado

P'ahé'žíde /p'ä-hä'-zhē'-dä/ *n.*, 1. the Kahokian Mounds, an ancient Native American civilization located in the present-day state of Illinois 2. the city of St. Louis, Missouri

P'ahéádi /p'ä-hä'-ä'-dē/ *n.*, on the hill

P'ahé mą́šì /p'ä-hä' moⁿ-shē'/ *n.*, high hill; *p'ahé mąšiát'a*, at the top of the hill

P'ahéšušudè /p'ä-hä'-shü-shü-dä/ *n.*, Badlands, refers to the badlands of South Dakota

P'ahéušúde /p'ä-hä'-ü-shü'-dä/ *n.*, the Great Smoky Mountains of North Carolina and Tennessee (Ponca oral history tells of the tribe once living in the East. Giving names to landmarks was common with the Ponca. Some anthropologists believe Eastern

Woodland culture is evident among the Ponca. The latest cultural identity, they believe, is Upper Plains culture.)

P'ahé žįgà /p'ä-hā'-zhēⁿ-gä/ *n.*, 1. small hill 2. proper name in the Mąk'ą́ clan of the Ponca people

P'áhì /p'ä'-hē'/ *n.*, neck, that part of the animal or human body that connects the head to the trunk

P'áhiugdè /p'ä'-hē-ü-gthä'/ *n.*, back of neck

P'aí'dadà /p'ä-ē'-thä-thä'/ *n.*, thorny, usu. refers to plants that have thorns, including sandbur, cocklebur, and "goat heads" or "stickers"

P'amáse /p'ä-mä'-sā/ *n.*, headcutters, another name for the Ponca warriors (The sign language symbol for *Ponca* is made by drawing the fingers, palm up, across the throat in a cutting motion.)

P'amáse /p'ä-mä'-sā/ *v.*, behead, decapitate, to behead or to cut off the head of the enemy

P'ánahò hétą egà /p'ä'-nä-hō' hā'-toⁿ ā-goⁿ/ *n.*, horned screech owl, of the genus *Megascops*

P'ąp'ą́de /p'oⁿ-p'oⁿ'-dä/ *v.*, vibrate, something inanimate that causes something to make small, rapid movements, as in the wind making an outdoor table with uneven legs rock

P'as'į́ /p'ä-s-ēⁿ/ *adj. phr.*, upside down, going or rolling over head first

P'ás'į̀ /p'ä'-s-ēⁿ/ *v.*, fall, to fall down head first

P'asiát'a /p'ä-sē'-ä'-t'ä/ *n.*, at the top, usu. refers to the top of a structure

P'asiát'à /p'ä-sēä-t'ä'/ *adj.*, tiptop, the highest point of something, such as a pinnacle or the top of a tree, house, or structure (he was working at the ~ part of the tower)

P'át'à /p'ä'-t'ä/ *adj.*, front, in front of (he sat in the ~ seat)

P'át'adišą̀ /p'ä'-t'ä-thē-shoⁿ/ *adv.*, front side, toward the front side of something or people

P'axdį́ /p'ä-xtheⁿ/ *n.*, nasal mucus, phlegm, usu. caused by some sort of infection in the nose, throat, sinuses, or lungs, which are lined with mucous membranes

P'áxdí daxù /p'ä-xthē' thä-xü/ *v.*, sniffling, to sniffle continuously because of a bad head cold, in order to prevent mucus from flowing out of the nose

P'ą́xe /p'oⁿ'-xä/ *n.*, radish, an edible root that is usually eaten raw, *Raphanus sativus* of the Brassicaceae family; *p'ą́xe židè*, red radish

P'áze /p'ä'-zä/ *n.*, evening, sunset, sundown, dusk

P'ázet'adišą̀ /p'ä'-zä-t'ä-thē-shoⁿ/ *prep.*, toward the evening

P'áze wadáte /p'ä'-zä wä-thä'-tā/ *n.*, supper, lit., evening meal, considered by some to be the main meal of the day, but could be a snack

P'é' /p'ä'/ *n.*, forehead, that part of the face above the eyebrows

P'ę́' /p'äⁿ/ *n./adv.*, adz or ax; in ancient times, a Ponca handheld tool made of flint, which could be attached to an elk horn for scraping

P'é'gazą́de /p'ä'-gä-zoⁿ'-dä/ *n.*, the Nez Perce Tribe of Native Americans

P'é'nąbà /p'ä'-noⁿ-bä/ (**P'é'dąbà** /p'ä'-thoⁿ-bä/) *n.*, seven, the number seven (7), lit., five and two (The Ponca count by fives and do not use the decimal system or tens.)

P'é't'ą̀ /p'ä'-t'oⁿ/ *n.*, sandhill crane, *Grus canadensis*

P'é'ut'áną /p'ä'-ü-t'ä'-noⁿ/ *n.*, forehead center, the center of the forehead

P'é'žį̀'bdá'skà /p'ä'-zhēⁿ-bthä'-skä'/ *n.*, perfume, Native American perfume, *Cogswellia daucifolia*

P'é'žį' ínąbdą' wažìde /p'ā́-zhēⁿ ē'-noⁿ-bthoⁿ' wä-zhē'-dā/ *n.*, perfume, Native American perfume, rose petals

P'é'ži'p'à /p'ā́-zhē-p'ä'/ *n.*, perfume, Native American perfume

P'é'ži'xút'à /p'ā́-zhē-xü'-t'ä'/ *n.*, sage, Native American cleansing sage, usu. used in prayers by burning the flat leaves, genus *Artemisia*

P'édá'bdì /p'ā́-thä'-bthē'/ *n.*, eight, lit., five and three, the number eight (8)

P'éde /p'ā́-dā/ *n.*, fire, refers to a fire that stands burning

P'éde /p'ā́-dā/ *n.*, matches, a small stick made of wood or hard paper coated on one end with a combustible substance and used to start fires

P'éde íganažì /p'ā́-dā ē'-gä-nä-zhē'/ *n.*, fire extinguisher, usu. a small, portable container that has special chemicals to put out fires

P'édeunéde /p'ā́-dā-ü-nä́-thā/ *n.*, stove, wood-burning stove

P'ehį́ ídišnà /p'ā́-hēⁿ ē'-thē-shnä'/ *n.*, tweezers, a small tool used to pick up small things or to remove small splinters; refers to a woman's tool for removing human hair from the eyebrows

P'énaxixè /p'ā́-nä-xē-xä'/ *n.*, eyebrow, the area of short delicate hairs above the eye

P'éniškà /p'ā́-nē-shkä'/ *n.*, tree frog, 1. a little green frog, *Hyla cinerea*, family Hylidae 2. a common male name among the Ponca people

P'étą /p'ā́-toⁿ/ *n.*, large crane, birds with long legs and long necks, one of many species of cranes

P'éxe /p'ā́-xā/ *n.*, gourd, one of various plants of the family Cucurbitasceae

P'éxehà /p'ā́-xā-hä'/ *n.*, bottle, lit., gourd hide, refers to glass bottles or other manmade containers for liquids

P'eží /p'ā-zhē'/ *adj.*, characteristic of something bad, old, and useless (Archival materials and a Ponca song refer to a boy by the name of Žįgá p'ežì, bad boy, who was afraid of the decapitated head of the enemy.)

P'ežigdé /p'ā-zhē-gthā'/ *pron./interj.*, something worthless or of no use, usu. a term used in name calling (*p'ežigdé!*, you are ~!)

P'í' /p'ē'/ *n.*, liver, a vital organ of humans and some animals

P'í' /p'ē'/ *v.*, *1st pers. sing.*, arrive, I ~ there; *1st pers. pres./past. p.*, I came there

P'í'dądà /p'ē'-thoⁿ-thoⁿ'/ *adv.*, again and again, a repeated behavior or action taken

P'í'denà /p'ē-thä-noⁿ'/ *v.*, repeat, try again, a command to try something again

P'í'gúdidądà /p'ē-gü'-dē-thoⁿ-thoⁿ'/ *adv.*, furthermore, in addition, more than that, usu. refers to an action or a verbal statement in response to another speaker's statement that is considered to be boring

P'í'uží' /p'ē'-ü-zhē'/ *v.*, refill, to fill up again, replenish

P'iáži gáxe /p'ēä́-zhē gä-xā/ *v.*, damage, ruin, spoil, or break something

P'ídądà /p'ē'-thoⁿ-thoⁿ'/ *adv.*, repeatedly, doing something over and over again

P'ídè /p'ē'-thā'/ *n.*, love between husband and wife (closer to eros love)

P'izá /p'ē-zä'/ *n.*, sand, granular material composed of rock and other mineral particles

P'izá'nik'à /p'ē-zä'-nē-k'ä'/ *n.*, lizard, suborder Lacertilia, includes gecko, chameleon, etc.

P'izá b'ahà /p'ē-zä' b-ä-hoⁿ'/ *n.*, sand dunes, refers to a hill in a desert formed by wind or the flow of water

P'izák'ą́de' /p'ē-zä'-k'oⁿ'-dā/ *n.*, sand plum, a small, round, edible fruit that grows abundantly in Oklahoma

P'izáugdą /p'ē-zä'-ü-gtho^n/ *n.*, gizzard, lit., has sand in it, also called the ventriculus, gastric mill, and gigerium, an organ in the digestive tract of waterfowl and other animals

P'ú' /p'ü'/ *interj.*, male exclamation, what the . . . , huh? . . .

P'ú'įdì /p'ü'-ē^n-thē'/ *n.*, humidity, humid, vapor in the air

Péde ní' /pā'-dä nē'/ *n.*, whiskey, lit., fire water, *p'éde*, fire, *ní'*, water, an alcoholic liquor

Púki /pü'-kē/ *n.*, a fluffy, downy thing

Púpúde /pü'-pü'-dä/ *n.*, loose dirt, dirt, or any substance that may be fine, like powder

Q

This letter is not included in the Ponca alphabet.

R

This letter is not included in the Ponca alphabet.

S

s /s/ twelfth consonant in the Ponca alphabet

š /sh/ thirteenth consonant in the Ponca alphabet

S'á'de /s-ä'-thä/ *adj.*, salty, having a slightly tart or bitter edge to a flavor

Š'eną'egà /sh-ā-no^n'-ē-go^n/ *adj.*, adequate, lit., just enough, enough, ample

Š'į'k'a /sh-ē^n'-k'ä/ *adj.*, uneven, something that has furrows and ridges, such as an uneven wooden board or a wrinkle in the nose

S'ihídubà /s-ē-hē'-dü-bä'/ *n.*, salamander, any of the species of amphibians within the order Caudata

Š'p'áiúni /sh-p'ä'-ē'-ü'-nē/ *n.*, Spaniard, corruption of *Spaniard*, a native or inhabitant of Spain

Šą /so^n/ *adj.*, shiny, gleaming, glistening

Šą' /sho^n/ *n.*, finish, the completion or finish of something (Also used in questions that connote what task has been completed, such as *šą'a?*, are you ready?, *wadáte tè, šą'a?*, is the food ready?)

Šą' /sho^n/ *n.*, it is ready, complete, set to go, done

Šą' éską edégąbažì /sho^n ā'-sko^n ā-thä'-go^n-bä-zhē'/ *adj.*, unaware, being unprepared or naïve about some possible impending danger

Šą'gaxè /sho^n'-gä-xä'/ *v.*, quit, stop doing, end the activity; *šą'p'axè*, I quit; *šą'škáxe*, you quit; *šą'gáxaì*, he/she/it/they quit

Šá'gaxè /shä'-gä-xä'/ *n.*, conclusion, bring to an end, close or finish

Šą'ną /sho^n'-no^n/ *adv.*, yet, even more, notwithstanding

Šá'p'è /shä'-p'ā'/ *n.*, six, the number six (6)

Šą't'ągà /sho^n'-t'o^n-gä'/ *n.*, wolf, *Canis lupus*, more often known as the gray wolf, a carnivore found mostly in the wilderness

Šą'xt'i k'igáxe /sho^n'-xt'ē k'ē-gä'-xä/ *n.*, success, favorable outcome of some task or undertaking

Šą'žįgà /sho^n'-zhē^n-gä'/ *n.*, pup, a young dog, *Canis lupus familiaris*

Šaą /shä-o^n'/ *n.*, the Sioux Tribe of Native Americans

Šaąxt'ì /shä-o^n-xt'ē'/ *n.*, Brule, Brule of the Teton Dakotas

Sabá'a /sä-bä'-ä/ (*fem.*) (**Sabá'aga** /sä-bä'-ägä/ [*masc.*]) *adj.*, cautious, as when commanded to be on the lookout for anything that might be a problem

Sabáži /sä-bä'-zhē/ *adj.*, sudden, abrupt and unexpected

Sabáži /sä-bä'-zhē/ *v.*, might, may, possibly, could, something that ~ happen in the future

Sábe /sä'-bā/ *adj.*, the color black, being the color of coal or carbon

Šábe /shä'-bā/ *adj.*, brown, 1. the color brown, dark 2. *v.*, darken, to make something a darker color

Sabé /sä-bā'/ *conj.*, in case, lest, for fear that

Sabé /sä-bā'/ *n.*, precaution, taking preventive measures or safeguards; *sabága*, you take measures against any possible trouble

Sábekidè /sä'-bā-kē-thā'/ *v.*, to make one's face black before going into battle

Sáda /sä'-dä/ *adj.*, ridged, stiff, usu. 1. refers to something extended, such as one's legs 2. flattened, as with a stiff collar

Šǫdádišè /shon-thä'-thēn-shä/ *v.*, you are all right, good, okay, refers to somebody stating that another will be all right, good, or okay given their condition of sickness, emotional condition, or status among family and friends

Šǫdé /shon-dä'/ *n.*, penis, the male organ for copulation and discharge of urine from the body

Sadé'gdè /sä-dä'-gthä'/ *n.*, brush arbor

Sadégde /sä-dä'-gthä/ *n.*, arbor, a Ponca shade made of upright poles with rafters made of smaller poles covered with small leafy branches

Šǫdési /shon-dä'-sē/ *n.*, scrotum, pouch that contains the testes in mammals

Šǫdíʃda /shon-thē'ʃ-thä/ *v.*, leave him/her/it alone, advice for another to avoid contact with somebody or something

Šǫdiʃdà (gà) /shon-thēʃ-thä' (gä')/ *v.t., fem./ masc.*, leave him alone, leave him/her/it alone

Sadú' /sä-thü'/ *n.*, rattlesnake, the name refers to a snake's rattle

Šadúha /shä-thü'-hä/ *v.*, following that, to say or do again, e.g., after someone makes a statement and then a person without regard rebuts what was said (~ *íye dǫǫ̀ži tè*, ~ you might get up and speak)

Šadúha /shä-thü'-hä/ *adv.*, again, usu. refers to saying something or repeating a behavior that could be characterized as good or bad

Šǫ́ge /shon'-gā/ *n.*, horse, *Equus caballus*, a large, hoofed, domesticated mammal with short hair, a long mane, and a long tail; *šǫ́ge nugà*, stallion, a male horse not gelded

Šǫ́ge't'ǫ́žįgà /shon'-gā-t'on-zhēn-gä'/ *n.*, colt, a young horse, usu. one less than a year old

Šǫ́ge'unǫ́ži /shon'-gā-ü-non'-zhē/ *n.*, barn, lit., where the horses stand

Šǫ́geágdį /shon'-gā-ä'-gthēn'/ *n./adv.*, horseback, sitting or riding on a horse

Šǫ́ge ágdì /shon'-gā ä'-gthē'/ *adj.*, equestrian, horseback, relates to riding on horses or horseback riding

Šǫ́ge gdežè /shon'-gā gthä-zhä'/ *n.*, pinto, pinto pony, usu. white marked with patches of another color

Šǫ́ge mǫt'ǫnǫhà /shon'-gā mon-t'on-non-hä'/ *n.*, mustang, wild horse, descended from horses brought to this continent by the Spanish

Šǫ́ge migà /shon'-gā mē-gä'/ *n.*, mare, adult female horse

Šǫ́ge mikáhe /shon'-gā mē-kä'-hä/ *n.*, currycomb, a comb with metal teeth for currying horses

Šǫ́ge nǫsé /shon'-gā non-sä'/ *n.*, horse hunter, 1. one who hunts and captures horses 2. male name in the Hísadà clan of the Ponca people

Šǫ́ge nǫ́xexidà /shon'-gā non-xä-xē-thä'/ *n.*, skittish horse, a horse that is nervous, jumpy, and edgy

Šą́genežè /shoⁿ'-gā-nā-zhā'/ *n.*, beer, lit., horse urine, an alcoholic beverage

Šą́ge šáge /shoⁿ'-gā shä'-gā/ *n.*, hoof, usu. refers to the hoof of a horse (The suffix -*šáge* is described as a nail or claw and may be applied to various mammals and fowl. A horse's hoof is composed of soft tissue and other keratinized structures.)

Šą́gešibè /shoⁿ'-gā-shē-bä'/ *n.*, worm, lit., horse intestine, usu. refers to a type of worm that appears above ground after a rain

Šą́get'ąžįgà /shoⁿ'-gā-t'oⁿ-zhēⁿ-gä'/ *n.*, foal, a horse that is one year old or younger, of mammals in the family Equidae

Šą́ge unąza /shoⁿ'-gā ü-noⁿ'-zä/ *n.*, corral, an enclosure to keep or confine livestock for loading, branding, and other such activities

Šą́ge unąžį /shoⁿ'-gā ü-noⁿ'-zhēⁿ/ *n.*, stable, a building where horses are kept

Šą́ge wadáte /shoⁿ-gā wä-thä'-tä/ *n.*, oatmeal, lit., horse food

Šą́ge wadaxt'à /shoⁿ'-gā wä-thä-xt'ä'/ *n.*, horsefly, lit., bites horses, a large female fly that sucks the blood of horses

Šą́ge waį /shoⁿ'-gā wä-ēⁿ'/ *n.*, horse blanket, a blanket to keep the horse warm or cool or to keep flies off

Šą́ge wánąkagdè /shoⁿ'-gā wä'-noⁿ-kä-gthä'/ *n.*, lantern, lit., horse lamp (In early Ponca history such lamps were used to light up an area where livestock were kept.)

Šą́ge žįgà /shoⁿ'-gā zhēⁿ-gä'/ *n.*, pony, lit., little horse

Sagí /sä-gē'/ *adj.*, hard, solid, firm

Sagí'gi'à /sä-gē'-gē-ä'/ (*fem.*) (**Sagí'gi'àgá'** /sä-gē'-gē-ä'-gä'/ [*masc.*]) *v.*, walk strong, lit., come walking strongly, commonly said to children in times when people had to walk great distances

Sagí'k'ida'á /sä-gē'-k'ē-thä-ä'/ (*fem.*) (**Sagí'k'ida'ágá'** /sä-gē'-k'ē-thä-ä'-gä'/ [*masc.*]) *v.*, encourage, lit., make yourself strong, a common saying to hearten someone or give them confidence

Sagí gáxe /sä-gē' gä'-xä/ *n.*, seal, something that makes a thing tight or airtight

Sáhį /sä'-hēⁿ/ *n.*, straw, stalks of threshed wheat, barley, or such used for weaving hats, baskets, etc.

Sahį́ /sä-hēⁿ'/ *n.*, grass, reeds that grow tall and slender near ponds

Sáhį wadáge /sä-hēⁿ wä-thä'-gā/ *n.*, straw hat, a brimmed head covering woven out of straw and worn during the summer for protection against the sun

Šahʃdà /shä-hʃ'-thä'/ *n.*, the Cheyenne Tribe of Native Americans

Sak'íba /sä-k'ē'-bä/ *prep.*, beside, animate or inanimate things close together or side by side; *sak'íbadì*, beside, 1. at the side of, nearby 2. usu. refers to something additionally said or done

Sáka /sä'-kä/ *interj.*, no more talking, something children say at bedtime (parents tell children to say ~), *archaic*, an expression said by children at bedtime, be silent, the absence of noise, usu. a word used to tell children at bedtime to be silent ("say *sáka*, you may not talk until morning")

Sáka /sä'-kä/ *n.*, silence, be silent, the absence of noise, an *archaic* expression used to tell children at bedtime to be silent (say *sáka*, you may not talk until morning)

Šą́ka /shoⁿ'-kä/ *n.*, nine, the number nine (9)

Sákadidè /sä'-kä-thē-dä'/ *n.*, watermelon, a large, round, sometimes elongated fruit with a hard green skin and sweet, juicy red or yellow flesh, *Citrullus lanatus* var. *lanatus*, of the family Curcurbitaceae

Sákadidè snúsnú /sä'-kä-thē-dä' snü'-snü'/ *n.*, muskmelon, a yellow or green fleshed, sweet-flavored fruit with a rough rind

Ṣǫkéda'(dagà) /shoⁿ-kā'-thä (thä-gä')/ *v.t.*, *sing.*, leave it alone, *fem/masc.*, advised to leave a thing alone, as in don't bother it

Sakíba /sä-kē'-bä/ *prep.*, adjacent, adjacent to something in particular

Sakíbadì /sä-kē'-bä-dē'/ *adv.*, alongside, next to, next to something nearby

Ṣǫméwadà (dagà) /shoⁿ-mā'-wä-thä' (thä-gä')/ *v.t.*, *pl.*, leave them alone, *fem./masc.*, advised to leave animate subject(s) in a particular state

Ṣǫmikè /shoⁿ-mē-kā'/ *adv.*, consequently, as a result, therefore (~, *bdé*, ~, I went on)

Ṣǫnak'ágde /shoⁿ-noⁿ-k'ä'-gthä/ *n.*, saddle, a seat used by a person riding on the back of a horse; *šánąk'ágde uží*, saddlebag; *šánąk'ágde ágašt'ągà*, saddle blanket

Ṣǫnak'agdè sí unáži /shoⁿ-noⁿ-k'ä-gthäⁿ' sē' ü-noⁿ'-zhēⁿ/ *n.*, stirrup, foot support on a saddle

Ṣǫnudà /shoⁿ-nü-dä/ *n.*, dog, refers to any breed of domestic dogs, *Canis lupus familiaris* (modern Ponca pronounciation is *šínudà*)

Ṣǫšą /shoⁿ-shoⁿ/ *adv.*, right away, without ado (When a task is completed or a crisis arises and further immediate action is required and a person or group leaves right away to follow up; *wadítą dišt'ąitedì ~ adái*, they finished the job and left ~)

Ṣǫšą́ /shoⁿ-shoⁿ/ *adv.*, always, perpetually, something that will go unchanged, as in certain cultural values that never change

Sąsą́ /soⁿ-soⁿ/ *adj.*, trembling, 1. somebody who is quivering or shaking, as in fear 2. *v.*, deliberate shaking of one's dance paraphernalia (bells or other clicking sound makers such as deer hooves) while dancing 3. *v.*, shiver, usu. caused by cold or cold wind hitting the body

Sąsą́ /soⁿ-soⁿ/ *adj.*, shimmering, glittering, iridescent

Ṣǫšą́da /shoⁿ-shoⁿ'-thä/ *adj.*, shaky, wobbly, something not sturdy

Šášáka /shä'-shä-kä/ *adv.*, unevenly, not level, not smooth, irregular, usu. refers to things made with the hands that are marked by ridges, uneven, or bumpy, mostly in reference to handiwork made with beads, quills, and other craft materials (*hįbé ukédi te hiská ádiaye te ~ xt'i gáxaì*, the beads are ~ placed on the moccasins)

Šášakà /shä'-shä-kä/ *adj.*, rough, marked by ridges, uneven, or bumpy, mostly refers to handiwork made with beads, quills, and other craft materials

Šą́skédégąžì /shoⁿ'-skä-thä'-goⁿ-zhē'/ *adv.*, did not think of it or did not think about it, refers to being preoccupied with something while a thing of importance occurred, being oblivious to something

Sát'ą /sä'-t'oⁿ/ *n.*, five, the number five (5)

Sát'ą'ìdawà /sä-t'oⁿ-ē-thä-wä'/ *n.*, five-dollar bill, U.S. currency

Ṣǫt'ągà hà' /shoⁿ-t'oⁿ-gä' hä'/ *n.*, wolf hide, an ancient piece of the Ponca Heدúškà dance paraphernalia (This symbolic piece, the head and entire hide of the wolf, was worn over the right shoulder of the dancer.)

Ṣǫt'ągà skà /shoⁿ-t'oⁿ-gä' skä'/ *n.*, white wolf, 1. *Canis lupus arctos*, species known by the Ponca in ancient times 2. male name in the Wašábe clan of the Ponca people

Ṣą́t'egažì /shoⁿ'-t'ä-gä-zhē'/ *interj.*, not likely to happen (he tried, but it's ~); any act or plan not thoroughly prepared and perceived as not likely to happen

Ṣą́t'egažì /shoⁿ'-t'ä-gä-zhē'/ *adj.*, improbable, doubtful, not likely to happen

Ṣǫtédà (dagà) /shoⁿ-tā'-thä' (thä-gä')/ *v.t.*, *pl.* leave them alone, *fem./masc.*, advised to leave specific inanimate objects unchanged in a particular state

Šátext'ì /shoⁿ-tā-xt'ē/ *adv.*, eventually, finally, in due course of time

Šáxt'igà /shoⁿ-xt'ē-goⁿ/ *adj.*, lackadaisical, halfhearted, casual, laid back

Šáxt'igà mądì /shoⁿ-xt'ē-goⁿ moⁿ-thēⁿ/ *v.*, amble, mosey, going at a slow pace in no particular direction

Šé /shā'/ *n.*, apple, a sweet fruit of the family Rosaceae, genus *Malus*; *šé hì*, apple tree

Sé' /sā'/ *v.*, cut, to separate a thing with a sharp tool, to penetrate with a sharp tool; *bisé'*, to cut by pressing a sharp instrument onto a thing; *gasé'*, to cut by using force with an instrument, such as an ax, cleaver, or long sword; *máse*, to cut something, usu. something like a rope, twine, thread; *máxạ*, to cut with a knife; *đisé'*, to cut by using the hands

Šé' /shā'/ *pron.*, that; *šé'áka*, that one, usu. refers to one particular person; *šé'ma*, refers to a group of people or animals; *šę'đą̀*, that round one, usu. refers to some specific place on the land; *šę'kè*, that one, usu. refers to one specific thing; *šé'te*, that one, usu. refers to a group of things; *šét'a*, refers to something standing away from the speaker

Šé'amà /shā'-ä-mä/ *pron.*, them, usu. refers to those things or that group of people standing away from the speaker; *đéámà*, those standing closest to the speaker; *duáma*, those standing slightly farther away from the speaker; *gááma*, those standing, running, speaking, sitting, eating, etc. out of sight of the speaker

Šę́'gą̀ /shāⁿ-goⁿ/ *adj.*, correct, lit., that's the way, usu. used when someone is working with someone who is doing something

Šé'gè /shā'-gā/ *pl. pron.* of *that*, those, refers to things placed close by; *šé'gešt'ì*, even ~ over there

Šę́'háí'mà /shāⁿ-hä'-ē'-mä/ *pl. pron.*, you, over there, usu. shouted out to get the attention of someone

Šé'higedì /shā'-hē-gā-dē/ *adv.*, in those scattered, unspecified places

Šé'k'i /shā'-k'ē/ *n.*, rattlesnake, the name refers to the snake's act of rattling

Šé'p'ahága /shā'-p'ä-hoⁿ-gä/ *n.*, first born, in the order of birth, the eldest or first child to be born

Šé't'adišą̀ /shā'-t'ä-thē-shoⁿ/ *adv.*, that way, toward that way, suggesting a place in sight across the room or the front yard

Šé'užégdą̀ /shā'-ü-zhā'-gthoⁿ/ *n.*, pie, baked fruit enclosed in pastry

Šé'žįgà /shā'-zhēⁿ-gä/ *n.*, newborn, a newborn, baby, infant

Šedą́ /shā-thoⁿ/ *v.*, break down, collapse, go kaput; *šešédá*, break down, the structure of something broken down in several places; *bišédạ*, break down by pressing; *bišéšédạ*, break down by continued pressing down; *đišédạ*, break down by use of the hands; *đišéšédạ*, break down by continued use of the hands; *gašédạ*, break down by force; *gašéšédạ*, break down by continuous use of force; *nạšédạ*, break down by stepping on or driving over something; *nạšéšédạ*, break down by continuously stepping or driving over something

Šedą́ /shā-thoⁿ/ *v.*, broken, something that was in one piece and has fallen apart; something that was running, e.g., an automobile, and is now broken down

Šédąkà /shā'-thoⁿ-kä/ *pl. pron.*, those, usu. refers to people, animals, or things within a short distance from the speaker; *gádạkà*, refers to people, animals, or things out of sight or in the mind

Šédạskaegą̀ /shā'-thoⁿ-skä-ä-goⁿ/ *adj.*, large, refers to the size of something; exaggerated, overly big size

Šédažì /shā'-thä-zhē'/ *adj.*, undaunted, fearless, showing no concern to him/her, usu. refers to a person whom somebody has something against

Šédažì /shā'-thä-zhē'/ *v.*, ignore, pay no attention to, pay no heed to him/her/it

Šédekì· /shā'-thä-kē'·/ *n.*, the Cherokee Tribe of Native Americans

Šédešt'iąžì /shā'-thä-sht'ē-oⁿ-zhē'/ *adj.*, unconcerned, indifferent, undaunted, nonchalant

Šédudì /shā'-thü-dē'/ *adv.*, 1. there, right there—pointing to something physical 2. in a speech, bringing attention to something

Šéga /shā'-goⁿ/ *conj.*, refers to something done in the same way or to performing some action in the same manner

Šégedì /shā'-gä-dē'/ *adv.*, there, to put, place, observe, remain at some physical location close by

Šéhaimà /shā'-hä-ē-mä'/ *n.*, a call to persons over there, refers to persons within hearing range or in sight of the speaker

Šéhiamà /shā'-hē-ä-mä'/ *n.*, them over there, refers to specific persons within hearing range or in sight of the speaker

Šéhidəát'a /shā'-hē-thəä-'t'ä/ *adv.*, yonder, a place within sight over there

Šéhįškubè /shā'-hēⁿ-shkü-bä'/ *n.*, peach, a fuzzy, sweet fruit; also nectarines

Šéhįškubèhì /shā'-hēⁿ-shkü-bä-hē'/ *n.*, peach tree, of the rose family, *Prunus persica*

Šémikè /shā'-mē-kā'/ *v. phr.*, there I was, refers to one in the middle of a predicament

Šémižįgà /shā'-mē-zhēⁿ-gä'/ *n.*, young woman, a female in the first years of womanhood, having the appearance of a woman

Šéną /shā'-noⁿ/ *adj.*, enough, sufficient amount (when something is given, the receiver says, "That's ~.")

Šéną /shā'-noⁿ/ *n.*, end of, no more, usu. refers to the exhausted supply of things (that's the ~ that)

Šénąskaegà /shā'-noⁿ-skä-ā-goⁿ/ *adj.*, gigantic, huge, immense, very big, relates to something that is very large for its kind

Šénąwadè /shā'-noⁿ-wä-thä'/ *n.*, eliminate, refers to the end of those who oppose each other in sports or in war; in war, means total elimination of the enemy

Šénąxt'ì /shā'-noⁿ-xt'ē'/ *adj.*, sufficient, a sufficient amount of things

Šénužįgà /shā'-nü-zhēⁿ-gä'/ *n.*, young men, usu. refers to young men who have come of age or are old enough to be married, provide for their family, and defend the camp (The Ponca use this term often in their Heдúškà dance songs, namely, going to meet the enemy.)

Sésasà /sā'-sä-sä'/ *v.*, trot, 1. the gait between a walk and run in humans 2. the slow gait of a four-legged animal

Sésasà wačígaxè /sā'-sä-sä' wä-chē'-gä-xä'/ *n.*, trot dance, a man's dance, a form of the Heдúškà dance

Šešé'dą /shā-shä-thoⁿ/ *adj.*, broken to pieces

Šét'adišą̀ /shā'-t'ä-thē-shoⁿ/ *prep./adv.*, over there, toward that direction, toward a space between the speaker and a point of reference such as the wall, auditorium, playing field

Šét'adišą̀ /shā'-t'ä-thē-shoⁿ/ *adv.*, yonder, designation of a place or thing closer to the speaker; over there within sight

Šetą́ /shā-toⁿ/ *n.*, end, finish, conclusion of something

Šetą́'žì /shā-toⁿ-zhē'/ *adj.*, endless, no end

Šetą́ną /shā-toⁿ-noⁿ/ *adv.*, still, refers to something that is always there or a condition that remains the same

Šéwaдažì /shā'-wä-thä-zhē'/ *adj.*, undaunted,

fearless, showing no concern about them, usu. refers to a person whom some people may have something against

Šéwadì /shā'-wä-dē/ *adv.*, there, indicates a place or position of a thing away from the speaker, usu. refers to distance from the speaker, as in an object across the room as opposed to an object close at hand, far away, out of sight

Šéwakidažì /shā'-wä-kē-thä-zhē'/ *adj.*, fearless, courageous, valiant, does not fear anyone

Šézi /shā'-zē/ *n.*, orange, a round citrus fruit with thick skin

Šéžidè /shā'-zhē-dä/ *adj./n.*, childish, an adult who displays childlike behavior following a disagreeable matter

Šéžįgà /shā'-zhēⁿ-gä/ *n.*, baby, a human baby

Šézi niúdiškì /shā'-zē nēü'-thē-shkē'/ *n.*, lemon, a small oval-shaped, bitter-tasting fruit, genus *Citrus* of the family Rutaceae; *šézi niúdiškì hì*, lemon tree

Šį́ /shēⁿ/ *n.*, fat, obese, corpulent, having too much fat or being overweight

Sí' /sē'/ *n.*, foot, the end of the human leg on which one stands and walks; the lower anatomical part of the human leg that includes toes and heel; *sí'te*, feet, plural of foot; *sihí'*, both feet

Sí' /sē'/ *n.*, kernel, seed, that part of a mature plant containing an embryo

Sí' /sē'/ *v.*, save, saving some or holding some back

Sí' /sē'/ *n.*, seed, an embryonic plant or the grain of plants

Šį́' /shēⁿ/ *adj.*, obese, fat, plump, corpulent

Ší' /shē'/ *conj.*, and, usu. used with a verbal clause (*edégąxt'ì égą gáxaì, ~ égą gáxaì*, he did it before, ~ he's doing it again)

Sí'dihà /sē'-dē-hä'/ *n.*, instep, the arch in the human foot

Šì'édąbà /shē-ā'-thoⁿ-bä/ *adv., prefix*, again, usu. used in an admonishing statement— (*~ gáxeažìgà*, never do this ~)

Sį́'gdè /sēⁿ'-gthä'/ *n.*, cricket, an insect that chirps, jumps, and bites, of the family Gryllidae

Si'hí /sē-hē'/ *n.*, foot bones, usu. refers to all parts of the feet, as in relating to pain

Ší'mąkà /shē'-moⁿ-koⁿ'/ *v.*, kneel, kneel down, to bend the knees to the ground

Ší'mąšadì /shē'-moⁿ-shä-dē'/ *v.*, kneel, kneeling down on one knee

Sí'nąuskída /sē'-noⁿ-ü-skē'-dä/ *n.*, arch, in anatomy, below the ~ of the feet

Sí'nąxixè /sē'-noⁿ-xē-xä/ *n.*, arch, in anatomy, the ~ of the foot

Sí'nié /sē'-nē-ā'/ *n.*, aching feet, 1. when a person stands all day on their feet 2. a person who may have medical issues with the feet

Sí'núkadį̀ /sē'-nü-kä-thēⁿ'/ *adj.*, barefooted, without shoes or foot covering of any kind

Sí'snejè'wagidè /sē'-snä-jä'-wä-gē-thä'/ *n.*, muskrat, a large rodent living in and near water, *Ondatra zibethicus*

Sí'úbahè /sē-ü'-bä-hä'/ *n.*, sides of the human foot

Sí'unąskida' /sē-ü-noⁿ'-skē-dä/ *n.*, the curve under the foot, the curve of the arches

Si'ušáge'wahì /sē-ü-shä'-gä-wä-hē'/ *n.*, toenails

Šíbè /shē'-bä'/ *n.*, intestines, bowels, or entrails; part of the digestive tract, used in processing food

Šíbe'užíga /shē'-bā-ü-zhē'-gä/ *n.*, small intestine

Sičáxu /sē-chä'-xü/ *n.*, the Teton Dakota people

Sída /sē'-dä/ *v.*, overripen, when produce becomes overripe and hard (Fresh corn, e.g., can be cooked or parched for eating and dehydrated for later use.)

Sidádi /sē-dä'-dē/ *n.*, yesterday, the day before today

Sidádi guádišą̀ /sē-dä'-dē güä'-thē-shoⁿ/ *n.*, yesterday, the day before yesterday

Sidádi guádišą̀ /sē-dä'-dē güä'-thē-shoⁿ/ *adv./n.*, two days before or the day before yesterday

Síde /sē'-thä/ *v.*, think, to think of something that happened or think of somebody (~ *nąmą́*, I ~ of you)

Sídè /sē'-thä/ *v.t./v.i.*, remember, retain an idea in the memory

Sį́de /sēⁿ'-dä/ *n.*, tail, the extended part of the rear end of the body of an animal, such as a monkey's tail, the tail feathers of a bird

Sį́de'ádį /sēⁿ-dä-ä'-thēⁿ/ *n.*, tails, lit., those who have tails, those with ~ (Refers to the warriors of the Đíxidà clan of the Ponca people, whose hairstyle involved shaving both sides of the head. The hair from the crown of the head was left long and was braided.)

Sidéde /sē-thä'-dä/ *n.*, heel, in human anatomy, the prominence of the calcaneus, or heel bone

Sį́de dihą̀ /sēⁿ'-dä thē-hoⁿ/ *n.*, tail, lifted tail, refers to the flash of the tail of the whitetail deer, *Odocoileus virginianus*, as it disappears into the bush

Sį́dé gdéškà /seⁿ-dä' gthä'-shkä/ *n.*, Spotted Tail, a Sioux war leader

Sį́déhi' /sēⁿ-dä'-hē/ *n.*, tailbone, the last bone at the bottom of the vertebral column, coccyx

Sidémąkà /sē-thä'-moⁿ-kä/ *n.*, a mythical creature told of in children's bedtime stories

Sį́de Skà /sēⁿ'-dä skä/ *n.*, White Tail (He was the principal chief of the Ponca, succeeding White Star, and a member of the Mąk'ą́ clan, who was subsequently succeeded by Wégasap'ì, Whip, a member of the Đíxidà clan.)

Sídewadažì /sē'-thä-wä-thä-zhē/ *adj.*, unthinkable, something undesirable to think about

Sídewadè /sē'-thä-wä-thä/ *adj.*, memorable, something that is unforgettable

Sidíze /sē-thē'-zä/ *n.*, step, footstep, stride, to take steps

Sídu'á' /sē'-dü-ä/ *adj.*, naked, nude; *hánuk'à*, naked, bare skinned; *nukádį̀*, unclothed

Sį́ga /sēⁿ'-gä/ *n.*, squirrel, a small animal with a bushy tail that lives in the trees, a rodent of the genus *Sciurus*

Šį́gažįgà /shēⁿ-gä-zhēⁿ-gä'/ *n.*, child, children

Šį́gažįgà wasésą /shēⁿ-gä-zhēⁿ-gä' wä-sä'-soⁿ/ *n.*, doll, a child's toy—figure of a human child or baby

Sigdé /sē-gthä'/ *n.*, footprint, track, 1. a foot mark made on the ground or grass by a person or animal 2. depressed grass, broken twigs, etc. also indicating a "footprint"

Sigdé /sē-gthä'/ *n.*, track, a mark left by an animate or inanimate moving thing, such as a footprint or a rut left by a wheel

Sigdé mąk'ą̀ /sē-gthä' moⁿ-k'oⁿ/ *n.*, *Plantago major*, a plant used for medicine, referred to in a children's story

Sigdé udúhe /sē-gthä' ü-thü'-hä/ *n./v.*, track, to track, to track a person or animal

Sihásabè /sē-hä'-sä-bä/ *n.*, the Blackfoot Tribe of Native Americans

Sihátą /sē-hä'-toⁿ/ *n.*, sole, in anatomy, the bottom of the foot

Sihí'dubà /sē-hē'-dü-bä/ *n.*, alligator, crocodile

Sihíbaxt'è /sē-hē'-bä-xt'ä/ *n./v.*, hobble, a device, usu. a thick wrap that is tied above the fetlock of the front legs to restrict the movement of a horse

Sik'ą /sē-k'oⁿ/ *n.*, ankle, the talocrural region; *sihí*, ankle

Šinąde /shē-noⁿ-dā/ *n.*, knee, the middle joint of the human leg

Sip'á /sē-p'ä/ *n., pl.*, toes; *sipáhi*, toe

Sip'áhi udíza /sē-p'ä'-hē ü-thē'-zoⁿ/ *n.*, middle toe

Sip'áhi ut'ąga /sē-p'ä'-hē ü-t'oⁿ-gä/ (*masc./fem.*) (**Sip'óho t'ągá** /sē-p'ō'-hō t'oⁿ-goⁿ/ [*masc.*]) *n.*, big toe

Sip'áhi užíga /sē-p'ä'-hē ü-zhēⁿ-gä/ (*masc./fem.*) (**Sip'úhu žíga** /sē-p'ü'-hü zhēⁿ-gä/ [*masc.*]) *n.*, little toe

Sip'aút'ągà uduáta /sē-p'äü'-t'oⁿ-gä ü-thüä'-toⁿ/ *n.*, second toe, the toe next to the big toe

Sip'áužíga udúatà /sē-p'ä'-ü-zhē'-gä ü-thü-ä-toⁿ/ *n.*, fourth toe, the toe next to the little toe

Šip'í /shē-p'ē/ *adv.*, again, once more, once again (do come ~)

Šip'í /shē-p'ē/ *v.*, repeat, do again

Šip'í udá /shē-p'ē' ü-thä/ *v.*, reiterate, to say something over and over again, to repeat something

Šíšígè /shē-shē-gä/ *n.*, dust, something of the nature of litter or small particles

Šíšt'ąnà /shē-sht'oⁿ-noⁿ/ *adv./n.*, again, something done all over again, usu. connotes something negatively done

Sit'áxì /sē-t'ä'-xē/ *n.*, ankle bone

Síúbažù /sē-ü'-bä-zhü/ *n.*, bunion, an enlargement of the joint at the base of the big toe, the hallux

Síwanidè /sē'-wä-nē-dä/ *n.*, rice, *Oryza sativa* (Asian rice) or *Oryza glaberrima* (African rice)

Síwanidè /sē'-wä-nē-dä/ *n.*, wild rice, of the genus *Zizania*

Sižú /sē-zhü/ *n.*, thigh, usu. refers to the upper part of the human leg, that area between the pelvis and knee

Šk'ąšk'ą /shk'oⁿ-shk'oⁿ/ *v.*, shake, tremble, shiver, to move with short and quick, jerky body movements, as in trembling in fear

Šką /shkoⁿ/ *v.*, motion, in motion, stir

Šką' /shkoⁿ/ *n.*, movement, the process of body movement, usu. refers to a person lying down or in a sitting position

Šká /skä/ *adj./n.*, white, the color white

Šką'áži /shkoⁿ-ä-zhē/ *v.*, does not move around, something or somebody is still, is inactive

Šką'ážì /shkoⁿ-ä-zhē/ *adj.*, motionless, still, at a standsill, stagnant, unmoving

Šká'dadà /shkä-thä-thä/ *adj.*, carefree, untroubled, cheerful, free from care, free as a lark

Šká'de /shkä-dä/ *n.*, event, a happening (This may include dances, ballgames, etc.)

Škáde /shkä-dä/ *n.*, play, social activities, as in games, dances, pow-wows, carnivals, circuses, sports, etc.

Šką·diá /shkoⁿ-thē-ä/ *n.*, sleep paralysis, a temporary inability to move and speak; a state between being awake and asleep

Skáskabè /skä-skä-bä/ *v.*, sticky, something that is gummy or gluey

Skážíde egà /skä-zhē-dä ä-goⁿ/ *n.*, pink, lit., a reddish-white color, a pale reddish color

Skéwą /skä-woⁿ/ *adv.*, always, usually, customarily, habitually, ordinarily (he ~ does that)

Skíde /skē-thä/ *adj.*, sweet, sugary; *skídeáži*, not sweet

Skíge /skē-gä/ *adj./n.*, heavy, a great amount of weight

Škúbe /shkü-bä/ *adj.*, deep, unfathomable, usu. refers to the depth of a river, lake, or any large body of water

Sná' /snä/ *n.*, scar, a mark on the flesh caused by a healed wound or burn

Šná'tigdágda /shnä'-tē-gthä'-gthä/ *adj.*, glittering, something reflecting light from small pieces causing a sparkling effect

Šnábe /shnä'-bā/ *adj.*, dirty, grimy, soiled; *ibišnabè*, make dirty or smear something on; *idébešnabè*, made his (something) dirty or smeared; *įdébišnabè*, made mine dirty or smeared

Snądá /snoⁿ-thä'/ *v.*, unravel, come loose, as in threads of seams in clothing

Snáde /snä'-thā/ *v.*, lubricate, oil or grease something; *wésnadè*, lubricant

Snáde /snä'-thā/ *v.*, to apply a substance on something, as in putting a salve on a wound, painting a house, greasing an automobile wheel axle

Šnahá' /shnä-hä'/ *adj.*, slippery, slick, as in ice on a sidewalk or highway

Snásną /snoⁿ'-snoⁿ/ *adj.*, level, usu. refers to topography of flatlands

Snedé /sna-dā'/ *adj.*, long, lengthy, extended, elongated

Snedé't'ągà /sna-dā'-t'oⁿ-gä/ *n.*, tall, refers to the height of somebody

Sni'égą /snē-ā'-goⁿ/ *adj.*, chilly, when the temperature is moderately cold

Šní'gdabaží /shnē'-gthä-bä-zhē'/ *v.*, doesn't take in coldness or does not feel the cold

Šníšnidè /shnē'-shnē-dā/ *adj.*, slippery, something being oily or greasy

Šnudáde /shnü-dä'-thā/ *v.*, come off, ~ on its own without help of human hands

Snúka /snü'-kä/ *v.*, curved, like a banana

Snúsnu /snü'-snü/ *adj.*, gelatinous, jellylike, gooey

Špáí'úni /shpäē'-ü'-nē/ *n.*, Mexican, corruption of *Spaniard*, a native or inhabitant of Mexico

Špášpa /shpä'-shpä/ *n.*, fragments, pieces that broke off or scattered pieces of something

Št'ągá /sht'oⁿ-gä'/ *adj.*, soft, supple, malleable

Št'ašt'áde /sht'ä-sht'ä'-dā/ *n.*, sides above hips

Št'íde /sht'ē'-dä/ *adj.*, warm, refers to warmth in a dwelling

Stáp'i /stä'-p'ē/ *adj.*, fashionable, stylish, smart (he was a ~ dresser)

Stáp'ì /stä'-p'ē'/ *adj.*, elegant, being stylish, well-dressed (used, e.g., if a suit fits perfectly and looks good on someone

Šú' /shü'/ *n.*, prairie chicken, *Tympanuchus cupido*

Šú'íbe'snedè /shü'-ē'-bā-snä-dā'/ *n.*, pheasant, Chinese ring-necked pheasant

Šu'wídąbè /shü-wēⁿ'-thoⁿ-bä'/ *v.*, charging, attacking, usu. done in warfare when the enemy is rushing inward

Šúde /shü'-dä/ *n.*, smoke, unburnt fuel, tiny particles that rise in the air from something burning

Šúde đip'áze /shü'-dä thē-p'ä'-zā/ *adj.*, dusty, dust raised by a moving vehicle

Šúde đip'áze /shü'-dä thē-p'ä'-zā/ *adj.*, smoky, usu. refers to something very smoky or making a lot of smoke from some source

Šúdemąhà /shü'-dä-moⁿ-hoⁿ'/ *n.*, fog, a vapor about the same density as clouds that sits near the ground

Šugá /shü-gä'/ *adj.*, thick, bulky

Šugá'žįgà /shü-gä'-zhēⁿ-gä'/ *n.*, dime, ten-cent piece

Šúšúdè /shü-shü'-dä/ *adj./n.*, dusty, something covered with dust

T

t /tə/ fourteenth consonant in the Ponca alphabet

T'ą́ /t'oⁿ/ *adj.*, lots of, many, masses of, large number of

T'á' /t'ä'/ *n.*, dehydrated meat, dried meat

T'ą́ /t'oⁿ/ *adj.*, plenty, lot of (*mázeskà adíte ~ áčą*, they have ~ of money)

T'ą́de /t'oⁿ-dä/ *n.*, ground, earth, dirt, soil

T'a'dé' /t'ä-dā'/ *n.*, wind, current of air or air-stream

T'ą́'de mąšą́dè /t'oⁿ'-dā moⁿ-shoⁿ'-dā/ *n.*, cellar, storm cellar, a place built to protect people from violent weather, such as tornadoes, cyclones, straight winds

T'a'gát'ubè' /t'ä-gä-t'ü-bā/ *n.*, pounded dry (dehydrated) meat, dehydrated meat, jerky, pemmican (dried meat pounded and sometimes mixed with nuts and dried berries)

T'a'žu /t'ä'-zhü/ *adj.*, meaty

T'á'žu /t'ä'-zhü/ *n.*, filet mignon, a choice cut of meat (beef) that is meaty, with less gristle and fat

T'abé /t'ä-bā'/ *n.*, ball, a round object used in many games, such as the Ponca game shinny, baseball, football, basketball, golf

T'abé'ą /t'ä-bā-oⁿ/ *n.*, baseball game, a favorite American game using a bat and ball and played by two teams of nine players

T'abé ganą́ge /t'ä-bā' gä-noⁿ'-gä/ *n.*, bowling, bowling game (The object of the game is to knock down ten pins at the end of a bowling lane with a bowling ball.)

T'abégasì /t'ä-bā'-gä-sē'/ *n.*, shinny, a Ponca men's game played four times every seven days during the springtime (The game is similar to hockey but is played on a field.)

T'abé į't̨į· /t'ä-bā' ē ⁿ'-teⁿ·/ *n.*, baseball bat, a club made of wood or metal and used to hit a baseball in a baseball game

T'abési /t'ä-bā'-sē/ *n.*, football, 1. an oval-shaped ball 2. a game played by two opposing teams on a rectangular field, involving kicking, passing, and running to take an oval-shaped ball across a goal line between two upright poles to make a score, while the opposing team tries to prevent them from achieving this goal

T'áč'inįgè /t'ä'-ch-ē-nēⁿ-gä'/(**T'áč'idįgè** /t'ä'-ch-ē-thēⁿ-gä'/) *n.*, meadowlark, a bird belonging to the genus *Sturnella*, a grassland bird

T'ačú'ge /t'ä-chü'-gä/ *n.*, pronghorn antelope

T'adą́he /t'ä-doⁿ'-hä/ *n.*, whirlwind, a vertical, fast-spinning column of air, a dust devil

T'ą́dai /t'oⁿ'-thä-ē/ *v.*, *archaic*, tanning, the process of softening animal skins for making clothing and other personal items, such as footwear and bags

T'áđazap'à /t'ä'-thä-zä-p'ä'/ *n.*, tick, a bloodsucking parasite of the superfamily Ixodoidea that attaches itself to warm-blooded animals

T'ádé'gaúbđį /t'ä-dā'-gä-ü'-bthēⁿ'/ *n.*, whirly wind, wind blowing in circles at an inner corner outside a building

T'adé'sagì' /t'ä-dā'-sä-gē'/ *n.*, windy, strong wind, blustery weather

T'adé'sagì't'ągà /t'ä-dā'-sä-gē'-t'oⁿ-gä'/ *n.*, tornado, a strong rotating column of air formed between the surface of the ground and a cumulonimbus cloud

T'adé'wégdi /t'ä-dā'-wä'-gthē/ *n.*, propane, butane, natural gas (ca. twentieth century)

T'ą́deáha hįbđíge /t'oⁿ'-dā-ä'-hä hēⁿ-bthēⁿ'-gä/ *n.*, ground beans

T'ą́deáhe /t'oⁿ'-dā-ä'-hä/ *v.*, hike, trek, to walk far (For most Native Americans, walking was the main mode for getting from one place to another; it was not done for pleasure or exercise.)

T'ą́dehanù /t'oⁿ'-dā-hä-nü/ *n.*, wild potatoes, American groundnut, a root with knots that resemble a potato

T'ą́deha hįbđíge /t'oⁿ'-dā-hä hēⁿ-bthēⁿ'-gä/ *n.*, mouse beans, lit., ground beans, wild beans collected by rodents and stored in their burrows, which meant they were planted

T'ą́de ígašpè /t'oⁿ'-dā ē'-gä-shpä'/ *n.*, pick, a tool with a pointed steel head attached to a wooden handle like an ax handle, used to break through hardened ground or clay

T'ą́deínąšpè /t'oⁿ-dā-ē'-noⁿ-shpā'/ *n.*, shovel, a tool for digging into the soil or other materials

T'ą́de mą̄šą́de užì /t'oⁿ-dā moⁿ-shoⁿ-dā ü-zhē'/ *n.*, October, lit., store food in caches, the tenth month in the year

T'ą́deudúdiudè /t'oⁿ-dā-ü-thü-thē-ü-dā'/ *n.*, auger, a drilling device to bore holes in soil, ice, or wood

T'ą́de wéədiudè /t'oⁿ-dā wā'ə-thē-ü-dā'/ *n.*, posthole digger, a hand or heavy equipment device used to dig holes in the ground

T'ą́di /t'oⁿ'-thē/ *v.*, run, to go faster (in speed) than a walk in such a manner that both feet leave the ground for each springing step

T'ą́dį ą́'sagì /t'oⁿ'-thēⁿ oⁿ'-sä-gē'/ *n.*, fast runner, someone who is a fast runner

T'ągá /t'oⁿ-gä'/ *adv.*, great, to a large degree, huge, immense, enormous, great big

T'ągá /t'oⁿ-gä'/ *adj.*, big, large

T'ągá' /t'oⁿ-gä'/ *adj.*, large, huge, immense, enormous, great big

T'ągá'ɖihà /t'oⁿ-gä-thē-hä'/ *n.*, large area, something that is widely extended or far ranging

T'ą́ga'xɖą̀ /t'oⁿ-gä-xthoⁿ'/ *n.*, fall, autumn, the season of the year that precedes winter, approximately three months (September, October, and November); *t'ą́gaxɖą̄ádi*, past fall; *t'ą́gaxɖą̄dą̀*, in the fall

T'ągá át'ašą̀ /t'oⁿ-gä' ä'-t'ä-shoⁿ'/ *adj.*, immense, massive

T'ągádihà /t'oⁿ-gä-thē-hä'/ *adv.*, greatly, to a larger degree or extent that reaches out

T'ą́gaxɖą̀'uską́skà /t'oⁿ'-gä-xthoⁿ'-ü-skoⁿ'-skä'/ *n.*, midfall, in the middle of fall

T'ą́gaxɖą́dą /t'oⁿ'-gä-xthoⁿ'-doⁿ'/ *prep. phr.*, in the fall

T'ą́gaxɖą̄dì /t'oⁿ'-gä-xthoⁿ-dē'/ *n.*, last fall

T'ą̄gáxt'iáži /t'oⁿ-gä'-xt'ē-ä'-zhē/ *adj.*, small, lit., not very large

T'áge /t'ä'-gā/ *n.*, nut (any)

T'áge't'ągà /t'ä'-gä-t'oⁿ-gä/ *n.*, black walnut, lit., big nut, family Juglandaceae (*t'áge t'ągà hì*, black walnut tree)

T'áge't'ągàhì /t'ä'-gä-t'oⁿ-gä-hē'/ *n.*, walnut tree, black walnut, *Juglans nigra*

T'áge'žįgà /t'ä'-gä-zhēⁿ-gä'/ *n.*, pecan, lit., small nut, an edible nut that grows in central and southern U.S. states and Mexico

T'àge'žįgàhì /t'ä'-gä-zhēⁿ-gä'-hē'/ *n.*, pecan tree, a species of hickory, *Carya illinoinensis*

T'áge bawégɖi /t'ä'-gā bä-wā'-gthē/ *n.*, peanut butter, a paste made from peanuts

T'áge ígaxixè /t'ä'-gā ē'-gä-xē-xä'/ *n.*, nutcracker, a device to crack nuts

T'ahá /t'ä-hä'/ *n.*, deer skin, buckskin, tanned deerskin

T'ahá'wagɖè /t'ä-hä'-wä-gthä'/ *n.*, shield, a piece of armor carried on the arm and used for protection against arrows and in hand-to-hand battles with war clubs

T'ą́he žįgà /t'oⁿ'-hä zhēⁿ-gä'/ *n.*, hot dog, wiener; commonly garnished with mustard, onions

T'ahį́ /t'ä-hēⁿ'/ *n.*, mane, the long hair that grows around the neck and head of certain animals, such as horses and lions

T'ahį́'wágɖą̀ /t'ä-hēⁿ'-wä-gthoⁿ'/ *n.*, roach, a headpiece made of deer tail and porcupine guard hair (some in an earlier period were composed of horsehair) worn by the Heɖúškà dancers

T'aí' /t'ä-ē'/ *n.*, that part of the skull located near the occipital bone, back of the head

T'aí'bažú /t'ä-ē'-bä-zhü'/ *n.*, the bone section that is located at the back bottom of the human skull

T'aídibút'a /t'ä-ē'-thē-bü'-t'ä/ *n.*, bun, a woman's hairstyle, a tight row of hair either braided or straight, worn in the back of the head

T'ak'ą́ /t'ä-k'oⁿ/ *n.*, muscle, in anatomy, a muscle's main function is to produce body movement as well as movement of the internal organs

T'ąk'į́'kiɗè /t'oⁿ-k'ēⁿ-kē-thã́/ *v.*, to do something that results in comfortable conditions, well-being, good fortune

T'ąk'į́'waɗaì /t'oⁿ-k'ēⁿ-wä-thä-ē/ *v.*, to cause us to possess from some other source, more often used in religious tones, as in "the Creator provides all good things for us."

T'aką́ hà /t'ä-koⁿ hä́/ *n.*, sinew, fibers of animal tendon, esp. of the American bison, used for thread and cordage for sewing or binding

T'ákįkį /t'ä'-kēⁿ-kēⁿ/ *v.*, totter, to walk unsteadily, to stagger, to have a wobbly gait

T'aní /t'ä-nē/ *n.*, soup, a liquid food usu. made with meat or vegetable stock

T'aní'uɗúgaɗúžè /t'ä-nē-ü-thü-gä-thü-zhã́/ *n.*, ladle, refers to a large long-handled spoon with a deep bowl used to serve soup, stew, and other foods

T'aniúze /t'ä-nēü-zā/ *n.*, au jus, from the French, the juice that comes from cooking or roasting beef

T'anúk'a máxąxà /t'ä-nü-k'ä mä'-xoⁿ-xoⁿ/ *n./v.*, butcher, to cut up meat

T'anúka /t'ä-nü-kä/ *n.*, meat, 1. edible animal flesh, namely, beef, pork, etc. 2. a proper male name in the Hísadà clan of the Ponca people

T'áši /t'ä'-shē/ *n.*, bump, result of swelling or contusion

T'áškà /t'ä'-shkä/ *n.*, acorn, the nut from an oak tree, genera *Quercus* and *Lithocarpus*, family Fasgaceae

T'áškahì nušiáha /t'ä'-shkä-hē nü-shēä-hä/ *n.*, blackjack oak (*Quercus marilandica*), a small oak tree; many are located in Osage County east of the Ponca reservation in Oklahoma

T'áškahì /t'ä'-shkä-hē/ *n.*, oak tree, one of many species of the genus *Quercus*

T'áškahì'nušíá'hà /t'ä'-shkä-hē-nü-shē-ä-hä́/ *n.*, scrub oak, *Quercus alba L.*

T'ašną́'gè'hì /t'ä-shnoⁿ-gä'-hē/ *n.*, ash tree, genus *Fraxinus* of the family Oleaceae

T'ašníga /t'ä-shnēⁿ-gä/ *n.*, chipmunk, a small striped rodent of the family Sciuridae

T'ašníge /t'ä-shnēⁿ-gä/ *n.*, mink, a carnivorous member of the family Mustelidae

T'asp'ą́ /t'ä-sp'oⁿ/ *n.*, persimmon, genus *Diospyros*, a small edible fruit that can be eaten only when completely ripe; the word *diospyros* means "the fruit of the gods"

T'asp'ą́hì /t'ä-sp'oⁿ-hē/ *n.*, persimmon tree

T'ašt'áde /t'ä-sht'ä-dä/ *n.*, flank, in human anatomy, that flesh on the sides of the lower ribcage

T'át'áši' /t'ä'-t'ä-shē/ *n.*, knobby, something covered with knobs

-t'atą /t'ä-toⁿ/ *prep.*, *suffix*, from; *máxet'atà*, from above; *hídet'atà*, from below; *šéket'atà*, from over there; *ɗéwadit'atà*, from here; *gáɗądìt'atà*, from somewhere over there; *Waxt'áwį niášigat'atà*, from the Ojibway people

T'atéga /t'ä-tä́-gä/ *n.*, flea, a small bloodsucking insect that feeds on warm-blooded animals

T'ą́wągɗà /t'oⁿ-woⁿ-gthoⁿ/ *n.*, clan, 1. clan, families who are related through a common ancestry 2. a village, city, community, a group of people living in houses in a particular location

T'ą́wągɗà /t'oⁿ-woⁿ-gthoⁿ/ *n.*, town, metropolis, city, clan; *t'ą́wągɗaàdi*, at or in the town; *t'ą́wągɗaadítą*, from the town; *t'ą́wągɗaát'a*, to the town; *t'ą́wągɗaát'áha*, toward town; *t'ą́wągdǝát'adišą̀*, toward or in the direction of town

T'ą́wągdą̀'t'ągà /t'onʸ-wonʸ-gthonʸ-t'onʸ-gä'/ *n.*, Oklahoma City, Oklahoma

T'ą́wągdą̀ iš'áge /t'onʸ-wonʸ-gthonʸ ēsh-ä'-gā/ *n.*, Arkansas City, Kansas, lit., old man town

T'áxe'čú' /t'ä'-xä-chü'/ *n.*, spittle, saliva, a fluid coming from salivary glands in the mouth

T'axp'í /t'ä-xp'ē'/ *n.*, crown, top of or crown of the head

T'áxt'ì /t'ä'-xt'ē'/ *n.*, deer, any of the ruminant mammals of the family Cervidae

T'áxt'ì k'ídixè /t'ä'-xt'ē' k'ē'-thē-xä'/ *n.*, rutting season, that time of the year when deer are in a state of sexual excitement

T'áxt'ì sį́de sábe /t'ä'-xt'ē' sēnʸ-dä sä'-bā/ *n.*, black antelope

T'áxt'ì sį́de sábe /t'ä'-xt'ē' sēnʸ-dä sä'-bā/ *n.*, black-tailed deer, *Odocoileus hemionus*; also known as mule deer

T'áxt'ì sį́de skà /t'ä'-xt'ē' sēnʸ-dä skä'/ *n.*, white-tailed deer, *Odocoileus virginianus*, a medium-sized deer native to most of the North American continent

T'áxt'ì Waú' /t'ä'-xt'ē' wä-ü'/ *n.*, Deer Woman, 1. is described as being very pretty and entices young men by her enchantment 2. young men are not to give in to her or something would happen to them, such as sickness (A mythological female who was said to have followed the Ponca to Indian Territory in 1876 and was said to have been seen by men in remote, lonely places.)

T'axúxe /t'ä-xü'-xä/ *n.*, lather, suds, soapsuds

T'ę̀ /t'änʸ/ *v.*, die, cease to live

T'é' /t'ä'/ *n.*, bison, a large, social animal with a large head, short horns, and a large hump above its shoulders that roamed the Great Plains before the coming of the Europeans

(Most historians use the term *buffalo* rather than *bison*.)

T'e'á /t'ä-ä'/ *n.*, forequarter, the front side of a bison (now beef, pork, etc.), usu. refers to the foreleg and shoulder

T'e'ázą't'asì /t'ä-ä'-zonʸ-t'ä-sē'/ *n.*, *archaic*, lit., bison kidneys, now the kidneys of domestic cattle

T'e'bdą́' /t'ä-bthonʸ'/ *n.*, daddy longlegs, an order of arachnids (Opiliones) that has a pill-like body and long legs

T'ę́'de /t'änʸ'-thä/ *v.*, kill, murder, take life

T'é'hà /t'ä-hä'/ *n.*, the hide of a bison

T'é' héup'agdą̀ /t'ä' hä-ü'-p'ä-gthonʸ'/ *n.*, buffalo-horn cap, a headpiece consisting of the head and horns of a buffalo bull

T'ę́'k'idè /t'änʸ'-k'ē-thä'/ *n.*, suicide, to take one's own life

T'e'ną́de /t'ä-nonʸ'-dä/ *n.*, heart, that edible organ of bovine cattle (orig. an archaic word for the heart of the American bison: *t'é'*, bison, *ną́de*, heart)

T'é'níxà /t'ä'-nē'-xä/ *n.*, tripe, the rubbery lining of the stomach of cattle, used as food

T'e'p'ì /t'ä-p'ē'/ *n.*, *archaic*, liver, lit., bison liver, *t'é'*, bison, *p'í*, liver; now applies to domestic cattle and other mammals

T'e'p'ìzi /t'ä-p'ē'-zē/ *n.*, gall; *t'é'*, bison, *p'ízi*, gall (bile); *archaic*, now applies to domestic cattle

T'é'šíbè /t'ä-shē'-bä/ *n.*, bovine intestine; orig. referred to bison intestines

T'é'sįdè /t'ä' sēnʸ-dä'/ *n.*, the tail of a bison

T'é'skà /t'ä'-skä/ *n.*, cattle, lit., white bison, large domesticated mammals, namely, cows and oxen

T'é'ska'mìgà /t'ä'-skä-mē-gä'/ *n.*, cow, a female member of domestic cattle or bovines

T'é'ska'núgà /t'ä'-skä-nü'-gä'/ *n.*, bull, a male member of domestic cattle or bovines

T'é'ska'žįgà /t'ā-skä-zhēⁿ-gä/ *n.*, calf, a young member of domestic cattle or bovines

T'é'ska basí' /t'ā'-skä bä-sē'/ *n.*, cowboy, lit., drives cattle, a hired hand whose responsibility is to tend to cattle for roundups and branding, driving them to some location

T'é'ska basí hįbé /t'ā'-skä bä-sē' hēⁿ-bä'/ *n.*, cowboy boots

T'é'ska hà /t'ā'-skä hä'/ *n.*, cowhide, the hide of the bovine — (Following Native American removal from their original homelands, European cattle were introduced as a source of food. The cowhide was used to make soles for moccasins and other personal or household necessities.)

T'é'štà /t'āⁿ'-shtoⁿ'/ *n.*, epilepsy, a neurological disorder whereby a person afflicted has seizures

T'é'unè /t'ā'-ü-nä/ *v.*, bison hunt (The Ponca had biannual bison hunts.)

T'é' waną́še /t'ā' wä-noⁿ'-shä/ *n.*, buffalo police, a security group for various Ponca activities, including the biannual Sun dance and annual bison hunt

T'é'xi /t'ā'-xē/ *adj.*, difficult, something hard to do, something hard to deal with

T'é'žéga /t'ā'-zhä'-gä/ *n.*, T-bone steak, a cut of beef from the loin region

T'é'žéga /t'ā'-zhä'-gä/ *n.*, hindquarter, the back quarter of a carcass of bison, beef, deer, moose, etc.

T'eá' /t'ā-ä'/ *n.*, tenderloin, any beef cut in the loin region

T'eát'at'à /t'ā-ä'-t'ä-t'ä'/ *n.*, praying mantis, family Mantidae, a predatory insect found throughout the world

T'ébià /t'ā'-bē-ä'/ *n.*, frog, amphibian without a tail of the order Anura

T'ébiàsnedè /t'ā'-bē-ä'-snä-dä/ *n.*, bullfrog

T'édawį /t'ā'-thä-wēⁿ/ *n.*, water lily, an edible aquatic plant with floating leaves and flowers

T'éde /t'ā-thä/ *v.*, save, put away, conserve

T'éga /t'ā-gä/ *adj.*, new, brand new

T'egá /t'ā-gä/ (**T'eyá** /t'ā-yä/) *n.*, loin, a prime cut of tender meat taken from the backbone and rib area of a bovine animal; also called *t'é'ną́k'ak'à*

T'ę́ gáxe /t'āⁿ gä-xä/ *n.*, ca. 1800s, feign death or pretend to be dead (The Ponca had a warrior society called **T'ę́ gáxe**, pretend to be dead, whose members, in battle, feigned death. To the surprise of the enemy, they would attack when the enemy came close.)

T'égidè /t'ā'-gē-thä/ *n.*, safeguard, save and keep, look after; *čégidè*, safeguard something special

T'ehé /t'ā-hä/ *n.*, spoon, lit., buffalo horn; *t'ehé žįgà*, teaspoon; *t'ehé t'ągà*, tablespoon

T'ehé t'ągà /t'ā-hä t'oⁿ-gä/ *n.*, tablespoon, used for serving food; a culinary measure, abbr. tbs. or tbsp., three teaspoons to one ~

T'ehé žįgà /t'ā-hä zhēⁿ-gä/ *n.*, teaspoon, abbr. tsp., a utensil usu. used for drinking tea or coffee and consuming desserts

T'éhįžidè /t'ā'-hēⁿ-zhē-dä/ *n.*, yarn belt, 1. an ornament of the Hedúškà dance paraphernalia 2. an ornament used on an infant's cradle

T'emíga /t'ā-mē'-gä/ *n.*, bison cow

T'ęą́ka baxú' /t'āⁿ-noⁿ'-kä bä-xü'/ *n.*, in carpentry, the ridge of the roof

T'ę́ ną́p'ažì /t'āⁿ' noⁿ'-p'ä-zhē/ *n.*, ca. 1800s, not afraid to die (The warrior society called **T'ę́ ną́p'ažì**, not afraid to die, were those Ponca men who staked themselves to the ground as the enemy approached. This was done to show that they would not back down or run from the enemy, even if death was imminent.)

T'eną́xdadè /t'ā-noⁿ'-xthä-dä/ *n.*, sweetbread, a culinary name for part of an animal stomach or belly

T'éná… gazáde wék'ąt'ą̀ /t'ä'-noⁿ'-zhēⁿ-hä' gä-zoⁿ'-dā wā'-k'oⁿ-t'oⁿ'/ *n.*, rope, braided rope made of hair from the head of a bison

T'eniúžihà /t'ä-nēü'-zhē-hä'/ *n.*, parfleche, a rawhide bag

T'é níxa /t'ä' nē'-xä/ *n.*, buffalo belly; edible parts include the rumen, or flat, smooth tripe; the reticulum, honeycomb tripe; and the omasum, the book or bible-leaf tripe

T'eníxaugdežè /t'ä-nē'-xä-ü-gthä-zhä'/ *n.*, omasum, the leaf-like, folded compartment in the bovine stomach

T'enúga /t'ä-nü'-gä/ *n.*, bison bull

T'enúga dádį /t'ä-nü'-gä thä'-thēⁿ/ *n.*, crazed bison (The Ponca tell stories of dangerous bison that became deranged because they ate certain plants.)

T'ep'ízi /t'ä-p'ē'-zē/ *n.*, bile, a fluid secreted by the liver that aids in digestive processes; a part of the liver that is edible

T'ešíbe ut'ága /t'ä-shē'-bä ü-t'oⁿ'-gä/ *n.*, large intestine

T'éska /t'ä'-skä/ *n.*, bovine, lit., white bison, relates to or resembles bovines, esp. the ox or cow

T'éskà'unáži /t'ä'-skä'-ü-noⁿ-zhē/ *n.*, barn, lit., where the cattle stand

T'éze /t'ä'-zä/ *n.*, waist, that part of the abdomen between the ribcage and hips

T'ežé bat'è /t'ä-zhä' bä-t'ä'/ *n.*, buffalo chip, 1. the waste product from bovine species that include domestic cattle, bison (buffalo), and others 2. the name of one of the men who accompanied Chief Standing Bear and testified in a landmark constitutional civil rights case for Native Americans in 1879 in Omaha, Nebraska

T'ežíga /t'ä-zhēⁿ'-gä/ *n.*, bison calf

T'i' /t'ē'/ *n.*, house, dwelling

T'í'a /t'ē'-ä/ *adj.*, rotten, decaying hides, cured leather, cloth of various grades

T'í'básihì /t'ē'-bä-sē-hē'/ *n.*, janitor, a person who does housecleaning and maintenance

T'í'bút'a /t'ē-bü'-t'ä/ *n.*, roundhouse — traditionally, a large, circular frame building that was used for tribal ceremonies and other gatherings, ca. 1910

T'í'gàxe /t'ē'-gä-xä/ *n./v.*, play, lit., make a house, usu. refers to children's play

T'í'hà /t'ē'-hä/ *n.*, canvas, lit., house hide, a covering for a dwelling, usu. the skin of an animal, now a heavy, thick fabric

T'í'hu'kà' /t'ē'-hü-koⁿ'/ *n.*, *pl.*, wind flaps at the top of the tipi that are used as a damper to control the draft inside the tipi

T'í'ídižà /t'ē'-ē-thē-zhä'/ *n.*, mop, a house implement made of absorbent material to clean floors

T'í'k'a'xúdè /t'ē'-k'ä-xü'-dä/ *n.*, silver fox, a variant of the red fox, *Vulpes vulpes*

T'í' p'ahášì /t'ē' p'ä-hä'-shē/ *n.*, upstairs, the second floor of a house or building

T'í'šì' /t'ē'-shē'/ *n.*, tipi poles, wooden poles that provide a frame for the structure to be covered with canvas (In their earlier history, the Ponca used bison hides to cover their tipis.)

T'í'sné'de /t'ē'-snä'-dä/ *n.*, tent, lit., long house

T'í'umíže wé'basihì /t'ē'-ü-mē'-zhä wä'-bä-sē-hē'/ *n.*, vacuum cleaner, lit., carpet cleaner

T'í'utáną /t'ē'-ü-tä'-noⁿ/ *n.*, street, lit., space between buildings, avenue, boulevard, alleyway, a public thoroughfare in a city or town

T'í'ut'áną /t'ē'-ü-t'ä'-noⁿ/ *n.*, alley, lit., in between houses, a narrow street in the back of buildings

T'i'žé'be'ganàge /t'ē-zhä'-bä-gä-noⁿ'-gä/ *n.*, revolving door

T'i'žébe /t'ē-zhä'-bä/ *n.*, door, entrance

T'i'žébe dik'ámą /t'ē-zhā'-bā thē-k'ä'-moⁿ/ *n.*, doorbell, a device that rings or chimes inside a house or building and is activated by a small button near the outside door frame

T'i'žébe udą́ /t'ē-zhā-bā ü-thoⁿ'/ *n.*, doorknob

T'í'žįgà /t'ē'-zhēⁿ-gä'/ *n.*, outhouse, lit., little house, a toilet constructed outdoors, usu. a small building built over a pit

T'iádį /t'ē-ä'-thēⁿ/ *n.*, House of the Hedúška, a designated place for meeting and dancing for the men's fraternal organization called the Hedúškà

T'iát'a /t'ē-ä'-t'ä/ *adv.*, indoors, in the house or building, at home; *t'iádi*, something or somebody in the house or building

T'idé' /t'ē-dā/ *v.*, to make a continuous rumbling sound something like thunder or heavy artillery in the distance

T'í gáxe /t'ē' gä'-xā/ *v.*, house building, constructing a house or any kind of building

T'íhabà /t'ē'-hä-bä'/ *n.*, mussel, a freshwater mollusk, a shell made round for use in costumes

T'í hídeát'a /t'ē' hē'-dā-ä'-t'ä/ *n.*, basement, room under the house

T'íhukà /t'ē'-hü-koⁿ'/ *n.*, vent, smoke hole, opening at the top of the tipi

T'ík'axudè /t'ē'-k'ä-xü-dä'/ *n.*, gray fox, *Urocyon cinereoargenteus*, a carnivorous mammal of the family Canidae

T'imą́te /t'ē-moⁿ'-tā/ *adj.*, indoor, inside, the interior of a house or building

T'í názat'à /t'ē' nä-zä-t'ä'/ *n.*, backyard, back of the house or dwelling

T'íúbixà /t'ē'-ü-bē-xoⁿ'/ *n.*, chimney swift, 1. a small, flocking bird that swarms near dwellings and rotting old trees 2. a personal male name in the Hísadà clan of the Ponca people

T'iúdip'ù /t'ēü'-thē-p'ü'/ *n.*, hut, a dome-shaped hut made with cut saplings bent together toward the center and covered with hides

T'iúdip'ù snedé /t'ēü'-thē-p'ü' snā-dā'/ *n.*, lodge, a large, elongated structure used for meetings or ceremonies for larger groups (The original covering for the lodge was bison hides, now it is canvas.)

T'iúdixdigè /t'ēü'-thē-xthē-gä'/ *n.*, ruins, the remains of a once-inhabited dwelling or house, usu. evidenced by piles of dirt and wood or a foundation

T'iúdixdigè /t'ēü'-thē-xthē-gä'/ *n.*, house foundation, refers to the dilapidated remains of a homestead

T'í udúšiát'a /t'ē' ü-thü'-shē-ä'-t'ä/ *n.*, front yard, lit., in front of the house or dwelling

T'í ugíp'i /t'ē' ü-gē'-p'ē/ *n.*, houseful, usu. refers to tribal ceremonies held in a tepee or similar dwelling, as in saying ~ *ą́gdį*, We were sitting in a ~

T'iúkedį /t'ē'-ü'-kā-thēⁿ/ *n.*, tipi, lit., common dwelling, a conical dwelling once covered with bison hides, now canvas

T'iúmižè /t'ē'-ü'-mē-zhā'/ *n.*, carpet, carpeting, rug, mat

T'iúp'è /t'ē-ü'-p'ā'/ *v.*, visit, to visit; *t'ápè*, *n.*, *archaic*, visit

T'iúži /t'ē'-ü'-zhē/ *n.*, family, family unit, relatives, kin

T'ižébeudą̀ /t'ē-zhā'-bā-ü-thoⁿ'/ *n.*, tipi door flap, doorknob

T'ú'sábe /t'ü-sä-bā/ *adj.*, dark blue, the color dark blue

T'ú'ze /t'ü'-zā/ *n.*, catfish (order Siluriformes), a freshwater fish with whiskers

T'ubáde /t'ü-bä-thā/ *v.*, crumble, to break into small pieces or tiny bits; *bit'úbe*, to crumble, crush, or grind by pressing down upon; *bit'út'úbe*, to continously crumble, crush by pressing down upon; *dit'úbe*, to crumble, crush, or grind with the use of the hands or hand tools; *gat'úbe*, to crumble something by force; *gat'út'úbe*, to continuously crumble something by force; *nąt'úbe*, to crumble, crush, or grind with machinery; *nąt'út'úbe*, to continuously crumble, crush, or grind something with machinery

T'úgdą /t'ü-gthoⁿ/ *v.*, haul, to carry things, usu. a load of a material goods, such as furniture, clothing, appliances, food

T'ušíge /t'ü-shēⁿ-gä/ *n.*, perfume, a modern fragrant liquid, a pleasant scent, usu. refers to women's perfume

T'ušníge /t'ü-shnēⁿ-gä/ *n.*, rainbow

T'uší' /t'ü-shē'/ *v.*, pop, the sound of something popping

T'úxa /t'ü'-xä/ *n.*, hump, bulge, lump

T'užíga /t'ü-zhēⁿ-gä/ *n.*, pawpaw, *Asimina triloba*, a temperate fruit tree, native to North America

Tą' /toⁿ/ *art.*, the, singular article (designates singular, standing, animate subjects) (*núžįgà ~ snędé t'ągà*, ~ boy is tall)

Té /tā/ *art.*, the, plural article (used with words that describe an inanimate thing or idea) (*t'í ~ é'gazizì'xtì gáxà bíkè*, they have built ~ houses in a row)

Ti'dą́bidè /tē-thoⁿ-bē-thä'/ *v.t.*, assail, sudden appearance of the enemy with intent to attack

Tí'de /tē'-thä/ *v.*, sent here, something sent to this place, such as a letter

Tidą́bidè /tē-thoⁿ-bē-thä'/ *adj.*, coming by suddenly, something or somebody coming by unexpectedly, usu. at high speed

Tidéde /tē-thä'-thä/ *v., sing.*, to start a song, usu. refers to somebody starting a tribal song

Tíxįdè /tē-xēⁿ-dä/ *n.*, ravine, a small valley that is larger than a gully, made by water or soil erosion; *tíxįdè*, arroyo, usu. a dry creekbed in the Southwest

Tú' /tü/ *adj.*, blue, the color of the sky

Tukáda /tü-kä-thä/ *n.*, warrior fraternity, an ancient war society of young Ponca men; P'adánik'ì, seasoned warriors of the Ponca tribe; T'ę́ nąp'ažì, not afraid to die Ponca warriors; T'ę́ gáxe, Ponca warriors who pretend to be killed; Wasná t'ągà, big belly, elderly Ponca warriors' organization (The elders of the Ponca people provided the names of these ancient warrior fraternities when the Ponca lived in the North Country.)

Tų́skà /tüⁿ'-skä/ *n.*, woodpecker, large red-headed woodpecker (family Picidae), a bird with a beak that hammers into wood to find insects

U

u /yü/ sixth vowel in the Ponca alphabet

ų /yüⁿ/ sixth nasalized vowel in the Ponca alphabet

U'ą́ /ü-oⁿ/ *v.*, place, to put in, as in to put a TV dinner in the microwave, to put another log in the heater

U'ą́dįgè /ü-oⁿ-thēⁿ-gä/ *adj.*, inactive, 1. unused, still, immobile 2. shiftless, not doing anything, just hanging around

Ú'čižè /ü'-chē-zhä/ *n.*, dilemma, condition of being in a sudden and unexpected predicament or quandary

U'číže /ü-chē'-zhä/ *n.*, deep weeds

Ú'dą̀ /ü-doⁿ/ *adj.*, good, fine, high quality, first rate

Ú'da'ék'idè /ü'-thä-ä'-k'ē-thä/ *n.*, humility, doing something to humble oneself

Ú'daedè /ü'-thä-ā-thä/ *adj.*, contrite, being repentent, sorry, and remorseful

Ú'daedè k'igáxe /ü'-thä-ā-thä' k'ē-gä'-xä/ *n.*, contrition, doing something in an apologetic manner

Ú'daxubè /ü'-thä-xü-bā'/ *n.*, accolade, a stated or public commendation or recognition of somebody for accomplishing something that seemed impossible; *wádaxubè*, to commend a group for an impossible task

Ú'dazè /ü'-thä-zā'/ *n./v.*, chime in, combine music harmoniously, refers to female background singers, women who sing at the drum with male singers at tribal dances (Female singers assist in singing in the "chorus" of the songs. They sit behind the men who sing around the drum at various Native American dance functions, including pow-wows. In the past women usu. "chimed in" after the beat of the drum in the middle of the song. Now women are called "chorus girls.")

Ú'di ì' /ü'-thē ē'/ *adj.*, gift, a gift to you

Ú'dit'à /ü'-thē-t'on/ *n.*, job, occupation, profession, vocation, something a person does to earn a living, ranging from manual labor to a position that requires specialized training and education

Ú'dižà /ü'-thē-zhä'/ *n.*, washtub, a tub for washing clothing, linens

U'gášudè /ü-gä-shü-dä'/ *adj.*, turbid, usu. refers to water that is stirred up with other matter, causing a clouded effect

Ú'gaxdè /ü'-gä-xthä'/ *n./v.*, facing, somebody or something that is oriented or positioned in a direction away from something else (*Mačú Nǫži, níkašigà wasésǫ kè, guádišǫ ~ nǫží*, the statue of Standing Bear is ~ the other way)

Ú'gdašigè /ü'-gthä-shē-gä'/ *v.*, complain, 1. expression of dissatisfaction, resentment, usu. done in airing one's personal feelings to another person 2. done in regard to one's feelings about some issue in a meeting

Ú'hǫšigdè /ü'-hon-shē-gthä'/ *n.*, cook helpers, food servers; those who help the main cook at feasts to serve food to the people (Orig. the servers were members of a Ponca Hedúškà organization.)

Ú'hiažì /ü'-hēä-zhē'/ *v.*, lose, be defeated in a game, to not win any money

U'hít'abažì /ü-hē'-t'ä-bä-zhē'/ *adj.*, eager, anxious for something to happen or to receive something

Ú'i /ü'-ē/ *n.*, gift, a gift to someone

Ú'i' /ü'-ē/ *v.*, loan, to loan or advance money to somebody; *ú'i*, *v.*, *past t.*, give, to loan or present something to somebody

Ú'ją /ü'-jon/ *adj.*, cute, pretty, attractive, adorable

Ú'kuhewadè /ü'-kü-hä-wä-thä'/ *n.*, a place that causes fear; a place that gives off an emotional concern, causing uncertainty and fear

Ú'niet'à /ü'-nē-ä-t'on/ *n.*, disease, a physical disorder or malady that prevents normal body functions, such as heart disease, diabetes, arthritis

Ú'p'ežì /ü'-p'ä-zhē'/ *n.*, trouble, dilemma, strife, disruption; somebody or something that agitates mentally, physically, or spiritually

U's'áde /ü-s-ä'-thä/ *adj.*, burning, as in a sensation caused by application of certain types of medication on the skin surface or by other sources, such as soap in the eyes

Ú'sągà /ü'-son-gä'/ *n.*, urgency, expectancy, the feeling that something is about to happen

Ú'šį'k'idè /ü'-shēn-k'ē-thä'/ *v.*, mislead oneself, to deceive oneself, to think that something was as one thought it to be even though it was not

Ú'šį'wadè /ü'-shēn-wä-thä'/ *n.*, quail, bobwhite, a small game bird native to North America in the order Galliformes, family Odontophoridae

Ų'šįdè /üⁿ-shēⁿ-thā'/ *v.*, deceive, "to be false to"; someone or something causing one to believe something that is not true

Ų'šįk'idè /üⁿ-shēⁿ-k'ē-thā'/ *v.*, deceived, deceived self or misinformed self

Ú'šįk'idè /ü-shēⁿ-k'ē-thā'/ *adj.*, confounded, someone confused or bewildered, as in somebody thinking he/she saw a person or an animal but was mistaken

Ú'šk'ą /ü-shk'oⁿ/ *n.*, situation, state of affairs

Ú'šk'adažì /ü-shk'ä-dä-zhē'/ *adj.*, 1. dauntless, fearless, resolute, confident 2. a man's name in the Wašábe clan of the Ponca people

Ú't'ąbedè /ü-t'oⁿ-bä-thā'/ *v.*, anticipating, knowing beforehand that something is going to happen or come to fruition

U't'ąnąadì /ü-t'ä-noⁿ-ä-dē'/ *v.*, left, lit., "left in between," to abandon or cast aside, used in reference to things being left somewhere (*wédihidè te, gá ~ ihé'daì*, they ~ their tools)

U't'ąnąahà /ü-t'ä-noⁿ-ä-hä'/ *v.*, lit., "in between or in the middle," usu. used in reference to something in the space between two structures, such as buildings, fences, or any space where a person can walk in between

Ú't'exì /ü-t'ä-xē'/ *n.*, difficulty, a perplexity; *ądágít'exì*, personally unable to think something clearly through; *wét'exì*, *pl.*, we can't think it clearly through; *í'git'exì*, he/she can't think it clearly through because his/her friend or relative is facing something difficult

Ú't'i /ü-t'ē/ *v.*, reside, to inhabit or live in a dwelling

U'wá'iyè /ü-wä'-ē-yä'/ *n.*, argue, argumentative; quarrelsome; a disagreement in which differing views are expressed

Ú'wadąbè /ü'-wä-doⁿ-bä'/ *n.*, lookout, sentry, sentinel

Ú'wa ì' /ü'-wä-ē'/ *adj.*, gift, a gift to us

Ú'wašką /ü-wä-shkoⁿ/ *v.*, help, a source of help that comes from within oneself by means of another person, thing, or deity

Ú'wį' /ü-wēⁿ/ *n.*, earrings, jewelry worn on the earlobes

U'wí'e /ü-wē'-ä/ *v.*, argue, to argue over something, to dispute, contend

Ú'wį'gazáde /ü'-wēⁿ-gä-zoⁿ-dä/ *n.*, necklace, a bead necklace made with the netted stitch of horse hair

U'xdážì /ü-xthä'-zhē/ *n.*, disability, lit., didn't catch up, intellectual disability, a genetic disorder, usu. a birth defect that causes some level of disability, as in Down's syndrome

Ú'xde /ü'-xthä/ *v.*, catch up, to catch up with

Ú'xt'adè /ü'-xt'ä-thä/ *adj.*, likeable, something that is pleasant or attractive to somebody

Ú'ži /ü-zhē/ *n.*, container, a receptacle, such as a box or a parfleche that holds or stores goods

Ú'ži /ü'-zhē/ *v.*, wish, want or desire for something, often refers to something to eat

Ú'ži /ü'-zhē/ *v.*, sow, to plant seeds

U'zí' /ü-zē'/ *n.*, rust, corrosion, oxidation

Ú'ži basnú /ü'-zhē bä-snü/ *n.*, dresser, chest of drawers, usu. a piece of bedroom furniture used for storing clothing

Ú'žihà /ü'-zhē-hä'/ *n.*, gunnysack, lit., leather container, a bag in which agricultural commodities were brought for payment for use of the Ponca's land and waterways in the North Country

Uą'digè /ü-oⁿ'-thēⁿ-gä'/ *prep phr.*, for no reason, something that someone does for no reason, sometimes done without thought

Uąhe /ü-oⁿ'-hä/ *n.*, cradle, a baby cradle (The Ponca usually made a soft mattress and placed it on a thin board about two feet long and about twelve to fourteen inches wide. The child was laid upon the cradle and wrapped tightly with a soft blanket.)

Uą́he šadú /ü-oⁿ-hä shä-thü'/ *n.*, cradle, a decorative baby cradle (The cradle was made with an additional foot- and head-board. Two decorative straps, which were decorated with either colorful porcupine quills or beads, were tied from the head-board to the foot. At the headboard were attached seashells that served as a noise-maker for the child.)

Uą́sidądą̀ /ü-oⁿ-sē-thoⁿ-thoⁿ/ *v.*, hopping, a person or animal jumping around sporadi-cally or at irregular intervals

Ubá'e /ü-bä'-ā/ *adj.*, crowded, congested, ~, where there is little space for people to move freely in a room or auditorium

Ubá'sni'snidè /ü-bä-snē-snē-dā'/ *v.*, inject, to inject continuously, as in getting a series of shots

Ubá'snidè /ü-bä-snē-dā'/ *v.*, inject, to in-ject a liquid into, as in giving a flu shot to a patient

Ubádą /ü-bä-doⁿ/ *v.*, tighten, to make tight, locking up something very tight; *ušp'ádą*, you tightened or locked; *ubádąì*, he/she tightened or locked; *ągú'ąbádąì*, we tight-ened or locked

Ubáhadì /ü-bä-hä-dē'/ *n.*, on the side, some-thing that is placed on the side of some-thing

Ubáhadì /ü-bä-hä-dē'/ *adj.*, next to, some-thing or somebody that is obviously near another person or thing

Ubáhadì /ü-bä-hä-dē'/ *adv.*, nearby, refers to something placed near anything (*edéšta adíte ~ it'eda bike*, he put those things ~)

Ubáhadì /ü-bä-hä-dē'/ *prep.*, beside, 1. some-thing or somebody being alongside of something or somebody 2. something or somebody being there but not necessarily

wanted in that place or situation (being in the way)

Ubáhat'adišą̀ /ü-bä-hä-t'ä-thē-shoⁿ/ *n. phr.*, edge, toward the edge

Ubáhe /ü-bä'-hā/ *n.*, edge, the border, perimeter, side of something

Ubásnè /ü-bä-snā/ *v.*, split, divide something lengthwise into parts; crack, as in to ~ an automobile window or glass tumbler

Ubášudè /ü-bä-shü-dā'/ *n.*, muddy, making muddy, usu. refers to something in liquid

Ubát'ądà /ü-bä-t'oⁿ-thä'/ *v.*, roll, rolling something over with a tool, such as a lever; *ubít'ądà*, roll something over by pressing

Ubát'ì /ü-bä-t'ē'/ *v.*, hang, to hang up, e.g., clothing, pictures, etc.

Ubát'i ináde /ü-bä-t'ē ē-noⁿ-thä/ *v.*, hang up, to hang something up, as in to hang a pic-ture on the wall or clothes on a clothesline

Úbatè /ü'-bä-tä'/ *n.*, seam, the stitching of thread joining two pieces of cloth or other material at their edges

Ubáudè /ü-bä'-ü-dä'/ *v.*, puncture, to pierce or make a hole with a pointed instrument

Ubáxą /ü-bä-xoⁿ/ *v.*, push in, as in to push a fork-ended stick into a log to extract a rabbit

Ubáxduxà /ü-bä-xthü-xä'/ *v.*, bore, 1. to make a hole in something 2. to make a ditch by passing something over the ground repeat-edly or by water flowing through

Ubáxp'adè /ü-bä-xp'ä-thä'/ *v.*, push off, push-ing something off of something, intention-ally or unintentionally

Ubázą /ü-bä-zoⁿ/ *n.*, corner, 1. the place where two intersecting edges come together 2. where two streets or roads cre-ate an intersection

Ubdáda /ü-bthä-thä/ *n.*, the Oglala band of the Lakota Nation

Ubésnì /ü-bä-snē'/ *v.*, discern, sense or notice

Ubétą /ü-bā'-toⁿ/ *v.*, wrap around or swaddle, to place a baby on a cradle board wrapped with appropriate blankets and woven belts to hold the infant in place; *idábetą̀*, to wrap something around a thing, as with a package

Ubí'xą /ü-bē'-xoⁿ/ *n./v.*, sprinkle, a sprinkling of rain before a rainstorm

Úbihą̀ /ü'-bē-hoⁿ/ *n.*, baking pan, a pan used for cooking breads, cakes, and other foods in an oven

Ubísądè /ü-bē'-soⁿ-dā/ *adj.*, packed, 1. being packed together, usu. refers to people sitting very close together 2. refers to a space between two structures 3. a male name in the Wažáž̀è clan of the Ponca people

Ubískì /ü-bē'-skē/ *v.*, tighten, to tighten by pressing down on, as in pressing down on clothing in a suitcase, fill to the brim, pack, cram, jam

Ubít'ą /ü-bē'-t'oⁿ/ *v.*, dip, to put something into liquid quickly

Učí'žè /ü-chē'-zhā/ *n.*, undergrowth, thick undergrowth and bushes

Účižè /ü'-chē-zhā/ *n.*, trouble, a state of distress or difficulty

Učíže /ü-chē'-zhā/ *n.*, brush, thicket, undergrowth, a dense patch of bushes, shrubs

Učíže ínąsedè /ü-chē'-zhā ē'-noⁿ-sā-thā/ *n.*, brush hog, a large rotary mower, usu. pulled or attached to a tractor to cut thick, deep weeds or brush

Udá /ü-thä'/ *v.*, tell, inform, divulge something that happened; *uwíbdà*, I told you; *uwída*, tell him/her; *úwagidà*, tell them

Udá /ü-thoⁿ/ *v.*, apprehend, to arrest somebody, capture (to ~ him, they gave chase)

Udą́ /ü-thoⁿ/ *v.*, catch, to hold on to, clutch, or grasp by taking hold of something

Udá' /ü-dä'/ *adj.*, icebound, something that is frozen within or covered with ice

Udą́' /ü-thoⁿ'/ *v.*, clutch, grasp, hold, grab, grip

Udą́ /ü-thoⁿ'/ *v.*, hold, 1. hold on to, to take hold of something 2. arrest (In modern times, the act of arresting someone.)

Udá'dadą̀ /ü-thä'-dä-thoⁿ/ *adj.*, become engrossed, absorbed, occupied, immersed in some activity

Udá'tą /ü-thä'-toⁿ/ *adj.*, next, after that, subsequently (~ *aká níkašigè snedé tągà*, the ~ person was tall)

Udą́be /ü-doⁿ'-bā/ *n.*, appearance, 1. the look or form of something 2. the look or form of a person

Udádadą̀ /ü-thä'-dä-thoⁿ/ *adj./v.*, accustomed or familiar to, to be committed to doing something that was tried, or to come together by strong interest

Udádadą̀ /ü-thä'-dä-thoⁿ/ *v.*, to involve oneself in some project or activity, to confirm one's involvement in an activity

Udádadą̀ /ü-thä'-dä-thoⁿ/ *v.*, congeal, solidify in any given situation that becomes customary or an involvement that leads to congealment

Udáde /ü-thä'-dä/ *n.*, adage, a saying that expresses a common experience, a proverb, a saying

Udáde /ü-thä'-dä/ *n.*, written rule, a written law, sayings, moral teachings, mores

Udáde'kè /ü-thä'-dä-kā/ *n.*, law, a decree, ruling, or written regulation, including mores

Údądehà /ü'-doⁿ-thä-hä/ *adj.*, well, refers to somebody recovering; *údątehà*, refers to something being completed in a skillful manner; *údąxt'ią̀*, very well, refers to anything from recovering to doing something skillfully

Udádekè /ü-thä'-dä-kā/ *n.*, rule, the written rule or law

Údaedè /ü'-thä-ā-thä'/ *v. phr.*, engaging in a humble and compassionate act to make things right

Udą́ga /ü-thoⁿ'-gä/ *v., 2nd pers. sing.*, hold, you hold, you clutch, you hang onto

Udáha /ü-thä'-hä/ *v.*, cling to, 1. to adhere to something in addition to something already in place 2. *n.*, something that is part of another thing, as in a lady's winter coat that comes with a scarf

Udáha /ü-thä'-hä/ *v.*, include, something that goes with or is attached to something

Udáha /ü-thä'-hä/ *v.*, attached, something that is attached to or connected to something

Udáha /ü-thä'-hä/ *v.*, along with, something attached to another thing

Udáhe /ü-thä'-hä/ *n.*, bit, the part of a pipe stem (modern pipe) that is held in the mouth

Udákiawatą̀ /ü-thä-kē-ä-wä-toⁿ'/ *v.*, 1. things that move past one after another 2. things that are placed in a sequence or in order 3. things lined up in order

Údaštè /ü'-thä-shtä'/ *n.*, leftovers, usu. food that is uneaten at a feast and taken home to be eaten later

Údąt'ehà /ü'-doⁿ-t'ä-hä'/ *v., 3rd pers. sing., masc.* expression, it (the situation) will be good

Údatèt'i /ü'-thä-tä'-t'ē/ *n.*, dining room, a room for eating food

Udázaè /ü-thä'-zä-ä'/ *n.*, reverberation, echo, noise in a large auditorium

Udázaì /ü-thä'-zä-ē'/ *n.*, women singers, lit., make loud sound, refers to women who sit and sing behind men singing at tribal dances (Orig. the women singers sang only the chorus of the song.)

Udázaì /ü-thä'-zäē'/ *n.*, reverberation, noise, echo, loud sound, the continuance of a sound after the initial sound is made

Udázązè /ü-thä'-zoⁿ-zä'/ *n.*, when hands or feet go to sleep, usu. caused by some physical malady

Údąžì /ü'-doⁿ-zhē'/ *adj.*, bad, 1. describes something that is not good (*šé' k'ip'íną̀gè kè ~*, that is a ~ car) 2. *adj.*, bad, morally no good (*níášigà ~ amà égą̀i*, he is a ~ person)

Udéwį /ü-thä'-wēⁿ/ *v.*, collect or amass, usu. refers to a collection of things, such as hobby items 2. to gather together, usu. refers to a group of people

Udí'edą̀ /ü-thē'-ā-thoⁿ/ *v.*, scattered, scattered in no order

Udíáge /ü-thē'-ä'-gä/ *adj.*, uncompromising, unbending, doesn't want to

Udíáge /ü-thē'-ä'-gä/ *v.*, refuse, declining to do a task or to do something that has been offered

Udiáge /ü-theä'-gä/ *v.*, won't, will not

Udíagè /ü-thē'-ä-gä/ *adj.*, unwilling, adverse, don't want to

Udíagè /ü-thē'-ä-gä'/ *v.*, resist, refusing to go along with

Udíaì /ü-thē'-ä-ē'/ *v.*, scatter, made into small pieces and scattered

Udíbdą̀ /ü-thē'-bthoⁿ/ *v.*, sniff, to draw air through the nose to smell or detect an odor that belongs to something desirable or undesirable, such as certain foods being prepared or animals being tracked as prey

Udídą /ü-thē'-doⁿ/ *v.*, lock, to fasten or secure with a latch

Udíde /ü-thē'-dä/ *v.*, cooperate, cooperation to accomplish something (they ~ and finish the job)

Udíde /ü-thē'-dä/ *adv.*, jointly, coming together to accomplish a task

Udíde /ü-thē'-dā/ *v.i.*, gang up, to join with another to accomplish any task

Udį́dį /ü-dēⁿ'-dēⁿ/ *adj.*, stiff, rigid, unbendable, usu. refers to the body, as in "his legs were ~"

Udíge /ü-thēⁿ'-gā/ *v.*, leave out, exclude, left out

Udį́·ge /ü-thēⁿ'·-gā/ *pron.*, nothing left, there was nothing left of many things

Udígudè /ü-thē'-gü-dā/ *v.*, to make a hole in something with the hands or a tool

Udík'ibà /ü-thē'-k'ē-bä/ *n.*, opening, making a slight opening with the hands and tools at a specific space or level on some structure

Udíp'up'ù /ü-thē'-p'ü-p'ü'/ *v.*, wrapped around, wrapping oneself tightly with a blanket or robe

Udíp'ušį̀ /ü-thē'-p'ü-shēⁿ'/ *adj.*, puff up, to cause something to expand in size, as with yeast in bread making

Udíšą /ü-thē'-shoⁿ/ *adv.*, around, to go around something

Udíšį /ü-thē'-shēⁿ/ *v.*, wrap, to ~ a thing (cloth or other substance) around something, as in covering or wrapping a gift

-udíšį /ü-thē'-shēⁿ/ *adj.*, *suffix*, unlikely, improbable, something not likely to occur

Údiskè /ü'-thē-skā/ *n.*, spider, arachnid, an eight-legged insect that spins webs to catch its prey

Údiske sábe /ü'-thē-skā sä'-bä/ *n.*, black widow, a poisonous female spider with an hourglass-shaped red mark on the abdomen

Údisket'ągà /ü'-thē-skā-t'oⁿ-gä/ *n.*, tarantula, a very large, hairy spider, an arachnid belonging to the Theraphosidae family

Udíski /ü-thē'-skē/ *v.*, tighten, to make tighter, as in tightening a nut on a bolt using a wrench

Udísną /ü-thē'-snoⁿ/ *v.*, affix, to attach something to something, to put something on something

Udísnà /ü-thē'-snoⁿ/ *v.*, attach, putting a thing onto something, as in threading a needle, putting a tire on, screwing a nut onto a bolt

Udísne /ü-thē'-snā/ *v.*, slit, 1. to cut apart, may refer to cloth or deerskin, e. g., that may be cut into strips 2. *n.*, a straight, narrow cut

Udíšp'ašp'à /ü-thē'-shp'ä-shp'ä'/ *v.*, crumble, to ~ or break into small pieces with the hands, as in cooking

Udísp'e /ü-thē'-sp'ā/ *v.*, withhold, to hold back something

Údit'ą̀ /ü'-thē-t'oⁿ/ *adj.*, 1. complicated, doing something that requires concentrated effort, something complex, intricate, or just plain thorny 2. *n.*, *3rd pers sing.*, work, he/she/it has work (*įtą ~ adì*, he has ~ now)

Udít'ubè /ü-thē'-t'ü-bä/ *v.*, to be milled, pulverized, or broken into pieces, usu. refers to hardened or dried food

Údįwit'ì /ü'-thēⁿ-wē-t'ē'/ *n.*, store, a place where merchandise is offered for retail sale

Údįwįt'ì't'ągà /ü'-thēⁿ-wēⁿ-t'ē'-t'oⁿ-gä'/ *n.*, Walmart, lit., a large building to buy, a corporation that has a chain of stores offering discount department store products, electronics, etc.

Údįwįt'ì adį̀ /ü'-thēⁿ-wē-t'ē' ä-theⁿ'/ *n.*, storekeeper, 1. one who sells merchandise 2. Ponca name for a white storekeeper named John Hron Sr. who lived on the reservation ca. 1910

Údįwįt'ì ázidądà /ü'-thēⁿ-wēⁿ-t'ē' ä-zhē-thoⁿ-thoⁿ'/ *n.*, shopping mall, a large enclosed building complex containing many stores and businesses

Udíxagà /ü-thē'-xä-gä'/ *v.*, to be chapped, being chapped on the face, hands, and lips

Udíxdaxdà /ü-thē'-xthä-xthä'/ *adj./v.*, loosen, to loosen something, such as a rope, a belt, a screw

Udíxidè /ü-thē'-xē-dä'/ *v.*, looking, looking at something or viewing the horizon for something

Udíxp'adè /ü-thē'-xp'ä-thä'/ *v.*, drop, release, let go of, let something drop from the hand

Údižà /ü'-thē-zhä'/ *n.*, tub, a broad, round, and open metal container, usu. used to wash clothing

Udíza /ü-thē'-zon/ *n.*, center, central point, the area or part of something centrally located in a circle or group of things

Udíza /ü-thē'-zon/ *prep.*, between, in the middle of where something or somebody is

Udízadi /ü-thē'-zon-dē/ *adj./n.*, middle, the center, the core of something or a group

Udízat'adišà /ü-thē'-zon-t'ä-thē-shon/ *prep. phr.*, middle, toward the ~

Udízat'atà /ü-thē'-zon-t'ä-ton/ *prep. phr.*, middle, from the ~

Údizè /ü'-thē-zä'/ *n.*, week, seven days

Udú'ábdaget'à /ü-thü'-ä'-bthä-gä-t'ä'/ *prep. phr.*, sheltered place, refers to a sheltered place where there is no wind

Udúadè /ü-thü'-on-thä'/ *adj.*, entangled, getting caught on something (the lawn mower was ~ with wire)

Udúadè /ü-thü'-on-thä'/ *v.*, ensnare, as in trapping an animal

Udúadè /ü-thü'-on-thä'/ *v.*, caught, being caught onto something

Udúagdè /ü-thü'-ä-gthä'/ *adv.*, often, frequently, repeatedly, over and over again

Udúbetà /ü-thü'-bä-ton/ *v.*, circle or circle around, more of a command to go around something

Udúbidà /ü-thü'-bē-don/ *v.*, dip, as to dip bread into soup or pastry into coffee

Udúdabaá(gá) /ü-thü'-don-bä-ä'(gä')/ *v.*, look into, investigate or research something first before jumping into it, taking it step by step

Udúdabè /ü-thü'-don-bä'/ *n.*, caution, looking into the matter before acting

Udúdabè /ü-thü'-don-bä'/ *v.*, investigate, to think about, examine, or deliberate over something, inspect

Udúdigè /ü-thü'-thēn-gä'/ *v.*, to be left out of something, usu. distribution of food or material goods

Udúdigè /ü-thü'-thēn-gä'/ *v.*, exclude, leave out, left out

Udúgahì /ü-thü'-gä-hē'/ *v.*, blend in, to stir something into another substance, usu. refers to cooking; *ígahì*, mix in

Udúgdà /ü-thü'-gthä'/ *v.*, regret, to be sorry for mistakes made, to be remorseful for being at fault

Udúhe /ü-thü'-hä'/ *v.*, follow, 1. to follow, to go behind 2. to go by or to follow the same pattern that was previously made by somebody; *udúkihè*, usu. refers to persons who are related in some form who follow immediately after one has left a room, a place, or even in death; *udúwihè*, I am following you; *udúdihè*, he/she/it is following you; *adúdihè*, we are following you; *udúgihè*, he followed his own (relative or pet); *adáwahè*, he/she/it/they followed me

Udúhi /ü-thü'-hē/ *v.*, reach, 1. to extend the arms and hands to grasp something, as in reaching for an apple on a tree 2. to pursue something that is reachable, such as higher education

Udúhi diáwadè /ü-thü'-hē thē-ä'-wä-thä'/ *adj.*, unattainable, not reachable, cannot be done, inaccessible

Udúk'ap'ì /ü-thü'-k'on-p'ē'/ *adj.*, suave, hand-

some, good or fine looking, being appropriately neat, as in "the suit fits perfectly and
looks good on him"

Udúkąp'ì /ü-thü'-koⁿ-p'ē'/ *adj.*, pleasing appearance, pleasant to look at, attractive

Udúki /ü-thü'-kē/ *v.*, defend, to support and
protect a person

Udúkiądè /ü-thü'-kē-oⁿ-thā'/ *v.*, 1. caught,
caught onto or into something (his shirt
got ~ on a protruding nail) 2. to meet up
with an unwanted situation that cannot
be avoided

Udúkihebè /ü-thü'-kē-hā-bā'/ *v.*, continue
a bit further

Udúkiąžì /ü-thü'-kē-noⁿ-zhē'/ *v.*, depend,
two persons or two groups depending upon
each other for support

Udúkižažè /ü-thü'-kē-zhä-zhä'/ *v.t.*, emulate,
try to do something that someone else was
successful in doing, try to be like, imitate,
copy

Udúmą /ü-thü'-moⁿ/ *adj.*, sorry, a feeling of
sorrow combined with anguish and torment over something said or done, or
something not said or done

Udúnąžì /ü-thü'-noⁿ-zhē'/ *n./v.*, reliance, to
rely upon or have confidence in

Udúnąžì /ü-thü'-noⁿ-zhē'/ *adj.*, dependable,
reliable, trustworthy, trusty, staunch

Udúnąžįwadažì /ü-thü'-noⁿ-zhēⁿ-wä-thä-
zhē'/ *adj.*, undependable, being unreliable
or unpredictable, usu. refers to a person,
weather conditions, old machinery

Udúši /ü-thü'-shē/ *prep.*, before, a position,
such as standing before

Udúšiát'a /ü-thü'-shē-ä-t'ä/ *adv.*, in front,
at or in the front

Udúšiát'a /ü-thü'-shē-ä-t'ä/ *prep./n.*, front,
in the front of (used when someone, e.g., is
honored and brought before the people and
is asked to sit in front of an audience)

Udút'adè /ü-thü'-t'ä-thā'/ *n.*, dislike, being
envious of somebody who accomplished
something and who is enjoying his/her
success

Udúxa /ü-thü'-xä/ *v.*, deceive, misinform,
trick, mislead, hoodwink; *wawéúxa*, to use
words and actions to deceive or lie

Udúxa /ü-thü'-xä/ *v.*, dupe, trick, pull the
wool over somebody's eyes

Ugá'e'e /ü-gä'-ā-ā/ *v.*, hanging, dangling or
hanging down

Ugába /ü-goⁿ'-bä/ *n.*, light, glow, luminosity,
illumination, usu. relates to light conditions at dusk, refers to emission of light in
conditions of semidarkness to darkness,
early or late light of the day

Ugába et'ádišą /ü-goⁿ'-bä-ä-t'ä'-thē-shoⁿ'/ *n.*,
dawn, lit., toward the light, first light

Ugádą /ü-gä'-doⁿ/ *v.*, nail, to fasten on with;
the process of using some sort of device
to pound something into something else,
such as a stake in the ground, a common
nail into a board

Ugáe'è' /ü-gä'-ā-ā/ *adj.*, dangling, hanging
loosely

Ugáha /ü-gä'-hä/ *v.*, drift, float, as a log floats
on the water, flowing downstream

Ugáhąnąpazè /ü-gä'-hoⁿ-noⁿ-pä-zā'/ *n.*, darkness, that which occurs at night, the absence of light

Ugánądà /ü-gä'-noⁿ-thä'/ *adj.*, overcast,
cloudy, gray sky

Ugánahąbazè ugdą́ /ü-gä'-nä-hoⁿ-bä-zā'
ü-gthoⁿ'/ *n.*, lit. put into darkness, put into
prison or jail, incarceration, imprisonment,
confinement

Ugánahąp'azè /ü-gä'-nä-hoⁿ-p'ä-zā'/ *n.*, jail,
lit., in the darkness, jail, detention center,
confinement

Ugás'į /ü-gä's-ēⁿ/ *v.*, peek, peek in or out

Ugášą /ü-gä'-shoⁿ/ *v.*, travel, 1. journey, trek,

tour 2. *archaic*, travel, to take a trek into enemy territory to take something

Ugášibè /ü-gä'-shē-bā/ *n.*, graduate, someone who has obtained a diploma or degree from a high school, school of technology, or college (Formerly the term referred to someone who "paid" or qualified themselves for a higher status in any of the Ponca ceremonies by doing or giving something significant to the community.)

Ugáški /ü-gä'-shkē/ *v.*, tie, tie to, fasten onto or strap on, as in to tie an animal up temporarily

Ugáški ináde /ü-gä'sh-kē ē-noⁿ'-thā/ *v.*, tether, tie, as in fastening a rope or chain to an animal to restrict its movement to a certain area

Ugásną /ü-gä'-snoⁿ'/ *v.*, lace, 1. to lace up 2. *n.*, cord, rope

Ugásnè /ü-gä'-snā/ *v.*, split, to split into two separate pieces by cutting, chopping, sawing

Ugásnè'žídè /ü-gä'-snä-zhē'-dä/ *n.*, braid yarn, yarn braided into the hair, worn by men

Ugásnì /ü-gä'-snē'/ *adj.*, cool, pleasantly cool

Ugásni žįgà /ü-gä'-snē zhēⁿ-gä'/ *n.*, breeze, light wind, current of cool air

Ugát'at'adà /ü-gä'-t'oⁿ-t'oⁿ-thä/ *n./v.*, tumble, an athletic movement; *ugát'at'adì*, something tumbling, as a tumbling weed

Ugáwįxè /ü-gä'-wēⁿ-xä/ *v.*, spiral, something moving downward through the air in circles

Ugáxdá'xdà /ü-gä'-xthä'-xthä/ *adj.*, loose fitting, baggy, saggy, clothing that is not tight fitting

Ųgáxdà užá'gè /üⁿ-gä'-xthoⁿ' ü-zhoⁿ'-gä'/ *n.*, *archaic*, passage, path of a migrating party

Ugáxdi /ü-gä'-xthē/ *n.*, Bressie Flats, several sections of land in Noble County, Oklahoma, on the Ponca Reservation ("Land grabbers" once acquired these lands. Hence the term *ugáxdi*, to grab with hands.)

Úgaxè /ü'-gä-xä/ *n.*, color, tint, shade

Ugáxedįgè /ü-gä'-xā-thēⁿ-gä/ *adj.*, refers to persons who have nothing to do or who do not do anything at all, such as vagrants or lazy people

Ugáxpè /ü-gä'x-pä/ *n.*, the Quapaw Tribe of Native Americans

Ugdá /ü-gthoⁿ'/ *v.*, put in, to deposit something into a thing, usu. refers to a thing that is connected to or was a part of a thing, as in resetting a stone in a ring

Ugdá' /ü-gthä'/ *v.*, tell of, to tell of or to give an account of something that happened; *ukígdà*, to tell of something about oneself

Ugdá'à' /ü-gthä-ä'/ *v.*, holler, yell loudly, shout, yell

Ugdáge /ü-gthoⁿ'-gä/ *v.*, submerge, go underwater, swim underwater

Úgdašigè /ü'-gthä-shē-gä/ *v.*, protest, make a complaint, object

Ugdé /ü-gthä'/ *n.*, opening, a small opening (*údiskè áka, ~ kè áhe ayádaì*, the spider escaped into/through the ~)

Ugdé /ü-gthä'/ *v.*, insert, as in placing a key into a lock

Ugdé' /ü-gthä'/ *n.*, small opening, as in a small opening to an animal's den or one that allows cold wind to come into a dwelling or house

Ugdéžažà /ü-gthä'-zhä-zhä/ *adj.*, very dirty body parts, usu. refers to lack of cleanliness (*núžįgà dįkè, p'áhi ké ~* the boy's neck is ~)

Ugdí' /ü-gthēⁿ'/ *n.*, seat, a place to sit, e.g., a place to sit on the ground, a bench, a chair, etc.

Ugdí' /ü-gthä'/ *v.*, occupy, live in, inhabit

Ugdí'íp'idagè /ü-gthēⁿ'-ē'-p'ē-thä-gä/ *n.*, seatbelt, in automobiles, a device that is used to restrain passengers

Ugd$\acute{\text{į}}$ ut'án$\acute{\text{a}}$hà /ü-gthē^n' ü-t'ä'-no^n-hä/ *n.*, aisle, a passageway, usu. refers to space between seats, as in a theater

Ugí'i /ü-gē'-ē/ *v.*, sprouting, the germination of a seed, esp. a perennial plant, which comes forth year after year

Ugígdispè /ü-gē'-gthē-spä'/ *v.*, cower, cringe in fear, somebody who lacks courage, a person who turns away from danger or trouble, as a dog puts its tail between its legs

Ugíket'$\acute{\text{a}}$ /ü-gē'-kä-t'o^n'/ *n.*, merit, the right to claim something accomplished, deserving respect and commendation

Ugíp'i /ü-gē'-p'ē/ *adj.*, full, filled, packed, occupied, full up

Ugíp'idè /ü-gē'-p'ē-thä'/ *v.*, fill, the process of filling something up

Uhá /ü-hä'/ *v.*, walk through, refers to walking through a certain passageway, such as walking through the woods, a forest, or a stream of water or along a lake or river; *uwáha*, I walked through

Úh$\acute{\text{a}}$ /ü'-ho^n/ *v.*, to cook, to roast, to bake, to grill, etc.

Úh$\acute{\text{a}}$'t'$\grave{\text{į}}$ /ü'-ho^n-t'ē^n'/ *n.*, kitchen, a room where meals are prepared

Úh$\acute{\text{a}}$'ud́úgaškè /ü'-ho^n-ü-thü'-gä-shkä'/ *n.*, tripod with a hanging pot for cooking

Uhá'ži'št'ì /ü-hä'-zhē-sht'ē'/ *n.*, detached, outsider, lit., even though I am not a part of it, removed, distant, far from it

Úh$\acute{\text{a}}$ágdè /ü'-ho^n-ä'-gthä'/ *n.*, grate, a grill, a metal frame of crossbars affixed over a fireplace for cooking

Uh$\acute{\text{á}}$ge /ü-ho^n'-gä/ *prep. phr.*, at the end of, something that comes at the end of other things, usu. refers to a structure at the end of others, such as houses, trees, streets, and may refer to the final episode of a play or persons presenting something to an audience

Uh$\acute{\text{á}}$ge hí'te /ü-ho^n'-gä hē'-tä/ *n.*, end, usu. refers to some activity that is coming to an end (at or toward the ~, our team won)

Úh$\acute{\text{a}}$šigdè /ü'-ho^n-shē-gthä'/ *n.*, those who serve food, orig. referred to men who served food at the Hed́úškà meetings and dances, now usu. refers to menfolk who serve food at feasts at tribal gatherings

Úh$\acute{\text{a}}$'kud̀è /ü'-ho^n-kü-thä'/ *n.*, microwave oven

Uhážištì /ü-hä'-zhē-shtē'/ *adj.*, freestanding, independent, esp. not being part of or affiliated with any group, usu. an introductory term used before a speech is given (being a ~ person, I . . .)

Uhé /ü-hä'/ *adj.*, insistent, adamant, unrelenting (~ *gád̀aì*, he is ~)

Uhé /ü-hä'/ *n.*, path, road, way (~ *wí gáxaì*, he made a ~ through the woods)

Uhé'dúbahà /ü-hä'-dü'-bä-hä'/ *n.*, highway, a four-lane highway

Uhé'wakid̀ažì /ü-hä'-wä-kē-thä-zhē'/ *v.*, obstruct, 1. obstruct, to prevent passage through 2. veto, disallowing a person to insist on their argument, forbid insistence 3. a Ponca male name

Uhé'wánasè /ü-hä'-wä-no^n-sä'/ *n.*, *archaic*, keeping them from passing by or "closing the escape route," usu. refers to an enemy attempting to escape

Uhéát$\acute{\text{a}}$ /ü-hä'-ä'-to^n/ *n.*, bridge, a structure built to span a river, crevice, or valley to allow passage

Uhéde /ü-hä'-thä/ *v.*, include, people or things that are brought in or involved

Uhégáxe /ü-hä'-gä-xä/ *n.*, path maker, pathfinder, 1. one who makes a pathway through unknown territories 2. a proper name of a male member of the Wašábe clan

Uhé sakíbadì /ü-hä' sä-kē'-bä-dē'/ *n.*, wayside, to be situated beside the road, street, or highway

Uhéwakiḍaẓì /ü-hā´-wä-kē-thä-zhé´/ *adj.*, impassable, lit., cannot pass here, 1. refers to an enemy trespassing tribally recognized territory 2. a proper male clan name 3. to not allow somebody to insist upon something

Úhi /ü´-hē/ *v.*, win, usu. to triumph or win in a competitive game; may refer to winning in other gambling games, such as dice, cards, or Indian dice; *uwáhi*, I won; *úḍahì*, you won; *éúhi*, they won; *é'ąwáhi*, he/she/they won from me

Uhí'aškà /ü-hē´-ä-shkä´/ *adj.*, short distance, not far, nearby, adjacent

Uhíaškà /ü-hē´-ä-shkä´/ *adv.*, close, near to something

Uhíaškà /ü-hē´-ä-shkä´/ *adj.*, nearby, the distance from one place to another

Úhiḍá /ü´-hē-thä´/ *n.*, bath, a large tub that a person can get into and wash their body

Úhiḍá t'í' /ü´-hē-thä´ t'ē´/ *n.*, bathroom, usu. refers to a room where there is a shower and bathtub

Uhíde /ü-hē´-thä/ *v.*, raise, rear, to raise up and nurture children

Uhít'aẓì /ü-hē´-t'ä-zhé´/ *adj.*, anxious, eager

Uhít'a'ẓì /ü-hē´-t'ä-bä-zhé´/ *n.*, anticipation; expectation, usu. excitedly expecting something good to happen

Úhuhù /ü´-hü-hü´/ *n./v.*, bark, the short, loud cry of a dog

Ujábe /ü-jä´-bä/ *adj.*, slight, 1. a small opening, such as a door left ajar, a window slightly opened 2. listening but hearing only a small part of the information passed on, usu. refers to gossip

Uk'áde /ü-k'ä´-dä/ *adv.*, aside, something aside of the main body of animate or inanimate things

Uk'áde /ü-k'ä´-dä/ *v.*, separate, not connected or attached to anything

Uk'ádeugḍà /ü-k'ä´-dä-ü-gtho^n/ *n.*, ca. 1900, the ace in a deck of playing cards

Uk'í'ket'à /ü-k'ē´-kā-t'o^n/ *v.*, acquired, to gain, accomplish, acquire for self, as in hard work to get a position on the job

Uk'í'p'ášnà /ü-k'ē´-p'ä-shno^n/ *adj.*, disproportionate, uneven, lopsided, a thing that does not come together as normal

Uk'í'tį /ü-k'ē´-tē^n/ *n.*, boxing, pugilism, the manly art of self-defense

Uk'íaḍè /ü-k'ē´-o^n-thä´/ *v.*, snag, to be caught or to be held by getting caught on something sharp

Uk'íba /ü-k'ē´-bä/ *n.*, opening, something not quite closed, e.g., a partially opened window

Uk'ígḍiagè /ü-k'ē´-gthē-ä-gä´/ *adj.*, lazy, indolent

Uk'íhi /ü-k'ē´-hē/ *adj.*, capable, can do, has the necessary talent to do something, equipped to do something

Uk'ík'íyè /ü-k'ē´-k'ē´-yā/ *n.*, dialogue, conversation between two or more people

Úk'ik'unéde /ü´-k'ē-k'ü-nä´-thä/ *n.*, organization, lit., come back to the fireplace, group, club, union, party

Úk'inaḍè /ü´-k'ē-no^n-thä´/ *adj.*, hidden, unseen, undetected, unobserved, not perceived or recognized among other things or people

Uk'ít'e /ü-k'ē´-t'ä/ *adj./n.*, alien, a description of or a person of another tribe, race, or nation

Uk'ít'e /ü-k'ē´-t'ä/ *n.*, orig., 1. enemy, foe, challenger 2. other tribe or nationality

Uk'íxde /ü-k'ē´-xthä/ *v.*, the point of disclosure of a person for some wrong that he had been doing for some time, in which he carelessly exposed the nature of the crime committed

Uką́ha /ü-ko^n´-hä/ *adj.*, apart, separated from

others, as a person who is present but never comes in to be involved

Uką́ha /ü-koⁿ'-hä/ *prep.*, beside, at the side of, near

Uką́ha /ü-koⁿ'-hä/ *v.*, adjoin, connect or be right next to (*waą́ niášigà mà ~ bažì*, he never even ~ himself to the singers)

Uką́ha /ü-koⁿ'-hä/ *n.*, 1. on the edge or a distance away from a group of people 2. never involved with any activity involving other people 3. alongside of any structure, usu. refers to someone walking by or something lying beside or being constructed with or close by

Uką́habažì /ü-koⁿ'-hä-bä-zhē'/ *v.*, uninvolved, being nearby but impassive, close by but not with or in (*niášigà ḍįkè ~*, the person was ~)

Uké't'ą /ü-kā'-t'oⁿ'/ *v.*, to attain, achieve, accomplish, to acquire something by effort

Ukédį /ü-kā'-thēⁿ/ *adj.*, common, general, familiar, as in somebody or something that is ordinary

Ukédįažì /ü-kā'-thēⁿ-ä-zhē'/ *adj.*, artificial, not the real thing, fake

Ukétą /ü-kā'-toⁿ/ *v.*, achieve, attain; *n.*, accomplishment, the completion of something

Ukí'gdè /ü-kē'-gthä'/ *v.*, join, to join in and become a part of the group or organization; *ukígdà*, to put oneself in without invitation

Ukí'mążà /ü-kē'-moⁿ-zhoⁿ'/ *n.*, heaven, in Judeo-Christian faith, the dwelling place of the creator—God or other heavenly being—and true Christians or believers

Ukíbašnà /ü-kē'-bä-shnoⁿ'/ *adj.*, uneven, as in carpentry where two boards do not meet evenly

Ukíe udį́šį /ü-kē'-ä ü-thēⁿ'-shēⁿ/ *adv. phr./n.*, not receptive to counseling, a person who will not listen to advice, counsel, or suggestion

Ukígdà /ü-kē'-gthä'/ *v.*, confess, admit, own up to something or make a confession

Ukíhi /ü-kē'-hē/ *adj.*, able, capable, can do

Ukíhi /ü-kē'-hē/ *v.*, can, be able to, be capable of, know how to; *uwákihì*, I ~; *uḍákihì*, you ~

Ukíhiáži /ü-kē'-hē-ä-'-zhē'/ *n.*, inability, lack of ability, the condition of not being able

Ukíhiwaḍè /ü-kē'-hē-wä-thä/ *v.*, enable, to make able or to give strength and power to do something

Ukíką /ü-kē'-koⁿ/ *v.*, cooperate, work or do something together, assist each other

Ukíką ḍiá' /ü-kē'-koⁿ thē-ä'/ *v.*, helpless, somebody who is unable to help him/herself, who is weak and dependent

Ukíkí'e /ü-kē'-kē'-ä/ *v.*, conversing, to exchange words or thoughts through speech

Ukíkínà /ü-kē'-kē'-nä/ *n.*, fighting over, fighting over something; *í'k'ik'inà*, fighting over some specific thing or things by two or more people, as in claiming an inheritance

Ukíkíye /ü-kē'-kē'-yā/ *v.*, communicate, to speak to each other, exchanging stories, ideas, information

Ukíkíži /ü-kē'-kē'-zhē/ *n.*, related, determining a relationship, usu. refers to stating that a person or persons are related to somebody through other relatives or through marriage

Úkinąḍì /ü'-kē-noⁿ-thē'/ *adj.*, obscure, indistinguishable, vague

Úkinąḍì /ü'-kē-noⁿ-thē'/ *v.*, to make indistinguishable, to mix an animate or inanimate subject with other things so that the subject becomes ~

Ukít'e /ü-kē'-t'ā/ *n.*, nationality, tribe, race of people

Ukít'e hébe /ü-kē'-t'ā hä'-bā/ *n.*, a designation of Ponca tribal members who are nonclan members born of other tribal descent (The Ponca tribe has a patrilineal clanship system.)

Úkixidà /ǘ-kē-xē-thä'/ *v.*, dispirit, dishearten, put a damper on something that
seems impossible to do

Úkizà /ǘ-kē-zä'/ *adj.*, vacant, unoccupied,
a place where no one is

Ukíži /ü-kē'-zhē/ *v.*, related, refers to persons
who are blood relatives or kinfolk

Umá'e /ü-mo^n-ā/ *n.*, groceries, provisions,
foodstuff, rations

Umá'snè /ü-mä-snä'/ *n.*, fried bread, lit., cut a
slit into, usu. a slit is cut into the dough as it
is prepared for frying

Umą́di /ü-mo^n-thē/ *n.*, domain, realm, area,
habitat, locale, environment, territory,
home; where humans or animals customarily live

Umą́di /ü-mo^n-thē/ *n.*, path, 1. route, track,
etc. 2. way of life 3. realm, domain, kingdom

Umą́dikà /ü-mo^n-thē-kä/ *n.*, year, the period
of 365 or 366 days

Umą́dikà'ą́mą /ü-mo^n-thē-kä-o^n'-mo^n/ *n.*,
yesteryear, last year, the year before this
year

Umą́dikà gdébą /ü-mo^n-thē-kä' gthä'-bo^n/
n., decade, a period of ten years

Umą́dikà gdébą hiwì /ü-mo^n-thē-kä' gthä'-
bo^n hē-wē'/ *n.*, century, lit., one hundred
years (Latin *centum*, one hundred)

Umą́dikà t'éga /ü-mo^n-thē-kä' t'ā'-gä/ *n.*,
new year (Sometime in the nineteenth century the first day of January in the modern
calendar was designated as the new year
The first few days of spring [*mé'p'ahągà*]
mark the Ponca new year.)

Umą́hą /ü-mo^n'-ho^n/ *n.*, the Omaha Tribe of
Native Americans

Úmąk'à /ǘ-mo^n-k'ä'/ *adj.*, easy, effortless,
uncomplicated, simple

Úmąkà /ǘ-mo^n-kä'/ *adj.*, cheap, inexpensive,
something that is not pricey or expensive

Umíže /ü-mē'-zhä/ *n.*, bedding, blanket,
sheets, etc. used for a bedcovering

Umížexáxáde /ü-mē'-zhä-xä-xä'-dä/ *n.*,
sheet, a bedsheet, usu. two pairs of thin
linen cloth, one used to cover a mattress
and the other to cover up the sleeper

Umúhunedè /ü-mü-hü-nä-thä'/ *n.*, flue, a
duct or chimney extending from a stove or
fireplace to the outdoors

Umúhunì /ü-mü-hü-nē'/ *n.*, damper, a plate
in a fireplace that regulates the flow of air
inside a chimney

Uná' /ü-nä'/ *v.*, borrow, to use, by agreement,
something that belongs to somebody else

Uná' /ü-nä'/ *v.*, rent, rental fee, lease

Uną́'ą /ü-no^n'-o^n/ *v.*, heard of, heard about
something

Unábdì /ü-nä'-bthē/ *v.*, perspire or sweat

Unágąbà /ü-nä'-go^n-bä/ *n.*, light, a light
coming from some source, causing illumination in a room, a building, or an open
area

Unágąbà /ü-nä'-go^n-bä/ *v.*, illuminate,
brighten, the effect of light away from the
main source

Uną́štą /ü-no^n'-shto^n/ *n.*, station, a place
where a public conveyance stops for passengers

Uną́xdùxda /ü-no^n'-xthü'-xthä/ *n.*, rut,
making a rut or groove on a dirt road after
rain

Uną́žį /ü-no^n'-zhē^n/ *n.*, shirt, usu. refers to
a man's garment for the upper part of the
body

Uną́žį /ü-no^n'-zhē^n/ *v.*, stand in, as in a child
playing and standing in a puddle

Uną́žį'čéškà /ü-no^n'-zhē^n-chä'-shkä/ *n.*,
jacket, a short coat

Uną́žį' màte /ü-no^n'-zhē^n mo^n'-tä/ *n.*, undershirt, T-shirt

Uną́žį'zizigè /ü-no^n'-zhē^n-zē-zē-gä/ *n.*,

sweater, usu. a knitted outergarment covering the upper body

Unážį t'ągà /ü-noⁿ-zhē̃ t'oⁿ-gä'/ *n.*, coat, usu. a full-length coat

Unážį xáxadè /ü-noⁿ-zhē̃ xä'-xä-dä'/ *n.*, blouse, usu. a lady's garment

Unážį xé'a /ü-noⁿ-zhē̃ xä'-ä/ *n.*, short-sleeved shirt

Uné' /ü-nä'/ *v.*, search, look for, seek out, to search for somebody or something that is missing; *uwáne*, I searched; *uɖáne*, you searched; *unái*, he/she/it searched; *uwíne*, I searched for you; *uɖíne*, he/she/it searched for you; *uɖínaì*, they searched for you; *unána*, searching, attempting to find something in different places

Unéde /ü-nä'-thä/ *n.*, fireplace, 1. hearth or fireplace 2. the fireplace of the Native American Church, namely, the ritual

Unéže /ü-nä'-zhä/ *n.*, urinal, a sanitary receptacle in which to urinate

Uníži /ü-nē̃'-zhē/ *adj.*, timid, without self-confidence and courage to do something

Úp'ežì /ü'-p'ā-zhē'/ *n.*, turmoil, something disrupting an event, chaos, mayhem

Úš'adįgè /üsh-ä-thē̃ⁿ-gä'/ *adj.*, presumptuous, not having proper social modesty in public, 1. someone who goes beyond what is right or who is not very proper 2. *n.*, one who acts and speaks unashamedly

Úš'k'ą údà /ü'-sh-k'oⁿ ü'-doⁿ'/ *adj.*, polite, gracious, courteous, well mannered

Úsągà /ü'-soⁿ-gä'/ *adj.*, critical, something that is life threatening, such as any sickness

Úsągà /ü'-soⁿ-gä'/ *adj.*, 1. life threatening, refers to something that is dangerous and perilous ("near the cliff, the car jumped the rail, causing a ~ situation) 2. critical, grave (very often used in relation to one who is critically ill or near death)

Usé' /ü-sā'/ *v.*, burn, to burn something up

Usésą /ü-sā'-soⁿ/ *n.*, mildew, something that spoils or turns to mold or fungi

Usésą /ü-sā'-soⁿ/ *adj.*, decomposed, refers to decomposition of foods, usu. something that has an unpleasant smell, esp. fats such as butter, noted by odor or taste and sometimes by sight

Úšį /ü'-shē̃ⁿ/ *v.*, mislead, an honest comment or thought to cause oneself or someone else to think or believe something that is not true

Úsihì /ü'-sē̃-hē̃'/ *adj.*, clean, unsoiled, spotless, immaculate, dirt free

Úšįkidè /ü'-shē̃ⁿ-kē̃-thä'/ *n.*, self-deception, a condition of an individual not being able to rationalize what is there in a logical way

-usk'ąska /ü-sk'oⁿ'-skä/ *adj.*, *suffix.*, mid, time of day, month, or year

Úšką /ü'-shkoⁿ'/ *n.*, action, event, something that happens, a happening or occurrence

Úšką /ü'-shkoⁿ'/ *n.*, culture, habits, behavior; in the social sciences, the way in which people develop social behavior in certain situations or conditions, resulting in varied habits, values, customs, arts, beliefs, established institutions, etc.

Úšką /ü'-shkoⁿ'/ *n.*, mores, the ways of life or customs of a particular group of people that include habits, manners, moral attitudes, unwritten laws

Úškap'iáži /ü'-shkoⁿ-p'ē̃-ä'-zhē̃/ *adj.*, unethical, unprincipled, wrong, bad, corrupt

Úškąúdą /ü'-shkoⁿ-ü'-doⁿ/ *adj.*, nice, refers to a person who has all the characteristics of being kind and polite in the social and cultural ways of the Native Americans and others

Úšką údą /ü'-sh-k'oⁿ ü'-doⁿ/ *adj.*, courteous, well mannered, a person who is polite and shows respect to everybody, kind, considerate, thoughtful, a good or benevolent nature

Uské' /ü-skā'/ *adj.*, full, usu. refers to people and other animate things in a tight place, jam packed, bursting at the seams

Uskíde /ü-skē'-thā/ *v.*, soured, to become spoiled or soured by fermentation, usu. refers to canned fruit or preserves in a jar

Uskúskè /ü-skü'-skā'/ *v.*, curdle, to turn sour, spoil, as in milk changing into curds

Ušnáha gáxe /ü-shnä'-hä gä'-xā/ *n.*, wallow, buffalo wallow, usu. refers to bison rolling on the ground and eventually leaving a large dusty depression on the ground

Usné' /ü-snā'/ *n.*, column, procession, in a row, in rank, in sequence

Usní' /ü-snē'/ *adj.*, cold, the state of coldness; having a low temperature

Usni'á't'adišą /ü-snē-ä'-t'ä-thē-shoⁿ'/ *adj.*, northerly, in a northerly direction

Usni'át'à /ü-snē-ä'-t'ä'/ *n.*, north, lit., where it is cold, one of the cardinal points on the compass

Uspé /ü-spä'/ *n.*, valley, dale, gully

Uspé' /ü-spä'/ *n.*, gully, a large ditch or small valley created or worn by running water after a heavy rain

Uspéádi /ü-spä'-ä'-dē/ *n.*, in the low place, low land

Ušt'ášt'a /ü-sht'ä'-sht'ä/ *n.*, remnants, pieces of things

Ušt'é' /ü-sht'ā'/ *n.*, left, left some items still there, refers to leaving food on the table, clothing on sale, or anything that can be bought, usu. things in short supply

Ušt'éte /ü-sht'ä'-tā/ *n.*, remainder, refers to particular things left over; *uštéke*, one thing left over

Ušté /ü-shtā'/ *adj.*, residual, left over, remaining, surplus

Ušté /ü-shtā'/ *n.*, remainder, something or things left over

Uštédą /ü-shtä'-thoⁿ/ *n.*, remainder, refers to one particular thing left in a horizontal position

Ušúde /ü-shü'-dā/ *adj.*, murky, muddy, turbid

Usúde /ü-sü'-dā/ *n.*, rash, outbreak on the surface of the skin, usu. red and itchy, usu. refers to diaper rash on babies

Ut'á' /ü-t'ä'/ *adj.*, wedged, lodged, stuck in between (his arm got ~ between two limbs on the tree)

Ut'a'nądì /ü-t'ä-noⁿ-dē'/ *prep.*, in between, 1. usu. refers to children being left alone between two or more homes of relatives 2. *n.*, something left lying around somewhere

Út'ąbedè /ü'-t'oⁿ-bä-thā'/ *adj.*, expectant, looking forward with anticipation to something that is likely to happen or anticipating something that will occur or is forthcoming

Út'ąbedè /ü'-t'oⁿ-bä-thā'/ *n./v.*, hoped, desired with expectation or desired with anticipation

Út'ąbedìgè /ü'-t'oⁿ-bä-theⁿ-gā'/ *n. phr.*, "no one to look to," no one to look forward to because of the death of the one who provided for one's needs and offered advice

Ut'áną /ü-t'ä'-noⁿ/ *n.*, gap, opening, a gap or aperture; an area between two structures or in the middle of something, e.g., the middle of a street

Út'i /ü'-t'ē/ *n.*, home, a residence of a family, families, or a single person

Út'i /ü'-t'ē/ *n.*, lair, a place or dwelling made by wild animals to rest or sleep

Utą́ /ü-toⁿ'/ *v.*, wear, put on, have on, be dressed in; *mą́'*, wore, *sing. past t.* of *wear*, I wore, to adorn oneself with clothing, shoes, etc.; *ą́'*, to wear or put on

Ųtį́ /ü-tēⁿ/ *v.*, hit, to hit or strike something or somebody with the hands or a weapon

Útihà /ü-tē-hä/ *adj.*, lonesome, forlorn

Utį́tį /ü-tēⁿ-tēⁿ/ *n.*, rap (*ebé etè, t'ižébekè ~*, somebody ~ped on the door)

Uwą́/ /ü-woⁿ/ *v.*, put in, usu. refers to putting firewood into a woodstove or fireplace, as in *žą́ ~'ga*, ~ wood or add wood

Úwadát'ą t'í /ü-wä-thä́-t'oⁿ t'ē'/ *n.*, saloon, bar, beer joint

Úwadáte t'ì /ü-wä-thä́-tä t'ē'/ *n.*, restaurant, cafe, a place where meals are cooked, sold, and served

Úwadit'ą̀ /ü-wä-thē-t'oⁿ'/ *n.*, employment, a contract between two parties to complete some sort of work or project in which one party is the employer and the other is the employee who does the work

Uwágda /ü-wä'-gthä/ *n.*, hardship, difficulty, conditions that are harsh

Uwágdà /ü-wä'-gthä'/ *n.*, poverty, neediness, destitution, hardship

Úwagidè /ü-wä-gē-thä'/ *v.*, inform, to tell or give information to a person or a group of people

Uwáha /ü-wä'-hä/ *v.*, walk through, refers to walking through a certain passageway, such as walking through the woods, forest, or a stream of water or along a lake or river

Uwáhąì /ü-wä'-hoⁿ-ē'/ *n.*, kinship, in Ponca kinship, how one is related to another, i.e., brother, sister, cousin, etc.

Uwą́he /ü-woⁿ-hä/ *n.*, shelter, refuge, sanctuary, safe haven

Uwą́he digè /ü-woⁿ-hä thē-gä'/ *adj.*, homeless, lit., no shelter, people who have no shelter, home, or permanent residence

Uwák'ą /ü-wä-k'oⁿ/ *v., 1st pers. sing., past t.*, helped, aided, assisted, helped out (*įdádą gáxaìke, ~ pí'*, I ~ in the project)

Úwak'ą́da wadahą̀ t'ì /ü'-wä-k'oⁿ-dä wä-thä-hoⁿ' t'ē'/ *n.*, church, house of worship, a place for public Christian worship

Uwák'igdižedà /ü-wä-k'ē-gthē-zhä-thä'/ *n./v.*, tired out, causing oneself to become mentally or physically fatigued, worn down, usu. caused by doing some activity, one who is tired out

Uwákihą̀ /ü-wä'-kē-hoⁿ'/ *adj.*, in addition to, following afterward or over this amount

Uwáną̀ą̀' /ü-wä'-noⁿ-oⁿ'/ *v.*, heard of, heard of us for something that we did or accomplished

Uwánądà /ü-wä'-noⁿ-thä'/ *adj.*, rare, limited, a thing that is in short supply or not available among us

Uwánądè /ü-wä'-noⁿ-thä'/ *adj.*, scarce, rarely found

Uwą́si /ü-woⁿ'-sē/ *v.*, departing, getting off a vehicle

Uwą́si /ü-woⁿ'-sē/ *v.*, jump, to jump, to hop

Uwą́sisì /ü-woⁿ'-sē-sē'/ *v.*, jumping, to jump up and down

Úwašką̀ /ü'-wä-shkoⁿ'/ *n./v.*, support, a source of encouragement and aid

Uwáwakét'ąì /ü-wä'-wä-kǟ-t'oⁿ-eⁿ'/ *n./v.*, gain, to gain or achieve something by somebody else's effort

Úwawešì /ü'-wä-wä-shē'/ *n.*, pay, compensation, recompense earned or paid for work performed

Úwawešì /ü'-wä-wä-shē'/ *v.*, earn, to receive something (e.g., money) in return for work services rendered

Uwéda /ü-wä'-thä/ *adj.*, scattered, any group of things that is sparsely or thinly distributed

Uwédąp'ì /ü-wä'-thoⁿ-p'ē'/ *n./v.*, excuse, pretext, ploy

Uwédi /ü-wä'-dē/ *n.*, heir, to be an heir of, one

who is entitled to receive the property of a deceased person

Uwét'a /ü-wā'-t'ä/ *n.*, claim, 1. considered to be the rightful owner 2. impregnation

Uwétakidè /ü-wā'-tä-kē-thā'/ *adj.*, impregnate, to make a female pregnant

Uwídąbè /ü-wē'-thoⁿ-bā'/ *adj.*, uphill, going up to higher ground from a lower level

Úwįgaządè /ü'-wēⁿ-gä-zoⁿ-dā'/ *n.*, choker, a short necklace, an ornament that is fastened closely around the neck and made of seed beads and horsehair using the netted stitch in the beadwork

Uwíhe /ü-wē'-hā/ *n.*, member, an associate, a constituent

Uwíhe /ü-wē'-hā/ *v.*, join, to become a part of an organization or a group

Uwíhe /ü-wē'-hā/ *v.*, participate, to take part, to involve oneself, to play a part of

Uwík'ą /ü-wē'-k'oⁿ/ *v.*, help, be of assistance, to support or provide a service to someone; *uwék'ą, 1st pers., past t.*, I ~; *uwáwak'ą, 1st pers., pres./past t.*, I ~ them

Uwíne /ü-wē'-nā/ *adj.*, burning, as in "the burning house"

Uwínedè /ü-wē'-nä-thā'/ *v.*, incinerate, burn, burn up, set fire to

Úxde /ü'-xthā/ *v.*, catch up with, to apprehend, to uncover some criminal misdeed, as in ~*áhi*, they caught up with him, indicating that he had committed some crime that was eventually uncovered

Uxdé' /ü-xthā'/ *adv.*, soon, shortly, in a little while, before long, as in ~ *t'í'ga*, come here

Uxdéá'ži /ü-xthā'-ä'-zhē/ *n.*, mentally deficient, ca. early twentieth century, having a disability such as Down's syndrome

Uxdéáhi /ü-xthā'-ä'-hē/ *v.*, to catch up to a person for a crime committed after a period of investigtion

Uxdəá'bážì /ü-xthəä'-bä'-zhē'/ *adv.*, secondary or inferior position

Uxdú'xdà /ü-xthü'-xthä/ *adj./n.*, concave, indented, cavernous, a hole in the surface of the road, a pothole, a ditch

Uxdúxa'há' /ü-xthü'-xä-hä'/ *n.*, bag, *archaic*, a bag to carry personal things

Uxdúxda /ü-xthü'-xthä/ *n.*, pothole, rut, hole, 1. a depression or dip on the road 2. a hole in a thing, such as a hollow log, a hole in the ground

Uxdúxda /ü-xthü'-xthä/ *adj.*, hollow, concave

Uxį́'e /ü-xēⁿ'-ä/ *v.*, disgruntled, a person who is displeased or discontented; usu. speaking unhappily because one feels one has been wronged or mistreated

Uxíjexčí ną́'ą́' /ü-xē'-jäx-chē' noⁿ-oⁿ'/ *v.*, hear of, hearing only a little bit of something

Uxp'áde /üx-p'ä'-thā/ *v.*, lose, misplace something, mislay, not be able to find something; *uxp'ádeadè*, I lost it; *uxp'ádedadè*, you lost it; *uxp'ádegidaì*, he/she/they lost it

Uxp'é /ü-xp'ä'/ *n.*, dish, plate, or saucer used esp. for serving food or holding something

Uxp'é t'ągà /üx-p'ä' t'oⁿ-gä'/ *n.*, platter, large plate, serving dish, tray

Uxp'é't'ągà /ü-xp'ä'-t'oⁿ-gä'/ *n.*, *archaic*, dishpan, a large pan used to wash dishes, pots, and tableware

Uxp'é'žįgà /ü-xp'ä'-zhēⁿ-gä'/ *n.*, cup, a container used to hold liquid drinks

Uxp'éibík'à /üx-p'ä'-ē-bē'-k'ä'/ *n.*, *archaic*, dish towel, an absorbent cloth used to dry dishes

Uxp'éužì /ü-xp'ä'-ü-zhē'/ *n.*, cupboard, cabinet for cups and plates, also used to store food and other crockery

Uxp'é wasésą /ü-xp'ä' wä-sä'-soⁿ/ *n.*, Chinaware, ceramic cups, dishes, saucers

Úxt'à /ü'-xt'ä'/ *adj.*, interesting, appealing, worthy of note

Úxt'ažì /ü'-xt'ä'-zhē'/ *adj.*, uninteresting, boring, dull, unexciting

Užą́' /ü-zhon'/ *n.*, bed, a piece of furniture used to sleep on

Užá't'à /ü-zhä'-t'ä'/ *n.*, The Mouth, a confluence of two rivers (This name is given to a geographic location on the Ponca reservation, where the Saltfork River flows into the Arkansas River in Kay County, Oklahoma.)

Užą́ge /ü-zhon'-gā/ *n.*, road, a known roadway

Užą́ge žát'a /ü-zhon'-gā zhä'-t'ä/ *n.*, junction, intersection, fork in the road

Užą́ ímuzà /ü-zhon' ē'-mü-zä'/ *n.*, bedstead, lit., poles that hold a bed, the framework of a bed

Užát'a /ü-zhä'-t'ä/ *n.*, fork, bifurcation, e.g., 1. the juncture where two or more things split off, as with the horns of a deer 2. a junction where two streams of water meet, forming one river 3. a junction where limbs of trees branch off

Užą́t'i /ü-zhon'-t'ē/ *n.*, bedroom, a room where people sleep through the night

Úžawà /ü'-zhä-wä/ *adj.*, festive, celebratory, delightful, connotes fun and merriment or revelry, enjoyment, something entertaining, usu. refers to activity such as an athletic event or a pow-wow and pow-wow dancing

Užéda /ü-zhä'-thä/ *adj./n.*, tired or tiredness, weary, worn out, etc.

Užéda /ü-zhä'-thä/ *v.*, to be exhausted, tired, worn out, weary, etc.

Úži /ü'-zhē/ *v.*, sow, to plant seeds in the ground to grow crops

Uží' /ü-zhē'/ *v.*, put in, to put something into a container, as in sugar into a cup, gas in a gas tank, etc.

Uží' /ü-zhē'/ *v.*, fill, to fill a container, to fill up

Úžibasnà /ü'-zhē-bä-snon'/ *n.*, chest of drawers, a dresser; a piece of furniture that has several drawers for storing or keeping clothing handy for use

Užíga /ü-zhēn'-gä/ *n.* a narrow grove of trees, usu. located in a low, small valley where a small stream of water flows

Úžihà /ü'-zhē-hä/ *n.*, sack, bag

Užú' /ü-zhü'/ *adj.*, genuine, traditional and authentic, the real thing

ə

Seventh vowel in the Ponca alphabet.

V

This letter is not included in the Ponca alphabet.

W

w /wə/ fifteenth consonant in the Ponca alphabet

Wá'bahì /wä-bä-hē'/ *v.*, elect, select, in Ponca politics, choose by ballot or vote for

Wá'baxù /wä-bä-xü'/ *v.t.*, pawn, hawk, to give something to someone or to a pawn shop for a loan

Wá'bazù /wä-bä-zü'/ *v.i.*, to point at a group of people or animals

Wá'datè /wä-thä-tā'/ *n.*, table, something to place food upon and eat; *wíádatè*, foodstuff; *wadáte*, eat, consume food

Wá'dazabažì /wä-thä-zä-bä-zhē'/ *v.*, harangue, a speech made to scold people in a public place

Wá'dixè /wä-thē-xā'/ *v.*, married—used in regard to women

Wá'dixè úškà /wä-thē-xā' ü'sh-kon'/ *n.*, matrimony, used in regard to women preparing for wedding nuptials

Wa'é /wä-ā'/ *v.*, cultivate, working on the land preparing to sow seeds and raise crops

Wá'gà /wä'-gä'/ *n.*, dress, to dress out meat, to clean and prepare for cooking or storing

Wą́'gidè /woⁿ'-gē-thä'/ *n.*, everyone, everybody in this particular group or gathering, refers to addressing everyone in attendance at a small or large gathering of any sort, usu. used in addressing attendees at meetings

Wa'į́' /wä-ēⁿ'/ *n.*, baggage, carried bags, gear, or bundles that contain one's belongings

Wa'į́'skígè /wä-ēⁿ'-skē'-gä'/ *v./n.*, heavy load, 1. to carry a heavy load (he has a ~ on his pickup truck) 2. to carry an emotional burden (being downhearted, he is carrying a ~)

Wa'į́'xudè /wä-ēⁿ'-xü-dä/ *n.*, Gray Robe Village, one of the three villages in present-day Nebraska where the Ponca lived before their removal to Indian Territory

Wa'į́' xúde /wä-ēⁿ' xü-dä/ *n.*, Gray Blanket, 1. a male ghost that followed the Ponca people to Indian Territory ca. 1876 and who still walks an old trail along the Arkansas River in Kay County, Oklahoma 2. a common gray blanket acquired by the Ponca ca. 1800s

Wa'į́' xúdè /wä-ēⁿ' xü'-dä/ *n.*, robe, lit., gray robe, made of furs taken from animals with gray fur

Wá'nąsè /wä'-noⁿ-sä/ *v.*, prohibit, bar, to keep someone or a group from passing through or doing something

Wá'nąxdè /wä'-noⁿ-xthä'/ *v.*, hide, hiding; *á'binąxdè*, hide, hiding a thing under something; *á'nąxdè*, hide, conceal, to hide something; *á'kinąxdè*, hiding; *í'kina'xdè*, hide, to hide self; *wénąxdè*, to hide themselves or something from us or them

Wá'spè /wä'-spä'/ *v.*, behave, to behave in a manner that is socially appropriate, esp.

by being polite, good-tempered, and self-controlled

Waą́ /wä-oⁿ'/ *n.*, song, a musical composition

Waą́ /wä-oⁿ'/ *v.*, sing, chant, hum

Waą́da /wä-oⁿ'-thä/ *v.*, leave, abandon, to leave some people or animals behind

Waą́ gáxe /wä-oⁿ' gä-xä/ *n.*, song maker, composer of songs, usu. refers to a person who composes a song concerning a significant deed or accomplishment of another

Waą́ niášigà /wä-oⁿ' nē-ä-shē-gä'/ *n.*, singer, lit., one who sings, usu. refers to a male person who sings or leads tribal songs at tribal ceremonies and church functions

Wabá'xu /wä-bä-xü/ *n.*, paper, newspaper, tablet (The term *waxį́ha* was used for paper in the 1800s.)

Wábagdà /wä'-bä-gthä'/ *adj.*, bashful, shy, self-conscious

Wabágdezè /wä-bä'-gthä-zä'/ *v.*, *archaic*, ca. nineteenth century, write, to write, writing

Wabáhi /wä-bä'-hē/ *v.*, pecking, as in chickens scratching and pecking on the ground for food

Wabáhi /wä-bä'-hē/ *v.*, graze, 1. nibble, forage (The prefix *wa* pluralizes the action of an individual or thing, as in *t'éská má ~ mądì*, the cattle are grazing) 2. to pick or picking, as in picking pecans in a pecan grove

Wabáhi /wä-bä'-hē/ *v.*, picking, 1. to harvest, as in picking pecans 2. pecking, as in chickens feeding on grain in the barnyard

Wábanà /wä-bä-noⁿ'/ *v.*, watch, to watch some activity, such as a movie, theatrical play, or pow-wow

Wabášedą /wä-bä'-shä-thoⁿ'/ *n.*, payment, the act of paying somebody for something

Wabásihì /wä-bä'-sē-hē/ *v.*, cleaning up, the act of cleaning up (he's ~ the place)

Wabásna /wä-bä'-snä/ *v.*, roast, cutting a

piece of meat and placing it over an open
fire with a green stick

Wabášnadè /wä-bä'-shnä-dā'/ *n.*, shinny, a
woman's shinny game played during the
spring that is similar to the men's shinny game

Wábatè /wä'-bä-tā'/ *n.*, ribbon, trimming,
a strip of fabric used to decorate another
piece of fabric

Wabáte /wä-bä'-tā/ *v.*, sew, stitch, seam; *baté,*
sew; *įdébatè,* you sewed it for me

Wabáxt'e /wä-bä'-xt'ā/ *n.*, bundle, things
that are tied or held together in a bag of a
sort (A bundle, whether large or small, usu.
contained medicines among the Ponca.
Sometimes the entire skin, tail, and head of
an otter was made into a bundle in which
to keep various medicines and related
articles.)

Wabáxu /wä-bä'-xü/ *n.*, book, manuscript,
paperback, hardback

Wabáxu /wä-bä'-xü/ *n.*, letter, mail, correspondence, communication between
people and businesses through the written
page or letter; now also refers to email

Wabáxu /wä-bä'-xü/ *n.*, omasum or "many-
piles," lit., book; leaf-like folds in the
bovine stomach

Wabáxu /wä-bä'-xü/ *n.*, writing, something
that has been written, as in a letter, newspaper, or any kind of document

Wabáxu'į /wä-bä'-xü-eⁿ'/ *n.*, mail carrier, lit.,
one who carries paper

Wabáxu'sagì /wä-bä'-xü-sä-gē'/ *n.*, fee
simple, lit., hard paper, ca. 1900, fee
patent, a legal requirement for removing
Indian lands from federal trust status that
gave Native Americans the right to sell
such lands

Wabáxu déde t'í' /wä-bä'-xü thä'-thä t'ē'/ *n.*,
post office, lit., sent the paper, refers to the
U.S. postal service

Wabáxu gáxaì kè /wä-bä'-xü gä'-xäē' kä'/ *n.*,
edition, one of a printing of the same newspaper or book

Wabáxu itéde /wä-bä'-xü ē-tä'-thä/ *n.*,
record, documents put away or stored

Wabáxu ugdą /wä-bä'-xü ü-gthoⁿ'/ *n.*, 1. envelope 2. mailbox

Wabáxu ugdę̀ /wä-bä'-xu ü-gthäⁿ'/ *n.*, mailbox, a rural mailbox or post office mailbox

Wabáxu wádadè ut'í' /wä-bä'-xü wä'-thä-dä'
ü-t'ē'/ *n.*, library, lit., reading house, library

Wábažą̀ /wä'-bä-zhoⁿ'/ *n.*, a ceremonial staff
used by an elder in the Pipe Dance ceremony of the Ponca

Wábazè /wä'-bä-zä'/ *n./v.*, scare, to scare
somebody; *wábazéát'ašą̀,* to scare somebody
extremely and suddenly

Wabdúga /wä-bthü'-gä/ *n.*, hominy, cooked
dried corn kernels

Wábinak'ą /wä'-bē-nä-k'oⁿ'/ *v.*, to flash light
upon, turning a light on people

Wabíšnudè /wä-bē'-shnü-dä'/ *v.*, hominy, lit.,
taking off, refers to the process of removing
the hull from grains of corn using ashes

Wábizedè /wä'-bē-zä-thä'/ *n.*, clothesline, a
type of rope, wire, or cord that is stretched
between two poles and on which clothes
are attached to dry

Wač'íška /wä-ch-ē'-shkä/ *n.*, creek, a narrow
channel or stream

Wač'íška níkašigà /wä-ch-ē'-shkä nē'-
kä-shē-gä/ *n.*, the Creek Tribe of Native
Americans

Wačéga /wä-chä'-gä/ *adj.*, tender, associated
with food, such as meat easily chewed

Wačí'gaxè /wä-chē'-gä-xä'/ *n./v.*, dance, general term for any kind of dancing, to dance

Wačǐ'škà'gdadì /wä-chē'-shkä'-gthä-dē'/ *n.*,
Chilocco School, lit., across the creek, Chilocco Indian School, Oklahoma

Wačíninik'à /wä-chē'-nē-nē-k'ä'/ *n.*, butterfly, an insect with brightly colored wings

Wačíninikà wažį́ga /wä-chē'-nē-nē-kä' wä-zhēⁿ'-gä/ *n.*, hummingbird, a tiny bird of the family Trochilidae

Wačíška žį́gá /wä-chē'-shkä zhēⁿ-gä'/ *n.*, brook, a small stream, rivulet

Wadá /wä-dä'/ *adj.*, prosperous, someone who has or possesses much

Wą́dą /woⁿ'-doⁿ/ *adv.*, both, usu. refers to performing a task together or doing the same thing

Wadá'edè /wä-thä'-ā-thä'/ *n.*, agape love (godly love)

Wadá'edè /wä-thä'-ā-thä'/ *adj.*, compassionate, one who shows compassion to others, who is empathetic and considerate

Wadá'edè /wä-thä'-ā-thä'/ *n.*, philio love (brotherly love)

Wadá'gè'púkì /wä-thä'-gä'-pü'-kē'/ *n.*, Russian, lit., big soft hat, Russian people, a native or inhabitant of Russia

Wadá't'ą̀ /wä-thä'-t'oⁿ'/ *v.*, to drink, drinking an alcoholic beverage

Wadá'zaì /wä-thä'-zä-ē'/ *n.*, guinea fowl, guinea hen

Wadą́besnedè /wä-doⁿ'-bä-snä-dä'/ *n./v.*, stare, 1. to look extendedly at somebody without moving the eyes 2. to constantly look at different people or things in a public place 3. one who stares

Wádádąbažì /wä'-thä'-thoⁿ-bä-zhē'/ *v.*, rake over the coals, reprove, tell off; usu. considered disrespectful to a hearer or hearers, esp. to people in a gathering

Wádadè /wä'-thä-dä'/ *v.*, to read something, usu. refers to reading some book, newspaper, or magazine

Wádaè' /wä'-thä-ā'/ *n.*, apron, a garment worn over the front of clothes in order to keep clean while cooking or doing other work

Wadáede /wä-thä'-ā-thä/ *adj.*, sympathetic; having an understanding, compassionate, or benevolent feeling or attitude toward someone in need

Wadáedè /wä-thä'-ā-thä'/ *adj.*, merciful, expressing or showing mercy and compassion

Wadáge /wä-thä'-gä/ *n.*, hat, a generic term for a headcovering worn for various purposes, including native headdresses worn for ceremonies, protection against the elements, war, or any reason or purpose

Wadáge bút'a /wä-thä'-gä bü'-t'ä/ *n.*, baseball cap, a cap formerly used by players in the game of baseball, now refers to any commonly worn cap

Wadáge sábe /wä-thä'-gä sä'-bä/ *n.*, neckerchief (Unlike cowboys, Ponca men wore a black scarf rolled up around the neck with the ends held together in the front with an ornament of some sort.)

Wadáge štą̀gà /wä-thä'-gä shtoⁿ-gä'/ *n.*, scarf, a headcovering or neck wrap, usu. used by women and girls

Wádagidè /wä'-thä-gē-thä'/ *v.*, gladden, to make somebody happy, delight, bring joy to somebody

Wádahà /wä'-thä-hä'/ *n.*, apparel, clothing, attire, garb, material worn on the human body

Wádahà /wä'-thä-hä'/ *n.*, attire, clothing, usu. refers to a certain type of clothing worn for a purpose

Wádahà /wä'-thä-hä'/ *v.*, wear, 1. putting on certain kinds of dancing paraphernalia (In the Ponca Hedúškà organization men, in addition to their deerskin shirt and leggings, wore symbols of war honors that included eagle feathers, skins of certain animals, bandoliers, hairpipe beads, or a roach, as well as other symbolic items.) 2. refers also to any uniformed clothing identifying persons, such as soldiers

Wádahidè /wä-thä-hē-dā/ *v.*, tease, saying or doing something comical in an annoying way to cause laughter

Wadáhut'à /wä-thä'-hü-t'o^n/ *v.*, to holler or screech, 1. usu. refers to an animal grasping or holding down its prey 2. a proper male name in the Wažáže clan

Wadáp'ip'ižè /wä-thä'-p'ē-p'ē-zhā/ *n.*, August, lit., corn is in silk, the eighth month of the year

Wádat'àį /wä'-thä-t'o^n-ē^n/ *v.*, revealed, 1. bringing something to light by someone (*ebéte*, ~, it was ~ to them by somebody) 2. caused to be revealed by speaking of something often

Wadátažì /wä-thä'-tä-zhē/ *v.*, fast, to not eat, a willful act of abstaining from food and drink

Wádaté /wä'-thä-tā/ *n.*, food, groceries, provisions, any edible produce

Wadáte /wä-thä'-tā/ *v.*, 1. to eat (*núžįgà dįkè ~ gdì*, the boy sat down ~) 2. food

Wádate'ádibdà /wä'-thä-tā-ä'-thē-bthä/ *n.*, tablecloth, usu. a cloth covering for the dining room table

Wadáte bí'zedè /wä-thä'-tā bē'-zā-thä/ *n.*, dehydrated food

Wadáte dįgè /wä-thä'-tā thē^n-gä/ *n.*, famine, no food, the scarcity of food, groceries, provisions, or any edible produce

Wadáwa /wä-thä'-wä/ *n.*, numbers, the sum of something, usu. represented by a word, symbol, or letter (In the Ponca language, it is represented in a word or words.)

Wadáwa /wä-thä'-wä/ *v.*, count, saying numbers beginning with the number one

Wadáwa dizè /wä-thä'-wä thē-zā/ *n.*, census, a procedure for taking a head count, getting information about a people in a given group

Wádažįgà /wä'-thä-zhē^n-gä/ *v.*, belittle, to be cocky, brashly overconfident, arrogant, saying something to or about another who is stronger physically (The term suggests taking liberties with words, which may incur negative consequences for the speaker.)

Wádažut'à /wä'-thä-zhü-t'o^n/ *v.*, to speak of a thing or something that ultimately will come to pass or be reached, achieved, accomplished, something like "self-fulfilled prophecy"

Wadį́ /wä-thē^n/ *n.*, wealth, to own much, usu. refers to material goods

Wadí'gdà digè /wä-thē'-gtho^n thē-gä/ *adj.*, foolish, thoughtless, unable to think

Wadíbabà /wä-thē'-bä-bä/ *n.*, playing cards, used to play various games, usu. for gambling (Each card is distinguished with a number from one to ten, with three additional cards called the jack, queen, and king. There are four sets of thirteen cards that are suited with a motif of hearts, diamonds, spades, and clubs.)

Wádidaxè /wä'-thē-dä-xä/ *v.*, scrape, 1. a bear making scratch or claw marks on a tree 2. a male name in the Wažáže clan of the Ponca people

Wadį́'hįsà /wä-thē^n'-hē^n-sä/ *v.*, to sting or bite, refers to flying insects such as wasps, mosquitoes, certain gnats

Wadíedà /wä-thē'-ä-tho^n/ *v.*, rummaging, to rummage through one's personal property, looking at one's personal property that has not been seen or touched over a long period of time

Wadígdà /wä-thē'-gtho^n/ *n.*, idea, plan, thought, the processes of mental activity

Wadígdà'á'ákikì /wä-thē'-gthoⁿ-ä'-ä'-kē-kē/ *n.*, *1st pers. sing.*, indecision; arguing with oneself; wavering

Wadígdą gáxe /wä-thē'-gthoⁿ gä'-xä/ *n.*, plan, idea, devise a plan of action to achieve a goal

Wádihì /wä'-thē-hē'/ *v.*, stir up, disturb, usu. refers to scaring up game

Wadíka /wä-thē'-kä/ *v.*, request, to ask somebody to help do something

Wadíp'i /wä-thē'-p'ē/ *adj.*, creative, a person who is ~ , imaginative, artistic; *waní'p'i, 2nd pers. sing.*, you are ~

Wadíp'i /wä-thē'-p'ē/ *n.*, magic, the supernatural; *v.*, connotes the ability to be creative or inventive

Wadíp'ì' /wä-thē'-p'ē'/ *n.*, talent, lit., one who knows how to do or make a thing, 1. talent, knack, aptitude 2. something done by a conjurer or magician

Wadíp'iáži /wä-thē'-p'ēä'-zhē/ *n.*, wrongdoing, illegal acts of behavior, a criminal act

Wadíse /wä-thē'-sä/ *v.*, tension, usu. refers to a toddler flexing all his/her muscles

Wadísi /wä-thē'-sē/ *n.*, *archaic*, giveaway, act of giving away following the funeral experience (This custom was practiced up to ca. 1933 and was done about six months after the interment of the deceased. Members of the family accumulated material goods to distribute to friends and other tribal members. No gift was given to family members. Ritual giving at funerals still exists but is done immediately after four days of other funeral customs.)

Wadíšna /wä-thē'-shnä/ *v.*, appear, something that becomes visible among other things; *ši'wadíšnà*, reappear, something that comes back to be seen visually

Wádišt'ąbažì /wä'-thē-sht'oⁿ-bä-zhē/ *v.t.*, detain, holding in custody

Wadíšup'à /wä-thē'-shü-p'ä/ *v.*, clean up, straighten things up, make tidy

Wadíʃde /wä-thē'-ʃ-thä/ *n.*, giveaway, the act of giving away to somebody who doesn't possess much, usu. done at ceremonial or ritual gatherings (as with the adage "~ to someone who doesn't possess much")

Wadít'ą /wä-thē'-t'oⁿ/ *v.*, work, to work, labor; *ú'dit'ą, n.*, job, to have a particular job

Wadít'ąt'ą̀ /wä-thē'-t'oⁿ-t'oⁿ/ *v.t.*, ransack, children (and some adults) getting into things or looking at private things in the home without permission

Wadít'ubè /wä-thē'-t'ü-bä/ *n.*, cornmeal, a flour ground from dehydrated or parched corn

Wádiwagazù /wä'-thē-wä-gä-zü/ *v.*, observe, to view or examine a situation or condition

Wadį́wį /wä-thēⁿ'-wēⁿ/ *v.*, shop, 1. to purchase something or some things 2. *n.*, purchases, things that have been bought

Wadį́wį úmąk'à /wä-thēⁿ'-wēⁿ ü'-moⁿ-k'ä'/ *n.*, sale, an auction, a garage sale

Wádixà̀ /wä'-thē-xoⁿ'/ *n.*, toy, a thing that children play with, such as games, models, dolls, a teddy bear

Wadíxt'i ihéde /wä-thē'-xt'ē ē-hä'-thä/ *adj.*, accessible, easy to get, reach, usu. refers to something valuable left out in the open so that it can be easily taken

Wadíxu /wä-thē'-xü/ *v.*, to draw, to sketch, to make a picture on a surface by using a pencil or pen

Wadíxu dip'ì /wä-thē'-xü thē-p'ē'/ *adj.*, artistic, usu. refers to somebody who excels at drawing and painting pictures

Wadíža /wä-thē'-zhä/ *v.*, launder, wash, to use water to wash clothes or linen

Wadížat'ì /wä-thē'-zhä-t'ē'/ *n.*, laundry, a place of business for washing clothes or a place in the home where clothes and linens are washed

Wadíze /wä-thē'-zā/ *v.*, payment, getting ~ for services provided (The first generation of Ponca living in Oklahoma leased their lands to white farmers, who made payments to the federal government's Indian agency. The Indian agency in turn made checks out to individual landowners. That individual was said to have gotten a check, *wadíze*; hence the word means to receive a check.)

Wadížu't'ą /wä-thē'-zhü-t'oⁿ'/ *v.*, grow crops, to grow plants, usu. refers to growing a variety of agricultural crops

Wadót'ada /wä-thō'-t'ä-dä/ (**Wadút'ada** / wä-thü'-t'ä-dä/) *n.*, the Otoe Tribe of Native Americans

Wadúdiažì /wä-thü'-dē-ä-zhē'/ *adj.*, far away, something, e.g., other lands, that are a long way from the speaker

Waé' /wä-ā'/ *v.*, farm, to cultivate, to till, farming or cultivating the land

Wága /wä'-gä/*n.*, meat-dehydrating process (The Ponca dehydrated meat by cutting thin layers of choice cuts with the grain of the meat and hanging them on a scaffold to dry in the sun.)

Wagáde /wä-gä'-thā/ *v.*, give away, to give something to somebody; relates to a personal act of giving something to a relative, friend, or anybody

Wagáxdą /wä-gä'-xthoⁿ/ *n.*, entourage, supporters, associates, usu. refers to any Ponca tribal ceremonial procession by those who assist, e.g., with the Pipe Dance ceremonial

Wagáxe /wä-gä'-xā/ *n.*, debt, something (money) that is owed to somebody, bound by verbal or written agreement

Wagáxe /wä-gä'-xā/ *v.*, credit, to finance, to buy something with promise to pay later

Wagáxe /wä-gä'-xā/ *n.*, gesture, 1. the sign language of Native Americans 2. gestures such as waving hands to get the attention of somebody

Wagáze /wä-goⁿ'-zā/ *v.*, learn, to be taught, to acquire knowledge

Wagáze t'í' /wä-goⁿ'-zā t'ē'/ *n.*, school, lit., house of teaching, a place to teach, train, educate

Wagáze ugášibè wabáxu /wä-goⁿ'-zā ü-gä'-shē-bā' wä-bä'-xü/ *n.*, diploma, a certificate issued by an educational institution verifying successful completion of a course of study in months or years; the term includes college degrees

Wagáze wádį /wä-goⁿ'-zā wä'-thēⁿ/ *n.*, teacher, the instructor, the tutor or educator

Wágazù /wä'-gä-zü'/ *adj.*, accurate, no errors, something that is without error, usu. refers to something that is passed along by word of mouth

Wágazù /wä'-gä-zü'/ *v.*, clarify, elucidate, e.g., to state exactly, to state clearly

Wágdą /wä'-gthoⁿ/ *n.*, brooch, set, pin, a piece of jewelry or other kind of decorative item attached to clothing

Wagdą úškà /wä-gthoⁿ' ü'sh-koⁿ'/ *n.*, matrimony, wedding, nuptials, marriage ceremony—used in regard to men

Wagdí' /wä-gthē'/ *n.*, maggot, larva of a fly of the order Diptera, more often applied to flies of the suborder Brachycera, or houseflies

Wagdíška /wä-gthē'-shkä/ *n.*, insects, 1. bugs 2. a proper male name in the Wažážè clan

Wagdíška hí'škubè /wä-gthē'-shkä hēⁿ'-shkü-bä/ *n.*, caterpillar, the larval form of members of the order Lepidoptera, usu. comprising butterflies and moths

Wagdíškasnedé /wä-gthē'-shkä-snä-dä'/ *n.*, centipede ("hundred feet"), arthropod belonging to the class Chilopoda

Wági /wä'-gē/ *v.*, came to get us (*wági ahì*, they ~)

Wágidè /woⁿ-gē-thä/ *n.*, refers to addressing everyone in attendance at a small or large gathering of any sort, usu. used in addressing attendees at meetings

Wagíka /wä-gē'-kä/ *v.*, request, to ask for something to be done

Wagít'ạbagà /wä-gē'-t'oⁿ-bä-gä/ *v.*, watch, keep vigil looking after us, usu. refers to a devout petition to Wak'ạda to keep watch over one who prays

Wahą́ /wä-hoⁿ'/ *v.*, encamp, 1. to set up a camp 2. to get one's belongings and move out and go somewhere to live

Wahą́ /wä-hoⁿ'/ *v.*, move, to relocate one's residence to another place

Wahą́' /wä-hoⁿ'/ *n.*, thread, 1. string, cord 2. *v.*, to move and camp out somewhere

Wahą́' /wä-hoⁿ'/ *v.*, relocate, move somewhere else, change place of residence

Wahába /wä-hä'-bä/ *n.*, corn on the cob

Wahába ídišp'è /wä-hä'-bä ē'-the-shp'ä/ *n.*, corn sheller (The corn-sheller devices used and known by the Ponca were handheld shellers. More recently, corn shellers were called *wahába íṇạšpè*, usu. a mechanized sheller.)

Wahába'ukéđì /wä-hä'-bä-ü-kä'-thē'/ *n.*, blue corn

Wahábe žé'ạhè /wä-hä'-bä zhä-oⁿ-hä'/ *n.*, parched corn, corn on the cob cooked on live coals; *watázi žé'ạhè*, parched corn

Wahą́đigè /wä-hoⁿ'-theⁿ-gä'/ *n.*, orphan, lit., no place to relocate, a child whose parents have died

Wahą́e /wä-hoⁿ'-ä/ *v.*, thank, express thanks, express gratitude, be grateful; *wíbđahà, 1st pers. sing.*, I ~ you

Wahą́e /wä-hoⁿ'-ä/ *v.*, pray, giving praise and thanks to God or making a devout petition for help

Wahą́e /wä-hoⁿ'-ä/ *v.*, plead, to implore, to plead to somebody or to a court in an earnest appeal for forgiveness or time; also a plea to an individual for forgiveness

Wahą́išigdè /wä-hoⁿ'-ē-shē-gthä/ *n.*, prayer, a person who prays for others, as he/she is often requested to do so (These people are known for praying for others and for better conditions for the people.)

Wahá sagí' /wä-hä' sä-gē'/ *n.*, rawhide, untanned animal hide; used for moccasin soles, shields

Wahé'ạ /wä-hä'-oⁿ/ *n.*, travois, sled made of two poles connected to the sides of an animal, usu. a horse or dog, to transport material goods; *wábahè*, travois

Wahéhe /wä-hä'-hä/ *adj.*, weak, fragile, flimsy, refers to something that can break easily, as in an old rotten step

Wahí' /wä-hē'/ *n.*, bone, the hard connecting parts of vertebrate skeletons; two principal parts of this material are collagen and calcium phosphate; *hí*, bone

Wahí'ni'é /wä-hē'-nē-ä'/ *n.*, arthritis, a joint disorder that involves pain and inflammation of the joints

Wahídagè /wä-hē'-thä-gä'/ *v.*, crippled, walking with a limp because of an injury or birth defect

Wahídaxà /wä-hē'-thä-xoⁿ/ *n.*, the Potawatomie Tribe of Native Americans

Wahút'ạdì /wä-hü'-t'oⁿ-thē'/ *n.*, gun, rifle, usu. refers to any kind of gun; a device that fires bullets

Wahút'ạdì čéška /wä-hü'-t'oⁿ-thē' chä'-shkä/ *n.*, pistol, revolver, handgun

Wahút'ạdì t'ạgà /wä-hü'-t'oⁿ-thē' t'oⁿ-gä/ *n.*, cannon, a large weapon mounted either on wheels, warships, or vehicles with a track

Waị /wä-ēⁿ/ *n.*, blanket, cover, mantle, something to cover up with when sleeping or keeping warm

Waị' /wä-ēⁿ/ *n.*, pack, bundle, things carried on the shoulders or back

Waị' /wä-ēⁿ/ *n.*, robe, usu. refers to tanned animal skins

Waị'ágdabe'sábe /wä-ēⁿ-ä'-gthä-bā-sä'-bä/ *n.*, a beaded, fringed black shawl, a popular Ponca shawl in the first half of the twentieth century

Waị'dadà /wä-ē'-thä-thä/ *adj.*, gossipy, a person who talks a lot about people

Waị'gabdà /wä-ēⁿ-gä-bthä/ *n.*, shawl, any open shawl

Waí'k'igdišt'ạ̀ /wä-ē'-k'ē-gthē-sht'oⁿ/ *v.t.*, prepare, to be ready beforehand for some purpose

Waí'k'igdišt'ạ̀ /wä-ē'-k'ē-gthē-shtoⁿ/ *adj.*, ready, to be prepared for something, to be complete and ready

Waịk'ạhazì /wä-ēⁿ-k'oⁿ-hä-zē/ *n.*, broadcloth, a red and blue broadcloth sewn together, said to be worn by women ca. 1800s; became a man's ceremonial blanket in later years (The blanket had a yellow- or gold-colored ribbon or cloth border.)

Waị púki /wä-ēⁿ pü'-kē/ *n.*, quilt, a blanket made of several layers of material, including cloth, cotton or wadding, and/or other woven material for the back

Waị skíge /wä-ēⁿ skē'-gä/ *n.*, burden, 1. load, something carried that is heavy 2. *v.*, to be oppressed with worry or something difficult to carry emotionally 3. *n.*, pack, package

Waị ukíbatè /wä-ēⁿ ü-kē'-bä-tä/ *n.*, broadcoth, usu. red and blue broadcloth sewn together (This imported, fine woven cloth had a likeness to deerskin. A closely woven or densely textured fabric, it is made of wool and has a lustrous

finish. The Ponca wore the blue section over the left shoulder based upon a lost ritual with the Osage people, who wore the red section over the left shoulder. A dark blue broadcloth sewn together with a white stripe down the center was also used by members of the Native American Church.)

Waị xdíxdị /wä-ēⁿ xthēⁿ-xthēⁿ/ *n.*, Pendleton blanket (These woolen blankets have Native American designs.)

Waíye udádá /wä-ē'-yä ü-thä'-thä/ *n.*, tattletale, tattler, gossiper

Wajép'a /wä-jä'-p'ä/ *n.*, town crier or herald, a person in the Osage Nation designated as one who makes public announcements in the camp and proclamations during ceremonies

Wak'ạ́ /wä-k'oⁿ/ *v.*, wager, bet, gamble, to take a chance in order to win something

Wak'ạ́da /wä-k'oⁿ-dä/ *n.*, God, orig. the great mystery, God the creator of the world

Wak'ạ́dagì /wä-k'oⁿ-dä-gē/ *n.*, a mythological creature that lived along the Missouri River, described as a water monster having a long body with horns on its head; Wak'ạdagi *mạšáde*, the dwelling place of the creature, a cavern somewhere along the Missouri River

Wak'ạ́da gíkạ /wä-k'oⁿ-dä gē'-koⁿ/ *v.*, cry to God, humbling self before God

Wak'ạ́da Íye /wä-k'oⁿ-dä ē'-yä/ *n.*, Holy Bible, the Word of God, the recorded text of the Old Testament history of the Hebrew people, which includes drama, poetry, philosophy, prophesy, and the New Testament history and words of Jesus, the Son of God, as well as letters or epistles written by followers of Jesus Christ

Wak'ạ́da íye unạ́ži /wä-k'oⁿ-dä ē'-yä ü-noⁿ-zhē/ *n.*, pulpit, a speaker's stand in the

Christian church from which a sermon is delivered by the minister

Wak'ą́da Ižį́gè /wä-k'oⁿ'-dä ē-zhēⁿ'-gā'/ *n.*, Son of God, Jesus Christ or the Anointed One, the Messiah

Wak'ą́da p'á'snedè /wä-k'oⁿ'-dä p'ä'-snä-dä'/ *n.*, elephant, large mammal of the family Elephantidae and the order Proboscidea; there are two species, the African elephant (*Loxodonta africana*) and the Asian elephant (*Elephas maximus*)

Wak'ą́da wadahą̀ /wä-k'oⁿ'-dä wä-thä-hoⁿ'/ *n.*, prayer, the act of speaking to God to praise him, giving thanks, making a confession, or making a petition to him

Wak'ą́da wadahą̀ níkašigà /wä-k'oⁿ'-dä wä-thä-hoⁿ' nē'-kä-shē-gä'/ *n.*, minister, 1. one who is authorized or ordained by church authorities to conduct religious worship, administer the holy sacraments, and teach the beliefs of the Christian church and is usu. referred to as the pastor or member of the clergy 2. the laity

Wak'ą́da wádahą̀ t'í' á'gdì /wä-k'oⁿ'-dä wä'-thä-hoⁿ' t'ē' ä'-gthēⁿ'/ *n.*, pews, church pews, usu. wooden benches arranged in rows facing the altar of a church

Wak'ą́da Waxúbe Wá'datè /wä-k'oⁿ'-dä wä-xü'-bä wä'-thä-tä'/ *n.*, communion table, a table in the Christian church on which the sacraments of bread and wine are placed for adherents who receive them according to a directive given by Jesus Christ, "Do in remembrance of me"

Wák'ù' /wä'-k'ü'/ *n.*, awl, a sharp, pointed tool for making marks or holes in leather

Wák'ù'žįgà /wä-k'ü'-zhēⁿ-gä'/ *n.*, needle

Waką́ /wä-koⁿ'/ *v.*, gamble, bet, wager

Waką́'užą́ge /wä-koⁿ'-ü-zhoⁿ'-gä/ *n.*, Milky Way, a myriad of stars, the galaxy that contains our solar system

Wak'ą́da Ižį́ge Ík'ip'ahą̀ /wä-k'oⁿ'-dä ē-zhēⁿ'-gä ē'-k'ē-p'ä-hoⁿ'/ *n.*, Christian, lit., one who knows the Son of God, Jesus

Wak'ą́da Ižį́ge Nít'a Agítedą̀dì /wä-k'oⁿ'-dä ē-zhē'-gä nē'-t'ä ä-gē'-tä'-thoⁿ-dē'/ *n.*, Easter, lit., when the Son of God arose from the dead

Wak'ą́da wadahą̀ /wä-k'oⁿ'-dä wä-thä-hoⁿ'/ *n.*, worship, a show of reverence, adoration, and devotion to Wak'ą́da, the Creator, that may include prayers, songs, readings, and other acts of worship

Wak'ą́dawadahą̀ Haská /wä-k'oⁿ'-dä-wä-thä-hoⁿ' hä-skä'/ *n.*, Christian flag, a white flag with a blue rectangular division in the top left corner with a red cross on it

Wak'ą́dawadahą̀ waą́ /wä-k'oⁿ'-dä-wä-thä-hoⁿ' wä-oⁿ'/ *n.*, hymns, Christian hymns

Wak'ą́dawadahą̀ waą́ wabáxu /wä-k'oⁿ'-dä-wä-thä-hoⁿ' wä-oⁿ' wä-bä'-xü/ *n.*, hymnal, a church songbook

Wak'ą́da wašiʃt'amà /wä-k'oⁿ'-dä wä-shē-ʃ'-t'ä-mä'/ *n.*, angels, lit., God's helpers, heavenly beings

Wak'ą́da waxúbe wadáte /wä-k'oⁿ'-dä wä-xü'-bä wä-thä'-tä/ *n.*, sacraments, bread and wine representative of the body and blood of Christ taken at the command of Christ, "Do this in remembrance of me"

Wak'ą́da žą́' waxúbe /wä-k'oⁿ'-dä zhoⁿ' wä-xü'-bä/ *n.*, cross, lit., sacred wood of God, the Christian cross upon which Jesus Christ was crucified

Wak'ą́didè /wä-k'oⁿ'-dē-thä'/ *n.*, anxiousness, uneasiness

Wakéga /wä-kä'-gä/ *adj.*, ill, sick, in poor health

Wakéga t'ì /wä-kä'-gä t'ē'/ *n.*, hospital, lit., house of the sick, sickbay, infirmary

Wakéga t'ì wadít'ąmà /wä-kä'-gä t'ē' wä-thē'-t'oⁿ-mä'/ *n.*, hospital staff, the people who work in the hospital, composed of medical doctors, nurses, medical specialists, aides, housekeeping personnel, etc.

Wakéga úsągà t'ì /wä-kā'-gä ü'-soⁿ-gä' t'ē'/ *n.*, emergency room of a hospital, refers to the reception of persons in need of immediate medical care or aid; includes the intensive or critical care unit

Wakéga užą́ t'ì /wä-kā'-gä ü-zhoⁿ' t'ē'/ *n.*, patient room, where care and treatment are given following a patient's entrance into the hospital and initial treatment

Wakéga wa'į̀ /wä-kā'-gä wä-ēⁿ'/ *n.*, ambulance, a motorized vehicle for transporting the sick or injured to a hospital or health facility

Wakíšnažixt'ì /wä-kē'-shnä-zhē-xt'ē'/ *v.*, most undeservedly, to receive something from a source that should otherwise have gone to another

Wamą́' /wä-moⁿ'/ *v.*, *1st pers.*, *past t.*, sang, to chant, croon, hum (I ~ at the pow-wow)

Wamą́'dą̀ /wä-moⁿ'-thoⁿ'/ *v.*, steal, to steal, to take property or something belonging to someone without permission, usu. done in secret

Wamą́dą̀št'ą̀ /wä-moⁿ'-thoⁿ-sht'oⁿ'/ *n.*, thief, somebody who habitually steals things

Wamą́he /wä-moⁿ'-hä/ *v.*, board, to live temporarily with some other family at their expense, but with willingness to help with household work or expenses

Wamáskè'násagè /wä-moⁿ'-skä'-nä'-sä-gä'/ *n.*, *s./pl.*, saltine crackers, crackers, a thin, crisp cracker sprinkled with salt

Wamáske'sì' /wä-moⁿ'-skä-sē'/ *n.*, wheat, seed wheat; *wamą́ske'hì*, wheat plant

Wamą́ske bdáskà /wä-moⁿ'-skä bthä'-skä'/ *n.*, pizza (To honor the queen consort of Italy on June 11, 1889, Raffaele Esposito created the pizza. It was made with tomatoes, mozzarella, and basil, representing the national colors on the Italian flag.)

Wamą́skè bút'à /wä-moⁿ'-skä' bü-t'ä'/ *n.*, hamburger, a sandwich made of a fried, grilled, or broiled flat patty of ground beef served on a bun with other ingredients, including mayonnaise or mustard, cheese, lettuce, tomatoes, and onions

Wamą́ske náxudedè /wä-moⁿ'-skä nä'-xü-dä-thä'/ *n.*, toast, a toasted slice of bread

Wamą́skè skíde /wä-moⁿ'-skä' skē'-thä/ *n.*, pastries, cake, cookies, sweet rolls

Wamí' /wä-mē'/ *n.*, blood, a bodily fluid that delivers necessary nutrients and oxygen to all parts of the body to maintain life and also transports waste from body cells

Wamí' skíde /wä-mē' skē'-thä/ *n.*, diabetes mellitus, a disease in which a person's pancreas does not regulate insulin, causing high or low levels of blood sugar

Wamíde /wä-mē'-dä/ *n.*, seeds, seeds stored for planting later

Wamídizè /wä-mē'-thē-zä'/ *n.*, transfusion, transferring whole blood from a healthy donor to somebody who has lost blood or who has a blood disorder

Wamiú't'è /wä-mēü'-t'ä'/ *n.*, bruise, usu. caused when a break occurs in the blood vessels near the surface of the skin whereby bits of blood cause discoloration

Wamúp'i /wä-mü'-p'ē/ *n.*, sharpshooter, a person who is skilled at shooting bullets from a rifle to hit a target

Wamúske /wä-müⁿ'-skä/ *n.*, 1. orig. bread made with powdered cornmeal 2. bread made with powdered wheat

Wamúske bdípe /wä-mü'-skä bthē'-pä/ *n.*, flour, a fine powder ground from wheat seeds for bread and other bakery products

Wamúske bit'út'ú'be /wä-müⁿ'-skä bē-t'ü'-t'ü'-bä/ *n.*, crumbs, bread crumbs

Wamúske ínat'ubède /wä-mü'-skā ē'-noⁿ-t'ü-bā'-thā/ *n.*, elevator, grain elevator, esp. for wheat in Texas, Oklahoma, and Kansas

Wamúske t'ubáde /wä-mü'-skā t'ü-bä'-thā/ *n.*, bread crumbs, small pieces of bread, usu. used in crumbing foods, casseroles, etc.

Wamúske ukédi /wä-mü'-skā ü-kā'-thē/ *n.*, lit., common bread biscuit, among the Ponca, a baked edible bread product made from flour

Wamúskè ukédi /wä-mü"-skā ü-kā'-thē/ *n.*, biscuits, lit., common bread

Wamúskeužì /wä-mü'-skā-ü-zhē'/ *n.*, flour bin, a container in which to keep flour

Waná' /wä-nä'/ *v.*, beg, beg for, ask for something to begin

Waná'áži /wä-noⁿ'-oⁿ'-zhē/ *n.*, deaf, lit., cannot hear

Waná'p'į /wä-noⁿ'-p'ēⁿ/ *n.*, necklace, an ornament of a sort worn around the neck

Waná'xe /wä-noⁿ'-xā/ *n.*, ghost, spirit, phantom, apparition

Waná'xe wačígaxè /wä-noⁿ'-xā wä-chē'-gä-xä'/ *n.*, ghost dance, one of the ritual dances of the Ponca

Wanábde't'agà /wä-noⁿ'-bthā-t'oⁿ-gä'/ *n.*, gluttony, someone who habitually eats too much

Wanádehidè /wä-noⁿ'-dā-hē-dā'/ *n.*, lit., interest from the heart, 1. refers to somebody willing to help others 2. *v.* to take an interest in and help with some worthy cause

Wanádehidè /wä-noⁿ'-dā-hē-dā'/ *adj./n.*, zealous, enthusiastic, 1. a passionate interest, usu. in a personal project one is pursuing 2. concern to aid another person in their human situation

Wanádehidè /wä-noⁿ'-dā-hē-dā'/ *v.*, concern, having a personal effect on from the heart

Wanáduzè /wä-noⁿ'-dü-zā'/ *adj.*, precarious, unstable, insecure, uncertain, unsafe, risky

Wanáduzè /wä-noⁿ'-dü-zā'/ *n.*, nervousness, a psycho/physiological state of feeling uncertain about something that may happen in a precarious situation

Wanágde /wä-nä'-gthā/ *n.*, domestic animals, refers to horses, dogs, cats, and bovines, esp. cows, oxen

Wanágde /wä-nä'-gthā/ *n.*, farm animals, namely cows, horses, pigs, etc.

Wanágdè /wä-nä'-gthā/ *n.*, pet, 1. a pet or household animal kept by a person 2. any domesticated animal, such as farm animals

Wanágde údatè /wä-nä'-gthā ü'-thä-tā'/ *n.*, trough, a feeding box, usu. to hold food or water for domestic animals

Wánakagdè /wä'-noⁿ-kä-gthā'/ *n.*, lamp, electric lights, gas light, etc.

Wanáp'a /wä-noⁿ'-p'ä/ *v.*, fear, to be afraid of something or somebody due to a sense of danger or a threat to secure feelings

Wanáp'ap'à /wä-noⁿ'-p'ä-p'ä'/ *v.*, to be fearful, afraid of a condition or situation

Wanáp'aži /wä-noⁿ'-p'ä-zhē'/ *adj.*, not fearful, not afraid

Wanáp'è /wä-noⁿ'-p'ä'/ *adj.*, afraid, frightened or apprehensive about something

Wanáse /wä-noⁿ'-sä/ *v.*, harvest, 1. reap, gather 2. to harvest game

Wanáše /wä-noⁿ'-shä/ *n.*, police, law enforcement, highway patrolman, military soldier

Wanásedè /wä-noⁿ'-sä-thā/ *n./v.*, harvesting, 1. the ~ or gathering of crops 2. ~ game (~ *ugí'p'ì*, the area is full of game)

Wanásede ugíp'ì /wä-noⁿ'-sä-thä ü-gē'-p'ē'/ *n.*, where game is plenteous, 1. usu. refers to places when certain animals returned to feed 2. a proper time to hunt certain animals

Wanáše t'í /wä-noⁿ'-shä t'ē'/ *n.*, police station, a building that houses police officers and cells for law offenders. See also *Ugánahap'azè*, jail.

Wanáše wačígaxè /wä-noⁿ-shā wä-chē'-gä-xā̱/ *n.*, soldier dance, a man's dance, a form of the Heⱡúškà dance

Wanášt'ą /wä-nä'-sht'oⁿ/ *n.*, beggar, one who habitually begs for something

Wanáštą /wä-nä'-shtoⁿ/ *n.*, Gypsy, one of a wandering group of people; *wanášt'ą*, beggars

Wanáxąxà /wä-nä'-xoⁿ-xoⁿ/ *n.*, lightning bug, firefly, a winged beetle of the family Lampyridae

Wanáxde /wä-noⁿ-xthā/ *adv.*, *archaic*, quickly, hurriedly (go now and return ~)

Wanáxdè /wä-noⁿ-xthā/ *v.*, *archaic*, hasten, rush; connotes making haste to a specific place and returning at once

Wánaxdè /wä-noⁿ-xthā/ *v.*, hide, hiding; *á'binąxdè*, hide, hiding a thing under something; *á'nąxdè*, hide, conceal, to hide something; *á'kinąxdè*, hiding; *í'kina'xdè*, hide, to hide oneself; *wénąxdè*, to hide themselves or something from us or them

Wanáxe /wä-nä'-xā/ *n.*, grains of corn cooked on a griddle, parched corn, usu. made from fresh-picked corn (A food staple for travelers.)

Wanáẑudè /wä-noⁿ-zhü-thā/ *n.*, combine, a machine that harvests grain crops

Wanáẑudè /wä-noⁿ-zhü-thā/ *v.*, thrash (thresh), to separate seeds from husks and straw

Wani'e /wä-nē'-ā/ *v.*, 1. hurt, to feel pain, ache, to be sore 2. *n.*, something that hurts or is emotionally painful

Waníde /wä-nē'-dā/ *n.*, gravy, the juices that come from cooking meats thickened with flour

Waníde /wä-nē'-thā/ *n.*, healer, 1. healer, usu. refers to Jesus, the Son of God 2. the Savior

Waníde /wä-nē'-thā/ *n.*, Savior, redeemer, the Son of God who saves or rescues one from unethical, unruly, corrupted living when one embraces the biblical truths of righteousness and establishes a standard of decency and honesty

Wanie íbahąžì /wä-nē'-ā ē'-bä-hoⁿ-zhēⁿ/ *adj.*, unknowing and unfeeling of a situation in which one does not know that he/she is unliked or unwanted in a group, or being oblivious to that condition

Wanít'à /wä-nē'-t'ä/ *n.*, animal, monster or creature

Wanít'a hà /wä-nē'-t'ä hä/ *n.*, pelt, the skin and fur of any animal

Wanít'a wáxa /wä-nē'-t'ä wä'-xä/ *n.*, African lion, *Panthera leo*, a large cat that has a yellow coat; the male members have a shaggy mane that is often referred to by the Ponca as *p'át'a hį́ škubè*, thick haired in the front

Waníte /wä-nē'-tä/ *adj.*, stingy, refers to somebody who doesn't give or spend and is not generous

Wap'áde /wä-p'ä'-dā/ *n.*, surgery, a medical procedure for operating or making an incision into the body for treating an injury or removing a disease

Wap'áde /wä-p'ä'-dā/ *v.*, butchering, cutting up or butchering the carcass of an animal

Wap'í' /wä-p'ē'/ *n.*, cache, store, reserve, collection

Wapúgahadà /wä-pü'-gä-hä-dä/ *n.*, burrowing owl, a small owl that lives in open landscapes such as open ranges, prairies, and farmlands and usu. makes its nests in prairie dog burrows and other burrows

Wás'pažì /wä's-pä-zhē'/ *v.*, misbehave, to behave inappropriately, esp. being naughty, bad, acting up

Wasábe /wä-sä'-bä/ *n.*, black bear, a black bear native to North America (*Ursus americanus*)

Wašábe /wä-shä'-bä/ *n.*, the Wašábe clan of the Ponca people, lit., old dark buffalo

Wašą́ge /wä-shoⁿ'-gä/ *n.*, corn pudding, made with ground, dehydrated corn

Wasé't'u' /wä-sä'-t'ü/ *n.*, blue clay, deposits composed of phyllosilicate minerals containing water in a mineral content in the soil that can cause clay to be various colors (The Ponca found this clay along the Missouri River.)

Wašé'xt'ì /wä-shä'-xt'ē/ *adj.*, ample, plenty, a lot, more than enough, usu. refers to the amount of food

Wasé'židè /wä-sä'-zhē-dä'/ *n.*, mescal bean, 1. a red-berry-producing tree found in the southern dry, arid lands; the berries were used as decorative beads on bandoliers 2. decorations made from the mescal bean, usu. hardened by heat

Wasé'židè /wä-sä'-zhē-dä'/ *n.*, red ocher, a reddish iron oxide

Waséką /wä-sä'-koⁿ/ *adj.*, spicy, peppery, refers to food or drink

Waséką /wä-sä'-koⁿ/ *adj.*, swift, fast, rapid

Waséką /wä-sä'-koⁿ/ *v.*, speed, to move faster with the use of the feet, as in driving some sort of vehicle or conveyance

Wasésą /wä-sä'-soⁿ/ *n.*, 1. ocher, a reddish or yellowish earthen iron oxide 2. clay 3. any earthen mixture or man-made materials prepared to create and construct various things, such as porcelain, children's toys, statues

Wasésą /wä-sä'-soⁿ/ *n.*, clay, porcelain, plastics, a wet, fine ground rock with other minerals that becomes solid when dry; also refers to other plastics, porcelain, ceramics, plaster, etc.

Wašéxtì /wä-shä'-xtē/ *adj.*, plentiful, abundant, much of, bountiful

Waší' /wä-shē'/ *n.*, servant, a helper not by force but by social standards, namely, among the Ponca people, to place oneself in a position of servitude in somebody's household where one is given shelter as a temporary guest; *archaic*, in an ancient period, an older child without parents might have been taken in by a household to live as one of their own children and might have served by hunting, planting, cutting wood, and carrying water

Wašį́ /wä-shēⁿ'/ *n.*, bacon, the meat from the back and sides of a hog

Wasí'síge /wä-sē'-sē'-gä/ *adj.*, energetic, lively, vigorous, active

Wašį́'užé'gdą /wä-sheⁿ'-ü-zhä'-gthoⁿ'/ *n.*, frybread, lit., cooked in fat (The earlier term was *umásnè*, to cut into.)

Wašíádi /wä-shē'-ä'-thē/ *n.*, helper, usu. one who helps at the direction of another

Wašínaxudè /wä-shē'-nä-xü-dä'/ *n.*, cracklings, pig rinds, pieces of rendered fried pork meat and skin

Wašką́ /wä-shkoⁿ'/ *v.*, strive, to try very hard to do or achieve something; *awáškà*, I tried hard; *wadáškà*, you tried hard; *wašką́i*, he/she/they tried hard

Wašką́ /wä-shkoⁿ'/ *v.*, persevere, maintain and persist in the task undertaken in spite of hardships and adversities

Wašką́'t'ągà /wä-shkoⁿ'-t'oⁿ-gä'/ *adj.*, muscular, being physically strong

Wašką́ dįgè /wä-shkoⁿ' thēⁿ-gä'/ *adj.*, weak, physically weak, a person who is physically weak or does not have the muscle power to accomplish a task

Wašką́t'ągà /wä-shkoⁿ'-t'oⁿ-gä'/ *adj.*, strong, physically strong and powerful, muscular

Wašką́xti /wä-shkoⁿ'-xtē/ *n.*, endurance, the ability to have strength or the power to endure hardship of any type or to complete a task

Waskíde /wä-skē'-thä/ *n.*, sweets, something that is sugary or that contains sugar, as in candies, cookies, pastries

Wašná' /wä-shnä'/ *n.*, belly, abdomen

Wašná't'ągà /wä-shnä'-t'oⁿ-gä/ *adj.*, big belly

Wasní'de /wä-snē'-dā/ *v.*, slow, lit., slow, late, to be late or overdue

Wašʃ't'amà /wä-shʃ-t'ä-mä/ *n.*, helpers, his/her/their helpers, hired workers or assistants (In Christian theology Wak'ą́da ~ refers to the angels of God.)

Wašt'agè /wä-sht'ä-gä/ *adj.*, easygoing, 1. describes a psychological behavioral pattern that is normal for a person who is gentle and calm or has a moderate temperament 2. refers to animals that have a moderate temperament, unlike, e.g., a spirited horse

Wašt'áge /wä-sht'ä'-gä/ *adj.*, tame, domesticated, docile, meek

Wašúše /wä-shü'-shä/ *adj.*, heroism, beyond bravery, fearlessness, great courage, devil-may-care acts

Wat'é /wä-t'ā'/ *n.*, a geographic location (probably near Genoa, Nebraska) where wild game, fruit, and other foodstuffs were plenteous and gathering food was good

Wat'ę́' /wä-t'āⁿ'/ *n.*, dead, the death of a person

Wat'ę́'de /wä-t'āⁿ'-thä/ *v.*, murder, to murder; taking the life of another person

Wat'ę́de /wä-t'āⁿ'-thä/ *v.*, killing, 1. to kill somebody, murder, take life 2. *n.*, refers to a person who kills

Wat'ę́ užá /wä-t'āⁿ' ü-zhoⁿ'/ *n.*, burial casket

Wat'úgdą /wä-t'ü'-gthoⁿ/ *n.*, carrier, any person, animal, or vehicle that carries cargo

Wat'úgdà /wä-t'ü'-gthoⁿ'/ *v.*, haul, to transport something in a vehicle

Watá' /wä-toⁿ'/ *n.*, pumpkin

Watá hášugà /wä-toⁿ' hä'-shü-gä/ *n.*, squash, an edible, round, thick-skinned squash, genus *Cucurbita*

Watá múxa /wä-toⁿ' mü'-xä/ *n.*, squash, straight-necked yellow squash, *Cucurbita pepo* var. *recticollis*

Watá níde'bazù /wä-toⁿ' nē'-dä-bä-zü/ *n.*, squash, an edible striped squash with a long neck, genus *Cucurbita*

Watą́zi /wä-toⁿ'-zē/ *n.*, corn, the grain of corn

Watą́zi'wažégdą̀ /wä-toⁿ'-zē wä-zhä'-gthoⁿ/ *n.*, cornbread

Watą́zinát'ušì /wä-toⁿ'-zē-nä'-t'ü-shē/ *n.*, popcorn, kernels of corn that pop open when heated

Watą́zi skídè /wä-toⁿ'-zē skē'-thä/ *n.*, sweet corn

Waté' /wä-tä'/ *n.*, 1. bounteous, *archaic*, abundant, overflowing, usu. refers to abundance of game, fruit, edible plants 2. the Elkhorn River in Nebraska

Waté' /wä-tä'/ *n.*, dress, a ladies' garment; *waté ukédį*, a homemade Native American dress; *wáxe waú waté*, white woman dress, refers to a store-bought dress

Waté'čéškà /wä-tä'-chä'-shkä/ *n.*, skirt, a ladies' outergarment, a skirt of any length or a half skirt

Waté'mątè /wä-tä'-moⁿ-tä/ *n.*, underskirt, a ladies' undergarment, slip

Watézeugdà̀ /wä-tä'-zä-ü-gthoⁿ/ *adj.*, pregnant, with child, expecting a baby

Waú' /wä-ü'/ *n.*, 1. woman, female 2. girlfriend (In modern times the term is used to denote some man's girlfriend.)

Waú'íye /wä-ü'-ē'-yä/ *n.*, lawyer, lit., woman talk, attorney (common pronounciation of the word is *waúwe* /wäü'-wä/)

Waú digè /wä-ü' thē-gä/ *n.*, bachelor, a single, unattached, man without a woman

Waú žįgá /wä-ü' zhēⁿ-gä/ *n.*, lit., little woman, old woman, a term of respect; venerable

Wáwaą̀ /wä'-wä-oⁿ/ *n.*, the ceremonial Pipe Dance

Wawé'bahą /wä-wā'-bä-hoⁿ'/ *n.*, witness, somebody who gives information about seeing or hearing something, usu. refers to legal matters

Wawé'giniè /wä-wā'-gē-nē-ā'/ *n.*, envy; resentfulness of another's advantages, possessions, or accomplishments (The Ponca term encompasses a dislike or hatred for one's status, but a kind of hatred toward the good of one's values. Individuals may hold these values as a high standard that they themselves have not yet achieved.)

Wawé'xaxà /wä-wā'-xä-xä'/ *v.*, ridicule, to deride, mock, or taunt somebody with laughter in their absence (This is considered to be bad behavior by the Ponca people.)

Wawédąbè /wä-wā'-doⁿ-bä'/ *v.*, show off, flaunt, to display something somebody thinks is worthy of showing in a flagrant way, such as a piece of jewelry, clothing, a car

Wawéəšt'aži /wä-wā'-ə-sht'ä-zhē/ *adj.*, immodest, no proper social reserve, has no modesty

Wawéət'adè /wä-wā'-ə-t'ä-thā'/ *n.*, jealousy, an inner, resentful emotional reaction to some people who have something that one believes should be one's own; *udút'adè*, being resentful toward a person who is enjoying his/her accomplishments, with thoughts that it should belong to the other person even though he/she did nothing to deserve such

Wawégaskądè /wä-wā'-gä-skoⁿ-thā'/ *v.*, imitate, attempting to do or act as somebody or to do what a group of people in their circle do

Waweíbahą /wä-wāē'-bä-hoⁿ'/ *n.*, eyewitness, one who has seen or observed an occurrence

Wawék'a /wä-wā'-k'ä/ *v.*, *3rd pers. sing.*, help, asking for help (*éi ~ atí*, he/she/it came asking for ~)

Wawékidè /wä-wā'-kē-thā'/ *v./n.*, discover, to find something for oneself, to find something unexpected and surprisingly delightful; discovery, the process of finding a thing

Wawémąxè /wä-wā'-moⁿ-xä'/ *v./n.*, questioned, interrogation, to get information concerning some matter, interview

Wawémąxè /wä-wā'-moⁿ-xä'/ *v.*, interrogate, question, interview, cross-examine, usu. refers to court proceedings

Wawéštaži /wä-wā'-shtä-zhē'/ *adj.*, unashamed, unembarrassed, blatant, ~ for it/them/anyone

Wawét'adè /wä-wā'-t'ä-thā'/ *v.*, resent, dislike, have bitter (borderline hateful) feelings toward a person or persons who have or accomplished something one has not; *udút'adè*, resentful or disliking somebody because he/she possesses something one does not have or because he/she has accomplished something one has not (The term is closely related to envy.) See *Wawé'giniè*, envy.

Wawét'ąį /wä-wā'-t'oⁿ-ēⁿ'/ *v.*, revealed, ~ to us specifically; *įwat'ąi*, ~ to me; *díwat'ąi*, ~ to you; *gíwat'ąi*, ~ to him/her/them; *wéwat'ąi*, it is clear to us or we understand the revelation of something shown

Wawík'a /wä-wē'-k'ä/ *v.*, *1st pers. sing.*, help, asking someone for help (~ *atí*, I come asking you for ~)

Wawiúxa /wä-wēü'-xä/ *v.*, deception, to do or show something to mislead, trick, hoodwink

Waxą'ha /wä-xoⁿ'-hä/ *n.*, husk, husk of corn

Waxága t'ągà /wä-xä'-gä t'oⁿ-gä'/ *n.*, cocklebur, a plant with thorny, long and slender spines

Waxága žįgà /wä-xä'-gä zhēⁿ-gä'/ *n.*, sandbur,

stickered weeds that grow in sandy soil, genus *Cenchrus*

Waxaí /wä-xäē'/ *v., past t.*, buried, burying the remains of several people

Waxáxa /wä-xoⁿ-xoⁿ/ *adj.*, sickly, always ailing, always sickly or hurting somewhere

Waxdá /wä-xthä'/ *n.*, milkweed, a flowering plant that secretes a milky substance

Waxdá' /wä-xthä'/ *n.*, cabbage, a leafy green vegetable

Waxdéxde /wä-xthä'-xthä/ *n.*, staff, an ornamented, feathered staff carried by a man of honor bestowing honors upon worthy recipients

Waxdí' /wä-xthē'/ *adj.*, jittery, on edge and nervous, or extremely nervous

Wáxe /wä'-xä/ *n.*, Creator, God, the Creator of the world and the universe (The Ponca believed in monotheism, the existence of one god. The attributes of the Creator, Wak'áda, were considered to be a mystery but knowable. As early as ca. 1870, a Ponca woman used the term *Wak'áda* in regard to her husband, who pursued the things of the Creator. She stated, "Nú wiwít'a, Wak'áda wádixè štiwà, ak'ík'abdà." [Even though my husband pursues the things of mystery, I want him back.] Though the term was used in that regard during that period, the term *Wak'áda* is used today in place of *Wáxe*.)

Waxé' /wä-xä'/ *v.*, bury, 1. lay to rest, inter 2. put in the ground

Wáxe ábitadè /wä'-xä ä'-bē-toⁿ-thä/ *n.*, a half-breed Native American who takes on the characteristics of white people (The term was predominantly used until ca. 1950s.)

Wáxegaxdà /wä'-xä-gä-xthoⁿ/ *n.*, conestoga, Conestoga wagon, prairie schooner, a large wagon covered with white canvas used by Caucasian people traveling west over Indian country in the nineteenth century

Wáxe hebè /wä'-xä hä-bä'/ *n.*, a designation for Ponca tribal members who are nonclan members of Caucasian descent (The Ponca have a patrilineal clanship system.)

Wáxe íye p'iáži /wä'-xä ē'-yä p'ē-ä'-zhē/ *v.*, cuss, lit., bad white man words, curse, swear

Waxíha /wä-xēⁿ'-hä/ *n.*, cloth, 1. textiles, fabric, material 2. *archaic* paper

Waxíha p'eži /wä-xēⁿ-hä p'ä-zhē/ *n.*, rag, an old piece of cloth

Waxíhaskà /wä-xēⁿ'-hä-skä/ *n.*, handkerchief, usu. a small piece of cloth for personal use, such as wiping one's hands or blowing one's nose (The Ponca refer to it as *p'áxdi íbikà*, snot wipe.)

Waxíha skà wà /wä-xēⁿ'-hä skä' wä-ēⁿ'/ *n.*, white blanket (The Ponca Sun dancers wore a white buckskin robe or wraparound from the waist to the ankles. Following contact with whites and trade goods, a white cloth sheet was worn, as shown in photographs from the late nineteenth to the early twentieth centuries.)

Waxp'ádi /wä-xp'ä'-thēⁿ/ *adj.*, destitute, impoverished, needy, penniless

Waxp'ádi k'igáxe /wäx-p'ä'-thēⁿ k'ē-gä'-xä/ *adj.*, apologetic, lit., causing oneself to feel sorrow or pity over something, usu. precipitated by some action or act, followed by a humbling act of compassion

Waxt'á hì /wä-xt'ä' hē'/ *n.*, fruit tree, any fruit-bearing tree

Waxt'á uxp'é /wäx-t'ä' ü-xp'ä'/ *n.*, vase, an open container used to hold flowers, usu. made of decorated glass or ceramics

Waxt'á' /wä-xt'ä'/ (**Wax'já'** /wäx-jä'/) *n.*, flowers, bouquet of flowers, any kind of flower

Waxt'á' /wä-xt'ä'/ *n.*, fruit, usu. refers to edible fruits from plants and trees, such as apples and oranges

Waxt'á' snedè /wä-xt'ä' snä-dā/ *n.*, banana, lit., long fruit, a slightly curved, edible, creamy, sweet, soft-fleshed fruit with a yellow skin; *waxt'á' snedè hí*, banana tree

Waxt'á užì /wä-xt'ä' ü-zhē/ *n.*, basket, a container for flowers or fruit

Waxt'áwį /wäx-t'ä'-wēⁿ/ *n.*, the Ojibwa Tribe of Native Americans (The term also applies to the Chippewa and Cree Nations of Native Americans and Canadian Natives.)

Waxúbe /wä-xü'-bä/ *adj.*, sacred, 1. *n.*, something sacred or holy 2. *n.*, refers to religious relics and certain practices in religious activities

Waxúbe gáxe /wä-xü'-bä gä'-xä/ *v.*, consecrate, to make something holy or sacred

Waxúbe užą́ge /wä-xü'-bä ü-zhoⁿ'-gä/ *n.*, *archaic*, holy way, an ancient term designating a way of life considered to be sacred, refers to 1. a person who led in spiritual ceremonials and who handled sacred paraphernalia and rites 2. living always in a compassionate, considerate, kindly manner that was prescribed by God 3. now applied to all Christian precepts

Wažá' /wä-zhä'/ *v.*, disbelieve, question, refers to questioning the facts or knowledge of something; *wéža*, to be skeptical or to question somebody's story

Wazáni /wä-zä'-nē/ *pron.*, everyone, relates specifically to every person present in a group to which one speaks

Wažáštą /wä-zhä'-shtoⁿ/ *v.*, doubts, somebody who habitually and always doubts others on any subject

Wažáže /wä-zhä'-zhä/ *n.*, the Osage Tribe of Native Americans

Wažážè /wä-zhä'-zhä/ *n.*, the Wažážè (Osage) clan of the Ponca people

Wažé'dįgè /wä-zhä'-thēⁿ-gä/ *adj.*, thankless, ungrateful, refers to somebody who shows no gratitude

Wazéde /wä-zā'-thä/ *n.*, doctor, orig. a Ponca man or woman who used natural medicines and remedies to effect cures for various illnesses, now a doctor, physician, doctor of medicine; *zéde*, *v.*, to doctor, treat

Wazéde waù' /wä-zā'-thä wä-ü'/ *n.*, nurse, a healthcare professional who, along with others, is responsible for the treatment and recovery of patients

Wazéde waù' t'iúnąžį /wä-zā'-thä wä-ü' t'ēü'-noⁿ-zhēⁿ'/ *n.*, nurses' station, that part of the hospital where medical personnel, esp. nurses, keep records of treatment, medicines and the progress of patients

Wažédįgè /wä-zhä'-thēⁿ-gä/ *adj.*, ungrateful, a person being unappreciative or thankless

Wažégdą uxp'é' /wä-zhä'-gthoⁿ ü-xp'ä'/ *n.*, baking pan, lit., pan for baking, for cooking breads, cakes, and other foods in an oven

Wazék'igdixè /wä-zā'-k'ē-gthē-xä/ *n.*, medical treatment, seeking medical aid from medical practitioners; *wazék'iđè*, *v.*, to treat oneself for some sickness, as in taking aspirin for a headache

Wažį́' /wä-zhēⁿ'/ *n.*, intelligence, psyche, mentality, awareness

Wažį́'áškà /wä-zhēⁿ'-ä'-shkä/ *adj.*, quick tempered, touchy, liable to become angry

Waží'áška /wä-zhēⁿ'-ä'-shkä/ *v.*, anger, lit., on the edge of anger, ready to express something with anger

Waží'de /wä-zhē'-dä/ *n.*, tomato, a round, red vegetable that can be eaten raw or cooked

Wažį́'íbahą /wä-zhēⁿ'-ē'-bä-hoⁿ'/ *n.*, psychologist, lit., one who knows the mind, one who studies and evaluates the behavior of people

Wažį́'k'udè /wä-zhēⁿ-k'ü-thā'/ *n./v.*, anger, to become quickly angered

Wažį́'kudè /wä-zhēⁿ'-kü-thā'/ *adv.*, easily incensed, 1. short-tempered 2. easily upset 3. quick to make a judgment

Wažį́'p'iáži /wä-zhēⁿ'-p'ē-ä'-zhē'/ *v.*, anger, lit., bad thoughts, fury, indignation

Wažį́'t'ù /wä-zhēⁿ'-t'ü'/ *n.*, blue bird, lit., blue anger, 1. refers to the bluejay 2. proper name in the Níkapášnà clan of the Ponca people

Wažį́'xídadì /wä-zhēⁿ'-xē'-dä-thē'/ *n.*, uncertainty, feeling of uncertainty, having reservations

Wazí'zi'jè /wä-zē'-zē-jā'/ *n.*, sparrow, a common small bird of the family Passeridae

Wažíbe /wä-zhē'-bā/ *n.*, marrow, lit., that of the leg, the tissue that is found in the interior of bones (Following the bison hunt the leg bone of the animal was roasted on live coals for the marrow.)

Wažįde /wä-zhēⁿ'-dā/ *n.*, buffalo berry, also called Nebraska currant, *Shepherdia argentea*, of the oleaster family, Elaeagnaceae

Wažį́ga /wä-zhēⁿ'-gä/ *n.*, bird, 1. any kind of fowl 2. a proper male name in the Hísadà clan of the the Ponca people

Wažį́ga'žìde /wä-zhēⁿ'-gä-zhē'-dā/ *n.*, chicken, lit., red bird, probably the breed Rhode Island Red

Wažį́ga'žìde út'i /wä-zhēⁿ'-gä-zhē'-dā ü'-t'ē/ *n.*, chicken coop, lit., chicken coop, a building where hens are kept to lay eggs in nest boxes

Wažį́ga íkidè /wä-zhēⁿ-gä ē'-kē-dā'/ *n.*, slingshot, lit., bird shooter, also called bean shooter, a homemade object used to shoot small projectiles, usu. rocks

Wažį́ga migà /wä-zhēⁿ'-gä mē-gä'/ *n.*, hen, refers to female chickens but may be applied to other poultry or game birds

Wažį́ga nugà /wä-zhēⁿ'-gä nü-gä'/ *n.*, rooster, usu. refers to chickens but may refer to other male birds

Wažį́gap'à /wä-zhē'-gä-p'ä'/ *n.*, pileated woodpecker, 1. a large North American woodpecker, *Dryocopus pileatus* 2. the name (Birdhead) of one of the last Northern Ponca Indian doctors

Wažį́ga ugdį̀ /wä-zhēⁿ'-gä ü-gthēⁿ'/ *n.*, aviary, a place or enclosure for birds, a coop, a birdcage

Wažį́gaúmą /wä-zhēⁿ'-gäü-moⁿ/ *n.*, 1. where the fowls of the air dwell 2. proper male name in the Đíxidą̀ clan of the Ponca people

Wažį́ga wadizè /wä-zhēⁿ'-gä wä-thē-zä'/ *n.*, Cooper's hawk, lit., gets chickens, commonly known as "chicken hawk," of the family Accipitridae, species *accipter* (Unofficially, there are three species of hawks called "chicken hawks": the Cooper's hawk is called a quail hawk, while the sharp-shinned hawk and the red-tailed hawk are called chicken hawks. Red-tailed hawks may hunt for free-range poultry more often.)

Wažį́ga žìde /wä-zhēⁿ'-gä zhē'-dā/ *n.*, cardinal, lit., red bird, passerine bird in the family Cardinalidae

Wažį́skà /wä-zhēⁿ'-skä'/ *adj./n.*, intelligent, lit., clear mind, 1. a person who is intellectual 2. a proper male name in the Đíxidą̀ clan of the Ponca people

Wažį́šte /wä-zhēⁿ'-shtä/ *v.*, brood, to be dejected, to feel self-pity, pout, to express sulky unhappiness about something

Wažį́xįdadì /wä-zhēⁿ'-xēⁿ'-dä-thē'/ *adj./n.*, doubtful, a state of being uncertain or unsure of a situation

Wažút'ą̀dè /wä-zhü'-t'oⁿ-thā'/ *n.*, produce, crops (vegetables, fruit, and grain) that are harvested, agricultural produce; *đižút'ą,* raising crops

Wažútą̀dè /wä-zhü'-toⁿ-thā'/ *n.*, produce, crops harvested, as in garden or farm products

Wé'basą̀dà /wā'-bä-soⁿ-thā'/ *n.*, spatula, a flat kitchen utensil; *wét'a íbisą̀dà,* egg turner

Wé'baxap'ì /wā'-bä-xä-p'ē'/ *n.*, fork, 1. an eating utensil 2. a pitchfork, a farming implement used for lifting hay

Wé'dabđì /wā'-thä-bthē'/ *adj.*, third, the third thing in a row of items or the third person or group of people coming in succession

Wé'dą̀žì /wā'-thä-zhē'/ *adj.*, blind, sightless; *n.*, refers to one who is blind

Wé'dihą̀ /wā'-the-hoⁿ'/ *n.*, block and tackle, a device using at least two pulleys with a rope to lift heavy loads

Wé'dubà /wā'-dü-bä'/ *adj.*, fourth, the fourth thing in a row of items or the fourth person or group of people coming in succession

Wé'e' /wā'-ā/ *n.*, hoe, orig. bison scapula used for hoeing; a metal garden implement

Wé'gą̀zè /wā'-goⁿ-zā'/ *n.*, measure, a system for determining the size, length, or extent of something, such as feet, yards, miles, pounds, bushels, acres

Wé'gdebą̀ /wā'-gthä-boⁿ'/ *adj.*, tenth, the tenth thing in a row of items or the tenth person or group of people coming in succession

Wé'gđì /wā'-gthē'/ *n.*, lard, 1. lard, a product from pig fat, also refers to canola oil (rapeseed [*brassica napus*] oil), vegetable oil 2. gasoline 3. oil

Wé'gđì't'ą̀wągđą̀ /wā'-gthē'-t'oⁿ-woⁿ-gthoⁿ'/ *n.*, Tulsa, Oklahoma, lit., oil town

Wé'gidè /wā'-gē-thā'/ *v.*, to eat at someone else's home; *n.*, a person who visits someone and stays until they are invited to eat

Wé'giną̀hì /wā'-gē-noⁿ-hē'/ *v., 3rd pers. sing.,* approve or sanction, approves it for them

Wé'į /wā'-ēⁿ/ *n.*, harness, usu. refers to a set of organized straps to harness horses and other animals in order to control something, as in pulling a wagon

Wé'į /wā'-ēⁿ/ *pron./v., 3rd pers. sing.,* he/she/ it carried us

Wé'i' /wā'-ē'/ *v., 3rd pers. sing.,* returned, giving back, to send back or restore something (~ *ahì,* he/she/it gave it back to us)

Wé'magixè /wā'-mä-gē-xā'/ *n.*, file, a tool for smoothing surfaces such as metal and wood

Wé'mąxè /wā'-moⁿ-xā'/ *v./n.*, query, question, inquiry, to ask a question

Wé'mubđazè /wā'-mü-bthä-zā'/ *n.*, bomb, an explosive device, such as dynamite, wartime explosives

Wé'ną̀bà /wā'-noⁿ-bä'/ *adj.*, second, a second thing in a row of items or the second person or group of people coming in succession

Wé'ną̀bđè /wā'-noⁿ-bthā'/ *n.*, pharynx, part of the throat that allows swallowed foods to pass down to the digestive system and allows air into the respiratory system

Wé'nądè /wā'-noⁿ-dā'/ *adj.*, full, stuffed, gorged, ate to the limit

Wé'ną̀hì /wā'-noⁿ-hēⁿ'/ *v.*, approve, endorse, agree, somebody approves with us

Wé'ną̀kihą̀ /wā'-noⁿ-kē-hoⁿ'/ *n.*, lever, a rigid bar or shaft that is placed on a fulcrum to lift or move heavy objects

Wé'ną̀xdè /wā'-noⁿ-xthä'/ *v.*, hidden from us, to hide something (*mázeskàte ~ itéđa bikè,* the money was ~)

Wé'ną̀žudè /wā'-noⁿ-zhü-thä'/ *n., archaic,* threshing machine (Now the term refers to the modern combine, a machine that separates seeds from husks and straw.)

Wé'nudąhągà /wā'-nü-doⁿ-hoⁿ-gä'/ *n.*, manager, director, supervisor, boss (A new term at the beginning of the twentieth century that is a derivative of the term for war leader, *nudáhągà*.)

Wé'p'é'nąbà /wā-p'ā'-noⁿ-bä'/ (**Wé'p'é'dąbà** /wā-p'ā'-thoⁿ-bä'/) *adj.*, seventh, the seventh thing in a row of items or the seventh person or group of people coming in succession

Wé'p'edábdį /wā'-p'ā-thä'-bthēⁿ/ *n.*, eighth, the eighth thing in a row of items or the eighth person or group of people coming in succession

Wé'sąka' /wā'-soⁿ-kä/ *n.*, ninth, the ninth thing in a row of items or the ninth person or group of people coming in succession

Wé'šap'è /wā'-shä-p'ā'/ *adj.*, sixth, the sixth thing in a row of items or the sixth person or group of people coming in succession

Wé'tį /wā'-tēⁿ/ *n.*, club, any kind of club used as a weapon, usu. a heavy stick, a war club

Wé'udá /wā-ü-thä'/ *n.*, something of any media that gives information or instructions to do something

Wé'užawà /wā'-ü-zhä-wä'/ *adj.*, joyful, to make something joyful

Wé'žahè /wā'-zhä-hä'/ *n.*, something to stab with, something to thrust forward with

Weádaskabè sábe /wā-ä'-thä-skä-bä' sä'-bä/ *n.*, asphalt, usu. used for surfacing roads; other uses include roofing shingles

Weának'ągdè ní /wā-ä'-nä-k'oⁿ-gthä' nē'/ *n.*, kerosene, lamp oil, etc.

Weánakągdè ugdè /wā-ä'-nä-koⁿ-gthä' ü-gthä'/ *n.*, wick, the spun or braided cotton fibers that draw up oil to burn in an oil lamp or candle

Wébabexį /wā'-bä-bä-xēⁿ/ *n.*, broom, a brush made of bristles and used to sweep floors and other surfaces, indoors or outdoors

Wébamą̀ /wā'-bä-moⁿ/ *n.*, a blunt pole tool for softening the hides of animals

Wébasadedè /wā'-bä-sä-dä-thä'/ *n.*, iron, a heated metal instrument used for pressing clothes

Wébasè /wā'-bä-sä'/ *n.*, saw, a tool to cut various materials, such as metal, plastics, wood

Wébasihì /wā'-bä-sē-hē'/ *n.*, cleaner, 1. any device used to clean something, such as a brush, sponge, or cloth; any liquid cleansing substance, soap 2. vacuum cleaner, mop, broom

Wébasną̀ /wā'-bä-snoⁿ/ *n.*, skewer, a stick or piece of metal used to roast meat or vegetables over a fire

Wébaù' /wā'-bä-ü'/ *n.*, scraper, an ancient Ponca tool for removing hair from the skin of bison, elk, deer, and other large mammals; a tool composed of an elkhorn handle and flint adz

Wébaudè /wā'-bä-ü-dä'/ *n.*, drill, a tool for drilling holes into or through various materials; now brace and bit

Wébaxù /wā'-bä-xü'/ *n.*, pen, pencil, or any writing instrument

Wébaxù udá /wā'-bä-xü' ü-thoⁿ'/ *v.*, sign, lit., to hold a writing instrument, to write one's signature, to make a "mark" on a document

Wébetą̀ /wā'-bä-toⁿ'/ *v.*, go around, to avoid by going around persons or things or circumnavigating the same

Wébiškì /wā'-bē-shkē'/ *n.*, washboard, a flat board with a metal corrugated surface used to clean and remove soil from clothing and other cloth products

Wédadè /wā'-dä-thä'/ *v.*, birth, giving birth

Wédaginąhì /wā'-thä-gē-noⁿ-hē'/ *v.*, *2nd pers. pl.*, permit, you giving permission

Wédawa'židè /wā'-thä-wä-zhē-dä'/ *n.*, penny, one cent

Wedázi /wā-dä'-zhē/ *pron.*, another way, a different direction (~ *adái*, he went ~)

Wedázi /wā-dä'-zhē/ *n.*, off course, a different direction, as in leaving the route and going in another direction

Wéde /wā'-thä/ *adj.*, *1st pers. pl.*, happy, we're happy, we are delighted, joyful, glad

Wé'de /wā'-thä/ *n./v.*, seeking, look for, usu. used in reference to finding appropriate wood or kindling for cooking or warming a dwelling

Wedéną /wā-dä'-noⁿ/ *n.*, half, one part of two equal parts, usu. refers to liquid

Wedénąskà /wā-dä'-noⁿ-skä'/ *adv.*, equally, equal share, same amount to each

Wedéšíte /wā-thä'-shē'-tä/ *v.*, help, you came to help when we needed it

Wedéta /wā-thä'-toⁿ/ *adv.*, this far, as when somebody or something came close to or close by in an approximate measurement from one's standpoint

Wedéta /wā-thä'-toⁿ/ *adv.*, that far from there to here, a comparative estimate of distance between known points of travel

Wedéta /wā-dä'-toⁿ/ *adv.*, this far, about halfway, more or less, in distance

Wedéta /wā-dä'-toⁿ/ *n.*, half, one part of two equal parts, 1. refers to the length of something solid 2. relative to distance, halfway to

Wédibdì /wā'-thē-bthē'/ *n.*, plow, an implement to turn the soil

Wédibexì /wā'-thēⁿ-bā-xēⁿ'/ *n.*, rake, a gardening tool used to gather grass or leaves and smooth soil in a garden; *v.*, *dibéxi*, the act of raking

Wédihà /wā'-thē-hoⁿ/ *adj.*, weigh or weight (~ *te ánqnià?*, how much do you weigh?)

Wédihà' /wā'-thē-hoⁿ/ *n.*, scale, a device to measure the weight of something

Wédihidè /wā'-thē-hē-dä/ *n.*, machine, mechanism, engine, contraption

Wédihidè /wā'-thē-hē-dä/ *n.*, tools, orig. something made to be used for some specific manual work, such as a hoe (*wé'e*) for gardening; now metal tools, motorized equipment, such as a forklift, earth mover, etc.

Wédihidè t'ągà /wā'-thē-hē-dä t'oⁿ-gä'/ *n.*, heavy equipment, bulldozer, earth mover, crane

Wédimà /wā'-thē-moⁿ'/ *n.*, whetstone, usu. a stone used to sharpen a thing; now a grinder, electric knife sharpener

Wédip'ì /wā'-thē-p'ē'/ *v.*, learned, learned from them

Wédišibè /wā'-thē-shē-bä'/ *n.*, key, lit., to open with, a metal instrument to unlock a door, car, padlock

Wédit'egà /wā'-thē-t'ā-gä'/ *n.*, detergent, liquid or powdered detergent for laundry

Wédit'egà /wā'-thē-t'ā-gä'/ *n.*, soap, a cleansing agent that comes in varied forms, such as bars, flakes, liquid, and granules

Wédit'ubè /wā'-thē-t'ü-bä'/ *n.*, mill, a device that breaks down larger or harder pieces of materials into smaller bits; *archaic*, a term for a hand coffee grinder or machinery for grinding grain

Wédiwì /wā'-thē-wēⁿ'/ *v.*, sell, the transfer of money for something, as in disposing of clothing, food, and other products for money

Wédixdì /wā'-thē-xthē'/ *n.*, brain, that part of the body that houses and governs the spirit of a human, his/her thoughts, intentions, and emotional responses to the world in which he/she lives

Wégasap'ì /wā'-gä-sä-p'ē'/ *n.*, Iron Whip, the principal chief of the Ponca people at the time of their forced removal from their homelands in what is now Nebraska and South Dakota, ca. 1876

Wégasap'ì /wā'-gä-sä-p'ē'/ *n.*, whip, 1. a device to lash at animals to keep them under control 2. proper male name in the Ðíxidǫ clan of the Ponca people

Wégasap'ì /wā'-gä-sä-p'ē'/ *n.*, Whip, principal chief of the Ponca people before their removal to Indian Territory, from the early nineteenth century through ca. 1868

Wégaskǫdè /wā'-gä-skoⁿ-thā'/ *v.*, mimic, to imitate something someone did, usu. to mimic somebody's voice and gestures in a deliberate or exaggerated way to amuse

Wégašt'ǫká' /wā'-gä-sht'oⁿ-kä'/ *v.*, tempt, using something to entice or appeal to somebody or a group of people to act or to say something

Wegáxe /wā-gä'-xā/ *adj./n.*, jesting, 1. a playful act mimicking something someone did seriously, namely, children (*níkašigà akà šį́gažįgàma ~aì, žǫníbut'à ɖizé' mǫɖí, į́déugɖǫ teɖǫdè*, the person pretended [jesting] before the children, when they got candy on Halloween) 2. a jest making a mockery of someone who did not complete or create something right

Wegáxe /wā-gä'-xā/ *adv.*, teasingly, teasing good-naturedly, teasing mischievously

Wégǫzè /wā'-goⁿ-zā/ *n.*, ruler, 1. a measuring device, tape measure, measuring stick 2. the distance from one point to another

Wegáze /wā-goⁿ'-zā/ *v.*, teach, to teach, show, or demonstrate

Wégdàè /wā'-gthä'-ā'/ *v.*, share, share out, one individual giving something to a specific group of people

Wégdaì /wā'-gthä-ē'/ *v.*, distribute, give out, dole out, hand out

Wégdì /wā'-gthē'/ *n.*, 1. oil (petroleum) 2. lard (white pork fat used for cooking) 3. any cooking oil, a blend of vegetable oils

Wégdì /wā'-gthē'/ *n.*, gasoline, petroleum, axle grease, engine oil, cooking oil

Wégdi /wā'-gthē/ *n.*, grease, fat, oil

Wégdisagì /wā'-gthē-sä-gē'/ *n.*, tallow, solid rendered fat of cattle

Wéginǫhì /wā'-gē-noⁿ-hē'/ *v.*, permit, let him/her/them do, to give permission to

Wéhusà /wā'-hü-sä'/ *v.*, to scold

Wék'ǫt'ǫ̀ /wā'-k'oⁿ-t'oⁿ'/ *n.*, string, refers to a strip of material (cord, rope, strap) used for tying up a package or for something like hobbling or tethering a horse

Wék'i'ǫ̀ /wā'-k'ē-oⁿ'/ *n.*, ornaments, 1. something that decorates or adds to something else, usu. refers to the Heɖúškà dancing paraphernalia 2. an assortment of things or objects that go with or are characteristic of something, as in medals on a soldier's uniform

Wék'išnǫ̀ /wā'-k'ē-shnoⁿ'/ *adj.*, thankful, to be thankful; *í'k'išnǫ̀*, to be personally thankful; *wǝ́ǫk'išnǫ̀*, we are personally thankful

Wék'išnǫ'wadè /wā'-k'ē-shnoⁿ-wä-thā'/ *adj./v.*, pleased, feeling satisfied about having done something or owning something

Wék'itè /wā'-k'ē-tā'/ *v., 3rd pers. pl.*, cheat, they cheated them

Wékiǫ̀ /wā'-kē-oⁿ'/ *n.*, dance paraphernalia, earned ornaments ("medals") worn by a Heɖúškà dancer

Wéku /wā'-kü/ *v., 1st pers. pl.*, invite, a call to come, usu. to a home or to some activity

Wémǫxè /wā'-moⁿ-xā/ *v./n.*, query, question, inquiry, to ask a question

Wénǫšè /wā'-noⁿ-shā'/ *v.*, take away, take possession of, 1. take from them, carry away from them 2. take or carry away from us

Wéni /wā'-nē/ *n.*, curer, somebody or something that cures or restores health to a person

Wénudą́hągà /wā̄-nü-doⁿ-hoⁿ-gä/ *n.*, boss, strawboss, team leader, somebody put in charge

Weógašè /wāō-gä-shā/ *v.*, encumber, to burden or hamper someone with something

Weógašè /wāō-gä-shā/ *n.*, inconvenience, somebody pushing somebody or something upon another without consideration

Wép'è /wā-p'ä/ *n.*, waiting, waiting on someone or others; *idágip'è*, waited for his

Wép'iáži /wā-p'ē-ä-zhē/ *n.*, troublemaker, connotes someone or something coming alongside causing unnecessary problems

Wép'iáži /wā-p'ē-ä-zhē/ *adj.*, disruptive, troublemaking, unruly, disturbing

Wépiáži /wā-pē-ä-zhē/ *adj.*, culpable, blameworthy, a person who deserves to be blamed as being wrong, evil, improper, or injurious among a group of people

Wés'à /wā's-ä/ *n.*, snake, 1. a reptile that is long and legless, such as a black snake, bull snake, or rattlesnake 2. a male name in the Wažážè clan among the Ponca people

Wés'à'sábe /wā's-ä-sä-bä/ *n.*, black snake, a nonvenomous snake of the species *colubridae*

Wésat'à /wā-sä-t'oⁿ/ *n.*, fifth, the fifth one; a thing, person, or people that stand(s) fifth in the row or in succession

Wéši /wā-shē/ *n.*, token, usu. an item or items used in a gambling game, 1. the Ponca used carved seeds or bone for counting scores in the "bowl dice game" 2. in the Ponca handgame, the handheld *wéši* are hidden from the guesser

Wéšną /wā-shnoⁿ/ *v.*, *past t.*, pleased, delighted, satisfied

Wéšną'wadè /wā-shnoⁿ-wä-thā/ *adj./v.*, pleased, 1. one who causes someone to feel pleased for gifts given to him/her 2. *n.*, proper female name

Wésnadè /wā-snä-thā/ *n.*, paint, a liquefied substance of different colors that may be applied to any surface; *v.*, *snáde*, paint, to paint something with a liquefied substance

Wét'à /wā-t'ä/ *n.*, egg, an edible product from chickens

Wét'ạ̀ /wā-t'oⁿ-ē/ *adj.*, apparent, something that is clear, understood, or able to be seen

Wét'ạ̀ /wā-t'oⁿ-ēⁿ/ *adj.*, noticeable, clear, visible, perceptible, obvious, in plain sight; *įwat'ạ̀*, I noticed; *díwat'ạ̀*, you noticed; *wéwat'ạ̀*, we noticed; *gíwat'ạ̀*, he/she/it noticed

Wét'ạ̀' /wā-t'oⁿ-ēⁿ/ *adj.*, obvious, clear, apparent

Wét'a ugášižè /wā-t'ä ü-gä-shē-zhä/ *v.*, hatch, a young fowl breaking out of an egg

Wét'a ugdè /wā-t'ä ü-gthä/ *n.*, nest, a structure of weeds and bird down made by fowl in which to lay and hatch their eggs

Wét'a uská' /wā-t'ä ü-skä/ *n.*, egg white, a substance whose purpose is to protect the yolk and provide nutrition for the growth of a fertilized embryo; an edible, nutritious food

Wét'a uzì /wā-t'ä ü-zē/ *n.*, yolk, the edible yellow internal part of an egg that is rich in protein and fat; the part that nourishes a developing embryo

Wét'ęt'ạ̀ /wā-t'äⁿ-t'oⁿ/ *n.*, funeral, a rite of showing respect and remembering or celebrating the life of a person who has died

Wét'ęt'ạ wédišedą̀ /wā-t'äⁿ-t'oⁿ wā-thē-shä-thoⁿ/ *n.*, Osage custom for ending their mourning

Wét'į /wā-t'ēⁿ/ *n.*, war club, 1. a club composed of a hard stone tied tightly at the end of a strong piece of wood with sinew 2. Wétįwį̀, Club Woman, proper female name in the Díxidą̀ clan of the Ponca people

Wétį /wā'-tēⁿ/ *n.*, whip, a flexible branch or stick or thin strips of leather attached to a handle and used to strike people or animals. Also see *Wé'tį,* club.

Weúdidą̀ /wā-ü'-thē-doⁿ/ *n.*, latch, a fastening device used to hold a door, gate, or cabinet closed

Weúdidą̀ /wāü'-thē-doⁿ/ *n.*, padlock, a device used to secure doors, cabinets, or gates, usu. a lock with a U-shaped bar that extends out to be hooked onto a staple affixed to the structure to be secured

Weúgąbà nąxé /wā-ü'-goⁿ-bä' noⁿ-xā'/ *n.*, pane, windowpane

Wéužawà /wā'-ü-zhä-wä'/ *n.*, to give entertainment, enjoyment, or amusement through some activity, such as dancing, singing, or just being a likable person to others (*ahííki, ~ adįáti,* his presence brought ~ enough)

Wéəbastà /wā'-ə-bä-stä'/ *n.*, patch, a piece of cloth or material to be sewn to another to repair a worn area or tear

Wí /wē'/ *pron.*, me, my, myself

Wí' /wē'/ *art.*, a/an, indefinite article (used to designate indefinite singular animate or inanimate objects; similar to the English *a* and *an*)

Wí' /wē'/ *n.*, one, relating to numerals, as in 1, 2, 3

Wí'bdugà /wē'-bthü-gä'/ *n.*, one-dollar bill

Wí'dądą̀ /wē'-thoⁿ-thoⁿ/ *adj.*, sparse, 1. scanty, scarce, skimpy 2. refers to individuals entering a place one at a time

Wí'dądądą̀ /wē'-thoⁿ-thoⁿ-doⁿ/ *pron.*, each, each one, apiece, two or more being considered one at a time

Wí'ke /wē'-kä/ *n.*, fact, reality, exactness, honesty, fidelity, etc.

Wi't'íni /wē-t'ē'-nē/ *n.*, daughter-in-law, a masculine word for daughter-in-law

Wi'žą́ge /wē-zhoⁿ'-gā/ *n.*, daughter (a man or woman saying, my ~)

Wiá'xčì'nà /wēä-xchē'-nä'/ *n.*, only one, only one thing left (The cardinal numbers are extended by adding *-nà* to each succeeding number, as in *~ uštè,* there is ~ left, or *dábdičì'nà uštè,* there are only three left.)

Wíágaškè /wē'-ä'-gä-shkä'/ *n.*, button, fastener, hook and eye

Wiáha /wē-ä'-hä/ *n.*, first, the first in a row or series

Wíáhidè /wē'-ä'-hē-dä'/ *adj.*, distant, far away or far off, something that is a great distance away

Wiákišną̀ /wēä'-kē-shnoⁿ/ *adj.*, grateful, being very appreciative for act(s) of kindness

Wiáxčì /wēä'-xchē'/ *n.*, one, refers to a thing that remains (*~ ušt'è, ~* left)

Wiáxčì'ą̀ /wēä'-xchē-oⁿ/ *adv.*, once, one time, to try something one time

Wíbdahą̀ /wē'-bthä-hoⁿ/ *interj.*, thank you, thanks, expression of gratitude for something; acknowledgement in gratitude for something

Wídądą̀ /wē'-thoⁿ-thoⁿ/ *n.*, ones, "by ones," as in they came in by ones or one at a time

Wigá'xdą̀ /wē-gä'-xthoⁿ/ *n.*, wife, my wife; *igáxdą̀,* his wife; *digáxdą̀,* your wife

Wihą́ga /wē-hoⁿ'-gä/ *n.*, *masc.*, sister-in-law (*duádikè ~,* this is my ~)

Wihé /wē-hä'/ *n.*, *masc./fem.*, sister, used to address a younger female sibling (this is my ~) (same as *winą́'*)

Wihé' /wē-hä'/ *n.*, younger sister (man or woman saying, my ~)

Wík'a /wē'-k'ä/ *v.*, help, assist, lend a helping hand, be of assistance

Wik'ą́ /wē-k'oⁿ/ *n.*, *masc./fem.*, grandmother, my grandmother; *gą̀hó',* male using abbreviated form addressing ~; *gą́ha,* female using abbreviated form addressing ~

Wíkażì /wē'-kä-zhē'/ *adj.*, untruthful, dishonest, or deceptive

Wíke /wē'-kä/ *adj.*, honest, frank, reliable, straightfoward, true, truth, truism

Wíkext'ì /wē'-kä-xt'ē'/ *adv.*, truly, beyond doubt, factually

Winą́żįgà /wē-noⁿ'-zhēⁿ-gä/ *n., masc.*, sister, refers to younger or "little" sister

Winísi /wē-nē'-sē/ *n.*, childen, lit., my little ones (my ~)

Wisą́'ga /wē-soⁿ'-gä/ *n.*, younger brother (man or woman saying, my ~)

Wisą́ga /wē-soⁿ'-gä/ *n., masc./fem.*, brother, a word to address a younger male sibling (this is my ~)

Wiší'e' /wē-shē'-ā/ *n.*, brother-in-law (woman saying, my ~)

Wišíką /wē-shē'-koⁿ/ *n., fem.*, sister-in-law (*duádikè* ~, this is my ~); *šiką́*, sister-in-law, used when addressing her

Wiʃwaą̀ /wēʃ'-wä-oⁿ'/ *pron.*, which one, inquiry as to which of several things or people

Wiʃwaą́št'i /wēʃ'-wä-oⁿ'-sht'ē/ *pron.*, whichever, usu. refers to a question asking for the selection of a thing among many things

Wít'a /wē'-t'ä/ *pron., sing.*, mine, something belonging to oneself; *pl./ emphatic, wíwít'a*, they are mine)

Wit'ą́de /wē-t'oⁿ'-dä/ *n.*, son-in-law (man or woman saying, my ~); in the Ponca kinship system, the relationship of father- and mother-in-law to son-in-law

Wit'ą́ge /wē-t'oⁿ'-gä/ *n., masc.*, sister, used to address an elder female sibling (this is my ~)

Wit'áhą /wē-t'ä'-hoⁿ/ *n.*, brother-in-law (man saying, my ~)

Wit'ą́škà /wē-t'oⁿ'-shkä/ *n., masc.*, nephew

Wit'ígą /wē-t'ē'-goⁿ/ *n., masc./fem.*, grandfather, my grandfather; *t'igą́'*, abbreviated form for ~; *t'igą́' ho*, male using abbreviated form addressing ~; *t'igą́ ha*, female using abbreviated form addressing ~

Wit'ími /wē-t'ē'-mē/ *n., masc./fem.*, aunt, father's sister

Wit'ínu /wē-t'ē'-nü/ *n., fem.*, elder brother, the feminine word for addressing an elder male sibling (this is my ~)

Wit'íżą /wē-t'ē'-zhoⁿ/ *n., masc.*, niece

Wit'ú'żągè /wē-t'ü'-zhoⁿ-gä/ *n., fem.*, niece

Wit'úškà /wē-t'ü'-shkä/ *n., fem.*, nephew

Wiú'ki'hą̀ /wēü'-kē-hoⁿ'/ *n.*, usu. black pepper, an eastern Indian plant ground with its husk and used as a condiment

Wíúdisą̀ /wē'-ü-thē-soⁿ'/ *n.*, skillet, a pan for frying or braising foods

Wiúgąbà /wēü'-goⁿ-bä'/ *n.*, window, lit., to brighten, a glass-covered opening, usu. on a building, house, or automobile

Wíúgąbà idágaxadè /wē'-ü-goⁿ-bä' ē-thä'-gä-xä-dā'/ *n.*, curtain, drapery, blind, shutter

Wiúgąbà nąxé /wēü'-goⁿ-bä' noⁿ-xä'/ *n.*, windowpane, a sheet of glass in a wooden or metal frame that is part of a window

Wiúhą /wēü'-hoⁿ/ *n.*, pan, saucepan

Wiúhą t'ągà /wē'-ü-hoⁿ t'oⁿ-gä'/ *n.*, kettle, a large metal vessel for cooking soup

Wiúhą t'ągá /wēü'-hoⁿ t'oⁿ-gä'/ *n.*, pot, a large cooking vessel

Wiúhą udúgaškè /wē-ü'-hoⁿ ü-thü'-gä-shkä'/ *n.*, tripod, a stand or support, usu. made of metal with three legs and used to support pots and pans

Wíúhe /wē'-ü-hā/ *v.*, follow, to follow behind somebody on a certain pathway

Wiúk'idabè /wēü'-k'ē-thä-bä'/ *n.*, potholder, a piece of quilted cloth used to hold hot kitchen cooking utensils

Wiúk'ihą̀ /wēü'-k'ē-hoⁿ'/ *n.*, pepper, usu. black pepper, now red pepper or any spice or spices added to cooking

Wiúk'ihąuží' /wēü'-k'ē-hoⁿ'-ü-zhē'/ *n.*, pepper shaker, a condiment holder, namely, for pepper

Wíúnabixą̀ /wē'-ü'-nä-bē-xoⁿ'/ *n.*, baking powder, leavening agent for baking cakes, breads, etc.

Wiúšį̇ /wēü'-shēⁿ/ *adj.*, useful, helpful, refers to something or someone that is helpful for certain things

Wiət'šíta /wēə-t'shē'-tä/ *n.*, the Wichita Tribe of Native Americans

Wižą́ɗe /wē-zhoⁿ'-thä/ *n., fem.*, sister, used to address an elder female sibling (*duáɗikè ~ wít'a*, this is my ~)

Wižį́ɗe /wē-zhēⁿ'-thä/ *n., masc.*, brother, the masculine word for addressing an elder male sibling (this is my ~)

Wižį́ge /wē-zhēⁿ'-gä/ *n., 1st pers. sing.*, son (man or woman saying, my ~); in the Ponca kinship system, the relationship of child to parent

Wəáda'ska'bè /wəä'-thä-skä-bā'/ *n.*, glue, superglue, an adhesive substance to bind together various surfaces; some usu. made of gelatin substances from animals, such as the hooves of horses, skins; *ákigɗaskabè*, two things glued or sticking to each other

Wəágaxadè /wə-ä'-gä-xä-dä'/ *n.*, lid, cover, cap; *idágaxadè*, using something to cover something

Wəáhidè /wəä'-hē-dä'/ *adv.*, far, faraway, distant from here

X

x /xə/ sixteenth consonant in the Ponca alphabet

X'á'ɗe /x'ä'-thä/ *adj.*, sour, bitter, tart; *us'áɗe*, refers to canned foods or drinks that become bitter, tart, or sour by standing too

long; may also be caused by overuse of spices

X'ą́xat'à /x'oⁿ'-xä-t'ä'/ *adv.*, away from, not near the people, at a distance from the main body of a group of things or people (*niášigà akà, ~ ną̇ží ną̀i*, the man always stands ~)

X'čáɗe /x'chä-thä'/ *v.*, like, to be more expressive in a gentler form, to like someone or something; *xt'áwaɗè*, I like (somebody or something)

X'wį́' /x'wēⁿ'/ *n./v.*, stink, horrible smell, unpleasant smell

Xą́ /xoⁿ'/ *v., past t.*, broke

Xa· /xä·/ *interj., fem.*, aha!, an expression indicating awareness or a discovery, e.g., catching someone in the act

Xá'gà /xä'-gä/ *v.*, chapped, refers to the skin becoming sore and rough

Xabáɗe /xä-bä'-thä/ *v. phr.*, peel off, something that comes off on its own accord, as with the bark of an old tree, the scab of a skinned knee

Xáda /xä'-thä/ *v.*, back, to go backward, a move backward

Xáda'dè /xä'-thä-thä'/ *v.*, going back, something being caused to go back, something that is put back to its position

Xáda'dè Užíga /xä'-thä-thä' ü-zhēⁿ'-gä/ *n.*, Going Back Small, lit., going back small, a creek named by the Ponca (This is a creek near Niobrara, Nebraska, known to back up when the Missouri River floods.)

Xáda dè /xä'-thä thä'/ *v.*, return, connotes returning and going again

Xáda dè /xä'-thä thä'/ *n.*, Going Back, lit., going back; a creek named by the Ponca (This is Bazile Creek, near Niobrara, Nebraska, known to back up when the Missouri River floods.)

Xádagɗè' /xä'-thä-gthä'/ *v.*, retreat, lit., going back, 1. an act of withdrawing from a situation that could be dangerous 2. refers to tributary creek water going back because of flooding from a larger river

Xáda gì /xä'-thä gē'/ *v.*, return, connotes going somewhere and returning or coming back; *gí'*, return

Xáde /xä'-dā/ *n.*, grass, weeds

Xáde /xä'-dā/ *n.*, hay, a herbaceous plant that is cut, baled, and used for animal food

Xą́·de /xoⁿ'·-dā/ *n.*, bunch, a group or cluster of things together, a group of people

Xą́·de /xoⁿ'·-dā/ *adv.*, collectively, together, as a group

Xáde banáną /xä'-dā bä-noⁿ'-noⁿ/ *n.*, buffalo grass, *Buchloe dactyloides*, a perennial grass that grows in clumps, as the Ponca word *banáną* suggests

Xádeídatè /xä'-dā-ē'-thä-tā'/ *n.*, weed eater, an electric- or gasoline-powered tool to trim grass along a walk or near a house or other structure

Xádeidizè /xä'-dā-ē-thē-zā'/ *n.*, pitchfork, a farm tool with a long handle and separated prongs used to lift and throw hay or other grass feed to animals

Xáde ígas / xä'-dā ē'-gä-sā'/ *n.*, weed cutter, a serrated double-edged cutting blade about fourteen by two inches attached to an approximately thirty-six-inch wooden handle for cutting moderately tall grass or weeds

Xáde íną sedè /xä'-dā ē'-noⁿ-sä-thä'/ *n.*, lawn mower

Xáde mąk'ą́ /xä'-dā moⁿ-k'oⁿ'/ *n.*, tea, lit., grass medicine

Xáde ubétą /xä'-dā ü-bā'-toⁿ/ *n.*, hay bale, baled hay, used to feed domesticated livestock

Xaéde /xä-ā'-thä/ *v.*, leak, seep out, trickle out

Xagé /xä-gä'/ *v.*, cry, weep, sob, shed tears

Xagé'št'à /xä-gä'-sht'oⁿ'/ *n.*, crybaby, lit., likes to cry

Xagéda'é /xä-gä'-thä'-ā'/ *v.*, wail, intensi-

fied crying, sad or mournful expression of sorrow

Xáxadè /xä-xä-dä'/ *adj.*, thin, thin garment or fabric, a material woven loosely; *unáži' x'áx'adè*, a woman's thin blouse; *máze x'áx'adè*, screen, a metal mesh frame

Xáxagà /xä-xä-gä'/ *adj.*, abrasive, rough, coarse, scratchy, refers to material causing irritation against the skin

Xą́xat'à /xoⁿ'-xä-t'ä'/ *adj.*, outer edges, standing on the ~ of a group (*niášigà akà, ~ ną́ží ną̀i*, the man always stands on the ~)

Xdá' /xthä'/ *adj.*, skinny, thin, lean, emaciated

Xdá' /xthä'/ *n.*, blossom, coming from a seed plant, the beginning of a plant

Xdábé /xthä'-bā/ *n.*, forest, woods, usu. refers to a large wooded area

Xdabé' /xthä'-bā/ *n.*, tree, 1. generally, a large woody plant having few branches on its lower part with many smaller branches on its upper parts 2. timber or forest

Xdabé'p'asi /xthä-bā'-p'ä-sē/ *n.*, treetop

Xdabé'p'asi'datè /xthä-bā'-p'ä-sē-thä-tä'/ *n.*, giraffe, lit., eat at the top of trees, a tall African mammal, *Giraffa camelopardalis*, of the family Giraffidae

Xdabéádi /xthä-bā'-ä'-dē/ *n.*, in the woods or forest, a place in the woods or forest

Xdát'a'bdúga'gabdà /xthä'-t'ä-bthü'-gä-gä-bthä'/ *n.*, budding out, plants that unfold

Xdažé /xthä-zhä'/ *v.*, to scream, to give a loud, high-pitched cry, yell, or scream, to shriek, usu. refers to someone who is in pain or is excited, as at a ball game

Xdažé /xthä-zhä'/ *n.*, yell, scream, shriek

Xdexdé /xthä-xthä'/ *n.*, tattoo, 1. *archaic*, refers to a tattoo ceremony or ritual for women 2. now refers to any tattoo

Xdį· /xtheⁿ'·/ *n./v.*, growl, a guttural sound made by dogs to give warning to trespassers

Xdí' /xthē'/ *n.*, pustule, abscess, a small bump under the skin filled with pus

Xdí't'ù /xthē'-t'ü'/ *adj.*, mean, small-minded, ill-tempered, malicious

Xdíáži /xthē'-ä'-zhē/ *adj.*, quiet, inaudible, in silence

Xdíážitigdaì /xthē'-ä'-zhē-tē-gthä-ē'/ *v.*, quieting, sudden quieting in a noisy, crowded place

Xdú'a /xthü-ä'/ *adj.*, hollow, as in something empty or void of substance

Xdudáde /xthü-dä'-thä/ *n.*, something that is no longer attached to, such as old boards off an old house, old house paint off an outside wall, bark off a tree

Xdudáde /xthü-dä'-thä/ *v. phr.*, *past t.*, peeled off, something coming off on its own, as in old paint on a house

Xé· /xā'·/ *interj.*, mistaken, a woman's vocal intonation indicative of a feeling of being mistaken

Xé· /xā'·/ *interj.*, expression, woman's expression of a mistake made or a misunderstanding of a statement

Xé'a /xā'-ä/ *adj.*, short, usu. refers to clothing, e.g., ~ skirt (The word is sometimes pronounced *xį'a*.)

Xé'de /xā'-thä/ *v.*, weep, to cause someone to weep (*isága etái đįkè xé'đaì*, he made his little brother cry)

Xé'gà /xā'-gä/ *adj./n.*, rotten, decaying substances such as wood or bones

X·ébe /x·ā'-bä/ *adj.*, shallow, not deep, as in a river or stream

Xéde /xā'-thä/ *v.*, make cry, cause to weep, sob, whimper, shed tears; *xéwađè*, to make them cry (*isága etái đįkè xé'đaì*, he made his little brother cry)

Xénahà /xā'-nä-hä'/ *interj.*, mistaken, a man's vocal intonation indicative of a feeling of being mistaken

Xénahà /xā'-nä-hä'/ *interj.*, expression, man's expression of a mistake made or a misunderstanding of a statement

Xéxe /xā'-xä/ *n./v.*, lullaby, to hum a repeated note to babies, lulling them to sleep (The Ponca mother usu. carries or rocks her baby in her arms and hums quietly and repeatly, "Ha-ú-ú-ú-ú-ú," until her baby sleeps.)

Xí'xiáda /xē'-xēä'-thä/ *v.*, to continuously fall for lack of support or strength, usu. refers to sickness

Xiáda /xēä'-thä/ *v.*, fall, go down, fall down, fall over; *baxiáda*, fall, go down, fall down, fall over by pushing; *đixiáda*, fall, go down, fall down, fall over by pulling with the hands; *gaxiáda*, fall, go down, fall down, fall over by force, chopping, or kicking with the feet; *nąxiáda* fall, go down, fall down, fall over by driving over or by stepping or standing on

Xidá' /xē-thä'/ *n.*, eagle, a large predatory bird of the Accipitridae family

Xidá'hągà /xē-thä'-hoⁿ-gä'/ *n.*, golden eagle (*Aquila chrysaetos*), the species of eagle that is honored or given high respect by the Ponca people

Xidá'mąšą̀ /xē-thä'-moⁿ-shoⁿ'/ *n.*, eagle feather

Xidá Skà /xē-thä' skä/ *n.*, White Eagle, 1. principal chief of the Ponca people at the time of forced removal to Indian Territory, ca. 1876 2. White Eagle Community, formerly Ponca Agency, in Kay County, Oklahoma

Xįhá /xēⁿ-hä'/ *n.*, complexion, color of skin, tone of skin

Xįhá'sábe /xēⁿ-hä'-sä'-bä/ *n.*, Negroid, lit., black complexion, people of African origin (also *Wáxe sábe*, the black white man)

Xįhá'skà /xēⁿ-hä'-skä'/ *n.*, Caucasoid, lit.,

white complexion, white-skinned people of European origin

Xįhá'ská' uké'đi /xēⁿ-hä'-skä' ü-kä'-thē/ *n.*, French person, lit., a common white person, a native or inhabitant of France

Xįhá'skà mása /xēⁿ-hä'-skä' moⁿ-sä/ *n.*, Briton, lit., an uppity (persnickity) white person, those who dwell in the country of England

Xįhá sabè /xēⁿ-hä' sä-bä/ *n.*, Afro-American, lit., black complexion, person of Negroid descent (The tribal usage of the term *wáxe sábe*, black white man, was common from ca. 1870 to the 1950s.)

Xįháska hébe /xēⁿ-hä'-skä hä'-bä/ *n.*, part white, refers to Native Americans, namely a Ponca whose father is Caucasian (Children whose fathers are non-Ponca are not clan members and are also sometimes referred to as "half-breeds." In the Ponca patrilineal clanship system, children whose fathers are of another tribe, race, or ethnicity, such as Asian or Mexican, cannot be a clan member. They are referred to as *ukíte hébe*, part other tribe.)

Xįháska íye /xēⁿ-hä'-skä ē'-yä/ *n.*, English language

Xíkidè /xē'-kē-thä'/ *n./v.*, dress up, 1. to put on special clothing, arrange and style the hair 2. to put on native Ponca paraphernalia for rituals or ceremonial dances

Xixáde /xē-xä'-thä/ *v.*, broken, usu. refers to glass, ceramics, etc. (The word is usu. used to refer to something that has been cracked.)

Xíxəáda /xē-xəä'-thä/ *v.*, falling, repeatedly falling down

Xíxįdà /xēⁿ'-xēⁿ-thä'/ *n.*, wrinkle, usu. refers to the skin

Xp'éga /xp'ä'-gä/ *adj.*, sallow, sickly, pale, ashen, pallid

Xp'éga /xp'ä'-gä/ *adj.*, listless, pallid, languid

Xt'ádažì /xt'ä'-thä-zhē'/ *v.*, dislike, doesn't like, has an aversion to

Xt'áde /xt'ä'-thä/ *v.*, like, to be fond of another person or thing, to be partial to something; *xt'áde*, I like; *íxt'amąžì*, I don't like; *đíxt'ažì*, you don't like; *xt'ádažì*, he/she/it doesn't like; *wé'xt'abaxì*, they don't like us

Xt'áwadábažì /xt'ä'-wä-thä-bä-zhē'/ *n.*, prejudice, lit., doesn't like us or them, a bad attitude toward an individual(s) with no good reason; *xt'ádažì*, doesn't like

Xubé /xü-bä'/ *n.*, supernatural powers, things that occur according to a set of principles apart from the laws of nature

Xúde /xü'-dä/ *n.*, gray, the color gray, ash color

Xué' /xü-ä'/ *v.*, roar, to emit a loud sound

Xúga /xü'-gä/ *n.*, badger, a short-legged omnivore in the subfamily Taxideinae of the family Mustelidae

Xuhį' /xü-hēⁿ'/ *adj.*, smelly, something that has an undesirable smell, usu. refers to a person

Xúk'à /xü'-k'ä'/ *n.*, drummers, drum and sing, usu. refers to singers (~ *mašé* . . . , you ~ . . .)

Xúka /xü'-kä/ *v.*, to drum and sing for dancers in any Native American dance experience

Y

y /yə/ seventeenth consonant in the Ponca alphabet

Yáda /yä'-thä/ *v.*, gape, looking intently with mouth open

Yəáda /yəä'-thä/ *v.*, yawn, to open the mouth and breathe deeply, usu. associated with sleepiness

Yʃnąxidà /yʃ'-noⁿ-xē-thä'/ *v.*, chase, to pursue, run after, go after, go in pursuit of, to engage in a fight or to battle

z

z /zə/ eighteenth consonant in the Ponca alphabet

ž /zhə/ nineteenth consonant in the Ponca alphabet

Žą́ /zhoⁿ/ *n.*, sleep, a period of time when consciousness is suspended

Žá' /zhä/ *n.*, greens, lit., weeds, usu. refers to spring greens, collard greens, poke, leafy greens

Žá' /zhä/ *n.*, weeds, plants that grow in their natural environment

Žą́' /zhoⁿ/ *n.*, wood, 1. a fibrous tissue found in trees and other plants, out of which boards and planks are made 2. wood used for fire to heat and cook

Žą́' /zhoⁿ/ *v.*, lie, lay, lain, the position of something that lies, such as a child's toy on a staircase

Žą́' ábasè /zhoⁿ ä'-bä-sä'/ *n.*, sawhorse, orig. a wooden, upright device used to support a log to be sawn

Žą'ábe /zhoⁿ'-ä'-bä/ *n.*, tree leaves; *ábe*, leaves

Žą'ábe /zhoⁿ'-ä'-bä/ *n.*, leaf; *žą́*, wood, *ábe*, leaf, the outgrowth of a tree or other plant

Žą'ádašnà /zhoⁿ'-ä'-thä-shnä/ *adj.*, icy, rain turning to ice, causing the land to be covered with ice (The Ponca term is derived from ice being on wood and trees.)

Žą́'bahút'ą /zhoⁿ'-bä-hü'-t'oⁿ/ *v.*, to play a fiddle or a violin

Žá'bè /zhä'-bä/ *n.*, beaver, a nocturnal, semi-aquatic rodent (The North American beaver, *Castor canadensis*, is native to North America.)

Žá'be't'ahì /zhä'-bä-t'ä-hē'/ *n.*, boxelder, *Acer negundo*, a choice tree for beavers to fell in northern Oklahoma along the Arkansas River

Žá'bè t'ą́wągdą̀ /zhä'-bä' t'oⁿ-woⁿ-gthoⁿ'/ *n.*, beaver dam, a dam built by beavers out of various sizes of branches as a place to live and to find protection against predators

Žą'dádįgè /zhoⁿ-dä-thēⁿ-gä/ *n.*, somniloquy, 1. *žą'dádįgè íye*, talking in one's sleep 2. sleepwalking or noctambulism

Žą́' gáse /zhoⁿ' gä-sä/ *n.*, wood cutting, the act of cutting wood

Žą́' gasnésne /zhoⁿ' gä-snä'-snä/ *n.*, split wood, usu. refers to blocks split with the grain of the wood

Žą'gášpe /zhoⁿ-gä-shpä/ *n.*, wood chips, small chips that come from cutting firewood and are used to start a fire

Žą́'gaxà /zhoⁿ'-gä-xä/ *n.*, tree branch, usu. refers to large branches reaching out

Žą́'gaxà /zhoⁿ'-gä-xä/ *n.*, limbs, the branches that extend up and outward from the main body of a tree

Zá'ge /zä'-gä/ *n.*, Sac (or Sauk) and Fox Tribes of Native Americans (Originally two separate tribes, who merged into a single tribe called the Sac and Fox.)

Žą́'hįbè /zhoⁿ'-hēⁿ-bä/ *n.*, shoes, lit., wooden shoes

Žą́'hidè /zhoⁿ'-hē-dä/ *n.*, tree trunk, the main or large base of a tree

Žą́' hidè /zhoⁿ' hē-dä/ *n.*, stump, the base part of a tree left in the ground after the tree is cut down

Žą́'i'bagizè /zhoⁿ'-ē'-bä-gē-zä/ *n.*, violin or fiddle, lit., making a wood squeak, a stringed musical instrument used to play classical music (violin) or country music (fiddle)

Žą́' íbamà /zhoⁿ' ē'-bä-moⁿ/ *n.*, rasp, wood rasp, a tool to smooth down rough edges

Žą́'íbasè /zhoⁿ'-ē'-bä-sä/ *n.*, saw, lit., wood cutter, a hand or power saw to cut wood or boards

Žą́'íbasedè /zhoⁿ'-ē'-bä-sä-thä/ *n.*, chainsaw,

a portable, mechanized saw for wood cutting that has a circular chain driven by a motor

Žą́’ímuzà /zhoⁿ’ ē’-mü-zä’/ *n.*, post, usu. refers to a corner fence post

Za’ní /zä-nē’/ *pron.*, everyone, a short form of *wazáni*

Žą́’p’à /zhä-p’ä’/ *n.*, chewing gum

Žą́’p’aí’dadàhì /zhoⁿ-p’ä-ē’-thä-thä’-hē’/ *n.*, thorny tree, any of the many species of thorny trees and bushes

Žą́’sagì /zhoⁿ’ sä-gē’/ *n.*, hardwood (The Ponca were acquainted with white elm, oak, ash, and walnut hardwoods.)

Žá’škúbe /zhä’-shkü-bā/ *n.*, weeds, refers to deep, thick weeds

Žą́’t’ę̀ /zhoⁿ’-t’ǟⁿ/ *adj.*, asleep, fast asleep or dead to the world

Žą́’ubáxą /zhoⁿ’-ü-bä’-xoⁿ/ *n.*, sliver, splinter, a small, slender, sharp piece of wood

Žą́’udúgasnè /zhoⁿ’-ü-thü’-gä-snä’/ *n.*, wedge, a metal tool, usu. thick on one end and tapering to a thin edge, used for splitting wood

Žą́’uxp’é’ /zhoⁿ’-ü-xp’ä’/ *n.*, wooden bowl

Žą́’wiúbasnà /zhoⁿ’-wē-ü’-bä-snoⁿ’/ *n.*, clothespin, a wooden (now plastic) clip used to hang clothing on a clothesline

Žą́’xdú’a /zhoⁿ’ xthü-ä/ *adj./n.*, hollow log, a large windfall (tree) that has lain upon the ground and been hollowed out by rot and digging by animals to use as a nesting or hiding place

Žą́’xegà /zhoⁿ’ xä-gä’/ *n.*, rotten wood (This type of wood was so named because of its uselessness for construction or burning, but it is useful for finding bait for fishing, as well as morels and other mushrooms, which grow near decaying wood and leaves.)

Žą́’xudèhì /zhoⁿ’-xü-dä’-hē’/ *n.*, hickory tree, small gray hickory tree, of the genus *Carya*

Za’zádè /zä-zä’-dä’/ *adj./n.*, raggedy, torn, worn to shreds, etc.

Žą́’žát’a /zhoⁿ’-zhä-t’ä/ *n.*, tree fork, where other limbs fork out from the main body of the tree

Žą́’žát’at’ągà /zhoⁿ’-zhä-t’ä-t’oⁿ-gä’/ *n.*, first forked limbs of a tree

Žą́’žįgà /zhoⁿ’ zhē̄n-gä’/ *n.*, sticks, twigs, a slender tree limb

Žąbdáska /zhoⁿ-bthä’-skä/ *n.*, board, lit., flat wood, a piece of wood formed into a flat or square piece

Žąbdáska ídiskebè /zhoⁿ-bthä’-skä ē’-thē-skä-bā’/ *n.*, hand plane, a hand-held woodworking tool with a sharpened cutting edge attached to the underside of the tool's body, which is used to shave and smooth the surface of wood boards

Žąbdáska ídiskebè /zhoⁿ-bthä’-skä ē’-thē-skä-bā’/ *n.*, plane, a tool in woodworking to smooth surfaces, usu. used to level two pieces of board to match or fit evenly

Žąbdáska t’ągà /zhoⁿ-bthä’-skä t’oⁿ-gä’/ *n.*, plank, wood ~, a large rectangular piece of flat wood used for the construction of ships, houses, bridges, and other structures; e.g., railroad ties

Žądá’dįgè /zhoⁿ-dä’-thē̄n-gä’/ *n.*, sleepwalking, noctambulism

Žądá’dįgè íye /zhoⁿ-dä’-thē̄n-gä’ ē’-yä/ *n.*, talking in one's sleep, somniloquy

Žądáha /zhoⁿ-thä’-hä/ *n.*, bark, the outer layer of a tree

Žądáte wagdíška /zhoⁿ-thä’-tä wä-gthē’-shkä/ *n.*, termite, any of the insects of the order Isoptera that feed on wood and are very destructive to buildings

Záde /zä-dä/ *adj./n.*, messy hair, loose hair strands, mussed-up hair, rumpled hair

Žądí’nągè /zhoⁿ-thē̄’-noⁿ-gä’/ *n.*, wagon, 1. horse-drawn wagon 2. child's wagon

Žądíną̨gè íbažą̀ /zhoⁿ-thē̄'-noⁿ-gā' ē'-bä-zhoⁿ'/ *n.*, *archaic*, the tongue of a horse-drawn wagon

Zaé /zä-ā'/ *adj.*, noisy, loud sounds, deafening

Žą gáse /zhoⁿ gä'-sä/ *v.*, chop wood, lit., cut wood

Žągáxa /zhoⁿ-gä'-xä/ *n.*, driftwood, pieces of wood piled up along the riverbank or floating in the river

Žagdáša waú /zhä-gthä'-shä wä-ü'/ *n.*, queen, queen of England

Žą́gdiškà /zhoⁿ'-gthē-shkä'/ *n.*, ant, a social insect of the family Formicidae that may be red, black, brown, or yellow and is found throughout the world in warmer climates

Žą́gdiškà sábe /zhoⁿ'-gthē-shkä' sä-bā/ *n.*, black ant, a species of carpenter ant, common ant in the United States

Žáhe /zhä'-hā/ *v.*, stab, pierce, gore, stick; to pierce or wound with a pointed weapon

Žáhe /zhä'-hā/ *v.*, sting, refers to an insect sting

Žą i'dadį̀ /zhoⁿ ē'-dä-thēⁿ'/ *v.*, going beyond the normal sleeping pattern, usu. refers to a person who sleeps far longer than he/she should

Žá ígasè /zhä' ē'-gä-sä'/ *n.*, scythe, a manually operated, long single-edged blade for cutting deep weeds, grass, or crops

Žą́imuzà /zhoⁿ-ē'-mü-zä'/ *n.*, fence post, wooden posts that are used to support fences

Žą́ką́ /zhoⁿ-koⁿ'/ *n.*, root, the part of a plant that spreads underground, absorbing water and nutrients from the earth for growth

Žąní' /zhoⁿ-nē'/ *n.*, sugar, lit., wood water (The term probably derived from the word for maple syrup.)

Žąní'hì /zhoⁿ-nē'-hē̄/ *n.*, sugarcane, a plant native to South Asia and Melanesia of the genus *Saccharum*, grass family Poaceae (Evidently the plant was grown in various parts of the United States, as the Ponca knew about it.)

Žąní'snu'snù /zhoⁿ-nē'-snü-snü/ *n.*, syrup, lit., slippery sugar, refers to all varieties, including corn syrup, maple syrup, glucose syrup, etc.

Žąní'uží' /zhoⁿ-nē'-ü-zhē'/ *n.*, sugar bowl, a condiment holder for sugar

Žąníbút'a /zhoⁿ-nē'-bü'-t'ä/ *n.*, candy, lit., round sugar

Žáp'à /zhä'-p'ä/ *n.*, gum, chewing gum (*Manilkara chicle* is a tropical evergreen tree in Mexico and Central America, from which gum is made.)

Žąsą́' /zhoⁿ-soⁿ'/ *n.*, sycamore tree, *Platanus occidentalis*, a tall, white-barked tree with yellow foliage in the fall

Zą́st'a /zoⁿ'-st'ä/ *n.*, bad smell, as in a baby diaper

Žą́ t'ągà /zhoⁿ' t'oⁿ-gä'/ *n.*, log, the large part of a tree, trunk of the tree, a large limb

Žą́təidįgè /zhoⁿ'-təē-thēⁿ-gä'/ *adj.*, sleepy, drowsy

Žą̀ uwą́ /zhoⁿ' ü-woⁿ'/ *v.*, stoke, add fuel, refers to putting firewood into a wood stove

Žąwáspažì /zhoⁿ-wä-spä-zhē'/ *n.*, restless sleeper, refers to one who doesn't sleep in one position but rolls around as he/she sleeps

Žą́waxúbe /zhoⁿ'-wä-xü'-bä/ *n.*, Sacred Pole, the Sacred Pole of the Omaha people

Žaxdá /zhä-xthä'/ *n.*, sunflower, *Helianthus x annus*

Žąxdą́'škà /zhoⁿ-xthoⁿ'-shkä'/ *n.*, grasshopper, a jumping/flying insect of the family Acrididae, which eats plants

Žą́xdudè /zhoⁿ'-xthü-dä'/ *v.*, snore, the making of harsh or coarse sounds while sleeping, caused by vibration of the upper mouth

Žáxudè /zhoⁿ'-xü-dā/ *n.*, 1. hickory tree 2. a proper male name in the Wašábe clan of the Ponca people

Žáządè /zoⁿ'-zoⁿ-dā/ *adv.*, together, collectively, groups of people or things in a scattered position in a large area; may also refer to individuals sitting in a row apart from each other

Záze /zoⁿ'-zā/ *n.*, a disgusting bad smell, generally from a bad piece of meat

Záze /zoⁿ'-zā/ *adj.*, rank, pungent, fetid, foul smelling

Žązí'hi /zhoⁿ-zē'-hē/ *n.*, Osage orange tree, commonly called hedge apple, horse apple, or bodark, *Maclura pomifera*

Žązí' mą́de /zhoⁿ-zē' moⁿ'-dā/ *n.*, Osage orange bow, made from the choice wood for making bows

Žązí'sabè /zhoⁿ-zē'-sä-bā/ *n.*, redbud tree, of the genus *Cercis*

Žązíhi /zhoⁿ-zē'-hē/ *n.*, bois d'arc tree, also known as Osage orange, horse apple, *Maclura pomifera* (The Ponca favor the wood to make bows.)

Žé' /zhā/ *n.*, bowel movement, feces

Žé'ąhè /zhā-oⁿ-hā/ *v.*, bake, 1. to cook in the oven 2. *watązi žé'ąhè*, to cook fresh corn on the cob over live coals

Zé'de /zā'-thā/ *v.*, treatment, medical treatment, to use medicines or therapy to cure sickness

Žeádigdą /zhā-ä'-dē-gthoⁿ/ *n.*, breechcloth, a cloth, orig. tanned buckskin, covering a man's lower body in place of shorts or the like

Zébe /zā'-bā/ *adj.*, shadowy, clouded, dark, dim

Žegá' /zhā-gä/ *n.*, hips and thighs, body parts of humans and animals

Žegá'skà /zhā-gä-skä/ *n.*, Chikaskia River, lit., white hips and thighs, the Chikaskia River in Oklahoma (The river was named by a woman of white descent. When jokingly told by a male relative how clear the Arkansas River was and that those residing nearby used it to bathe in, she responded, "We white hips and thighs bathe in a river equally clear.")

Žégdą /zhā'-gthoⁿ/ *v.*, roast, to roast something on embers; now to cook or bake in the oven

Žémusnadè /zhā'-mü-snä-dā/ *v.*, squat, to sit on one's heels

Žéži /zhā'-zhē/ *v.*, fry, refers to food that is cooked in fat or oil; *wažéži*, to fry something

Zí' /zē'/ *n.*, mustard, the yellow powder from the seeds of the mustard plant, used as a condiment

Zí' /zē'/ *n.*, yellow, the color yellow

-ží' /zhē'/ *suffix*, denotes something negative, as in *údą~*, not good, *adá~*, didn't go

Ží'de /zhē'-dā/ *adj.*, red, the color red; *žíde egą*, reddish; *žíde gáxe*, redden or make red

Zi'žíde /zē'-zhē'-dā/ *adj.*, orange, lit., yellow-red, orange or orange color

Žįáx'čì /zhēⁿ-ä'x-chē/ *adj.*, very small, miniature, very little in size

Žįáxčį /zhēⁿ-ä'-xchēⁿ/ *adj.*, minuscule, very small, tiny, minute

Žįáxčiáčą /zhēⁿ-ä'-xchē-ä'-choⁿ/ *adj.*, minuscule, tiny, minute

Žíbe /zhē'-bā/ *n.*, leg, a limb of a human being used for walking, standing, etc.; also a limb of other animals

Žíbe'ut'ága /zhē'-bā-ü-t'oⁿ'-gä/ *n.*, femur, in anatomy, the thigh bone

Žíbe ni'é /zhē'-bā nē-ä'/ *n.*, leg ache, usu. refers to overuse of the legs, namely, by children

Žídą /zhē'-doⁿ/ *n.*, dew, moisture from the air condensed on outdoor things, esp. at night

Žįgá /zhēⁿ-gä'/ *adj.*, little, small, 1. small in stature, height 2. small in size 3. may refer to children, as in *žįgá mà*, the little ones

Žįgá' /zhēⁿ-gä'/ *adj.*, small, 1. small, little, etc. 2. *n.*, little ones, children (your ~ ones are growing up.)

Ziúbidà /zēü'-bē-doⁿ/ *n.*, bugle/bugler, a bugle or one who blows a bugle (The Ponca acquired some musical instruments during the 1800s and used them in and around the drum. A person blew the bugle in a certain part of the Hedúškà song.)

Žįžį'íye /zhēⁿ-zhēⁿ'-ē'-yä/ *v.*, whisper, speak softly

Zizí'je'íyè /zē-zē'-jä-ē'-yä/ *v.*, undertone, whisper, to speak in a low voice

Zízigè /zē'-zē-gä/ *adj.*, elastic, stretchy, as a sweater, *unáži'zizigè*

Zízigè /zē'-zē-gä/ *adj./n.*, stretchable, something that can be stretched

Zizík'à /zē-zē-k'ä'/ *n.*, turkey, a large game bird, *Meleagris gallopavo*

Žú' /zhü'/ *n.*, flesh, the substance or tissue that covers the body of humans and animals, mainly made up of muscles and fat

Žú'dį́gigì /zhü-thēⁿ-gē-gē'/ *n.*, palsy, uncontrolled movements of the body

Žúáži /zhü'-ä'-zhē/ *n. phr.*, doesn't have physical stamina, usu. refers to a person who doesn't have the strength or even the ability to do a job

Žuáži /zhü-ä'-zhē/ *adj.*, frail, lit., not strong, usu. refers to a person who is critically ill or in poor health

Žuáži /zhü-ä'-zhē/ *adj.*, weak, physically weak, being ill or deathly ill

Zúbe /zü'-bä/ *adj./n.*, pointed, an object, such as a stick, pole, knife, etc., that has an end that comes to a point

Zudé' /zü-dä'/ *v.*, whistle, to produce a high-pitched sound by blowing through the teeth and lips

Žúga /zhü'-gä/ *n.*, body, entails the entire human body system or physical structure

Žúga'uhè /zhü'-gä-ü-hä'/ *v.*, shudder or tremble from fear, to shiver with fear

Žúgadišįǝgi /zhü'-gä-thē-shēⁿ'-ǝ-gē/ *v.*, tremble, twitch, usu. refers to a medical condition that involves an involuntary contraction of muscles in the upper part of the body, esp. the shoulder area

Žúgauhè /zhüⁿ'-gä-ü-hä'/ *n.*, fearful, a feeling of fright with chills, to make one's nerves tingle, to make one's hair stand on end

Žúgauxp'áde /zhü'-gä-üx-p'ä'-thä/ *adj.*, failing health, physical breakdown, an affliction causing an individual to physically deteriorate

Žúgdè /zhü'-gthä'/ *prep.*, with, in the company of, together with

Žúhè /zhü'-hä'/ *v.*, wade, to wade; to walk in water

Žúk'igdè /zhü'-k'ē-gthä'/ *adv.*, together, 1. jointly (the pipes fit ~) 2. mutually (the crowd agreed ~) 3. as partners (the man and the woman were ~, the boys were ~)

Žunákadè /zhü-nä'-kä-dä'/ *n.*, fever, lit., hot flesh, the increase of body temperature, usu. due to illness of some sort

Žút'ą /zhü'-t'oⁿ/ *v.*, grow, 1. refers to plants coming up 2. in modern times, used in connection with raising children

Žút'ą /zhü'-t'oⁿ/ *v.*, raise, to grow crops

Žuži'dè /zhü-zhē'-dä'/ *n.*, measles, also called rubeola

English to Ponca

A

abandoned **Ádiudè** /ä'-thē-ü-dā'/ *v.t., past t.*, abandoned, left somebody behind

abduct **Adį́'ayáda** /ä-thēⁿ'-ä-yä'-thä/ *v.t.*, abduct, make off with, to snatch, usu. refers to taking somebody away

ability **Đihį́de** /thē-hēⁿ'-dā/ *n.*, ability, capacity or ability to do something with the hands, such as repairing or making something

ablaze **Ná'xdį̀** /nä'-xthēⁿ'/ *adj.*, ablaze, aflame, usu. refers to wood burning in the fireplace or the wick on an oil lamp

able **Ukíhi** /ü-kē'-hē/ *adj.*, able, capable, can do

above **Á'mustà** /ä'-mü-stä/ *prep.*, above, over—*á'mustà'ta, prep.*, from above

above **Bahášiat'à** /bä-hä'-shē-ä-t'ä/ *adv.*, above, indicates something that is on top of or overhead

above the brow **Héə'bažà** /hä'-ə-bä-zhoⁿ'/ *n.*, above the brow, lit., where the horns stick out (The expression designates an area of the face analogous to where the horns of the American bison are, slightly above a man's or woman's brow)

abrasive **Xáxagà** /xä'-xä-gä'/ *adj.*, abrasive, rough, coarse, scratchy

absent **Ahíbažì** /ä-hē'-bä-zhē'/ *adj.*, absent, not present, not present at a certain place

absorb **Ánaxihidè** /ä'-nä-xē-hē-thä'/ *v.*, absorb, taking in or taking up the rays of sunshine, as in basking in the sun

absurd **Égažiáčạ'** /ä'-goⁿ-zhē-ä'-choⁿ/ *adj.*, absurd or absurdity, something that is unreasonable or even foolish

abundant **Íše** /ē'-shä/ *adj.*, abundant, usu. refers to some things that are available in abundance

abuse **Đinágdè** /thē-nä'-gthä'/ *n.*, abuse, lit., handle as a captive, ill treatment, but not violent

accessible **Wadíxt'i ihéde** /wä-thē'-xt'ē ē-hä'-thä/ *adj.*, accessible, easy to get, reach, usu. refers to something valuable left out in the open so that it can be easily taken

accidental **Mạnạ́di** /moⁿ-noⁿ'-thē/ *adj.*, accidental, unintentional, inadvertent

accolade **Ú'đaxubè** /ü'-thä-xü-bä/ *n.*, accolade, a stated or public commendation or recognition of somebody for accomplishing something that seemed impossible; *wádaxubè*, to commend a group for an impossible task

accurately **Gap'í** /gä-p'ē'/ *adv.*, accurately (Suggests something that is done exactly the right way. The prefix *ga* usu. indicates something done by force, as in striking or by wind. ~ then, may refer to someone hitting a baseball at a precise place on the bat, causing the ball to travel a great distance.)

accuse **Á'gda** /ä'-gthä/ *v.i.*, to accuse, to put blame on

accustom **Égipiạ̀'** /ä'-gē-pēoⁿ'/ *v.*, accustom, adjust to, adapt to, to get used to or become familiar with something or to people, to become accustomed to any condition

accustomed **Udádadà** /ü-thä'-dä-dä-thoⁿ'/ *adj./v.*, accustomed to, to be committed to doing something that was tried, or to come together by strong interest

accumulate **Áhigedè** /ä'-hē-gä-thä'/ *v.*, accumulate, accrue, amass, to gather or collect

accurate **Wágazù** /wä'-gä-zü'/ *adj.*, accurate, no errors, something that is without error, usu. refers to something that is passed along by word of mouth

ace **Uk'ádeugdà** /ü-k'ä'-dä-ü-gthoⁿ'/ *n.*, ca. 1900, the ace in a deck of playing cards

achieve **Ukétạ** /ü-kä'-toⁿ/ *v.*, achieve, attain;

n., accomplishment, the completion of something

aching feet **Sí'nié** /sē-nē-ā'/ *n.*, aching feet, 1. when a person stands all day on their feet 2. a person who may have medical issues with the feet

acorn **T'áškà** /t'ä'-shkä'/ *n.*, acorn, the nut from an oak tree, genera *Quercus* and *Lithocarpus*, family Fasgaceae

acquired **Uk'í'ket'ą̀** /ü-k'ē'-kä-t'oⁿ'/ *v.*, acquired, to gain, accomplish, acquire for self, as in hard work to get a position on the job

across **Ádit'à** /ä'-thē-t'ä'/ *adv.*, across (*úwe kè ~ adái*, he is going ~ the field)

across **Ák'í'p'azà** /ä'-k'ē'-p'ä-zoⁿ'/ *prep.*, across, facing something or somebody across an intervening space

across **Gdadį́'** /gthä-dēⁿ'/ *adv.*, across, refers to something lying across one's pathway, roadway, or, e.g., laying an object horizontally on something vertical, forming a 90° angle

action **Úšką̀** /ü'-shkoⁿ'/ *n.*, action, event, something that happens, a happening or occurrence

adage **Udáde** /ü-thä'-dā/ *n.*, adage, a saying that expresses a common experience, a proverb, a saying

adequate **Š'eną́'egà** /sh-ā-noⁿ'-ē-goⁿ'/ *adj.*, adequate, lit., just enough, enough, ample

adjacent **Sakíba** /sä-kē'-bä/ *prep.*, adjacent, adjacent to something in particular

adjoin **Uką́ha** /ü-koⁿ'-hä/ *v.*, adjoin, connect or be right next to (*waą́ niášigà mà ~ bazì*, he never even ~ himself to the singers)

admonish **Í'nitè** /ē'-nē-tä/ *v.*, admonish, reprimand and caution somebody concerning something; *wénitè*, to admonish or reprimand two or more

adverse **Ágdadè** /ä'-gthä-thä/ *adj.*, adverse, unfavorable, undesirable, or harmful

adz **P'ę́'** /p'āⁿ'/ *n.*, adz or ax; in ancient times, a Ponca handheld tool made of flint, which could be attached to an elk horn for scraping

affix **Udísną** /ü-thē'-snoⁿ/ *v.*, affix, to attach something to something, to put something on something

afraid **Wanáp'è** /wä-noⁿ'-p'ä'/ *adj.*, afraid, frightened or apprehensive about something

African lion **Wanít'a wáxa** /wä-nē'-t'ä wä'-xä/ *n.*, African lion, *Panthera leo*, a large cat that has a yellow coat; the male members have a shaggy mane that is often referred to by the Ponca as *p'át'a hį́ škubè*, thick haired in the front

Afro-American **Xįhá sabè** /xēⁿ-hä' sä-bä'/ *n.*, Afro-American, lit., black complexion, person of Negroid descent (The tribal usage of the term *wáxe sábe*, black white man, was common from ca. 1870 to the 1950s.)

afterward **Ágahadì** /ä'-gä-hä-dē'/ *adv.*, afterward, later on or subsequently, usu. refers to something being done after something has started

afterward **Đišt'ą́tedì** /thē-sht'oⁿ'-tä-dē'/ *adv.*, afterward, subsequent to, or something that will happen after something has been completed

afternoon **Mí'dą mą́ši ákihą̀** /mē'-thoⁿ moⁿ'-shē ä'-kē-hoⁿ'/ *n.*, afternoon, the time between noon and evening

again **Đeną́'** /thä-noⁿ'/ *adv.*, again, "do it again," connotes an action taken one more time

again **Šadúha** /shä-thü'-hä/ *adv.*, again, usu. refers to saying something or repeating a behavior that could be characterized as good or bad

again **Ši'édąbà** /shē-ä'-thoⁿ-bä/ *adv.*, prefix, again, usu. used in an admonishing statement (*~ gáxeažigà*, never do this ~)

again **Šip'í** /shē-p'ḗ/ *adv.*, again, once more, once again (do come ~)

again **Šíšt'ąnà** /shē'sh-t'oⁿ-noⁿ'/ *adv./n.*, again, something done all over again, usu. connotes something negatively done

again and again **P'í'dądà** /p'ḗ'-thoⁿ-thoⁿ'/ *adv.*, again and again, a repeated behavior or action taken

agape love **Wadá'edè** /wä-thä'-ā-thä'/ *n.*, agape love (godly love)

agent **Idádidaì** /ē-thä'-dē-thä-ē'/ *n.*, agent, refers to U.S. government agents on Indian reservations; *idádidait'à*, agency, the office of the agent

aggravated **Baskíde** /bä-skē'-thä/ *adj.*, aggravated, irritated, provoked

agree **Ínąhì** /ē'-noⁿ-hēⁿ'/ *v.*, agree, agree to, to consent, acquiesce

aha! **Xa·** /xä·/ *interj.*, *fem.* aha!, an expression indicating awareness or a discovery, e.g., catching someone in the act

ahead of **É't'ądì** /ā'-t'oⁿ-thē'/ *prep.*, ahead of, earlier than or sooner than others

air conditioner **Mąze'ugásni gáxè** /moⁿ'-zā-ü-gä'-snē gä'-xä'/ *n.*, air conditioner, ca. mid-twentieth century, lit., metal that makes cool

aircraft **Mądé'giá'** /moⁿ-dā'-gē-oⁿ'/ *n.*, aircraft, lit., flying canoe, airplane, or jet-propelled aircraft

airport **Mądé'giá' unášt'à** /moⁿ-dā'-gē-oⁿ' ü-noⁿ'-sht'oⁿ'/ *n.*, airport, a facility where flights take off and land that includes a control tower for incoming and outgoing aircraft

aisle **Ugdí ut'ánhà** /ü-gthēⁿ' ü-t'ä'-noⁿ-hä'/ *n.*, aisle, a passageway, usu. refers to space between seats, as in a theater

akin **É'kidè** /ā'-kē-thä/ *adj.*, usu. 1. persons related by blood 2. things that have a common origin

alien **Uk'ít'e** /ü-k'ḗ'-t'ä/ *adj./n.*, alien, a description of or a person of another tribe, race, or nation

alight **Á'idą** /ä'-ē-thoⁿ'/ *v.*, alight, to descend from the air and come to rest, as a bird comes to rest on a limb of a tree

alight **Ídą** /ḗ'-thoⁿ/ *v.*, alight, to land, to descend from the air onto the ground or water (a duck can ~ on the water)

alive **Nít'a** /nē'-t'ä/ *adj.*, alive, a living thing; *aní't'à*, *1st pers. sing.*, I am alive; *đaní't'a*, you are alive; *nít'aì*, he/she/they are alive; *ąnít'a*, we are alive

all **Bdúga** /bthü'-gä/ *pron.*, all, the whole of, entirety

all **É'ną** /ā'-noⁿ'/ *pron.*, all, the total amount, everything, the entire (~ *ušté*, that's ~ that's left)

all **Gdúba** /gthü'-bä/ *pron.*, all, refers to a specific group of people or things

all day **Ába'idàugdè** /oⁿm'-bä-ē-thä'-ü-gthä'/ *prep. phr.*, all day, refers to doing something throughout the day, as in walking throughout the day on a journey

all day **Ába ídawà** /oⁿ'-bä ē'-thä-wä'/ *n./adv.*, all day, all the day long

alley **T'í'ut'áną** /t'ē'-ü-t'ä'-noⁿ/ *n.*, alley, lit., in between houses, a narrow street in the back of buildings

alligator **Sihí'dubà** /sē-hē'-dü-bä'/ *n.*, alligator, crocodile

all night **Hą́'idàugdè** /hoⁿ'-ē-thä'-ü-gthä'/ *prep. phr.*, throughout the night

allow **Gídik'à** /gē'-thē-k'oⁿ'/ *v.*, allow, making or granting a way clear for somebody, may be a social issue or passageway

almost **Ą́dinà** /oⁿ'-thē-noⁿ'/ *adv.*, almost, nearly, just about, not quite

alone **Enąxčì** /ā-noⁿ'-xchē'/ *pron.*, alone, something or somebody being by itself

alone **Ešną́** /ā-shnoⁿ'/ *adj.*, alone, refers to a

person (or group) who did or wanted to do something alone

alongside Sakíbadì /sä-kē'-bä-dē'/ *adv.*, alongside, next to, next to something nearby

along with Udáha /ü-thä'-hä/ *v.*, along with, something attached to another thing

also Edábe /ā-dä'-bä/ *adv.*, also, in addition, included, usu. refers to adding another one of something

alternately Át'ak'idada̖ /ä'-t'oⁿ-k'ē-thoⁿ-thoⁿ'/ *adv.*, alternating, interchanging, to repeatedly interchange

although Ða̖ža̖ /thoⁿ-zhoⁿ'/ *conj.*, although, used to show that something does not happen without something else happening

always Idá'ugdè /ē-thä'-ü-gthä'/ *adv.*, always, often, frequently, time and again, regularly

always Ša̖ša̖ /shoⁿ'-shoⁿ'/ *adv.*, always, perpetually, something that will go unchanged, as in certain cultural values that never change

always Skéwa̖ /skä'-woⁿ/ *adv.*, always, usually, customarily, habitually, ordinarily (he ~ does that)

ambivalent É'šte'a̖'a̖' /ā'-shtä-oⁿ'-oⁿ'/ *adj.*, ambivalent, unsure, mixed feelings, conflicting feelings about something

amble Ša̖xt'igà ma̖dì /shoⁿ'-xt'ē-goⁿ' moⁿ-thēⁿ'/ *v.*, amble, mosey, going at a slow pace in no particular direction

ambulance Wakéga wa'ì̖ /wä-kä'-gä wä-ēⁿ'/ *n.*, ambulance, a motorized vehicle for transporting the sick or injured to a hospital or health facility

American Ma̖hi t'a̖gà /moⁿ'-hē t'oⁿ'-gä/ *n.*, American, lit., big knife (circa 1800s)

amid Gaza̖ /gä-zoⁿ'/ *prep.*, amid, mid, middle

amid Gaza̖át'a /gä-zoⁿ'-ä'-t'ä/ *adv.*, amid, "way out there" in the middle

among Gaza̖di̖ /gä-zoⁿ'-dēⁿ/ *prep.*, among, amid, "right there" in the middle

ample Wašé'xt'ì /wä-shä'-xt'ē'/ *adj.*, ample, plenty, a lot, more than enough, usu. refers to the amount of food

ancient P'aha̖gadìta̖ /p'ä-hoⁿ'-gä-dē'-toⁿ/ *adj.*, ancient, lit., something from the beginning, antiquated

and Kí' /kē'/ *conj.*, and, in addition to (*gdéba̖ na̖bá ~ wí*, twenty ~ one)

and Ší' /shē'/ *conj.*, and, usu. used with a verbal clause (*edéga̖xt'ì éga̖ gáxaì, ~ éga̖ gáxaì,* he did it before, ~ he's doing it again)

and then Ga̖'ki /goⁿ'-kē/ *conj.*, and (*T'áwa̖gda̖ta ahí ~ t'í ke t'á agda̖i,* they went to the city ~ went home)

angels Wak'a̖da wašiʃt'amà /wä-k'oⁿ'-dä wä-shē-ʃ'-t'ä-mä/ *n.*, angels, lit., God's helpers, heavenly beings

anger Baskíde /bä-skē'-thä/ *v.*, anger, being incensed or infuriated

anger Waží'áška /wä-zhē'-ä'-shkä/ *v.*, anger, lit., on the edge of anger, ready to express something with anger

anger Waží'k'ude̖ /wä-zhēⁿ'-k'ü-thä'/ *n./v.*, anger, to become quickly angered

anger Ważí̖'p'iáži /wä-zhēⁿ'-p'ē-ä'-zhē'/ *v.*, anger, lit., bad thoughts, fury, indignation

anguished Ná̖dèwaxp'ádi /noⁿ'-dä'-wäx-p'ä'-thē/ *n.*, anguished, emotional distress because of something that has happened

animal Wanít'à /wä-nē'-t'ä'/ *n.*, animal, monster or creature

ankle Sik'a̖ /sē-k'oⁿ'/ *n.*, ankle, the talocrural region; *sihí*, ankle

ankle bone Sit'áxì /sē-t'ä'-xē'/ *n.*, ankle bone

annoy Áma̖k'ažì /ä'-moⁿ-k'ä-zhē'/ *v.*, annoy, to irritate, aggravate, or get on one's nerves, tired of, to grow disgusted with something or somebody, sick of it or him;

ámąk'ažiwaɖè, something that a person can get tired of

another way **Wedáži** /wā-dä'-zhē/ *pron.*, another way, a different direction (~ *aɖái*, he went ~)

ant **Žą́gdiškà** /zhoⁿ'-gthē-shkä'/ *n.*, ant, a social insect of the family Formicidae that may be red, black, brown, or yellow and is found throughout the world in warmer climates

anticipating **Ú't'ąbedè** /ü'-t'oⁿ-bā-thä'/ *v.*, anticipating, knowing beforehand that something is going to happen or come to fruition

anticipation **Uhít'a'žì** /ü-hē'-t'ä-zhē'/ *n.*, anticipation; expectation, usu. excitedly expecting something good to happen

antisocial **Et'áhažì** /ā-t'ä'-hä-zhē'/ *adj.*, antisocial, unwilling to associate in a normal or friendly way with other people, responds disruptively to the established social order, has bad ways

anxious **Uhít'ažì** /ü-hē'-t'ä-zhē'/ *adj.*, anxious, eager

anxiousness **Waką́didè** /wä-koⁿ'-dē-thä'/ *n.*, anxiousness, uneasiness

anybody **Ebédįkeštiwà** /ā-bā-thēⁿ-kä-shtē-woⁿ'/ *pron.*, anybody, anybody who is somebody (of importance or fame) or an average person

anyone **Ebé'štiwà** /ā-bā'-shtē-woⁿ'/ *pron.*, anyone, any one person

anything **Įdádąštiwà** /ēⁿ-dä'-doⁿ-shtē-woⁿ'/ *pron.*, anything, any kind of thing, whatever

anytime **Atą́štiwà** /ä-toⁿ'-shtē-woⁿ'/ *pron.*, anytime, whenever, at any time

apart **Uką́ha** /ü-koⁿ'-hä/ *adj.*, apart, separated from others, as a person who is present but never comes in to be involved

ape **Išt'ínikè t'ągá** /ē-sht'ē'-nē-kä' t'oⁿ-gä'/ *n.*, ape, refers to any of the large primates; does not include humans

apologetic **Waxp'ádį k'igáxe** /wäx-p'ä'-thēⁿ k'ē-gä'-xä/ *adj.*, apologetic, lit., causing oneself to feel sorrow or pity over something, usu. precipitated by some action or act followed by a humbling act of compassion

Appaloosa **Nį́de ská** /nēⁿ'-dā skä'/ *n.*, Appaloosa, a breed of horse with a spotted coat, striped hooves, and other identifying features (These horses were supposedly developed by the Shoshone people.)

apparel **Wádahà** /wä-thä-hä'/ *n.*, apparel, clothing, attire, garb, material worn on the human body

apparent **Wét'ąì** /wä-t'oⁿ-ē'/ *adj.*, apparent, something that is clear, understood, or able to be seen

appear **Wadíšna** /wä-thē'-shnä/ *v.*, appear, something that becomes visible among other things; *ši'wadíšnà*, reappear, something that comes back to be seen visually

appearance **Udą́be** /ü-doⁿ'-bā/ *n.*, appearance, 1. the look or form of something 2. the look or form of a person

appear **Édąbè** /ā'-thoⁿ-bā/ *v.*, appear, come into sight, become visible

appease **Gašt'ą́k'a** /gä-sht'oⁿ'-k'ä/ *v.*, appease, pacifying somebody to get something from them; bribe, to get something from or to make a person do something by offering something desirable to them

applaud **Nąbé gačáčakì** /noⁿ-bā' gä-chä'-chä-kē'/ *n./v.*, applaud, an expression of approval made by clapping the hands

apple **Šé** /shä'/ *n.*, apple, a sweet fruit of the family Rosaceae, genus *Malus*; *šé hì*, apple tree

apply **K'ią́** /k'ē-oⁿ'/ *v.t.*, apply, refers to the Ponca practice of putting on or applying ocher or charcoal on the face in preparation for battle (*įdé'sabèàde*, I make my face black)

apprehend **Udą́** /ü-thoⁿ'/ *v.*, apprehend, to

arrest somebody, capture (to ~ him, they gave chase)

apprehensive **Idák'uhè** /ē-thä'-k'ü-hā'/ *adj.*, apprehensive, for fear that, uneasy about something

approach **A·í'** /ä··ē'/ *v.*, approach, coming toward where I am or where we are, to draw closer to us; *aíbadà*, they are approaching us

approve **Ínahì** /ē'-noⁿ-hē'/ *v.*, approve, somebody approves; *idánahì, 1st pers.*, I approved of; *ídanahì, 2nd pers.*, you approved something; agree to, to consent, acquiesce

approve **Wé'nahì** /wā'-noⁿ-hēⁿ'/ *v.*, approve, endorse, agree, somebody approves with us

approves **Wé'ginahì** /wā'-gē-noⁿ-hē'/ *v., 3rd pers. sing.*, approve or sanction, he/she/it approves it

apricot **K'áde híškubè** /k'oⁿ'-dā hēⁿ'-shkü-bā'/ *n.*, apricot, a small, round, fuzzy fruit from the genus *Prunus*

April **Nąží'štà** /noⁿ-zhēⁿ'-shtoⁿ'/ *n.*, April, lit., constant or recurring rain, the fourth month in the year

apron **Wádaè'** /wä'-thä-ā'/ *n.*, apron, a garment worn over the front of clothes in order to keep clean while cooking or doing other work

Arapaho **Mąxpíat'à** /moⁿ-xpē'-ä-t'oⁿ'/ *n.*, the Arapaho Tribe of Native Americans, "Stands on the clouds" (A variant meaning or pronounciation among the Ponca is *mąxpíat'ù*, blue cloud)

arbor **Sadégde** /sä-dā'-gthā/ *n.*, arbor, a Ponca shade made of upright poles and with rafters made of smaller poles covered with small leafy branches

arborvitae **Má'zi bdáska** /mä'-zē bthä'-skä/ *n.*, arborvitae, a flat-leaf evergreen of the genus *Thuja*

arch **Sí'náuskída** /sē'-noⁿ-ü-skē'-dä/ *n.*, arch, in anatomy, below the ~ of the feet

arch **Sí'náxixè** /sē'-noⁿ-xē-xä'/ *n.*, arch, in anatomy, the ~ of the foot

argue **U'wá'iyè** /ü-wä'-ē-yä'/ *n.*, argue, argumentative; quarrelsome; a disagreement in which differing views are expressed

argue **U'wí'e** /ü-wē'-ä/ *v.*, argue, to argue over something, to dispute, contend

argue over **Íye ákikì** /ē'-yā ä'-kē-kē'/ *v.*, argue over, to argue over some specific thing

arid **Mąbíze** /moⁿ-bē'-zā/ *adj.*, arid, very dry, bone dry, usu. refers to parts of the country that have very little water or rainfall

Arikara **P'ádi pizà** /p'ä'-thēⁿ pē-zä'/ *n.*, Arikara Tribe of Native Americans, lit., sand Pawnee

arise **Nąží'** /noⁿ-zhēⁿ'/ *v.*, arise, stand

arise **Nąží'á** /noⁿ-zhēⁿ'-ä'/ *v., fem.*, arise, stand up

arise **Nąží'gà** /noⁿ-zhēⁿ'-gä'/ *v., masc.*, arise, stand up

arise **P'áha** /p'ä'-hoⁿ/ *v.*, arise, usu. refers to telling someone to get up out of bed

Arkansas City ᴋꜱ **T'áwągdà iš'áge** /t'oⁿ'-woⁿ-gthoⁿ' ēsh-ä'-gä/ *n.*, Arkansas City, Kansas, lit., old man town

Arkansas River **Ní'skà** /nē'-skä/ *n.*, Arkansas River, lit., crystal-clear water (The Ponca who came to Indian Territory in the nineteenth century said the river was "crystal clear." It later became polluted following oil exploration, due to discharge from a refinery and to raw sewage.)

arm **Á'** /ä'/ *n.*, arm

arm **Á'hidè** /ä'-hē-dä'/ *n.*, lower arm

arm **Á'ut'ága** /ä'-ü-t'oⁿ'-gä/ *n.*, upper arm

armband **Á'ubísną** /ä'-ü-bē'-snoⁿ/ *n.*, an armband or wrist ornament of the Hedúškà dance paraphernalia

armpit **Nusí'** /nü-sē'/ *n.*, armpit, the axilla or oxter

around **Bút'audíş̣ą** /bü-t'ä-ü-thē'-shoⁿ/ *adv.*, around (he circled ~ the building)

around **Udíş̣ą** /ü-thē'-shoⁿ/ *adv.*, around, to go around something

arrive **Atí'** /ä-tē'/ *v.*, *3rd pers. sing./pl.*, arrive/s, he/she/it/they ~ here

arrive **Đatí'** /thä-tē'/ *v.*, *2nd pers. sing.*, arrive, you ~ here

arrive **P'í'** /p'ē'/ *v.*, *1st pers. sing.*, arrive, I ~ there; *1st pers. pres/past. part.*, I came there

arrived **Ahí'** /ä-hē'/ *v.*, *3rd pers. pl.*, *past part.*, arrived, they ~ there

arrogant **Mą́'sa'** /moⁿ'-sä/ *adj.*, arrogant, conceited, pompous, egotistical

arrowhead **Mą́'** /moⁿ'/ *n.*, a projectile point such as an arrowhead or spearhead

arrow shaft **Mą́'dehì** /moⁿ'-dā-hē'/ *n.*, arrow shaft, usually made of lightweight wood (One end of the arrowhead is attached and the other end is feathered and nocked, accommodating the bowstring of the bow.)

artery **K'ą́'** /k'oⁿ'/ *n.*, artery, blood vessel, the vessel that carries blood throughout the body, coming from the heart

arthritis **Wahí'ni'é** /wä-hē'-nē-ā'/ *n.*, arthritis, a joint disorder that involves pain and inflammation of the joints

artificial **Ukédįažì** /ü-kā'-thēⁿ-ä-zhē'/ *adj.*, artificial, not the real thing, fake

artistic **Wadíxu đip'ì** /wä-thē'-xü thē-p'ē'/ *adj.*, artistic, usu. refers to somebody who excels at drawing and painting pictures

as **Šégą** /shä'-goⁿ/ *conj.*, refers to something done in the same way or to performing some action in the same manner

ashamed **Í'št'è** /ē'-sht'ä'/ *adj.*, ashamed, ashamed of, feeling shame, guilt, or disgrace because of some foolish act or statement made; *idák'iaštè*, *1st pers.*, ashamed of something; *ík'ištaì*, *3rd pers.*, ashamed of something

ashes **Mąxúde** /moⁿ-xü'-dä/ *n.*, ashes, residue, cinders

ashes **Nąxdę́** /noⁿ-xthāⁿ'/ *n.*, ashes, the residue of something after burning

ash tree **T'ašną́'gè'hì** /t'ä-shnoⁿ'-gä'-hē'/ *n.*, ash tree, genus *Fraxinus* of the family Oleaceae

aside **Uk'áde** /ü-k'ä'-dä/ *adv.*, aside, something aside of the main body of animate or inanimate things

ask **Ímąxè** /ē'-moⁿ-xä/ *v.*, ask, asking an individual about a person, place, or thing; *wémąxè*, asking a group of people about a person, place, or thing; *ądámąxaì*, asking me personally about something

ask for **Ná** /nä'/ *v.*, ask for, to ask for something from somebody, such as a favor or material goods; *giná*, to ask for something back

asleep **Žą́'t'ę̀** /zhoⁿ'-t'āⁿ/ *adj.*, asleep, fast asleep or dead to the world

asphalt **Weádaskabè sábe** /wā-ä'-thä-skä-bā' sä'-bä/ *n.*, asphalt, usu. used for surfacing roads; other uses include roofing shingles

aspirin **Mąká bút'a** /moⁿ-koⁿ' bü-t'ä/ *n.*, aspirin, a medicine that relieves pain and is known as acetylsalicylic acid

assail **Ti'dą́bidè** /tē-thoⁿ'-bē-thä'/ *v.t.*, assail, sudden appearance of the enemy with intent to attack

assist **Gík'à** /gē'-k'ä'/ *v.*, assist, help, to ask for help or support

assortment **Á'židądą̀** /ä'-zhē-thoⁿ-thoⁿ'/ *n.*, assortment, lit., different things, a variety of things, hodgepodge

astride **Ágažadè** /ä'-gä-zhä-dä/ *adv.*, astride, straddling, as in horseback riding with legs on both sides of the horse

at **-at'a** /ä-t'ä/ *prep.*, *suffix*, at, as in *gáat'à*, ~ that place over there, *usniát'a*, ~ the place where it is cold at **Et'á** /ā-t'ä'/ *prep.*, at, denotes a presence or occurrence on or near something

ate **Ą'wą́dataì** /oⁿ-woⁿ'-thä-tä-ē'/ *v.*, 1st pers. pl., past t., ate, we ate

atop **Ágahà** /ä'-gä-hä'/ *prep.*, atop, on top of

attach **Ábaxą̀** /ä'-bä-xoⁿ'/ *v.*, attach, pin, as in sticking something into the hair, such as an ornament or a hair clasp

attach **Udísną̀** /ü-thē'-snoⁿ'/ *v.*, attach, putting a thing onto something, as in threading a needle, putting a tire on, screwing a nut onto a bolt

attached **Udáha** /ü-thä'-hä/ *v.*, attached, something that is attached to or connected to something

attain **Uké't'ą̀** /ü-kä'-t'oⁿ'/ *v.*, to attain, achieve, accomplish, to acquire something by effort

attire **Wádahà** /wä'-thä-hä'/ *n.*, attire, clothing, usu. refers to certain type of clothing worn for a purpose

auger **T'ą́deudúdiudè** /t'oⁿ'-dä-ü-thü'-thē-ü-dä'/ *n.*, auger, a drilling device to bore holes in soil, ice, or wood

August **Wadáp'ip'ižè** /wä-thä'-p'ē-p'ē-zhä'/ *n.*, August, lit., corn is in silk, the eighth month of the year

au jus **T'aniúze** /t'ä-nē-ü'-zä/ *n.*, au jus, from the French, the juice that comes from cooking or roasting beef

aunt **Wit'ími** /wē-t'ē'-mē/ *n.*, *masc./fem.*, aunt, father's sister

aurora borealis **Níka nąxè** /nē'-kä noⁿ-xä'/ *n.*, aurora borealis, lit., the spirit of man, northern lights

automobile **K'ip'ínągè** /k'ē-p'ē'-noⁿ-gä'/ *n.*, automobile, auto, car

autumn **T'ą́ga'xdą̀** /t'oⁿ'-gä-xthoⁿ'/ *n.*, autumn, fall, that period of time between summer and winter, approximately three months (September, October, and November); *t'ą́gaxdą́ádi*, past fall; *t'ą́gaxdądą̀*, in the fall

aviary **Wažíga ugdį̀** /wä-zhēⁿ'-gä ü-gthēⁿ'/ *n.*, aviary, a place or enclosure for birds, a coop, a birdcage

awake **Í'kidè** /ē'-kē-thä'/ *v.*, awake, conscious, up

awaken **Đi·xí** /thē·-xē'/ *v.*, awaken, to awaken somebody from sleep, to rouse somebody from sleep

awaken **Í'kip'ahą̀** /ē'-kē-p'ä-hoⁿ'/ *v.*, awaken, waking up following a period of being comatose or unconscious

away from **Gaxát'a** /gä-xä'-t'ä/ *adv.*, away from a particular thing or place; *prefix* for a proper male name in the Wašábe clan of the Ponca people (The name Gaxát'a nąží' implies a bison standing apart from the herd.)

away from **X'ą́xat'à** /xoⁿ'-xä-t'ä'/ *adv.*, away from, not near the people, at a distance from the main body of a group of things or people (*niášigà akà, ~ nąží̀ nài*, the man always stands ~)

awl **Wák'ù'** /wä-k'ü'/ *n.*, awl, a sharp, pointed tool for making marks or holes in leather

ax **Mą́ze'p'è** /moⁿ'-zä-p'ä'/ *n.*, lit., metal adz, ax

B

baby **Šéžįgà** /shä'-zhēⁿ-gä'/ *n.*, baby, a human baby

bachelor **Waú đigè** /wä-ü' thē-gä'/ *n.*, bachelor, a single, unattached man without a woman

back **Ną́ka** /noⁿ'-kä/ *n.*, the back area of a vertebrate animal's body

back **Xáda** /xä'-thä/ *v.*, back, to go backward, a move backward

back of head **T'aí'** /t'ä-ē'/ *n.*, that part of the skull located near the occipital bone, back of head back of neck **P'áhiugdè** /p'ä'-hē-ü-gthä'/ *n.*, back of neck

back of shin **Hí'usági** /hē'-ü-sä'-gē/ *n.*, back of the shin, the calf, the back part of the leg below the knee

back side **Názat'à** /nä'-zä-t'ä'/ *n.*, back side, the part that is farthest from the front, at the rear of something (~ of a teepee or a building)

back up **Názahà** /nä'-zä-hä'/ *v.*, back up, to go backward or move something backward

back up **Níst'ù** /nē's-t'ü'/ *v.*, back up, to move oneself backward, usu. done when exiting a place that is considered holy or of a religious nature

backwater **Niúgašúp'a** /nē-ü'-gä-shü'-p'ä/ *n.*, backwater, refers to water backed up from a main river that stands apart after a flood

backyard **T'í názat'à** /t'ē' nä'-zä-t'ä'/ *n.*, backyard, back of the house or dwelling

bacon **Wašį́** /wä-shēⁿ'/ *n.*, bacon, the meat from the back and sides of a hog

bad **Údąžì** /ü'-doⁿ-zhē'/ *adj.*, bad, 1. describes something that is not good (*šé' k'ip'ínągè kè* ~, that is a ~ car) 2. *adj.*, bad, morally no good (*níášigà* ~ *amà égài*, he is a ~ person)

badger **Xúga** /xü'-gä/ *n.*, badger, a short-legged omnivore in the subfamily Txideinae of the family Mustelidae

Badlands **P'ahéšušudè** /p'ä-hä'-shü-shü-dä'/ *n.*, Badlands, refers to the badlands of South Dakota

bag **Uxdúxa'há'** /ü-xthü'-xä-hä'/ *n.*, bag, *archaic*, a bag to carry personal things

baggage **Wa'į́'** /wä-ēⁿ'/ *n.*, baggage, carried bags, gear, or bundles that contain one's belongings

bake **Žé'ąhè** /zhä'-oⁿ-hä'/ *v.*, bake, 1. to cook in the oven 2. *watázi žé'ąhè*, to cook fresh corn on the cob over live coals

baking pan **Úbihạ̀** /ü'-bē-hoⁿ'/ *n.*, baking pan, a pan used for cooking breads, cakes, and other foods in an oven

baking pan **Wažégdą uxp'é'** /wä-zhä'-gthoⁿ ü-xp'ä'/ *n.*, baking pan, lit., pan for baking, for cooking breads, cakes, and other foods in an oven

baking powder **Wíúnabixạ̀** /wē'-ü'-nä-bē-xoⁿ'/ *n.*, baking powder, leavening agent for baking cakes, breads, etc.

bald **Nąškí šnahá** /noⁿ-shkē' shnä-hä'/ *adj.*, bald, bald headed, somebody who has no hair on his/her scalp; *t'axp'í šnà*, being bald at the crown of the head

bald eagle **P'ásą** /p'ä'-soⁿ/ *n.*, bald eagle, a bird of prey in North America, *Haliaeetus leucocephalus*

baling wire **Mázebdązè** /moⁿ'-zä-bthoⁿ-zä'/ *n.*, baling wire (This type of wire was used for agricultural and industrial purposes.)

ball **T'abé** /t'ä-bä'/ *n.*, ball, a round object used in many games, such as the Ponca game shinny, baseball, football, basketball, golf

banana **Waxt'á' snedè** /wä-xt'ä' snä-dä'/ *n.*, banana, lit., long fruit, a slightly curved, edible, creamy, sweet, soft-fleshed fruit with a yellow skin; *waxt'á' snedè hí*, banana tree

bandage **Ádi'stà** /ä'-thē-stä'/ *v.*, bandage, as in bandaging a wound

bandolier **Nusí'axdadè** /nü-sē'-ä-xthä-dä'/ *n.*, bandolier, orig. a leather strap worn over the shoulders and across the chest to support a pouch or some type of article, 1. a belt with small pockets for storing cartridges that was worn over the shoulders and across the chest 2. in the early twentieth century, a representation of the cartridge belt worn by dancers in the Ponca Hedúškà organization, consisting of hairpipe and metal and glass beads

banishment **Đédewakidè** /thā'-thā-wā-kē-thā'/ *n.*, banishment, expulsion (Among the Ponca, banishing from the reservation a person who violates tribal moral codes too often, including those who commit murder. They are not welcomed back.)

Bannock **Bánikì** /bä'-nē-kē'/ *n.*, Bannock Tribe of Native Americans

baptism **Níʼágaxtʼa̧dè** /nē'-ä'-gä-xt'oⁿ-thä'/ *n.*, baptism, Christian baptism, refers to sprinkling or pouring water upon the individual being baptised

barbed wire **Ma̧ze baídadà** /moⁿ'-zä bä-ē'-thä-thä'/ *n.*, barbed wire, usu. two twisted fencing wires with sharp points set at varied intervals used to fence farmland and other types of property to keep something in or out

barber **Na̧žíha disè'** /noⁿ-zhē'-hä thē-sä'/ *n.*, barber, lit., hair cutter, a person who cuts and styles boys' and men's hair

barefooted **Síʼnúkadi̧** /sē-nü'-kä-thēⁿ'/ *adj.*, barefooted, without shoes or foot covering of any kind

barely **Na̧žiškexčʼì** /noⁿ'-zhē-shkäx-ch-ē'/ *adv.*, barely, not quite (~ *akí*, he ~ got home)

barely **Na̧ži̧xčì** /noⁿ'-zhēⁿ-xchē'/ *adv.*, barely, just about, by very little or to a very small extent

bark **Úhuhù** /ü'-hü-hü'/ *n./v.*, bark, the short, loud cry of a dog

bark **Ža̧dáha** /zhoⁿ-thä'-hä/ *n.*, bark, the outer layer of a tree

barn **Ša̧geʼuná̧ži** /shoⁿ'-gä-ü-noⁿ'-zhē/ *n.*, barn, lit., where the horses stand

barn **Tʼéskàʼuná̧ži** /t'ä'-skä'-ü-noⁿ'-zhē/ *n.*, barn, lit., where the cattle stand

barn swallow **Niškúʼškù** /nē-shkü'-shkü'/ *n.*, barn swallow, of the species *Hirundo rustica*

barrette **Na̧žíhaʼ idádisa̧dè** /noⁿ-zhē'-hä ē-thä'-thē-soⁿ-dā'/ *n.*, barrette, a clip or clasp to hold hair in place

barrier **Áʼna̧ʼsè** /ä'-noⁿ-sä'/ *n.*, a barrier to prevent something or someone from passing through, a shutter

baseball **Tʼabé** /t'ä-bā'/ *n.*, baseball, baseballs have a rubber or cork center, wrapped with yarn and covered with two pieces of horse or cowhide

baseball bat **Tʼabé i̧ʼti̧·** /t'ä-bā' ēⁿ'-teⁿ·/ *n.*, baseball bat, a club made of wood or metal and used to hit a baseball in a baseball game

baseball cap **Wadáge bútʼa** /wä-thä'-gä bü'-t'ä/ *n.*, baseball cap, a cap formerly used by players in the game of baseball, now refers to any commonly worn cap

baseball game **Tʼabéʼa̧** /t'ä-bā'-oⁿ/ *n.*, baseball game, a favorite American game using a bat and ball and played by two teams of nine players

basement **Tʼí hídeátʼa** /t'ē' hē'-dä-ä'-t'ä/ *n.*, basement, room under the house

bashful **Wábagdà** /wä'-bä-gthä'/ *adj.*, bashful, shy, self-conscious

basket **Waxtʼá užì** /wä-xt'ä' ü-zhē'/ *n.*, basket, a container for flowers or fruit

bass **Huhú ítʼa̧gà** /hü-hü' ē'-t'oⁿ-gä/ *n.*, bass, large-mouth bass, *Micropterus salmoides*

bat **Gada̧** /gä-doⁿ'/ *v.*, bat, to hit something away, as in striking a baseball away

bath **Úhidá** /ü'-hē-thä'/ *n.*, bath, a large tub that a person can get into and wash their body

bathe **Hidá'** /hē-thä'/ *v.*, bathe 1. to bathe, wash, cleanse, clean, etc. 2. to swim

bathroom **Úhidá tʼí'** /ü'-hē-thä' t'ē'/ *n.*, bathroom, usu. refers to a room where there is a shower and bathtub

battery **Na̧gdíze** /noⁿ-gthē'-zä/ *n.*, battery, a

device that has electrochemical cells and makes electrical energy

Bazile Creek **Xáda dè užį́gà** /xä'-thä thä' ü-zhēⁿ'-gä/ *n.*, lit., small going back (A small creek known for flowing back when the Missouri R. floods)

bead **Hįská** /hēⁿ-skä/ *n.*, bead, a very small to large rounded piece of glass, wood, or plastic that is pierced for stringing to make a necklace or other kinds of jewelry

beaded belt **Íp'iɖagè á'baè** /ē'-p'ē-thä-gä' ä'-bä-ä/ *n.*, beaded belt, *íp'iɖagè hįská ábaè*, belt covered with beads; *hįbé ábaè*, moccasins covered with beads

beans **Hibɖį́gè** /hē-bthēⁿ'-gä/ *n.*, beans, any type of bean

bean seeds **Hibɖį́si** /hē-bthēⁿ'-sē/ *n.*, bean seeds, usu. saved for planting

bear **Mąčú'** /moⁿ-chü'/ *n.*, bear, a large omnivorous animal, usu. refers to the grizzly bear, *Ursus arctos horribilis*

bearclaw necklace **Mąčúšagè** /moⁿ-chü'-shä-gä/ *n.*, bearclaw necklace (The Ponca made these necklaces from the claws of the grizzly bear.)

beard **Įdé hį́ škúbe** /ēⁿ-dä' hēⁿ' shkü'-bä/ *n.*, beard, lit., thick hair on the face

beat **Gaxɖí'** /gä-xthē'/ *v.*, beat, whip, flog, batter, etc.

beaver **Žá'bè** /zhä'-bä/ *n.*, beaver, a nocturnal, semiaquatic rodent (The North American beaver, *Castor canadensis*, is native to North America.)

beaver dam **Žá'bè t'ą́wągɖą̀** /zhä-bä t'oⁿ'-woⁿ-gthoⁿ'/ *n.*, beaver dam, a dam built by beavers out of various sizes of branches as a place to live and to find protection against predators

become **Égą ahí** /ä'-goⁿ ä-hē'/ *v.*, become, to come to be; *égą hít'įkè*, I will come to be; *égą*

šít'anikè, you will come to be; *égą ahít'akà*, he/she/it will come to be; *égą ągáhit'atè*, we will come to be; *égą sít'amašè*, you (all) will come to be; *égą ahít'amà*, they will come to be

bed **Užą́'** /ü-zhoⁿ'/ *n.*, bed, a piece of furniture used to sleep on

bedding **Umíže** /ü-mē'-zhä/ *n.*, bedding, blanket, sheets, etc. used for a bedcovering

bedew **Áżidą̀** /ä'-zhē-doⁿ'/ *v. phr.*, bedew, becoming wet from dew overnight

bedroom **Užą́t'i** /ü-zhoⁿ'-t'ē/ *n.*, bedroom, a room where people sleep through the night

bedstead **Užą́ ímuzà** /ü-zhoⁿ' ē'-mü-zä/ *n.*, bedstead, lit., poles that hold a bed, the framework of a bed

bee **K'igɖą́xe** /k'ē-gthoⁿ'-xä/ *n.*, bee, any kind of bee of the family Apoidea

beer **Šą́genežè** /shoⁿ'-gä-nä-zhä/ *n.*, beer, lit., horse urine, an alcoholic beverage

beeswax **Kigɖą́xe įgɖè** /kē-gthoⁿ'-xä ēⁿ-gthä'/ *n.*, beeswax, wax made by honeybees of the genus *Apis*

before **E't'ą́diàt'a** /ä-t'oⁿ'-thē-ä-t'ä/ *adv.*, before, earlier than, usu. refers to a task or duty to be there or do something before it is due

before **Ét'ąì** /ä'-t'oⁿ-ē'/ *adv.*, before, usu. used to begin an activity in advance of others (*ukíte amà ~ wak'iɖà*, start in this battle ~ the enemy acts)

before **P'ahą́'gà** /p'ä-hoⁿ'-gä/ *adj.*, before, first, primary, earliest, standing in front of

before **Uɖúši** /ü-thü'-shē/ *prep.*, before, a position such as standing before

befriend **Ikágek'iɖè** /ē-kä'-gä-k'ē-thä'/ *n.*, friendship, companionship, a special relationship between two or more people; an interpersonal bond

beg **Waná'** /wä-nä'/ *v.*, beg, beg for, ask for something to begin beggar **Wanášt'ą** /wä-nä'-sht'oⁿ/ *n.*, beggar, one who habitually begs for something

beg off **Í'íge** /ēⁿ'-ēⁿ'-gä/ *v.*, beg off, reject, doesn't want something viewed or offered

behave **Wá'spè** /wä'-spä'/ *v.*, behave, to behave in a manner that is socially appropriate esp. by being polite, good-tempered, and self-controlled

behead **P'amáse** /p'ä-mä'-sä/ *v.*, behead, decapitate, to behead or to cut off the head of the enemy

behind **Ánazatą** /ä'-nä-zä-toⁿ/ *adv.*, behind, "from behind"

behind **Uxdəá'báži** /ü-xthəä'-bä'-zhē'/ *adv.*, secondary or inferior position

believe **Nądè'ąwągdegą** /noⁿ-dä'-oⁿ-woⁿ'-gthä-goⁿ'/ *v.*, believe, lit., because it is in my heart (The Ponca understanding or truth of a thing was based upon the premises of investigation, practice, and tradition. The truth of God was having confidence in something unseen but experienced in the real world they lived in, so they maintained that proposition or premise that, in turn, solidified their religious belief.)

belittle **Đaxt'áži** /thä-xt'ä'-zhē/ *v.*, belittle, degrade, put down, usu. refers to something done, performed

belittle **Đižúážigą** /thē-zhü-ä'-zhē-goⁿ/ *v.*, belittle, lit., he/she belittled you, put down, discredit, or disgrace

belittle **Wádažįgà** /wä'-thä-zhēⁿ-gä/ *v.*, belittle, to be cocky, brashly overconfident, arrogant, saying something to or about another who is stronger physically (The term suggests taking liberties with words, which may incur negative consequences for the speaker.)

bellow **Hút'ą** /hü'-t'oⁿ/ *v.*, bellow, usu. refers to the bellow of a large animal; *nisúde đihút'ą*, to cause sound to come from an in-strument or whistle, a horn, the whistle of a train

bells **Máze'k'amà'** /moⁿ'-zä-k'ä-moⁿ'/ *n.*, bells, lit., clanging metal, sleighbells

belly **Wašná'** /wä-shnä'/ *n.*, belly, abdomen

below **Híde** /hē'-dä/ *adv.*, below; *hideát'a*, at a certain place below

belt **Í'p'idagè** /ē'-pē-thä-gä/ *n.*, belt, usu. refers to a strip of leather worn around the waist to hold the trousers up; refers to any material around the waist such as a cummerbund or sash

belt buckle **Í'p'idagè idágaškè** /ē'-p'ē-thä-gä' ē-thä'-gä-shkä'/ *n.*, belt buckle

bench **Á'gđì'snedè** /ä'-gthē'-snä-dä'/ *n.*, couch, divan, sofa, settee, bench

bend **Bibđí'bđi'dà** /bē-bthē'-bthē-thä'/ *v.*, to continuously bend, turn, or twist a thing by use of a tool

bend **Bibđį'dà** /bē-bthēⁿ'-thä'/ *v.*, to bend, turn, twist by use of a tool

bend **Đibđí'dà** /thē-bthē'-thä'/ *v.*, to bend, as in bending a wire or turning a handle of a door by use of the hands

beneath **Gihá** /gē-hä'/ *adv.*, beneath; *gigđát'a*, indicates that something is below or beneath another thing

benefit from **Í'giudà** /ē'-gē-ü-doⁿ/ *prep. phr.*, lit., to get better from something, benefit from, suggests getting better through some sort of aid in times of sickness or other hardship

bent **Đigúže** /thē-gü'-zhä/ *adj.*, bent, curved, crooked, not straight—recently applied to people who are dishonest or are involved in criminal activity; *đigúgúže*, zigzag, more than one curve or bend in a thing

berth **E'wáš'nągè užą́** /ā-wä'sh-noⁿ-gä' ü-zhoⁿ/ *n.*, berth, usu. refers to a sleeping bed on a train

beside **Sak'íba** /sä-k'ē'-bä/ *prep.*, beside, animate or inanimate things close together or side by side; *sak'íbadì*, beside, 1. at the side of, nearby 2. usu. refers to something additionally said or done

beside **Ubáhadì** /ü-bä'-hä-dē'/ *prep.*, beside, 1. something or somebody being alongside of something or somebody 2. something or somebody being there but not necessarily wanted in that place or situation (being in the way)

beside **Ukáha** /ü-koⁿ-hä/ *prep.*, beside, at the side of, near

best **Enáúdą** /ā-noⁿ'-ü'-doⁿ/ *adj.*, best, usu. refers to something that is higher or to one who is utmost in perfection

bet **Giší'** /gē-shē'/ *v.*, bet, betting something in a Ponca gambling game (Historically, tribal members bet a variety of personal items in a gambling game, such as a necklace, earrings, moccasins, and now, money.)

between **Ídąbeádi** /ē'-doⁿ-bä-ä'-dē/ *prep.*, between, flanked by, in the middle where something or somebody can be seen

between **Udízą** /ü-thē'-zoⁿ/ *prep.*, between, in the middle of where something or somebody is

bewitch **Gdáxe** /gthoⁿ'-xä/ *v.*, bewitch, to affect somebody with a spell causing sickness (The Ponca people used medicines to cure people of sickness. This term may have been adapted from white people who practiced witchcraft. The Ponca word means rotten or rancid.)

bewitched **Íxt'à** /ē'-xt'ä'/ *v.*, bewitched, somebody determined to be ~

beyond **Ákihà** /ä'-kē-hoⁿ/ *adv.*, beyond, further than, past from where you are; *uwák'ihà*, *n.*, often refers to generations, as in designating a relationship of parents to future generations

biceps **Aú'k'ąt'à** /äü'-k'oⁿ-t'oⁿ/ *n.*, biceps, muscle in the upper arm

big **T'ągá** /t'oⁿ-gä'/ *adj.*, big, large

big belly **Wašná't'ągà** /wä-shnä'-t'oⁿ-gä'/ *adj.*, big belly

Big Dipper **Míxasì t'ągà** /mē'-xä-sē' t'oⁿ-gä'/ *n.*, Big Dipper (Ursa Major), lit., big duck's feet, seven stars resembling a duck's feet

bigfoot **Ídá'dįgè** /ēⁿ-dä'-thēⁿ-gä'/ *n.*, no father, lit., has no father, a mythological character described as a large hairy being, sometimes called Bigfoot or Sasquatch (Searches for such a being have been inconclusive in modern times.)

bigheaded **Niášigà íye wadéga** /nē-ä'-shē-gä' ē'-yā-wä-dā'-gä/ *n.*, bigheaded, a person who speaks as though he/she knows everything; a "know it all"

bighorn sheep **Haxúde'hé't'ągà** /hä-xü'-dä-hā'-t'oⁿ-gä'/ *n.*, bighorn sheep

big toe **Sip'áhi ut'ága** /sē-p'ä'-hē ü-t'oⁿ-gä/ (*masc./fem.*) (**Sip'óho t'ągá** /sē-p'ō-hō t'oⁿ-goⁿ'/ [*masc.*]) *n.*, big toe (The first term is *masc./fem.* The second is *masc.*)

bile **T'ep'ízi** /t'ä-p'ē'-zē/ *n.*, bile, a fluid secreted by the liver that aids in digestive processes; a part of the liver that is edible

binoculars **Mąze wédąbè** /moⁿ'-zā wä'-doⁿ-bä'/ *n.*, binoculars, also called field glasses, used to magnify objects in the distance

bird **Wažíga** /wä-zhēⁿ'-gä/ *n.*, bird, 1. any kind of fowl 2. a proper male name in the Hísadà clan of the the Ponca people

birth **Wédadè** /wā'-dä-thā'/ *v.*, birth, giving birth

birthed **Í'da** /ē'-dä/ *v.*, *past t.*, birthed, gave birth

birthday **Àba ída** /oⁿ'-bä ē'-dä/ *n.*, birthday, a day celebrating the anniversary of one's date of birth

biscuit **Wamúske ukédi** /wä-mü'-skä ü-kā'-

thē/ *n.*, lit., common bread biscuit, among the Ponca, a baked edible bread product made from flour

bison **T'é'** /t'ā/ *n.*, bison, a large, social animal with a large head, short horns, and a large hump above its shoulders that roamed the Great Plains before the coming of the Europeans (Most historians use the term *buffalo* rather than *bison*.)

bison bull **T'enúga** /t'ā-nü'-gä/ *n.*, bison bull

bison calf **T'ežíga** /t'ā-zhēⁿ'-gä/ *n.*, bison calf

bison cow **T'emíga** /t'ā-mē'-gä/ *n.*, bison cow

bison hide **T'é'hà** /t'ā'-hä/ *n.*, the hide of a bison

bison hunt **T'é'unè** /t'ā'-ü-nä/ *v.*, bison hunt (The Ponca had biannual bison hunts.)

bison tail **T'é'sįdè** /t'ā' sēⁿ-dā'/ *n.*, the tail of a bison

bit **Mázedahè** /moⁿ'-zā-thä-hā/ *n.*, bit, the metal part of a bridle that goes into the horse's mouth to control the animal

bit **Udáhe** /ü-thä'-hä/ *n.*, bit, the part of a pipe stem (modern pipe) that is held in the mouth

bite **Đáxt'à** /thä'x-t'ä'/ *v.*, to bite (*šánudà áka, niášìgà ḍįkè ~ì*, the dog ~ the man); *đaxà*, to break something by biting; *gđáxt'à*, to bite himself as in biting his lip or tongue

bite off **Đašp'é** /thä-shp'ä'/ *n.*, bite off, biting off a piece of food, such as a cookie

bitter **P'á'** /p'ä'/ *adj.*, bitter, pungent

black **Sábe** /sä'-bä/ *adj.*, the color black, being the color of coal or carbon

black ant **Žágđiškà sábe** /zhoⁿ'-gthē-shkä' sä'-bä/ *n.*, black ant, a species of carpenter ant, common ant in the United States

black antelope **T'áxt'ì sįde sábe** /t'ä'-xt'ē' sēⁿ-dä sä'-bä/ *n.*, black antelope

black bear **Wasábe** /wä-sä'-bä/ *n.*, black bear, a black bear native to North America (*Ursus americanus*)

black duck **Míxa gdáxe** /mē'-xä gthoⁿ'-xä/ *n.*, black duck, refers to a little black duck that elders say is "not good to eat"

black eagle feather **Mášạ'šabè** /moⁿ'-shoⁿ-shä-bä/ *n.*, black eagle feather, orig. worn in the hair by new young members of the Heđúškà organization

blacken **Bisábe** /bē-sä'-bä/ *v.*, blacken, to make something black by pressing down on

blacken **Násabède** /nä'-sä-bä-thä'/ *v.*, blacken, 1. to make something black, either by burning or by painting 2. *įdé sabeđè*, to blacken the face, refers to the apperance of Ponca warriors on a war journey

blacken face **Įdé sábe'ág'idè** /ēⁿ-dä' sä'-bä-ä'-g-ē-thä'/ *v. phr.*, I blackened my face, refers to Ponca warriors who painted their faces black before they went to war, meaning they were prepared to die if necessary

Blackfoot **Sihásabè** /sē-hä'-sä-bä/ *n.*, the Blackfoot Tribe of Native Americans

blackhaw fruit **Nášạmà** /noⁿ'-shoⁿ-moⁿ'/ *n.*, blackhaw fruit, a small, flat seed covered with a sweet-tasting hull (*nášạmàhì*, blackhaw tree, *Viburnum rufidulum*, is a flowering shrub that grows on the Ponca reservation along the Arkansas Rover in northern Oklahoma.)

blackjack oak tree **T'áškahì nušiáha** /t'ä'-shkä-hē' nü-shēä'-hä/ *n.*, blackjack oak (*Quercus marilandica*), a small oak tree; many are located in Osage County east of the Ponca reservation in Oklahoma

black panther **Įgdága** /ēⁿ-gthoⁿ'-gä/ *n.*, black panther, the panther, cougar, or mountain lion (This variety of large cat roamed along the rivers in Oklahoma and has been seen by tribal members many times along the banks of the Arkansas River, running along the east boundary of the Ponca reservation)

black pepper **Wiú'ki'hạ** /wēü'-kē-hoⁿ'/ *n.*,

usu. black pepper, an eastern Indian plant ground with its husk and used as a condiment

black shawl **Waį'ágdabe'sábe** /wä-ēⁿ-ä'-gthä-bā-sä'-bā/ *n.*, a beaded, fringed black shawl, a popular Ponca shawl in the first half of the twentieth century

black snake **Wés'à'sábe** /wā's-ä'-sä'-bā/ *n.*, black snake, a nonvenomous snake of the species *colubridae*

black-tailed deer **T'áxt'ì síde sábe** /t'ä'-xt'ē' sēⁿ'-dā sä'-bā/ *n.*, black-tailed deer, *Odocoileus hemionus*; also known as mule deer

black walnut **T'áge't'ągà** /t'ä'-gä-t'oⁿ-gä'/ *n.*, black walnut, lit., big nut, family Juglandaceae (*t'áge t'ągà hì*, black walnut tree)

Blackwell ok **Nisní'sabè** /nē-snē'-sä-bā/ *n.*, Blackwell, Oklahoma

black widow **Údiske sábe** /ü-thē-skä sä'-bā/ *n.*, black widow, a poisonous female spider with an hourglass-shaped red mark on the abdomen

blame **Ágda** /ä'-gthä/ *v.*, blame, hold responsible

blanket **Waį** /wä-ēⁿ/ *n.*, blanket, cover, mantle, something to cover up with when sleeping or keeping warm

blend **Í'kidibdą** /ē'-kē-thē-bthoⁿ/ *v.*, blend, to mix together, mixture

blend in **Udúgahì** /ü-thü'-gä-hē'/ *v.*, blend in, to stir something into another substance, usu. refers to cooking; *ígahì*, mix in

blind **Wé'daⁿì** /wā'-thä-zhē'/ *adj.*, blind, sightless; *n.*, refers to one who is blind

blink **Đip'įze** /thē-p'ēⁿ'-zā/ *v.*, blink, blink the eyes; *įšt'á đip'įze*, blink the eyes

blister beetle **Niúžiwadè** /nē-ü'-zhē-wä-thä'/ *n.*, blister beetle, any of the beetles (Coleoptera) that bite or secrete a blistering agent, causing redness and blisters on the skin

blizzard **Máde gašúde** /mä'-thä gä-shü'-dä/

n., blizzard, a strong, cold wind driving snow, a snowstorm

block **Ánąsądè** /ä'-noⁿ-soⁿ-dä'/ *v.*, block, block a door with one's body by leaning against it or placing a foot at the bottom of the door to keep it from opening

block **Ánąsè** /ä'-noⁿ-sä'/ *n./v.*, block, to block, barrier, blockade, barricade

block and tackle **Wé'dihą̀** /wā'-thē-hoⁿ'/ *n.*, block and tackle, a device using at least two pulleys with a rope to lift heavy loads

blond **Nąžíha zì** /noⁿ-zhē'-hä zē'/ *adj.*, blond, blond hair; *n.*, refers to a person who is blond as "that blond"

blood **Wamí'** /wä-mē'/ *n.*, blood, a bodily fluid that delivers necessary nutrients and oxygen to all parts of the body to maintain life and also transports waste from body cells

bloodletting **Ágaxù** /ä'-gä-xü'/ *n./v.*, bloodletting, a medical procedure for drawing blood for relief, bleed or to draw blood

blood vessel **K'ą́** /k'oⁿ'/ *n.*, blood vessel, artery, the vessel that carries blood throughout the body, coming from the heart

bloom **Gabdá** /gä-bthä'/ *v.*, bloom, to come into flower, refers to flowers opening

blossom **Xdá'** /xthä'/ *n.*, blossom, coming from a seed plant, the beginning of a plant

blouse **Uną́žį xáxadè** /ü-noⁿ-zhēⁿ xä'-xä-dä'/ *n.*, blouse, usu. a lady's garment

blow **Bixą́** /bē-xoⁿ'/ *v.*, 1. to inflate by blowing, to blow up a balloon, to air up a tire 2. to blow on embers to start a fire

blow a horn **Bihút'ą̀** /bē-hü'-t'oⁿ'/ *v.*, to blow a horn or whistle; *bihúhut'ą̀*, to continuously blow a horn or whistle 2. pressing down on the horn in an automobile

blow away **Gahį́'da** /gä-hēⁿ'-thä/ *v.*, to blow away, as in anything not secured on a windy day

blowing wind **Gaúdibdį** /gä-ü'-thē-bthēⁿ/ *v.*, blowing wind, something or somebody causing things or debris to blow upon something or on people

blow nose **P'á' gažį'** /p'ä' gä-zhēⁿ/ *v.*, blow nose, to expel mucus from the nose

blown on **Ágabdį** /ä'-gä-bthēⁿ/ *n./v.*, blow on, something blown upon

blow smoke **Đašúde** /thä-shü'-dä/ *v.*, blow smoke, as in smoking a pipe, cigarette, etc.

blue **Tú'** /tü'/ *adj.*, blue, the color of the sky

blue bird **Wažį't'ù** /wä-zhēⁿ'-t'ü'/ *n.*, blue bird, lit., blue anger, 1. refers to the blue jay 2. proper name in the Níkapášnạ clan of the Ponca people

blue clay **Wasé't'u'** /wä-sä'-t'ü/ *n.*, blue clay, deposits composed of phyllosilicate minerals containing water in a mineral content in the soil that can cause clay to be various colors (The Ponca found this clay along the Missouri River.)

blue corn **Wahába'ukédì** /wä-hä'-bä-ü-kä'-thē'/ *n.*, blue corn

blue knife **Mą́hi t'ú** /moⁿ'-hē t'ü'/ *n.*, blue knife (Mentioned by elders of the tribe, a blue flint was quarried to make knives and other usable implements.)

bluff **P'a'dáge** /p'ä-thä'-gä/ *n.*, bluff, a particular, known place in Nebraska where individual battles were fought

blur **Ádixudè** /ä'-thē-xü-dä'/ *n.*, blur, something that is unclear or fuzzy

blur **Įšt'á ádixudè** /ēⁿ-sht'ä' ä-thē-xü-dä'/ *n.*, blur, visual problems causing things to be seen as obscure or indistinct

board **Wamą́he** /wä-moⁿ'-hä/ *v.*, board, to live temporarily with some other family at their expense, but with willingness to help with household work or expenses

board **Žạbdáska** /zhoⁿ-bthä'-skä/ *n.*, board,

lit., flat wood, a piece of wood formed into a flat or square piece

bobcat **Įgdą́ga'mą́t'anạhà** /ēⁿ-gthoⁿ'-gä-moⁿ'-t'ä-no-hä/ *n.*, bobcat, *Lynx rufus* of the cat family Felidae 2. tiger, following the introduction of exotic animals to America

body **Žúga** /zhü'-gä/ *n.*, body, entails the entire human body system or physical structure

boil **Ábixạ̀** /ä'-bē-xoⁿ/ *v.*, boil, simmer, bubble, e.g., water changing from a liquid to a vapor with the addition of heat

boiled **Ná't'u'bè** /nä-t'ü-bä/ *v.*, boiled, cooked to pieces, usu. something boiled, e.g., meat, potatoes

Bois D'Arc Creek **Níp'à** /nē-p'ä/ *n.*, Bois D'Arc Creek, in Kay County, Oklahoma, a small tributary entering the Salt Fork River — referred to in Ponca as "bitter water"

Bois D'Arc tree **Žạzíhi** /zhoⁿ-zē'-hē/ *n.*, bois d'arc tree, also known as Osage orange, horse apple, *Maclura pomifera* (The Ponca favor the wood to make bows.)

bolt **Mą́ze udúgaškè** /moⁿ'-zä ü-thü'-gä-shkä'/ *n.*, bolt, a round metal bar with threads of various lengths used with a nut to fasten two or more pieces of solid material together

bomb **Wé'mubdazè** /wä'-mü-bthä-zä'/ *n.*, bomb, an explosive device, such as dynamite, wartime explosives

bone **Wahí'** /wä-hē'/ *n.*, bone, the hard connecting parts of vertebrate skeletons; two principal parts of this material are collagen and calcium phosphate; *hí*, bone

bone joints **Hí'úkitè** /hē'-ü'-kē-tä'/ *n.*, joints or bone joints, a place where bones of humans and other vertebrate animals are connected

book **Wabáxu** /wä-bä'-xü/ *n.*, book, manuscript, paperback, hardback

bore **Ubáxduxà** /ü-bä'-xthü-xä/ *v.*, bore, 1. to make a hole in something 2. to make a ditch by passing something over the ground repeatedly or by water flowing through

borrow **Uná'** /ü-nä'/ *v.*, borrow, to use, by agreement, something that belongs to somebody else

boss **Wénudáhągà** /wä'-nü-doⁿ'-hoⁿ-gä/ *n.*, boss, strawboss, team leader, somebody put in charge

both **É'dąbà** /ä'-thoⁿ-bä/ *pron.*, both, as in both were present

both **Wádą** /woⁿ'-doⁿ/ *adv.*, both, usu. refers to performing a task together or doing the same thing

bother **Biná'gdè** /bē-nä'-gthä/ *v.*, to bother and annoy another person or an animal

both sides **Agdákahą** /ä-gthoⁿ'-kä-hoⁿ/ *adv.*, on both sides, on each side of something

bottle **P'éxehà** /p'ä'-xä-hä/ *n.*, bottle, lit., gourd hide, refers to glass bottles or other man-made containers for liquids

bottom **Hídeát'a** /hē'-dä-ä'-t'ä/ *n.*, bottom, at the lowest place or bottommost part of something; *hidéát'à't'adižą*, toward the bottom of something

bounteous **Waté'** /wä-tä'/ *n.*, 1. bounteous, *archaic*, abundant, overflowing, usu. refers to abundance of game, fruit, edible plants 2. the Elkhorn River in Nebraska

bovine **T'éska** /t'ä'-skä/ *n.*, bovine, lit., white bison, relates to or resembles bovines, esp. the ox or cow

bovine intestine **T'é'šíbè** /t'ä'-shē'-bä/ *n.*, bovine intestine; orig. referred to bison intestines

bow **Bip'ámąxè** /bē-p'ä'-moⁿ-xä/ *v.*, bow, making somebody bow by pressing down on their head

bow **Haxúde hé t'ągà máde** /hä-xü'-dä hä'

t'oⁿ-gä' moⁿ'-dä/ *n.*, bow, lit., bow made of "big horn sheep horns" and wood

bow **Máde** /moⁿ'-dä/ *n.*, bow, a weapon for shooting arrows, usu. made of wood from the Osage Orange tree

bow **P'á'máxe** /p'ä'-moⁿ-xä/ *v.*, bow, 1. to bow the head as in reverence during a prayer 2. to sit with a bowed head when in a state of emotional distress over something

bowel movement **Žé'** /zhä/ *n.*, bowel movement, feces

bowl **Uxp'é't'ągà** /ü-xp'ä'-t'oⁿ-gä/ *n.*, bowl, a large bowl for mixing flour, vegetables; a serving bowl

bowling **T'abé ganáge** /t'ä-bä' gä-noⁿ'-gä/ *n.*, bowling, bowling game (The object of the game is to knock down ten pins at the end of a bowling lane with a bowling ball.)

box **K'ú'gè** /k'ü'-gä/ *n.*, box, trunk, chest, case, crate

boxelder **Žá'be't'ahì** /zhä-bä-t'ä-hē/ *n.*, boxelder, *Acer negundo*, a choice tree for beavers to fell in northern Oklahoma along the Arkansas River

boxing **Uk'í'tį** /ü-k'ē'-tēⁿ/ *n.*, boxing, pugilism, the manly art of self-defense

box turtle **G'é'gdé'ze** /g-ä'-gthä'-zä/ *n.*, box turtle, terrapin, family Emydidae, a land turtle that has a moveable hinge on the lower shell that allows it to retract in the shell and close up

boy **Núžigà** /nü'-zhēⁿ-gä/ *n.*, boy, young male, a youngster

brace **Ábat'ù** /ä'-bä-t'ü/ *v.*, brace, to hold or prop something up

bracelet **Axíbe** /ä-xē'-bä/ *n.*, bracelet

bracing **Idábat'ù** /ē-thä'-bä-t'ü/ *adj.*, bracing, holding, or propping something up

brag **Đažáwa** /thä-zhä'-wä/ *v.*, brag, to brag or boast about somebody's accomplishments; *wáḓažawà*, to brag or boast about a group; *k'igḓížawà*, to brag or boast about oneself

braid **Áskù** /ä'-skü'/ *n.*, braid, a singular braid worn by the Ðíxidą and Níkapášną clansmen (The braid was part of the "mohawk" hairstyle, where the short hair was cut to the crown of the head and the rest of the hair grew long and was braided into a single braid by the Ðíxidą. The Níkapášną did not have the braid but tied eagle feathers where the hair grew long below the crown of the head.)

braid **Gasądè** /gä-soⁿ-dä/ *n.*, braid, three separate strands of human hair in an intertwined arrangement (This was a Ponca hair fashion worn by men and women as well as children. Men and boys wore the braids over the front of the shoulders while women and young girls wore theirs over the back.)

braided yarn **Ugásnè'žídè** /ü-gä'-snä'-zhē'-dä'/ *n.*, braid yarn, yarn braided into the hair, worn by men

brain **Wédixdì** /wä'-thē-xthē'/ *n.*, brain, that part of the body that houses and governs the spirit of a human, his/her thoughts, intentions, and emotional responses to the world in which he/she lives

branching horn **Hé'šádagè** /hä'-shä'-thä-gä'/ *n.*, 1. branching horn of the bull elk 2. proper male name among the Ponca people

brand **Náxudè** /nä'-xü-thä'/ *v.*, brand, to burn a mark or symbol on cattle

brassiere **Ðíʃmątè** /thē'-ʃ-moⁿ-tä'/ *n.*, brassiere, bra, a woman's undergarment that covers and supports the breasts

brazen **Úš'adįgè** /ü'sh-ä-thēⁿ-gä'/ *adj.*, brazen, bold and unashamed, shameless, impudent; lacking modesty

bread **Ní'dè** /nē'-dä'/ *n.*, light bread, wheat bread, dinner rolls, or any other commercially prepared bread

bread **Wamúske** /wä-müⁿ-skä/ *n.*, 1. orig. bread made with powdered cornmeal 2. bread made with powdered wheat

bread **Wamúskè ukédi** /wä-müⁿ-skä' ü-kä'-thē/ *n.*, biscuits, lit., common bread

bread crumbs **Wamúske t'ubáde** /wä-müⁿ-skä t'ü-bä-thä/ *n.*, bread crumbs, small pieces of bread, usu. used in crumbing foods, casseroles, etc.

break **Bixą'** /bē-xoⁿ'/ *v.*, break, to cause something to come to pieces; *bixą'xą̀*, pressing down on something, breaking it into pieces by use of the hands; *baxą'*, to break something by pushing down; *baxą́xą*, to continue to break something to pieces by pushing down; *ḓixą́*, to break something with the hands; *ḓixą́'xą̀*, break, continue to break something to pieces with the hands; *gaxą́'*, to break something to pieces by force; *gaxą́'xą*, break, to continue breaking something to pieces by force; *nąxą́'*, to break something to pieces by running over it or by stepping on it; *nąxą́'xą*, to continue to break something to pieces by running over or stepping on it

break down **Šedą́** /shä-thoⁿ'/ *v.*, break down, collapse, go kaput; *šešédą́*, break down, the structure of something broken down in several places; *bišédą*, break down by pressing; *bišéšédą*, break down by continued pressing down; *ḓišédą*, breakdown by use of hands; *ḓišéšédą*, break down by continued use of the hands; *gašédą*, to break down by force; *gašéšédą*, break down by continuous use of force; *nąšédą*, break down by stepping on or driving over something; *nąšéšédą*, break down by continuously stepping or driving over something

breakout **K'ináṣibè** /k'ē-noⁿ-shē-bā'/ *v.*,
1. break out, usu. refers to animals, such as
horses or cattle 2. take flight from, as a person may escape from confinement

breast **Mązé** /moⁿ-zā'/ *n.*, breast, the upper
front part of the female human body, the
ventral region

breastfeed **Mązé'į** /moⁿ-zā'-ēⁿ/ *v.*, breastfeed,
to feed an infant with breast milk from
female breasts

breathe **Niú'** /nē-ü'/ *v.*, breathe, to inhale and
exhale

breathing **Niúdizè** /nē-ü'-thē-zā'/ *v.*, breathing, inhalation, gulp of air

breathless **Gaskí** /gä-skē'/ *adj.*, breathless, out of
breath, gasping, winded, fighting for breath

breechcloth **Žeádigdą** /zhā-ä'-dē-gthoⁿ/ *n.*,
breechcloth, a cloth, orig. tanned buckskin,
covering a man's lower body in place of
shorts or the like

breed **K'ídixè** /k'ē'-thē-xā'/ *n.*, breed, breeding partners in animals

Bressie Flats **Ugáxdi** /ü-gä'-xthē/ *n.*, Bressie
Flats, several sections of land in Noble
County, Oklahoma, on the Ponca Reservation ("Land grabbers" once acquired these
lands. Hence the term *ugáxdi*, to grab with
hands.)

breeze **Ugásni žįgà** /ü-gä'-snē zhēⁿ-gä'/ *n.*,
breeze, light wind, current of cool air

brick **Í'e náẓidedè** /ē'-ā nä'-zhē-dä-thä'/
n., brick, a made or baked block of clay
or other material that is used to build
buildings

bridge **Uhéátą** /ü-hä'-ä'-toⁿ/ *n.*, bridge, a
structure built to span a river, crevice, or
valley to allow passage

bridge of nose **P'á'uskída** /p'ä'-ü-skē'-dä/ *n.*,
bridge of the nose

bridle **Mąze'dahè** /moⁿ-zā-thä-hä'/ *n.*, bridle,
a harness for a horse's head

bring **Adígià(gá)** /ä-thēⁿ'-gēä'(gä')/ *v.*, bring,
a command to bring; *adíáhi*, brought something to that place

bring **Agdádį atì** /ä-gthä'-theⁿ ä-tē'/ *v. phr.*,
bring, to ~ his own

bring **Agímądía(gá)** /ä-gē'-moⁿ-thēⁿ'-ä(gä')/
v., bring, fetch, go and get (*mąkásabè
dúba* ~, ~ some coffee)

bringing **Adíágadį** /ä-thēⁿ'-oⁿ'-gä-thēⁿ/
v., bringing, bringing a specific thing
(*uxp'éte* ~, we are ~ the dishes)

Briton **Xįhá'skà mąsa** /xēⁿ-hä'-skä' moⁿ-sä/
n., Briton, lit., an uppity (persnickity) white
person, those who dwell in the country of
England

broadcloth **Waįk'ąhazì** /wä-ēⁿ'-k'oⁿ-hä-zē'/
n., broadcloth, a red and blue broadcloth
sewn together, said to be worn by women
ca. 1800s; became a man's ceremonial blanket in later years (The blanket had a yellow-
or gold-colored ribbon or cloth border.)

broadcloth **Waį ukíbatè** /wä-ēⁿ' ü-kē'-
bä-tä'/ *n.*, broadcoth, usu. red and blue
broadcloth sewn together (This imported,
fine woven cloth had a likeness to deerskin. A closely woven or densely textured
fabric, it is made of wool and has a lustrous finish. The Ponca wore the blue
section over the left shoulder based upon
a lost ritual with the Osage people, who
wore the red section over the left shoulder. A dark blue broadcloth sewn together
with a white stripe down the center was
also used by members of the Native
American Church.)

broke **Xą́** /xoⁿ'/ *v., past t.*, broke

broken **Bixą́í'** /bē-xoⁿ'-ē'/ *v., past t.*, to be broken, fractured, cracked, caused something
to separate into pieces

broken **Šedą́** /shä-thoⁿ'/ *v.*, broken, something that was in one piece and has fallen

apart; something that was running, e.g., an automobile, and is now broken down

broken **Šešé'dą** /shā-shā'-thoⁿ/ *adj.*, broken to pieces

broken **Xixáde** /xē-xä'-thā/ *v.*, broken, usu. refers to glass, ceramics, etc. (The word is usu. used to refer to something that has been cracked.)

brooch **Wágdą** /wä'-gthoⁿ/ *n.*, brooch, set, pin, a piece of jewelry or other kind of decorative item attached to clothing

brood **Wažį́šte** /wä-zhēⁿ'-shtā/ *v.*, brood, to be dejected, to feel self-pity, pout, to express sulky unhappiness about something

brook **Wačíška žįgá** /wä-chē'-shkä zhēⁿ-gä'/ *n.*, brook, a small stream, rivulet

broom **Wébabexį̀** /wā'-bä-bä-xēⁿ'/ *n.*, broom, a brush made of bristles and used to sweep floors and other surfaces, indoors or outdoors

brother **Wisą́ga** /wē-soⁿ'-gä/ *n., masc./fem.*, brother, a word to address a younger male sibling (this is my ~)

brother **Wit'ínu** /wē-t'ē'-nü/ *n., fem.*, brother, the feminine word for addressing an elder male sibling (this is my ~)

brother **Wižį́de** /wē-zhēⁿ'-thā/ *n., masc.*, brother, the masculine word for addressing an elder male sibling (this is my ~)

brother-in-law **Wišį́e'** /wē-shē'-ä/ *n.*, brother-in-law, (woman saying: my ~)

brother-in-law **Wit'áhą** /wē-t'ä'-hoⁿ/ *n.*, brother-in-law, (man saying: my ~)

brought **Adį́ áti** /ä-thēⁿ' ä'-tē/ *v. past t., past part.* of "to bring"

brought here **Adiáti** /ä-thēä'-tē/ *v., past t.*, brought here, to bring a specific thing to this place

brow **Hé'úbažą̀** /hā'-ü-bä-zhoⁿ'/ *n.*, brow, lit., where the horns are—above right and left of the brow or forehead, the area at the hairline

brown **Šábe** /shä'-bā/ *adj.*, brown, 1. the color brown, dark 2. *v.*, darken, to make something a darker color

bruise **Wamiú't'è** /wä-mēü'-t'ä'/ *n.*, bruise, usu. caused when a break occurs in the blood vessels near the surface of the skin whereby bits of blood cause discoloration

Brule **Šaą́xt'ì** /shä-oⁿ'-xt'ē'/ *n.*, Brule, Brule of the Teton Dakotas

brush **Učíže** /ü-chē'-zhä/ *n.*, brush, thicket, undergrowth, a dense patch of bushes, shrubs

brush arbor **Sadé'gdè** /sä-dā'-gthä'/ *n.*, brush arbor

brush hog **Učíže įnąsedè** /ü-chē'-zhä ē'-noⁿ-sä-thä'/ *n.*, brush hog, a large rotary mower, usu. pulled or attached to a tractor to cut thick, deep weeds or brush

budding out **Xdát'a'bdúga'gabdà** /xthä'-t'ä-bthü'-gä-gä-bthä'/ *n.*, budding out, plants that unfold

buffalo belly **T'é níxa** /t'ä' nē'-xä/ *n.*, buffalo belly; edible parts include the rumen, or flat, smooth tripe; the reticulum, honeycomb tripe; and the omasum, the book or bible-leaf tripe

buffalo berry **Wažį́de** /wä-zhēⁿ'-dä/ *n.*, buffalo berry, also called Nebraska currant, *Shepherdia argentea*, of the oleaster family Elaeagnaceae

buffalo carp **Hužíde** /hü-zhē'-dä/ *n.*, buffalo carp from the family Catostomidae of the genus *Ictiobus*

buffalo chip **T'ežé bat'è** /t'ā-zhä' bä-t'ä'/ *n.*, buffalo chip, 1. the waste product from bovine species that include domestic cattle, bison (buffalo), and others 2. the name of one of the men who accompanied Chief Standing Bear and testified in a landmark constitutional civil rights case for Native Americans in 1879 in Omaha, Nebraska

buffalo grass **Xáde banáṇa** /xä'-dā bä-noⁿ'-
noⁿ/ *n.*, buffalo grass, *Buchloe dactyloides*, a
perennial grass that grows in clumps, as the
Ponca word *banáṇa* suggests

buffalo-horn cap **T'é' héúp'agdà** /t'ā' hā'-ü'-
p'ä-gthoⁿ/ *n.*, buffalo-horn cap, a headpiece consisting of the head and horns of a
buffalo bull

buffalo police **T'é' wanášhe** /t'ā' wä-noⁿ'-shā/
n., buffalo police, a security group for various Ponca activities, including the biannual
Sun dance and annual bison hunt (Other
documents show that most historians use
buffalo for bison.)

bugle/bugler **Ziúbidà** /zēü'-bē-doⁿ'/ *n.*, bugle/
bugler, a bugle or one who blows a bugle
(The Ponca acquired some musical instruments during the 1800s and used them
in and around the drum. A person blew
the bugle in a certain part of the Heđúškà
song.)

build a fire **Né'de** /nā'-thā/ *v.*, to build a fire

bull **Nugá'** /nü-gä'/ *n.*, bull, any adult breed
of mammals or fowl including domestic
cattle, seals, chickens, etc.

bull **T'é'ska'núgà** /t'ā'-skä-nü'-gä'/ *n.*, bull, a
male member of domestic cattle or bovines

bullet **Mázemà** /moⁿ'-zä-moⁿ/ *n.*, bullet, lit.,
metal projectile point, shell, ammunition

bullfrog **T'ébiàsnedè** /t'ā'-bē-ä'-snä-dā/ *n.*,
bullfrog

bumblebee **K'igđáxet'àgà** /k'ē-gthoⁿ'-xä-t'oⁿ-
gä'/ *n.*, bumblebee, a large black and yellow bee of the genus *Bombus*, in the family
Apidae

bump **Ámàtì** /ä'-moⁿ-tēⁿ'/ *v.*, bump, to bump
into something; *ákimàtè*, to bump into each
other

bump **T'áshi** /t'ä'-shē/ *n.*, bump, result of
swelling or contusion

bumping **Ámàtìtì** /ä'-moⁿ-tēⁿ'-tēⁿ'/ *v.*, bump-

ing, e.g., when a shutter continuously
bumps against the wall or window

bumpy **Ámàtìtì** /ä'-moⁿ-tēⁿ'-tēⁿ'/ *adj.*, bumpy,
e.g., refers to something that bumps and
jolts along a roadway while riding in some
kind of vehicle

bun **T'aídibút'a** /t'ä-ē'-thē-bü'-t'ä/ *n.*, bun, a
woman's hairstyle, tight row of hair either
braided or straight, worn in the back of the
head

bunch **Xą·de** /xoⁿ'-dā/ *n.*, bunch, a group or
cluster of things together, a group of people

bundle **Wabáxt'e** /wä-bä'-xt'ä/ *n.*, bundle,
things that are tied or held together in a
bag of a sort (A bundle, whether large or
small, usu. contained medicines among the
Ponca. Sometimes the entire skin, tail, and
head of an otter was made into a bundle in
which to keep various medicines and related articles.)

bundle up **K'igđíp'up'ù** /k'ē-gthē'-p'ü-p'ü'/ *v.*,
bundle up, usu. refers to wrapping oneself
up with blankets or, as in times past, robes

bunion **Síúbažù** /sē'-ü'-bä-zhü'/ *n.*, bunion, an
enlargement of the joint at the base of the
big toe, the hallux

burden **Waį skíge** /wä-ēⁿ' skē'-gā/ *n.*, burden, 1. load, something carried that is heavy
2. *v.*, to be oppressed with worry, or something difficult to carry emotionally 3. *n.*,
pack, package

burial casket **Wat'é užą́** /wä-t'äⁿ' ü-zhoⁿ'/ *n.*,
burial casket

buried **Waxaí** /wä-xäē'/ *v.*, *past. t.*, buried,
buried the remains of several people

burn **Usé'** /ü-sä'/ *v.*, burn, to burn something up

burned **Ągúwài** /oⁿ-gü'-woⁿ-ē'/ *v.*, *1st pers. pl.*,
we burned it

burned **Ní'dè** /nē'-dä'/ *v.*, 1. burn, usu. a person getting burned 2. used when food is
ready, is cooked

burning **Uwíne** /ü-wē'-nā/ *adj.*, burning, as in "the burning house"

burning **U's'áde** /ü-s-ä'-thā/ *adj.*, burning, as in a sensation caused by application of certain types of medication on the skin surface or by other sources, such as soap in the eyes

burnish **Badią'ba-bà** /bä-thē-oⁿ-bä-bä'/ *v.*, burnish, to polish, make shine

burnt **Náxudè** /nä'-xü-dā/ *v.*, burnt, scorched, usu. refers to cooked food

burn up **Ná'dįgè** /nä'-thēⁿ-gā'/ *v.*, burn up, something consumed by fire

burro **Nit'át'ągà núšíáha** /nē-t'ä'-t'oⁿ-gä' nü'-shē'-ä'-hä/ *n.*, burro, a small donkey found in Latin America

burrow **Mąšáde** /moⁿ-shoⁿ'-dä/ *n.*, burrow, a tunnel or a hole dug into the ground by an animal for habitation

burrowing owl **Wapúgahadà** /wä-pü'-gä-hä-dä'/ *n.*, burrowing owl, a small owl that lives in open landscapes such as open ranges, prairies, and farmlands and usu. makes its nests in prairie dog burrows and other burrows

burst **Gabdáze** /gä-bthä'-zā/ *v.*, burst, to break open, to rupture something

bury **Waxé'** /wä-xā'/ *v.*, bury, 1. lay to rest, inter 2. put in the ground

bus **K'ip'ínągè t'ągà** /k'ē-p'ē'-noⁿ-gā' t'oⁿ-gä'/ *n.*, bus, a long motor vehicle with many seats, usu. for fare-paying passengers

bus depot **K'ip'ínągè t'ągà uną'št'ą̀** /k'ē-p'ē'-noⁿ-gā t'oⁿ-gä' ü-noⁿ'-sht'oⁿ'/ *n.*, bus depot

but **Éde** /ä'-dā/ *conj.*, but, excepting that, since

but **Égądążą̀** /ä'-goⁿ-thoⁿ-zhoⁿ'/ *conj.*, but, lit., that may be, ~ or except that

butcher **T'anúk'a máxąxà** /t'ä-nü'-k'ä mä'-xoⁿ-xoⁿ'/ *n./v.*, butcher, to cut up meat

butchering **Wap'áde** /wä-p'ä'-dä/ *v.*, butchering, cutting up or butchering the carcass of an animal

butter **Bawégdì** /bä-wä'-gthē'/ *n.*, butter, lit., churning to butter, a soft, creamy spread

butterfly **Wačíninik'à** /wä-chē'-nē-nē-k'ä'/ *n.*, butterfly, an insect with brightly colored wings

buttocks **Níde** /nē'-dā/ *n.*, 1. buttocks 2. rump

button **Wíágaškè** /wē'-ä'-gä-shkä'/ *n.*, button, fastener, hook and eye

buy **Điwį́'** /thē-wēⁿ'/ *v.*, buy, pay money for, purchase; *bdį́wį̀*, I buy or bought; *nį́wį̀*, you buy or bought; *ądį́wį̀*, we bought; *ądį́wį̀t'ągatà*, we will have bought

buzzard **Héga** /hā'-gä/ *n.*, buzzard, 1. a North American vulture 2. a proper name in the Wažážè clan among the Ponca people

by **Ešą́di** /ā-shoⁿ'-dē/ *prep.*, by, something or somebody is close to something or somebody

by now **Đétądąhì** /thā'-toⁿ-doⁿ-hē'/ *adv.*, by now, something that happened or was required to happen at or before a particular time

bypass **Íbetą̀** /ē'-bā-toⁿ'/ *v.*, bypass, go around

C

cabbage **Waxdá'** /wä-xthä'/ *n.*, cabbage, a leafy green vegetable

cache **Wap'ḗ'** /wä-p'ē'/ *n.*, cache, store, reserve, collection

cacophony **Įgdéze** /ēⁿ-gthä'-zā/ *n.*, cacophony, a meaningless mixture of sounds, as in cackles, wails

Caddo **P'a'ú'de** /p'ä-ü'-dä/ *n.*, the Caddo Tribe of Native Americans, lit., nose pierced

calendar **Mí'ídawà** /mē-ē'-thä-wä/ *n.*, calendar, lit., month counter, 1. a system of keeping track of the time in a year (The Ponca counted twelve moons in a year and recognized each moon by natural occurrences.)

2. monthly, refers to something happening every month (~ *a'tí nái*, he comes here ~)

calf **T'é'ska'žįgà** /t'ä'-skä-zhēⁿ-gä/ *n.*, calf, a young member of domestic cattle or bovines

call **Gíbą** /gē'-boⁿ/ *v.*, call, summon, or yell to someone to come

calm **Ábdagè** /ä'-bthä-gä/ *n.*, calm, on the sheltered side of a windbreak, usu. refers to a place where people are standing or sitting at an outdoor event or activity

calm **Ágdabè** /ä'-gthä-bä/ *adj.*, calm, tranquil, peaceful, serene, usu. refers to people's conditions of life and living

calumet **Niní'ba** /nē-nē'-bä/ *n.*, calumet, a ceremonial pipe

came **Ahí'** /ä-hē'/ *v.*, came, came there, came to that place; *atí'*, came here; *šuhí'*, they came there; *šiáhi*, they came there again; *šup'í'*, I came there

camera **Įdéwabaxù ídizè** /ēⁿ-dä'-wä-bä-xü' ē'-thē-zä/ *n.*, camera, a device for taking photographs

camp circle **Húdugà** /hü'-thü-gä/ *n.*, camp circle, orig. referred to the circle of dwellings, usu. tipis (Ca. 1850s, photos show the Ponca encampment scattered with *mąit'i* and *t'i ukédi*, earthen lodges and tipis.)

can **Ukíhi** /ü-kē'-hē/ *v.*, can, be able to, be capable of, know how to; *uwákihì*, I ~; *udákihì*, you ~

candy **Žąníbút'a** /zhoⁿ-nē'-bü'-t'ä/ *n.*, candy, lit., round sugar

cane **Hímągdè** /hē'-moⁿ-gthä/ *n.*, cane, a walking cane, usu. made of wood, now aluminum

cannon **Wahút'ądì t'ągà** /wä-hü'-t'oⁿ-thē' t'oⁿ-gä/ *n.*, cannon, a large weapon mounted either on wheels, warships, or vehicles with a track

canoe **Mądé'** /moⁿ-dä/ *n.*, canoe, boat, ship

can't **Điá'** /thē-ä'/ *v.*, can't, contraction of *cannot*; *bđí'a*, I can't; *ní'a*, you can't; *điá'i*, he/she/it/they can't

canvas **T'í'hà** /t'ē'-hä/ *n.*, canvas, lit., house hide, a covering for a dwelling, usu. the skin of an animal, now a heavy, thick fabric

cap **Wadáge bút'a** /wä-thä'-gä bü-t'ä/ *n.*, cap, a head covering with a visor, usu. close fitting to the head

capable **Uk'íhi** /ü-k'ē'-hē/ *adj.*, capable, can do, has the necessary talent to do something, equipped to do something

captive **Nágdè** /nä'-gthä/ *n.*, captive, one held as a prisoner or kept within bounds

cardinal **Wažíga žíde** /wä-zhēⁿ'-gä zhē'-dä/ *n.*, cardinal, lit., red bird, passerine bird in the family Cardinalidae

care **Á'ądè** /ä'-oⁿ-thä/ *v.*, care, to be concerned; to become involved or do something to keep something or somebody safe

carefree **Šká'dadà** /shkä'-thä-thä/ *adj.*, carefree, untroubled, cheerful, free from care, free as a lark

caring **Wanádehidè** /wä-noⁿ'-dä-hē-dä/ *adj.*, caring, usu. refers to a person who has a loving, kind, and helpful spirit

carnival **Íškadè gáxe** /ē'-shkä-dä' gä'-xä/ *n.*, carnival, circus, and other kinds of fun gatherings, making fun things to see and do

carp **Hubdá'ska** /hü-bthä'-skä/ *n.*, carp (*Cyprinus carpio*), a freshwater fish with scales

carpet **T'íúmižè** /t'ē'-ü'-mē-zhä/ *n.*, carpet, carpeting, rug, mat

carrier **Wat'úgdą** /wä-t'ü'-gthoⁿ/ *n.*, carrier, any person, animal, or vehicle that carries cargo

carrot **Mąščíge wadatè** /moⁿ-shchēⁿ'-gä wä-thä-tä/ *n.*, carrot, an orange, tubular, edible root vegetable (a ~ is considered rabbit food)

carry **Adį́ágadà** /ä-thēⁿ'-ä'-gä-thä'/ v., carry, to carry away something openly; *áigadà*, to carry something openly

carry **Į́** /ēⁿ'/ v., carry, to hold while moving, as in ~ a box up the stairs

carry **Wé'į** /wä'-ēⁿ/ *pron./v.*, *3rd pers. sing.*, he/she/it carried us

carve **Máxu** /mä'-xü/ v., carve, artistic carving into wood by cutting and shaping something; engraving

cash **Mázeskà wadíšnà** /moⁿ'-zä-skä' wä-thē'-shnä'/ n., cash, the actual physical form of money, dollars and cents

cat **Įgdą́ga** /ēⁿ'-gthoⁿ'-gä/ n., cat, any domesticated cat (The Ponca Boarding School, where Ponca children learned to speak English, was established ca. 1884. The children were not allowed to speak Ponca. Employees of the school used the term *pussy*. The children used a corruption of the English version, saying *b'ú'sì*. The term became standard use even when speaking Ponca.)

catch **Udą́** /ü-thoⁿ'/ v., catch, to hold on to, clutch, or grasp by taking hold of something

catch up **Ú'xde** /ü'-xthä'/ v., catch up, to catch up with

caterpillar **Wagdíška hį́'škubè** /wä-gthē'-shkä hēⁿ'-shkü-bä'/ n., caterpillar, the larval form of members of the order Lepidoptera, usu. comprising butterflies and moths

catfish **T'ú'ze** /t'ü'-zä/ n., catfish (order Siluriformes), a freshwater fish with whiskers

cattle **T'é'skà** /t'ä'-skä/ n., cattle, lit., white bison, large domesticated mammals, namely, cows and oxen

Caucasoid **Xįhá'skà** /xēⁿ-hä'-skä/ n., Caucasoid, lit., white complexion, white-skinned people of European origin

caught **Ąwádąì** /oⁿ-woⁿ'-thoⁿ-ē'/ v., they caught me, to apprehend, to get caught doing something; *udídąì*, they caught you; *uwádąì*, they caught us

caught **Udúądè** /ü-thü-oⁿ-thä'/ v., caught, being caught onto something

caught **Udúkiądè** /ü-thü-kē-oⁿ-thä'/ v., 1. caught, caught onto or into something (his shirt got ~ on a protruding nail) 2. to meet up with an unwanted situation that cannot be avoided

cause **Éwą** /ä'-woⁿ/ n., cause, the source of something that happens

caused by **Éwawà** /ä'-wä-woⁿ'/ n., caused by, attributable to something or somebody

caused to **-k'idè** /k'ē-thä'/ v., *suffix*, caused to, an action made by oneself, as in *íyek'idè*, to talk or speak; *xúbek'idè*, to prepare oneself to use one's own spiritual powers; *k'iák'ik'íde*, to prepare oneself for war by putting on war paint, usu. black paint

caution **Udúdąbè** /ü-thü'-doⁿ-bä'/ n., caution, looking into the matter before acting

cautious **Sabá'a** /sä-bä'-ä/ (*fem.*) (**Sabá'aga** /sä-bä'-ä-gä/ [*masc.*]) *adj.*, cautious, as when commanded to be on the lookout for anything that might be a problem

cave **Mąšáde** /moⁿ-shoⁿ'-dä/ n., cave, 1. a hollow place in the ground big enough for a man to enter 2. a small hollow tunnel made by small burrowing animals

cedar **Mázi** /mä'-zē/ n., cedar, the leaves of a coniferous tree that are stiff needlelike shoots—the shoots are burned to cause smoke that is used in some rituals and ceremonies

cedar tree **Má'zihì** /mä'-zē-hē'/ n., any cedar or coniferous tree

cellar **T'ą́de mąšą́dè** /t'oⁿ'-dä moⁿ-shoⁿ'-dä'/ n., cellar, storm cellar, a place built to protect people from violent weather, such as tornadoes, cyclones, straight winds

cell phone **Máze'í'udà žįgà** /moⁿ'-zā-ē'-ü-thä' zheⁿ-gä'/ *n.*, cell phone, cellular phone

cemetery **Míxe** /mē'-xä/ *n.*, cemetery, a place where dead people are buried, a graveyard, a burial ground

census **Wadáwa ɖizè** /wä-thä'-wä thē-zä'/ *n.*, census, a procedure for taking a head count, getting information about a people in a given group

center **Ídąbè** /ē'-doⁿ-bä'/ *n.*, center, usu. relates to something that is seen in the middle of a group of things or people

center **Udízą** /ü-thē'-zoⁿ/ *n.*, center, central point, the area or part of something centrally located in a circle or group of things

centipede **Wagɖíškasnedé** /wä-gthē'-shkä-snä-dä'/ *n.*, centipede ("hundred feet"), arthropod belonging to the class Chilopoda

century **Umáɖikà gɖébą hiwì** /ü-moⁿ'-thē-kä' gthä'-boⁿ hē-wē'/ *n.*, century, lit., one hundred years (Latin *centum*, one hundred)

chainsaw **Žą́'íbasedè** /zhoⁿ'-ē'-bä-sä-thä'/ *n.*, chainsaw, a portable, mechanized saw for wood cutting that has a circular chain driven by a motor

chair **Á'gɖį** /ä'-gthēⁿ'/ *n.*, chair, seat, stool

challenge **Ákiɖà** /ä'-kē-thä'/ *v.*, challenge, contest, match, as in fighting

change **Ðiáži** /thē-ä'-zhē/ *v.*, change, alter, modify

chap **Dí'xe** /dē'-xä/ *v.*, chap, to become sore and cracked by exposure to wind or cold

chapped **Udíxagà** /ü-thē'-xä-gä'/ *v.*, chapped, being chapped on the face, hands, and lips

chapped **Xá'gà** /xä'-gä'/ *v.*, to be chapped, refers to the skin becoming sore and rough

chapped lips **Íha uxága** /ē'-hä ü-xä'-gä/ *v.*, chapped lips, lips that become dry and sometimes cracked because of a lack of moisture; also referred to as cheilitis simplex or common cheilitis

char **Náxudè** /nä'-xü-dä'/ *v.*, char, 1. to darken something, e.g., wood, by burning 2. to scorch food

charcoal **Nąxdé** /noⁿ-xthä'/ *n.*, charcoal, a black form of carbon produced by heating or burning wood until it is black

charging **Šu'wídąbè** /shü-wēⁿ'-thoⁿ'-bä'/ *v.*, charging, attacking, usu. done in warfare when the enemy is rushing inward

chase **Ðixé'** /thē-xä'/ *v.*, chase, to pursue, to follow something or somebody in order to capture or overtake

chase **Yʃnąxidà** /yʃ'-noⁿ-xē-thä'/ *v.*, chase, to pursue, run after, go after, go in pursuit of, to engage in a fight or to battle

cheap **Úmąkà** /ü'-moⁿ-kä'/ *adj.*, cheap, inexpensive, something that is not pricey or expensive

cheat **Ík'itè** /ē'-k'ē-tä'/ *v.* cheat, to cheat him/ her

cheat **Wék'itè** /wä-k'ē-tä'/ *v.*, *3rd pers. pl.*, cheat, they cheated them

cheek **Ðéxądè** /thä'-xoⁿ-dä'/ *n.*, cheek, the part of the face that is soft below the eyes; *ɖéxądè wahí*, cheekbone

cheerful **Gíɖi** /gē'-thē/ *adj.*, cheerful, jolly, joyful, merry, in good spirits

cheese **Bawé'gɖì'sagì** /bä-wä'-gthē'-sä-gē'/ *n.*, cheese, solid food made from milk from mammals

Cherokee **Šéɖekì·** /shä'-thä'-kē'·/ *n.*, the Cherokee Tribe of Native Americans

chest **Mą́ge** /moⁿ'-gä/ *n.*, chest, thorax, that part of the human body between the throat and abdomen

chest of drawers **Úžibasnà** /ü'-zhē-bä-snoⁿ'/ *n.*, chest of drawers, a dresser; a piece of furniture that has several drawers for storing or keeping clothing handy for use

chew **Ðaškí'** /thä-shkē'/ *v.*, chew, to chew, gnaw on food with teeth chewing gum **Žá'p'à** /zhä'-p'ä/ *n*., chewing gum

Cheyenne **Šahʃdà** /shä-hʃ'-thä/ *n*., the Cheyenne Tribe of Native Americans

chick **K'ip'áda (ja)** /k'ē-p'ä'-dä (jä)/ *n*., chick, a baby chicken, hatchling

chicken **Wažįga'žìde** /wä-zhēⁿ'-gä-zhē'-dā/ *n*., chicken, lit., red bird, probably the breed Rhode Island Red

chicken coop **Wažįga'žìde út'i** /wä-zhēⁿ'-gä-zhē'-dā ü'-t'ē/ *n*., chicken coop, lit., chicken coop, a building where hens are kept to lay eggs in nest boxes

chieftain **Níka'gahì** /nē'-kä-gä-hē'/ *n*., chieftain, lit., person who is above all, tribal chief, chief, group leader, etc.

Chikaskia River **Žegá'skà** /zhä-gä'-skä/ *n*., Chikaskia River, lit., white hips and thighs, the Chikaskia River in Oklahoma (The river was named by a woman of white descent. When jokingly told by a male relative how clear the Arkansas River was and that those residing nearby used it to bathe in, she responded, "We white hips and thighs [bathe in a river equally clear]."

child **Šįgažįgà** /shēⁿ'-gä-zhēⁿ-gä/ *n*., child, children

childish **Šéžidè** /shä'-zhē-dā/ *adj./n.*, childish, an adult who displays childlike behavior following a disagreeable matter

children **Winísi** /wē-nē'-sē/ *n*., childen, lit., my little ones

chilly **Sni'égą** /snē-ä'-goⁿ/ *adj*., chilly, when the temperature is moderately cold

Chilocco School **Wačí'škà'gdadì** /wä-chē'-shkä'-gthä-dē'/ *n*., Chilocco School, lit., across the creek, Chilocco Indian School, Oklahoma

chime in **Ú'dazè** /ü'-thä-zä/ *n./v.*, chime in, combine music harmoniously, refers to women who sing at the drum with male singers at tribal dances (In the past women usu. "chimed in" after the beat of the drum in the middle of the song. Now women are called "chorus girls.")

chimney swift **T'íúbixà** /t'ē'-ü-bē-xoⁿ/ *n*., chimney swift, 1. a small, flocking bird that swarms near dwellings and rotting old trees 2. a personal male name in the Hísadà clan of the Ponca people

chin **Įkì** /ēⁿ'-kē/ *n*., chin, in human anatomy, that part of the face protruding under the lips

Chinaware **Uxp'é wasésą** /ü-xp'ä' wä-sä'-soⁿ/ *n*., Chinaware, ceramic cups, dishes, saucers

Chinese **Ásku snedè** /ä'-skü snä-dä/ *n*., Chinese, lit., a long single braid, a native of China

chip **Gašp'é** /gä-shp'ä/ *v*., chip, as in cutting off, chipping, a piece of wood from a log; *dišp'é*, to tear off a piece using the hands; *dašp'é*, to bite off a piece of food; *nąšp'é*, to chip off by stepping on or driving over

chipmunk **T'ašníga** /t'ä-shnēⁿ'-gä/ *n*., chipmunk, a small striped rodent of the family Sciuridae

choke **Núde dit'ą** /nü'-dä thē-t'oⁿ/ *v*., choke, to block breathing, to obstruct breathing by hindering the air passageway to the lungs (The elders said this was not the proper way of taking the life of the enemy. The Ponca were known as or called P'á máse, "decapitators," in hand-to-hand combat. Otherwise, they used the bow and arrow.)

chokecherry **Nąp'a** /noⁿ'-p'ä/ *n*., chokecherry, an edible berry that grows in clusters on a large shrub, usu. the Ponca people found them in Nebraska and South and North Dakota, *Prunus virginiana*, var. *demissa*, western chokecherry

choker **Úwįgaządè** /ü'-wēⁿ-gä-zoⁿ-dä/ *n*.,

choker, a short necklace, an ornament that is fastened closely around the neck and made of seed beads and horsehair using the netted stitch in the beadwork

choose **E'ą̀št'iwì dizá(ga)** /ä-o^n-sht'ē-wē' thē-zä'(gä)/ *v.*, choose, select, or decide to get from several things

chop **Gasé** /gä-sä'/ *v.*, chop, chop by using a tool such as an ax

chopping **Gasása** /gä-sä'-sä/ *v.*, chopping, chopping continuously by using a tool such as an ax

chop wood **Žą gáse** /zho^n gä'-sä/ *v.*, chop wood, lit., cut wood

Christian **Wak'ą́da Ižį́ge Ík'ip'ahą̀** /wä-k'o^n-dä ē-zhē^n'-gä ē'-k'ē-p'ä-ho^n'/ *n.*, Christian, lit., one who knows the Son of God, Jesus

Christian flag **Wak'ą́dawadahą̀ Haská** /wä-k'o^n'-dä-wä-thä-ho^n' hä-skä'/ *n.*, Christian flag, a white flag with a blue rectangular division in the top left corner with a red cross on it

Christmas Day **Ą̀ba'waxúbe't'ągà** /o^{n}m'-bä-wä-xü'-bä t'o^{n}gä'/ *n.*, Christmas Day

church **Úwak'ą́da wadahą̀ t'ì** /ü'-wä-k'o^n-dä wä-thä-ho^n' t'ē'/ *n.*, church, house of worship, a place for public Christian worship

cigarette **Niní** /nē-nē'/ *n.*, cigarette, or any kind of product that uses tobacco leaves

circle **Bút'a udíšą** /bü'-t'ä ü-thē'-sho^n/ *v.*, circle, go around

circle **Udúbetą̀** /ü-thü'-bä-to^n'/ *v.*, circle or circle around, more of a command to go around something

circular **Bút'a** /bü'-t'ä/ *adj.*, circular, round, spherical, rotund

circumnavigate **Íbetą̀** /ē'-bä-to^n'/ *v.*, circumnavigate, circle, go around something or somebody to get to the other side of them

claim **Uwét'a** /ü-wä'-t'ä/ *n.*, claim, 1. considered to be the rightful owner 2. impregnation

clamp **Mą́ze weánąsądè** /mo^n'-zä wä-ä'-no^n-so^n-dä'/ *n.*, clamp, vise, a device used to hold or fasten two things together

clan **Đíxidą̀** /thē'-xē-do^n'/ *n.*, the Đíxidą̀ clan of the Ponca people (Đíxidą̀ men were considered "shock troops," along with the Níkapášną̀ clan. The Đíxidą̀ men wore a hairstyle with a single braid at the back of the head and were also referred to as *sį́de adį̀*, those who have tails.)

clan **Hísadà** /hē'-sä-dä'/ *n.*, the Hísadà clan of the Ponca people, lit., straight legs (Alice Fletcher and Francis LeFlesche said the term meant "stretched, referring to the stretch of the legs in running" [(1911)1972: 41–42]. J. O. Dorsey called them "thunder people" [1891:331–32]. They are known by the Ponca as "rain makers.")

clan **Mą́k'ą́** /mo^n-k'o^n'/ *n.*, the Mą́k'ą́ clan of the Ponca people, lit., medicine

clan **Níkapášną̀** /nē'-kä-pä'-shno^n'/ *n.*, the Níkapášną̀ clan of the Ponca people, lit., man with bald head (The warriors of this clan shaved their hair, wearing a "Mohawk"-style haircut. They tied a symbolic feather at the tail or back of the head. They, along with the Đíxidą̀ clansmen, were considered "shock troops.")

clan **Né'št'à** /nä'-sht'ä'/ *n.*, the now extinct Nèšta clan of the Ponca people, lit., places of water

clan **Núxe** /nü'-xä/ *n.*, the Núxe clan of the Ponca people, lit., ice,

clan **T'ą́wągdà** /t'o^n'-wo^n-gtho^n'/ *n.*, clan, 1. clan, families who are related through a common ancestry 2. a village, city, community, a group of people living in houses in a particular location

clan **Wašábe** /wä-shä'-bä/ *n.*, the Wašábe clan of the Ponca people, lit., old dark buffalo clan **Wažážè** /wä-zhä'-zhä'/ *n.*, the Wažážè (Osage) clan of the Ponca people

clang **K'amą́** /k'ä-moⁿ'/ *v./n.*, clang, to make a ringing sound when two pieces of metal hit each other (hear the bells ~)

clanging **Gak'ák'ámą̀** /gä-k'ä'-k'ä'-moⁿ'/ *v./n.*, clanging, to make a clanging sound repeatedly

clarify **Wágazù** /wä'-gä-zü'/ *v.*, clarify, elucidate, e.g., to state exactly, to state clearly

clay **Wasésą** /wä-sä'-soⁿ'/ *n.*, clay, porcelain, plastics, a wet, fine ground rock with other minerals that becomes solid when dry; also refers to other plastics, porcelain, ceramics, plaster, etc.

clean **Đisíhi** /thē-sē'-hē/ *v.*, clean, to clean something with the hands

clean **Úsihì** /ü'-sē-hē'/ *adj.*, clean, unsoiled, spotless, immaculate, dirt free

cleaner **Wébasihì** /wä'-bä-sē-hē'/ *n.*, cleaner, 1. any device used to clean something, such as a brush, sponge, or cloth; any liquid cleansing substance, soap 2. vacuum cleaner, mop, broom

cleaning up **Wabásihì** /wä-bä'-sē-hē'/ *v.*, cleaning up, the act of cleaning up (he's ~ the place)

clean up **K'igdíšup'à** /k'ē-gthē'-shü-p'ä'/ *v.*, clean up, clean one's dwelling or rooms up

clean up **Wadíšup'à** /wä-thē'-shü-p'ä'/ *v.*, clean up, straighten things up, make tidy

clear **Đišnáp'a** /thē-shnä'-p'ä/ *adj./v.*, clear, rid of any or all physical material—clearing debris, grass, or weeds from the ground; after hair cutting, leaving one nearly bald

clear **K'ú'gdì** /k'ü'-gthē'/ *adj.*, clear, crystal clear, translucent (The Arkansas River was said to be crystal clear when the Ponca first came to this land in Indian Territory in 1878.)

clear sky **G'éda** /g-ä'-thä/ *n.*, clear sky, a sky with no clouds, usu. said following cloudy skies

clear up **Gasíhi** /gä-sē'-hē/ *v.*, clear up, clearing up (the sky clearing after a storm)

cleft palate **Íhasè'** /ē'-hä-sä'/ *n.*, cleft palate, a defect in newborn babies where the tissues of the lip or palate do not fuse normally

cliff **Mąá'** /moⁿ-ä'/ *n.*, cliff, precipice, crag (A Ponca Heđúškà song refers to *mąá zì*, which refers to the yellow cliffs along the north bank of the Missouri River in South Dakota.)

climb **Ádiškabè** /ä'-thē-shkä-bä'/ *v.*, climb, to climb using hands and feet

cling to **Uđáha** /ü-thä'-hä/ *v.*, cling to, 1. to adhere to something in addition to something already in place 2. *n.*, something that is part of another thing, as in a lady's winter coat that comes with a scarf

clip **Đisé** /thē-sä'/ *v.*, clip, to cut or trim something, as in trimming the hair with shears

clock **Mí'íđąbè** /mē'-ē'-doⁿ-bä'/ *n.*, clock, lit., a sun-seeing device, a device used to measure time, may refer to a sundial, wrist watch, or other device

close **Ánąsè** /ä'-noⁿ-sä'/ *v.*, close, to close or fasten shut, block, to block, barrier, blockade, barricade

close **Áškà** /ä'-shkä'/ *v.*, close, refers to nearly reaching a point; came close but not quite there

close **Égià** /ā'-gē-oⁿ'/ *v.*, close, close it (*t'ižébe kè ~gà*, ~ the door)

close **Ešnáadi** /ā-shnoⁿ'-ä-dē/ *adj.*, close, close by, nearby

close **Ešną́'ahà** /ā-shoⁿ'-ä-hä'/ *adj.*, close, refers to being close to a particular thing or group; *ešą́'ahàbažì*, did not come around or close to a thing or group, as in tribal gatherings

close **Ešną́'ahàhà** /ā-shnoⁿ'-ä-hä'-hä'/ *adj.*, close, always being close by or near

close **Í'biskì** /ē'-bē-skä'/ *v.*, close, usu. refers to somebody being or sitting very close to somebody

close **Uhíaškà** /ü-hē'-ä-shkä'/ *v.*, close, the distance between two places

closed eyes **Į'štá dipį́že** /ēⁿ-shtä' thē-pēⁿ'-zhä/ *adj.*, closed eyes

closer **Dúdahà** /dü'-dä-hä'/ *adj.*, closer, to come closer or bring the self and/or something closer

closer **Edídą̀dą̀** /ā-dē'-thoⁿ'-thoⁿ'/ *adj.*, closer, coming closer little by little or bit by bit

closest **Ešáxt'ì** /ā-shä'-xt'ē'/ *adj.*, closest, very close by

cloth **Waxį́ha** /wä-xēⁿ'-hä/ *n.*, cloth, 1. textiles, fabric, material 2. *archaic* paper

clothesline **Wábizedè** /wä'-bē-zä-thä'/ *n.*, clothesline, a type of rope, wire, or cord that is stretched between two poles and on which clothes are attached to dry

clothespin **Žą́'wiúbasnà** /zhoⁿ'-wē-ü'-bä-snoⁿ'/ *n.*, clothespin, a wooden (now plastic) clip used to hang clothing on a clothesline

clothing **Háde** /hä'-thä/ *n.*, clothing, refers to a covering of garments for people; clothes

cloud **Mąxp'í'** /moⁿx-p'ē'/ *n.*, cloud, clouds, general term for clouds

cloudburst **Nążį́ ák'išugà** /noⁿ-zhēⁿ' ä'-k'ē-shü-gä'/ *n.*, cloudburst, usu. rain with hail and thunder

cloudy **Ámąxp'ì** /ä'-moⁿx-p'ē'/ *adj.*, cloudy, refers to scattered clouds of any type

cloudy **Gamáxp'i** /gä-moⁿ'-xp'ē'/ *adj./n.*, cloudy, clouds forming or wind blowing up clouds

club **Wé'tį** /wā'-tēⁿ/ *n.*, club, any kind of club used as a weapon, usu. a heavy stick, a war club

clump **Bat'é** /bä-t'ä'/ *n.*, clump, as in a thicket or a clump of grass

clumps **Bat'éte** /bä-t'ä'-tā/ *n.*, clumps, as in clumps of bushes and trees growing scattered out in the prairie; *banáną*, clumps

cluster **Bat'é** /bä-t'ä'/ *n./v.*, cluster, a group of things or people that are tightly connected (*niášigà ma ~ gdiáma*, the people were sitting in a ~)

clutch **Udą́'** /ü-thoⁿ'/ *v.*, clutch, grasp, hold, grab, grip

coals **Nąxdé** /noⁿ-xthä'/ *n.*, coals, the black residue on burnt wood (Ponca men used this residue to blacken their faces when they went to meet the enemy in battle. The color was symbolic of death.)

coat **Unážį t'ągà** /ü-noⁿ'-zhēⁿ t'oⁿ-gä'/ *n.*, coat, usu. a full-length coat

coccyx **Níde wahì** /nē'-dā wä-hē'/ *n.*, coccyx, referred to as the tailbone, the final segment of the vertebral column, composed of three to five separate or fused vertebrae below the sacrum

cocklebur **Waxága t'ągà** /wä-xä'-gä t'oⁿ-gä'/ *n.*, cocklebur, a plant with thorny, long and slender spines

cocky **Wadážįgà** /wä-thä'-zhēⁿ-gä'/ *adj.*, cocky, brashly overconfident, arrogant

coffee **Mąką́ sábe** /moⁿ-koⁿ' sä-bä/ *n.*, coffee, lit., black medicine, the ground seeds from the coffee tree used to make a stimulating drink, drunk with or without sugar and cream

coffee bean tree **Ną́t'it'ahì** /noⁿ'-t'ē-t'ä-hē'/ *n.*, coffee bean tree, *Gymnocladus dioicus*, a tree in the subfamily Caesalpinioideae of the pea family Fabaceae; a thorny tree with pods

coffee grinder **Mąką́ sábe ínąt'ubè** /moⁿ-koⁿ' sä-bä ē'-noⁿ-t'ü-bä'/ *n.*, *archaic*, coffee grinder, nineteenth- and early twetieth-century product used by the Ponca

coffee grounds **Mąką́ sábe nąxdé** /moⁿ-koⁿ' sä-bā noⁿ-xthä'/ *n.*, coffee grounds coffee pot **Mąką sábe udúhą** /moⁿ-koⁿ' sä-bā ü-thü'-hoⁿ/ *n.*, coffeepot, a pot to brew coffee in

coiled snake **K'igdíbut'à** /k'ē-gthē'-bü-t'ä'/ *n.*, 1. coiled snake, usu. refers to a snake that is ready to strike 2. proper male name in the Wažážè clan of the Ponca people

cold **Usní'** /ŭ-snē'/ *adj.*, cold, the state of coldness; having a low temperature

collapse **Idágaspè** /ē-thä'-gä-spä'/ *v.*, collapse, to cause something to sink in or to be weighed down by excess covering

collapse **Šedą́** /shā-thoⁿ'/ *v.*, collapse, give way, crumble, come apart

collar bone **Mą́ge'wahì** /moⁿ'-gā-wä-hē'/ *n.*, collarbone, in human anatomy the clavicle, the bone over the top of the chest

collect **Udéwį** /ü-thä'-wēⁿ/ *v.*, collect or amass, usu. refers to a collection of things, such as hobby items 2. to gather together, usu. refers to a group of people

collectively **Xą́·de** /xoⁿ'-·dā/ *adv.*, collectively, together, as a group

collision **Ákinągè** /ä'-kē-noⁿ-gā'/ *n./v.*, collision, crash into, as in two automobiles colliding

color **Úgaxè** /ü'-gä-xā'/ *n.*, color, tint, shade

colt **Šą́ge't'ą'žìgà** /shoⁿ'-gä-t'oⁿ-zhēⁿ-gä'/ *n.*, colt, a young horse, usu. one less than a year old

columbine **Mąk'ą́ ínąbdą̀'k'idè** /moⁿ-k'oⁿ' ē'-noⁿ-bthoⁿ-k'ē-thä'/ *n.*, columbine, Native American man's perfume, lit., black medicine perfume, *Aquilegia canadensis* L. See Howard 1965:69.

column **Usné'** /ü-snä'/ *n.*, column, procession, in a row, in rank, in sequence

Comanche **P'ádak'à** /p'ä'-dä-k'ä'/ *n.*, the Comanche Tribe of Native Americans

comatose **Í'k'ib'ahąžì** /ē'-k'ē-b-ä-hoⁿ-zhē'/ *adj.*, comatose, being in a state of coma, being unconscious

comb **Gahé** /gä-hä'/ *v.*, to comb, the act of combing hair

comb **Mik'áhe** /mē-k'ä'-hā/ *n.*, comb, an instrument to run through and untangle hair

combine **Waną́žudè** /wä-noⁿ'-zhü-thä'/ *n.*, combine, a machine that harvests grain crops

come **Gí'** /gē'/ *v.*, come, get nearer, approach

come after **Agí'ki** /ä-gē'-kē/ *v. phr.*, come after, one coming to get something that belongs to him/her

come back **Agdí'** /ä-gthē'/ *v.*, come back, he/she/it/they come back, returning to a previously occupied place or station, 1. came home, refers to a person who had been away and has now come home 2. refers to the seasons and animals, as in the winter has returned or the geese have returned

come back **Gíga** /gē'-gä/ *v.*, 2nd pers. sing. (fem., *giá*), come back, come back to here, move back to here, get back to here; *gí'iga*, *pl.* (*fem.*, *gí'iá*), come back, come back to here, move back to here, get back to here

come here **Dúda** /dü'-dä/ *v.*, come here, expression made to somebody by the one who is speaking, usu. made to a child

come off **Šnudáde** /shnü-dä'-thä/ *v.*, come off, ~ on its own without help of human hands

comical **Í'xetewadè** /ē'-xā-tā-wä-thä'/ *adj.*, comical, lit., someone or something that makes one laugh, is comical, funny, humorous

coming **Aí badą̀** /ä-ē' bä-doⁿ'/ *v. phr.*, coming, "they are or somebody is ~ because" of wanting something or wanting to do something

coming **Aít'amà** /ä-ē'-t'ä-mä/ *v.*, coming,

"they are coming" as we anticipate their arrival

coming back **Agdít'amà** /ä-gthē'-t'ä-mä'/ *v. phr.*, coming back, he/she/it/they "will come back" (*míxa amà ~*, the ducks are ~)

coming by suddenly **Tidą́bidè** /tē-thonⁿ'-bē-thä'/ *adj.*, coming by suddenly, something or somebody coming by unexpectedly, usu. at high speed

coming days **Ą́ba adáikedì** /onⁿm'-bä ä-thä'-ē-kä-dē'/ *adj.*, coming days, the days that follow today or the future that follows from now on

command **Ágažì** /ä'-gä-zhē'/ *v.*, command, to command or to order somebody to do something; *áwigažì*, I ordered or commanded you; *wá'agažì*, I ordered or commanded them; *áwadagažì*, you ordered or commanded me; *wą́dagažì*, you ordered or commanded them; *ádigažì*, he ordered or commanded you; *wą́ąga'gažì*, we ordered or commanded them

common **Ukédį** /ü-kä'-thēⁿ/ *adj.*, common, general, familiar, as in somebody or something that is ordinary

common cold **Húxp'è** /hü-xp'ä'/ *n.*, common cold, a viral infection that causes coughing, sneezing, fever, etc.

communicate **Ukíkíye** /ü-kē'-kē'-yā/ *v.*, communicate, to speak to each other, exchanging stories, ideas, information

communion table **Wak'ą́da Waxúbe Wá'datè** /wä-k'onⁿ'-dä wä-xü'-bä wä'-thä-tä'/ *n.*, communion table, a table in the Christian church on which the sacraments of bread and wine are placed for adherents who receive them according to a directive given by Jesus Christ, "Do in remembrance of me"

compact disc (CD) **Mą́ze bdáskà wą́** /monⁿ'-zä bthä'-skä' wä-onⁿ/ *n.*, compact disc (CD),

a disc used to store digital data, such as recorded music

compassionate **Wadá'edè** /wä-thä'-ä-thä'/ *adj.*, compassionate, one who shows compassion to others, who is empathetic and considerate; philia love (brotherly love)

compel **Įtédi** /ēⁿ-tä-dē/ *v.*, compel, to cause somebody to do something that he/she should have done after he/she disregarded the matter

compete **Ákikidà** /ä'-kē-kē-thä'/ *v.*, compete, struggle to win, as in sports such as football, basketball, baseball, boxing; *ákidà*, to compete with one opponent

complain **Ú'gdašigè** /ü'-gthä-shē-gä'/ *v.*, complain, 1. expression of dissatisfaction, resentment, usu. done in airing one's personal feelings to another person 2. done in regard to one's feelings about some issue in a meeting

complexion **Xįhá** /xēⁿ-hä'/ *n.*, complexion, color of skin, tone of skin

complicated **Údit'ą̀** /ü'-thē-t'onⁿ'/ *adj.*, 1. complicated, doing something that requires concentrated effort, something complex, intricate or just plain thorny 2. *n.*, *3rd pers sing.*, work, he/she/it has work (*ítą ~ adì*, he has ~ now)

computer **Mą́zè wédixdì** /monⁿ'-zä' wä'-thē-xthē'/ *n.*, computer, lit., metal brain, processor, PC

concave **Uxdú'xdà** /ü-xthü'-xthä'/ *adj./n.*, concave, indented, cavernous, a hole in the surface of the road, a pothole, a ditch

conceal **Ánąxdè** /ä'-nonⁿ-xthä'/ *v.*, conceal, to hide a person or something, to hide feelings or facts

conceivable **Edégąwadè** /ā-thä'-gonⁿ-wä-thä'/ *adj.*, conceivable, something that is possible or plausible concern **Waną́dehidè** /wä-non'-dā-hē-dā'/ *v.*, concern, having a personal effect on from the heart

conclusion **Šá'gaxè** /shä'-gä-xä'/ *n.*, conclusion, bring to an end, close or finish

condition of **Eą́'a** /ā-on'-ä/ *n.*, the condition, quality, or degree of something in question

conestoga **Wáxegaxdą̀** /wä'-xä-gä-xthon'/ *n.*, conestoga, conestoga wagon, prairie schooner, a large wagon covered with white canvas used by Caucasian people traveling west over Indian country in the nineteenth century

confess **Ukígdà** /ü-kē'-gthä'/ *v.*, confess, admit, own up to something or make a confession

confident **Gíxek'à bažì** /gē'-xä-k'ä' bä-zhē'/ *adj.*, confident, not apprehensive, not anxious, not fearful

confounded **Ú'šįk'idè** /ü'-shēn-k'ē-thä'/ *adj.*, confounded, someone confused or bewildered, as in somebody thinking he/she saw a person or an animal but was mistaken

confusion **Đagdégdešnà** /thä-gthä'-gthä-shnä'/ *adj.*, confusion, disorder—making a mess out of speech or song, esp. of certain subjects

congeal **Udádadą̀** /ü-thä'-dä-thon'/ *v.*, congeal, solidify in any given situation that becomes customary or an involvement that leads to congealment

consciousness **Ík'ip'ahą̀** /ē'-k'ē-p'ä-hon'/ *n.*, consciousness, to come back from a period of unconsciousness

consecrate **Waxúbe gáxe** /wä-xü'-bä gä'-xä/ *v.*, consecrate, to make something holy or sacred

consequently **Šą́mikè** /shon'-mē-kä/ *adv.*, consequently, as a result, therefore (~, *bdé*, ~, I went on)

consider **Udúdąbè** /ü-thü'-don-bä'/ *v.*, consider, to think about it, examine or deliberate over something

constant **Égą šášą** /ä'-gon shon'-shon/ *adj.*, constant, continuous, likely to continue on and on, refers to a situation or condition that will always be the same

container **Ú'ži** /ü'-zhē/ *n.*, container, a receptacle, such as a box or a parfleche that holds or stores goods

contemplate **Đáškadadà** /thä'-shkä-thä-thä'/ *v.*, contemplate, cause to contemplate or "stir up in their minds"

contend **Ákidà** /ä'-kē-thä'/ *v., 2nd pers. sing.*, contend, to vie in a contest or rivalry against another

content **Đáxt'ì** /thon'-xt'ē'/ *adj.*, content, a condition of being happy, satisfied, comfortable

content **Edážegą̀** /ā-thä'-zhä-gon'/ *adj.*, content, well-being, the condition of someone or a group being contented

contentment **Ną́de ísawadè** /non'-dā ē'-sä-wä-thä'/ *n.*, contentment, content, pleasantness, usu. refers to a physical location of a place, home, or land and its topography (*mążą́ ke ~*, the land is a place of ~)

contentment **Ną́de'ísawadèxt'ì** /non'-dā-ē'-sä-wä-thä'-xt'ē'/ *n.*, a place of contentment or one pleasing or to one's liking (*mążą́ ke*, ~ *ągdí*, we live in the land that is a place of great ~)

continue **Udúkihebè** /ü-thü'-kē-hä-bä'/ *v.*, continue a bit further

continuous **Idúagdè** /ē-thü'-ä-gthä'/ *adj.*, continuous, endless, perpetual

contrite **Ú'daedè** /ü'-thä-ä-thä'/ *adj.*, contrite, being repentent, sorry, and remorseful

contrition **Ú'daedè k'igáxe** /ü'-thä-ä-thä' k'ē-gä'-xä/ *n.*, contrition, doing something in an apologetic manner

control **Í'digdą̀** /ē'-thē-gtho^n/ v., control, manage, regulate, direct

conversing **Ukíki'e** /ü-kē'-kē'-ä/ v., conversing, to exchange words or thoughts through speech

cook **Úhą** /ü'-ho^n/ v., to cook, to roast, to bake, to grill, etc.

cooked **Ní'dè'dè** /nē'-dā'-thā'/ n., cooked, food that has been prepared to consume (*Úhą* is a term that is also used to denote prepared food.)

cook helpers **Ú'hąšigdè** /ü'-ho^n-shē-gthā'/ n., cook helpers, food servers; those who help the main cook at feasts to serve food to the people (Orig. the servers were members of a Ponca Hedúškà organization.)

cooking tripod **Úhą'udúgaškè** /ü'-ho^n-ü-thü'-gä-shkā'/ n., tripod with a hanging pot for cooking

cook stove **Mą́ze unéde** /mo^n'-zä ü-nä'-thä/ n., *archaic*, cookstove, lit., metal fireplace, refers to a wood-burning range; *weúhą unéde*, cooking stove or gas or electric range

cool **Ugásnì** /ü-gä'-snē'/ adj., cool, pleasantly cool

cool down **Ásnidè** /ä'-snē-thä'/ adj., cool down, to make cool as with food, a room, and other conditions or things that retain heat

cooperate **Udíde** /ü'-thē'-dä/ v., cooperate, cooperation to accomplish something (they ~ and finish the job)

cooperate **Ukíką** /ü-kē'-ko^n/ v., cooperate, work or do something together, assist each other

Cooper's hawk **Wažį́ga wadizè** /wä-zhē^n'-gä wä-thē-zā'/ n., Cooper's hawk, lit. gets chickens, commonly known as "chicken hawk," of the family Accipitridae, species *accipter* (Unofficially, there are three species of hawks called "chicken hawks": the Cooper's hawk is called a quail hawk, while the sharp-shinned hawk and the red-tailed hawk are called chicken hawks. Red-tailed hawks may hunt for free-range poultry more often.)

corn **Wahába** /wä-hä'-bä/ n., corn on the cob

corn **Wanáxe** /wä-nä'-xä/ n., grains of corn cooked on a griddle, parched corn, usu. made from fresh-picked corn

corn **Watą́zi** /wä-to^n'-zē/ n., corn, the grain of corn

cornball dumpling **Bibdúbdúga** /bē-bthü'-bthü'-gä/ n., cornball dumpling, finely ground corn cooked with beans

cornbread **Watą́zi'wažégdą̀** /wä-to^n'-zē-wä-zhā'-gtho^n/ n., cornbread

corner **Ubázą** /ü-bä'-zo^n/ n., corner, 1. the place where two intersecting edges come together 2. where two streets or roads create an intersection

corner of the eye **Įšt'ádedè** /ē^n-sht'ä'-thä-dä'/ n., corner of the eye

corner of the mouth **Ídedè** /ē'-thä-dä'/ n., corner of the mouth

corn hill **Mą́'gdągè** /mo^n'-gtho^n-gä'/ n., corn hill, the ancient ground preparation for planting corn, building a small hill with a depression where the seed corn was placed and covered

cornmeal **Wadít'ubè** /wä-thē'-t'ü-bä/ n., cornmeal, a flour ground from dehydrated or parched corn

corn pudding **Wašą́ge** /wä-sho^n'-gä/ n., corn pudding, made with ground, dehydrated corn

corn sheller **Wahába ídišp'è** /wä-hä'-bä ē'-thē-shp'ä'/ n., corn sheller (The corn-sheller devices used and known by the Ponca were handheld shellers. More recently, corn shellers were called *wahába ínąšpè*, usu. a mechanized sheller.)

corral **Šáge unáza** /shoⁿ'-gä ü-noⁿ'-zä/ *n.*, corral, an enclosure to keep or confine livestock for loading, branding, and other such activities

correct **Đawágazù** /thä-wä'-gä-zü/ *adj.*, correct, to tell something or say something correctly, as in ~ *uwídagà*, tell it ~ly to him

correct **Égą** /ä'-goⁿ/ *v.*, to be correct, right, exact

correct **Šę́'gà** /shäⁿ'-goⁿ/ *adj.*, correct, lit., that's the way, usu. used when someone is working with someone who is doing something

correctly **Nąp'í** /noⁿ-p'ē'/ *adv.*, correctly, doing something ~ or something running ~

corrugated tin **Mą́ze đibébés'į** /moⁿ'-zä thē-bä'-bä'-s-ēⁿ/ *n.*, corrugated tin, tin roofing

cost **Í'đawà** /ē'-thä-wä'/ *v.*, cost, charge, rate, the value of something in terms of currency

cotton **Híxp'e** /hēⁿ'-p'ä/ *n.*, cotton, a fluffy fiber from the cotton plant of the genus *Gossypium*, family Malvaceae

cottonwood **Má'a'** /mä'-ä/ *n.*, cottonwood, refers to the cottonwood tree, genus *Populus*

cottonwood tree **Má'ahì** /mä'-ä-hē'/ *n.*, cottonwood tree, genus *Populus*, found on the Ponca reservation in Oklahoma

cough **Đašnúde** /thä-shnü'-dä/ *v.*, cough, to extract phlegm from the chest or cough up phlegm

cough **Húx'p'è** /hü'x-p'ä'/ *v.*, cough, a release of air through the windpipe and mouth, often expelling an obstruction, namely, phlegm

cough **Húx'p'è gaštą́žì** /hü'x-p'ä' gä-shtoⁿ'-zhē'/ *v.*, hacking cough

could have **Edé'gą** /ä-dä'-goⁿ/ *aux. v.*, could have, refers to something that somebody ~ done because it was the correct or right thing to do when it availed itself

council **Gahí'e** /gä-hē'-ä/ *n.*, council, usu. refers to the tribal council of the Ponca people

councilman **Gahí'e niášigà** /gä-hē'-ä nē-ä'-shē-gä/ *n.*, councilman, 1. a person who is a member of the tribal council 2. a politician in any government

count **Đawá** /thä-wä'/ *v.*, count, to engage in the act of counting (~ *ukíhi*, he can ~)

count **Kigđáwa** /kē-gthä'-wä/ *v.*, count, to count his own

count **Wađáwa** /wä-thä'-wä/ *v.*, count, saying numbers beginning with the number one

country **Mążą́** /moⁿ-zhoⁿ'/ *n.*, country, a section or region in the world that has its own government, geographic boundaries, and citizens

court **Mí'idáp'e** /mē-ē-thä'-p'ä/ *v.*, court, adulate, to flatter and adore, seeking the love or affection of a girl

courteous **Úšką úđą** /ü'sh-k'oⁿ ü'-doⁿ/ *adj.*, courteous, well-mannered, a person who is polite and shows respect to everybody, kind, considerate, thoughtful, a good or benevolent nature

cover **Ágasp'è** /ä'-gä-sp'ä'/ *v.*, cover, 1. hide from view, put out of sight, connotes something that either has been hidden deliberately or was found under something 2. in a ritual Ponca giveaway, used to indicate that an individual was honored with much material goods, usu. the placing of many Pendleton blankets or shawls upon or covering the person in the ritual dance

cover **Ágaxadè** /ä'-gä-xä-dä/ *v.*, cover, to cover up something (to use a lid to ~ the food); *idágigđaxadè*, covered his own

covering **-abaè'** /ä-bä-ä'/ *n.*, *suffix*, covering, 1. something laid or covered over a thing, esp. embellished decorations on Ponca ceremonial garb, e.g., moccasins covered with beads, as in *hìbé* ~ 2. a breakout of the skin, cause by a sickness, such as measles, chicken pox, etc. (his arm has a ~ of red bumps)

covering **Idágaxadè** /ē-thä'-gä-xä-dä'/ *n.*, covering, something used to cover something of any size

cover with **Į'žą** /ēⁿ-zhoⁿ/ *v.*, cover with, something used to sleep under, such as a blanket used to cover or sleep under

cow **T'é'ska'migà** /t'ä'-skä-mē-gä'/ *n.*, cow, a female member of domestic cattle or bovines

cowboy **T'é'ska basí'** /t'ä'-skä bä-sē'/ *n.*, cowboy, lit., drives cattle, a hired hand whose responsibility is to tend to cattle for roundups, branding, driving them to some location

cowboy boots **T'é'ska basí hįbé** /t'ä'-skä bä-sē' hēⁿ-bä'/ *n.*, cowboy boots

cower **Ugígdispè** /ü-gē'-gthē-spä'/ *n.*, cower, cringe in fear, somebody who lacks courage, a person who turns away from danger or trouble, as a dog puts its tail between its legs

cowhide **T'é'ska hà** /t'ä'-skä hä'/ *n.*, cowhide, the hide of the bovine (Following Native American removal from their original homelands, European cattle were introduced as a source of food. The cowhide was used to make soles for moccasins and other personal or household necessities.)

coyote **Mík'asì** /mē-k'ä-sē'/ *n.*, coyote (*Canis latrans*), a carnivorous canine related to the wolf

crack **Bašíšižè** /bä-shē'-shē-zhä'/ *v.*, to crack, crumble, or crush a solid substance continuously

crack **Bašížè** /bä-shē'-zhä'/ *v.*, to crack, crumble, or crush with the use of the hands by pressing

crack **Baxíxe** /bä-xē'-xä/ *v.*, crack, to crack by applying pressure

crack **Đašíže** /thä-shē'-zhä/ *v.*, crack, to ~ with the teeth

crack **Gadúxe** /gä-dü'-xä/ *v.*, crack, to crack something open, such as an egg

crack **Gašíšižè** /gä-shē'-shē-zhä'/ *v.*, to crack something with an instrument by hitting or striking continuously

crack **Gašížè** /gä-shē'-zhä'/ *v.*, to crack something with an instrument by hitting or striking

crack **Gaxíxe** /gä-xē'-xä/ *v.*, crack or break, usu. refers to glass or ceramics cracking; *gaxíxixè*, to continuously crack

cracking sound **Đat'á'xì** /thä-t'ä'-xē'/ *v.*, to make a loud cracking sound with the teeth while eating nuts

cracklings **Wašínaxudè** /wä-shē'-nä-xü-dä'/ *n.*, cracklings, pig rinds, pieces of rendered fried pork meat and skin

cradle **Uą́he** /ü-oⁿ'-hä/ *n.*, cradle, a baby cradle (The Ponca usually made a soft mattress and placed it on a thin board about two feet long and about twelve to fourteen inches wide. The child was laid upon the cradle and wrapped tightly with a soft blanket.)

cradle **Uą́he šadú** /ü-oⁿ'-hä shä-thü'/ *n.*, cradle, a decorative baby cradle (The cradle was made with an additional foot- and headboard. Two decorative straps, which were decorated with either colorful porcupine quills or beads, were tied from the headboard to the foot. At the headboard were attached seashells that served as a noisemaker for the child.)

cramps **Đik'ú'** /thē-k'ü'/ *n.*, cramps, an involuntary, painful muscle contraction

crane **Bdé'xe** /bthä'-xä/ *n.*, small crane, one of many species of cranes

crane **P'étą** /p'ä'-to^n/ *n.*, large crane, birds with long legs and long necks, one of many species of cranes

cranium **Nąškì'wahì** /no^n-shkē'-wä-hē'/ *n.*, cranium, skull, the part of the skeleton that encloses the brain

crash **Gačíže** /gä-chē'-zhä/ *v.*, crash, a loud sound made by something banging or striking against something else, such as a falling tree hitting the ground; *ígačìžè*, something that falls against something with a loud crashing sound

crave **É'saxt'ì** /ä'-sä-xt'ē'/ *interj.*, crave, thirst after, be consumed with desire, as in "Boy! I'd like to have soda right now!"

crave **Gą́'da áčą** /go^n'-thä ä'-cho^n/ *v.*, crave, *3rd pers. pl.*, yearn for, desire, long for, hunger after

crawdad **Mą́škà** /mo^n'-shkä'/ *n.*, crawdad, same as crayfish, freshwater crustacean with large claws like a lobster

crawl **Midá'dà** /mē-dä'-dä'/ *v.*, crawl away, to move quickly along on hands and knees, as if fleeing

crawl **Midé'** /mē-dä'/ *v.*, crawl, to crawl (*šéžįgà dįkè ~ ukíhi*, the baby can ~)

crazed bison **T'enúga dádį** /t'ā-nü'-gä thä'-thē^n/ *n.*, crazed bison (The Ponca tell stories of dangerous bison that became deranged because they ate certain plants.)

creative **Wadíp'i** /wä-thē'-p'ē/ *adj.*, creative, a person who is ~ , imaginative, artistic; *waní'p'i*, *2nd pers. sing.*, you are ~

Creator **Wáxe** /Wä'-xä/ *n.*, Creator, God, the Creator of the world and the universe (The Ponca believed in monotheism, the existence of one god. The attributes of the Creator, Wak'ą́da, were considered to be a mystery but knowable. As early as ca. 1870, a Ponca woman used the term *Wak'ą́da* in regard to her husband, who pursued the things of the Creator. She stated, "Nú wiwít'a, Wak'ą́da wádixè štiwà, ak'ík'ąbdà." [Even though my husband pursues the things of mystery, I want him back.] Though the term was used in that regard during that period, the term *Wak'ą́da* is used today in place of *Wáxe*.)

creak **Gizé** /gē-zä'/ *v.*, creak, something that makes a grating or squeaking sound; *gígíze*, to continuously make a creaking sound; *bigíze*, make a creaking sound by pressing down

credit **Wagáxe** /wä-gä'-xä/ *v.*, credit, to finance, to buy something with promise to pay later

creek **Wač'íška** /wä-ch-ē'-shkä/ *n.*, creek, a narrow channel or stream

Creek **Wač'íška níkašigà** /wä-ch-ē'-shkä nē'-kä-shē-gä/ *n.*, the Creek Tribe of Native Americans

creep **Bisp'áspà** /bē-sp'ä'-spä/ *v.*, creep, to move along with the body bent and close to the ground

cricket **Sį́'gdè** /sē^n'-gthä/ *n.*, cricket, an insect that chirps, jumps, and bites, of the family Gryllidae

crippled **Wahídagè** /wä-hē'-thä-gä/ *v.*, crippled, walking with a limp because of an injury or birth defect

crispy **Ná'sagì** /nä'-sä-gē'/ *adj.*, 1. crispy, usu. refers to something that is ~, such as crackers 2. refers to something that has been overcooked or burned to a crisp

critical **Úsągà** /ü'-so^n-gä/ *adj.*, critical, something that is life threatening, such as any sickness

crooked **Bažą́žą́** /bä-zho^n'-zho^n/ *adj.*, crooked, anything that appears to be or is ~ or uneven, as in a ~ board, land that has many knolls, a bumpy road

crooked **Đigúže** /thē-gü'-zhä/ *adj.*, crooked,

curved, not straight; *đigúgúže*, zigzag, more than one curve or bend in a thing

cross **Ákidit'à** /ä'-kē-thē-t'ä'/ *v.*, cross, traverse, to pass through or go across, as in crossing a field

cross **Wak'ǫ́da žǫ́' waxúbe** /wä-k'oⁿ'-dä zhoⁿ' wä-xü'-bä/ *n.*, cross, lit., sacred wood of God, the Christian cross upon which Jesus Christ was crucified

cross-eyed **Ǐšt'á' gđák'ǫ̀** /ēⁿ-sht'ä' gthä-k'oⁿ'/ *adj./n.*, cross-eyed, strabismus, a condition that prevents a person from directing both eyes at the same time toward the same point, resulting in double vision

crouch **Bisp'é** /bē-sp'ä'/ *n.*, crouch, act of bending low close to the ground

crow **K'á'xe** /k'ä'-xä/ *n.*, crow, a large black bird with a loud cry, of the genus *Corvus*, family Corvidae

Crow **K'á'xe ník'ašigà** /k'ä'-xä nē'-k'ä-shē-gä'/ *n.*, the Crow Tribe of Native Americans (The tribe is also referred to as Húp'a't'i)

crowbar **Máze íđišnudè** /moⁿ'-zā ē'-thē-shnü-dä'/ *n.*, crowbar, a tool made of steel, usually flattened on both ends, with one end bent to be used as a lever to remove nails or other materials affixed to a structure

crowbelt **K'á'xemįgđà** /k'ä'-xä-mēⁿ-gthoⁿ'/ *n.*, the crowbelt; a part of a Ponca Heđúškà member's dance paraphernalia consisting of the feathers of four predator birds: eagle, hawk, owl, and crow

crowd **Á'ki'é** /ä'-kē-ä'/ *n.*, crowd, usu. used in connection with a throng of people present at a gathering

crowded **Ubá'e** /ü-bä-ä/ *adj.*, crowded, congested, ~, where there is little space for people to move freely in a room or auditorium

crowded **Ubísądè** /ü-bē'-soⁿ-dä'/ *adj.*,

crowded, usu. 1. refers to seating and/or standing room only 2. male name in the Wažážè clan of the Ponca people

crow feathers **K'á'xe hà ínąp'į̀** /k'ä'-xä hä' ē'-noⁿ-p'ē²'/ *n.*, crow feathers, the entire skin and feathers, including the head, of the crow (This ancient symbolic piece of Ponca Heđúškà paraphernalia was worn over the left shoulder.)

crown **T'axp'í** /t'ä-xp'ē'/ *n.*, crown, top of or crown of the head

crumble **T'ubáde** /t'ü-bä'-thä/ *v.*, crumble, to break into small pieces or tiny bits; *bit'úbe*, to crumble, crush, or grind by pressing down upon; *bit'út'úbe*, to continuously crumble, crush by pressing down upon; *đit'úbe*, to crumble, crush, or grind with the use of the hands or hand tools; *gat'úbe*, to crumble something by force; *gat'út'úbe*, to continuously crumble something by force; *nąt'úbe*, to crumble, crush, or grind with machinery; *nąt'út'úbe*, to continuously crumble, crush, or grind something with machinery

crumble **Uđíšp'ašp'à** /ü-thē'-shp'ä-shp'ä'/ *v.*, crumble, to ~ or break into small pieces with the hands, as in cooking

crumbs **Wamúske bit'út'ú'be** /wä-müⁿ'-skä bē-t'ü'-t'ü'-bä/ *n.*, crumbs, bread crumbs

crutch **Hí'mągdè** /hē'-moⁿ-gthä'/ *n.*, crutch, cane, a support to help the lame in walking—one end fits under the armpit, with a crosspiece and a handle at mid length that can be held by the hands

cry **Áxa** /ä'-xä/ *v.*, cry, to cry for, as in a child crying for something

cry **Xagé** /xä-gā'/ *v.*, cry, weep, sob, shed tears

crybaby **Xagé'št'ǫ̀** /xä-gā'-sht'oⁿ'/ *n.*, crybaby, lit., likes to cry

cry out **Hú't'ǫ̀** /hü'-t'oⁿ'/ *v.*, 1. to cry out, as a trapped animal crying out 2. Wađáhut'ǫ̀, proper male name in the Wažáže clan of the Ponca people

cry to God **Wak'ą́da gíką** /wä-k'oⁿ'-dä gē'-koⁿ/ *v.*, cry to God, humbling self before God

cucumber **K'uk'úmi** /k'ü-k'ü-mē/ *n.*, cucumber, 1. a long green vegetable with white inner flesh, usu. eaten in salads 2. pickle, a cucumber that is flavored with dill and preserved with vinegar and other preservatives

cuddle **Ákinè** /ä'-kē-nä'/ *v.*, cuddle, two persons holding each other affectionately, to hug tenderly

culpable **Wépiáži** /wä-pē-ä'-zhē'/ *adj.*, culpable, blameworthy, a person who deserves to be blamed as being wrong, evil, improper, or injurious among a group of people

cultivate **Wa'é** /wä-ä'/ *v.*, cultivate, working on the land preparing to sow seeds and raise crops

culture **Úšką** /ü'-shkoⁿ'/ *n.*, culture, habits, behavior; in the social sciences, the way in which people develop social behavior in certain situations or conditions, resulting in varied habits, values, customs, arts, beliefs, established institutions, etc.

cumulus clouds **Mąxp'í' bat'á't'à** /moⁿx-p'ē' bä-t'ä'-t'ä'/ *n.*, cumulus clouds

cup **Uxp'é'žįgà** /ü-xp'ä'-zhēⁿ-gä'/ *n.*, cup, a container used to hold liquid drinks

cupboard **Uxp'éuži** /ü-xp'ä'-ü-zhē'/ *n.*, cupboard, cabinet for cups and plates, also used to store food and other crockery

curdle **Uskúskè** /ü-skü'-skä'/ *v.*, curdle, to turn sour, spoil, as in milk changing into curds

cure **Níde** /nē'-thä/ *v.*, to cure, make well, restore to health

cured **Í'nidè** /ē'-nē-thä'/ *v.*, to get cured by or with medicine or something else (The Ponca believed that some physical activity, such as dancing, could make a person well.)

curer **Wéni** /wä'-nē/ *n.*, curer, somebody or something that cures or restores health to a person

curl **Đišá'ge** /thē-shä'-gä/ *v.*, curl, to make, as with hair, a curved shape, wave

current **Ágaxdè** /ä'-gä-xthä'/ *v.*, current, flowing with the wind, tide

current **Ágaxdè** /ä'-gä-xthä'/ *n. phr.*, current, the flow of the wind or current of the wind (the flaps at the top of a tepee serve as a damper for the inner ~ of air)

currycomb **Šáge mikáhe** /sho ⁿ'-gä mē-kä'-hä/ *n.*, currycomb, a comb with metal teeth for currying horses

curtain **Wiúgąbà idágaxadè** /wēü'-goⁿ-bä' ē-thä'-gä-xä-dä'/ *n.*, curtain, drapery, blind, shutter

curved **Snúka** /snü'-kä/ *v.*, curved, like a banana

cushion **Įbehì št'ągá** /ēⁿ'-bä-hēⁿ' sht'oⁿ-gä'/ *n.*, cushion, a soft pad or pillow used for sitting, kneeling, or lying down

cuss **Wáxe íye p'iáži** /wä-xä ē'-yä p'ē-ä'-zhē/ *v.*, cuss, lit., white man's bad words, curse, swear

cut **Đisné** /thē-snä'/ *n.*, cut, a minor cut made on the skin by an animal, a scratch made by coming into contact with a sharp object

cut **Sé'** /sä'/ *v.*, cut, to separate a thing with a sharp tool, to penetrate with a sharp tool; *bisé'*, to cut by pressing a sharp instrument onto a thing; *gasé'*, to cut by using force with an instrument, such as an ax, cleaver, or long sword; *máse*, to cut something, usu. something like a rope, twine, thread; *máxą*, to cut with a knife; *đisé'*, to cut by using the hands

cute **Nájegda'wadè** /noⁿ'-jä-gthä-wä-thä'/ *adj.*, cute; adorable (This term is a derivative of the word *nádegdàwadè*, unsightly, unpleasant, unlikeable. But it is assigned to cuteness in babies, puppies, and other small animals or things.)

cute **Ú'ją** /ü'-joⁿ/ *adj.*, cute, pretty, attractive, adorable

cut off **Ámašp'è** /ä-mä-shp'ä'/ *v.*, to cut off a piece of something; *ímašpè*, cut off a piece for me; *đimašpè*, cut off a piece for you; *wémašpè*, cut off a piece for them, as with food

cut off **Gí'masè** /gē'-mä-sä'/ *v.*, cut off, 1. to cut something off someone, as in *mą́de k'ą́ kè*, ~(*ai*), he ~ his bow string 2. a surgical procedure to remove a limb of the human body or to have a person's limb cut off in battle

cutting **Bisá'sa** /bē-sä'-sä/ *v.*, to cut to pieces by pressing a sharp instrument onto a thing; *nąsása*, to cut to shreds by stepping on continuously or driving over continuously

cutting **Másasà** /mä'-sä-sä'/ *v.*, cutting, to cut into strips or pieces with a knife

cut up **Basása** /bä-sä'-sä/ *n.*, something that is cut up, 1. segmented, something that has been divided up in pieces, as with a log 2. partition, usu. refers to real estate, namely, inherited fractionalized land (*mąžą́ basása*, lands held in trust by the federal government and inherited by succeeding generations of the original allottee's family)

cut with **Í'gasè** /ē'-gä-sä'/ *v.*, cut with, the instrument used to, as in *mąhí et'áike* ~, he used his knife to ~

D

daddy longlegs **T'e'bđą́'** /t'ä-bthoⁿ'/ *n.*, daddy longlegs, an order of arachnids (Opiliones) that has a pill-like body and long legs

daily **Ą́ba ídawà** /oⁿ'-bä ē'-thä-wä'/ *adv./adj.*, daily, every day; something done every day

damage **P'iáži gáxe** /p'ēä'-zhē gä-xä/ *v.*, damage, ruin, spoil, or break something

damp **Bízext'iáži** /bē-zä-xt'ē-ä'-zhē/ *adj.*, damp, slightly wet, said of something that still has some moisture in it

damper **Umúhunì** /ü-mü'-hü-nē'/ *n.*, damper, a plate in a fireplace that regulates the flow of air inside a chimney

dance **Heđúška'wačí'gaxè** /hä-thü'-shkä-wä-chē'-gä-xä'/ *n.*, a dance commonly called the "war dance," a man's dance held in conjunction with the Heđúškà organization

dance **Wačí'gaxè** /wä-chē'-gä-xä'/ *n./v.*, dance, general term for any kind of dancing, to dance

dance paraphernalia **Wékią̀** /wä-kē-oⁿ'/ *n.*, dance paraphernalia, earned ornaments ("medals") worn by a Heđúškà dancer

dangling **Ugáe'è'** /ü-gä'-ä-ä'/ *adj.*, dangling, hanging loosely

dappled **Gdežé'** /gthä-zhä'/ *adj.*, dappled, spotted, speckled (*šáge ~ wì àgđì*, he rode a ~ horse)

dark blue **T'ú'sábe** /t'ü'-sä-bä/ *adj.*, dark blue, the color dark blue

darken **Ná'šabeđè** /nä-shä-bä-thä'/ *v.*, darken, usu. refers to making deerskin darker in color

darkness **Ágahąnąp'azè** /ä'-gä-hoⁿ-noⁿ-p'ä-zä'/ *n.*, darkness, state of dimness or darkness caused by covering or turning off lights in a room

darkness **Ugáhąnąpazè** /ü-gä'-hoⁿ-noⁿ-pä-zä'/ *n.*, darkness, that which occurs at night, the absence of light

daughter **I'žáge** /ē-zhoⁿ'-gä/ *n.*, daughter, lit., his/her daughter, relationship of female child to parent

daughter **Wi'žáge** /wē-zhoⁿ'-gä/ *n.*, daughter (a man or woman saying, my ~)

daughter-in-law **Mí'wađixè** /mē'-wä-thē-xä'/

n., daughter-in-law (a man or woman may say, "my ~")

daughter-in-law **Wi't'íni** /wē-t'ē'-nē/ *n.*, daugher-in-law, a masculine word for daughter-in-law

dauntless **Ú'šk'adaži** /ü-shk'ä-dä-zhē'/ *adj.*, 1. dauntless, fearless, resolute, confident 2. a man's name in the Wašábe clan of the Ponca people

dawn **Ába et'ádišà** /oⁿm'-bä ā-t'ä'-thē-shoⁿ'/ *n.*, dawn, toward the morning; dawn of the day

dawn **Ugába et'ádišà** /ü-goⁿ'-bä ā-t'ä'-thē-shoⁿ'/ *n.*, dawn, lit., toward the light, first light

day **Ába** /oⁿm'-bä/ *n.*, day, daytime, daylight; *e'sidádi*, the day before a certain day; *e'gasądì*, on the morrow after a certain day; *e'hądi*, on the night before; *e'sidádi guádišà*, two days before or on the second day before

day after **Ába udúhe** /oⁿm'-bä ü-thü'-hä/ *n.*, *archaic*, day after, the day after today

day after **Égasądì** /ā'-gä-soⁿ-thē'/ *n.*, the day after of any other day, a past or future day

daybreak **Ába édạbè** /oⁿm'-bä ä'-thoⁿ-bä/ *n.*, daybreak, sunrise, sunup

daytime **Ábadà** /oⁿm'-bä-doⁿ'/ *n.*, daytime, during the day

dead **Wat'ę'** /wä-t'äⁿ'/ *n.*, dead, the death of a person

deaf **Waną́áži** /wä-noⁿ'-oⁿ'-zhē/ *n.*, deaf, lit., cannot hear

debate **Íye ákikída** /ē'-yā ä'-kē-kē'-thä/ *v.*, debate, usu. refers to a contentious viewpoint of some concern; a formal argument in public

debt **Wagáxe** /wä-gä'-xä/ *n.*, debt, something (money) that is owed to somebody, bound by verbal or written agreement

decade **Umádikà gdébạ** /ü-moⁿ'-thē-kä' gthä'-boⁿ/ *n.*, decade, a period of ten years

deceive **Udúxa** /ü-thü'-xä/ *v.*, deceive, misinform, trick, mislead, hoodwink; *wawéúxa*, to use words and actions to deceive or lie

deceive **Ú'šịdè** /üⁿ'-shēⁿ-thä'/ *v.*, deceive, "to be false to"; or someone or something causing one to believe something that is not true

deceived **Ú'šịk'idè** /üⁿ'-shēⁿ-k'ē-thä'/ *v.*, deceived, deceived self or misinformed self

December **Máde oskáska** /mä'-thä ō-skoⁿ'-skä/ *n.*, December, lit., middle of the time when it snows, the twelfth month of the year

deception **Wawiúxa** /wä-wē-ü'-xä/ *v.*, deception, to do or show something to mislead, trick, hoodwink

decisive **Á'šiáda** /ä'-shēä'-thä/ *adj.*, decisive, as in making a definite choice quickly without consideration for the outcome of the situation

decomposed **Usésą** /ü-sä'-soⁿ/ *adj.*, decomposed, refers to decomposition of foods, usu. something that has an unpleasant smell, esp. fats such as butter, noted by odor or taste and sometimes by sight

decorate **Á'ba'è** /ä'-bä-ä/ *v.*, to decorate lavishly, e.g., *hịbé'á'baè*, moccasins that are entirely beaded

decry **Đašíge** /thä-shē'-gä/ *v.*, decry, to say something in response to what someone says about a report or tale that is unbelievable

deep **Škúbe** /shkü'-bä/ *adj.*, deep, unfathomable, usu. refers to the depth of a river, lake, or any large body of water

deep weeds **U'číže** /ü-chē'-zhä/ *n.*, deep weeds

deer **T'áxt'ì** /t'ä'-xt'ē'/ *n.*, deer, any of the ruminant mammals of the family Cervidae

deerskin **T'ahá'** /t'ä-hä'/ *n.*, deer skin, buckskin, tanned deerskin

deerskin dress **Háwatè** /hä'-wä-tā/ *n.*, deerskin dress, lit., dress made from animal skins, 1. buckskin or leather dress, a woman's garment 2. a proper name of a female member of the Hísadà clan of the Ponca people

Deer Woman **T'áxt'i Waú'** /t'ä'-xt'ē wä-ü'/ *n.*, Deer Woman, a mythological character first appearing to young Ponca men in the North Country. Usually appearances are to young men. (Some young men still claim to see her in lonely places.)

defend **Udúki** /ü-thü'-kē/ *v.*, defend, to support and protect a person

defrost **Náskądè** /nä'-skonⁿ-thä'/ *v.*, defrost, thaw out, unfreeze

dehydrate **Bí'zedè** /bē'-zä-thä'/ *v.*, dehydrate, dry, to remove water from to make dry

dehydrated food **Wadáte bí'zedè** /wä-thä'-tä bē'-zä-thä'/ *n.*, dehydrated food

dehydrated meat **T'á'** /t'ä'/ *n.*, dehydrated meat, dried meat

delightful **Úžawà** /ü'-zhä-wä'/ *adj.*, delightful, connotes fun and merriment or revelry; festive, celebratory

deliver **Adiáhi** /ä-thēä'-hē/ *v.*, deliver, to take or carry something to a person or place

demand **Áhušigè** /ä'-hü-shē-gä'/ *v.*, demand, insist, ask for something forcefully

demean **Đižuáži** /thē-zhü-ä'-zhē/ *v.*, demean, put down, to debase somebody

demolish **Đišédą** /thē-shä'-thonⁿ/ *v.*, demolish, to break or tear down by hand, machinery, or other forces

denied **Á'ąbažì** /ä'-onⁿ-bä-zhē'/ *adj.*, denied, an indication of a negative response to a request made about something or somebody

dense **Á'k'išugà** /ä'-k'ē-shü-gä'/ *adj.*, dense, 1. intense, as in a downpour of rain 2. refers to people crowded close together

dentist **Hi'wádit'ą̀** /hē-wä'-thē-t'onⁿ/ *n.*, dentist, a person who is a trained practioner in the branch of medicine that deals with treatment of the teeth and related conditions

depart **Ągádè't'è** /onⁿ-gä'-thä-t'ä'/ *v.t.*, *1st pers. pl.*, depart, let us depart, let us go; *agádaì*, we are departing or going

departed **Kigdái** /kē-gthä'-ē/ *v.t.*, *3rd pers. pl.*, departed, people have left an area to go to their own home or village

departing **Uwąsi** /ü-wonⁿ'-sē/ *v.*, departing, getting off a vehicle

depend **Udúkinąžì** /ü-thü'-kē-nonⁿ-zhē'/ *v.*, depend, two persons or two groups depending upon each other for support

dependable **Udúnąžì** /ü-thü'-nonⁿ-zhē'/ *adj.*, dependable, reliable, trustworthy, trusty, staunch

depend upon **Ák'inąžì** /ä-k'ē-nonⁿ-zhē'/ *v.*, depend upon, to rely or place trust in another for one's well-being (Although used more for family members and friends, it was historically part of the Ponca Heđúškà fraternal organization of men who defended the camp and did good deeds.)

deplete **Nądíge** /nonⁿ-thēⁿ'-gä/ *v.*, deplete, to decrease or use up the supply of things or a thing that causes the loss of something

derogatory **Đadábažì** /thä-thonⁿ'-bä-zhē'/ *v.*, derogate, put down, to make a remark to or about another person in an insulting or critical manner

descend **Gawíxe** /gä-wēnⁿ'-xä/ *v.*, descend, lit., to fly close by, usu. refers to birds flying low above housetops; refers also to low-flying aircraft

desirable **Gądawadè** /gonⁿ-thä-wä-thä'/ *n.*, desirable, something attractive, worthy of desire

desire **Gądaxtì** /gonⁿ-thä-xtē'/ *v.*, desire, yearning, longing

despise **Í't'ade'áčąi** /ē'-t'ä-thä-ä'-choⁿ-ē'/ *v.t.*, despise, to look at with contempt or scorn

destitute **Waxp'ádį** /wä-xp'ä'-thēⁿ/ *adj.*, destitute, impoverished, needy, penniless

destroy **Mú'šedą** /mü'-shä-thoⁿ/ *v.*, destroy, blow to pieces, obliterate, demolish

detached **Uhá'ži'št'ì** /ü-hä'-zhē-sht'ē'/ *adj.*, detached, outsider, lit., even though I am not a part of it, removed, distant, far from it

detain **Wádišt'ąbažì** /wä-thē-sht'oⁿ-bä-zhē'/ *v.t.*, detain, holding in custody

detergent **Wédit'egà** /wä'-thē-t'ä-gä'/ *n.*, detergent, liquid or powdered detergent for laundry

detriment **Ágdadè** /ä'-gthä-thä'/ *n.*, detriment, something causing detriment, disadvantage, harm or loss

devil **Náxe p'éži** /noⁿ'-xä p'ä'-zhē/ *n.*, devil, Satan (In the Judeo-Christian faith Satan is a fallen angel who opposes all that is good, often referred to as the adversary.)

devour **Đasní** /thä-snē'/ *v.*, devour, eating something up, nothing left

dew **Žídą** /zhē'-doⁿ/ *n.*, dew, moisture from the air condensed on outdoor things, esp. at night

diabetes **Wamí' skíde** /wä-mē' skē'-thä/ *n.*, diabetes mellitus, a disease in which a person's pancreas does not regulate insulin, causing high or low levels of blood sugar

dialogue **Uk'ík'íyè** /ü-k'ē'-k'ē'-yä'/ *n.*, dialogue, conversation between two or more people

diamond willow tree **Đíxutibdą́bdąxèhì** / thē'-xü-tē-bthoⁿ'-bthoⁿ-xä'-hē'/ *n.*, diamond willow tree, a willow known by the Ponca in Nebraska that grows in the north country (The wood is deformed into diamond-shaped segments with alternating colors of red and white when debarked.)

diapers **Nídeágdè** /nē'-dä-ä'-gthä'/ *n.*, dia-pers, a square piece of cloth or absorbent material worn by babies as underwear

diaphragm **Điʃ'xdú'a** /thē-ʃⁿ-xthü'-ä/ *n.*, diaphragm or chest cavity

diarrhea **B'áxet'à** /b-ä'-xä-t'ä'/ *n.*, diarrhea, complications causing frequent bowel movements

dice **K'ą́si** /k'oⁿ'-sē/ *n.*, dice, lit., plum seed, orig. used in a Ponca family game called Indian dice, now refers to dice, two small cubes with one to six spots marked on the sides, used in a gambling game

die **T'è** /t'äⁿ/ *v.*, die, cease to live

different **Á'žì** /ä'-zhē/ *adj.*, different, not the same kind

different **Égą àži** /ä'-goⁿ ä'-zhē/ *adj.*, different, differing in form or quality

difficult **T'é'xi** /t'ä'-xē/ *adj.*, difficult, something hard to do, something hard to deal with

difficulty **Ú't'exì** /ü'-t'ä-xē'/ *n.*, difficulty, a perplexity; *ądą́gį́t'exì*, personally unable to think something clearly through; *wét'exì*, *pl.*, we can't think it clearly through; *í'git'exì*, he/she can't think it clearly through because his/her friend or relative is facing something difficult

dig **E'** /ä'/ *v.*, dig, excavate

dig **Mąé'** /moⁿ-ä'/ *v.*, dig, lit., dig ground, dig the ground, as with hands or tools

digestive problems **Ną́dewádaskabè** /noⁿ'-dä-wä'-thä-skä-bä'/ *n.*, *archaic*, digestive problems, usu. refers to a long-term illness (This word may have referred to acid reflux/heartburn.)

dignity **K'igdí'ežubà** /k'ē-gthē'-ä-zhü-bä'/ *n.*, dignity, to dignify self, the state of being worthy of respect or holding a position of respect

dilemma **Ú'čižè** /ü'-chē-zhä'/ *n.*, dilemma, condition of being in a sudden and unexpected predicament or quandary dime **Šugá'žįgà** /shü-gä'-zhēⁿ-gä'/ *n.*, dime, ten-cent piece

dining room **Údatèt'i** /ü'-thä-tā'-t'ē/ *n.*, dining room, a room for eating food

dinner **Mídą mą́ši wadáte** /mē'-thoⁿ moⁿ-shē wä-thä'-tā/ *n.*, dinner, the most important or main meal of the day, which can be served at noon or in the evening

dip **Ubít'ą** /ü-bē'-t'oⁿ/ *v.*, dip, to put something into liquid quickly

dip **Udúbidą̀** /ü-thü'-bē-doⁿ/ *v.*, dip, as to dip bread into soup or pastry into coffee

diploma **Wagą́ze ugášibe wabáxu** /wä-goⁿ'-zä ü-gä'-shē-bä' wä-bä'-xü/ *n.*, diploma, a certificate issued by an educational institution verifying successful completion of a course of study in months or years; the term includes college degrees

dipper **Ní'idát'ą̀** /nē'-ē-thä'-t'oⁿ/ *n.*, dipper, a dipper for drinking water

direction **E't'ádišą̀** /ā-t'ä'-thē-shoⁿ/ *n.*, direction, in the direction of something

direction **Gáket'adišą̀** /gä-kä-t'ä-thē-shoⁿ/ *n.*, direction, the direction of something spoken of

direction **Gát'adišą̀** /gä-t'ä-thē-shoⁿ/ *n.*, direction, generally toward an unspecified direction

dirty **Šnábe** /shnä'-bä/ *adj.*, dirty, grimy, soiled; *ibišnabè*, make dirty or smear something on; *idébešnabè*, made his (something) dirty or smeared; *įdébišnabè*, made mine dirty or smeared

disappear **Đįgeátiagdè** /thēⁿ-gä-ä'-tē-ä-gthä'/ *v.*, disappear, to go away suddenly

disassemble **Đišédą** /thē-shä'-thoⁿ/ *v.t.*, disassemble, the process of taking something apart; dismantle, to take apart or take to pieces

disbelieve **Wažá'** /wä-zhä'/ *v.*, disbelieve, question, refers to questioning the facts or knowledge of something; *wéža*, to be skeptical or to question somebody's story

discard **Ą́da** /oⁿ'-thä/ *v.*, discard, dispose of, throw away, get rid of

discern **Ubésnì** /ü-bä'-snē'/ *v.*, discern, sense or notice

discharge **Mút'úši** /mü'-t'ü'-shē/ *v.*, discharge, go off, as in the use of a gun; *t'uší'*, the popping or cracking sound of a cartridge being fired

discontent **Ną́de ísawadàžì** /noⁿ'-dä ē'-sä-wä-thä'-zhē'/ *n.*, discontent, dissatisfied, not to one's liking

discourtesy **Úškąp'iáži** /ü'-shkoⁿ-p'ē-ä'-zhē/ *n.*, discourtesy, lack of courtesy, impoliteness, incivility

discover **Wawékidè** /wä-wä'-kē-thä'/ *v./n.*, discover, to find something for oneself, to find something unexpected and surprisingly delightful; discovery, the process of finding a thing

discussion **Ga'íye** /gä-ē'-yä/ *n.*, discussion, consideration given by argument, comment, etc., not restricted to but usu. a term used in reference to a committee meeting, esp. one concerning looking for, finding, or exploring solutions

disease **Ú'niet'ą̀** /ü'-nē-ä-t'oⁿ/ *n.*, disease, a physical disorder or malady that prevents normal body functions, such as heart disease, diabetes, arthritis

disgruntled **Uxį́'e** /ü-xēⁿ'-ā/ *v.*, disgruntled, a person who is displeased or discontented; usu. speaking unhappily because one feels one has been wronged or mistreated

dish **Uxp'é** /ü-xp'ä'/ *n.*, dish, plate, or saucer used esp. for serving food or holding something

disheartening **Ą'wą́'gí't'exì** /oⁿ-woⁿ'-gē'-t'ä-xē'/ *v.*, disheartening, *1st pers. sing.*, I am grieved, disturbed, troubled, disconcerted over something that has happened

dishpan **Uxp'é't'ągà** /ü-xp'ä'-t'oⁿ-gä/ *n.*, *archaic*, dishpan, a large pan used to wash dishes, pots, and tableware

dish towel **Uxp'éibík'à** /üx-p'ä'-ē-bē'-k'ä/ *n.*, *archaic*, dish towel, an absorbent cloth used to dry dishes

disintegrate **Mú'dįgè** /mü'-thēⁿ-gä/ *v.*, disintegrate, fall to pieces or apart and be gone by implosion

dislike **Idá't'abdè** /ē-thä'-t'ä-bthä/ *pron./v.*, dislike, *1st pers. sing., pres. t.*, lit., I don't like, to dislike an animate thing—humans or lower animals

dislike **Í't'adè** /ē'-t'ä-thä/ *n.*, dislike, objectionable, being erroneous in some unwanted act or behavior (~*wadéxt'ì p'áxe*, I did an unlikeable or objectional thing) where the act is not purposeful; *wawéət'ade*, disliking a person for what he/she accomplished (the term is closely related to envy)

dislike **Í'xt'amąžì** /ēⁿ'-xt'ä-moⁿ-zhē/ *pron./v.*, dislike, *1st pers. sing., pres. t.*, I don't like it, to dislike an inanimate thing or activity, not caring for the activity, object or thing, such as a car, a hunting experience, or watching a sporting event

dislike **Udút'adè** /ü-thü'-t'ä-thä/ *n.*, dislike, being envious of somebody who accomplished something and is enjoying his/her success

dislike **Xt'ádažì** /xt'ä'-thä-zhē/ *v.*, dislike, doesn't like, has an aversion to

dismantle **Đišédą** /thē-shä'-thoⁿ/ *v.t.*, dismantle, to take apart or take to pieces

disobedient **Íye wáną'ąžì** /ē'-yä wä'-noⁿ-oⁿ-zhē/ *adj.*, disobedient, lit., one who does not listen, rebellious, defiant, behaving badly

disparage **Đažúbažì** /thä-zhü'-bä-zhē/ *v.*, disparage, ridicule, criticize, putting somebody down

dispirit **Úkixidà** /ü-kē-xē-thä/ *v.*, dispirit, dishearten, put a damper on something that seems impossible to do

dispiritedness **Nąde waxp'ádi** /noⁿ-dä wä-xp'ä'-thē/ *n.*, dispiritedness, lit., heart made poor, the state of being discouraged or disheartened by someone

display **Bahá** /bä-hä'/ *v.*, display, to show

disproportionate **Uk'í'p'ášną** /ü-k'ē'-p'ä'-shnoⁿ/ *adj.*, disproportionate, uneven, lopsided, a thing that does not come together as normal

dispute **Íye ákikidà** /ē'-yä ä'-kē-kē-thä/ *v.*, dispute, to question or disagree about something, leading to argument

disruptive **Wép'iáži** /wä-p'ē-ä'-zhē/ *adj.*, disruptive, troublemaking, unruly, disturbing

dissatisfied **Gíšąžì** /gē'-shoⁿ-zhē/ *adj.*, dissatisfied with some plan, decision, activity, etc.

dissimilar **Égąxt'iáži** /ä'-goⁿ-xt'ē-ä'-zhē/ *adj.*, dissimilar, unlike, not really comparable

dissolve **Niúgaskądè** /nēü'-gä-skoⁿ'-thä/ *adj.*, dissolve, to soften and liquefy in water

distant **Wíáhidè** /wē'-ä'-hē-dä/ *adj.*, distant, far away or far off, something that is a great distance away

distressed **Gít'exì** /gē'-t'ä-xē/ *adj.*, distressed, usu. associated with suffering by being distraught, worried, bothered

distribute **Wégdaì** /wä'-gthä-ē/ *v.*, distribute, give out, dole out, hand out

disunite **Ákip'azà** /ä'-kē-p'ä-zoⁿ/ *v.*, disunite, to disunite or make a boundary (This can be an unwanted thing. Sometimes a person in a tribal gathering would separate himself or herself from other family members in a "give-away" and do his or her own thing.)

dive **Gdáge** /gthoⁿ'-gä/ *v.*, dive, plunge into the water headfirst with arms and hands extended forward divide **Ak'íwahà** /ä-k'ē'-wä-hä/ *v.*, divide, share, usu. refers to an activity between two individuals or to dividing up between two groups or persons

divorce **K'iáda** /k'ē-oⁿ-thä/ *n.*, divorce, separation, dissolving or legally ending a marriage

dizziness **Náxeskàži'** /noⁿ-xä-skä'-zhē/ *n.*, dizziness, a condition caused by something being wrong with one's spatial perception

do **Gáxe** /gä'-xä/ *v.*, do, did, done

doctor **Wazéde** /wä-zä'-thä/ *n.*, doctor, orig. a Ponca man or woman who used natural medicines and remedies to effect cures for various illnesses, now a doctor, physician, doctor of medicine; *zéde*, *v.*, to doctor, treat

dog **Šánudà** /shoⁿ-nü-dä/ *n.*, dog, refers to any breed of domestic dogs, *Canis lupus familiaris* (the modern Ponca pronunciation is *šínudà*)

dogwood tree **Mása'xt'i'hì** /moⁿ-sä-xt'ē-hē'/ *n.*, dogwood tree, lit., the tree that became proud, the dogwood tree, genus *Cornus*

doll **Šígažįgà wasésą** /shēⁿ-gä-zhēⁿ-gä' wä-sä'-soⁿ/ *n.*, doll, a child's toy—figure of a human child or baby

domain **Umádį** /ü-moⁿ-thēⁿ/ *n.*, domain, realm, area, habitat, locale, environment, territory, home; where humans or animals customarily live

domestic animals **Wanágde** /wä-nä'-gthä/ *n.*, domestic animals, refers to horses, dogs, cats and bovines, esp. cows, oxen

door **T'i'žébe** /t'ē-zhä'-bä/ *n.*, door, entrance

doorbell **T'i'žébe dik'ámą** /t'ē-zhä'-bä thē-k'ä'-moⁿ/ *n.*, doorbell, a device that rings or chimes inside a house or building and is activated by a small button near the outside door frame

doorknob **T'i'žébe udą́** /t'ē-zhä'-bä ü-thoⁿ/ *n.*, doorknob

Dorsey, James O. **Đási** /thä'-sē/ *n.*, James O. Dorsey, Ponca corruption of the name *Dorsey* (James Owen Dorsey, October 31, 1848–February 4, 1895, was an Episcopalian missionary and linguist who recorded the Ponca language ca. 1870–71 while working with the Ponca near current Niobrara, Nebraska.)

double **Nąbáha** /noⁿ-bä'-hä/ *adv.*, double, two together

doubt **Gíža** /gē'-zhä/ *v.*, doubt, to doubt him/her, have reservations, disbelief or simply not believing him/her; *wéža*, doesn't believe him/her/it; *wažá*, doesn't believe or doubts what he/she hears; *į̀·ža*, doesn't believe or doubts me; *đíža*, doesn't believe or doubts you

doubtful **Wažįxįdadì** /wä-zhēⁿ-xēⁿ-dä-thē'/ *adj./n.*, doubtful, a state of being uncertain or unsure of a situation

doubts **Wažášťą** /wä-zhä'-shtoⁿ/ *v.*, doubts, somebody who habitually and always doubts others on any subject

downhearted **Náde ísazì** /noⁿ-dä ē'-sä-zhē'/ *adj.*, downhearted, unhappy or in low spirits

downhill **P'a'mú'** /p'ä-mü/ *adv.*, downhill, downward

drag **Đisnú'** /thē-snü'/ *v.*, to drag, pulling by sliding or dragging an object on the ground, floor, or any flat surface

drain **Đixt'á** /thē-xt'oⁿ/ *v.*, drain, to draw off (drain) water from the sink

draw **Wadíxu** /wä-thē'-xü/ *v.*, to draw, to sketch, to make a picture on a surface by using a pencil or pen

drawing **Đixú** /thē-xü'/ *n.*, a drawing, a sketch, a picture made with the use of a pencil or pen

dread **Idákuhè** /ē-thä'-kü-hä/ *v.*, dread, to be anxious about, worried about disappointment dreading **Égà'idák'uhè** /ä'-goⁿ'-ē-thä'-k'ü-hā'/ *n.*, dreading, feeling anxiety over something that happened or could happen

dream **Háde** /hoⁿ'-thä/ *n.*, dream, images that come to mind while sleeping; sometimes real and imaginary places, people, and events are seen in the sleeping condition

dreamed **Idáhabdè** /ē-thä'-hoⁿ-bthä/ *v.*, *past. t.*, dreamed, lit., I dreamed; *ídahabè*, you dreamed; *íhabdaì*, he/she/they dreamed

dress **Wá'gà** /wä'-gä/ *n.*, dress, to dress out meat, to clean and prepare for cooking or storing

dress **Waté'** /wä-tā'/ *n.*, dress, a ladies' garment; *waté ukédi*, a homemade Native American dress; *wáxe waú waté*, white woman dress, refers to a store-bought dress

dresser **Ú'ži basnú** /ü'-zhē bä-snü'/ *n.*, dresser, chest of drawers, usu. a piece of bedroom furniture used for storing clothing

dress up **Xíkidè** /xē'-kē-thä'/ *n./v.*, dress up, 1. to put on special clothing, arrange and style the hair 2. to put on native Ponca paraphernalia for rituals or ceremonial dances

dried **Ábizè** /ä'-bē-zā'/ *n.*, something dried, as in dried up in the sun

dried, pounded meat **T'a'gát'ube'** /t'ä-gä'-t'ü-bā/ *n.*, dried, pounded meat, dehydrated meat, jerky, pemmican—dried meat pounded and sometimes mixed with nuts and dried berries

drift **Ugáha** /ü-gä'-hä/ *v.*, drift, float, flowing downstream

driftage **Nidá'gaxá'** /nē-doⁿ'-gä-xä'/ *n.*, driftage, usu. in reference to driftwood and other debris that piles up by the force of a flood

driftwood **Žagáxa** /zhoⁿ-gä'-xä/ *n.*, driftwood, pieces of wood piled up along the riverbank or floating in the river

drill **Wébaudè** /wä'-bä-ü-dä'/ *n.*, drill, a tool for drilling holes into or through various materials; now brace and bit

drink **Ðat'á** /thä-t'oⁿ'/ *v.*, drink, to drink any liquid beverage; *í'dat'à*, something to drink from—dipper, cup, hands

drink **Wadá't'à** /wä-thä'-t'oⁿ/ *v.*, to drink, drinking an alcoholic beverage

drip **Niúga'é'é** /nē-ü'-gä-ä'-ä'/ *v.*, drip, liquid falling in drops

dripping wet **Ágamù** /ä'-gä-mü'/ *adj.*, dripping wet, getting wet from rain, sopping wet, or sodden from some source

drip upon **Ágamuxt'à** /ä'-gä-mü-xt'oⁿ'/ *v.*, drip upon, causing water to drip upon or be sprayed upon them or us or on something

drive **Baší** /bä-shē'/ *v.*, to drive, steer, chauffeur, etc.

drone **Gaxát'à wadábe** /gä-xä-t'ä wä-doⁿ'-bä/ *n.*, drone, unmanned aerial vehicle (UAV) (A drone is a controlled device, situated apart from a main body, with the capability of monitoring varied conditions in the community and providing security surveillance for home and country. Other uses include film making, filming sports, monitoring livestock, conducting rescue missions, etc.)

drop **Ðišná** /thē-shnoⁿ'/ *v.*, drop or dropped, fumble, something slipping from the hands

drop **Udíxp'adè** /ü-thē'-xp'ä-thä'/ *v.*, drop, release, let go of, let something drop from the hand

drought **Nážiáži** /noⁿ-zhēⁿ-ä'-zhē/ *n.*, drought, when it does not rain in various places on earth for an extended period of time

drown **Niút'è** /nē-ü'-t'āⁿ'/ *v.*, drown, lit., die in the water

drugstore **Maká údiwit'ì** /moⁿ-koⁿ' ü-thē-wēⁿ-t'ē'/ *n.*, drugstore, a store that has a pharmarcy and sells miscellaneous medical products and a variety of household and personal items

drum **Gak'úge** /gä-k'ü'-gā/ *v.*, drum, to beat and hear the sound of a drum with a drumstick; *kúge utį̀*, one striking or hitting a drum, as a member of a singing group at a tribal dance

drum **K'úge** /k'ü'-gā/ *n.*, ca. twentieth century, drum, a percussion instrument made of a hollow cylinder with the hide of a bovine or bison stretched over both sides; *k'úge t'ą̀gà*, ceremonial drum, usu. used for various dances and other activities; *mąk'ą́datè k'úge*, Native American Church drum

drum **Néxe** /nā'-xā/ *n.*, *archaic*, drum, may be called a "percussion instrument"

drum fish **Hubđáska** /hü-bthä'-skä/ *n.*, drum fish, also called freshwater drum, *Aplodinotus grunniens*

drum hide **K'úge hà** /k'ü'-gā hä'/ *n.*, drum hide (The original hides for making drums were bison hides. The hide used for drums was considered a revered and sacred item in the Ponca Heđúškà organization.)

drummers **Xúk'à** /xü-k'ä'/ *v.*, drummers, drum and sing, usu. refers to singers (*~ mašé . . .*, you *~ . . .*)

drumming **Néxe'gak'ú'** /nā'-xā-gā-k'ü'/ *v.*, *archaic*, drumming, to drum, to beat upon a drum

drunkard **Dádiamà** /dä'-thē-ä-mä'/ *n.*, drunkard, those who habitually drink alcoholic beverages; *xúbe* (The term *xúbe* originally was used in relation to those who possessed medicines that were considered sacred as well as relics that were also kept sacred by the people. In the early twentieth century the term was applied to those who imbibed too often. A man was said to have sat by the trail that led into a city, waiting for a free ride on a wagon. After he sat for a very long time, a man saw him lift his arms up, probably stretching, and said of him jokingly, "Xúbe k'igáxaìte . . ." [He is making himself use mysterious powers to catch a ride.] Being overheard, the term *xubé* became commonly used for those who drink much.)

dry **Bí'ze** /bē'-zā/ *adj.*, used to describe dry substances, including land that has very little water; *bi'bí'ze*, *v.*, dry, to make dry by pressing down and wringing out with the hands; *bízeđè*, *v.*, dry, to let dry, or to dry by a mechanical device; *gabíze*, *v.*, to dry by flapping in the wind, e.g., clothes on the clothesline; *nąbíze*, *v.*, dry, 1. to dry by using a modern dryer 2. to dry caused by driving an auto over a wet, muddy road

dry cleaners **Háde đisíhi t'ì** /hä'-thä thē-sē'-hē t'ē'/ *n.*, dry cleaners, establishment for professional cleaning of various types of garments

duck **Míxa** /mē'-xä/ *n.*, duck, the common name for a large number of species in the Anatidae family of swimming birds

dull **Baí'áži** /bä-ē'-ä'-zhē/ *adj.*, dull, not sharp, not finely honed

dull **Búšna** /bü'-shnä/ *adj.*, dull, something that is rounded, blunted, such as a knife or spear point

dull sound **Gapúki** /gä-pü'-kē/ *v.*, dull sound, 1. to strike something, making a dull sound 2. something falling, making a dull sound

dumpling **Ą́ba'gđè** /oⁿm'-bä-gthä'/ *n.*, corn dumpling, a Ponca food made from corn

dung beetle **Įgđé'babút'à** /ēⁿ-gthä'-bä-bü'-t'ä'/ *n.*, dung beetle, from the insect order Coleoptera

dupe **Uđúxa** /ü-thü'-xä/ *v.*, dupe, trick, pull the wool over somebody's eyes duplicate **Ékigà gáxe** /ā'-kē-goⁿ' gä'-xā/ *n.*, duplicate, copy, replica, reproduction

dust **Šíšígè** /shē'-shē'-gā/ *n.*, dust, something of the nature of litter or small particles

dust storm **Mągášudè** /moⁿ-gä'-shü-dā/ *adj.*, dust storm, consisting of hard-blowing dust from the ground, rising and then settling in or on the ground, people, or things

dusty **Á'múšudè** /ä'-mü-shü-dā/ *v.*, dusty, making dust come over them or us

dusty **Nąšúde** /noⁿ-shü'-dā/ *adj.*, dusty, making dust by driving over a dirt or gravel road

dusty **Šúde dip'áze** /shü-dā thē-p'ä'-zā/ *adj.*, dusty, dust raised by a moving vehicle

dusty **Šúšúdè** /shü'-shü'-dā/ *adj./n.*, dusty, something covered with dust

E

each **Wí'dądà** /wē'-thoⁿ-thoⁿ/ *pron.*, each, each one, apiece, two or more being considered one at a time

eager **U'hít'abažì** /ü-hē'-t'ä-bä-zhē/ *adj.*, eager, anxious for something to happen or to receive something

eagle **Xidá'** /xē-thä/ *n.*, eagle, a large predatory bird of the Accipitridae family

eagle feather **Xidá'mąšą̀** /xē-thä'-moⁿ-shoⁿ/ *n.*, eagle feather

ear **Nąxíde** /noⁿ-xē'-dā/ *n.*, ear, the inner ear, labyrinth, a part that also senses the state of one's equilibrium

ear **Nit'á'** /nē-t'ä/ *n.*, ear, the external or outer part of the ear composed mostly of cartilage and skin

earache **Nąxíde'ni'é** /noⁿ-xē'-dā-nē-ā'/ *n.*, earache, a sometimes sharp to dull pain that can last for a short span of time or be a long-term condition, referred to as otalgia, and not always associated with inner

ear diseases, may be caused by other conditions

earlobe **Nąxídehidè** /noⁿ-xē'-dā-hē-dā'/ *n.*, earlobe, the fleshy lower part of the external ear

earn **Úwawešì** /ü-wä-wä-shē'/ *v.*, earn, to receive something (e.g., money) in return for work services rendered

earrings **Ú'wį̀'** /ü'-wēⁿ'/ *n.*, earrings, jewelry worn on the earlobes

earth **Mążą́** /moⁿ-zhoⁿ'/ *n.*, earth, land

earthen lodge **Mąíti** /moⁿ-ē'-tē/ *n.*, earthen lodge, mound dwelling, a circular dwelling composed of wooden poles and a thatched roof covered with dirt

easily **Ą́dixčìègą̀** /oⁿ-thē-xchē-ā'-goⁿ/ *adv.*, easily, without difficulty, without problems, simply, effortlessly

easily incensed **Wažį́'kudè** /wä-zhēⁿ'-kü-thä'/ *adv.*, easily incensed, 1. short-tempered 2. easily upset 3. quick to make a judgment

east **Mí'édąbèt'à** /mē-ä'-thoⁿ-bä-t'ä'/ *n.*, east, lit., where the sun comes and shows itself, one of the cardinal points on the compass

Easter **Wak'ą́da Ižį́ge Nít'a Agítedądì** /wä-k'oⁿ'-dä ē-zhēⁿ'-gä nē'-t'ä ä-gē'-tä-thoⁿ-dē'/ *n.*, Easter, lit., when the Son of God arose from the dead

easterly **Mí'édąbè't'adišą̀** /mē'-ä'-thoⁿ-bä'-t'ä-thē-shoⁿ/ *adj./adv.*, in an easterly direction, toward the east

easy **Úmąk'à** /ü'-moⁿ-k'ä'/ *adj.*, easy, effortless, uncomplicated, simple

easygoing **Wašt'áge** /wä-sht'ä'-gā/ *adj.*, easygoing, 1. describes a psychological behavioral pattern that is normal for a person who is gentle and calm or has a moderate temperament 2. refers to animals that have a moderate temperament, unlike, e.g., a spirited horse

eat **Ðaté'** /thä-tā'/ *v.*, eat, to eat, to consume food

eat **Wadáte** /wä-thä'-tä/ *v.*, 1. to eat (*núži̧gà di̧kè ~ gði*, the boy sat down to eat) 2. food

edge **Ubáhat'adišà̧** /ü-bä'-hä-t'ä-thē-shoⁿ/ *n. phr.*, edge, toward the edge

edge **Ubáhe** /ü-bä'-hä/ *n.*, edge, the border, perimeter, side of something

edition **Wabáxu gáxaì kè** /wä-bä'-xü gä'-xäē' kä'/ *n.*, edition, one of a printing of the same newspaper or book

egg **Wét'à** /wä'-t'ä'/ *n.*, egg, an edible product from chickens

egg white **Wét'a uská'** /wä'-t'ä ü-skä'/ *n.*, egg white, a substance whose purpose is to protect the yolk and provide nutrition for the growth of a fertilized embryo; an edible, nutritious food

eh **Háhe** /hä'-hä/ *interj.*, eh?, an expression of confirmation or agreement for something said

eight **P'édá'bði** /p'ä-thä'-bthē'/ *n.*, eight, lit., five and three, the number eight (8)

eighth **Wé'p'edábði** /wä'-p'ä-thä'-bthēⁿ/ *n.*, eighth, the eighth thing in a row of items or the eighth person or group of people coming in succession

either **Áwadikešt'iwà̧** /ä'-wä-thē-kä-sht'ē-woⁿ/ *n.*, either, a word that connects two situations, one of which may be eliminated or may be included

elastic **Zízigè** /zē'-zē-gä'/ *adj.*, elastic, stretchy, as a sweater, *uná̧ži'zizigè*

elasticity **Bazí'zi** /bä-zē'-zē/ *n.*, elasticity, flexibility

elbow **Ast'úhi** /ä-st'ü'-hē/ *n.*, elbow, the elbow joint between the upper and lower arm

elbow joint **Á'ukíte** /ä'-ü-kē'-tä/ *n.*, elbow joint, a hinge joint between the humerus in the upper arm and radius and ulna in the forearm

elder **Iš'áge** /ēsh-ä'-gä/ *n.*, elder or aged man, an old man; *waú'ži̧gà*, lit., little woman, elder or aged woman, an old woman

elder brother **Wit'ínu** /wē-t'ē'-nü/ *n., fem.*, elder brother, the feminine word for addressing an elder male sibling (woman saying: my ~)

elder brother **Wižį́de** /wē-zheⁿ'-thä/ *n., masc.*, elder brother, the masculine word for addressing an elder male sibling (man saying: my ~)

elderly **Ną́ áma** /noⁿ' ä'-mä/ *n.*, elderly, the elderly; *íš'áge*, elderly (The term originally referred to both men and women. The generations of the early twentieth century began to apply the term to men only.)

elder sister **Ižą́de** /ē-zhoⁿ'-thä/ *n.*, elder sister, lit., the eldest of two or more sisters, usu. refers to the one who is older

elder sister **Wit'ą́ge** /wē-t'oⁿ'-gä/ *n.*, elder sister, *masc.* for addressing an elder female sibling (man saying: my ~)

elder sister **Wižą́de** /wē-zhoⁿ'-thä/ *n.*, elder sister, *fem.* for addressing an elder sister (*duáðikè ~ wít'a*, this is my ~)

elect **Wá'bahì** /wä'-bä-hē'/ *v.*, elect, select, in Ponca politics, choose by ballot or vote for

electrical storm **Ðigí'gðizè** /thē-gē'-gthē-zä'/ *n.*, electrical storm, usu. refers to extreme continuous lightning

electricity **Ðigdíze** /thē-gthē'-zä/ *n.*, electricity, a phenomenal form of energy that is descriptive in electric charge, current, field, electromagnetic wave, chemistry, circuits, power, electronics, etc.

elegant **Stáp'ì** /stä-p'ē'/ *adj.*, elegant, being stylish, well-dressed (used, e.g., if a suit fits perfectly and looks good on someone)

elephant **Wak'ą́da p'á'snedè** /wä-k'oⁿ'-dä p'ä'-snä-dä'/ *n.*, elephant, large mammal of the family Elephantidae and the order Proboscidea; there are two species, the African elephant (*Loxodonta africana*) and the Asian elephant (*Elephas maximus*)

elevate **Đimą́ši** /thē-moⁿ'-shē/ *v.*, elevate, to raise, to lift up with the use of the hands or with machinery, to lift something upward from a lower level to a higher level

elevator **Níka'dihą̀** /nē'-kä-thē-hoⁿ'/ *n.*, elevator, lit., lift people, a machine that carries people up and down to various floors in tall buildings

elevator **Wamúske ínąt'ubède** /wä-mü'-skä ē'-noⁿ-t'ü-bā'-thā/ *n.*, elevator, grain elevator, esp. for wheat in Texas, Oklahoma, and Kansas

eliminate **Šénąwadè** /shā'-noⁿ-wä-thā'/ *n.*, eliminate, refers to the end of those who oppose each other in sports or in war; in war, means total elimination of the enemy

elk **Ą̀'pą̀** /oⁿ'-poⁿ'/ *n.*, elk, a large North American deer (*Cervus canadensis*) that lives in herds

elk **He'xága** /hā-xä'-gä/ *n.*, elk, lit., rough horn, a large deer (*Cervus canadensis*) native to western North America

elm tree **É'žą̀hì** /ā'-zhoⁿ-hē'/ *n.*, elm tree (Three varieties are located on the Ponca reservation in Oklahoma: the red elm, *é'žą̀ žíde* or *žą́šídehì*, the white elm, *é'žą̀ skà*, and the Chinese elm, no Ponca name, of the genus *Ulmus*

elsewhere **Áwakedìstewą̀** /ä'-wä-kä-dē'-shtä-woⁿ'/ *adv.*, elsewhere, in another or different place

embarrassed **Í'štewadè** /ē'-shtä-wä-thā'/ *adj.*, embarrassed, ashamed of, the feeling of shame, guilt, embarrassment for unbecoming behavior

embellish **Điá't'ašą̀** /thē-ä'-t'ä-shoⁿ'/ *v.*, embellish, lit., more than, blown up, adding to something—native dance clothing,

dancing, or any personal act of speaking or singing

embrace **Áne** /ä'-nā/ *v.*, embrace, to give a hospitable or loving embrace, hug, cuddle

embracing **Á'k'inè** /ä'-k'ē-nā/ *n.*, embracing, hugging each other affectionately

emerge **Gašíbe** /gä-shē'-bā/ *v.*, emerge, to come out of or come forth into view

emergency room **Wakéga úsągà t'ì** /wä-kā'-gä ü'-soⁿ-gä' t'ē'/ *n.*, emergency room of a hospital, refers to the reception of persons in need of immediate medical care or aid; includes the intensive or critical care unit

emphasize **Á'dazabaži** /ä'-thä-zä-bä-zhē'/ *v.*, emphasize, to state or stress, to give special wording to something the speaker wishes to convey

emphasize **Đadéxt'ì** /thä-dā'-xt'ē'/ *v.*, emphasize, lit., say again (strongly), to stress or put emphasis on something to somebody

employment **Úwadit'ą̀** /ü'-wä-thē-t'oⁿ'/ *n.*, employment, a contract between two parties to complete some sort of work or project in which one party is the employer and the other is the employee who does the work

empty **Bašą́da** /bä-shoⁿ'-thä/ *v.*, to empty, to pour out any substance, liquid or solid, from a container

emulate **Udúkižažè** /ü-thü'-kē-zhä-zhä'/ *v.t.*, emulate, try to do something that someone else was successful in doing, try to be like, imitate, copy

enable **Ukíhiwadè** /ü-kē'-hē-wä-thā'/ *v.*, enable, to make able or to give strength and power to do something

encamp **Wahą́** /wä-hoⁿ'/ *v.*, encamp, 1. to set up a camp 2. to get one's belongings and move out and go somewhere to live

encourage **Sagí'k'ida'á** /sä-gē'-k'ē-thä-ä'/ (*fem.*) (**Sagí'k'ida'ágá'** /sä-gē'-k'ē-thä-ä'-

gä'/ [*masc.*]) *v.*, encourage, lit., make yourself strong, a common saying to hearten
someone or give them confidence

encumber **Weógašè** /waõ'-gä-shä'/ *v.*, encumber, to burden or hamper someone with
something

end **Šetą́** /shä-ton'/ *n.*, end, finish, conclusion
of something

end **Uhą́ge hí'te** /ü-hon'-gä hē'-tā/ *n.*, end,
usu. refers to some activity that is coming
to an end (at or toward the ~, our team won)

ending **Í'dišedà** /ē'-thē-shä-thä'/ *n.*, ending,
at the conclusion, usu. something that happens or is a part of the ceremonial dances
or gatherings that precede the closing

endless **Šetą́žì** /shä-ton'-zhē'/ *adj.*, endless,
no end

end of **Šéną** /shä'-non/ *n.*, end of, no more,
usu. refers to the exhausted supply of
things (that's the ~ that)

endurance **Wašką́xti** /wä-shkon'-xtē/ *n.*, endurance, the ability to have strength or the
power to endure hardship of any type or to
complete a task

enemy **Uk'ít'e** /ü-k'ē'-t'ä/ *n.*, orig., 1. enemy,
foe, challenger 2. other tribe or nationality

energetic **Wasí'síge** /wä-sē'-sē'-gä/ *adj.*, energetic, lively, vigorous, active

English language **Xįháska íye** /xēn-hä'-skä
ē'-yā/ *n.*, English language

engrossed **Udá'dadą̀** /ü-thä'-dä-thon'/ *adj.*,
become engrossed, absorbed, occupied,
immersed in some activity

enlarge **Đit'ą́ga** /thē-t'on'-gä/ *v.*, enlarge, to
make bigger or increase size with the hands

enough **Šéną** /shä'-non/ *adj.*, enough, sufficient amount (when something is given,
the receiver says, "That's ~.")

ensnare **Udúą̀dè** /ü-thü'-on-thä'/ *v.*, ensnare,
as in trapping an animal

entangled **Udúą̀dè** /ü-thü'-on-thä'/ *adj.*, en-

tangled, getting caught on something (the
lawn mower was ~ with wire)

enter **É'gihà** /ä'-gē-hä'/ *v.*, enter, to go into a
house or building as some animals go into
burrows

entourage **Wagáxdą** /wä-gä'-xthon/ *n.*, entourage, supporters, associates, usu. refers to
any Ponca tribal ceremonial procession by
those who assist, e.g., with the Pipe Dance
ceremonial

envelope **Wabáxu ugdą̀** /wä-bä'-xü ü-gthon'/
n., 1. envelope 2. mailbox

envy **Wawé'giniè** /wä-wä'-gē-nē-ä'/ *n.*,
envy; resentfulness of another's advantages, possessions, or accomplishments
(The Ponca term encompasses a dislike
or hatred for one's status, but a kind of
hatred toward the good of one's values.
Individuals may hold these values as a
high standard that they themselves have
not yet achieved.)

epilepsy **T'ę́štą̀** /t'ān'-shton'/ *n.*, epilepsy, a
neurological disorder whereby a person
afflicted has seizures

equally **Wedénąskà** /wä-dä'-non-skä'/ *adv.*,
equally, equal share, same amounts to each

equestrian **Šą́ge ágdì** /shon'-gä ä'-gthē'/ *adj.*,
equestrian, horseback, relates to riding on
horses or horseback riding

erase **Đįgé gáxe** /thēn-gä' gä'-xä/ *v.*, erase, lit.,
cause to be gone, to remove, to wipe away

ermine **Ičą́gaskà** /ē-chon'-gä-skä'/ *n.*, ermine,
1. the common name for a white north-
ern weasel that has a small long body with
short legs and tail (*Mustela erminea*) 2. white
weasel, a male Ponca name

erratic **Ést'eą'ą̀** /ä'-st'ä-on-on/ *adj.*, erratic, 1.
usu. refers to things going wrong, lack of
consistency or uniformity 2. modern usage
may refer to how an automobile performs

erroneous **Ną́de** /non'-thā/ *adj.*, erroneous,

thoughts or ideas that contain error, incorrect or wrong answers

error Đašną /thä-shnoⁿ/ *n.*, error, the act of not speaking or singing correctly, an unintentional mistake

escalator Átą đimą́ši /ä́-toⁿ thē-moⁿ-shē/ *n.*, escalator, lit., steps that lift

escape K'iną́šibè /k'ē-noⁿ-shē-bä/ *v.*, escape, break out, coming out of something by force

esophagus Đéškaxđú'a /thä́-shkä-xthü-ä/ *n.*, esophagus, a muscular tube through which food passes from the pharynx to the stomach

established Đą́xt'i /thoⁿ-xt'ē/ *v.*, established, settled, settled down or became peaceful

esteem Ą́xt'idè /oⁿ-xt'ē-thä/ *n.*, esteem, high regard

eternity Nít'a'uháge đįgè /nē-t'ä-ü-hä́-gä theⁿ-gä/ *n.*, eternity, infinity, lit., life without end

evening P'áze /p'ä́-zä/ *n.*, evening, sunset, sundown, dusk

event Šká'de /shkä́-dä/ *n.*, event, a happening (This may include dances, ballgames, etc.)

eventually Šą́text'ì /shoⁿ-tä-xt'ē/ *adv.*, eventually, finally, in due course of time

ever Šą́šą /shoⁿ-shoⁿ/ *adv.*, ever, always, perpetually

ever since Atą́dità /ä-toⁿ-dē-toⁿ/ *adv.*, ever since, ever since when, from then to now

every day Ą́ba ék'iną /oⁿ-bä ä́-k'ē-noⁿ/ *n./ adv.*, every day, day after day, daily, usu. refers to a certain number of days or a period of time

everyone Wą́'gidè /woⁿ-gē-thä/ *pron.*, everyone, everybody in this particular group or gathering, refers to addressing everyone in attendance at a small or large gathering of any sort, usu. used in addressing attendees at meetings

everyone Wazáni /wä-zä́-nē/ *pron.*, everyone, relates specifically to every person present in a group to which one speaks

everyone Za'ní /zä-nḗ/ *n.*, everyone, a short form of *wazáni*

everything Įdáđą bđúga /ēⁿ-dä́-doⁿ bthǘ-gä/ *pron.*, everything, the whole lot, entirety

everywhere Águdì'štì'dąđà /ä́-gü-dē-shtḗ-thoⁿ-thoⁿ/ *adv.*, everywhere, here and there

evict Ą́ši ą́da /ä́-shē oⁿ-thä/ *v.*, evict, thrown out, force a person out of

exaggerate -á't'ašą̀ /ä́-t'ä-shoⁿ/ *v.*, *suffix*, exaggerate, exceed, overdo it, too much

exaggerated Đaá't'ašą̀ /thä-ä́-t'ä-shoⁿ/ *v.*, exaggerated, overstated, refers to bragging about the performance of a person's accomplishments; *điá't'ašą̀*, performing or doing something over and beyond what is necessary

examine Điwágazù /thē-wä́-gä-zü/ *v.*, examine, scrutinize, scan, inspect

exasperate Baskíde /bä-skḗ-thä/ *v.*, exasperate, upset, to be beside yourself, irritate

exasperated Ą́baskidè /oⁿm-bä-skē-thä/ *v.*, *1st pers. sing.*, exasperated, irritated, "I am ~."

excellent Á't'à /ä́-t'ä/ *adj.*, excellent, first rate, superior, high quality, etc.

except that Ę́gądązà /äⁿ-goⁿ-thoⁿ-zhoⁿ/ *prep.*, except, but, as in "that's the way it was ~"

exchange Ík'ik'awadè /ḗ-k'ē-k'ä-wä-thä/ *v.*, exchange, 1. to part with in order to receive something of the same value 2. trade, to give something and receive something of the same value

exclamation Í'ji'jì! /ḗ-jē-jḗ!/ *interj.*, exclamation, an exclamation upon touching something hot

exclude Uđúđįgè /ü-thǘ-theⁿ-gä/ *v.*, exclude, leave out, left out

excuse **Uwédạp'ì** /ü-wä'-thoⁿ-p'ē'/ *n./v.*, excuse, pretext, ploy

exhaust **Ðadíge** /thä-thēⁿ'-gä/ *v.*, exhaust, to make an exceptional verbal display of words to keep somebody from saying more, usu. making another person's words seem less than important

exhaust **Ðidíge** /thē-thēⁿ'-gä/ *v.*, exhaust, deplete, use up, as in there isn't anything left; *gadíge*, use up by hitting, as in hitting limbs of a tree to remove nuts; *nạdíge*, use up, as in running out of gasoline; *wénạdịgè*, to use theirs up

exhausted **Gask'í** /gä-sk'ē'/ *v.*, exhausted, tired out, all-in, tiredness after running a long distance or from doing heavy labor; being completely out of breath

exhausted **Užéda** /ü-zhä'-thä/ *v.*, to be exhausted, tired, worn out, weary, etc.

expectant **Út'ạbedè** /ü'-t'oⁿ-bä-thä/ *adj.*, expectant, looking forward with anticipation to something that is likely to happen or anticipating something that will occur or is forthcoming

expert **Ðip'iát'ašạ** /thē-p'ē'-ä'-t'ä-shoⁿ'/ *n.*, expert, a skilled person in some field, a specialist

explode **Mút'ušì** /mü'-t'ü-shē'/ *v.*, explode, self-explosion, e.g., when a gun with a "hair-trigger" expends a cartridge with a slight touch

explosion **Múbdazè** /mü'-bthä-zä'/ *n.*, explosion, blast, detonation

express gratitude **K'iwáhạ̀ì** /k'ē-wä'-hoⁿ-ē'/ *v.*, express gratitude, to thank others

expression **Bə** /bə/ *interj.*, expression, an expression that connotes the element of surprise over some action or statement made by another; also the element of surprise in seeing something unusual or different

expression **Ei'ná** /ā-nä'/ *interj.*, expression, a woman's expression of strong feelings denoting dislike for another's behavior in speech or action, usu. directed to the individual

expression **Xé·** /xä'·/ *interj.*, expression, woman's expression of a mistake made or a misunderstanding of a statement

expression **Xénahà** /xä'-nä-hä'/ *interj.*, expression, man's expression of a mistake made or a misunderstanding of a statement

extend **Ðisnéde** /thē-snä'-dä/ *v.*, extend, to lengthen, to make longer

extinquish **Biná'ži** /bē-nä'-zhē/ *v.*, extinguish, to put out, quench, douse a fire by pressing down on it with something in the hands, as in using a wet cloth to put out a small fire; *dináži*, to turn off a light switch; *ganáži*, wind (~ a kerosene lamp, ~ a grass fire with a wet gunnysack)

extravagant **Á't'ašạ** /ä'-t'ä-shoⁿ'/ *adj.*, extravagant, exaggerated or beyond something that is within reason

extreme **Ðiát'ašạ** /thē-ä'-t'ä-shoⁿ'/ *adj./v.*, extreme, doing or making something immoderate

eye **Ịštá'** /ēⁿ-shtä'/ *n.*, eye or eyes, the organ of vision

eyeball socket **Ịštá'úgdè** /ēⁿ-shtä-ü'-gthä'/ *n.*, eyeball socket, that cavity in the skull where the eye is situated

eyebrow **P'á'uskída** /p'ä'-ü-skē'-dä/ *n.*, eyebrow, that opening between the eyebrows

eyebrow **P'énaxixè** /p'ä'-nä-xē-xä'/ *n.*, eyebrow, the area of short delicate hairs above the eye

eye drops **Ịšt'á ugáxt'ạ̀** /ēⁿ-sht'ä' ü-gä-xt'oⁿ'/ *n.*, eye drops, a solution of liquid drops for eyes, such as lubricants, eyewashes

eyeglasses **Mạ́ze ịšt'á'ugdạ̀** /moⁿ'-zä ēⁿ-sht'ä'-ü-gthoⁿ'/ *n.*, eyeglasses, lit., metal on the eye, eyeglasses, spectacles, glasses, etc.

eyelashes **Įštáhį** /ēⁿ-shtä'-hēⁿ/ *n.*, eyelashes

eyelids **Įštáhà** /ēⁿ-shtä'-hä'/ *n.*, eyelids, that thin fold of skin that covers and protects the eye

eye mucus **Įšt'áxdį** /ēⁿ-sht'ä'-xthēⁿ/ *n.*, eye mucus, a slimy substance that lubricates and protects the mucous membranes, associated with the eyes when awakening in the morning

eyewitness **Waweíbahà** /wä-wāē'-bä-hoⁿ/ *n.*, eyewitness, one who has seen or observed an occurrence

F

fable **Híga** /hē'-gä/ *n.*, fable, usu. children's stories of anthropomorphized animals that have a moral

face **Įdé'** /ēⁿ-dä/ *n.*, face, the front part of the head from the top of the forehead to the base of the chin

face **K'íbaxdà** /k'ē'-bä-xthä'/ *v.*, face, to stand facing toward somebody or something

facing **Ú'gaxdè** /ü'-gä-xthä'/ *n./v.*, facing, somebody or something that is oriented or positioned in a direction away from something else (*Mačú Nąži, níkašigà wasésą kè, guádišą ~ nąží*, the statue of Standing Bear is ~ the other way)

fact **Wí'ke** /wē'-kā/ *n.*, fact, reality, exactness, honesty, fidelity, etc.

failing health **Žúgauxp'áde** /zhü'-gä-üx-p'ä'-thä/ *adj.*, failing health, physical breakdown, an affliction causing an individual to physically deteriorate

faithful **Gíwikè** /gē'-wē-kā/ *adj.*, faithful, loyal, devoted, committed

fall **P'ás'į'** /p'ä'-s-ēⁿ/ *v.*, fall, to fall down head first

fall **T'ága'xdà** /t'oⁿ'-gä-xthoⁿ/ *n.*, fall, autumn, the season of the year that precedes winter, approximately three months (September, October, and November); *t'ágaxdąádi*, past fall; *t'ágaxdądà*, in the fall

fall **Xiáda** /xēä-thä/ *v.*, fall, go down, fall down, fall over; *baxíáda*, fall, go down, fall down, fall over by pushing; *đixíáda*, fall, go down, fall down, fall over by pulling with the hands; *gaxíáda*, fall, go down, fall down, fall over by force, chopping, or kicking with the feet; *nąxíáda*, fall, go down, fall down, fall over by driving over or by stepping or standing on

fall from **K'igdéže** /k'ē-gthä'-zhā/ *v.i.*, fall from or become less, as in lowering of self-esteem after doing or accomplishing something of worth

falling star **Miká'e uxp'áde** /mē-kä'-ā üx-p'ä'-thä/ *n.*, falling star, a name for a meteorite entering the earth's atmosphere, becoming visible to the human eye

fall plum **K'ąde x'áde** /k'oⁿ'-dā x'ä'-thä/ *n.*, fall plum, lit., sour plum, a plum tree that bears fruit in the late summer and early fall (*k'ąde x'áde hì*, fall plum tree)

false **Égąžì** /ā'-goⁿ-zhē/ *adj.*, false, incorrect, not in line with the facts, erroneous, untrue, inaccurate, flawed

family **T'íúži** /t'ē'-ü'-zhē/ *n.*, family, family unit, relatives, kin

famine **Wadáte đįgè** /wä-thä'-tä thēⁿ-gä'/ *n.*, famine, no food, the scarcity of food, groceries, provisions, or any edible produce

fan **Ášudè** /ä'-shü-dä'/ *v./n.*, fan, to ceremonially fan using an eagle tail to ~ the smoke of cedar upon a person or persons

fan **Ganí'** /gä-nē'/ *v.*, to fan, to use an eagle-feathered fan to fan a person ceremonially, usu. done in the home, but often done in the Native American Church; *wegáni*, to fan more than one person

fan **Įdéaganì** /ēⁿ-dä-ä'-gä-nē'/ *n.*, fan, 1. a

handheld device for producing a flow of air to one's face 2. the feathers of various fowl that form a feathered fan, esp. eagle tail feathers

fan **Kigđáni** /kē-gthä'-nē/ *v.*, fan, to cool oneself by using a fan

far **Wəáhidè** /wəä'-hē-dä'/ *adv.*, far, faraway, distant from here

far away **Wadúdiazì** /wä-thü'-dē-ä-zhē'/ *adj.*, far away, something, e.g., other lands, that are a long way from the speaker

fare **Í'nągè** /ē'-noⁿ-gä'/ *n.*, fare, cost of ticket, money for gasoline and food

farm **Waé'** /wä-ā'/ *v.*, farm, to cultivate, to till, farming or cultivating the land

farm animals **Wanágđe** /wä-nä'-gthä/ *n.*, farm animals, namely, cows, horses, pigs, etc.

farmer **Mążą́ unà** /moⁿ-zhoⁿ' ü-nä'/ *n.*, farmer, lit., land borrower, leaser of land (commonly used for the person who leases land, namely, farmer)

farther **Ákihą̀** /ä'-kē-hoⁿ'/ *adv.*, farther, 1. in travel, to go farther, refers to going past a place or going beyond the destination 2. in buying, to get more

farther **Et'áha** /ā-t'ä'-hä/ *adv.*, farther, farther than

fashionable **Stáp'i** /stä'-p'ē/ *adj.*, fashionable, stylish, smart (he was a ~ dresser)

fast **Wadátazì** /wä-thä'-tä-zhē'/ *v.*, fast, to not eat, a willful act of abstaining from food and drink

fast **Waséką** /wä-sä'-koⁿ/ *v.*, fast, speedy, rapid, hasty, breakneck speed

faster **Điwásekà** /thē'-wä-sä-koⁿ'/ *v.*, to go faster, to make something go faster

fasten **Ágaškè** /ä'-gä-shkä'/ *v.*, fasten, to attach, clasp, secure something from opening

fast runner **Ą́'sagì** /oⁿ'-sä-gē'/ *adj.*, fast runner, quick and speedy on the feet

fat **Šį́** /shēⁿ'/ *n.*, fat, obese, corpulent, having too much fat or being overweight

fatality **Gat'ę́** /gä-t'äⁿ'/ *n.*, fatality, fatal accident, death resulting from disaster, highway crash

father **Įdádi** /ēⁿ-dä'-dē/ *n.*, father, *mas./fem.* male parent (my ~ works every day); *iđádi*, his father; *įdádi*, my father; *điá'di*, your father

father **Idádidaì** /ē-thä'-dē-thä-ē'/ *n.*, father, 1. refers to someone saying "his father," as related in the Ponca kinship system 2. refers to the government agent at the reservation-level office

fault **Éwakià'** /ā'-wä-kē-oⁿ'/ *n.*, fault, an unfortunate situation or something that a person brought upon him/herself, being responsible for one's own failure, one's own fault; *điʃwađakià*, you brought it upon yourself

faux pas **Đip'íbazì** /thē-p'ē'-bä-zhē'/ *n.*, faux pas, blunder, a social blunder, as in arriving too early at a formal gathering

fear **Waną́p'a** /wä-noⁿ'-p'ä/ *v.*, fear, to be afraid of something or somebody due to a sense of danger or a threat to secure feelings

fearful **K'úhe** /k'ü'-hä/ *v.*, fearful, fearful of ghosts

fearful **Waną́p'ap'à** /wä-noⁿ'-p'ä-p'ä'/ *v.*, fearful, to be fearful, afraid of a condition or situation

fearful **Žúgauhè** /zhüⁿ'-gäü-hä'/ *n.*, fearful, a feeling of fright with chills, to make one's nerves tingle, to make one's hair stand on end

fearless **Šéwakiđazì** /shä'-wä-kē-thä-zhē'/ *adj.*, fearless, courageous, valiant, does not fear anyone

fearless **Waną́p'azì** /wä-noⁿ'-p'ä-zhē'/ *adj.*, not fearful, not afraid fearsome **Ną́p'ewadè** /noⁿ'-p'ä-wä-thä'/ *adj.*, fearsome, formidable, causing intense or extreme fear

feather **Mą́šą** /moⁿ'-shoⁿ/ *n.*, feather, plumage on birds; *Įbe*, tail feathers of birds; *xidá mą́šą*, eagle feathers; *xidá íbe*, tail feathers of an eagle; *xidá hįxp'é*, eagle plume; *xidá áhį*, eagle wings

feathered headdress **Mą́šą'p'agdà** /moⁿ'-shoⁿ-p'ä-gthoⁿ'/ *n.*, feathered headdress, eagle-feathered headdress, sometimes referred to as warbonnets (*Warbonnet* is a misnomer. The headdress was worn by leaders of men in most tribes at important meetings and other special occasions.)

February **Mí'udúnąžiwadażì** /mē'-ü-thü'-noⁿ-zhē-wä-thä-zhē'/ *n.*, February, lit., undependable moon, the second month of the year (The elders also used *míxa agdáike*, when the ducks go back [north])

feces **Įgdé'** /ēⁿ-gthä'/ *n.*, feces, solid waste from the body

feed **Ídišį** /ē'-thē-shēⁿ'/ *v.*, feed, usu. refers to providing a meal for somebody but is also used to refer to feeding an animal; *iwadišį*, to feed them

feel **Đit'ą́** /thē-t'oⁿ'/ *v.*, feel, to feel or touch with the hands

feeling of **É'saxt'ì** /ä'-sä-xt'ē'/ *n./prep.*, feeling of, an emotional sensation not connected to sight, hearing, taste, or smell but thought of want or desire

fee simple **Wabáxu'sagì** /wä-bä'-xü-sä-gē'/ *n.*, fee simple, lit., hard paper, ca. 1900, fee patent, a legal requirement for removing Indian lands from federal trust status that gave Native Americans the right to sell such lands

fell **Baxíáda** /bä-xē'-ä'-thä/ *v.*, fell, push down by force or the body or machinery

fell **Đixíáda** /thē-xē'-ä'-thä/ *v.*, fell, pushed down by force, by use of the hands

fell **Nąxíáda** /noⁿ-xē'-ä'-thä/ *v.*, fell, push down by force, by use of the feet or machinery

fell **Gaxíáda** /gä-xē'-ä'-thä/ *v.*, fell, as in cutting down a tree (connotes use of an instrument to fell a tree or high winds felling a structure)

female **Migá'** /mē-gä'/ *n.*, female of any adult breed of mammals or fowl, including cattle, seals, moose, chickens, etc.

femur **Žíbe'ut'ą́ga** /zhē'-bä-ü-t'oⁿ'-gä/ *n.*, femur, in anatomy, the thigh bone

fence **Ną́za** /noⁿ'-zä/ *n.*, fence, 1. barrier, railing, enclosure 2. a fortified enclosure (The Ponca people, descendents of the eastern culture, namely, the Middle Mississippian culture, built fortified villages. The last such fort was built in current Knox County, Nebraska. The fort was called Ną́za by historians.)

fence post **Žą́imuzà** /zhoⁿ-ē'-mü-zä'/ *n.*, fence post, wooden posts that are used to support fences

ferocious **Ną́p'ewadè** /noⁿ'-p'ä-wä-thä'/ *adj.*, ferocious, brutal, extremely fierce

festive **Úžawà** /ü'-zhä-wä'/ *adj.*, festive, celebratory, delightful, connotes fun and merriment or revelry

festivities **Íškade'gàxe** /ē'-skä-dä-gä'-xä/ *n.*, festivities, a place where play activities are happening, carnival

fever **Žunákadè** /zhü-nä'-kä-dä/ *n.*, fever, lit., hot flesh, the increase of body temperature, usu. due to illness of some sort

fifth **Wésat'ą̀** /wä'-sä-t'oⁿ'/ *n.*, fifth, the fifth one; a thing, person, or people that stand(s) fifth in the row or in succession

fifty-cent piece **Mąsą́'dihà** /moⁿ-soⁿ'-thē-hä'/ *n.*, fifty-cent piece, half dollar (A U.S. coin no longer in circulation.)

fifty-dollar bill **Gdébạ'sat'ạ'ídawà** /gthä'-boⁿ-sä-t'oⁿ-ē'-thä-wä/ *n.*, fifty-dollar bill, U.S. currency

fight **K'ína** /k'ē'-nä/ *v.*, fight, to engage in a fight

fighting **K'ík'ína** /k'ē-k'ē'-nä/ *v.*, fighting, engaging in a physical fight between two people or in combat

fighting over **Ukíkínà** /ü-kē'-kē'-nä/ *n.*, fighting over, fighting over something; *i'k'ik'inà*, fighting over some specific thing or things by two or more people, as in claiming an inheritance

file **Wé'magixè** /wä'-mä-gē-xä'/ *n.*, file, a tool for smoothing surfaces such as metal and wood

filet mignon **T'á'žu** /t'ä'-zhü/ *n.*, filet mignon, a choice cut of meat (beef) that is meaty, with less gristle and fat

fill **Ugíp'idè** /ü-gē'-p'ē-thä'/ *v.*, fill, the process of filling something up

fill **Uží'** /ü-zhē'/ *v.*, fill, to fill a container, to fill up

fin **Hú'įbe** /hü-ēⁿ'-bä/ *n.*, fin (of a fish)

find **Í'de** /ē'-thä/ *v.*, find, to locate something that was lost; *idáde*, I found it; *idadè*, you found it; *idaì*, he/she/it found it

fingernail bone **Nạbé'šáge'wahì** /noⁿ-bä'-shä'-gä-wä-hē'/ *n.*, fingernail bone, that part of the human anatomy under the fingernails called the phalanx bone

fingernails **Nạbé' šágè** /noⁿ-bä' shä'-gä'/ *n.*, fingernails, that part of the human anatomy that covers the tips of the fingers, composed of keratin

fingers **Nạbé'** /noⁿ-bä'/ *n.*, fingers, in anatomy, the five digits of the hand

fingertips **Nạbé'p'asì** /noⁿ-bä'-p'ä-sē'/ *n.*, fingertips

finish **Đišt'ạ̀** /thē-sht'oⁿ'/ *v.*, finish, quit, end, bring to an end or close

finish **K'igdíštạ̀** /k'ē-gthē'-shtoⁿ'/ *n.*, finish, a single person or a group completing a task

finish **Šạ́'** /shoⁿ'/ *n.*, finish, the completion or finish of something (Also used in questions that connote what task has been completed, such as *šạ́'a?*, are you ready?, *wadáte tè, šạ́'a?*, is the food ready?)

fire **P'éde** /p'ä'-dä/ *n.*, fire, refers to a fire that stands burning

fire extinguisher **P'éde íganažì** /p'ä'-dä ē'-gä-nä-zhē'/ *n.*, fire extinguisher, usu. a small, portable container that has special chemicals to put out fires

fireplace **Unéde** /ü-nä'-thä/ *n.*, fireplace, 1. hearth or fireplace 2. the fireplace of the Native American Church, namely, the ritual

first **Adúha** /ä-thü'-hä/ *adj.*, first, to be the first to act, to initiate something before others do

first **P'ahạ́ga** /p'ä-hoⁿ'-gä/ *n./adj.*, first, at first, beginning, primary, earliest, usu. refers to beginning something

first **Wiáha** /wē-ä'-hä/ *n.*, first, the first in a row or series

first born **Šé'p'ahạ́ga** /shä'-p'ä-hoⁿ'-gä/ *n.*, first born, in the order of birth, the eldest or first child to be born

fish **Hugáse** /hü-gä'-sä/ *v.*, fish, to go fishing

fish **Huhú'** /hü-hü'/ *n.*, fish, generic term, a vertebrate that lives in water and has fins, scales, and gills

fishing tackle **Huwégasì** /hü-wä'-gä-sē'/ *n./v.*, fishing tackle, any sort of device used to catch fish, fishing equipment such as lures, baits, hooks, lines, sinkers

fish scales **Huhúsịse** /hü-hü'-sēⁿ'-sä/ *n.*, fish scales (Some fish, such as salmon and carp, are covered with cycloid scales, while perch have ctenoid scales, and sturgeon and gars have ganoid scales.)

Fish Smell Village **Hubdạ́** /hü-bthoⁿ'/ *n.*, Fish

Smell Village, lit., the smell of fish, the name of an ancient Ponca tribal village in Nebraska (This village site was one of the last three Ponca villages near the confluence of the Niobrara and Missouri Rivers before the Ponca's forced removal to Indian Territory)

fist **Ną̄bé'šą́k'à** /noⁿ-bā́-shoⁿ'-k'ä'/ *n.*, fist, the fingers tightly curled into the hand

fit **Énąskà** /ā́'-noⁿ-skä'/ *v.*, to fit, to be the proper size or shape of clothing for somebody

five **Sát'ą** /sä́'-t'oⁿ/ *n.*, five, the number five (5)

five-dollar bill **Sát'ą́idawà** /sä́'-t'oⁿ-ē-thä-wä'/ *n.*, five-dollar bill, U.S. currency

fix **Đip'í·** /thē-p'ḗ'·/ *v.*, fix, repair, mend, put right, put back into working order

flag **Haská** /hä-skä'/ *n.*, flag, lit., white hide or soft deerskin (orig. carried by Ponca and members of other tribes as a symbol of peace), a rectangular piece of cloth with symbols that designate the identity of a nation

flagpole **Haská ímuzà** /hä-skä' ḗ'-mü-zä'/ *n.*, flagpole, a pole on which a flag is hoisted

flame **Ná'xdį̀** /nä́'-xthēⁿ'/ *n.*, flame, from something burning

flank **T'ašt'áde** /t'ä-sht'ä'-dä/ *n.*, flank, in human anatomy, that flesh on the sides of the lower ribcage

flapping sound **Gasásap'ì** /gä-sä́-sä-p'ē'/ *adj.*, flapping sound, something blowing and flapping in the wind, such as cloth

flash **Bináką tigdè** /bē-nä́-koⁿ tē-gthä'/ *v.*, flash, to give off light suddenly from some source

flashlight **Bináką** /bē-nä́-koⁿ/ *n.*, flashlight, 1. a handheld device with batteries and bulb to make light 2. *v.*, to cause a light to come on

flat **Bdáska** /bthä'-skä/ *adj.*, flat, plane

flatlands **Mąžą́ snásną́** /moⁿ-zhoⁿ' snoⁿ'-snoⁿ'/ *n.*, flatlands, composed of lands that are nearly level (In the early years in Indian Territory, certain families were allotted good farmlands, *mąžą́ snásną́*. The elders said that these lands were given to the "half breeds." The real Ponca got rough lands.)

flat-leaf evergreen **Mázibdáska** /mä-zē-bthä'-kä/ *n.*, flat-leaf evergreen, arborvitae

flat nose **P'á'šį̀** /p'ä'-shēⁿ'/ *n.*, flat nose (Authorities say this condition may come from a long range of causes, including skeletal abnormalities. Individuals born with this condition are rare among the Native American people.)

flatten **Bibdá'skà** /bē-bthä'-skä'/ *v.*, flatten, to cause something to become flat by pressing down with the hands

flatten **Đibdá'skà** /thē-bthä'-skä'/ *v.*, flatten, to flatten out by the use of the hands only

flatten **Gabdá'skà** /gä-bthä'-skä'/ *v.*, flatten, to flatten out or smash by striking with an object

flatten **Gastá'** /gä-stä'/ *v.*, flatten, to flatten by striking or stepping on, usu. refers to weeds or grass

flatten **Nąbdá'skà** /noⁿ-bthä'-skä'/ *v.*, flatten, to flatten something that contains air, usu. a tire on an automobile

flatten **Nąst'á** /noⁿ-st'ä'/ *v.*, flatten, to flatten something with the feet or wheels, as with grass flattened by walking over it or driving over it repeatedly

flat tire **Nąną́ge bdáska** /noⁿ-noⁿ'-gä bthä'-skä/ *n.*, flat tire, when a tire on a vehicle goes flat or is deflated

flaunt **K'ip'áhahà** /k'ē-p'ä'-hä-hä'/ *v.*, flaunt, show off, show off shamelessly, try to make an impression

flavorful **Azé** /ä-zä'/ *n.*, something that is flavorful, food that has a very pleasing taste, delectable, usu. refers to certain meat dishes

flea **T'atéga** /t'ä-tā'-gä/ *n.*, flea, a small blood-sucking insect that feeds on warm-blooded animals

flee **Áhe** /oⁿ-hä/ *v.*, flee, get away from, usu. from coming disaster (~ from the tornado); *gí'ąhè*, to flee from somebody

flesh **Žú'** /zhü'/ *n.*, flesh, the substance or tissue that covers the body of humans and animals, mainly made up of muscles and fat

flirt **Midígdą** /mē-thē'-gthoⁿ/ *v.*, flirt, usu. a male's playful act to show that he is attracted to a female

float **Ugáha** /ü-gä'-hä/ *v.*, float, as a log floats on the water

flood **Nidą́** /nē-doⁿ/ *n.*, flood, the rising and overflow of water from a river or stream onto dry land

floor **Nąde** /noⁿ-dä/ *n.*, floor, that part of a building or house that is walked or stood on

flounce **Nąsą́sądè(jè)** /noⁿ-soⁿ'-soⁿ-dā'(jā')/ *v.*, flounce, to move about or walk about in a jerky or bouncy motion in addition to jerking the shoulders, usu. applied to women

flour **Wamúske bdípe** /wä-mü'-skä bthē'-pä/ *n.*, flour, a fine powder ground from wheat seeds for bread and other bakery products

flour bin **Wamúskeužì** /wä-mü'-skä-ü-zhē'/ *n.*, flour bin, a container in which to keep flour

flow **Múxt'ą žąi** /mü'-xt'oⁿ zhoⁿ'-ē/ *v.*, flow, stream, run, water or some liquid moving in a stream

flowers **Waxt'á'** /wä-xt'ä'/ (**Wax'já'** /wäx-jä'/) *n.*, flowers, bouquet of flowers, any kind of flower

flow swiftly **Gasúse** /gä-sü'-sä/ *v.*, flow swiftly, usu. a small stream of fast-flowing water

flue **Umúhunedè** /ü-mü'-hü-nä-thä'/ *n.*, flue, a duct or chimney extending from a stove or fireplace to the outdoors

flute **Nisúde** /nē-sü'-dä/ *n.*, flute, lit., whistle, understood in the context of a statement (*núžìgà áka, ~ kè, mížìgà dįké gią́ ahì*, the boy went to play his ~ for the girl)

fly **Gią́'** /gē-oⁿ'/ *v./adj.*, fly, flying

flyswatter **Hą́t'ęgà'ígaxdì** /hoⁿ-t'ǟⁿ-gä-ē'-gä-xthē'/ *n.*, flyswatter, a fly-killing instrument also used for controlling other flying insects

foal **Šą́get'ążįgà** /shoⁿ-gä-t'oⁿ-zhēⁿ-gä'/ *n.*, foal, a horse that is one year old or younger, mammals in the family Equidae

fog **Šúdemąhà** /shü'-dä-moⁿ-hoⁿ'/ *n.*, fog, a vapor about the same density as clouds that sits near the ground

fold **Betą́'** /bä-toⁿ'/ *v.*, fold, to bend a piece of paper, cloth, a flag, clothing, etc. over itself

follow **Udúhe** /ü-thü'-hä/ *v.*, follow, 1. to follow, to go behind 2. to go by or to follow the same pattern that was previously made by somebody; *udúkihè*, usu. refers to persons who are related in some form who follow immediately after one has left a room, a place, or even in death; *udúwihè*, I am following you; *udúdihè*, he/she/it is following you; *ądúdihè*, we are following you; *udúgihè*, he followed his own (relative or pet); *ądą́wąhè*, he/she/it/they followed me

follow **Wíúhe** /wē'-ü-hä/ *v.*, follow, to follow behind somebody on a certain pathway

following that **Šadúha** /shä-thü'-hä/ *v.*, following that, to say or do again, e.g., after someone makes a statement and then a person without regard rebuts what was said (~ *íye dạnąžì tè*, ~ you might get up and speak)

food **Wádaté** /wä'-thä-tä/ *n.*, food, groceries, provisions, any edible produce

foolish **Wadí'gdą digè** /wä-thē'-gthoⁿ thē-gā′/ *adj.*, foolish, thoughtless; unable to think

foot **Sí'** /sē′/ *n.*, foot, the end of the human leg on which one stands and walks; the lower anatomical part of the human leg that includes toes and heel; *sí'te*, feet, plural of foot; *sihí'*, both feet

football **T'abési** /t'ä-bā′-sē/ *n.*, football, 1. an oval-shaped ball 2. a game played by two opposing teams on a rectangular field, involving kicking, passing, and running to take an oval-shaped ball across a goal line between two upright poles to make a score, while the opposing team tries to prevent them from achieving this goal

foot bones **Si'hí** /sē-hē′/ *n.*, foot bones, usu. refers to all parts of the feet, as in relating to pain

footprint **Sigdé** /sē-gthā′/ *n.*, footprint, track, 1. a foot mark made on the ground or grass by a person or animal 2. depressed grass, broken twigs, etc., also indicating a "footprint"

force **Mú'** /mü′/ *n.*, *prefix*, force, indicates force from within

forearm **Á'hidè** /ä′-hē-dä′/ *n.*, forearm, that part of the human arm between the elbow and the wrist

forehead **P'é'** /p'ā′/ *n.*, forehead, that part of the face above the eyebrows

forehead center **P'é'ut'áną** /p'ā′-ü-t'ä′-noⁿ/ *n.*, forehead center, the center of the forehead

forequarter **T'e'á** /t'ā-ä′/ *n.*, forequarter, the front side of a bison (now beef, pork, etc.), usu. refers to the foreleg and shoulder

forest **Xdábé** /xthä-bä′/ *n.*, forest, woods, usu. refers to a large wooded area

forget **Gisídeáži** /gē-sē′-thä-ä′-zhē/ *v.t./v.i.*, forget, cannot remember an idea or a thing

forgot **Gisídeəbaži** /gē-sē′-thä-ə-bä-zhē′/ *v.t./ v.i.*, forgot, *past t.* of *gisídeáži*, forget

fork **Užát'a** /ü-zhä-t'ä/ *n.*, fork, bifurcation, e.g., 1. the juncture where two or more things split off, as with the horns of a deer 2. a junction where two streams of water meet, forming one river 3. a junction where limbs of trees branch off

fork **Wé'baxap'ì** /wä′-bä-xä-p'ē′/ *n.*, fork, 1. an eating utensil 2. a pitchfork, a farming implement used for lifting hay

forming clouds **Gamáxp'i** /gä-moⁿ′-xp'ē/ *adj./n.*, forming clouds, weather conditions developing suddenly

fortunate **Gížu** /gē′-zhü/ *adj.*, fortunate, lucky, chance happening, good fortune, windfall

found **Idá'dè** /ē-thä′-thä′/ *v.*, *1st pers. sing.*, I found

four **Dú'ba** /dü′-bä/ *n.*, four, the number four (4)

Four Eyes **Ịšt'á'dú'ba** /ēⁿ-sht'ä′ dü-bä/ *n.*, Four Eyes, lit., an aboriginal short dog with long hair and small spots above the eyes (now extinct), hence "four eyes" (Four Eyes is one of the oldest Ponca family names.)

fourth **Wé'dubà** /wä′-dü-bä′/ *adj.*, fourth, the fourth thing in a row of items or the fourth person or group of people coming in succession

fourth born **Asážịgà** /ä-sä′-zhēⁿ-gä/ *n.*, fourth born, usu. a name given to a fourth-born female child

fourth toe **Sip'áužíga udúatą̀** /sē-p'ä′-ü-zhē′-gä ü-thü′-ä-toⁿ′/ *n.*, fourth toe, the toe next to the little toe

fox **Mądí'k'a'šižè** /moⁿ-thē′-k'ä-shē-zhä′/ *n.*, fox, a general term used for various breeds of small omnivorous animals of the Canidae family

fragile **Wahéhe** /wä-hä′-hä/ *adj.*, fragile, flimsy, refers to something that can break easily, as in an old rotten step fragments **Špášpa** /shpä'-shpä/ *n.*, fragments, pieces that broke off or scattered pieces of something

frail **Žuáži** /zhü-ä'-zhē/ *n.*, frail, lit., not strong, usu. refers to a person who is critically ill or in poor health

free **Ðišt'ą** /thē-sht'oⁿ/ *adj./v.*, free, let go, release, liberate, unleash

freestanding **Uhážištì** /ü-hä'-zhē-sht'ē'/ *adj.*, freestanding, independent, esp. not being part of or affiliated with any group, usu. an introductory term used before a speech is given (being a ~ person, I . . .)

freeze **Dá'** /dä'/ *v.*, freeze, ice up, usu. refers to anything that becomes frozen by extreme cold temperature

French people **Xįhá'ská' uké'di** /xēⁿ-hä-skä' ü-kä-thē/ *n.*, French person, lit., a common white person, a native or inhabitant of France

frequently **Idáúgdè** /ē-thä'-ü'-gthä'/ *adv.*, frequently, often, recurrently, habitually

Friday **Ą́ba'wé'sat'ą̀** /oⁿm'-bä-wä'-sä-t'oⁿ'/ *n.*, Friday, lit., day number five

fried bread **Umá'snè** /ü-mä'-snä'/ *n.*, fried bread, lit., cut a slit into, usu. a slit is cut into the dough as it is prepared for frying

friend **Ikágè** /ē-kä'-gä'/ *n.*, friend, buddy, pal

friendship **Ikágek'idè** /ē-kä'-gä-k'ē-thä'/ *n.*, friendship, companionship, a special relationship between two or more people; an interpersonal bond

fringes **Gasné'snè** /gä-snä'-snä'/ *n.*, fringes, tassel

frog **T'ébià** /t'ä'-bē-ä'/ *n.*, frog, amphibian without a tail of the order Anura

from **Edítą** /ā-dē'-toⁿ/ *prep.*, from, starting; the source from which something comes or from where a race begins

from **-t'atą** /t'ä'-toⁿ/ *prep.*, *suffix*, from; *mą́xet'atą̀*, from above; *hídet'atą̀*, from below; *šéket'atą̀*, from over there; *ɖéwadit'atą̀*, from here; *gáɖądìt'atą̀*, from somewhere over there; *Waxt'áwį niášigat'atą̀*, from the Ojibway people

from behind **Á'nazeatą̀** /ä'-nä-zā-ä-toⁿ'/ *prep. phr.*, from behind, something coming from behind

from here **Ðédudítą'** /thä'-thü-dē'-toⁿ/ *prep. phr.*, from here (~ this time or place); *edítą*, from there

front **P'át'à** /p'ä'-t'ä'/ *adj.*, front, in front of (he sat in the ~ seat)

front **Uɖúšiát'a** /ü-thü'-shē-ä'-t'ä/ *prep./n.*, front, in the front of (used when someone, e.g., is honored and brought before the people and is asked to sit in front of an audience)

front yard **T'í uɖúšiát'a** /t'ē' ü-thü'-shē-ä'-t'ä/ *n.*, front yard, lit., in front of the house or dwelling

frozen **Mądá** /moⁿ-dä/ *adj.*, frozen, icy, ice covered, usu. refers to the ground

fruit **Waxt'á'** /wä-xt'ä'/ *n.*, fruit, usu. refers to edible fruits from plants and trees, such as apples and oranges

fruit tree **Waxt'á hì** /wä-xt'ä' hē'/ *n.*, fruit tree, any fruit-bearing tree

fry **Žéži** /zhä'-zhē/ *v.*, fry, refers to food that is cooked in fat or oil; *wažéži*, to fry something

frybread **Wašį́'užé'gdą̀** /wä-sheⁿ'-ü-zhä'-gthoⁿ'/ *n.*, frybread, lit., cooked in fat (The earlier term was *umásnè*, to cut into.)

fulfilled **Gíšą́xt'ì** /gē'-shoⁿ'-xt'ē'/ *v.*, fulfilled, overly satisfied

full **Ugíp'i** /ü-gē'-p'ē/ *adj.*, full, filled, packed, occupied, full up

full **Uské'** /ü-skä'/ *adj.*, full, usu. refers to people and other animate things in a tight place, jam packed, bursting at the seams

full **Wé'nadè** /wā'-noⁿ-dā'/ *adj.*, full, stuffed, gorged, ate to the limit

funeral **Wét'et'à** /wā-t'āⁿ-t'oⁿ'/ *n.*, funeral, a rite of showing respect and remembering or celebrating the life of a person who has died

funeral casket **Wat'é užą́** /wä-t'āⁿ' ü-zhoⁿ'/ *n.*, burial casket, coffin

furious **Ábaskíde** /ä'-bä-skē'-thä/ *adj./v.*, furious, to be furious or incensed

further **Ákihà** /ä'-kē-hoⁿ'/ *adv.*, further, more, added, 1. in travel, to go farther 2. in buying, to get more

furthermore **P'i'gúdidadà** /p'ē-gü'-dē-thoⁿ-thoⁿ'/ *adv.*, furthermore, in addition, more than that, usu. refers to an action or a verbal statement that is considered to be boring

future **Ą́ba et'ądeát'a** /oⁿ'-bä ā-t'oⁿ'-thä-ä'-t'ä/ *n.*, future, lit., the days yet to come

G

gain **Uwáwakét'ą** /ü-wä'-wä-kä-t'oⁿ'/ *n./v.*, gain, to gain or achieve something by somebody else's effort

gall **T'e'p'ìzi** /t'ä-p'ē'-zē/ *n.*, gall; *t'é*, bison, *p'ízi*, gall (bile); *archaic*, now applies to domestic cattle

gallop **Bat'úidáda** /bä-t'ü'-ē-thä'-thä/ *v.*, gallop at the gait of a horse

gamble **Waką́** /wä-koⁿ'/ *v.*, gamble, bet, wager

gamble with **Ík'ikà** /ē'-k'ē-koⁿ'/ *v. phr.*, gamble with, traditionally the Ponca gamble material goods in their gambling games

game pieces **Wéši** /wā'-shē/ *n.*, game pieces, handgame stones, other handheld game pieces such as dice

gang up **Udíde** /ü-thē'-dä/ *v.i.*, gang up, join with another to accomplish any task

gap **Ut'áną** /ü-t'ä'-noⁿ/ *n.*, gap, opening, a gap or aperture; an area between two structures or in the middle of something, e.g., the middle of a street

gape **Yáda** /yä'-thä/ *v.*, gape, looking intently with mouth open

gar **Hu'p'á'si'snedè** /hü-p'ä'-sē-snä-dä/ *n.*, gar, 1. a freshwater fish with a long head and teeth (family Lepisosteidae) 2. sturgeon (family Acipenseridae)

garden hose **Ní'idá'umúbixà** /nē'-ē-thä'-ü-mü'-bē-xoⁿ'/ *n.*, garden hose, sprinkler

garter **Hídawì** /hē'-thä-wē'/ *n.*, garter, an elastic band to hold socks or stockings in place

gasoline **Wégdì** /wā'-gthē'/ *n.*, gasoline, petroleum, axle grease, engine oil, cooking oil

gas range **Úhą unéde** /ü'-hoⁿ ü-nä'-thä/ *n.*, gas range, an appliance for cooking

gather **Udéwį** /ü-thä'-wēⁿ/ *v.*, gather, 1. to collect, accumulate 2. assemble, congregate, meet

gelatinous **Snúsnu** /snü'-snü/ *adj.*, gelatinous, jellylike, gooey

gentle **Wašt'áge** /wä-sht'ä'-gä/ *n.*, gentle, temperate, peaceable, easy mannered, usu. refers to domesticated animals as in "a ~ horse"

gently **Í·digdà** /ē'-- thē-gthoⁿ'/ *adv.*, gently, quietly, lightly, smoothly, soothingly, tenderly

genuine **Užú'** /ü-zhü'/ *adj.*, genuine, traditional and authentic, the real thing

German people **Í'e'dašádu** /ē'-ä-thä-shä'-thü/ *n.*, German people, lit., speaks with guttural sounds, a native or inhabitant of Germany

gesture **Wagáxe** /wä-gä'-xä/ *n.*, gesture, 1. the sign language of Native Americans 2. gestures such as waving hands to get the attention of somebody

get **Agí'de** /ä-gē'-thā/ *v. phr.*, get, to go and get a specific thing

get **Ɖizé** /thē-zā'/ *v.*, get, obtain, acquire

getting wet **Ganáxe** /gä-nä'-xā/ *adj.*, getting wet, rained upon, sprinkled upon

ghost **Waną́'xe** /wä-noⁿ'-xā/ *n.*, ghost, spirit, phantom, apparition

ghost dance **Waną́'xe wačígaxè** /wä-noⁿ'-xā wä-chē'-gä-xā'/ *n.*, ghost dance, one of the ritual dances of the Ponca

gift **Ąwą́ i'** /oⁿ-woⁿ' ē/ *adj.*, gift, a gift to me

gift **Ú'di i'** /ü'-thē ē'/ *adj.*, gift, a gift to you

gift **Ú'i** /ü'-ē/ *n.*, gift, a gift to someone

gift **Ú'wa i'** /ü'-wä ē'/ *adj.*, gift, a gift to us

gigantic **Šénaskaegà** /shä'-noⁿ-skä-ä-goⁿ'/ *adj.*, gigantic, huge, immense, very big, relates to something that is very large for its kind

giggle **Íxačačà** /ē'-xä-chä-chä'/ *v.*, giggle, chuckle, laugh nervously

giraffe **Xdabé'p'asi'datè** /xthä-bā'-p'ä-sē thä-tä'/ *n.*, giraffe, lit., eat at the top of trees, a tall African mammal, *Giraffa camelopardalis*, of the family Giraffidae

girl **Mížįgà** /mē'-zhēⁿ-gä/ *n.*, girl, a young female, an adolescent female

give **Í'** /ē'/ *v.*, to give, offer, present, bestow, grant; *a·í'*, I give/gave; *ɖi·í'*, he/she/it gives/gave to you; *ą·í'*, he/she/it gives/gave to me; *ú'i*, they give/gave to them

giveaway **Gadé** /gä-thä'/ *n.*, giveaway, refers to the act of giving something away

giveaway **Wadíʃde** /wä-thēⁿ'-ʃ-thä'/ *n.*, giveaway, the act of giving away to somebody who doesn't possess much, usu. done at ceremonial or ritual gatherings (as with the adage "~ to someone who doesn't possess much")

giveaway **Wadísi** /wä-thē'-sē/ *n.*, *archaic*, giveaway, act of giving away following the funeral experience (This custom was practiced up to ca. 1933 and was done about six months after the interment of the deceased. Members of the family gathered material goods to distribute to friends and other tribal members. No gift was given to family members. Ritual giving at funerals still exists but is done immediately after four days of other funeral customs.)

give away **Wagáde** /wä-gä-thä'/ *v.*, give away, to give something to somebody; relates to a personal act of giving something to a relative, friend, or anybody

gizzard **P'izáugɖà** /p'ē-zä'-ü-gthoⁿ'/ *n.*, gizzard, lit., has sand in it, also called the ventriculus, gastric mill, and gigerium, an organ in the digestive tract of waterfowl and other animals

gladden **Wádagidè** /wä'-thä-gē-thä'/ *v.*, gladden, to make somebody happy, delight, bring joy to somebody

glance **Basták'ì** /bä-stä'-k'ē'/ *v.*, glance, to glance off of the body of somebody or of an animal; *bisták'ì*, to glance off after pressing down on an object; *ɖisták'ì*, to glance off of something by use of the hands; *gasták'ì*, to glance off of something by force; *nąsták'ì*, to glance off of the feet or a wheel

glass **Ną́'xe** /noⁿ'-xā/ *n.* glass, any kind of glass, a drinking glass, tumbler, glass jar

glide **Gawíxe** /gä-wēⁿ'-xā/ *v.*, glide, to move as an eagle glides or sails over the treetops

glittering **Šná'tigdágda** /shnä'-tē-gthä'-gthä/ *adj.*, glittering, something reflecting light from small pieces causing a sparkling effect

gloves **Nąbé'udí'šì** /noⁿ-bā'-ü-thē'-shēⁿ'/ *n.*, gloves, a protective covering for the hands

glue **Wəáda'ska'bè** /wəä'-thä-skä-bä'/ *n.*, glue, superglue, an adhesive substance to bind together various surfaces; some usu. made of gelatin substances from animals, such as the hooves of horses, skins; *ákigɖa-*

skabè, two things glued or sticking to each other

gluttony **Waną́bde't'ągà** /wä-noⁿ-bthä-t'oⁿ-gä'/ *n.*, gluttony, someone who habitually eats too much

gnat **Náhągežįgà** /nä-hoⁿ-gä-zhēⁿ-gä'/ (**Ðáhągežįgà** /thä-hoⁿ-gä-zhēⁿ-gä'/) *n.*, gnat, a small, annoying biting fly of the Dipterid suborder Nematocera (The prefix of this word, *ná/ɖá*, is differently pronounced by tribal members. No information is available as to why this is done.)

go **Ðé'** /thä'/ *v.*, go, to go; *aɖái*, went, *past t.* of *go*

go **Mądíga(à)** /moⁿ-theⁿ'-gä(ä')/ *v.*, *masc./fem.*, go, a command to go

go around **Í'betà** /ē'-bä-toⁿ/ *v.*, go around, circle, circumnavigate, to walk close by in such a way as to avoid meeting something or someone, or to drive an automobile in such a way as to avoid another automobile or any structure

go around **Wébetà** /wä'-bä-toⁿ/ *v.*, go around, to avoid by going around persons or things or circumnavigating the same

goat **He'sak'í'bà** /hä-sä-k'ē'-bä/ *n.*, goat, lit., between two horns, an animal with backward-curved horns, straight hair, and a short tail; *he'sak'í'bà nugà*, billy goat, a male goat; *he'sak'í'bà migà*, nanny goat, a female goat; *he'sak'í'bà žįgà*, kid goat

goatee **Íkihì** /ēⁿ'-kē-hēⁿ'/ *n.*, goatee, lit., hair on chin, a style of hair growth on the chin (Historically, Ponca men grew a long goatee and a mustache that hung downward.)

go back **Gdé'** /gthä'/ *v.*, go back, went back or returned to where one came from

God **Níkawasà** /nē-kä-wä-sä'/ *n.*, God, *archaic* ca. 1800s, a deity of God, a spiritual presence of the essence of God in ritual healing

God **Wak'ą́da** /wä-k'oⁿ'-dä/ *n.*, God, orig. the great mystery, God the creator of the world

go first **Adúhagà** /ä-thü-hä-gä'/ *v. phr.*, go first, usu. a command to proceed ahead of others; to act before others on specific things

going **Bdé** /bthä'/ *v.*, *1st pers. sing.*, going, I'm going (over there or someplace)

going back **A'gdé'** /ä-gthä'/ *v.*, *1st pers. sing.*, going back, "I'm leaving and returning to a certain place"

going back **Xáda'dè** /xä-thä-thä'/ *v.*, going back, something being caused to go back, something that is put back to its position

Going Back **Xáda'dè** /xä-thä-thä'/ *n.*, Going Back, lit., going back, a creek named by the Ponca (This is Bazile Creek, near Niobrara, Nebraska, known to back up when the Missouri River floods.)

Going Back Small **Xáda'dè Užíga** /xä-thä-thä' ü-zhēⁿ'-gä/ *n.*, Going Back Small, lit., going back small, a creek named by the Ponca (This is a creek near Niobrara, Nebraska, known to back up when the Missouri River floods.)

golden eagle **Xidá'hągà** /xē-thä'-hoⁿ-gä'/ *n.*, golden eagle (*Aquila chrysaetos*), the species of eagle that is honored or given high respect by the Ponca people

gone **Ðigé'** /thēⁿ-gä'/ *adj.*, gone, 1. used up, consumed, spent; *gadíge*, used up by means of striking or being windblown, usu. refers to pecan and other nut trees; *nądíge*, used up, usu. refers to running out of gas 2. refers to the deceased

good **Ú'dà** /ü'-doⁿ'/ *adj.*, good, fine, high quality, first rate

good vision **Įšt'áska** /ēⁿ-sht'ä'-skä/ *n.*, good vision, lit., white eyes, a person with exceptional vision

goose **Míxat'ągà** /mē'-xä-t'oⁿ-gä/ *n.*, goose,

lit., big duck, any of various domesticated or wild geese, such as the Canada goose

gooseberry **B'ézi** /b-ā'-zē/ *n.*, gooseberry, a small, round fruit of the family Grossulariaceae, genus *Ribes*

goshawk **Gde'dą́ áhįšut'à** /gthā-doⁿ ä'-hēⁿ-shü-t'ä/ *n.*, goshawk, a large hawk, the North American goshawk

gossip **Íye'udàdà** /ē'-yā-ü-thä'-thä/ *n.*, gossip, to gossip; to spread a rumor

gossipy **Waí'dadà** /wä-ē'-thä-thä/ *adj.*, gossipy, a person who talks a lot about people

got **Đizái** /thē-zä'-ē/ *v.*, *3rd pers.*, *past part.*, to get, got, he/she/it/they got

gourd **P'éxe** /p'ä'-xä/ *n.*, gourd, one of various plants of the family Cucurbitasceae

grab **Đixdą́** /thē-xthoⁿ'/ *v.*, grab, grabbing something in bunches

graduate **Ugášibè** /ü-gä-shē-bā/ *n.*, graduate, someone who has obtained a diploma or degree from a high school, school of technology, or college (Formerly the term referred to someone who "paid" or qualified themselves for a higher status in any of the Ponca ceremonies by doing or giving something to the community.)

grandchild **It'úš'p'à** /ē-t'ü'-sh-p'ä/ *n.*, *3rd pers. sing./pl.*, grandchild (a man or woman saying, his/her ~); *t'ú'šp'à hó*, *1st pers. sing.*, male using abbreviated form addressing ~; *t'ú'šp'à hà*, *1st pers. sing.*, female using abbreviated form addressing ~

grandfather **It'ígą** /ē-t'ē'-goⁿ/ *n.*, *masc./fem.*, grandfather, his/her grandfather

grandfather **Wit'ígą** /wē-t'ē'-goⁿ/ *n.*, *masc./fem.*, grandfather, my grandfather; *t'igą́'*, abbreviated form for ~; *t'igą́' ho*, male using abbreviated form addressing ~; *t'igą́ ha*, female using abbreviated form addressing ~

grandmother **Ik'ą́** /ē-k'oⁿ'/ *n.*, *masc./fem.*, grandmother, his/her grandmother

grandmother **Wik'ą́** /wē-k'oⁿ'/ *n.*, *masc./fem.*, grandmother, my grandmother; *gą̨hó'*, male using abbreviated form addressing ~; *gą́ha*, female using abbreviated form addressing ~

grape **Házi** /hä'-zē/ *n.*, grape, an edible fruit that grows in clusters on woody vines, the species of the *Vitis* genus known and eaten by the Ponca; term now applies to any species of grape

grasp **Udą́** /ü-thoⁿ'/ *v.*, grasp, take hold of

grasp with mouth **Đahé** /thä-hä'/ *v.*, grasp with mouth, hold onto with mouth, hold with mouth, as a dog may carry a stick in its mouth

grass **Sahį́** /sä-hēⁿ'/ *n.*, grass, reeds that grow tall and slender near ponds

grass **Xáde** /xä'-dā/ *n.*, grass, weeds

grasshopper **Žąxdą́'škà** /zhoⁿ-xthoⁿ'-shkä'/ *n.*, grasshopper, a jumping/flying insect of the family Acrididae, which eats plants

grate **Úhąágdè** /ü-hoⁿ-ä'-gthä'/ *n.*, grate, a grill, a metal frame of crossbars affixed over a fireplace for cooking

grateful **Wiákišnà** /wēä'-kē-shnoⁿ'/ *adj.*, grateful, being very appreciative for act(s) of kindness

grave **Ísabè** /ē'-sä-bä'/ *adj.*, grave, refers to a person who is in serious to critical condition due to sickness or injury

grave **Míxe** /mē'-xä/ *n.*, grave, a burial site

gravy **Waníde** /wä-nē'-dä/ *n.*, gravy, the juices that come from cooking meats thickened with flour

gray **Xúde** /xü'-dä/ *n.*, gray, the color gray, ash color

Gray Blanket **Wa'į́' xúde** /wä-ēⁿ' xü'-dä/ *n.*, Gray Blanket, 1. a male ghost that followed the Ponca people to Indian Territory ca. 1876 and who still walks an old trail along the Arkansas River in Kay County, Oklahoma 2. a common gray blanket acquired by the Ponca ca. 1800s

gray fox **T'ík'axudè** /t'ē'-k'ä-xü-dā'/ *n.*, gray fox, *Urocyon cinereoargenteus*, a carnivorous mammal of the family Canidae

Gray Robe Village **Wa'į'xudè** /wä-ēⁿ'-xü-dā'/ *n.*, Gray Robe Village, one of the three villages in present-day Nebraska where the Ponca lived before the removal to Indian Territory

graze **Wabáhi** /wä-bä'-hē/ *v.*, graze, 1. nibble, forage (The prefix *wa* pluralizes the action of an individual or thing, as in *t'éská má ~ mąđì*, the cattle are grazing) 2. to pick or picking, as in picking pecans in a pecan grove

grease **Wégđi** /wä'-gthē/ *n.*, grease, fat, oil

greasy **Šníšnidè** /shnē'-shnē-dā'/ *adj.*, greasy, oily, slippery, slimy

great **T'ągá** /t'oⁿ-gä'/ *adv.*, great, to a large degree, huge, immense, enormous, great big

greatly **T'ągádihà** /t'oⁿ-gä'-thē-hä'/ *adv.*, greatly, to a larger degree or extent that reaches out

green **Č'ú'** /ch-ü'/ *n.*, green, the color green (*pézit'ù* is an Omaha reference to the color green, from a blue-tinted plant)

greens **Žá'** /zhä'/ *n.*, greens, lit., weeds, usu. refers to spring greens, collard greens, poke, leafy greens

greeting **Ahó'** /ä-hō'/ *interj./n.*, greeting, a Ponca male greeting, as in "hello" or "hi"

greeting **Nąbé bazú** /noⁿ-bā' bä-zü'/ *v.*, greeting, the Plains Native American sign language greeting of rubbing hands together upon seeing a friend or relative after a long period of time, indicating delight and happiness over meeting again

groceries **Umą́'e** /ü-moⁿ'-ā/ *n.*, groceries, provisions, foodstuff, rations

groom **G'igdístubè** /g-ē-gthē'-stü-bā'/ *v.*,

groom, to spruce up, trim, usu. refers to animals that clean their feathers with the beak or clean their fur with the tongue

ground **Bit'úbe** /bē-t'ü'-bā/ *v.*, ground, to grind or to crumble

ground **Bit'ú'tubè** /bē-t'ü'-tü-bā'/ *v.*, ground, to grind or crumble continuously

ground **Gat'ú'be** /gä-t'ü'-bā/ *v.*, ground, to grind or break up by striking with an instrument

ground **Nąt'ú'be** /noⁿ-t'ü'-bā/ *v.*, ground, to grind by use of the feet or machinery

ground **T'ą́de** /t'oⁿ'-dā/ *n.*, ground, earth, dirt, soil

ground beans **T'ą́deáha hįbđíge** /toⁿ'-dä-ä'-hä hēⁿ-bthēⁿ'-gä/ *n.*, ground beans

ground squirrel **Hé'xđì** /hā'-xthē'/ *n.*, ground squirrel, a little squirrel that lives underground

group **Gđúba** /gthü'-bä/ *n.*, group, a splinter group, unit, a specific small part of a larger party, usu. people or things

grow **Žút'ą** /zhü'-t'oⁿ/ *v.*, grow, 1. refers to plants coming up 2. in modern times, used in connection with raising children

grow crops **Wadížu't'ą̀** /wä-thē'-zhü-t'oⁿ'/ *v.*, grow crops, to grow plants, usu. refers to growing a variety of agricultural crops

growl **Xđį́** /xtheⁿ'/ *n./v.*, growl, a guttural sound made by dogs to give warning to trespassers

grumble **Edéšt'e'à** /ā-dā'-sht'ä-ä'/ *v.*, grumble whine, bellyache, to continue to complain in an annoying way; *n.*, someone who grumbles and complains, usu. because of discontent

guess **Égà'ebdégà** /ā'-goⁿ'-ā-bthā'-goⁿ'/ *v.*, guess, suppose, or suppose something; conjecture

guinea fowl **Wadá'zaì** /wä-thä'-zä-ē'/ *n.*, guinea fowl, guinea hen gully **Uspé′** /ü-spä′/ *n.*, gully, a large ditch or small valley created or worn by running water after a heavy rain

gum **Žáp′à** /zhä′-p′ä′/ *n.*, gum, chewing gum (*Manilkara chicle* is a tropical evergreen tree in Mexico and Central America from which gum is made.)

gum disease **Hižú′niè** /hē-zhü′-nē-ā′/ *n.*, gum disease, gingivitis and periodontitis — affects the tissue housing of the roots of the teeth

gums **Hižú′** /hē-zhü′/ *n.*, gums, the flesh that surrounds the roots of the teeth

gun **Wahút′ądì** /wä-hü′-t′oⁿ-thē′/ *n.*, gun, rifle, usu. refers to any kind of gun; a device that fires bullets

gunny sack **Ú′žihà** /ü′-zhē-hä′/ *n.*, gunnysack, lit., leather container, a bag in which agricultural commodities were brought for payment for use of the Ponca's land and waterways in the North Country

gun powder **Mąxúde** /moⁿ-xü′-dä/ *n.*, gunpowder, a chemical substance that explodes on impact

gush **Mú′xt′à** /mü′-xt′oⁿ/ *v.*, gush, to gush out by force, refers to liquid flowing out, pouring out

guttural **Đašádu** /thä-shä′-thü/ *adj.*, guttural, gruff sounding, a deep, raspy sound

Gypsy **Wanáštà** /wä-nä′-shtoⁿ/ *n.*, Gypsy, one of a wandering group of people; *wanášt′à*, beggars

H

habitat **Umądi** /ü-moⁿ-thē/ *n.*, habitat, locale, environment, territory, home

hackberry tree **Gubé′hì** /gü-bä′-hē′/ *n.*, hackberry tree, of the genus *Celtis*

haggard **Đaéga** /thä-ā′-gä/ 1. *adj.*, haggard, worn down, gaunt 2. *n.*, someone who has an exhausted appearance

hail **Mási** /mä-sē/ *n.*, hail, frozen rain, small pellets of ice

hair **Hị′** /hēⁿ′/ *n.*, hair, body hair, hair that develops on the human body other than hair on the head

hair **Nąžíha** /noⁿ-zhē′-hä/ *n.*, hair, hair on the head, tresses, locks

hair brush **Nąžíha wébagahè** /noⁿ-zhēⁿ′-hä wä′-bä-gä-hä′/ *n.*, hair brush (Orig. brushes were made from needlegrass awns [probably *Hesperostipa curtiseta*, a Canadian needlegrass] tied in bundles.)

hair clasp **Nąžíha ábaxdadè** /noⁿ-zhē′-hä ä′-bä-xthä-dä′/ *n.*, hair clasp, a device to hold a girl's or woman's hair in place, such as a barrette

haircut **Nąžíha disé** /noⁿ-zhē′-hä thē-sä′/ *n.*, haircut, the act of trimming or styling the hair; *nąžíha wádisè*, barber

hairpin **Nąžíha ábaxà** /noⁿ-zhē′-hä ä′-bä-xoⁿ/ *n.*, hairpin, a piece of wire or some such used to hold a person's hair in place, usu. used by women to fasten up the hair or hold something on the hair

hair pulling **Đip′áze** /thē-p′ä′-zä/ *v.*, pulling hair, tousled, usu. refers to women fighting and pulling the other's hair, causing their hair to be disheveled

hair ties **Nąžíha ík′ąt′à** /noⁿ-zhēⁿ′-hä ē′-k′oⁿ-t′oⁿ/ *n.*, hair ties, usu. hair beads, jewelry, especially stringed beads attached to the braids of girls and women

hairy **Hị′škúbe** /hēⁿ′-shkü′-bä/ *adj.*, hairy, furry, covered with hair

half **Wedéną** /wä-dä′-noⁿ/ *n.*, half, one part of two equal parts, usu. refers to liquid

half **Wedétą** /wä-dä′-toⁿ/ *n.*, half, one part of two equal parts, 1. refers to the length of something solid 2. relative to distance, halfway to half cooked **Nídažì** /nē'-dä-zhē'/ *adj.*, half cooked, any food that is poorly prepared or not cooked to proper, healthy standards, such as meats that are rare, vegetables still hard, so-called half-boiled eggs

Halloween **Į'déugdą** /ēⁿ-dä'-ü-gthoⁿ'/ *n.*, Halloween, lit., put mask on, a festive time when Ponca children and adults put on masks and celebrate (Considered to be "all saints day" or "all saints eve" by the Europeans, when children played pranks on others. Joining in, the Ponca people usu. have parties at home and at church for a fun time. Other activities include Native American dances and contests for most comically dressed persons.)

halter **Įdé'udíšą** /ēⁿ-dä'-ü-thē-shoⁿ'/ *n.*, halter, unlike a bridle, a type of a headgear used to lead horses and other animals

hamburger **Wamáskè bút'à** /wä-moⁿ'-skä' bü-t'ä'/ *n.*, hamburger, a sandwich made of a fried, grilled, or broiled flat patty of ground beef served on a bun with other ingredients including mayonnaise or mustard, cheese, lettuce, tomatoes, and onions

hame **Đéška ídidà** /thä'-shkä ē'-thē-doⁿ'/ *n.*, hame, one of two curved pieces placed on the collar of an animal harness to which the traces are attached

hammer **Į'wetį** /ēⁿ'-wä-tēⁿ'/ *n.*, hammer, 1. a tool, usu. used for driving nails into wood surfaces 2. a tool used to deliver an impact to flatten or shape an object or to break up objects

hand **Nąbé** /noⁿ-bä'/ *n.*, hand, in human anatomy, that part of the body that has a palm, fingers, and thumb and is located at the end of the arm

handgame **Į'ųtį** /ēⁿ'-üⁿ-tēⁿ'/ *n.*, handgame (A Plains Indian social guessing game where two persons each hide an object in either of their hands and a person attempts to guess which hand the objects are in. Two opposing teams participate, along with scorekeepers.)

handkerchief **Waxįhaskà** /wä-xēⁿ'-hä-skä'/ *n.*, handkerchief, usu. a small piece of cloth for personal use, such as wiping one's hands or blowing one's nose (The Ponca refer to it as *p'áxđì íbikà*, snot wipe.)

handle **Íkądè** /ē'-koⁿ-thä'/ *n.*, handle, 1. grip, knob, a device used to hold on to something by hand 2. a device used to attach something to something else

hand lotion **Nąbé í'snadè** /noⁿ-bä' ē'-snä-thä'/ *n.*, hand lotion, a commercial product to help keep skin soft and smooth, usu. used by women (The term applies to all body creams and lotions.)

hand over **Gá'** /gä'/ *v.*, hand over, to give something to somebody

hand plane **Žąbdáska ídiskebè** /zhoⁿ-bthä'-skä ē'-thē-skä-bä'/ *n.*, hand plane, a hand-held woodworking tool with a sharpened cutting edge attached to the underside of the tool's body, which is used to shave and smooth the surface of wood boards

handshake **Nąbéúdą** /noⁿ-bä'-ü-thoⁿ/ *n.*, handshake, a greeting by two people grasping right hand to right hand and pumping with an up-and-down movement

handsome **Udúk'ąp'ì** /ü-thü'-k'oⁿ-p'ē'/ *adj.*, handsome, good or fine looking

hang **Ubát'ì** /ü-bä'-t'ē'/ *v.*, hang, to hang up, e.g., clothing, pictures, etc.

hanging **Ugá'e'e** /ü-gä'-ä-ä/ *v.*, hanging, dangling or hanging down

hang up **Ubát'i inąde** /ü-bä'-t'ē ē-noⁿ'-thä/ *v.*, hang up, to hang something up, as in to hang a picture on the wall or clothes on a clothesline

haphazardly **Đip'íp'iažì** /thē-p'ē'-p'ē-ä-zhē'/

adv., haphazardly, chaotically, not uniformly, done without concern for neatness or correctness

happiness **Ną́de' gíudą̀** /noⁿ-dā gē-ü-doⁿ/ *n.*, happiness, includes fulfillment (I feel good about this)

happy **Á'gidè** /ä'-gē-thā/ *v.*, to be happy, to be happy over somebody or something

happy **Gíde** /gē'-thā/ *n.*, happiness, cheerfulness, gladness, bliss, etc.

happy **Į́·de** /ēⁿ'--thā/ *v.*, *1st pers. sing.*, happy, I'm happy, I'm joyful

happy **Wéde** /wā'-thā/ *adj.*, *1st pers. pl.*, happy, we're happy, we are delighted, joyful, glad

harangue **Wá'dazabažì** /wä'-thä-zä-bä-zhē'/ *v.*, harangue, a speech made to scold people in a public place

harbor **Mądé uną́št'ą** /moⁿ-dā' ü-noⁿ'-sht'oⁿ/ *n.*, harbor, a place where boats dock

hard **Sagí** /sä-gē'/ *adj.*, hard, solid, firm

harden **Gasági** /gä-sä'-gē/ *v.*, harden, usu. refers to a heavy wind blowing upon something

harden **Nąsági** /noⁿ-sä'-gē/ *v.*, harden, harden by stepping on something; *unąsagì*, harden by continuously stepping on or driving over

hardship **Uwágda** /ü-wä'-gthä/ *n.*, hardship, difficulty, conditions that are harsh

hardware store **Mą́ze údiwįt'ì** /moⁿ'-zä ü'-thē-wēⁿ-t'ē'/ *n.*, hardware store, a store that sells tools, utensils, locks, hinges, wire

hardwood **Žą́' sagì** /zhoⁿ' sä-gē'/ *n.*, hardwood (The Ponca were acquainted with white elm, oak, ash, and walnut hardwoods.)

harness **Wé'į** /wä'-ēⁿ/ *n.*, harness, usu. refers to a set of organized straps to harness horses and other animals in order to control something, as in pulling a wagon

harvest **Waną́se** /wä-noⁿ'-sä/ *v.*, harvest, 1. reap, gather 2. to harvest game

harvesting **Waną́sedè** /wä-noⁿ'-sä-thä'/ *n./v.*,

harvesting, 1. the ~ or gathering of crops 2. ~ game (~ *ugí'p'ì*, the area is full of game)

has **Adį́'** /ä-thēⁿ'/ *v.*, *3rd pers. sing.*, *pres./past t.*, has, he/she/it has

has **Agdádį** /ä-gthä'-thēⁿ/ *v.*, has, he/she has his/her own or possesses his/her own

Haskell **Hidəát'à** /hē-dəä-t'ä/ *n.*, Haskell, Haskell Indian School, Lawrence, Kansas, now Haskell University

hasten **Waną́xdè** /wä-noⁿ-xthä/ *v.*, *archaic*, hasten, rush; connotes making haste to a specific place and returning at once

hat **Wadáge** /wä-thä'-gā/ *n.*, hat, a generic term for a headcovering worn for various purposes, including native headdresses worn for ceremonies, protection against the elements, war, or any reason or purpose

hatch **Wét'a ugášižè** /wä-t'ä ü-gä'-shē-zhä/ *v.*, hatch, a young fowl breaking out of an egg

hatchet **Mą́zepè žįgà** /moⁿ'-zä-pä' zhēⁿ-gä/ *n.*, hatchet, a small, short ax that has the head of a hammer opposite the blade

hate **Í't'adè át'ašą̀** /ē'-t'ä-thä' ä'-t'ä-shoⁿ/ *v.*, hate, abhor, detest

haul **T'úgdą̀** /t'ü'-gthoⁿ/ *v.*, haul, to carry things, usu. a load of a material goods, such as furniture, clothing, appliances, food

haul **Wat'úgdą̀** /wä-t'ü'-gthoⁿ/ *v.*, haul, to transport something in a vehicle

haunt **K'úhewadè** /k'ü'-hä-wä-thä/ *v./n.*, to haunt, a place that a spirit or ghost makes scary

have **Adį́** /ä-thēⁿ/ *v.*, have, to have; *abdí*, *1st pers. sing.*, I have; *aní'*, *2nd pers. sing.*, you have; *adí'*, *3rd pers. sing.*, he/she/it has; *ągádį̀*, *1st pers. pl.*, we have; *aní'i*, *2nd pers. pl.*, you all have; *adí'i*, *3rd pers. pl.*, they have

have **Ągádįt'ągatà** /oⁿ-gä'-thēⁿ-t'oⁿ-gä-toⁿ/ *v.*, *1st pers. pl.*, *future perfect tense*, we will have had havoc **Á'gdadè** /ä'-gthä-thä'/ *n.*, havoc, a condition of havoc or chaos caused by somebody or something, usu. said to have happened to a person

hawk **Gdedą́'** /gthä-do^n/ *n.*, hawk, any hawk of the genus *Accipiter*

hay **Xáde** /xä'-dä/ *n.*, hay, a herbaceous plant that is cut, baled, and used for animal food

hay bale **Xáde ubétą** /xä-dä ü-bä'-to^n/ *n.*, hay bale, baled hay, used to feed domesticated livestock

hazel nuts **Á'žįgà** /o^n'-zhē^n-gä'/ *n.*, hazelnuts, *Corylus avellana*

he **Éi'** /ā'/ *n.*, he, 1. he/she/it 2. he's/she's/it's the one 3. that's it

head **Nąšk'í** /no^n-shk'ē'/ *n.*, head, that part of the body that has a face—eyes, nose, ears, etc.—and has a cavity for the brain

head **P'á'** /p'ä'/ *n.*, head, 1. head, the top part of the body of humans and other animals 2. nose, in anatomy, that part of the head that projects out in front of the face and is used to smell and to breathe in and exhale air in conjunction with the mouth

headache **Nąškí'ni'é** /no^n-shkē'-nē-ä'/ *n.*, headache, a pain in the head or neck (This includes any type of headache, such as migraines.)

headcutters **P'amáse** /p'ä-mä'-sä/ *n.*, headcutters, another name for the Ponca warriors (The sign language symbol for *Ponca* is made by drawing the fingers, palm up, across the throat in a cutting motion.)

head first **Bas'į́'** /bä-s-ē^n'/ *adv.*, head first, usu. refers to falling forward with the head down

head louse **Hé'** /hä'/ *n.*, head louse (*Pediculus humanus capitis*) that causes infestation (These parasites spend their entire life on the human scalp, feeding on human blood.)

heal **Níde** /nē'-thä/ *v.*, heal, get well, restore to good health, cure

healed **Giní** /gē-nē'/ *v.*, heal, restore to health, get well from sickness

healed us **Niáwagidadè** /nē-ä'-wä-gē-thä-thä'/ *v.*, healed us, 1. somebody using medicines cured us 2. refers to Wak'ą́da healing the physical body and spirit or soul of man

healer **Waníde** /wä-nē'-thä/ *n.*, healer, 1. healer, usu. refers to Jesus, the Son of God 2. the Savior

healthy **Nié dįgè** /nē-ä' thē^n-gä'/ *adj.*, healthy, in good health, able-bodied

heap **Bat'é'** /bä-t'ä'/ *n.*, heap, pile, things that are thrown atop one another in no order

hear **Ną'ą́** /no^n-o^n'/ *v.*, hear, having the sense of hearing

heard of **Uną́ą** /ü-no^n'-o^n/ *v.*, heard of, heard about something

heard of **Uwáną'ą́'** /ü-wä'-no^n-o^n'/ *v.*, heard of, heard of us for something that we did or accomplished

hear of **Uxíjexčí ną'ą́'** /ü-xē'-jäx-chē' no^n-o^n'/ *v.*, hear of, hearing only a little bit of something

heart **Ną́de** /no^n'-dä/ *n.*, heart, in anatomy, the organ that pumps blood through blood vessels in humans and animals

heart **T'e'ną́de** /t'ä-no^n'-dä/ *n.*, heart, that edible organ of bovine cattle (Orig. an archaic word for the heart of the American bison: *t'é'*, bison, *ną́de*, heart)

heart disease **Ną́dewakéga** /no^n-dä-wä-kä'-gä/ *n.*, heart disease, refers to any heart ailment, cardiac problems

heaven **Ukí'mążą̀** /ü-kē'-mo^n-zho^n'/ *n.*, heaven, in Judeo-Christian faith, the dwelling place of the creator—God or other heavenly being—and true Christians or believers

heavy **Skíge** /skē'-gā/ *adj./n.*, heavy, a great amount of weight

heavy equipment **Wédihidè t'ǫgà** /wā'-thē-hē-dā' t'oⁿ-gä'/ *n.*, heavy equipment, bull-dozer, earth mover, crane

heavy load **Wa'į'skígè** /wä-ēⁿ'-skē'-gä'/ *v./n.*, heavy load, 1. to carry a heavy load (he has a ~ on his pickup truck) 2. to carry an emotional burden (being downhearted, he is carrying a ~)

Heđúškà **Heđúškà** /hā-thü'-shkä'/ *n., archaic*, a fraternal organization of the Ponca people consisting of good, upright men who offered ethical teachings to boys (six or seven years old and up), went on hunting expeditions to provide food for widows and the aged, and defended the village in warfare; the term is Heđóška when pronounced in song (The Heđúškà organizations ca. 1900 among the Southern Ponca included Heđúškà wanáxe, Heđúškà wahǫ́đįgè, Heđúškà wasísíge, and Heđúškà gđą́đi.)

heel **Sidéde** /sē-thā'-dā/ *n.*, heel, in human anatomy, the prominence of the calcaneus, or heel bone

height **Đétąha** /thā'-toⁿ-hä/ *n.*, height, stature, "this tall"

heir **Uwédi** /ü-wā'-dē/ *n.*, heir, to an heired of, one who is entitled to receive the property of a deceased person

hello **Ahó'** /ä-hō'/ *interj.*, hello, male greeting, Ponca greeting or salutation between men (In an archaic usage, *ahó'* was interjected by a man relating a story, as in "okay…" or "all right…" in the middle of a sentence. In modern times, the term is often used at many different tribal gatherings, esp. at intertribal dances to denote "thank you," a usage said to be of Kiowa origin.)

help **Ú'waškà** /ü-wä-shkoⁿ'/ *v.*, help, a source of help that comes from within oneself by means of another person, thing, or deity

help **Uwík'ą** /ü-wē'-k'oⁿ/ *v.*, help, be of assistance, to support or provide a service to someone; *uwék'ą*, 1st pers., past. t., I ~; *uwáwak'ą*, 1st pers., pres./past t., I ~ them

help **Wawék'a** /wä-wā'-k'ä/ *v., 3rd pers. sing.*, help, asking for help (*éi ~ atí*, he/she/it came asking for ~)

help **Wawík'a** /wä-wē'-k'ä/ *v., 1st pers. sing.*, help, asking someone for help (*~ atí*, I come asking you for ~)

help **Wedéšite** /wä-thā'-shē'-tā/ *v.*, help, you came to help when we needed it

help **Wík'a** /wē'-k'ä/ *v.*, help, assist, lend a helping hand, be of assistance

helped **Uwák'ą** /ü-wä'-k'oⁿ/ *v., 1st pers. sing., past t.*, helped, aided, assisted, helped out (*įdáđą gáxaìke, ~ pí'*, I ~ in the project)

helper **Wašíáđi** /wä-shē'-ä'-thē/ *n.*, helper, usu. one who helps at the direction of another

helpers **Wašʃ't'amà** /wä-shʃ-t'ä-mä'/ *n.*, helpers, his/her/their helpers, hired workers or assistants (In Christian theology Wak'ą́da ~ refers to the angels of God.)

helpless **Ukíką điá'** /ü-kē'-koⁿ thē-ä'/ *v.*, helpless, somebody who is unable to help him/her self, who is weak and dependent

hen **Wažíga migà** /wä-zhēⁿ'-gä mē-gä'/ *n.*, hen, refers to female chickens but may be applied to other poultry or game birds

here **Đédu** /thā'-thü/ *adv.*, here, refers to something in this place, namely, a house, building, land, country, and sometimes our walk of life, as in *đédu ąmą́đi kedì*, where we live our lives

here **Đéduadì** /thā'-thü-ä-dē'/ *adv.*, here, refers to something in or at this place near where the speaker stands here **Ðé′gedì** /thä′-gä-dē′/ *adv.*, here, stating something about a short distance from where you stand

here **Dúádạdì** /dü′-ä′-thoⁿ-dē′/ *adv.*, here, stating something about this place closer to where one is or close at hand

here **Edí** /ä-dē′/ *adv.*, here, a response to a question about where a person or thing is (*núžįgà tạ̀ ~ à?*, is the boy ~?; answer: *núžįgà tạ̀ ~*, the boy is ~)

here **Gá′** /gä′/ *adv.*, here, refers to somebody giving or showing somebody something, offering something to someone

here **Gá′dạdì** /gä′-thoⁿ-dē′/ *adv.*, here, at this place, may refer to a place out of sight of where you speak

here **Šéwadì** /shä′-wä-dē′/ *adv.*, here, farther away, farther than something close at hand

hereditary **Gigdé′t′ạ** /gē-gthä′-t′oⁿ/ *adj.*, hereditary, refers to having characteristic traits of a parent or other relatives and ancestors

heroism **Wašúše** /wä-shü′-shä/ *adj.*, heroism, beyond bravery, fearlessness, great courage, devil-may-care acts

hesitant **Ágabagdaì** /oⁿ′-gä-bä-gthä-ē′/ *v.*, *3rd pers. pl.*, to be hesitant, we hesitate; being uncertain, diffident (as in "we do not like to ask for a favor"); to feel uncertain or being not sure about something

hesitate **Ábagdà** /ä′-bä-gthä′/ *v.*, hesitate, hold back because of doubt or indecision

hex **Í′xt′à** /ē′-xt′ä′/ *n.*, hex, a spell, a curse; *v.t.*, hexed (*núžįgà akà ~ akà*, the boy was ~)

hickory nuts **Nạsi** /noⁿ′-sē/ *n.*, hickory nuts, genus *Carya* of the Juglandaceae family, that grow within an outer husk

hickory tree **Nạsi′hì** /noⁿ′-sē-hē′/ *n.*, hickory tree, of the genus *Carya*

hickory tree **Žạ́xudè** /zhoⁿ′-xü-dä′/ *n.*, 1. hickory tree 2. a proper male name in the Wašábe clan of the Ponca people

hickory tree **Žạ́′xudèhì** /zhoⁿ′-xü-dä′-hē′/ *n.*, hickory tree, small gray hickory tree, of the genus *Carya*

hidden **Úk′inạdè** /ü′-k′ē-noⁿ-thä′/ *adj.*, hidden, unseen, undetected, unobserved, not perceived or recognized among other things or people

hide **Há′** /hä′/ *n.*, hide, rawhide, the untanned hide of an animal

hide **Wánạxdè** /wä-noⁿ-xthä′/ *v.*, hide, hiding; *á′binạxdè*, hide, hiding a thing under something; *á′nạxdè*, hide, conceal, to hide something; *á′kinạxdè*, hiding; *í′kina′xdè*, hide, to hide oneself; *wénạxdè*, to hide themselves or something from us or them

high **Basnáde** /bä-snä′-dä/ *adj.*, high, elevated, far above ground, usu. refers to somebody or something standing high above

high **Mạšiádì** /moⁿ-shēä′-dē′/ *adj.*, high, a place that is towering, such as a high mountain

high **Mạšiáhà** /moⁿ-shēä′-hä′/ *adj.*, high, anything that relates to height (*t′inạ́k′a ké ~*, the roof is high)

high hill **P′ahé mạ́šì** /p′ä-hä′ moⁿ′-shē′/ *n.*, high hill; *p′ahé mạšiát′a*, at the top of the hill

highway **Uhé′dúbahà** /ü-hä′-dü-bä-hä′/ *n.*, highway, a four-lane highway

hike **T′ạ́deáhe** /t′oⁿ′-dä-ä′-hä/ *v.*, hike, trek, to walk far (For most Native Americans, walking was the main mode for getting from one place to another; it was not for pleasure or exercise.)

hill **P′ahé′** /p′ä-hä′/ *n.*, hill, knoll, mound, butte

hilly **P′ahą́hạ** /p′ä-hoⁿ′-hoⁿ/ *adj.*, hilly, rolling hills (*mạžạ́ ké ~*, the land is ~)

hindquarter **T'é'žéga** /t'ā-zhä'-gä/ *n.*, hind-quarter, the back quarter of a carcass of bison, beef, deer, moose, etc.

hips and thighs **Žegá'** /zhä-gä/ *n.*, hips and thighs, body parts of humans and animals

his **E't'ái** /ā-t'ä'-ē/ *poss. pron.*, his/hers/its/theirs, something belonging or attributed to him/her/it

hit **Gadą́** /gä-doⁿ/ *v.*, hit, to hit or strike something with the hands or with something in the hand, e.g., using a baseball bat

hit **Gap'í** /gä-p'ē'/ *v.*, hit, hitting something at the right place, as in to ~ a baseball far away

hit **Ųtį́** /ü-tēⁿ/ *v.*, hit, to hit or strike something or somebody with the hands or a weapon

hobble **Sihíbaxt'è** /sē-hē'-bä-xt'ä'/ *n./v.*, hobble, a device, usu. a thick wrap that is tied above the fetlock of the front legs to restrict the movement of a horse

hoe **Wé'e'** /wā'-ā/ *n.*, hoe, orig. bison scapula used for hoeing; a metal garden implement

hoist, block and tackle **Wé'nąkihà** /wā'-noⁿ-kē-hoⁿ/ *n.*, block and tackle hoist, a device that has two or more pulleys with a rope or chain threaded through them to lift heavy material

hold **Udą́** /ü-thoⁿ/ *v.*, hold, 1. hold on to, to take hold of something 2. arrest (In modern times, the act of arresting someone.)

hold **Udą́ga** /ü-thoⁿ-gä/ *v.*, *2nd pers. sing.*, hold, you hold, you clutch, you hang onto

hold down **Ánąsądè** /ä'-noⁿ-soⁿ-dä'/ *v.*, hold down, squeezing, to hold in place with the feet; *ábasądè*, hold in place by using one's own body; *ábisądè*, hold in place by pressing down

hold with mouth **Đahé'** /thä-hä'/ *v.*, hold with the mouth, as a dog may carry a stick in its mouth

hole **Mąšáde** /moⁿ-shoⁿ-dä/ *n.*, hole, den, burrow, lair (*mądíxudè dįké ~ ke égihà adái*, The prairie dog went into a ~)

holler **B'ą́'** /b-oⁿ/ *v.*, holler, to call out to somebody

holler **Ugdá'à'** /ü-gthä-ä'/ *v.*, holler, yell loudly, shout, yell

hollering **B'ą́bą** /b-oⁿ'-boⁿ/ *v.*, hollering, to continuously holler

hollow **Uxdúxda** /ü-xthü'-xthä/ *adj.*, hollow, concave

hollow **Xdú'a** /xthü'-ä/ *adj.*, hollow, as in something empty or void of substance

hollow echo **Gat'ámą** /gä-t'ä'-moⁿ/ *v.*, hollow echo (A modern term, ca. 1800s, refers to sound coming from a metal barrel.)

hollow log **Žá' xdú'a** /zhoⁿ' xthü'-ä/ *adj./n.*, hollow log, a large windfall (tree) that has lain upon the ground and been hollowed out by rot and digging by animals to use as a nesting or hiding place

Holy Bible **Wak'ą́da Íye** /wä-k'oⁿ'-dä ē'-yä/ *n.*, Holy Bible, the Word of God (The recorded text of the Old Testament history of the Hebrew people, which includes drama, poetry, philosophy, prophesy, and the New Testament history and words of Jesus, the Son of God, as well as letters or epistles written by followers of Jesus Christ.)

Holy Communion **Wak'ą́da waxúbe wadáte** /wä-k'oⁿ'-dä wä-xü'-bä wä-thä'-tä/ *n.*, sacraments, bread and wine representative of the body and blood of Christ taken at the command of Christ, "Do this in remembrance of me"

Holy Spirit **Ną́xe xubè** /noⁿ'-xā xü-bä'/ *n.*, Holy Spirit, the third person of the holy trinity in Christianity (The Holy Spirit is also referred to as the Comforter, Healer, Friend, Advocate, Teacher, etc.)

holy way **Waxúbe užą́ge** /wä-xü'-bä ü-zhoⁿ'-gä/ *n.*, *archaic*, holy way, an ancient term designating a way of life considered to be sacred, refers to 1. a person who led in spiritual ceremonials and who handled sacred paraphernalia and rites 2. living always in a compassionate, considerate, kindly manner that was prescribed by God 3. now applied to all Christian precepts

home **Út'i** /ü'-t'ē/ *n.*, home, a residence of a family, families, or a single person

homelands **Mažą iš'áge** /mä-zhoⁿ ēsh-ä'-gā/ *n.*, homelands, refers to original lands of the Ponca that covered hundreds of thousands of acres of land west of the Missouri to western parts of the current state of Nebraska (Information about village sites of the Ponca may be read in Howard 1970.)

homeless **Uwą́he digè** /ü-woⁿ'-hā thē-gā'/ *adj.*, homeless, lit., no shelter, people who have no shelter, home, or permanent residence

homeward **Gdé'** /gthā'/ *v.*, homeward, to go back; *agdé*, I'm going homeward or back; *agdái*, he/she/it/they went homeward or went back; *ągágdaì*, we are going homeward or back

hominy **Wabdúga** /wä-bthü'-gā/ *n.*, hominy, cooked dried corn kernels

hominy **Wabíšnudè** /wä-bē'-shnü-dā/ *v.*, hominy, lit., taking off, refers to the process of removing the hull from grains of corn using ashes

homosexual **Mixúga** /mē-xü'-gā/ *n.*, homosexual, gay, usu. refers to a male person feeling sexual attraction toward another male; a person who is sexually attracted to a person of the same sex

honest **Wíke** /wē'-kā/ *adj.*, honest, frank, reliable, straightfoward, true, truth, truism

honey **K'igdą́xe** /k'ē-gthoⁿ'-xā/ *n.*, honey, a syrupy sweet food made by bees of the genus *Apis*

honeybee **K'igdą́xe** /k'ē-gthoⁿ'-xā/ *n.*, honeybee, a bee of the the genus *Apis* that gathers nectar from wildflowers and produces sweet food called honey

honk **Đihút'ą** /thē-hü'-t'oⁿ/ *v.*, honk, to honk the horn of a vehicle

honor **Ą́xt'idè** /oⁿ'-xt'ē-thā'/ *n./v.*, honor, respect, mark of respect, reverence, hold in highest regard; *áxt'idè* respect to one person; *áxt'iwadè*, respect to more than one person; *áxt'ikidè*, self admiration or personal pride; *áxt'iwidè*, I respect and hold you in high regard, usu. refers to God, Wak'ą́da

hoof **Šą́ge šáge** /shoⁿ'-gā shä'-gā/ *n.*, hoof, usu. refers to the hoof of a horse (The suffix *-šáge* describes a nail or claw and may be applied to various mammals and fowl. A horse's hoof is composed of soft tissue and other keratinized structures.)

hope **Út'ąbedè** /ü-t'oⁿ-bā-thā'/ *n./v.*, hope, desire with expectation or desire with anticipation

hopping **Uą́sidą̀dą̀** /ü-oⁿ'-sē-thoⁿ-thoⁿ'/ *v.*, hopping, a person or animal jumping around sporadically or at irregular intervals

horn **Hé'** /hā'/ *n.*, horn, a pointed projection made of hardened protein over bone on the head of some animals, such as cattle, deer, sheep

horned screech owl **P'ánahò héta egà** /p'ä'-nä-hō' hā'-toⁿ ā-goⁿ'/ *n.*, horned screech owl, of the genus *Megascops*

horned toad **Hádewadą̀bè** /hä'-dā-wä-doⁿ-bā'/ *n.*, horned toad, an insect-eating lizard with spikes on its head, of the genus *Phrynosoma* (The Ponca name is derived from the placement of the eyes, which are located on the side of the skull, giving the ability to see in varied directions.)

horse **Šą́ge** /shoⁿ'-gā/ *n.*, horse, *Equus cabal-*

lus, a large, hoofed, domesticated mammal with short hair, a long mane, and a long tail; *šáge nugà*, stallion, a male horse not gelded

horseback **Šágeágdi̧** /shon-gā-ä'-gthēn/ *n./adv.*, horseback, sitting or riding on a horse

horse blanket **Šáge wa̧i̧** /shon-gā wä-ēn/ *n.*, horse blanket, a blanket to keep the horse warm or cool or to keep flies off

horse collar **Núde wéi̧** /nü'-dā wā'-ēn/ *n.*, horse collar, lit., neck harness, part of the harness that fits around the horse's neck and shoulders, allowing it to pull a wagon and other loads

horsefly **Šáge wadaxt'à** /shon'-gā wä-thä-xt'ä'/ *n.*, horsefly, lit., bites horses, a large female fly that sucks the blood of horses

horse hunter **Šáge na̧sé** /shon'-gā non-sä'/ *n.*, horse hunter, 1. one who hunts and captures horses 2. male name in the Hísadà clan of the Ponca people

horseshoe **Máze siúgadà** /mon'-zā sē-ü'-gä-don'/ *n.*, horseshoe, a U-shaped piece of metal nailed to the hooves of horses

hospital **Wakéga t'ì** /wä-kā'-gä t'ē'/ *n.*, hospital, lit., house of the sick, sick bay, infirmary

hospital staff **Wakéga t'ì wadít'a̧mà** /wä-kā'-gä t'ē' wä-thē'-ton-mä'/ *n.*, hospital staff, the people who work in the hospital, composed of medical doctors, nurses, medical specialists, aides, housekeeping personnel, etc.

hot **Nák'adè** /nä'-k'ä-dä'/ *adj.*, hot, may refer to a hot day, hot water

hot dog **T'áhe ži̧gà** /t'on'-hä zhēn-gä'/ *n.*, hot dog, wiener; commonly garnished with mustard, onions

house **T'í'** /t'ē'/ *n.*, house, dwelling

housefly **Há̧t'egà** /hon'-t'ä-gä/ *n.*, housefly, an insect of the family Muscidae, a fly that lives around human beings and is capable of spreading disease

house foundation **T'iúdixɖigè** /t'ēü'-thē-xthē-gä'/ *n.*, house foundation, refers to the dilapidated remains of a homestead

houseful **T'í ugíp'i** /t'ē' ü-gē'-p'ē/ *n.*, houseful, usu. refers to tribal ceremonies held in a tepee or similar dwelling, as in saying, ~ *a̧gɖi̧*, we were sitting in a ~

how **Áwategà** /ä'-wä-tä-gon'/ *adv.*, how, introduces a question about how something is done or happens

however **Ða̧žá** /thon-zhon'/ *adv.*, however, though, nevertheless

howl **Hú·** /hü'·/ *v.*, howl, to cry out (*šánudà áka ~ gɖì*, the dog ~ed)

huddle **Bat'é** /bä-t'ä'/ *n./v.*, huddle, a group of people who are crowded together (*Niášigà ma ~ gɖiáma*, The people ~ together)

hug **Á'nè** /ä'-nä'/ *v.*, hug, to hug, to ~ somebody affectionately or to put your arms around something

human **Níka** /nē'-kä/ *n.*, human being, person, being, mankind

human-like **P'á'snut'à** /p'ä'-snü-t'ä'/ *n.*, human-like, lit., long, curved head, a real or mythological human-like creature who lived in ancient times and was said to have an elongated head

humidity **P'ú'i̧ɖì** /p'ü'-ēn-thē'/ *n.*, humidity, humid, vapor in the air

humility **Ú'da'ék'idè** /ü'-thä-ä'-k'ē-thä'/ *n.*, humility, doing something to humble oneself

humming bird **Wačíninikà waží̧ga** /wä-chē'-nē-nē-kä' wä-zhēn-gä/ *n.*, hummingbird, a tiny bird of the family Trochilidae

hump **T'úxa** /t'ü'-xä/ *n.*, hump, bulge, lump

humpback **Náxahì t'úxà** /non'-xä-hē' t'ü'-xä'/ *n.*, humpback, a crooked back caused by injury or kyphosis

hundred **Gɖébą'hi̧wì'** /gthä'-bon-hēn-wē'/ *n.*, hundred, Roman numeral C, Latin term *centum*

hundred-dollar bill **Gdébą hiwì ídawà** /gthā'-boⁿ hē-wē' ē'-thä-wä'/ *n.*, one-hundred-dollar bill, U.S. currency

hungry **Nąp'éhì** /noⁿ-p'ā'-hē'/ *adj.*, hungry, ravenous, famished

hunker **Bispé** /bē-spā'/ *v.*, hunker, to sit on one's heels, squat down; *bispáspa*, to continually crouch, walking close to the ground

hunt **Ábaè** /ä'-bä-ā'/ *v.*, hunt, to hunt, stalk, or to seek out prey

hunter **Ábaè** /ä'-bä-ā'/ *n.*, hunters (~ *mà ágdì*, the ~ have returned)

hunting party **Gaxdą́** /gä-xthoⁿ'/ *n., archaic*, hunting party, a large hunting party, usu. including families

hurricane **Ní't'ągà t'adésagì t'ągà** /nē'-t'oⁿ-gä' t'ä-dā'-sä-gē' t'oⁿ-gä'/ *n.*, hurricane, lit., big wind of the ocean, a powerful, destructive wind in the Western Hemisphere that usu. occurs along the eastern coast of the United States and the Gulf of Mexico

hurry **Ðikúde** /thē-kü'-thä/ *v./n.*, hurry, rush, usu. the urgency to get something done

hurry **Hidék'idè** /hē-thā'-k'ē-thā'/ *v./n.*, hurry, usu. refers to rushing to get ready to go someplace

hurt **Ną́ka** /noⁿ'-kä/ *v./n.*, hurt, injured

hurt **Niégáxe** /nē-ā'-gä'-xä/ *v.*, hurt, harmed, injured by something

hurt **Waní'e** /wä-nē'-ā/ *v.*, 1. hurt, to feel pain, ache, to be sore 2. *n.*, something that hurts or is emotionally painful

husband **É'gdągè** /ā'-gthoⁿ-gä'/ *n.*, husband, the male partner in the marriage of a man and woman

husk **Waxą́'ha** /wä-xoⁿ'-hä/ *n.*, husk, husk of corn

hut **T'iúdip'ù** /t'ēü'-thē-p'ü'/ *n.*, hut, a dome-shaped hut made with cut saplings bent together toward the center and covered with hides

hymnal **Wak'ą́dawadahą̀ waą́ wabáxu** /wä-k'oⁿ'-dä-wä-thä-hoⁿ' wä-oⁿ' wä-bä-xü/ *n.*, hymnal, a church songbook

hymns **Wak'ą́dawadahą̀ waą́** /wä-k'oⁿ'-dä wä-thä-hoⁿ' wä-oⁿ'/ *n.*, hymns, Christian hymns

hysterical **Íxagaskí t'ę** /ē'-xä-gä-skē' t'āⁿ/ *adj.*, hysterical, a fit of uncontrolled laughter or crying

hysterics **Íxa dašt'ą́žì** /ē'-xä thä-sht'oⁿ'-zhē'/ *n.*, hysterics, condition of laughing or crying

I

ice **Núxe** /nü'-xä/ *n.*, ice, 1. frozen water 2. male name in the Núxe clan of the Ponca people

icebound **Udá'** /ü-dä'/ *adj.*, icebound, something that is frozen within or covered with ice

ice cream **Núxe bawégdi** /nü'-xä bä-wä'-gthē/ *n.*, ice cream, a dessert made from milk and cream along with other ingredients and various flavorings

ice pick **Núxe ígašižè** /nü'-xä ē'-gä-shē-zhä'/ *n.*, ice pick, an awl-like tool to crack or chip ice

icy **Žą́'ádašnà** /zhoⁿ-ä'-thä-shnä'/ *adj.*, icy, rain turning to ice, causing the land to be covered with ice (The Ponca term is derived from ice being on wood and trees.)

idea **Wadígdą̀** /wä-thē'-gthoⁿ'/ *n.*, idea, plan, thought, the processes of mental activity

if **Kí'** /kē'/ *n.*, if, stipulation, usu. used after a verb (*ìtą adái kí', nąp'í' ahì t'akà*, if he goes now, he'll get there right on time)

igloo **Núxe t'ì** /nü'-xä t'ē'/ *n.*, igloo, lit., ice

house, Inuit word meaning snow house or
hut

ignorant **Íbahąžì** /ē'-bä-hoⁿ-zhē'/ *n./adj.*,
ignorant, lit., does not know, a person untaught, uneducated, illiterate

ignore **Šédažì** /shā'-thä-zhē'/ *v.*, ignore, pay
no attention to, pay no heed to him/her/it

ill **Wakéga** /wä-kā'-gä/ *adj.*, ill, sick, in poor
health

illegitimate **Et'ádįgè** /ā-t'ä'-thēⁿ-gā'/ *adj.*,
illegitimate, lit., belonging to none, a child
born to a woman not married

illness **Ú'nièt'ą** /ü'-nē-ā-t'oⁿ/ *n.*, illness, the
state of having an illness or sickness from
an infection

illuminate **Unágąbä** /ü-nä'-goⁿ-bä/ *v.*, illuminate, brighten, the effect of light away from
the main source

ill-willed **Ímądà** /ē'-moⁿ-thä'/ *v.*, ill-willed, to
have or harbor enmity or hostile feelings
against somebody; *wémądà*, having or harboring enmity or hostile feelings against
more than one person

imagine **Edégą** /ā-thä'-goⁿ/ *v.*, imagine, think
of, bring to mind, forming a mental image
of something

imitate **Wawégaskądè** /wä-wä'-gä-skoⁿ-thä'/
v., imitate, attempting to do or act as somebody or to do what a group of people in
their circle do

immediately **Đegáádi** /thä-goⁿ'-ä'-dē/ *adv.*,
immediately, at once, without delay

immense **T'ągá át'ašą** /t'oⁿ-gä' ä'-t'ä-shoⁿ'/
adj., immense, something that is massive

immerse **Ní' ubít'ą** /nē' ü-bē'-t'oⁿ/ *v.*, immerse, dip, dunk (to ~ something or some-
body completely in water)

immodest **Wawéəšt'aži** /wä-wä'-ə-sht'ä-zhē/
adj., immodest, no proper social reserve,
has no modesty

impassable **Uhéwakidažì** /ü-hä'-wä-kē-thä-
zhē'/ *adj.*, impassable, lit., cannot pass here,
1. refers to an enemy trespassing tribally
recognized territory 2. a proper male clan
name 3. to not allow somebody to insist
upon something

impetuous **Ábačižè** /ä'-bä-chē-zhä'/ *adj.*, impetuous, hasty, rash, charaterized by doing
something without thinking

implode **Mút'ušì** /mü-t'ü-shē'/ *v.*, implode,
an explosion from forces within

impregnate **Uwétakidè** /ü-wä'-tä-kē-thä'/ *v.*,
impregnate, to make a female pregnant, to
fertilize

improbable **Šą́t'egažì** /shoⁿ'-t'ä-gä-zhē'/ *adj.*,
improbable, doubtful, not likely to happen

impudent **Úš'a'dįgè** /ü'sh-ä-thēⁿ-gä'/ *adj.*, impudent, lacking modesty, brazen, bold and
unashamed, shameless

in **Mą́te** /moⁿ'-tä/ *prep.*, in, usu. refers to
somebody or something inside a particu-
lar place

inability **Ukíhiáži** /ü-kē'-hē-ä'-zhē/ *n.*, inability, lack of ability, the condition of not
being able

inaccessible **Udúhi điáwadè** /ü-thü'-hē thē-
ä'-wä-thä'/ *adj.*, inaccessible, not reachable

inactive **U'ą́dįgè** /ü-oⁿ-thēⁿ-gä'/ *adj.*, inactive,
1. unused, still, immobile 2. shiftless, not
doing anything, just hanging around

in between **Ut'a'nądì** /ü-t'ä-noⁿ-dē'/ *prep.*, in
between, 1. usu. refers to children being
left alone between two or more homes of
relatives 2. *n.*, something left lying around
somewhere

in case **Sabé** /sä-bä'/ *conj.*, in case, lest, for fear
that

incensed **Baskíde** /bä-skē'-thä/ *adj.*, incensed, being aroused with anger within
although not expressed openly (A person in

such a state may suddenly act upon his/her emotions.)

incinerate **Uwínedè** /ü-wē'-nā-thā'/ *v.*, incinerate, burn, burn up, set fire to

incisors **Hí'u'špedì** /hē'-ü-shpā-dē'/ *n.*, incisors, the sharp-edged front teeth used for cutting food

include **Edábe** /ē-dä'-bā/ *v.*, include, being included (*ugášạ aḍái kí ~ aḍį̣ aḍái*, he was ~ in the trip)

include **Udáha** /ü-thä'-hä/ *v.*, include, something that goes with or is attached to something

include **Uhéde** /ü-hä'-thä/ *v.*, include, people or things that are brought in or involved

inconsequential **Ịdádạ̀žì** /ēⁿ-dä'-doⁿ-zhē'/ *adj.*, inconsequential, of no concern or nothing to worry about

inconvenience **Weógašè** /wāō'-gä-shä'/ *n.*, inconvenience, somebody pushing somebody or something upon another without consideration

incorrect **Égạ̀žì** /ä'-goⁿ-zhē'/ *adj.*, incorrect, false, not in line with the facts, erroneous, untrue, inaccurate, flawed

incubate **Nážutạdè** /nä'-zhü-toⁿ-thä'/ *v.*, incubate, fowl hatching eggs by keeping them warm by sitting on them or carefully maintaining controlled heat

incubator **Nákạ nážutạwadè** /nä'-koⁿ nä'-zhü-toⁿ-wä-thä'/ *n.*, incubator, an apparatus to hatch eggs artificially

indecision **Wadígdą̣'á'ákikì** /wä-thē'-gthoⁿ'-ä'-ä'-kē-kē'/ *n.*, indecision, arguing with oneself, wavering

Indian agent **Idádidaì** /ē-thä-dē-thäē'/ *n.*, Indian agent, a person who was authorized by the federal government to interact with Native Americans and to approve or disapprove their land leases and land sales

Indian commissioner **I't'ígạdà žịgà** /ē-t'ē'-goⁿ-thä' zhēⁿ-gä'/ *n.*, Indian commissioner, refers to the U.S. commissioner of Indian affairs

indistinguishable **Úkinạdì** /ü-kē-noⁿ-thē'/ *v.*, to make indistinguishable, to mix an animate or inanimate subject with other things so that the subject becomes ~

indoor **T'imạ́te** /t'ē-moⁿ'-tä/ *adj.*, indoor, inside, interior of a house or building

indoors **T'iát'a** /t'ē-ä'-t'ä/ *adv.*, indoors, in the house or building, at home; *t'iádi*, something or somebody in the house or building

ineffective **Í'giúdạ̀žì** /ē'-gēü'-doⁿ-zhē'/ *adj.*, ineffective, futile, usu. refers to medicines taken

inept **Edíạk'íhiažì** /ā-dē'-ə-k'ē'-hē-ä-zhē'/ *adj.*, inept, lacking ability, ineffectual

infect **Á'ạdà** /ä'-oⁿ-thä'/ *v.*, infect, lit., to pass something on to somebody, to contaminate, refers, e.g., to passing a common cold to somebody else

inflate **Múbixạ́** /mü-bē-xoⁿ'/ *v.*, inflate, to inflate a balloon, pump up a tire

inform **Úwagidè** /ü'-wä-gē-thä'/ *v.*, inform, to tell or give information to a person or a group of people

information **Á'ạ'wà** /ä'-oⁿ-wä'/ *n.*, information, 1. a phrase used to acquire information about the identity or nature of somebody or about the purpose of something 2. an inquiry concerning a consequence, outcome, or end result, as in "what happened to …"

in front **Udúšiát'a** /ü-thü'-shē-ä'-t'ä/ *adv.*, in front, at or in the front

inhale **Đahúni** /thä-hü'-nē/ *v.*, inhale, to breathe in air

inhabit **Ú't'ì** /ü'-t'ē'/ *v.*, inhabit, occupy, reside

inject **Ubá'snidè** /ü-bä'-snē-dā'/ *v.*, inject, to inject a liquid into, as in giving a flu shot to a patient inject **Ubá'sni'snidè** /ü-bä'-snē-snē-dä/ *v.*, inject, to inject continuously, as in getting a series of shots

injure **Nąka** /noⁿ'-kä/ *v.*, injure, hurt; *ínąk'à*, to be hurt by; *nák'ak'idè*, to hurt oneself; *nák'awadài*, to hurt them

inner **Mạteát'a** /moⁿ'-tä-ä'-t'ä/ *adj.*, inner, inside (*hiská te, ~ itédaì*, she put the beads in the ~ part of the box); *mạteát'a, n.*, inner recesses, as in a hollow place like a wall, niche, or inner place

inner ear **Nạxíde** /noⁿ-xē'-dä/ *n.*, inner ear, the organ of hearing

insects **Wagdíška** /wä-gthē'-shkä/ *n.*, insects, 1. bugs 2. a proper male name in the Wažážè clan

insert **Ugdé** /ü-gthä/ *v.*, insert, as in placing a key into a lock

inside **Mạteádi** /moⁿ'-tä-ä'-dē/ *n.*, inside (*t'í'te ~ adaì*, he went ~ the house)

insist **Áhušigè** /ä-hü-shē-gä/ *v.*, insist, as in to "keep asking for something"

insistent **Uhé** /ü-hä/ *adj.*, insistent, adamant, unrelenting (*~ gádaì*, he is ~)

instep **Sí'dihà** /sē'-dē-hä/ *n.*, instep, the arch in the human foot

intelligence **Wažį́'** /wä-zhēⁿ/ *n.*, intelligence, psyche, mentality, awareness

intelligent **Wažį́skà** /wä-zhēⁿ'-skä/ *adj./n.*, intelligent, lit., clear mind, 1. a person who is intellectual 2. a proper male name in the Đíxidà clan of the Ponca people

interest **Á'ạdè** /ä'-oⁿ-thä/ *n./v.*, interest, be of interest; take interest to help with somebody's dilemma or situation; *á'ạdext'ì*, having deep concern or interest in somebody's dilemma or situation

interest **Idáhidè** /ē-thä'-hē-dä/ *v.*, interest, to come into interest through a noticeable situation, or to be called to attention or awareness of a situation

interesting **Úxt'à** /ü-xt'ä/ *adj.*, interesting, appealing, worthy of note

internal **Điſmạtè** /thēʃ-moⁿ-tä/ *n.*, internal, in anatomy, refers to that area inside the human form that houses the organs from the heart to the stomach area

interpreter **Íyeskà** /ē'-yä-skä/ *n.*, interpreter, 1. one who translates a language unknown to others 2. proper feminine name in the Hísadà clan of the Ponca people

interrogate **Wawémạxè** /wä-wä'-moⁿ-xä/ *v.*, interrogate, question, interview, cross-examine, usu. refers to court proceedings

intestines **Šíbè** /shē'-bä/ *n.*, intestines, bowels, or entrails; part of the digestive tract, used in processing food

intoxicant **Mạk'ą́'p'ežì** /moⁿ-k'oⁿ'-p'ä-zhē/ *n.*, intoxicant, intoxicating beverages; new, mind-altering drugs

intoxicated **Dá'dį** /dä'-theⁿ/ *adj./v.*, intoxicated, drunk, drunken

intoxicated by **Į́'dadì** /ēⁿ'-dä-thä/ *v.*, to be intoxicated, to get intoxicated by some alcoholic beverage

invariably **Égą šą́šą** /ä'-goⁿ shoⁿ'-shoⁿ/ *adv.*, invariably, something that is consistent, continually, always the same

investigate **Udúdạbè** /ü-thü'-doⁿ-bä/ *v.*, investigate, to think about, examine, or deliberate over something, inspect

invite **Wéku** /wä-kü/ *v.*, *1st pers. pl.*, invite, a call to come, usu. to a home or to some activity

inward **Mạtáta** /moⁿ-tä'-tä/ *adv.*, inward, on the inside

inwardly **Mạteádi** /moⁿ-tä-ä'-dē/ *adv.*, inwardly, innermost self, privately

Iowa **Máxudè** /mä'-xü-dä/ *n.*, Iowa, the Iowa Tribe of Native Americans

iron **Násadedè** /nä'-sä-dä-thä/ *v.*, iron, to flatten or press something flat with heat iron **Wébasadedè** /wā'-bä-sä-dā-thā'/ *n.*, iron, a heated metal instrument used for pressing clothes

Iron Whip **Wégasap'ì** /wā'-gä-sä-p'ē'/ *n.*, Iron Whip, the principal chief of the Ponca people at the time of their forced removal from their homelands in what is now Nebraska and South Dakota, ca. 1876

irrigate **Ní'ámuxt'ą** /nē'-ä'-mü-xt'oⁿ'/ *v.*, irrigate, cause water to cover an area, to flood an area with water

is **Aké'** /ä-kā'/ *v.*, *prefix*, is, *3rd pers. sing.* of *be*

island **Niúdąt'à** /nē-ü'-thoⁿ-t'ä'/ *n.*, island, isle, atoll

itch **Đa'í'í'da** /thä-ē'-ē'-thä/ *n.*, itch, prickling, tingling, itchiness

I was there **Edí'bđì** /ä-dē'-bthē'/ *v.*, *1st pers. sing.*, *past t.*, I was there

J

jacket **Unążį'čéškà** /ü-noⁿ'-zhēⁿ-chā'-shkä/ *n.*, jacket, a short coat

jackrabbit **Mąščį'skà** /moⁿsh-chēⁿ'-skä'/ *n.*, jackrabbit, *Lepus californicus* (A jackrabbit is a hare, not a rabbit.)

jail **Ugánahąp'azè** /ü-gä'-nä-hoⁿ-p'ä-zā'/ *n.*, jail, lit., in the darkness, jail, detention center, confinement

janitor **T'í'básihì** /t'ē'-bä'-sē-hē'/ *n.*, janitor, a person who does housecleaning and maintenance

January **Mí' núxe dá-tedè** /mē' nü'-xā dä'-tā-thā'/ *n.*, January, lit., moon when ice begins to form, the first month of the year (The elders also used the following for January: *má'spą̀*, snow melts, *t'áxt'i má' anągè*, when deer paw the snow, i.e., in search for food.)

Japanese people **Įštá'mu'sna'dè** /ēⁿ-sht'ä'-mü-snä-dā'/ *n.*, Japanese people, lit., slanted eyes, a person of Japanese descent, a native of Japan

jar **Gap'ą́de** /gä-p'oⁿ'-dā/ *v./n.*, to jar, a physical jolt, to give a violent jerk or bump; *gap'ą́p'ą́de*, to continuously violently jerk or bump

jar **Gap'ą́dedą̀** /gä-p'oⁿ'-dā-thoⁿ'/ *v.*, jar, something that is put down or falls down with a violent jerk or bump; a person who sits down ungracefully with a jerk or bump

jaw **Đébahì** /thä'-bä-hē'/ *n.*, jaw, that part of the facial structure where teeth are set, either the mandible or the maxilla

jealous **Mi'wá'da** /mē-wä'-dä/ *adj.*, jealous, refers to a man who is jealous

jealous **Ną́wązì** /noⁿ'-woⁿ-zē'/ *adj.*, jealous, refers to a woman who is jealous

jealousy **Wawéət'adè** /wä-wä'-ə-t'ä-thā'/ *n.*, jealousy, an inner, resentful emotional reaction to some people who have something that one believes should be one's own; *udút'adè*, being resentful toward a person who is enjoying his/her accomplishments, with thoughts that it should belong to the other person even though he/she did nothing to deserve such

jerk **Đidą́'agì** /thē-doⁿ'-ä-gē'/ *v./n.*, to jerk, 1. something jerked or yanked away from some source 2. refers to something that is moving and jerking, such as an auto that misfires

jerk **Điš'í'agì** /thē-sh-ē'-ä-gē'/ *v.*, jerk, to move involuntarily (Usu. refers to jerking related to some cause, such as Parkinson's disease or other neurological conditions.)

jerking **Đidą́'agìgi** /thē-doⁿ'-ä-gē'-gē/ *v.*, jerking, refers to something that is moving, an auto that misfires

jerking **Điš'í'ágìgì** /thē-sh-ē'-ä'-gē-gē'/ *v.*, jerking continuously, involuntary movement (Usu. refers to jerking continuously

related to some cause, such as Parkinson's
disease and other neurological conditions.)

jesting **Wegáxe** /wā-gä'-xā/ *adj./n.*, jesting, 1.
a playful act mimicking something some-
one did seriously, namely, children (*níkašigà akà šígažįgàma ~aì, žąníbut'à đizé'
mądí, į'đeugđà teđàdè*, the person pretended
[jesting] before the children, when they
got candy on Halloween) 2. a jest making a
mockery of someone who did not complete
or create something right

Jesus **Jísasà** /jē'-sä-sä'/ *n.*, Jesus, the Son of
God, Jesus of Nazareth, the second person
in the trinity, the Messiah (The one who
came into the world offering immortality to
all who believe that he was resurrected and
is the Son of God.)

jet aircraft **Mądégià waséką** /moⁿ-dā'-gē-
oⁿ' wä-sā'-koⁿ/ *n.*, jet aircraft, an aircraft
powered with jet engines or jet propulsion

jingle **Mą́ze gat'át'amą** /moⁿ'-zā gä-t'ä'-t'ä-
moⁿ'/ *n.*, jingle, a clinking sound, usu. made
by small bells; *gat'át'amą̀*, jingle; *gaj'áj'amą̀*,
tinkle, usu. refers to baby toys and some
women's dance paraphernalia that includes
tiny bells and small seashells

jittery **Waxđí'** /wä-xthē'/ *adj.*, jittery, on edge
and nervous, or extremely nervous

job **Ú'đit'ą̀** /ü'-thē-t'oⁿ'/ *n.*, job, occupation,
profession, a job or vocation, ranging from
manual labor to a position that requires
specialized training and education

join **Ukí'gđè** /ü-kē'-gthä'/ *v.*, join, to join in
and become a part of the group or organization; *ukígđà*, to put oneself in without invitation

join **Uwíhe** /ü-wē'-hā/ *v.*, join, to become a
part of an organization or a group

joint **Hiúk'itè** /hēü'-k'ē-tā/ *n.*, joint, a place
in the skeletal structure where bones meet
and are connected

joint **-'k'ite'** /k'ē-tā/ *n.*, *suffix*, a place in the
skeletal structure where bones meet and
are connected; *á'* ~, arm ~; *astúhi* ~, elbow ~;
šinądeu ~, knee ~

jointly **Udíde** /ü-thē'-dā/ *adv.*, jointly, coming
together to accomplish a task

joking **K'í'ška'dè** /k'ē'-shkä-dā'/ *n.*, joking, to
do or say something causing laughter and
amusement, 1. to joke with 2. to do something with intention

joyful **Wé'užawà** /wā'-ü-zhä-wä'/ *adj.*, joyful,
to make something joyful

July **Mé' oską́ska** /mā' ō-skoⁿ'-skä/ *n.*, July,
lit., middle of the summer, the seventh
month in the year

jump on **Á'ą'sì** /ä'-oⁿ-sē'/ *v.*, to jump on, to
leap upon

jump **Uwási** /ü-woⁿ'-sē/ *v.*, jump, to jump, to
hop

jumping **Uwą́sisì** /ü-woⁿ'-sē-sē'/ *v.*, jumping,
to jump up and down

junction **Užą́ge žát'a** /ü-zhoⁿ'-gā zhä'-t'ä/ *n.*,
junction, intersection, fork in the road

June **Mąšté p'ahą́ga** /moⁿ-shtä' p'ä-hoⁿ'-gä/
n., June, lit., beginning of sunny days, the
sixth month in the year

just right **Égìdà** /ā'-gē-doⁿ'/ *adj.*, just right,
1. usu. refers to the size of a thing that fits
appropriately, as in clothing 2. something
that is appropriate for a person (*nikášigà
đįkè, údit'ą̀ te* ~, the job is ~ for that person); *égiją̀*, just right, usu. refers to the fit
of girls', women's, and babies' clothing

just right **Égijà** /ā'-gē-joⁿ'/ *adj.*, just right, usu.
refers to the size of a cute thing for children
that fits appropriately, as in clothing

K

Kahokian Mounds **P'ahé'žíde** /p'ä-hā'-zhē'-
dā/ *n.*, 1. the Kahokian Mounds, an ancient

Native American civilization located in the present-day state of Illinois 2. the city of St. Louis, Missouri

Kaw **Ką́ze** /koⁿ'-zā/ *n.*, the Kaw Tribe of Native Americans

keep **Adį́'** /ä-thēⁿ'/ *v.*, keep, reserved for future use; *agdádį*, has or keeps in reserve; *akígdadì*, keeping something always

keep **Agdádį** /ä-gthä'-thēⁿ/ *v.*, keep, to have one's own in one's possession

kernel **Sí'** /sē'/ *n.*, kernel, seed, that part of a mature plant containing an embryo

kerosene **Weának'ągdè ní** /wä-ä'-nä-k'oⁿ-gthä' nē'/ *n.*, kerosene, lamp oil, etc.

kettle **Wíúhą t'ągà** /wē'-ü-hoⁿ t'oⁿ-gä/ *n.*, kettle, a large metal vessel for cooking soup

key **Wédišibè** /wä'-thē-shē-bä'/ *n.*, key, lit., to open with, a metal instrument to unlock a door, car, padlock

kick **Nąté** /noⁿ-tä'/ *v.*, kick, 1. boot, punt 2. dance

Kickapoo **Hígabù** /hē'-gä-bü'/ *n.*, the Kickapoo Tribe of Native Americans

kidneys **Áząt'asì** /ä'-zoⁿ-t'ä-sē'/ *n.*, kidneys, the organs of humans and other vertebrate animals that process waste matter

kidneys **T'e'ázą t'asì** /t'ä-ä'-zoⁿ-t'ä-sē'/ *n.*, *archaic*, lit., bison kidneys, now the kidneys of domestic cattle

kill **T'ę́de** /t'āⁿ'-thä/ *v.*, to kill, murder, take life

killed **Gat'ę́** /gä-t'āⁿ'/ *v.*, killed, got killed (*k'ip'íŋągè kedí ~ biámà*, he was ~ in a car accident)

killing **Wat'ę́de** /wä-t'āⁿ'-thä/ *v.*, killing, 1. to kill somebody, murder, take life 2. *n.*, refers to a person who kills

kin **É'kidè** /ä'-kē-thä'/ *n.*, kin, kindred, relatives, family members

kind **Úšką údą** /ü'sh-koⁿ ü'-doⁿ/ *adj.*, kind, considerate, thoughtful, a good or benevolent nature

kindling **Ínedè** /ē'-nä-thä'/ *n.*, kindling, material to start a fire, usu. small sticks and wood chips

kinship **Uwáhąì** /ü-wä'-hoⁿ-ē'/ *n.*, kinship, in Ponca kinship, how one is related to another, i.e., brother, sister, cousin, etc.

kinsmen **Įdádąwagidè** /ēⁿ-dä'-doⁿ-wä-gē-thä'/ *n.*, kinsmen, a term for addressing a group of kinsmen of varied relations, as in, "Kinsmen!/Relatives!, I would speak to you."

Kiowa **K'áiwà** /k'ä'-ē-wä'/ *n.*, the Kiowa Tribe of Native Americans

kiss **Í'ákigdà** /ē'-ä'-kē-gthä'/ *v.*, kiss, to caress with the lips

kitchen **Úhą't'į** /ü'-hoⁿ-t'ēⁿ'/ *n.*, kitchen, a room where meals are prepared

knee **Šinądé** /shē-noⁿ'-dä/ *n.*, knee, the middle joint of the human leg

kneel **Ší'mąkà** /shē'-moⁿ-koⁿ'/ *v.*, kneel, kneel down, to bend the knees to the ground

kneel **Ší'mąšadì** /shē'-moⁿ-shä-dē'/ *v.*, kneel, kneeling down on one knee

knew **Í'b'ahąì** /ē'-b-ä-hoⁿ-ē'/ *v.*, *3rd pers. sing.*, knew, *past and pres. t.* of *to know*

knife **Mą́hį** /moⁿ'-hēⁿ/ *n.*, knife, 1. blade, table knife, carving knife, cook's knife, dagger, stiletto, etc. 2. proper name of a nonclan member of the Ponca people

knob **T'áši** /t'ä'-shē/ *n.*, knob, a bump, a bulge, a protuberance

knobby **T'át'áši** /t'ä-t'ä'-shē/ *n.*, knobby, something covered with knobs

knock **Gakúge** /gä-kü'-gä/ *v.*, knock, to strike something, as a door; *gakúkugè*, to continually knock or strike, as in knocking on a door

knock down **Gabdíže** /gä-bthē'-zhä/ *v.*, knock down, to knock down with force, usu. refers to somebody being pushed or knocked down by somebody or something

knock down **Gaxiáda** /gä-xēä'-thä/ *v.*, knock down, to cause to fall by striking with an instrument; knock down in boxing

knocking sound **Gat'á'xì** /gä-t'ä'-xē'/ *v.*, to make a knocking sound by striking, falling, spinning, etc.

knock off **Gašnúde** /gä-shnü'-dä/ *v.*, to knock off, as in removing a bolt from something by striking it; *gašnúšnúde*, to knock off continuously, as in removing a bolt from something by striking it

knock out **Gazą́įhédè** /gä-zoⁿ-ēⁿ'-hä'-thä/ *v.*, to knock out, to make unconscious (~ in the manly art of self-defense, i.e., boxing)

knoll **P'ahą́'** /p'ä-hoⁿ'/ *n.*, knoll, hill, mound

knoll **P'ahą́hą** /p'ä-hoⁿ'-hoⁿ/ *n.*, knoll, being hilly, usu. refers to small hills

know **Í'bahà** /ē'-bä-hoⁿ'/ *v.*, to know, *idáp'ahą*, I know; *íšp'ahą*, you know; knowing; *i'bahą'ì*, they know; *i'bahąì*, he/she/it knows; *ądą́'bahą'ì't'ągatà*, we will have known

knuckles **Nąbé ukíte** /noⁿ-bä' ü-kē'-tä/ *n.*, knuckles, the joints in the fingers

L

lace **Ugásnà** /ü-gä'-snoⁿ'/ *v.*, lace, 1. to lace up 2. *n.*, cord, rope

lackadaisical **Šąxt'igà** /shoⁿ-xt'ē-goⁿ/ *adj.*, lackadaisical, halfhearted, casual, laid back

ladle **T'aní'udúgadúžè** /t'ä-nē'-ü-thü'-gä-thü'-zhä/ *n.*, ladle, refers to a large long-handled spoon with a deep bowl used to serve soup, stew, and other foods

lair **Út'i** /ü'-t'ē/ *n.*, lair, a place or dwelling made by wild animals to rest or sleep

lake **Né t'ągà** /nä' t'oⁿ-gä/ *n.*, lake, a large body of fresh water that is surrounded by land

lamp **Wánąkagdè** /wä'-noⁿ-kä-gthä'/ *n.*, lamp, electric lights, gas light, etc.

lance **Mą́'dèhì** /moⁿ'-dä-hē/ *n.*, lance, a spear or lance, a weapon made of wood sharpened at one end or with an attached flint projectile point (The lance was primarily used by Comanche warriors in the old days. A one-time battle with the Ponca resulted in a trade of Ponca bows and arrows for Comanche horses in a peace agreement.)

land **Mą́žą́** /moⁿ-zhoⁿ'/ *n.*, land, ground, terra firma

landmark **Mą́žą́ baxú** /moⁿ-zhoⁿ' bä-xü'/ *n.*, landmark (To the Ponca, this refers to unique features of the landscape, including rivers and other land features, such as Niagara Falls, Kohokian Mounds, the Mississippi River, Pike's Peak, and mountain ranges and great rivers that were recognizable, especially ones that enabled them to identify their location.)

lantern **Šáge wánąkagdè** /shoⁿ'-gä wä'-noⁿ-kä-gthä'/ *n.*, lantern, lit., horse lamp (In early Ponca history such lamps were used to light up an area where livestock were kept.)

lard **Wé'gdì** /wä'-gthē'/ *n.*, lard, 1. lard, a product from pig fat, also refers to canola oil (rapeseed [*brassica napus*] oil), vegetable oil 2. gasoline 3. oil

large **Šédąskaegà** /shä'-thoⁿ-skä-ä-goⁿ'/ *adj.*, large, refers to the size of something; exaggerated, overly big size

large **T'ągá'** /t'oⁿ-gä'/ *adj.*, large, huge, immense, enormous, great big

large area **T'ągá'dihà** /t'oⁿ-gä'-thē-hä'/ *n.*, large area, something that is widely extended or far ranging

large intestine **T'ešíbe ut'ą́ga** /t'ä-shē'-bä ü-t'oⁿ'-gä/ *n.*, large intestine

laryngeal prominence **Nú'de t'á'ši** /nü'-dä t'ä'-shē/ *n.*, laryngeal prominence (Adam's apple), a large bump on the neck, formed by the angle of the thyroid cartilage, that is most noticeable on adult men

lash **Gasáp'i** /gä-sä'-p'ē/ *v.*, lash, to whip with a stinging blow

last **Adúhagè** /ä-thü'-hä-gä'/ *adj.*, last, the last of some people or animals coming

last **Háši** /hä'-shē/ *adj.*, last, end, after everything else

latch **Weúdidạ̀** /wā-ü'-thē-doⁿ'/ *n.*, latch, a fastening device used to hold a door, gate, or cabinet closed

later **Gáčegà** /goⁿ'-chä-goⁿ'/ *adj./adv.*, later, refers to doing something later on or afterward

lather **T'axúxe** /t'ä-xü'-xä/ *n.*, lather, suds, soapsuds

laugh **Í'xa** /ē'-xä/ *v.*, to laugh

laugh at **Í'xa'xà** /ē'-xä-xä'/ *v.*, laugh at, laugh to scorn, sneer at, make fun of, mock, jeer

launder **Wadíža** /wä-thē'-zhä/ *v.*, launder, wash, to use water to wash clothes or linen

laundry **Wadížat'ì** /wä-thē'-zhä-t'ē'/ *n.*, laundry, a place of business for washing clothes, or a place in the home where clothes and linens are washed

law **Udáde'kè** /ü-thä'-dä-kä'/ *n.*, law, a decree, ruling, or written regulation, including mores

lawn mower **Xáde ínạsedè** /xä'-dä ē'-noⁿ-sä-thä'/ *n.*, lawn mower

lawyer **Waú'íye** /wä-ü'-ē'-yä/ *n.*, lawyer, lit., woman talk, attorney (common pronounciation of the word is *waúwe* /wäü'-wä/)

lay aside **Ihéde** /ē-hä'-thä/ *v.*, lay aside, to put something down horizontally; *itéde, v., pl.*, lay aside, to put things down horizontally

lazy **Uk'ígdiagè** /ü-k'ē'-gthē-ä-gä'/ *adj.*, lazy, indolent

lead **Adúha** /ä-thü'-hä/ *v.*, lead, to go first; to do something first or to lead in a task to be done; *adúhagà*, you go first

leader **Hágạ** /hoⁿ'-gä/ *n.*, leader, usu. refers to a male person up front, at the head of, the one up front

leaf **Ábe** /ä'-bä/ *n.*, leaf or leaves

leaf **Žá'ábe** /zhoⁿ'-ä'-bä/ *n.*, leaf; *žá*, wood, *ábe*, leaf, the outgrowth of a tree or other plant

leak **Xaéde** /xä-ä'-thä/ *v.*, leak, seep out, trickle out

lean **Á'kạ̀** /ä'-koⁿ'/ *v.*, lean, to lean on

learn **Wagáze** /wä-goⁿ'-zä/ *v.*, learn, to be taught, to acquire knowledge

learned **Wédip'ì** /wä-thē-p'ē'/ *v.*, learned, learned from them

lease **Mạžá uná** /moⁿ-zhoⁿ'-ü-nä/ *n.*, lease, 1. usu. refers to a lease of land, the authorized signing of a lease agreement between the Bureau of Indian Affairs and an Indian landowner 2. refers to one (a farmer) who wants to lease land

leather **Há'** /hä'/ *n.*, leather, the skin of any animal, usu. softened or dressed for use

leave **Waáda** /wä-oⁿ'-thä/ *v.*, leave, abandon, to leave some people or animals behind

leave him alone **Šạdiʃdà (gà)** /shoⁿ-theʃ'-thä' (gä')/ *v.t.*, leave him alone, *fem./masc.*, leave him/her/it alone

leave it alone **Šạkéda'(dagà)** /shoⁿ-kä'-thä (thä-gä')/ *v.t.*, *sing.* leave it alone, *fem./masc.*, advised to leave a thing alone, as in don't bother it

leave them alone **Šạméwadà (dagà)** /shoⁿ-mä'-wä-thä' (thä-gä')/ *v.t.*, *pl.*, leave them alone, *fem./masc.*, advised to leave animate subject(s) in a particular state

leave them alone **Šạtédà (dagà)** /shoⁿ-tä'-thä' (thä-gä')/ *v.t.*, *pl.*, leave them alone, *fem./masc.*, advised to leave specific inanimate objects unchanged in a particular state

leaving **A'gdá'i** /ä-gthä'-ē/ *v.*, *3rd pers. sing.*, leaving, he/she/it is leaving

leech **Gisná** /gē-snä'/ *n.*, leech, a bloodsucking aquatic worm that lives in the water, from the class Hirudinea, used by some tribes as medicine

left **Ayádaì** /ä-yä'-thä-ē'/ *v., 3rd pers. sing./pl.*, left, to go away from one place to another

left **Điúdą** /thē-ü'-doⁿ/ *v.*, left, to leave a place or site in a clean condition

left **Ušt'é'** /ü-sht'ä'/ *n.*, left, left some items still there, refers to leaving food on the table, clothing on sale, or anything that can be bought, usu. things in short supply

left behind **Ádiudà** /ä'-thē-ü-doⁿ/ *adv.*, left behind, as in being present when all have left a place that was once crowded and is now empty of people, but clean and clear of debris

left handed **Đá't'a** /thä'-t'ä/ *adj.*, left handed, the dominant use of the left hand, anything done with the left hand

left out **Udúdįgè** /ü-thü'-thēⁿ-gä'/ *v.*, to be left out of something, usu. distribution of food or material goods

leftovers **Údaštè** /ü'-thä-shtä'/ *n.*, leftovers, usu. food that is uneaten at a feast and taken home to be eaten later

left side **Đá't'àt'adišà** /thä'-t'ä-t'ä-thē-shoⁿ'/ *adj.*, left side, toward the left of a person

leg **Žíbe** /zhē'-bä/ *n.*, leg, a limb of a human being used for walking, standing, etc.; also a limb of other animals

leg ache **Žíbe ni'é** /zhē'-bä nē-ä'/ *n.*, leg ache, usu. refers to overuse of the legs, namely, by children

leggings **Há'utà** /hä'-ü-toⁿ'/ *n.*, leggings, men's leather leggings, usu. made from the skin of a deer; two pieces of clothing that covered the legs of men like the legs of trousers

lemon **Šézi niúdiškì** /shä'-zē nēü-thē-shkē'/ *n.*, lemon, a small oval-shaped, bitter-tasting fruit, genus *Citrus* of the family Rutaceae (*šézi niúdiškì hì*, lemon tree)

length **Đetą́** /thä-toⁿ'/ *n.*, length, extent of distance from here to there; an estimated ~, as in "this long"

lesbian **Mixúga waù** /mē-xü'-gä wä-ü'/ *n.*, lesbian, a female homosexual; homosexual, refers to a female who feels sexually attracted to another female

lessen **Đihébe** /thē-hä'-bä/ *v.*, to lessen, to decrease or minimize

let **-akidé** /ä-kē-thä'/ *v., suffix*, let, consent to (*Heđúškà wačígaxè* ~, I ~ him Heđúškà dance)

letter **Wabáxu** /wä-bä'-xü/ *n.*, letter, mail, correspondence, communication between people and businesses through the written page or letter; now also refers to email

lettuce **Mąščíge wadatè** /moⁿsh-chēⁿ'-gä wä-thä-tä'/ *n.*, lettuce, an edible broadleaf vegetable (~ is considered rabbit food)

level **Bdáda** /bthä'-thä/ *adj.*, level, being horizontal, something that is even with the ground—the Niobrara River in Nebraska, e.g., is called Niúbdáda because of its flat or level appearance in the landscape

level **Snásną** /snoⁿ'-snoⁿ/ *adj.*, level, usu. refers to topography of flatlands

library **Wabáxu wádadè ut'í'** /wä-bä'-xü wä'-thä-dä ü-t'ē'/ *n.*, library, lit., reading house, library

Library of Congress **I't'í'gąde'àt'à wabáxu ité'daikè t'í** /ē-t'ē'-goⁿ-thä-ä'-t'ä' wä-bä-xü ē-tä'-thä-ē-kä' t'ē'/ *n.*, the Library of Congress in Washington DC

lick **Đasní'bè** /thä-snē'-bä/ *v.*, lick, to lick

lid **Wəágaxadè** /wə-ä'-gä-xä-dä'/ *n.*, lid, cover, cap; *iđágaxadè*, using something to cover something

lie **Đi'zwé žą́** /thē-zwä' zhoⁿ'/ *v.*, lie, to stay at rest in a horizontal position, to put oneself in a prostrate position on the ground or on a bed

lie **Íʼuʼsiʼštʼa̱** /ē'-ü-sē-sht'oⁿ/ v., lie, to fabricate, to say an untruth, to deceive, to make a false statement

lie **Ža̱ʼ** /zhoⁿ/ v., lie, lay, lain, the position of something that lies, such as a child's toy on a staircase

lied **Ídaúsiʼštʼa̱** /ē'-thä-ü-sē-sht'oⁿ/ v., 2nd pers. sing., pres. t., you fabricated a story, you lied

lie on **Áža̱** /ä'-zhoⁿ/ v., lie on, to lie upon something, such as a bed, a bench, or grass

life threatening **Úsa̱ga̱** /ü'-soⁿ-gä/ adj., 1. life threatening, refers to something that is dangerous and perilous (near the cliff, the car jumped the rail, causing a ~ situation) 2. critical, grave (very often used in relation to one who is critically ill or near death)

lift **Đihą́** /thē-hoⁿ'/ v., to lift, elevate, lift up, hoist

lift **Đimą́ši** /thē-moⁿ'-shē/ v., lift with the use of hands or with machinery, to lift something upward from a lower level to a higher level

light **Háhadè** /hä'-hä-dä/ adj., light, refers to weight — buoyant, feathery

light **Náka̱** /nä'-koⁿ/ n., light, bright, radiated light from a source such as a lightbulb

light **Náka̱dè** /nä'-koⁿ-thä/ v., light, to light a lamp, to turn the lights on

light **Ugá̱ba** /ü-goⁿ'-bä/ n., light, glow, luminosity, illumination, usu. relates to light conditions at dusk, refers to emission of light in conditions of semidarkness to darkness, early or late light of the day

light **Unágabà** /ü-nä'-goⁿ-bä/ n., light, a light coming from some source, causing illumination in a room, a building, or an open area

lightning **Đią́ba** /thē-oⁿm'-bä/ n., lightning, a flash of light in the sky when there is a thunderstorm

lightning bug **Wanáxa̱xà** /wä-nä'-xoⁿ-xoⁿ/ n., lightning bug, firefly, a winged beetle of the family Lampyridae

light post **Náka̱ ímuzà** /nä-koⁿ ē'-mü-zä/ n., light post, usu. refers to streetlights, yard lights

like **Xʼčáde** /x'chä-thä/ v., like, to be more expressive in a gentler form, to like someone or something; *xtʼáwadè*, I like (somebody or something)

like **Xtʼáde** /xt'ä-thä/ v., like, to be fond of another person or thing, to be partial to something; *xtʼáde*, I like; *i̱xtʼama̱ži̱*, I don't like; *đíxtʼaži̱*, you don't like; *xtʼádaži̱*, he/she/it doesn't like; *wéʼxtʼabaxì*, they don't like us

likeable **Úʼxtʼadè** /ü'-xt'ä-thä/ adj., likeable, something that is pleasant or attractive to somebody

like this **Đéga̱** /thä'-goⁿ/ adv., like this, like so, as in *déga̱ gáxaga̱*, do it in this manner

limbs **Ža̱ʼgaxà** /zhoⁿ'-gä-xä/ n., limbs, the branches that extend up and outward from the main body of a tree

Lincoln NE **Niskíʼde tʼa̱wa̱gda̱** /nē-skē'-thä t'oⁿ-woⁿ-gthoⁿ'/ n., Lincoln, Nebraska, lit., salt city (The city was so named because of the salt plains found nearby.)

lion **Wanítʼa wáxa** /wä-nē'-t'ä wä-xä/ n., African lion *Panthera leo*, a large cat that has a yellow coat; the male members have a shaggy mane that is often referred to by the Ponca as *pʼátʼa hi̱ škubè*, thick haired in the front

lips **Íha** /ē'-hä/ n., lips (The upper and lower lips are referred to as labium superius oris and labium inferius oris, respectively.)

lipstick **Íha ížidedè** /ē'-hä ē'-zhē-dä-thä/ n., lipstick, a cosmetic product of varied colors applied to the lips

listen **Áʼna̱ʼa̱** /ä'-noⁿ-oⁿ/ v., listen, to listen

or hear, being attentive and mindful when another offers advice; paying serious attention to another

listen **Í'e ák'iną'ą̀** /ē'-ā ä'-k'ē-noⁿ-oⁿ/ *v.*, listen, when two or more persons or entities listen to each other in seriousness

listless **Xp'éga** /xp'ā'-gä/ *adj.*, listless, pallid, languid

little **Hé'ga** /hā'-gä/ *adj.*, little, a small amount, usu. refers to a small amount of things

little **Žįgá** /zhēⁿ-gä/ *adj.*, little, small, 1. small in stature, height 2. small in size 3. may refer to children as in *žįgá mà*, the little ones

little bit **Hegá** /hā-gä/ *pron.*, little bit, a small amount of something

Little Dipper **Míxa sì žįgà** /mē'-xä sē' zhēⁿ-gä/ *n.*, Little Dipper (*Ursa Minor*), lit., little duck's feet, seven stars resembling a duck's feet

little father **Įdá'di'žįgà** /ēⁿ-dä'-dē-zhēⁿ-gä/ *n.*, little father (man or woman saying, my ~) (In the patrilineal kinship system of the Ponca, one designates one's father's younger brother as "little father")

little finger **Nąbéhi užįgà** /noⁿ-bā'-hē ü-zhēⁿ'-gä/ (*masc./fem.*) (**Nąbúhu žįga** /noⁿ-bü'-hü zhēⁿ'-gä/ [*masc.*]) *n.*, little finger

little mother **Ínahà'žįgà** /ē'-nä-hä'-zhēⁿ-gä/ *n.*, little mother (man or woman saying, my ~) (In the patrilineal kinship system of the Ponca, one designates one's mother's younger sister or one's mother's brother's daughter as "little mother.")

little toe **Sip'áhi užįga** /sē-p'ä'-hē ü-zhēⁿ-gä/ (*masc./fem.*) (**Sip'úhu žįga** /sē-p'ü'-hü zhēⁿ'-gä/ [*masc.*]) *n.*, little toe

live in **Wamáhe** /wä-moⁿ'-hä/ *v.*, to live temporarily with some other family at their expense, but with willingness to help in the household work or expenses

live on **Nądáha** /noⁿ-dä'-hä/ *v.*, live on, live on well, a spiritual word that connotes hope for individual(s) to carry on their lives with good health, emotional stability, and prosperity

liver **P'í'** /p'ē'/ *n.*, liver, a vital organ of humans and some animals

liver **T'e'p'ì** /t'ā-p'ē'/ *n.*, *archaic*, liver, lit., bison liver, *t'é*, bison, *p'í*, liver; now applies to domestic cattle and other mammals

livestock **Wanágde** /wä-nä'-gthä/ *n.*, livestock, farm animals, domestic animals

lizard **P'izá'nik'à** /p'ē-zä'-nē-k'ä'/ *n.*, lizard, suborder Lacertilia, includes gecko, chameleon, etc.

loan **Ú'i'** /ü'-ē/ *v.*, loan, to loan or advance money to somebody; *ú'i*, *v.*, *past t.*, give, to loan or present something to somebody

lock **Ánąsè** /ä'-noⁿ-sä/ *v.*, lock, to prevent use by unauthorized persons; to stop something from passing through, as in turning the water off

lock **Udídą** /ü-thē'-doⁿ/ *v.*, lock, to fasten or secure with a latch

locus **Đé anážįtè** /thā' ä-noⁿ-zhēⁿ-tā/ *n.*, locus, lit., "here I stand" (In ancient Ponca philosophy, an individual sees his/her position at the center of all things created, so his/her position in the universe is at the center, below the zenith and above the nadir. However, he/she oftens says in communications with the Creator, *Ebé bđį máži*, I am nothing/nobody.)

lodge **T'iúdip'ù snedé** /t'ēü'-thē-p'ü' snä-dä'/ *n.*, lodge, a large, elongated structure used for meetings or ceremonies for larger groups (The original covering for the lodge was bison hides, now it is canvas.)

log **Žą́ t'ągà** /zhoⁿ' t'oⁿ-gä/ *n.*, log, the large part of a tree, trunk of the tree, a large limb

loin **T'egá** /t'ā-gä/ (**T'eyá** /t'ā-yä'/) *n.*, loin,

a prime cut of tender meat taken from the backbone and rib area of a bovine animal, also called *t'é'nák'ak'à*

lonesome **Útihà** /ü'-tē-hä/ *adj.*, lonesome, forlorn

long **Snedé** /snä-dä'/ *adj.*, long, lengthy, extended, elongated

long ago **P'ahą́'gadì** /p'ä-hon'-gä-dē'/ *n.*, long ago, at the beginning, start, first

long for **Éskąnà** /ā'-skon'-non'/ *v.*, long for, longed, wished

long time **K'áši** /k'ä'-shē/ *n.*, long time, a lengthy period of time, ages, for years and years

long-winded **Éya snedè** /ā'-yä snä-dä/ *adj.*, long-winded, overtalkative, verbose

look at **Ábanà** /ä'-bä-non'/ *v.*, *sing.*, to look at or gaze at an individual person or thing

look cross **Đixúxu** /thē-xü'-xü/ *v.*, look cross, to make an unpleasant face

looking **Udíxidè** /ü-thē'-xē-dä/ *v.*, looking, looking at something or viewing the horizon for something

lookout **Ú'wadąbè** /ü'-wä-don-bä/ *n.*, lookout, sentry, sentinel

loose fitting **Ugáxdá'xdà** /ü-gä'-xthä'-xthä'/ *adj.*, loose fitting, baggy, saggy, clothing that is not tight fitting

loosen **Udíxdaxdà** /ü-thē'-xthä-xthä'/ *adj./v.*, loosen, to loosen something, such as a rope, a belt, a screw

lopsided **Ádikà** /ä'-thē-kon/ *adj.*, lopsided, uneven, unbalanced

lose **Ú'hiażì** /ü'-hēä-zhē'/ *v.*, lose, be defeated in a game, to not win any money

lose **Uxp'áde** /üx-p'ä'-thä/ *v.*, lose, misplace something, mislay, not be able to find something; *uxp'ádeadè*, I lost it; *uxp'ádedadè*, you lost it; *uxp'ádegidaì*, he/she/they lost it

lots of **T'ą́** /t'on'/ *adj.*, lots of, many, masses of, large number of

lotion **Nąbé ísnadè** /non-bä' ē'-snä-thä'/ *n.*, lotion, usu. refers to women's hand and body lotions to smooth, moisturize, and soften the skin

loudly **Đahé'gażì** /thä-hä'-gä-zhē'/ *adv.*, loudly, to voice words loudly or deafeningly in order to be heard above other sounds

loudly **Đasági** /thä-sä'-gē/ *adv.*, loudly, usu. refers to words that are strong enough to make an impression on another or a group (Term also describes scolding children.)

love **Dą́dè** /don'-thä/ *v.*, love, expression of extreme love or liking for a man or woman or between a boy and girl; a love or liking of a person that interferes with other matters in life

love **Đaéde** /thä-ä'-thä/ *n.*, love, 1. agape love (God love) 2. philia love (love for family, friends, etc.)

love **P'ídè** /p'ē'-thä/ *n.*, love between husband and wife (closer to eros love)

lower **Đihí·de** /thē-hē'·-dä/ *v.*, lower, let down, refers to lowering a thing or dimming the light, as in *nákąkè, đihídagà*, turn the light down

lower **Hídedéde** /hē'-dä-thä'-thä/ *v.*, lower, lowering something with some sort of device

lower arm **Á'hidè'** /ä'-hē-dä'/ *n.*, lower arm, forearm, that part of the arm where the ulna and radius are located

Lower Brule **Kúda wičáša** /kü'-dä wē-chä'-shä/ *n.*, Lower Brule Band of the Dakota Nation

lubricate **Snáde** /snä'-thä/ *v.*, lubricate, oil or grease something; *wésnadè*, lubricant

lucky **Gížu** /gē'-zhü/ *adj.*, lucky, good fortune

ludicrous **Á·dinà** /on'·-thē-non'/ *adj.*, ludicrous, absurd, ridiculous, nonsensical, laughable, as in something obviously absurd

lukewarm **Nášta** /nä'-shtä/ *adj.*, lukewarm, usu. refers to water or a drink; tepid

lullaby **Xéxe** /xā'-xā/ *n./v.*, lullaby, to hum a repeated note to babies, lulling them to sleep (The Ponca mother usu. carries or rocks her baby in her arms and hums quietly and repeatly, "Ha-ú-ú-ú-ú-ú," until her baby sleeps.)

lumpy **Bažúžu** /bä-zhü'-zhü/ *adj.*, lumpy, like something having lumps, not smooth or even

lungs **Đáxe** /thä'-xā/ *n.*, lungs, the two organs that breath is taken into; *t'é'đáxè*, bison or bovine lungs

M

machine **Wéđihidè** /wā'-thē-hē-dā'/ *n.*, machine, mechanism, engine, contraption

maggot **Wagđí'** /wä-gthē'/ *n.*, maggot, larva of a fly of the order Diptera, more often applied to flies of the suborder Brachycern, or houseflies

magic **Wađíp'i** /wä-thē'-p'ē/ *n.*, magic, the supernatural; *v.*, connotes the ability to be creative or inventive

magpie **Mągí'xt'à't'ągà** /moⁿ-gē'-xt'ä'-t'oⁿ-gä'/ *n.*, magpie, a bird of the genus *Pica*; ~ *áhįšut'à* or *įbe snedè*, magpie (A bird of the crow family with black and white feathers and a long, wedge-shaped tail.)

maiden **Šémižįgà** /shä'-mē-zhēⁿ-gä'/ *n.*, maiden, a young girl

mailbox **Wabáxu ugđè** /wä-bä'-xu ü-gthäⁿ'/ *n.*, mailbox, a rural mailbox or post office mailbox

mail carrier **Wabáxu'į** /wä-bä'-xü-ēⁿ'/ *n.*, mail carrier, lit., one who carries paper

make **Gáxe** /gä'-xā/ *v.*, make, to make; *p'áxe*, I made; *škáxe*, you made; *gáxaì*, he made

make **Gáxe'** /gä'-xā/ *v.*, make, to make, cre-ate; *p'áxe*, I made; *škáxe*, you made; *gáxaì*, he made

make cry **Xéde** /xā'-thā/ *v.*, make cry, cause to weep, sob, whimper, shed tears; *xéwađè*, to make them cry (*isága etái đįkè xé'đaì*, he made his little brother cry)

make faces **P'ađį́šį** /p'ä-thēⁿ'-shēⁿ/ *v.*, make faces, lit., to crimp up the nose, to twist or contort the face to take on an unnatural or grotesque shape

male **Nugá** /nü-gä'/ *adj.*, 1. male, relates to the sex that produces sperm to fertilize female eggs 2. proper male name in the Mąk'ą́ clan of the Ponca people

mallard **Míxa p'áhį t'ú'** /mē'-xä p'ä'-hēⁿ t'ü'/ *n.*, mallard, a wild male duck that has a dark green head with a white ring around its neck

mama's boy **Įhầt'ągà** /ēⁿ-hoⁿ'-t'oⁿ-gä'/ *adj./n.*, mama's boy, a little boy or teenage boy who clings to his mother (The term does not relate to the Freudian oedipus complex. A boy may also cling to his father in the same manner.)

mama's girl **Įhầt'ągà** /ēⁿ-hoⁿ'-t'oⁿ-gä'/ *adj./n.*, mama's girl, a little girl or teenage girl who clings to her mother (The term does not relate to the Freudian electra complex. A girl may also be close to her father in the same manner.)

man **Nú'** /nü'/ *n.*, 1. man 2. potato, a root vegetable; *nú' skíde*, sweet potato

manage **Nągedè** /noⁿ'-gä-thä'/ *v.*, manage, oversee, 1. to manage a business 2. to direct a religious ceremony or service

manager **Wé'nudąhągà** /wā'-nü-doⁿ-hoⁿ-gä'/ *n.*, manager, director, supervisor, boss (A new term at the beginning of the twentieth century that is a derivative of the term for war leader, *nudáhągà*.)

Mandan **Mawádanì** /mä-wä'-dä-nē'/ *n.*, the Mandan Tribe of Native Americans

mane **T'ahį́** /t'ä-hēⁿ'/ *n.*, mane, the long hair that grows around the neck and head of certain animals, such as horses and lions

manner **Gą́'** /goⁿ'/ *n.*, manner, a way of doing something, a method or style; *égą*, in that manner

many **Áhigè** /ä'-hē-gä'/ *adj.*, many, lot of, plentiful

map **Mą̨žą́baxù** /moⁿ-zhoⁿ'-bä-xü'/ *n.*, map, lit., land drawing; mapping

marble **Į́'e gajabè** /ēⁿ'-ä gä-jä-bä'/ *n.*, marble, a small glass ball used in a game of marbles

March **Míxa agdáikedì** /mē'-xä ä-gthä'-ē-kä-dē'/ *n.*, March, lit., when the waterfowl returns home, the third month in the year (The elders also used *įštá ukiadà*, sore eyes [caused by snow glare].)

mare **Šą́ge migà** /shoⁿ'-gä mē-gä'/ *n.*, mare, adult female horse

mark **Ábaxù** /ä'-bä-xü'/ *v.*, mark, in the sense of marking upon something, such as paper or any other surface

mark **Baxú** /bä-xü'/ *v.*, mark, to ~ a line or make a visible impression on the surface of something

marrow **Wažíbe** /wä-zhē'-bä/ *n.*, marrow, lit. that of the leg, the tissue that is found in the interior of bones (Following the bison hunt the leg bone of the animal was roasted on live coals for the marrow.)

marry **Mí'gdą̀** /mē'-gthoⁿ'/ *v.*, married—used in regard to men

marry **Wá'dixè** /wä'-thē-xä'/ *v.*, married—used in regard to women

mash **Baxdíxdi** /bä-xthē'-xthē'/ *v.*, mash, usu. refers to food, as in potato salad or a purée

mask **Įdéugdą̀** /ēⁿ-dä'-ü-gthoⁿ'/ *n.*, mask, usu. refers to using a mask at a masquerade

match **Égidà** /ä'-gē-dä'/ *v.*, match, match with something or somebody, combine well with something; *égijà*, matching with something or somebody cute

matches **P'éde** /p'ä'-dä/ *n.*, matches, a small stick made of wood or hard paper coated on one end with a combustible substance and used to start fires

mating **K'ídixè** /k'ē'-thē-xä'/ *v.*, mating, in the case of horses, when a mare is sexually receptive toward a stallion and physically prepared for conception

matrimony **Wádixè úšką̀** /wä'-thē-xä' ü'sh-koⁿ'/ *n.*, matrimony, used in regard to women preparing for wedding nuptials

matrimony **Wagdą́ úškà** /wä-gthoⁿ' ü'sh-koⁿ'/ *n.*, matrimony, wedding, nuptials, marriage ceremony—used in regard to men

May **Mé' p'ahága** /mā' p'ä-hoⁿ'-gä/ *n.*, May, lit., the beginning of summer, the fifth month in the year

me **-bdį́'** /bthēⁿ'/ *pron./suffix*, me, commonly used with *wiʃbdį*, it's ~, or *é·bdį̀*, it's ~

me **Wí** /wē'/ *pron.*, me, my, myself

meadowlark **T'áč'inįgè** /t'ä'-ch-ē-nēⁿ-gä'/ (**T'áč'idįgè** /t'ä'-ch-ē-thēⁿ-gä'/) *n.*, meadowlark, a bird belonging to the genus *Sturnella*, a grassland bird

mean **Mą̨dą́ xdí't'ù** /moⁿ-thoⁿ' xthē'-t'ü'/ *adj.*, mean, to be malicious underhandedly, secretly, and sneakily

mean **Xdí't'ù** /xthē'-t'ü'/ *adj.*, mean; small-minded, ill-tempered, malicious

meanwhile **Éditedądì** /ā-dē'-tä-thoⁿ-dē'/ *adv.*, meanwhile, at that time, during that period

measles **Žuži'dè** /zhü-zhē'-dä/ *n.*, measles, also called rubeola

measure **Wé'gązè** /wā'-goⁿ-zä'/ *n.*, measure, a system for determining the size, length, or extent of something, such as feet, yards, miles, pounds, bushels, acres

meat **T'anúka** /t'ä-nü'-kä/ *n.*, meat, 1. edible

animal flesh, namely, beef, pork, etc. 2. a proper male name in the Hísadà clan of the Ponca people

meaty **T'a'žu** /t'ä-zhü/ *adj.*, meaty

medical treatment **Wazék'igdixè** /wä-zä'-k'ē-gthē-xä/ *n.*, medical treatment, seeking medical aid from medical practitioners; *wazék'idè*, to treat oneself for some sickness, as in taking aspirin for a headache

medicine **Mąk'ą́** /moⁿ-k'oⁿ/ *n.*, medicine, drug, tablet, pill, medication

meet **Ák'ip'à** /ä-k'ē-p'ä'/ *v.*, meet, encounter, meet up with; *á'ak'ip'à*, 1st pers. sing., past part., I met

meet **Ák'ip'anà** /ä-k'ē-p'ä-noⁿ'/ *v.*, meet, coming toward each other on the path or roadway

meeting **Gahí'e** /gä-hē'-ä/ *n.*, meeting, talks, consultation; a committee coming together to discuss some topic or topics, usu. in a formal setting (The word probably is a derivative of *gaíye*.)

melon **Đáxe** /thä'-xä/ *n.*, melon, the edible, fleshy part of the melon, of the family Cucurbitaceae

melt **Náskà** /nä-skoⁿ/ *v.*, melt, usu. refers to something unfreezing, as in ice changing to water; to change from a solid to a liquid state, esp. by heating

member **Uwíhe** /ü-wē'-hä/ *n.*, member, an associate, a constituent

memorable **Sídewadè** /sē'-thä-wä-thä'/ *adj.*, memorable, something that is unforgettable

mentally deficient **Uxdéá'ži** /ü-xthä'-ä'-zhē/ *n.*, mentally deficient, ca. early twentieth century, having a disability such as Down's syndrome

merciful **Wadáedè** /wä-thä'-ä-thä'/ *adj.*, merciful, expressing or showing mercy and compassion

merit **Ugíket'ą̀** /ü-gē'-kä-t'oⁿ'/ *n.*, merit, the right to claim something accomplished, deserving respect and commendation

mescal bean **Wasé'židè** /wä-sä'-zhē-dä/ *n.*, mescal bean, 1. a red-berry-producing tree found in the southern dry, arid lands; the berries were used as decorative beads on bandoliers 2. decorations made from the mescal bean, usu. hardened by heat

messy **Čáza** /chä'-zä/ *adj.*, messy, untidy, cluttered, in disarray

messy hair **Záde** /zä'-dä/ *adj./n.*, messy hair, loose hair strands, mussed-up hair, rumpled hair

metal **Mą́ze** /moⁿ'-zä/ *n.*, metal, iron

meteorite **Miká'e uxp'áde** /mē-k'ä'-ä üx-p'ä'-thä/ *n.*, meteorite, 1. a meteorite on the ground 2. a meteorite falling (The one significant meteorite known to the Ponca was located in the area of Keyapaha, South Dakota. It was call *į́'ę dihą́dądì*, which was also the name of a temporary village site for games. The location was called *į́'ę dihą́dądì*. The term means "where they lifted the rock.")

meteor shower **Mikáe uxp'ádetedądì** /mē-kä'-ä üx-p'ä'-thä-tä-thoⁿ-dē'/ *n.*, meteor shower (Refers to the great meteor shower that occured ca. 1833. That date was often used as a mark of time for various events, such as birth dates that occurred before or after the meteor shower. The Ponca named a village site for that celestial event.)

Mexican **Špáí'úni** /shpäē'-ü'-nē/ *n.*, Mexican, corruption of *Spaniard*, a native or inhabitant of Mexico

mice and rats **Ičą́ga** /ē-choⁿ'-gä/ *n.*, general term for mice and rats

microwave oven **Úhą'kudè** /ü'-hoⁿ-kü-thä'/ *n.*, microwave oven

mid **-usk'ą́ska** /ü-sk'oⁿ'-skä/ *adj.*, *suffix.*, mid, time of day, month, or year

middle **Udízɑdi** /ü-thē'-zoⁿ-dē/ *adj./n.*,
middle, the center, the core of something
or a group

middle **Udízɑt'adišɑ̨** /ü-thē'-zoⁿ-t'ä-thē-
shoⁿ'/ *prep. phr.*, middle, toward the ~

middle **Udízɑt'atɑ̨** /ü-thē'-zoⁿ-t'ä-toⁿ'/ *prep.
phr.*, middle, from the ~

middle finger **Nɑbé'wé'dabdì** /noⁿ-bā'-wä-
thä-bthē'/ *n.*, middle finger, third finger

middle toe **Sip'áhi udízɑ̨** /sē-p'ä'-hē ü-thē'-
zoⁿ/ *n.*, middle toe

midnight **Hɑ̨'uskɑ́ska** /hoⁿ'-ü-skoⁿ'-skä/ *n.*,
midnight, twelve o'clock at night

midsummer **Nugé'úskɑ́'skà** /nü-gä'-ü'-skoⁿ'-
skä'/ *n.*, midsummer, summer solstice, usu.
refers to the longest day of the year

midwinter **Má'dè'uskɑ́skà** /mä'-thä'-ü-skoⁿ'-
skä'/ *n.*, midwinter, winter solstice, usu.
refers to the shortest day of the year

midfall **T'ɑ̨gaxdɑ̨'uskɑ́skà** /t'oⁿ'-gä-xthoⁿ'-ü-
skoⁿ'-skä'/ *n.*, midfall, in the middle of fall

might **Sabáži** /sä-bä'-zhē/ *v.*, might, may, possibly, could, something that ~ happen in the
future

mildew **Usésɑ̨** /ü-sä'-soⁿ/ *n.*, mildew, something that spoils or turns to mold or fungi

milk **Mɑzé'ni** /moⁿ-zä'-nē/ *n.*, milk

milkweed **Waxdá** /wä-xthä'/ *n.*, milkweed,
a flowering plant that secretes a milky
substance

Milky Way **Wakɑ́'užɑ́ge** /wä-koⁿ'-ü-zhoⁿ'-gä/
n., Milky Way, a myriad of stars, the galaxy
that contains our solar system

mill **Wédit'ubè** /wä'-thē-t'ü-bä'/ *n.*, mill, a
device that breaks down larger or harder
pieces of materials into smaller bits; *archaic*, a term for a hand coffee grinder or
machinery for grinding grain

milled **Udít'ubè** /ü-thē'-t'ü-bä'/ *v.*, to be
milled, pulverized, or broken into pieces,
usu. refers hardened or dried food

mimic **Wégaskɑdè** /wä'-gä-skoⁿ-thä'/ *v.*, mimic,
to imitate something someone did, usu. to
mimic somebody's voice and gestures in a
deliberate or exaggerated way to amuse

mine **Wít'a** /wē-t'ä/ *pron.*, *sing.*, mine, something belonging to oneself; *pl./emphatic*,
wíwít'a, they are mine

minister **Wakɑ́da wadahɑ̨ níkašigà** /wä-
k'oⁿ'-dä wä-thä-hoⁿ' nē'-kä-shē-gä'/ *n.*, minister, 1. one who is authorized or ordained
by church authorities to conduct religious
worship, administer the holy sacraments,
and teach the beliefs of the Christian
church and is usu. referred to as the pastor
or member of the clergy 2.the laity

mink **T'ašɪ́ge** /t'ä-shēⁿ'-gä/ *n.*, mink, a carnivorous member of the family Mustelidae

minuscule **Žɪ̨áxčɪ̨** /zhēⁿ-ä'-xchēⁿ'/ *adj.*, minuscule, very small, tiny, minute

mirror **Níú'k'igdas'ɪ̨** /nē'-ü-k'ē-gthä-s-ēⁿ'/
n., mirror, lit., look into the water at self,
reflect

misbehave **Wás'pažì** /wä's-pä-zhē'/ *v.*, misbehave, to behave inappropriately, esp.
being naughty, bad, acting up

mischievous **Nɑxíde dɪge** /noⁿ-xē'-dä thēⁿ-
gä'/ *adj.*, mischievous, lit., has no ear, behaves badly, does not listen to good advice

miser **Niášigà waníte** /nēä'-shē-gä' wä-nē'-
tä/ *n.*, miser, somebody who is stingy, not
generous, tight

miserable **Gít'exì** /gē'-t'ä-xē'/ *adj.*, miserable,
an uneasy feeling that precedes becoming
ill; *ɑdɑ́gít'exì*, personally feeling bad, as
in after eating something disagreeable;
í'git'exì, as in, he's not feeling well after he
ate that food

mislead **Úšɪ̨** /ü'-shēⁿ/ *v.*, mislead, an honest
comment or thought to cause oneself or
someone else to think or believe something
that is not true

mislead self **Úʼšįʼkʼidè** /ü-shēⁿ-kʼē-thā′/ *v.*, mislead oneself, to deceive oneself, to think that something was as one thought it to be even though it was not

miss **Gašną** /gä-shnoⁿ′/ *v.*, miss, failing to hit something with something in the hands or with the hand, as when using a bat to try to hit a ball

miss **Múšną** /mü-shnoⁿ′/ *v.*, miss, to fail to hit a target with a gun, bow and arrow, or stone; *muášną*, *pers. pron.*, I missed the target

miss **Nąšną** /noⁿ-shnoⁿ′/ *v.*, miss, usu. 1. refers to missing the correct passageway or roadway 2. misalignment of two or more boards or poles when building a structure

Missouria **Níʼutʼási** /nē-ü-tʼä′-sē/ *n.*, Missouria, the Missouria Tribe of Native Americans

mistake **Mąnądį** /moⁿ-noⁿ′-thēⁿ/ *v.*, mistake, 1. wrongly understood, wrong or incorrect in understanding, perception, or opinion of a thing or idea 2. to do something unintentionally 3. wander away

mistaken **Anąbdì** /ä-noⁿ′-bthē′/ *v.*, *1st pers. sing.*, mistaken, I am (was) mistaken

mistaken **Awąnądì** /oⁿ-woⁿ′-noⁿ-thē′/ *v.*, *1st pers. pl.*, mistaken, we are (were) mistaken

mistaken **Đanąnì** /thä-noⁿ′-nē′/ *v.*, *2nd pers. sing.*, mistaken, you are (were) mistaken

mistaken **Đanąnį** /thä-noⁿ′-nē-ēⁿ′/ *v.*, *2nd pers. pl.*, mistaken, you all are (were) mistaken

mistaken **Mąnániáčą** /moⁿ-noⁿ′-nē-ä′-choⁿ′/ *v.*, mistaken, "you are badly ~"

mistaken **Nądį** /noⁿ′-thēⁿ/ *v.*, *3rd pers. sing./pl.*, he/she/it/they (was/were) mistaken

mistaken **Xé·** /xä′·/ *interj.*, mistaken, a woman's vocal intonation indicative of a feeling of being mistaken

mistaken **Xénahà** /xä′-nä-hä′/ *interj.*, mistaken, a man's vocal intonation indicative of a feeling of being mistaken

mistreat **Ágdaʼadį** /ä′-gthä-ä-thēⁿ′/ *v.*, mistreat, abuse somebody, treat badly; *ágdawádį*, 1. treated them badly, as in prisoners 2. to be beating the other team or winning by a large score in sports

mix **Íʼkʼidibdą** /ē′-kʼē-thē-bthoⁿ′/ *v.*, mix, to make a mixture or to combine things into one mass or collection of things

moan **Ígatʼą** /ē′-gä-tʼoⁿ′/ *v.*, moan in pain because of some illness or injury

moccasins **Hįbéʼukédį** /hēⁿ-bä-ü-kä-thēⁿ/ *n.*, moccasins, Native American "shoe" made of deerskin or other soft leather from moose and elk; the soles were made from the tough hide of the bison

mock **Íʼgązè** /ē′-goⁿ-zä′/ *v.*, mock, ridicule or make fun of

molars **Híʼutʼága** /hē′-ü-tʼoⁿ′-gä/ *n.*, molars, twelve large back teeth used for chewing and grinding food

mole **Mądíga** /moⁿ-thēⁿ′-gä/ *n.*, mole, a small burrowing animal that lives underground, digging tunnels in search of food

Monday **Ábaʼwaxúbe dištʼáki** /oⁿm-bä-wä-xü′-bä thē-shtʼoⁿ′-kē/ *n.*, Monday, the second day of the week, the day after holy day, Sunday

money **Mázeʼskà** /moⁿ′-zä-skä′/ *n.*, money, lit., white metal, currency

monkey **Éʼštʼínikè** /ä′-shtʼē′-nē-kä′/ *n.*, monkey, refers to some primates that have tails or are tailless (It is thought that the original Ponca term referred to the North American river otter, *Lontra canadensis*, because of its playful behavior. Hence the term *éʼštʼínikè*, so, that's the way you are.)

month **Míʼ** /mē′/ *n.*, month, 1. the period between new moons 2. a month as calculated according to the Gregorian calendar moodiness **É'št'eą̀'ą̀** /ā'-sht'ā-oⁿ'-oⁿ'/ *n.*, moodiness, inconstancy, instability

moon **Nią́ba** /nē-oⁿ'-bä/ *n.*, moon, the natural satellite of earth

Moonhead **Nią́ba wédixdì** /nē-oⁿ'-bä wā'-thē'-xthē'/ *n.*, Moonhead, spiritual leader of the Caddo Tribe of Native Americans, known primarily by the Osage Tribe of Native Americans

moonlight **Nią́ba** /nē-oⁿ'-bä/ *n.*, moonlight, light from the sun that strikes the surface of the moon and is reflected to earth

mop **T'í'ídiz̧à** /t'ē'-ē'-thē-zhä/ *n.*, mop, a house implement made of absorbent material to clean floors

more **Áhigidè** /ä'-hē-gē-thä/ *adj.*, more, somebody adding or saving an additional amount of something

more **Á'ki'hą̀** /ä'-kē-hoⁿ/ *adj.*, 1. more, additional 2. further, go farther on

morel **Mikáexdì** /mē-kä'-ā-xthē'/ *n.*, morel, genus *Morchella*, a pitted, cone-shaped edible fungi (*morel* comes from *L. maurus*, meaning brown) usu. found in the early spring (Resembling the lining of the stomach, ~ is also called *t'eníxa ugdéže*. This term is believed to be of Omaha origin. The term *t'eníxa ugdéže*, in Ponca, refers to part of the stomach of the American bison.)

moreover **B'igúdidą̀dà** /b-ē-gü'-dē-thoⁿ-thoⁿ'/ *adv.*, moreover, furthermore, what is more, additionally

mores **Úšką̀** /ü'-shkoⁿ/ *n.*, mores, the ways of life or customs of a particular group of people that include habits, manners, moral attitudes, unwritten laws

Morman **Mǫmána** /mōⁿ-mä'-nä/ *n.*, Morman, a member of a religious sect saved by the Ponca (According to the elders, this group of people were starving and in "pitiful condition" when they came to the Ponca asking for help. The Ponca allowed them to stay on Ponca property for about two or three years, and then they went on their way.)

morning **Hą́'egačè** /hoⁿ'-ā-goⁿ-chä/ *n.*, *adj.*, morning, daybreak, sunup

mosquito **Náhą̧gè** /nä'-hoⁿ-gā'/ (**Đáhą̧gè** /thä'-hoⁿ-gā'/) *n.*, mosquito, a small flying insect that feeds on blood (The pronunciation of words such as this could vary from village to village. *Đáhą̧gè* is now used at the discretion of the speaker.)

mosquito net **Náhą̧gè uk'íą̧dè** /nä'-hoⁿ-gā' ü-k'ē'-oⁿ-thä/ *n.*, mosquito net, a thin netting used to cover a bed or window for protection against mosquitoes (alternative pronounciation, *Đáhą̧gè uk'íą̧dè* /thä'-hoⁿ-gā' ü-k'ē'-oⁿ-thä/)

mother **Ínahà** /ē'-nä-hä/ *n.*, *masc./fem.*, mother (my ~ is a caring person)

motherless **Íhą́ ḑigè** /ē'-hoⁿ' thēⁿ-gā'/ *adj.*, motherless, having no living mother or having no known mother

motion **Gayázazà** /gä-yä'-zä-zä/ *n.*, motion, something moving to and fro from the wind; *k'igdíyazazà*, causing oneself to rock or move steadily, as in a rocking chair

motion **Šką́** /shkoⁿ/ *v.*, motion, in motion, stir

motionless **Šką́'áz̧ì** /shkoⁿ'-ä-zhē/ *adj.*, motionless, still, at a standsill, stagnant, unmoving

mountain **P'ahé't'ą̧gà** /p'ä-hā'-t'oⁿ-gä/ *n.*, mountain, 1. the surface of the earth higher in elevation than a hill 2. proper male name in the Đíxidą̀ clan of the Ponca people

mountain lion **Įgdą́'si'snedè** /ēⁿ-gthoⁿ'-sē-snä-dä/ *n.*, mountain lion, cougar, puma

mourn **Gík'ą** /gē-k'oⁿ/ *v.*, mourn, to express sadness over somebody's death by weeping openly

mouse **Įčą́gaz̧įgà** /ēⁿ-choⁿ'-gä-zhēⁿ-gä/ *n.*, mouse, a small rodent

mouse beans **T'ǫ́deha hįbdíge** /t'oⁿ'-dā-hä hēⁿ-bthēⁿ'-gā/ *n.*, mouse beans, lit., ground beans, wild beans collected by rodents and stored in their burrows, which meant they were planted

mouth **Í'** /ē'/ *n.*, mouth, the oral cavity in which humans and animals take food

Mouth **Užá't'à** /ü-zhä'-t'ä'/ *n.*, The Mouth, a confluence of two rivers (This name is given to a geographic location on the Ponca reservation where the Saltfork River flows into the Arkansas River in Kay County, Oklahoma.)

mouthwash **Hí'ídižà** /hē'-ē'-thē-zhä'/ *n.*, mouthwash or mouth rinse, usu. a flavored antiseptic solution for cleansing the mouth and freshening the breath

mouthy **Íye'wadéga** /ē'-yā-wä-dä'-gä/ *adj./v.*, mouthy, refers to a person who speaks as though he/she knows everything yet speaks with shallow words

move **Wahą́** /wä-hoⁿ'/ *v.*, move, to relocate one's residence to another place

movement **Šką́'** /shkoⁿ'/ *n.*, movement, the act or process of body movement, usu. refers to a person lying down or in a sitting position

move over **Et'áha** /ā-t'ä'-hä/ *adv.*, move over, a function word that indicates position and distance, as in telling someone to move a little farther over or away (~ *gdíga*, ~ that way)

movies **Įdé'wabaxù'škà** /ēⁿ-dä'-wä-bä-xü'-shkoⁿ'/ *n.*, movies, lit., moving pictures

moving **Ágaxdè** /ä'-gä-xthä'/ *adj.*, moving, something or somebody moving with the current of the water or wind

mower **Mąhį́ ínąsède** /moⁿ-hēⁿ' ē'-noⁿ-sä'-thä/ *n.*, mower, a push mower or a gas-powered lawn mower

much **-čábe** /chä'-bä/ *adj.*, *suffix*, much; *usní-čabè*, much cold, very cold

much **He'gá'bažì** /hā-gä'-bä-zhē'/ *adj.*, much, lit., not a small amount or not a little

much **Íše** /ē'-shä/ *adj.*, much, usu. a large amount of something desirable to possess

mud **Mądí'xdi'bè** /moⁿ-thē'-xthē-bä'/ *n.*, mud, mud on shoes and clothing from walking on muddy paths

mud **Mąská'ska'be** /moⁿ-skä'-skä-bä/ *n.*, mud, muddy, sludge, mire

muddled **Đagdégdešnà** /thä-gthä'-gthä-shnä'/ *v.*, muddled, messed up, mixed up, refers to mixing the nature of stories or songs confusedly

muddy **Ubášudè** /ü-bä'-shü-dä/ *n.*, muddy, making muddy, usu. refers to something in liquid

mudhen **Đaxp'ą́'** /thä-xp'oⁿ'/ *n.*, mudhen, the American coot

mulberry **Mázi'žù** /mä'-zē-zhü/ *n.*, mulberry, a small, edible, sweet fruit

mulberry tree **Mázi'žùhì** /mä-zē-zhü-hē'/ *n.*, mulberry tree, genus *Morus* in the family Moraceae

mule **Nit'á't'ągà** /nē-t'ä'-t'oⁿ-gä/ *n.*, mule, the offspring of a horse and donkey that is sterile and has long ears and a short mane

mumps **Núde íba** /nü'-dä ē'-bä/ *n.*, mumps, also known as epidemic parotitis, noted by the swelling of the parotid glands

murder **Wat'ę́'de** /wä-t'äⁿ'-thä/ *v.*, murder, to murder; taking the life of another person

murky **Ušúde** /ü-shü'-dä/ *adj.*, murky, muddy, turbid

murmur **Íye tigdè** /ē'-yä tē-gthä'/ *n.*, murmur, something said quietly, as somebody speaking in a low, indistinct voice; more than a whisper

muscle **T'ak'ą́** /t'ä-k'oⁿ'/ *n.*, muscle, in anatomy, a muscle's main function is to produce body movement as well as movement of the internal organs

muscular **Wašką't'ągà** /wä-shkoⁿ-t'oⁿ-gä'/ *adj.*, muscular, being physically strong

mush **Wašą́ge** /wä-shoⁿ-gä/ *n.*, mush, ground corn cooked in water, a porridge

muskmelon **Sákadidè snúsnú** /sä-kä-thē-dä' snü'-snü'/ *n.*, muskmelon, a yellow or green fleshed, sweet-flavored fruit with a rough rind

muskrat **Sí'snejè'wagidè** /sē'-snā-jä'-wä-gē-thä'/ *n.*, muskrat, a large rodent living in and near water, *Ondatra zibethicus*

mussel **T'íhabà** /t'ē'-hä-bä'/ *n.*, mussel, a freshwater mollusk, a shell made round for use in costumes

mustache **Íhį̀** /ē'-hēⁿ'/ *n.*, mustache, the hair growth on a man's upper lip, usu. grown long to drape down on each side of the lips — now such hair is grown to trim and style

mustang **Šą́ge mąt'ąnąhà** /shoⁿ'-gä moⁿ-t'oⁿ-noⁿ-hä'/ *n.*, mustang, wild horse, descended from horses brought to this continent by the Spanish

mustard **Zí'** /zē'/ *n.*, mustard, the yellow powder from the seeds of the mustard plant, used as a condiment

mythological creature **Gisná** /gē-snä'/ *n.*, a mythological creature, said to have lived in a lake that never froze during the coldest months of the year and described as looking like a leech or bloodsucker

mythological creature **Įgdą́'** /ēⁿ-gthoⁿ'/ *n.*, a mythological creature that dwells in clouded, stormy skies (The word for the sound of thunder comes from the name of this astronomical creature.)

mythological creature **Mąną́diwadè** /moⁿ-noⁿ'-thē-wä-thä'/ *n.*, a mythological creature, lit., leads astray, a creature that has the appearance of a dwarf or midget who moves about during the early morning, at sundown, and on foggy days and who has powers to lead a person away

mythological creature **T'áxt'ì Waú'** /t'ä'-xt'ē'-wä-ü'/ *n.*, Deer Woman, 1. is described as being very pretty and entices young men by her enchantment 2. young men are not to give in to her or something would happen to them, such as sickness (A mythological female who was said to have followed the Ponca to Indian Territory in 1876 and was said to have been seen by men in remote, lonely places.)

mythological creature **Wak'ą́dagì** /wä-k'oⁿ'-dä-gē/ *n.*, a mythological creature that lived along the Missouri River, described as a water monster having a long body with horns on its head; *Wak'ą́dagi mąšą́de*, the dwelling place of the creature, a cavern somewhere along the Missouri River

N

nail **Ugádą** /ü-gä'-doⁿ/ *v.*, nail, to fasten on with; the process of using some sort of device to pound something into something else, such as a stake in the ground, a common nail into a board

nails **Mą́ze'udúgadą̀** /moⁿ'-zä-ü-thü'-gä-doⁿ'/ *n.*, nails

naked **Sídu'á'** /sē'-dü-ä'/ *adj.*, naked, nude; *hánuk'à*, naked, bare skinned; *nukádį̀*, unclothed

name **Ižáže** /ē-zhä'-zhā/ *n.*, name, a person's name, identity, as in a brand; *ižáže đadè*, to call the name of somebody at a gathering for some purpose; *ižáže'í*, to name somebody or something

name calling **Gdą́gdą** /gthoⁿ'-gthoⁿ/ *n.*, name calling, the use of offensive words toward another, usu. occuring in an argument

nape **P'á'hiugdè** /p'ä'-hē-ü-gthä'/ *n.*, nape,

back of the neck, the indented center in the back of the neck

narrow **Bdá'ze** /bthon'-zā/ *adj.*, narrow, thin, slender

narrow escape **Hádizàha** /hä'-thē-zä'-hä/ *n.*, narrow escape, just barely got away from danger or trouble

Narrow Grave **Míxe Bdáze** /mē'-xā bthon'-zā/ *n.*, Narrow Grave, an ancient village site near Ponca, Nebraska, where the Ponca people once lived

nasalize **Ðat'íze** /thä-t'ēn'-zā/ *n.*, nazalize, talk through the nose

nasal mucus **P'axdí'** /p'ä-xthen'/ *n.*, nasal mucus, phlegm, usu. caused by some sort of infection in the nose, throat, sinuses, or lungs, which are lined with mucous membranes

nasal passage **P'á'xdugè** /p'ä'-xthü-gā'/ *n.*, nasal passage, the interior parts of the nasal cavity

National Archives **I't'í'gade'àt'à wabáxu ité'daikè ut'í'** /ē-t'ē'-gon-thä-ä'-t'ä' wä-bä'-xü ē-tä'-thä-ē-kä' ü-t'ē'/ *n.*, the National Archives in Washington DC

nationality **Ukít'e** /ü-kē'-t'ā/ *n.*, nationality, tribe, race of people

Native American **Níkašigà'uké'di** /nē'-kä-shē-gä'-ü-kā'-thē'/ *n./adj.*, Native American, lit., common people, the indigenous people of North America (The term *Native American* has existed for many years, e.g., for the Native American Church, and is now commonly used in some public places and in modern writings beginning ca. 1970s. The term *Indian* is the original name Europeans gave to the inhabitants of North America; they used *Plain Indians* for those who lived on the Great Plains of America. *Indian* is still widely used by Native peoples.)

Native American Church **Makádatè** /mon-kon'-thä-tā'/ *n.*, lit., eats medicine, Native American Church

Native American traditional Christian hymns **Niášigà ukédi Wak'áda wádahà waá** /nē-ä'-shē-gä' ü-kä'-then wä-k'on'-dä wä'-thä-hon' wä-on'/ *n.*, Native American traditional Christian hymns, Native hymns composed by early Ponca Christians using ancient tunes applied to Christian principles

natural gas **T'adé'wégdi** /t'ä-dā'-wä'-gthē/ *n.*, natural gas, butane, propane (ca. twentieth century)

navel **Ðét'a** /thä'-t'ä/ *n.*, navel, umbilicus, or belly button, a small depression in the center of a person's belly where the umbilical cord detached after birth

near **Ešá'** /ā-shon'/ *adj/adv.*, near, close at hand, very close, adjacent

near **K'áge** /k'on'-gā/ *adv.*, near, usu. refers to the time of day—close to noon, almost night, near morning; approaching destination, as in ~ly there

nearby **Ubáhadì** /ü-bä'-hä-dē'/ *adv.*, nearby, refers to something placed near anything (*edéšta adíte ~ it'eda bike*, he put those things ~)

nearer **Dúdihà** /dü-dē-hä'/ *adv.*, this way, come closer, or draw near

nearly **Ádinà** /on'-thē-non'/ *adv.*, approximately, just about, nearly, not quite, came near

nearly new **Áwazì** /ä'-won-zhē'/ *adj.*, nearly new, refers to clothing that has hardly been worn

Nebraska **Ní' bdáska** /nē' bthä'-skä/ *n.*, Nebraska, the state of Nebraska (The name probably originated from the Ponca's name for the Platte River, Ní' bdáska, flat river, because the river was very often level with the topography in many places.)

neck **P'áhì** /p'ä'-hē/ *n.*, neck, that part of the animal or human body that connects the head to the trunk

neckerchief **Wadáge sábe** /wä-thä'-gä sä'-bā/ *n.*, neckerchief (Unlike cowboys, Ponca men wore a black scarf rolled up around the neck with the ends held together in the front with an ornament of some sort.)

necklace **Ú'wį'gazą́de** /ü'-wēⁿ'-gä-zoⁿ'-dä/ *n.*, necklace, a bead necklace made with the netted stitch of horse hair

necklace **Waną́'p'į** /wä-noⁿ'-p'ēⁿ/ *n.*, necklace, an ornament of a sort worn around the neck

needle **Wák'ù'žįgà** /wä-k'ü'-zhēⁿ-gä/ *n.*, needle

negative **-ží'** /zhē/ *suffix*, denotes something negative, as in *údą~*, not good, *ađá~* didn't go

neglect **Á'ki'hidažì** /ä'-kē-hē-dä-zhē/ *v.*, neglect, to be inattentive, to disregard

neglected **Dą́'beđįgè** /doⁿ'-bä-theⁿ-gä/ *adj.*, neglected, lacking care, usu. refers to someone who is homebound without care or is disabled and not visited

Negroid **Xįhá'sábe** /xēⁿ-hä'-sä'-bā/ *n.*, Negroid, lit. black complexion, people of African origin (also referred to as *Wáxe sábe*, the black white man)

nephew **Wit'ą́škà** /wē-t'oⁿ'-shkä'/ *n., masc.*, nephew

nephew **Wit'úškà** /wē-t'ü'-shkä'/ *n., fem.*, nephew

nervousness **Waną́duzè** /wä-noⁿ'-dü-zä'/ *n.*, nervousness, a psycho/physiological state of feeling uncertain about something that may happen in a precarious situation

nest **Wét'a ugdè** /wä'-t'ä ü-gthä'/ *n.*, nest, a structure of weeds and bird down made by fowl in which to lay and hatch their eggs

nestle **G'igdíp'úp'u** /g-ē-gthē'-p'ü'-p'ü/ *v.*, nestle, to settle snugly or to lie in a shel-tered way, wrapping up in a blanket to keep warm and comfy

new **T'éga** /t'ä'-gä/ *adj.*, new, brand new

newborn **Šé'žįgà** /shä-zhēⁿ-gä'/ *n.*, newborn, a newborn, baby, infant

Newkirk OK **Hú'đugà** /hü'-thü-gä'/ *n.*, Newkirk, Oklahoma

new year **Umą́dikà t'éga** /ü-moⁿ'-thē-kä' t'ä'-gä/ *n.*, new year (Sometime in the nineteenth century the first day of January in the modern calendar was designated as the new year. The first few days of spring [*mé'p'ahągà*] mark the Ponca new year.)

next **Udá'tą** /ü-thä'-toⁿ/ *adj.*, next, after that, subsequently (~ *aká níkašigè snedé tągà*, the ~ person was tall)

next to **Ubáhadì** /ü-bä'-hä-dē/ *adj.*, next to, something or somebody that is obviously near another person or thing

Nez Perce **P'é'gazą́de** /p'ä'-gä-zoⁿ'-dä/ *n.*, the Nez Perce Tribe of Native Americans

Niagara Falls **Ní'uxp'áde** /nē-üx-p'ä'-thä/ *n.*, Niagara Falls, a natural wonder in North America—(The Ponca people, before their migration to the north central plains, considered the falls a landmark.)

nice **Úškąúdą** /ü-shkoⁿ-ü'-doⁿ/ *adj.*, nice, refers to a person who has all the characteristics of being kind and polite in the social and cultural ways of the Native Americans and others

nickel **Bdé'k'ažįgà** /bthä'-k'ä-zhēⁿ-gä/ *n.*, nickel, 1. five-cent piece 2. proper female name in the Đíxidą̀ clan of the Ponca people

niece **Wit'ížą** /wē-t'ē'-zhoⁿ/ *n., masc.*, niece

niece **Wit'ú'žągè** /wē-t'ü'-zhoⁿ-gä'/ *n., fem.*, niece

night **Hą́'** /hoⁿ'/ *n.*, night; darkness; *hą́'ádi*, last night; *hą́'đi*, tonight; *hą́'ádi guáđišà*, the night before last; *hą́'ámąt'à*, the other night; *e'hąádi guáđišą̀*, on the second night before nightfall **Hą́dą ahítedì** /hon'-don ä-hē'-tā-dē'/ *n.*, nightfall, lit., when it comes to night, at the close of the day

nighttime **Hą́'dą** /hon'-don/ *n.*, nighttime, at night, nocturnal

Níkapášną̀ **Níkapášną̀** /nē-kä-pä-shnon'/ *n.*, the Níkapášną̀ clan of the Ponca people, lit., man with a bald head (The warriors of this clan shaved their hair, wearing a "Mohawk"-style haircut. They tied a symbolic feather at the tail or back of the head. They, along with the Ðíxidą̀ clansmen, were considered "shock troops.")

nine **Šą́ka** /shon'-kä/ *n.*, nine, the number nine (9)

nineteen **Agdį́šą̀kà** /ä-gthēn'-shon-kä'/ *n.*, nineteen

ninety **Gdébąšą̀kà** /gthä'-bon-shon-kä'/ *n.*, ninety

ninety-nine **Gdébąšą̀kà k'í šą́ka** /gthä'-bon-shon'-kä' k'ē' shon'-kä/ *n.*, ninety-nine

ninth **Wé'sąka'** /wä'-son-kä/ *n.*, ninth, the ninth thing in a row of items or the ninth person or group of people coming in succession

Niobrara River **Niú'bdáda** /nē-ü'-bthä'-thä/ *n.*, Niobrara River, Nebraska, lit., flat, wide, or broad water

nipple **Mązé'p'à** /mon-zä'-pä/ *n.*, nipple, tip of the mammary gland

nit **Hesą́'** /hä-son'/ *n.*, nit, the egg of a parasitic insect, the egg of a louse

no **Ą́'k'ažì** /on'-k'ä-zhē'/ *n.*, no, never, refusal, no way; *ą́k'ažit'ìą̀, ~*, not at all, by ~ means

nobody **Ebábišt'iwą̀zì** /ä-bä-bē-sht'ē-won-zhē'/ *n.*, nobody, finding there really wasn't anyone there after thinking there was a person present

nobody **Ebébišt'iwą̀zì** /ä-bä-bē-sht'ē-won-zhē'/ *n.*, nobody, refers to a person who is a nobody

nobody **Ebéšt'iwą̀zì** /ā-bä-sht'ē-won-zhē'/ *n./pron.*, nobody, not anyone, refers to nobody being there

nod **P'agás'į** /p'ä-gä's-ēn/ *v./n.*, nod, 1. *v.*, concur or agree 2. *n.*, the okay or go-ahead sign 3. *v.*, a baby's nod to parents

no father **Įdá'dįgè** /ēn-dä-thēn-gä'/ *n.*, no father, lit., no father, a mythological character described as a large, hairy being, sometimes called Bigfoot or Sasquatch (Searches for such a being have been inconclusive in modern times.)

noise **Biza'e** /bē-zä'-ā/ *n.*, noise, a loud rattling, smacking noise; *biza'za'è, v.*, to continuously making a loud rattling, smacking noise

noise **K'adą́** /k'ä-thon'/ *n.*, noise, a noise caused by metal hitting or being hit by some other object; *k'ak'ádą*, a continuous noise made by metal hitting or being hit by some other object

noisy **Zaé** /zä-ā'/ *adj.*, noisy, loud sounds, deafening

none **Ęną́** /ā-non'/ *pron.*, none, no more of something, as in that's all or not any

noon **Mí'dą mą́ši** /mē'-thon mon'-shē/ *n.*, noon, lit., when the sun is high, noon hour

Norfolk NE **Nipúki** /nē-pü'-kē/ *n.*, Norfolk, Nebraska

north **Usni'át'à** /ü-snē-ä'-t-ä/ *n.*, north, lit., where it is cold, one of the cardinal points on the compass

northeast **Í't'at'à** /ē'-t'ä-t'ä/ *n.*, northeast, lit., touching here and there, one of the nautical points on the compass

northeasterly **Í't'at'à't'adišą̀** /ē'-t'ä-t'ä'-t'ä-thē-shon'/ *n./adj.*, northeasterly, in a northeasterly direction

northerly **Usni'á't'adišą̀** /ü-snē-ä'-tä-thē-shon'/ *adj.*, northerly, in a northerly direction

North Star **Miká'e škáažì** /mē-kä'-ā shkoⁿ-ä-zhē'/ *n.*, North Star, lit., the star that does not move, also called the polestar

northwest **I't'áxeát'a** /ē-t'ä'-xā-ä'-t'ä/ *n.*, northwest, one of the nautical points on the compass

northwesterly **I't'áxeá't'adišà** /ē-t'ä'-xā-ä'-t'ä-thē-shoⁿ'/ *n./adj.*, northwesterly, in a northwesterly direction

nose **P'á'** /p'ä'/ *n.*, nose, in anatomy, the organ of smell that projects out in front of the face

nosebleed **P'á'šudáde** /p'ä-shü-dä'-thā/ *n.*, nosebleed, epistaxis, an occurrence of bleeding from the nose

nose bridge **P'á'uskídà** /p'ä'-ü-skē'-dä/ *n.*, nose bridge, the upper bony part of the nose

notch **Máxu** /mä'-xü/ *n.*, notch, score with a tool, cut into wood to make a mark (A~ is made at the end of an arrow.)

nothing **Įdádąšt'iáži** /ēⁿ-dä'-doⁿ-sht'ē-ä'-zhē/ *pron.*, nothing, "it's nothing at all"

nothing left **Udį·ge** /ü-thēⁿ'-·gä/ *pron.*, nothing left, there was nothing left of many things

noticeable **Wét'àį** /wā'-t'oⁿ-ēⁿ'/ *adj.*, noticeable, clear, visible, perceptible, obvious, in plain sight; *įwat'àį*, I noticed; *díwat'àį*, you noticed; *wéwat'àį*, we noticed; *gíwat'àį*, he/she/it noticed

not likely **Á'xt'à** /ä'-xt'oⁿ'/ *adj.*, not likely, not viable, out of the question

not likely to happen **Šą́t'egaži** /shoⁿ'-t'ä-gä-zhē'/ *interj.*, not likely to happen (he tried, but it's ~); any act or plan not thoroughly prepared and perceived as not likely to happen

November **Osní' əhą́ge** /ō-snē' ə-hoⁿ'-gä/ *n.*, November, lit., the beginning of cold (weather), the eleventh month of the year

now **Ðegą́di** /thä-goⁿ'-dē/ *adv.*, now, at the present time or moment (go there ~)

now **Į́'tą** /ēⁿ'-toⁿ/ *adv.*, now, at the moment, at this time, at this instant, etc. (~ you can hear it); *į́'čą*, now

nowhere **Águdišt'iwąžì** /ä'-gü-dē-sht'ē-woⁿ-zhē'/ *adv.*, nowhere, at no place; a place that doesn't exist

now what **Į́'tą'wà** /ēⁿ'-toⁿ'-woⁿ'/ *adv./interj.*, now what?, an expression used as a remark about a statement made or an action taken, usu. said in questioning one's honesty or directness

nudge **Bisp'á** /bē-sp'oⁿ'/ *v.*, nudge, 1. to press on or poke somebody gently 2. *đisp'á*, to nudge somebody gently with the hands; *basp'á*, to nudge somebody with the arm, elbow, or knee

numbers **Wadáwa** /wä-thä'-wä/ *n.*, numbers, the sum of something, usu. represented by a word, symbol, or letter (In the Ponca language, it is represented in a word or words.)

nurse **Wazéde waù'** /wä-zā'-thä wä-ü'/ *n.*, nurse, a healthcare professional who, along with others, is responsible for the treatment and recovery of patients

nurses' station **Wazéde waù' t'iunáží** /wä-zā'-thä wä-ü' t'ēü-noⁿ'-zhēⁿ/ *n.*, nurses' station, that part of the hospital where medical personnel, esp. nurses, keep records of treatment, medicines, and the progress of patients

nut **T'áge** /t'ä'-gä/ *n.*, nut (any)

nutcracker **T'áge ígaxixè** /t'ä'-gä ē'-gä-xē-xä'/ *n.*, nutcracker, a device to crack nuts

nuts and bolts **Mą́ze'udúgaškè** /moⁿ'-zā-ü-thü'-gä-shkä'/ *n.*, nuts and bolts, metal fasteners such as nuts, bolts, and screws

O

oak tree **T'áškahì** /t'ä́-shkä-hē̄/ *n.*, oak tree, one of many species of the genus *Quercus*

oatmeal **Šáge wadáte** /shonⁿ-gä wä-thä́-tä/ *n.*, oatmeal, lit., horse food

obedient **Íye wáną'ą** /ē̄-yä wä́-nonⁿ-onⁿ/ *adj.*, obedient, lit., "one who listens," refers to a young person who practices good social behavior

obese **Šį́'** /shēⁿ/ *adj.*, obese, fat, plump, corpulent

obscure **Úkiną̀dì** /ǖ-kē-nonⁿ-thē̄/ *adj.*, obscure, vague

observe **Wádiwagazù** /wä́-thē-wä-gä-zǖ/ *v.*, observe, to view or examine a situation or condition

obstinate **Đizáde** /thē̄-zonⁿ-dä/ *adj.*, obstinate, sitting obstinately proud

obstruct **Uhé'wakiđažì** /ü-hä́-wä-kē-thä-zhē̄/ *v.*, obstruct, 1. obstruct, to prevent passage through 2. veto, disallowing a person to insist on their argument, forbid insistence 3. a Ponca male name

obtain **Đizé'** /thē̄-zä́/ *v.*, obtain, get, take

obvious **Wét'ą́ì** /wä́-t'onⁿ-ē̄ⁿ/ *adj.*, obvious, clear, apparent

occasional **At'ą́štì** /ä́-t'onⁿ-shtē̄/ *adv.*, occasional

occasionally **Atą́'šti'dą̀dà** /ä-tonⁿ-shtē-thonⁿ-thonⁿ/ *adv.*, occasionally, on different occasions, from time to time, now and then, every so often, etc.

occipital **T'aí'** /t'ä-ē̄/ *n.*, that part of the skull located near the occipital bone, back of the head

occipital bone **T'aí'bažú** /t'ä-ē̄-bä-zhǖ/ *n.*, the bone section that is located at the back bottom of the human skull

occupy **Ugdí'** /ü-gthē̄/ *v.*, occupy, live in, inhabit

occupation **Ú'dit'ą̀** /ǘ-thē-t'onⁿ/ *n.*, occupation, profession, something a person does to earn a living

ocean **Ní't'ą̀gà** /nē̄-t'onⁿ-gä/ *n.*, ocean, sea

ocher **Wasésą** /wä-sä́-sonⁿ/ *n.*, 1. ocher, a reddish or yellowish earthen iron oxide 2. clay 3. any earthen mixture or man-made materials prepared to create and construct various things, such as porcelain, children's toys, statues

October **T'ą́de mą̀šáde užì** /t'onⁿ-dä monⁿ-shonⁿ-dä ü-zhē̄/ *n.*, October, lit., store food in caches, the tenth month in the year

odoriferous **Bdą́'** /bthonⁿ/ *adj.*, odoriferous, giving off an odor, sometimes morally offensive, sometimes a pleasant smell

off course **Wedáži** /wä-dä́-zhē/ *n.*, off course, a different direction; as in leaving the route and going in another direction

often **Udúagdè** /ü-thǘ-ä-gthä/ *adv.*, often, frequently, repeatedly, over and over again

Oglala **Ubđáđà** /ü-bthä́-thä/ *n.*, the Oglala band of the Lakota Nation

oil **Wégdì** /wǟ-gthē̄/ *n.*, 1. oil (petroleum) 2. lard (white pork fat used for cooking) 3. any cooking oil, a blend of vegetable oils

oilcloth tablecloth **Ní'ága'šnahà** /nē̄-ä́-gä-shnä-hä/ *n.*, oilcloth tablecloth, a tablecloth with vinyl covering; *archaic*, a close-woven cotton fabric coated with boiled linseed oil to make it waterproof

Ojibwa **Waxt'áwį** /wäx-t'ä́-wēⁿ/ *n.*, the Ojibwa Tribe of Native Americans (The term also applies to the Chippewa and Cree Nations of Native Americans and Canadian Natives.)

Oklahoma City OK **T'ą́wągdą̀'t'ą̀gà** /t'onⁿ-wonⁿ-gthonⁿ-t'onⁿ-gä/ *n.*, Oklahoma City, Oklahoma

old **It'ą́điàdi** /ē̄-t'onⁿ-thē-ä́-dē/ *n.*, old, something that has been used for a long time, usu. showing wear and tear

old; older **Ną́** /noⁿ/ *adj.*, old or older, refers to the age of a person (*núẓį̇gà aka, eí ~i*, the boy is ~)

old man **Iš'áge** /ēsh-ä'-gā/ *n.*, old man, a term of respect; venerable

Old Man Bear **Mąčú Iš'áge** /moⁿ-chü' ēsh-ä'-gā/ *n.*, Old Man Bear, the name of a legendary dog who fought the enemy with the Ponca

old woman **Waú ẓį̇gá** /wä-ü' zhēⁿ-gā/ *n.*, lit., little woman, old woman, a term of respect; venerable

omasum **T'eníxaugdeẓè** /t'ā-nē'-xä-ü-gthā-zhā'/ *n.*, omasum, the leaf-like, folded compartment in the bovine stomach

omasum **Wabáxu** /wä-bä'-xü/ *n.*, omasum or "many-piles," lit., book; leaf-like folds in the bovine stomach

Omaha **Umą́hą** /ü-moⁿ'-hoⁿ/ *n.*, the Omaha Tribe of Native Americans

on **Gahá'** /gä-hä'/ *prep.*, on, suggests something atop or positioned at the top

once **Wiáxči'ą̀** /wēä-xchē-oⁿ'/ *adv.*, once, one time, to try something one time

one **-aké'** /ä-kā'/ *n.*, *suffix*, one, denotes a particular person or thing, as in that's the one; *dé̇ke*, this one closest to me; *duáke*, this one; *gáke*, speaking of a particular thing; *še'akè*, that one; *ámąkè*, the other one

one **Wí'** /wē'/ *n.*, one, relating to numerals as in 1, 2, 3

one **Wiáxčì** /wēä-xchē'/ *n.*, one, refers to a thing that remains (~ *ušt'è*, ~ left)

one-dollar bill **Wí'bɖugà** /wē'-bthü-gä'/ *n.*, one-dollar bill

one hundred **Gdébą'hiwì'** /gthä'-boⁿ-hē-wē'/ *n.*, one hundred; Roman numeral C; Latin term *centum*

one-hundred-dollar bill **Gdébą hiwì ídawà**

/gthä'-boⁿ hē-wē' ē'-thä-wä'/ *n.*, one-hundred-dollar bill, U.S. currency

one only **Enáxčì** /ā-noⁿ'-xchē'/ *adj.*, one only, refers to a solitary person, a single play in sports, or a thing (~ *ušté*, ~ person was left)

ones **Wídąɖà** /wē'-thoⁿ-thoⁿ'/ *n.*, ones, "by ones," as in they came in by ones or one at a time

one thousand **K'ú'gewì** /k'ü'-gā-wē'/ *n.*, one thousand (The number one thousand was called *gdébą'hiwì' t'ągà*, big one hundred. The Ponca received $1,000 in payment from the government for passing over their lands and usage of the Missouri River. The payment was brought to them in a box, *k'úge*, containing one thousand dollars. The term *k'úge*, box, came to mean one thousand.)

one-thousand-dollar bill **K'ú'ge'hį̇wį'ídawà** /k'ü'-gā-hēⁿ-wēⁿ-ē'-thä-wä'/ *n.*, one-thousand-dollar bill, U.S. currency

ongoing **Nądáha** /noⁿ-dä'-hä/ *adj.*, ongoing, long-lasting, enduring, usu. refers to continuing life in good health, happiness, contentment, etc.

onion **Mąẓáxe** /moⁿ-zhoⁿ'-xä/ *n.*, onion, a round, pungent, edible bulb that can be eaten raw or cooked

only one **Wiá'xčì'nà** /wēä'-xchē'-nä/ *n.*, only one, only one thing left (The cardinal numbers are extended by adding *-nà* to each succeeding number, as in ~ *uštè*, there is ~ left, or *dábɖičì'nà uštè*, there are only three left.)

On Our Side **Đégihà** /thä'-gē-hä/ *n.*, on our side, 1. used when a Ponca addresses members of the Ponca Tribe 2. refers to the five tribes, namely, the Kaw, Omaha, Osage, Ponca, and Quapaw, who speak the same language

on target **Ádut'ą̀** /ä'-thü-t'oⁿ'/ *adj.*, on target, on course, doing or saying something just right

oodles **Đijá'** /thē-jo^n'/ *n.*, oodles, plenty, lots of, loads (usu. used in jest, referring to one getting money, but can be used for other things received in excess)

oops **H'ái** /h-o^n'-ē/ *interj.*, oops!, a male expression of one's own clumsiness, mistake, or blunder; used more often when something is accidentally dropped

ooze **Á'snuè** /ä'-snü-ā'/ *n./v.*, ooze, to flow or leak slowly, usu. refers to a liquid substance

open **Bašíbe** /bä-shē'-bā/ *adj./v.*, to open by pushing, usu. used when something, such as a door, could not be normally opened (*t'ižébe ké ~ dédaì*, he ~ the door)

open **Bašíšíbe** /bä-shē'-shē'-bā/ *adj./v.*, to open continuously by pushing (*t'ižébe té ~ dédaì*, he continuously ~ the doors)

open **Baiáxa** /bäē-ä'-xä/ *v./adj.*, open, as in a door left open intentionally or unintentionally (*t'ižébe ké ~ itédaì*, he left the door ~)

open **Điáxa** /thē-ä'-xä/ *v./adj.*, open, an open door or a door left open

open **Đišíbe** /thē-shē'-bā/ *v./adj.*, open, to unlock a door or gate with a key, or to ~ some device with the hands

open **K'íza** /k'ē'-zä/ *adj.*, open, open or clear of people and things, a sense of emptiness due to a lack of people and things

opening **Udík'ibà** /ü-thē'-k'ē-bä'/ *n.*, opening, making a slight opening with the hands and tools at a specific space or level on some structure

opening **Ugdé** /ü-gthä'/ *n.*, opening, a small opening (*údiskè áka, ~ kè áhe ayádaì*, the spider escaped into/through the ~)

opening **Uk'íba** /ü-k'ē'-bä/ *n.*, opening, something not quite closed, e.g., a partially opened window

opening **Ut'áną** /ü-t'ä'-no^n/ *n.*, opening, refers to the middle of something, e.g., the middle of a street

operate **Đináge** /thē-no^n'-gā/ *v.*, operate, 1. to make something function (~ an automobile) 2. to operate a mechanical device with the hands

operative **Nąúdą** /no^n-ü'-do^n/ *adj.*, operative, lit., runs good, run, refers to machinery, as in an automobile engine

opinionated **Í'yèk'idè** /ē'-yä'-k'ē-thä'/ *adj.*, opinionated, lit., cause himself to speak, speaking to a gathering from his/her point of view

opossum **Įšt'į'p'à** /ē^n-sht'ē^n'-p'ä/ *n.*, opossum, a marsupial commonly seen in the Western Hemisphere

opposite **Ámat'adišą** /o^n'-mo^n-t'ä-thē-sho^n'/ *adv.*, opposite, on the other side or ~ side of something

opposite **K'íbaxdą** /k'ē'-bä-xtho^n'/ *adj.*, opposite, facing another person located directly across from one

orange **Šézi** /shä'-zē/ *n.*, orange, a round citrus fruit with thick skin

orange **Zi'žíde** /zē-zhē'-dā/ *adj.*, orange, lit., yellow-red, orange or orange color

orate **Íye'ną žį'** /ē'-yä-no^n-zhē^n'/ *v.*, orate, to lecture; to give a speech, oration

order **Ágažì** /ä'-gä-zhē'/ *v.*, order, command, to order somebody to do something

ordinary **Ukédi** /ü-kä'-thē/ *adj.*, ordinary, common, familiar

organization **Úk'ik'unéde** /ü-k'ē-k'ü-nä'-thä/ *n.*, organization, lit., come back to the fireplace, group, club, union, party

original **P'ahága gáxekè** /p'ä-ho^n'-gä gä'-xä-kä'/ *n.*, original, the first of something that was made

oriole **Mągí'xt'à** /mo^n-gē'-xt'ä'/ *n.*, 1. oriole, a small black bird, probably Bullock's oriole (The bird known by the Ponca is probably of the species *icterus*, family Icteridae. The males are black and orange, while females are plain.) 2. any black birds, e.g., common grackle

ornaments **Wék'i'à** /wä'-k'ē-oⁿ'/ *n.*, ornaments, 1. something that decorates or adds to something else, usu. refers to the Heḏúškà dancing paraphernalia 2. an assortment of things or objects that go with or are characteristic of something, as in medals on a soldier's uniform

orphan **Waháḏiḡè** /wä-hoⁿ'-thēⁿ-gä'/ *n.*, orphan, lit., no place to relocate, a child whose parents have died

Osage **Wažáže** /wä-zhä'-zhä/ *n.*, the Osage Tribe of Native Americans

Osage orange bow **Žạzí' máde** /zhoⁿ-zē' moⁿ'-dä/ *n.*, Osage orange bow, made from the choice wood for making bows

Osage orange tree **Žạzí'hi** /zhoⁿ-zē'-hē/ *n.*, Osage orange tree, commonly called hedge apple, horse apple, or bodark, *Maclura pomifera*

other **Ámà** /oⁿ'-moⁿ'/ *adj.*, other, another, another one (~ *kè ạ'íḏagà*, hand me the ~ one)

other **Ážiamà** /ä'-zhē-ä-mä/ *adj.*, other, as in another person or persons

other side **Ámạt'adišà** /oⁿ'-moⁿ-t'ä-thē-shoⁿ'/ *adj.*, other side, flip side, backside, reverse side

other side **Mạsáḏi** /moⁿ-soⁿ'-thē/ *adj.*, other side, something usu. described as being over or across a thing, such as a river, lake, or ocean (*ní't'ạgà ~-at'à aḏái*, he went to the ~ of the ocean)

other way **Gédišà** /gä'-thē-shoⁿ'/ *prep.*, other way, around the ~

Otoe **Waḏót'ada** /wä-thō'-t'ä-dä/ (**Waḏút'ada** /wä-thü'-t'ä-dä/) *n.*, the Otoe Tribe of Native Americans

otter **Nušṇá'** /nü-shnoⁿ'/ *n.*, otter, a fish-eating water animal, subfamily Lutrinae

otter skin **Nušṇá'ha** /nü-shnoⁿ'-hä/ *n.*, otter skin (The skin has many uses, such as medicine bags, dance paraphernalia of the Heḏúškà, caps. In the past, it was worn only by men who had knowledge of medicines and healing.)

otterskin cap **Nušṇáha waḏagè** /nü-shnoⁿ'-hä wä-thä-gä'/ *n.*, otter-skin cap, a man's cap, now worn at Heḏúškà dances

ouch **Á'nạnà·** /oⁿ'-noⁿ-noⁿ'·/ *interj.*, ouch, an expression of pain or injury; *áḏəḏù*, expression of pain

ours **Ạgút'a** /oⁿ-gü'-t'ä/ *pron.*, ours, our, something belonging to us

out **Ná'ži** /nä'-zhē/ *adv.*, out, something no longer burning or lit, 1. fire is no long burning 2. lightbulb has gone out (Most homes until ca. 1950 had oil lamps. The lamp was put out [*bináži*] by blowing on it.)

outer ear **Nit'á'** /nē-t'ä'/ *n.*, outer ear, that part of the ear that extends on the side of the head, consisting of the pinna or auricle

outer edges **Xáxat'à** /xoⁿ'-xä-t'ä'/ *adj.*, outer edges, standing on the ~ of a group (*niášigà akà, ~ nạžį́ nài*, the man always stands on the ~)

outgushing **Gamú'i** /gä-mü'-ē/ *n.*, outgushing, pouring out in profusion

outhouse **T'í'žiḡà** /t'ē'-zhēⁿ-gä'/ *n.*, outhouse, lit., little house, a toilet constructed outdoors, usu. a small building built over a pit

out of **Gašíbeát'a** /gä-shē'-bää'-t'ä/ *adv.*, out of, not in, implies getting oneself out of something

outside **Ágahat'à** /ä'-gä-hä-t'ä/ *n.*, outside, exterior, the outer surface, such as walls

outside **Ášiadì** /ä'-shē-ä-dē'/ *adv.*, outside, 1. an indication of something outside at a certain place 2. sombody outside of a group or crowd of people outside **Ášiat'à** /ä'-shē-ä-t'ä'/ *adv.*, happening outside, exterior, usu. refers to something outside of a building, dwelling, or house

outside of **Gašíbeàt'a** /gä-shē'-bä-ä'-t'ä/ *adv.*, outside of, being ~ something that one was involved in or locked up in

overcast **Ugánạdà** /ü-gä'-noⁿ-thä'/ *adj.*, overcast, cloudy, gray sky

overlook **Điwágazubažì** /thē-wä'-gä-zü-bä-zhē'/ *v.*, overlook, to miss seeing or determining something, usu. through inspection

overripe **Sída** /sē'-dä/ *v.*, overripen, when produce becomes overripe and hard (Fresh corn, e.g., can be cooked or parched for eating and dehydrated for later use.)

overseas **Ní't'ạgà mạsạ́dihà** /nē'-t'oⁿ-gä' moⁿ-soⁿ'-thē-hä'/ *n.*, overseas, refers to countries beyond the Atlantic and Pacific Oceans

oversee **Ákihidè** /ä'-kē-hē-dä'/ *v.*, oversee, 1. to take care of someone or something 2. to oversee and protect someone or something

overshadow **Ágahanạp'áze** /ä'-gä-hä-noⁿ-p'ä'-zä/ *v.*, overshadow, to cast a shadow over something, as in heavy clouds casting a shadow over the land

overshoes **Hịbé uwákihà** /hēⁿ-bä' ü-wä'-kē-hoⁿ'/ *n.*, overshoes, galoshes, a large kind of rubber shoe or boot that fits over shoes for protection from water, mud, or snow

over there **Gáhidè** /gä'-hē-thä'/ *prep./adv.*, over there, in that direction that is out of sight from the speaker

over there **Gát'adižạ̀** /gä'-t'ä-thē-shoⁿ'/ *adv.*, over there, 1. to indicate a place out of sight, toward a position away from the speaker 2. that way, toward no particular place or direction (stand over ~) 3. to indicate that a statement close to an idea or plan could have or should have been included in one's speech or presentation

over there **Šét'adižạ̀** /shä'-t'ä-thē-shoⁿ'/ *prep./adv.*, over there, toward that direction, toward a space between the speaker and a point of reference such as the wall, auditorium, playing field

overturn **Ákigdažạ̀** /ä'-kē-gthä-shoⁿ'/ *v.*, overturn, tip over, capsize

owl **Bánahò(hù)** /bä'-nä-hō'(hü')/ *n.*, owl

own **Etái** /ā-tä'-ē/ *v.t./adj.*, *3rd pers.* he/she/it/they own/s, possess, belonging to them, as in property

P

pack **Waị'** /wä-ēⁿ'/ *n.*, pack, bundle, things carried on the shoulders or back

packed **Ubísạdè** /ü-bē'-soⁿ-dä'/ *adj.*, packed, 1. being packed together, usu. refers to people sitting very close together 2. refers to a space between two structures 3. a male name in the Wažážè clan of the Ponca people

padlock **Weúdidạ̀** /wäü'-thē-doⁿ'/ *n.*, padlock, a device used to secure doors, cabinets, or gates, usu. a lock with a U-shaped bar that extends out to be hooked onto a staple affixed to the structure to be secured

pail **Néxe** /nä'-xä/ *n.*, pail, bucket

pail **Ní'idagè** /nē'-ē-thä-gä'/ *n.*, *archaic*, pail to carry water with

pain **Í'niedè** /ē'-nē-ä-thä'/ *n.*, pain, something that causes pain, as in brushing a hand against a sharp object

pain **Ni'é** /nē-ä'/ *n*, pain, 1. physical pain 2. emotional pain

paint **K'i'ạ́** /k'ē-oⁿ'/ *v.*, paint, to put paint on the face, usu. among those who would be going into battle with the enemy

paint **Wésnadè** /wä'-snä-thä'/ *n.*, paint, a liquefied substance of different colors that may be applied to any surface; *snáde*, *v*., paint, to paint something with a liquefied substance

pair **Nąbáha** /noⁿ-bä'-hä/ *n*., pair, duo, two of a kind, two things that are identical or similar

pairs **Nąbádądą̀** /noⁿ-bä'-thoⁿ-thoⁿ/ *n*., pairs, two by two (they passed by in ~)

palate **Kąbdáde** /koⁿ-bthä'-dä/ *n*., palate, the roof of the mouth

pallid **Kú'zi** /kü'-zē/ *adj*, pallid, having a pale complexion

palm **Nąbéudúdą** /noⁿ-bä'-ü-thü'-doⁿ/ *n*., palm, the surface of the open hand

palsy **Žú'dįgigì** /zhü-thēⁿ'-gē-gē'/ *n*., palsy, uncontrolled movements of the body

pan **Wiúhą** /wēü'-hoⁿ/ *n*., pan, saucepan

pane **Weúgąbà nąxé** /wä-ü'-goⁿ-bä' noⁿ-xä'/ *n*., pane, windowpane

panty **Nídeudíšį́ mą́te** /nē'-dä-ü-thē'-shēⁿ moⁿ'-tä/ *n*., panty, panties, a type of undergarment designed for women and girls; may also refer to men's undergarments

paper **Wabá'xu** /wä-bä'-xü/ *n*., paper, newspaper, tablet (The term *waxího* was used for paper in the 1800s.)

paraphernalia **Wék'ią̀** /wä-k'ē-oⁿ'/ *n*., paraphernalia, an assortment of things or objects that go with or are characteristic of something, as in all things that are worn on the Hedúškà dance outfit

paraplegic **Mądiáži** /moⁿ-thēä'-zhē/ *n*., paraplegic, lit., cannot walk, someone who cannot move both legs and thus cannot walk because of some kind of sickness or injury

parched corn **Wahábe žé'ąhè** /wä-hä'-bä zhä'-oⁿ-hä'/ *n*., parched corn, corn on the cob cooked on live coals; *watázi žé'ąhè*, parched corn

parched corn **Wanáxe** /wä-nä'-xä/ *n*., parched

corn, usu. grains of corn parched on a griddle (A food staple for travelers.)

parfleche **T'eniúžihà** /t'ä-nēü'-zhē-hä'/ *n*., parfleche, a rawhide bag

parking lot **K'ip'ínągè uną́štą** /k'ē-p'ē'-noⁿ-gä' ü-noⁿ'-shtoⁿ/ *n*., parking lot, a parking lot for automobiles

parsimonious **Gíwašt'ažì** /gē'-wä-sht'ä-zhē'/ *adj*., parsimonious, not willing to part with resources, frugal, thrifty

participate **Uwíhe** /ü-wē'-hä/ *v*., participate, to take part, to involve oneself, to play a part of

partition **Basé** /bä-sä'/ *n./v*., partition, divider, something that separates two or more things; *mą̨zá bašè*, partition of acreage of land

part of **Điskébe** /thē-skä'-bä/ *n*., part of, used in negative tones (~ *íbahąbažì*, he doesn't know even ~ it)

part of **Hebádi** /hä-bä'-dē/ *adj*., part of, part of the way, refers to something that was incomplete (~*xčí ahí*, he went only ~ the way)

part of **Hébe** /hä-bä'/ *n*., part of, partial, a piece of something

part white **Xįháska hébe** /xēⁿ-hä'-skä hä'-bä/ *n*., part white, refers to Native Americans, namely a Ponca whose father is Caucasian (Children whose fathers are non-Ponca are not clan members and are also sometimes referred to as "half-breeds." In the Ponca patrilineal clanship system, children whose fathers are of another tribe, race, or ethnicity, such as Asian or Mexican, cannot be a clan member. They are referred to as *Ukíte hébe*, part other tribe.)

pass **Gaxá'** /gä-xä'/ *v*., pass, get ahead of another traveler

passage **Ųgáxdą̀ užą́'gè** /üⁿ-gä'-xthoⁿ' ü-zhoⁿ'-gä'/ *n*., *archaic*, passage, path of a migrating party

pass by **Ígadizè** /ḗ'-gä-dē-zā'/ *v.*, pass by, refers to passing through or by the village dwellings in a ritualistic manner during the Ponca Sun dance ceremony (*Ígadizè waą́*, songs, were sung during the ritual of riders on horseback dragging the sacred pole through the village before the Sun dance commenced. These songs were slow, mournful supplications of a prayerful nature that called for the crowd to be quiet.)

passed by **Ána'ù** /ä'-nä-ü'/ *v.*, *past t.*, passed by, went close by it or somebody

passed by me **Íną'ù** /ḗⁿ-noⁿ-ü'/ *v.*, *past t.*, passed by me, went close by me

pass the buck **Ábašibè** /ä'-bä-shē-bā'/ *v.*, pass the buck, avoid responsibility by passing it on to someone else

pass through **Íhe** /ḗ'-hā/ *v.*, pass through, go through, lead through, cross through

past **Ák'usądè** /ä'-k'ü-soⁿ-dā'/ *prep.*, past, went past, went beyond, further than

pastries **Wamą́skè skíde** /wä-moⁿ'-skä' skē'-thä/ *n.*, pastries, cake, cookies, sweet rolls

past time **Edítą** /ā-dē'-toⁿ/ *v. phr.*, past time, since then or of a ~

patch **Ábastà** /ä'-bä-stä'/ *v.*, patch, to patch a piece of cloth or material to another to repair or cover a tear or worn area

patch **Wéəbastà** /wä'-ə-bä-stä'/ *n.*, patch, a piece of cloth or material to be sewn to another to repair a worn area or tear

path **Uhé** /ü-hā'/ *n.*, path, road, way (*wí gáxaì*, he made a ~ through the woods)

path **Umą́di** /ü-moⁿ'-thē/ *n.*, path, 1. route, track, etc. 2. way of life 3. realm, domain, kingdom

pathetic **Đa'é'tewadè** /thä-ä'-tä-wä-thä'/ *adj.*, pathetic, pitiable

path maker **Uhégáxe** /ü-hä'-gä-xā/ *n.*, path maker, pathfinder, 1. one who makes a pathway through unknown territories

2. a proper name of a male member of the Wašábe clan

patient room **Wakéga užą́ t'ì** /wä-kā'-gä ü-zhoⁿ' t'ē'/ *n.*, patient room, where care and treatment are given following a patient's entrance into the hospital and initial treatment

pawn **Wá'baxù** /wä'-bä-xü'/ *v.*, pawn, hawk, to give something to someone or to a pawn shop for a loan

Pawnee **P'ádį** /p'ä'-thēⁿ/ *n.*, the Pawnee Tribe of Native Americans

pawpaw **T'užíga** /t'ü-zhēⁿ'-gä/ *n.*, pawpaw, *Asimina triloba*, a temperate fruit tree, native to North America

pay **Úwawešì** /ü'-wä-wä-shē'/ *n.*, pay, compensation, recompense earned or paid for work performed

pay for **Bašédą** /bä-shä'-thoⁿ/ *v.*, pay for, pay for something

payment **Wabášedą̀** /wä-bä'-shä-thoⁿ'/ *n.*, payment, the act of paying somebody for something

payment **Wadíze** /wä-thē'-zā/ *v.*, payment, getting ~ for services provided (The first generation of Ponca living in Oklahoma leased their lands to white farmers, who made payments to the government's Indian agency. The Indian agency in turn made checks out to individual landowners. That individual was said to have gotten a check, *wadíze*; hence, the word means to receive a check.)

peach **Šéhįškubè** /shä'-hēⁿ-shkü-bä'/ *n.*, peach, a fuzzy, sweet fruit; also nectarines

peach tree **Šéhįškubèhì** /shä'-hēⁿ-shkü-bä-hē'/ *n.*, peach tree, of the rose family, *Prunus persica*

peanut **Ą́žįgà** /oⁿ'-zhēⁿ-gä'/ *n.*, peanut, also called the groundnut, *Arachis hypogaea*

peanut butter **T'áge bawégdi** /t'ä'-gä bä-wä-gthē/ *n.*, peanut butter, a paste made from peanuts

pear **Mǎčú** /moⁿ-chü'/ *n.*, pear, orig. European, an edible fruit of the genus *Pyrus* (The Ponca, during the first white contact, heard the English word for pear and mistakenly thought it to be *bear*. They applied the Native word for bear to the fruit, hence *mǎčú*, pear)

peas **Hibdígè bút'à** /hē-bthēⁿ-gā' bü-t'ä/ *n.*, peas, a seed that grows in a pod and is edible, a fruit of the plant *Pisum sativum*

pebble **Í'e žįgà** /ēⁿ'-ā zhēⁿ-gä/ *n.*, pebble, small rock (The Ponca also referred to the *wéši* in the handgame as a "little rock.")

pecan **T'áge'žįgà** /t'ä-gä-zhēⁿ-gä/ *n.*, pecan, lit., small nut, an edible nut that grows in central and southern U.S. states and Mexico

pecan tree **T'àge'žįgàhì** /t'ä'-gä-zhēⁿ-gä-hē'/ *n.*, pecan tree, a species of hickory, *Carya illinoinensis*

pecking **Wabáhi** /wä-bä'-hē/ *v.*, pecking, as in chickens scratching and pecking on the ground for food

peek **Ugás'į** /ü-gä's-ēⁿ/ *v.*, peek, peek in or out

peel **Baxdúde** /bä-xthü'-dā/ *v.*, peel, to peel by pushing apart

peel **Baxdú'xdu'dè** /bä-xthü'-xthü-dā'/ *v.*, peel, to continuously peel by pushing apart

peel **Đixábe** /thē-xä'-bā/ *v.*, peel, to remove with hands, as in peeling a banana

peel **Đixáxábe** /thē-xä'-xä'-bā/ *v.*, peel, to continuouly peel with hands, as in peeling a banana

peel **Gaxábe** /gä-xä'-bā/ *v.*, peel, as in removing or taking off the bark of a tree by striking it with an instrument

peeled off **Xdudáde** /xthü-dä'-thä/ *v. phr.*, *past t.*, peeled off, something coming off on its own, as in old paint on a house

peel off **Xabáde** /xä-bä'-thä/ *v. phr.*, peel off, something that comes off on its own accord, as with the bark of an old tree, the scab of a skinned knee

pelican **Hu'dáte** /hü-thä'-tä/ *n.*, pelican, a web-footed bird of the family Pelecanidae that has an expanding beak used to catch and store fish

pelt **Wanít'a hà** /wä-nē'-t'ä hä/ *n.*, pelt, the skin and fur of any animal

pen **Wébaxù** /wā'-bä-xü/ *n.*, pen, pencil, or any writing instrument

Pendleton blanket **Waį xdíxdí** /wä-ēⁿ' xthēⁿ'-xthēⁿ/ *n.*, Pendleton blanket (These woolen blankets have Native American designs.)

penis **Šądé** /shoⁿ-dä'/ *n.*, penis, the male organ for copulation and discharge of urine from the body

penitentiary **Í'ę'gadádą̀** /ēⁿ'-äⁿ-gä-dä'-thoⁿ/ *n.*, penitentiary, lit., break rocks, prison

penny **Wédawa'židè** /wä'-thä-wä-zhē-dä'/ *n.*, penny, one cent

pepper **Wiúk'ihą̀** /wēü'-k'ē-hoⁿ'/ *n.*, pepper, usu. black pepper, now red pepper or any spice or spices added to cooking

pepper shaker **Wiúk'ihąuží'** /wēü'-k'ē-hoⁿ'-ü-zhē'/ *n.*, pepper shaker, a condiment holder, namely, for pepper

perfect hit **Gap'í'** /gä-p'ē'/ *adj./v.*, perfect hit, to hit, strike, punch, smack something or somebody perfectly

perfume **Í'nąbdą̀'k'idè** /ē'-noⁿ-bthoⁿ'-k'ē-thä'/ *n.*, perfume, Native American man's perfume, derived from the plant *Thalictrum purpurascens*

perfume **Mąk'ą́ ínąbdą̀ k'idè** /moⁿ-k'oⁿ' ē'-noⁿ-bthoⁿ' k'ē-thä'/ *n.*, perfume, columbine, a Native American man's perfume, lit., black medicine perfume, *Aquilegia canadensis L.* See Howard 1965:69.

perfume **Nubdą́'** /nü-bthoⁿ'/ *n.*, perfume,

lit., the smell of man, namely, in the use of "Indian" perfume

perfume **P'é'žį'bdá'skà** /p'ä'-zhēⁿ-bthä'-skä'/ *n.*, perfume, Native American perfume, *Cogswellia daucifolia*

perfume **P'é'žį' ínąbdą' wažìde** /p'ä'-zhēⁿ ē'-noⁿ-bthoⁿ wä-zhē'-dä/ *n.*, perfume, Native American perfume, rose petals

perfume **P'é'ži'p'à** /p'ä'-zhē-p'ä'/ *n.*, perfume, Native American perfume

perfume **T'ušįge** /t'ü-shēⁿ-gä/ *n.*, perfume, a modern fragrant liquid, a pleasant scent, usu. refers to women's perfume

period **K'áši** /k'ä'-shē/ *n.*, period, time, long time, long period of time (~ *wit'ába mąžì*, I haven't seen you for a ~ of time)

periodically **Atą́štidądą** /ä-toⁿ-shtē-thoⁿ-thoⁿ/ *adv.*, periodically, from time to time, once in a while

permanent **Égą šą́šą** /ä'-goⁿ shoⁿ-shoⁿ/ *adj.*, permanent, usu. refers to a situation or condition that will always be the same

permission **Wéginąhì** /wä'-gē-noⁿ-hē'/ *v.*, permit, let him/her/them do, to give permission to

permit **Íginąhì** /ē'-gē-noⁿ-hē'/ *v.*, permit, let him/her/it do something, permit somebody to do something

permit **Wédaginąhì** /wä'-thä-gē-noⁿ-hē'/ *v.*, *2nd pers. pl.*, permit, you all giving permission

persevere **Wašką́** /wä-shkoⁿ'/ *v.*, persevere in spite of hardships and adversities, maintain and persist in the task undertaken

persimmon **T'asp'ą́** /t'ä-sp'oⁿ'/ *n.*, persimmon, genus *Diospyros*, a small, edible fruit that can be eaten only when completely ripe (The word *diospyros* means "the fruit of the gods.")

persimmon tree **T'asp'ą́hì** /t'ä-sp'oⁿ'-hē'/ *n.*, persimmon tree

persist in **Edíʃ'sà** /ā-dē'-ʃ-sä/ *v.*, persist in, continue, carry on, go on, persevere with

person **Níkašigà** /nē'-kä-shē-gä/ *n.*, person; *niášigà* (alternate pronunciation), person

perspire **Unábdì** /ü-nä'-bthē'/ *v.*, perspire or sweat

pet **Wanágdè** /wä-nä'-gthä'/ *n.*, pet, 1. a pet or household animal kept by a person 2. any domesticated animal, such as farm animals

pews **Wak'ą́da wádahą̀ t'í' ágdį** /wä-k'oⁿ'-dä wä'-thä-hoⁿ' t'ē' ä'-gthēⁿ'/ *n.*, pews, church pews, usu. wooden benches arranged in rows facing the altar of a church

peyote **Mąk'ą́** /moⁿ-k'oⁿ'/ *n.*, peyote, *Lophophora williamsi*

peyote drum **Mąk'ą́datè k'úge** /moⁿ-k'oⁿ'-thä-tä' k'ü'-gä/ *n.*, peyote drum (The drum is composed of an iron kettle measuring usu. 9½ inches at the top and about 8 inches deep. A fitted wet deerskin placed over the top is tied tightly with a cotton rope. Water is also put into the kettle.)

pharynx **Wé'nąbdè** /wä-noⁿ'-bthä'/ *n.*, pharynx, part of the throat that allows swallowed foods to pass down to the digestive system and allows air into the respiratory system

pheasant **Šú'íbe'snedè** /shü'-ē'-bä-snä-dä'/ *n.*, pheasant, Chinese ring-necked pheasant

philio love **Wadá'edè** /wä-thä'-ä-thä'/ *n.*, philio love (brotherly love)

philosophy **Íbahą̀'waną́dehidè** /ē'-bä-hoⁿ'-wä-noⁿ'-dä-hē-däⁿ'/ *n.*, philosophy, love of wisdom

pick **Bahí** /bä-hē'/ *v.*, pick, to harvest, as in to pick pecans, to pick up items dropped on the floor

pick **T'ą́de ígašpè** /t'oⁿ'-dä ē'-gä-shpä'/ *n.*, pick, a tool with a pointed steel head attached to a wooden handle like an ax handle, used to break through hardened ground or clay

picking **Wabáhi** /wä-bä'-hē/ *v.*, picking, 1. to harvest, as in picking pecans 2. pecking, as in chickens feeding on grain in the barnyard

pickle **K'uk'úmi** /k'ü-k'ü-mē/ *n.*, pickle, a cucumber preserved in vinegar or brine

pickup truck **K'ip'ínągè wat'ú'gdą** /k'ē-p'ē'-noⁿ-gä' wä-t'ü'-gthoⁿ/ *n.*, pickup truck

picture **Įdé wábaxù** /ēⁿ-dä' wä-bä-xü/ *n.*, picture, photograph, portrait; an image made by painting, by drawing, with a camera

pie **Šé'užégdą** /shä-ü-zhä'-gthoⁿ/ *n.*, pie, baked fruit enclosed in pastry

piece **Hébe** /hä'-bä/ *n.*, piece, part of, fraction, a piece or bit of something

pig **K'úkusì** /k'ü'-kü-sē'/ *n.*, pig, hog, swine

pigeon **Đít'a t'ągà** /thē'-t'ä t'oⁿ-gä'/ *n.*, pigeon, of the family Columbidae (There are two birds: pigeons, the larger bird, and doves, the smaller bird. They feed on fruits, seeds, and plants.)

pigsty **K'úk'úsi' unáži** /k'ü'-k'ü-sē ü-noⁿ'-zhē/ *n.*, pigsty, lit., where the pigs stand, pigpen

Pike's Peak **P'ahé'žé'egà** /p'ä-hä'-zhä'-ä-goⁿ'/ *n.*, *archaic*, ca. 1600s, lit. the likeness of the phallus, a place near Colorado Spings, Colorado

pile **Bat'é** /bä-t'ä'/ *v.*, pile, to pile something or lay something one upon another, as with a pile of clothing or papers

pillow **Íbehì** /ēⁿ'-bä-hēⁿ/ *n.*, pillow, head support, a bag filled with feathers or other soft material used to cushion the head during sleep or for sitting upon

pillowcase **Íbehì udíšį** /ēⁿ'-bä-hēⁿ' ü-thēⁿ'-shēⁿ/ *n.*, pillowcase, a sacklike, removable cotton covering for a pillow

pin **Wágdą'** /wä'-gthoⁿ'/ *n.*, pin, a piece of jewelry or other kinds of decorative items attached to clothing

pinch **Đit'úbè** /thē-t'ü'-bä/ *v.*, 1. pinch, tweak, nip, squeeze 2. to break off a piece with the hands

pine needles **Mázì** /mä'-zē/ *n.*, needles of the cedar tree used in tribal rituals and ceremonies

pink **Skážíde egà** /skä-zhē'-dä ä-goⁿ'/ *n.*, pink, lit., a reddish-white color, a pale reddish color

pink conch shell **Níkidè** /nē'-kē-dä/ *n.*, pink conch shell, a marine shell made round and polished for use in the Heđúškà dance paraphernalia

pinto **Šą́ge gdežè** /shoⁿ'-gä gthä-zhä'/ *n.*, pinto, pinto pony, usu. white marked with patches of another color

Pipe Dance staff **Niní'bažą̀** /nē-nē'-bä-zhoⁿ'/ *n.*, the Pipe Dance staffs, one of which had seven bald eagle feathers attached to the tip and the other that had ten golden eagle feathers attached at the tip

Pipe Dance **Wá'wą** /wä'-woⁿ'/ *n.*, the ceremonial Pipe Dance

pipe stem **Niní'ba žą̀** /nē-nē'-bä zhoⁿ'/ *n.*, pipe stem, the stem of a tobacco pipe

pistol **Wahút'ądì čéška** /wä-hü'-t'oⁿ-thē' chä'-shkä/ *n.*, pistol, revolver, handgun

pitchfork **Xádeidizè** /xä'-dä-ē-thē-zä'/ *n.*, pitchfork, a farm tool with a long handle and separated prongs used to lift and throw hay or other grass feed to animals

pitiful **Đaétewadè** /thä-ä'-tä-wä-thä'/ *v.*, to be pitiful, pitiable, unfortunate, sad, poor

pity **Đaéde** /thä-ä'-thä/ *v.*, pity, to have sympathy for or feel sorry for, to have compassion for someone who is suffering or unhappy

pizza **Wamáske bđáskà** /wä-moⁿ'-skä bthä'-skä/ *n.*, pizza (To honor the queen consort of Italy on June 11, 1889, Raffaele Esposito created the pizza. It was made with tomatoes, mozzarella, and basil, representing the national colors on the Italian flag.)

place **Á'ạhè** /ä'-oⁿ-hä'/ *v.*, place, to place upon

place **U'ạ́** /ü-oⁿ'/ *v.*, place, to put in, as in to put a TV dinner in the microwave, to put another log in the heater

placed **Inạ́daì** /ē-noⁿ'-thäē'/ *v.*, *past t.*, placed, to put, place, stand or lie something specifically somewhere

plan **Wadígdạ gáxe** /wä-thē'-gthoⁿ gä'-xä/ *n.*, plan, idea, devise a plan of action to achieve a goal

plane **Žạbdáska ídiskebè** /zhoⁿ-bthä'-skä ē'-thē-skä-bä'/ *n.*, plane, a tool in woodworking to smooth surfaces, usu. used to level two pieces of board to match or fit evenly

plank **Žạbdáska t'ạgà** /zhoⁿ-bthä'-skä t'oⁿ-gä'/ *n.*, plank, wood ~, a large rectangular piece of flat wood used for the construction of ships, houses, bridges, and other structures; e.g., railroad ties

Plantago major **Sigdé mạk'ạ̀** /sē-gthä' moⁿ-k'oⁿ'/ *n.*, *Plantago major*, a plant used for medicine, referred to in a children's story

platter **Uxp'é t'ạgà** /üx-p'ä' t'oⁿ-gä'/ *n.*, platter, large plate, serving dish, tray

Platte River **Níbdá'ska** /nē-bthä'-skä/ *n.*, Platte River, lit., flat water, the Platte River in the present-day state of Nebraska

play **Íškadè gáxe** /ē'-shkä-dä' gä'-xä/ *n.*, play, lit., make play activities, e.g., rides in a carnival; refers to other fun activities, as in a circus or at dances, pow-wows, or rodeos

play **Škáde** /shkä'-dä/ *n.*, play, social activities, as in games, dances, pow-wows, carnivals, circuses, sports, etc.

play **T'í'gàxe** /t'ē'-gä'-xä/ *n./v.*, play, lit., make a house, usu refers to children's play

playing cards **Wadíbabà** /wä-thē'-bä-bä'/ *n.*, playing cards, used to play various games,

usu. for gambling (Each card is distinguished with a number from one to ten, with three additional cards called the jack, queen, and king. There are four sets of thirteen card that are suited with a motif of hearts, diamonds, spades, and clubs.)

plead **Wahạ́e** /wä-hoⁿ'-ä/ *v.*, plead, to implore, to plead to somebody or to a court in an earnest appeal for forgiveness or time; also a plea to an individual for forgiveness

pleased **Wék'išnạ'wadè** /wä-k'ē-shnoⁿ-wä-thä'/ *adj./v.*, pleased, feeling satisfied about having done something or owning something

pleased **Wéšnạ** /wä'-shnoⁿ/ *v.*, pleased, delighted, satisfied

pleased **Wéšnạ'wadè** /wä-shnoⁿ-wä-thä'/ *adj./v.*, pleased, 1. one who causes someone to feel pleased for gifts given to him/her 2. *n.*, proper female name

pleasing appearance **Udúkạp'ì** /ü-thü'-koⁿ-p'ē'/ *adj.*, pleasing appearance, pleasant to look at, attractive

plentiful **Wašéxtì** /wä-shä'-xtē'/ *adj.*, plentiful, abundant, much of, bountiful

plenty **Áhigè** /ä'-hē-gä'/ *adv.*, plenty, lots, much

plenty **Íše** /ē'-shä/ *adj.*, plenty, usu. refers to particular things, specific things

plenty **T'ạ́'** /t'oⁿ'/ *adj.*, plenty, lot of (*mázeskà adíte ~ áčạ*, they have ~ of money)

pliers **Mạ́ze'ídisè** /moⁿ-zä-ē'-thē-sä'/ *n.*, pliers, a hand tool with hinged arms and a jaw to grip something or remove something, such as a bolt

plod **Nạpéza** /noⁿ-pä'-zä/ *v.*, plod, tread wearily, to walk heavily and laboriously

plop **Gaškáp'ì** /gä-shkä'-p'ē/ *v.*, plop, somebody or something falling down heavily on the ground or floor

plow **Đibđí** /thē-bthē'/ *v.*, plow, to till the

ground or plow up, as in plowing up a field to sow grain

plow **Wédibdì** /wā'-thē-bthē'/ *n.*, plow, an implement to turn the soil

plum **K'ą́de'** /k'oⁿ'-dā/ *n.*, plum, a small, round, edible fruit (*k'ą́de'hì*, plum tree and plum bush, genus *Prunus*)

plume **Hį̀xpé'** /hēⁿ-xpā'/ *n.*, plume, the fluffy undertail feathers of an eagle (The Ponca attached this plume of the eagle, considered to be sacred, to the hair for those who were set aside in the Wáwą̀ ceremony to serve the people. This item has now become an ornamental part of modern Native American women's dance paraphernalia.)

plump **B'ų́šį̀** /b-üⁿ'-shēⁿ'/ *adj.*, plump, 1. chubby, fleshy, or fat 2. refers to something more round or spherical

pocket knife **Mą́hi žį̀gà** /moⁿ'-hē zhēⁿ'-gä/ *n.*, pocketknife, penknife, switchblade

pods **Ną́t'i't'à** /noⁿ-t'ē-t'ä'/ *n.*, pods, e.g., pods that hold black seeds from a thorn tree

point **Á'bazù** /ä'-bä-zü'/ *v.t.*, point, to point at a particular inanimate thing

point **Wá'bazù** /wä'-bä-zü'/ *v.i.*, to point at a group of people or animals

pointed **Zúbe** /zü'-bā/ *adj./n.*, pointed, an object, such as a stick, pole, knife, etc., that has an end that comes to a point

pointing finger **Ną̀bé'wé'bazù** /noⁿ-bā'-wä'-bä-zü'/ *n.*, pointing finger, refers to the index finger, trigger finger, forefinger

police **Waną́še** /wä-noⁿ'-shā/ *n.*, police, law enforcement, highway patrolman, military soldier

police station **Waną́še t'í** /wä-noⁿ'-shā t'ē'/ *n.*, police station, a building that houses police officers and cells for law offenders. See also *Ugánahąp'azè*, jail.

polish **Ba'ɖią́ąbà** /bä-thē-oⁿ'-oⁿ-bä'/ *v.*, polish, buff, shine and sparkle

polish **Ba'ɖią́'babà** /bä-thē-oⁿ'-bä-bä'/ *v.*, polish, buff to make something shine and sparkle

polish **Bit'éga** /bē-t'ä'-gä/ *adj.*, polish, lit., to cause to be new, refers to putting a new gloss, luster, or smoothness on an old surface

polite **Úš'k'ą údą̀** /üsh-k'oⁿ ü'-doⁿ'/ *adj.*, polite, gracious, courteous, well-mannered

Ponca **P'ą́c'a** /p'oⁿ'-k'ä/ *n.*, the Ponca Tribe of Native Americans

Ponca **P'a'máse'** /p'ä-mä'-sā/ *n.*, Ponca, *archaic*, lit., those who cut off the heads of enemies, usu. refers to warriors of the Ponca people

Ponca Creek **Ní'udít'è̀ wačíškà** /nē'-ü-thē'-t'äⁿ wä-chē'-shkä'/ *n.*, Ponca Creek, lit, the water to kill in creek, Knox County, Nebraska

Ponca Fort **Ną́za** /noⁿ'-zä/ *n.*, Ponca Fort (The Ponca Fort site is the location of a once-fortified earth-lodge village in Knox County, Nebraska, approximately eight miles west of Niobrara. It was a post palisade fort. The area covered approximately three acres of land. "The fort was well situated from a defensive point of view, being located on a prominence, one of the bluffs of the Missouri, some 50 or 60 feet above the floor of the valley of Ponca Creek" [Howard 1965].)

pond **Né'** /nā'/ *n.*, pond, pool

pony **Šą́ge žį̀gà** /shoⁿ'-gä zhēⁿ'-gä'/ *n.*, pony, lit., little horse

pop **Ná't'u'šì** /nä'-t'ü-shē'/ *v.*, pop, popping sound made by heat, e.g., popcorn, fireworks

pop **T'uší'** /t'ü-shē'/ *v.*, pop, the sound of something popping

popcorn **Watą́zinát'uši** /wä-toⁿ'-zē-nä'-t'ü-shē'/ *n.*, popcorn, kernels of corn that pop open when heated

popsicle **Núxe snì** /nü'-xā snē'/ *n.*, popsicle, lit., cold ice, also snow cone

popping sound **Gat'ú'šì** /gä-t'ü'-shē'/ *v.*, to make a popping or cracking sound using some instrument of force

population **Áną** /ä'-noⁿ/ *n.*, population, lit., how many, refers to the number of things or people

porcupine **B'aí'** /b-ä-ē'/ *n.*, porcupine, a large rodent with quills of the order Rodentia, family Erethizontidae

possess **Adí'** /ä-thē'/ *v.*, possess, to own, to own something, as in property, money

possum grapes **Házi bdáze** /hä'-zē bthoⁿ'-zā/ *n.*, possum grapes, a woody vine with very small grapes, *Ampelopsis cordata*

post **Žą' ímuzà** /zhoⁿ' ē'-mü-zä/ *n.*, post, usu. refers to a corner fence post

posthole digger **T'ą́de wéədiudè** /t'oⁿ'-dā wä'-ə-thē-ü-dā'/ *n.*, posthole digger, a hand or heavy equipment device used to dig holes in the ground

post office **Wabáxu déde t'í'** /wä-bä'-xü thä'-thä t'ē'/ *n.*, post office, lit., sent the paper, refers to the U.S. postal service

pot **Wiúhą t'ągá** /weü'-hoⁿ t'oⁿ'-gä/ *n.*, pot, a large cooking vessel

potato **Nú'** /nü'/ *n.*, potato, *Solanum tuberosum*

Potawatomie **Wahídaxà** /wä-hē'-thä-xoⁿ'/ *n.*, the Potawatomie Tribe of Native Americans

potholder **Wiúk'idabè** /weü'-k'ē-thä-bä'/ *n.*, potholder, a piece of quilted cloth used to hold hot kitchen cooking utensils

pothole **Uxdúxda** /ü-xthü'-xthä/ *n.*, pothole, rut, hole, 1. describing a depression or dip on the road 2. a hole in a thing, such as a hollow log, a hole in the ground

pounded dry meat **T'a'gát'ubè'** /t'ä-gä'-t'ü-bä'/ *n.*, pounded dry (dehydrated) meat, dehydrated meat, jerky, pemmican (dried meat pounded and sometimes mixed with nuts and dried berries)

pour **Bixt'ą́** /bē-xt'oⁿ'/ *v.*, to pour, to cause to flow, to cause to drain out of something

pour **Bixt'ą́'xt'ą** /bē-xt'oⁿ'-xt'oⁿ'/ *v.*, to pour, to cause to continuously flow, to cause to continuously drain out of something

pour **Gamú'** /gä-mü'/ *v.*, pour, 1. to pour the contents of something into a container at once 2. rain coming down in a downpour, as in *Nążí akà ~ tigdài*, the rain came down in a down ~

pour out **Bašą́da** /bä-shoⁿ'-thä/ *v.*, to pour out, to empty

pour out **Gamúe** /gä-mü'-ā/ *v.*, pour out, 1. refers to any kind of liquid being poured out suddenly 2. refers to any solid substance being poured out, e.g., gravel from a dump truck

poverty **Uwágdà** /ü-wä'-gthä/ *n.*, poverty, neediness, destitution, hardship

powdery **Bdípe** /bthē'-pā/ *n.*, something that is powdery, chalky, a fine grind, reduced to powder or dust

prairie chicken **Šú'** /shü'/ *n.*, prairie chicken, *Tympanuchus cupido*

prairie dog **Mądík'a xudè** /moⁿ-thē'-k'ä xü-dä'/ *n.*, prairie dog, a burrowing rodent that has light brown fur

prairie schooner **Wáxegaxdà** /wä'-xā-gä-xthoⁿ'/ *n.*, prairie schooner, a large wagon covered with white canvas used by Caucasian people traveling west over Indian country in the nineteenth century, a Conestoga wagon

praise **Đahą́** /thä-hoⁿ'/ *v.*, to praise, 1. to glorify, make expressions of worshipping God 2. *n.*, giving honor to somebody who did something praiseworthy

praiseworthy **Đahą́wadè** /thä-hoⁿ'-wä-thä'/ *adj.*, praiseworthy, laudable, usu. refers to

Wak'ą́da (God) or Wak'ą́da Ižíge (Son of God)

prance **Nąstáp'i** /nonⁿ-stä-p'ē/ *v.*, prance, strut, as in the horse began to ~

pray **Wahą́e** /wä-honⁿ-ā/ *v.*, pray, giving praise and thanks to God or making a devout petition for help

prayer **Wahą́išigdè** /wä-honⁿ-ē-shē-gthā/ *n.*, prayer, a person who prays for others, as he/she is often requested to do so (These people are known for praying for others and for better conditions for the people.)

prayer **Wak'ą́da wadahà** /wä-k'onⁿ-dä wä-thä-honⁿ/ *n.*, prayer, the act of speaking to God to praise him, giving thanks, making a confession, or making a petition to him

prayer and fasting **Nǫ́žižą̀** /nonⁿ-zhē-zhonⁿ/ *adj.*, prayer and fasting (~ *adá biáma*, he went to pray and fast) (The Ponca people who studied the art of healing and solving social and psychological problems went into the wilderness to search in nature for the answers.)

praying mantis **T'eát'at'à** /t'ā-ä-t'ä-t'ä/ *n.*, praying mantis, family Mantidae, a predatory insect found throughout the world

pray for **Gíwahą̀i** /gē-wä-honⁿ-ē/ *v.t.*, to pray to God for somebody

precarious **Waną́duzè** /wä-nonⁿ-dü-zā/ *adj.*, precarious, unstable, insecure, uncertain, unsafe, risky

precaution **Sabé** /sä-bā/ *n.*, precaution, taking preventive measures or safeguards; *sabága*, you take measures against any possible trouble

pregnant **Watézeugdą̀** /wä-t'ā-zā-ü-gthonⁿ/ *adj.*, pregnant, with child, expecting a baby

prejudice **Xt'áwadábaží** /xt'ä-wä-thä-bä-zhē/ *n.*, prejudice, lit., doesn't like us or them, a bad attitude toward an indivi-

dual(s) with no good reason; *xt'ádaží*, doesn't like

prepare **Et'ą́dikidè** /ä-t'onⁿ-thē-kē-thā/ *v.*, prepare, to put things in order, to devise a plan to be ready for something that may happen

prepare **Waí'k'igdišt'ą̀** /wä-ē-k'ē-gthē-sht'onⁿ/ *v.t.*, prepare, to be ready beforehand for some purpose

present **E'dí** /ā-dē/ *n.*, present, here, in attendance, at hand, etc.

presently **Đegádi** /thä-gonⁿ-dē/ *adv.*, presently, at this moment, right now

president **I't'ígądè** /ē-t'ē-gonⁿ-thā/ *n.*, the president of the United States of America

presidential medals **It'ígądè wanáp'į** /ē-t'ē-gonⁿ-thā wä-nonⁿ-p'ēⁿ/ *n.*, presidential medals (These medals were presented to Native American leaders who went the U.S. capital for tribal matters.)

press **Bistá** /bē-stä/ *v.*, press, press down, bear down on

press **Nąstá** /nonⁿ-stä/ *v.*, press, being pressed down while being walked on repeatedly, usu. refers to grass

pressed **Bisáda** /bē-sä-dä/ *v.*, pressed, to remove unwanted creases from a piece of cloth using a hot iron

presumptuous **Úš'adįgè** /ü'sh-ä-thēⁿ-gā/ *adj.*, presumptuous, not having proper social modesty in public, 1. someone who goes beyond what is right or who is not very proper 2. *n.*, one who acts and speaks unashamedly

pretentious person **Niášigà mąščį́žįgè** /nē-ä-shē-gä monⁿ-shchēⁿ-zhēⁿ-gā/ *adj.*, a pretentious person who acts as though he/she knows something that no one else knows

prevent passage **Uhé'wakidaží** /ü-hā-wä-kē-thä-zhē/ *v.*, to prevent passage, 1. as in preventing an individual trying to cross a border 2. a proper male name among the Ponca people

previously **Atą'xt'iadì** /ä-toⁿ'-xt'ē-ä-dē'/ *adv.*, previously, when something occurred in the past

prison **Í'e gadadą** /ē'-ä gä-dä-thoⁿ'/ *n.*, prison, lit., breaking rocks, penitentiary, penal complex

prisoner **Ná'gdè** /nä'-gthä'/ *n.*, prisoner, namely, a war prisoner

proceed **Égą'gà** /ä'-goⁿ-gä'/ *v.*, proceed, go ahead or begin what you intend to do

prod **Bažíde** /bä-zhēⁿ'-dä/ *v.*, prod, to poke, thrust

produce **Wažútądè** /wä-zhü'-toⁿ-thä'/ *n.*, produce, crops harvested, as in garden or farm products

produce **Wažút'ądè** /wä-zhü'-t'oⁿ-thä'/ *n.*, produce, crops (vegetables, fruit, and grain) that are harvested, agricultural produce; *dižút'ą*, raising crops

profanity **Wáxe íye p'iáži** /wä-xä ē'-yä p'ē-ä'-zhē/ *v.*, profanity, lit., bad white man words, foul language, cussing, obscenities

prohibit **Wá'nąsè** /wä-noⁿ-sä'/ *v.*, prohibit, bar, to keep someone or a group from passing through or doing something

prohibit passage **Uhé'wánąsè** /ü-hä'-wä'-noⁿ-sä'/ *n.*, *archaic*, keeping them from passing by or "closing the escape route," usu. refers to an enemy attempting to escape

prompt **Á'gažì** /ä'-gä-zhē'/ *v.*, prompt, to prompt someone to say or do something

pronghorn antelope **T'ačú'ge** /t'ä-chü'-gä/ *n.*, pronghorn antelope

propane **T'adé wégdì** /t'ä-dä' wä'-gthē'/ *n.*, propane, butane, natural gas (ca. twentieth century)

property **Įdádą adį** /ēⁿ-dä'-doⁿ ä-thēⁿ'/ *n.*, property, possessions, belongings, stuff

prosperous **Wadá** /wä-dä'/ *adj.*, prosperous, someone who has or possesses much

protest **Úgdašigè** /ü-gthä-shē-gä'/ *v.*, protest, make a complaint, object

protocol **Íhudà** /ē'-hü-thä'/ *n.*, protocol, process, taking steps through something or some person or entity in order to reach or speak to someone

proud **Í'kižù** /ē'-kē-zhü'/ *adj.*, proud, pleased and satisfied, usu. about some new possession, such as clothing or jewelry

provisions **Umą́'e** /ü-moⁿ'-ä/ *n.*, groceries, provisions, foodstuff, rations

provoked **Ą́bak'à** /oⁿm-bä-k'ä'/ *v.*, provoked, being provoked to do something in retaliation

pry **Baxdúde** /bä-xthü'-dä/ *v.*, pry, to pull apart or open with a tool, such as a lever or crowbar

psychiatric disorder **Gdą́dį** /gthoⁿ'-thēⁿ/ *n.*, psychiatric disorder, the emotionally disabled, those who do not show good sense or behavior

psychological examination **Ną́xe'diwágazù** /noⁿ'-xä-thē-wä'-gä-zü/ *n.*, psychological examination or evaluation

psychologist **Wažį́'íbahà** /wä-zhēⁿ'-ē'-bä-hoⁿ'/ *n.*, psychologist, lit., one who knows the mind, one who studies and evaluates the behavior of people

public **Gaé'** /gä-ä'/ *adj.*, public, something open to view; *gaé' itéde*, *v.*, to place something out in the open or make it accessible

pudding **Ą́bagdè** /oⁿ'-bä-gthä'/ *n.*, pudding, sweetened ground corn cooked in water

puddle **Niúži** /nēü'-zhē/ *n.*, puddle, water puddle

puff **Í'dašudè** /ē'-thä-shü-dä'/ *v.*, puff, using the peace pipe to draw and blow smoke

puff up **Udíp'ušį** /ü-thē'-p'ü-shēⁿ'/ *adj.*, puff

up, to cause something to expand in size, as with yeast in bread making

pull **Đidą́** /thē-doⁿ/ *v.*, pull, tow, to draw or pull along behind

pull **Đisnù** /thē-snü/ *v.*, pull, to pull with use of the hands or a mechanical device, usu. sliding on the floor or ground

pull hair **Đip'á'zè** /thē-p'ä'-zā/ *v.*, pull hair, refers to hair pulling between women fighting

pulpit **Wak'ą́da íye uną́ži** /Wä-k'oⁿ'-dä ē'-yä ü-noⁿ'-zhē/ *n.*, pulpit, a speaker's stand in the Christian church from which a sermon is delivered by the minister

pulverize **Nąt'úbe** /noⁿ-t'ü'-bā/ *v.t.*, pulverize, to make something small by crushing or beating by mechanical means or by stepping on

pump **Ní' ubíxt'ą** /nē' ü-bē'-xt'oⁿ/ *v.*, pump, to pump water

pumpkin **Watą́'** /wä-toⁿ'/ *n.*, pumpkin

puncture **Ubáudè** /ü-bä'-ü-dā/ *v.*, puncture, to pierce or make a hole with a pointed instrument

pup **Šą́'žįgà** /shoⁿ'-zhēⁿ-gä/ *n.*, pup, a young dog, *Canis lupus familiaris*

pupil **Įštá'ušábedą̀** /ēⁿ-shtä'-ü-shä'-bā-thoⁿ/ *n.*, pupil, lit., the dark circular opening in the center of the eye, pupil of the eye

purple **Házi** /hä'-zē/ *adj.*, purple, the color purple, also lavender, violet (*T'ú'žíde*, reddish-blue, is also used to describe the color purple.)

purposely **É'sa'xt'ì** /ā'-sä-xt'ē'/ *adv.*, purposely, with intent, calculatingly

purse **Mázeska uží'** /moⁿ'-zä-skä ü-zhē'/ *n.*, purse, a handbag women carry filled with many things; billfold, a man's small folded flat case for carrying a couple of dollars

push **Badą́** /bä-doⁿ'/ *v.*, push, shove, move forward

push **Baną́ge** /bä-noⁿ'-gā/ *v.*, push, to push something on wheels, such as a wagon or wheelbarrow

push **Basnú** /bä-snü/ *v.*, push, pushing and sliding something on a flat surface

push **Bat'ą́t'ądį̀** /bä-t'oⁿ'-t'oⁿ-thēⁿ/ *v.*, push, connotes causing a person to walk fast, as in a stumbling fashion, repeatedly holding and pushing (*udą́i kí, waną́še amà ~ adí adái*, arresting him, the police, ~ing him, took him)

push apart **Baxdúde** /bä-xthü'-dā/ *v.*, push apart, an action of pushing with an instrument to remove a covering from something (he used a tool to ~ the bark from the trees to make teepee poles)

push away **Bahé** /bä-hā'/ *v.*, push away, to push someone or something away from them; *bahé déde*, to push aside

pushed down **Baxiáda** /bä-xēä'-thä/ *v.*, pushed down, to push down something, usu. refers to an upright structure (he ~ a rotten tree)

push in **Ubáxą** /ü-bä'-xoⁿ/ *v.*, push in, as in to push a fork-ended stick into a log to extract a rabbit

push off **Ubáxp'adè** /ü-bä'-xp'ä-thä/ *v.*, push off, pushing something off of something, intentionally or unintentionally

push open **Bašíbe** /bä-shē'-bä/ *v.*, push open, as in to ~ a door with the weight of the body

push up **Bamą́ši** /bä-moⁿ'-shē/ *v.*, push up, as in pushing a thing above the head to a shelf

pustule **Xdí'** /xthē'/ *n.*, pustule, abscess, a small bump under the skin filled with pus

put aside **Ihéde** /ē-hä'-thä/ *v.*, put aside, lay aside, set down, put down

put in **Ugdą́** /ü-gthoⁿ'/ *v.*, put in, to deposit something into a thing, usu. refers to a thing that is connected to or was a part of a thing, as in resetting a stone in a ring put in **Uwą** /ü-wonⁿ/ *v.*, put in, usu. refers to putting firewood into a woodstove or fireplace, as in *žą́'~'ga*, ~ wood or add wood

put in **Uží'** /ü-zhē/ *v.*, put in, to put something into a container, as in sugar into a cup, gas in a gas tank, etc.

putrid **Bdą́ p'iáži** /bthonⁿ p'ēä'-zhē/ *adj.*, putrid, as in something that smells rotten, decaying, rank, decomposing

Q

quail **Ú'šį'wadè** /ü-shēⁿ-wä-thä'/ *n.*, quail, bobwhite, a small game bird native to North America in the order Galliformes, family Odontophoridae

quandary **Ú'čižè** /ü'-chē-zhä'/ *n.*, quandary, predicament, in the middle of uncertainty as to what to do in a difficult situation

Quapaw **Ugáxpè** /ü-gä'x-p'ä'/ *n.*, the Quapaw Tribe of Native Americans

quarrel **Íye ákikidà** /ē'-yä ä'-kē-kē-thä'/ *n.*, quarrel, a verbal dispute or conflict between two entities

quarry **Idábaè** /ē-thä'-bä-ä'/ *n.*, quarry, an animal or human being hunted, pursued—usu. refers to waiting for the enemy to come by after carrying out the chase—(~ *gą̄įte*, he waited for the enemy)

quarter **Miká'ídawà** /mē-kä'-ē'-thä-wä'/ *n.*, quarter, lit., the price of a racoon, a quarter of a dollar

queen **Mąšiát'a mądì waú** /monⁿ-shēä'-t'ä monⁿ-thē' wä-ü'/ *n.*, queen, lit., woman who walks above, refers to women monarchs of foreign countries

queen **Žagdáša waú** /zhä-gthä'-shä wä-ü'/ *n.*, queen, queen of England

queer **É·xt'iáži** /ä'-·xt'ēä'-zhē/ *adj.*, queer, different in some way, not quite the same thing, questionable

query **Wémąxè** /wä'-monⁿ-xä'/ *v./n.*, query, question, inquiry, to ask a question

question **Gíža** /gē'-zhä/ *v./n.*, question, having reservations about a thing or a situation

questioned **Wawémąxè** /wä-wä'-monⁿ-xä'/ *v/n.*, questioned, interrogation, to get information concerning some matter, interview

quickly **Waną́xde** /wä-nonⁿ'-xthä/ *adv.*, archaic, quickly, hurriedly (go now and return ~)

quicksand **Mąníni** /monⁿ-nē'-nē/ *n.*, quicksand, a mixture of water and sand

quick-tempered **Wažį́'áškà** /wä-zhēⁿ'-ä'-shkä'/ *adj.*, quick tempered, touchy, liable to become angry

quiet **Xdíáži** /xthē'-ä'-zhē/ *adj.*, quiet, inaudible, in silence

quieting **Xdíážitigdaì** /xthē'-ä'-zhē-tē-gthä-ē'/ *v.*, quieting, sudden quieting in a noisy, crowded place

quietude **Gaxdíáži** /gä-xthē'-ä'-zhē'/ *n.*, quietude, the state of quiet, usu. refers to stillness or calmness after a storm

quills **B'aí'** /b-ä-ē'/ *n.*, quills, lit., sharp, refers to the quills of a porcupine

quilt **Waį púki** /wä-ēⁿ' pü'-kē/ *n.*, quilt, a blanket made of several layers of material, including cloth, cotton or wadding, and/or other woven material for the back

quit **Šą́'gaxè** /shonⁿ-gä-xä'/ *v.*, quit, stop doing, end the activity; *šą́'p'axè*, I quit; *šą́'škáxe*, you quit; *šą́'gáxaì*, he/she/it/they quit

quiver **Mą́žihà** /monⁿ-zhē-hä'/ *n.*, quiver, arrow quiver, a case made from the hide of a bison to hold arrows

R

rabbit **Mąščį́'gè** /monⁿsh-chēⁿ'-gä'/ *n.*, rabbit, cottontail

race **Ki'kíbanà** /kē-kē'-bä-nonⁿ'/ *v.*, race, compete, competition usu. in running on foot or on horseback, but the term is also appropriate for any type of race on wheels; *kíbaną̀*, race between two people

raccoon **Miká'** /mē-kä'/ *n.*, raccoon, a nocturnal animal of the genus *Prolcyon*

radio **Mą́ze íudà** /moⁿ'-zā ē'-ü-thä'/ *n.*, radio, an early electronic device that receives news and music from a transmitter or radio station, now may receive a broadcast from a satellite

radio **Mą́ze wa'ą́** /moⁿ'-zā wä-oⁿ'/ *n.*, radio, lit., metal that sings, refers to a radio or any modern device that provides music

radish **P'ą́xe** /p'oⁿ'-xā/ *n.*, radish, an edible root that is usually eaten raw, *Raphanus sativus* of the Brassicaceae family; *p'ą́xe židè*, red radish

rag **Waxíha p'ežì** /wä-xēⁿ'-hä p'ā-zhē'/ *n.*, rag, an old piece of cloth

raggedy **Za'zádè** /zä-zä'-dä/ *adj./n.*, raggedy, torn, worn to shreds, etc.

railroad track **E'wáś'ną̀gè uhè** /ā-wä'sh-noⁿ-gä' ü-hä'/ *n.*, railroad track

rain **Ną̀ží** /noⁿ-zhē'/ *v./n.*, rain, water that is formed in the clouds and falls to earth

rainbow **T'ušníge** /t'ü-shnēⁿ'-gä/ *n.*, rainbow

raining consistently **Ną̀žíną̀štą́žį** /noⁿ-zhēⁿ'-noⁿ-shtoⁿ'-zhēⁿ/ *v.*, rain consistently, refers to rainy days during spring

rain on **Áną̀žį̀** /ä'-noⁿ-zhēⁿ'/ *v.*, rain on, to get rained on

rainstorm **Ną̀žį́' ákišugà** /noⁿ-zhēⁿ' ä'-kē-shü-gä'/ *n.*, rainstorm, deluge, cloudburst

rainy **Ną̀žíśt'ą̀** /noⁿ-zhē'-sh'toⁿ'/ *adj.*, rainy, rain that comes often

raise **Uhíde** /ü-hē'-thä/ *v.*, raise, rear, to raise up and nurture children

raise **Žút'ą** /zhü'-t'oⁿ/ *v.*, raise, to grow crops

raisin **Házi bdą́ze** /hä'-zē bthoⁿ'-zā/ *n.*, raisin, a dried grape, said to have health benefits

rake **Wédįbexį̀** /wā'-thēⁿ-bä-xēⁿ'/ *n.*, rake, a gardening tool used to gather grass or leaves and smooth soil in a garden; *v.*, *dįbéxį̀*, act of raking

rancid **Gdą́xe** /gthoⁿ'-xā/ *adj.*, rancid, smelling of decomposing fats and oils, usu. in meats

rank **Zą́ze** /zoⁿ'-zā/ *adj.*, rank, pungent, fetid, foul smelling

ransack **Wadít'ą̀** /wä-thē'-t'oⁿ-t'oⁿ'/ *v.t.*, ransack, children (and some adults) getting into things or looking at private things in the home without permission

rap **Utį́tį** /ü-tēⁿ'-tēⁿ/ *n.*, rap (*ebé etè, t'ižébekè ~*, somebody ~ped on the door)

rapidly **Gišką́át'ašą̀** /gē-shkoⁿ'-ä'-t'ä-shoⁿ'/ *adv.*, rapidly, to go rapidly, swiftly, briskly

rare **Uwáną̀dà** /ü-wä'-noⁿ-thä'/ *adj.*, rare, limited, a thing that is in short supply or not available among us

rash **Usúde** /ü-sü'-dä/ *n.*, rash, outbreak on the surface of the skin, usu. red and itchy, usu. refers to diaper rash on babies

rasp **Žą́' íbamą̀** /zhoⁿ' ē'-bä-moⁿ'/ *n.*, rasp, wood rasp, a tool to smooth down rough edges

raspberry **A'gdą́'ka'mą̀gè** /ä-gthoⁿ'-kä-moⁿ-gä'/ *n.*, raspberry, a perennial plant of the genus *Rubus*

rat **Įčą́t'ągà** /ēⁿ-choⁿ'-t'oⁿ-gä'/ *n.*, rat, a large, long-tailed rodent of the Muridae family

rattle **Đisá'du** /thē-sä'-thü/ *v.*, rattle, to rattle an instrument or an object with the hands

rattle **Đisá'sadù** /thē-sä'-sä-thü'/ *v.*, rattle, to continuously rattle an instrument or an object with the hands

rattle **Gasá'du** /gä-sä'-thü/ *v.*, rattle, to rattle an instrument or object, e.g., shaking a gourd using force to cause it to rattle

rattle **Gasá'sadù** /gä-sä'-sä-thü'/ *v.*, rattle, to continuously rattle an instrument or object, e.g., using force to cause a gourd to rattle

rattle **Nạsá'du** /noⁿ-sä'-thü/ v., rattle, to rattle something with the foot or legs, e.g., a Hedúškà dancer rattling the deer hooves that are wrapped around his lower legs or a Creek women's stomp dancer shaking shells wrapped around her lower legs

rattle **Nạsá'sadù** /noⁿ-sä'-sä-thü/ v., rattle, to continuously rattle something with the foot or legs, e.g., a Hedúškà dancer rattling the deer hooves wrapped around his lower legs or a Creek stomp dancer shaking shells

rattlesnake **Sadú'** /sä-thü'/ n., rattlesnake, the name refers to a snake's rattle

rattlesnake **Šé'k'i** /shä-k'ē/ n., rattlesnake, the name refers to the snake's act of rattling

rattling **Bisá'du** /bē-sä'-thü/ v., rattling, to make a rattling noise by pressing down on something

rattling **Bisá'sadù** /bē-sä'-sä-thü/ v., rattling, to make a continuous rattling noise by pressing down on something

raven **K'áxe** /k'ä'-xä/ n., raven, a large crow with glossy black feathers, *Corvus corax*

ravine **Tíxįdè** /tē-xēⁿ-dä'/ n., ravine, a small valley that is larger than a gully, made by water or soil erosion; *tíxįdè*, arroyo, usu. a dry creekbed in the Southwest

raw **Nídažì** /nē'-dä-zhē'/ adj., raw, usu. refers to uncooked food

rawhide **Wahá sagí'** /wä-hä' sä-gē'/ n., rawhide, untanned animal hide; used for moccasin soles, shields

reach **Udúhi** /ü-thü'-hē/ v., reach, 1. to extend the arms and hands to grasp something, as in reaching for an apple on a tree 2. to pursue something that is reachable, such as higher education

reach in **Đižįde** /thē-zhēⁿ'-dä/ v., reach in, reaching in one's pockets

read **Á'dadè** /ä'-thä-dä/ v., to read, recite, interpret some written material

read **Wádadè** /wä'-thä-dä/ v., to read something, usu. refers to reading some book, newspaper, or magazine

ready **Šą́'** /shoⁿ'/ n., it is ready, complete, set to go, done

ready **Waí'k'igdišt'ą̀** /wä-ē'-k'ē-gthē-sht'oⁿ'/ adj., ready, to be prepared for something, to be complete and ready

rear **Ną́·de** /noⁿ'·-dä/ n., rear, in the back part, at the rear of something, the part that is farthest from the front

rebellious **Íye wánạ'ạ̀žì** /ē'-yä wä'-noⁿ-oⁿ-zhē'/ adj., rebellious, unruly, defiant, deliberately will not listen to someone in authority

recede **Gasp'é** /gä-sp'ä'/ v., recede, 1. to become less or ebb, as after the flooding of a river 2. clearing of any liquid (e.g., water) when debris goes to the bottom of a container

receive **Đizé** /thē-zä'/ v., receive, to receive or to own for oneself something that was offered or given

recent **Į́'cạxt'ì** /ēⁿ'-choⁿ-xt'ē'/ adj., recent, just a while ago, a short time ago

recently **Į́'cạxt'iàdi** /ēⁿ'-choⁿ-xt'ē-ä'-dē/ adv., recently, something that occurred recently at a certain day or time

record **Wabáxu itéde** /wä-bä'-xü ē-tä'-thä/ n., record, documents put away or stored

recover **K'igdázu** /k'ē-gthä'-zü/ v., recover, that point of recovering from a state of sickness—something like awakening from being comatose, the start of recovery

recovered **Gdíze** /gthē'-zä/ v., pres./past t., recover, get back, to get something back that had been taken

recovered **Giní** /gē-nē'/ v., past t., recovered, got well

red **Ží'de** /zhē'-dä/ adj., red, the color red; *žíde egà*, reddish; *žíde gáxe*, redden or make red redbud tree **Žązí'sabè** /zhoⁿ-zē'-sä-bä'/ *n.*, redbud tree, of the genus *Cercis*

redeem **K'igdíp'ì** /k'ē-gthē'-p'ē'/ *v.*, redeem, to extricate oneself from something detrimental

red elm tree **É'žą'žíde** /ä'-zhoⁿ-zhē'-dā/ *n.*, red elm tree

red fox **Mąžą́ha** /moⁿ-zhoⁿ'-hä/ *n.*, red fox

red haired **Nąžíha žíde** /noⁿ-zhē'-hä zhē'-dā/ *adj.*, red haired; *n.*, refers to a person with red hair

red ocher **Wasé'židè** /wä-sā'-zhē-dā/ *n.*, red ocher, a reddish iron oxide

refill **P'í'uži'** /p'ē'-ü-zhē'/ *v.*, refill, to fill up again, replenish

refinish **Bit'éga** /bē-t'ä'-gä/ *v.*, refinish, as in to sand and polish old furniture

refuse **K'ídikąži'udíšį** /k'ē-thē-koⁿ-zhē-ü-thē'-shēⁿ/ *v.*, refuse, will not accept help or aid; *k'ídikąžiwadè*, would not be able to help or aid following a refusal of offered help

refuse **Udíage** /ü-thē'-ä'-gä/ *v.*, refuse, declining to do a task or to do something that has been offered

regret **Udúgdà** /ü-thü'-gthä'/ *v.*, regret, to be sorry for mistakes made, to be remorseful for being at fault

regurgitate **Í'gdebè** /ē'-gthä-bä'/ *v.*, regurgitate, vomit, to expel partly digested food from the stomach back to the mouth and out

rehearse **Íkigdaskądè** /ē'-kē-gthä-skoⁿ-thä'/ *v.*, rehearse, practice, to do over and over before presentation

rein **Íkididą̀** /ē'-k'ē-thē-doⁿ/ *n.*, rein, a strap or straps attached to the bit of a bridle by which a rider controls the horse

reincarnation **P'ahą́gadì išáge** /p'ä-hoⁿ'-gä-dē' ēsh-ä'-gä/ *n.*, reincarnation, lit., old man who lived before, philosophy or religious belief that some children had lived a previous life because of their talk of things past

reiterate **Šip'í udá** /shē-p'ē' ü-thä'/ *v.*, reiterate, to say something over and over again, to repeat something

reject **Gą́daži** /goⁿ-thä-zhē'/ *v.*, reject, decline, to refuse to accept something; *gą́da'baži*, refers to somebody who doesn't want something when offered, something that is turned down

reject **Į́'įgè** /ēⁿ-ēⁿ-gä'/ *v.*, reject, not wanting a thing or things that are unappealing

rejoice **Á'gidè** /ä'-gē-thä'/ *v.*, rejoice, to be glad or to take delight in

related **Éde** /ä'-thä'/ *n.*, relations, family, kin; *e'kidè*, refers to people who are related

related **Ukíkízi** /ü-kē'-kē-zhē/ *n.*, related, determining a relationship, usu. refers to stating that a person or persons are related to somebody through other relatives or through marriage

related **Ukízi** /ü-kē'-zhē/ *v.*, related, refers to persons who are blood relatives or kinfolk

relatives **Į́'dádąwagidè** /ēⁿ-dä'-doⁿ-wä-gē-thä'/ *n.*, relatives, addressing a crowd of people with whom the speaker may be a kinsman

relatives **K'igdét'ą** /k'ē-gthä'-t'oⁿ/ *n.*, relatives, refers to a person who has one or more relatives whom he/ she favors in personal behavior and looks

relax **Ą́zegidaì** /oⁿ-zā-gē-thäē'/ *v.*, 3rd pers. pl., they relaxed

release **Đištą́ déde** /thē-shtoⁿ' thä'-thä/ *v.*, release, to set free from confinement or bondage

reliance **Udúnąží** /ü-thü'-noⁿ-zhē'/ *n./v.*, reliance, to rely upon or have confidence in

relieve **Gídik'ą̀** /gē-thē-k'oⁿ'/ *v.*, relieve, to free or aid somebody from an unpleasant or painful situation

relocate **Wahą́'** /wä-hoⁿ'/ *v.*, relocate, move somewhere else, change place of residence remainder **Ušté** /ü-shtä'/ *n.*, remainder, something or things left over

remainder **Uštédą** /ü-shtä'-thoⁿ/ *n.*, remainder, refers to one particular thing left in a horizontal position

remainder **Ušt'éte** /ü-sht'ä'-tā/ *n.*, remainder, refers to particular things left over; *uštéke*, one thing left over

remarkable **Đaxúbe** /thä-xü'-bā/ *v.*, to be remarkable, recognizing a person who does something extraordinary or significantly noteworthy

remember **Awądísidè** /oⁿ-woⁿ'-thē'-sē-thä'/ *v.*, *1st pers. pl.*, remember, to remember some people; *wegísidè*, *1st pers. sing.*, I ~ you

remember **Gisíde** /gē-sē'-thä/ *v.*, remember, to remember something

remember **Sídè** /sē'-thä/ *v.t./v.i.*, remember, retain an idea in the memory

remnants **Ušt'ášt'a** /ü-sht'ä'-sht'ä/ *n.*, remnants, pieces of things

remove **Bašnú'de** /bä-shnü'-dä/ *v.*, remove, to remove by prying, as in removing a sealed lid; *bašnú'šnudè*, to take off hurriedly by prying, piece by piece

remove **Đišnúde** /thē-shnü'-dä/ *v.*, remove, to remove by use of hands and hand tools; *đišnúšnudè*, to remove with hands and hand tools repeatedly

rend **Babđáze** /bä-bthä'-zā/ *v.*, rend, tear, shred

rent **Uná'** /ü-nä'/ *v.*, rent, rental fee, lease

repair **Đip'í·** /thē-p'ē'·/ *v.*, repair, to fix, patch up, restore something close to its original condition

repeat **P'í'denà** /p'ē'-thä-noⁿ/ *v.*, repeat, try again, a command to try something again

repeat **Šip'í'** /shē-p'ē'/ *v.*, repeat, do again

repeatedly **P'ídądà** /p'ē'-thoⁿ-thoⁿ/ *adv.*, repeatedly, doing something over and over again

reprove **Wádadąbažì** /wä'-thä-thoⁿ-bä-zhē'/ *v.*, reprove, tell off, rake over the coals

repulse **Nądegdà** /noⁿ'-dä-gthä'/ *v.*, repulse, disgust, revolt, nauseate

repulsive **Nądegdàwadè** /noⁿ'-dä-gthä'-wä-thä'/ *adj.*, repulsive, disgusting, nauseating, gross, abhorrent

resemble **Ábitądè** /ä'-bē-toⁿ-thä'/ *v.*, resemble, semblance, bear a resemblance to, similarity, akin to, be like (he ~s his grandfather)

resemble **Égąigà** /ä'-goⁿ-ēⁿ-goⁿ'/ *v.*, resemble, to have a likeness to another thing

resent **Wawét'adè** /wä-wä'-t'ä-thä'/ *v.*, resent, dislike, have bitter (borderline hateful) feelings toward a person or persons who have accomplished something one has not; *udút'adè*, resentful or disliking somebody because he/she possesses something one does not have or because he/she has accomplished something one has not (The term is closely related to envy.) See *Wawé'giniè*, envy.

reserved **Gí'dikądè** /gē'-thē-koⁿ-thä'/ *v.*, reserved, making a place or opening for somebody in a situation where others may be seated, speaking, standing, applying for, etc.

reside **Ú't'i** /ü'-t'ē/ *v.*, reside, to inhabit or live in a dwelling

residual **Ušté** /ü-shtä'/ *adj.*, residual, left over, remaining, surplus

resist **Udíagè** /ü-thē'-ä-gä'/ *v.*, resist, refusing to go along with

rest **Ázegidè** /oⁿ'-zä-gē-thä'/ *v.*, rest, relax, take a break, recess

restaurant **Úwadáte t'ì** /ü'-wä-thä'-tä t'ē'/ *n.*, restaurant, cafe, a place where meals are cooked, sold, and served

restrained **Ądáwądišp'egà** /oⁿ-thoⁿ'-wä-thē-shp'ä-gä'/ *n.*, state of being restrained, lit., "as I am kept back or ~ from speaking or doing something on account of it," an expression of being kept back or restrained on account of something

retardation **U'xdáẓì** /ü-xthä'-zhē'/ *n.*, disability, lit., "didn't catch up," intellectual disability, a genetic disorder, usu. a birth defect that causes some level of disability, as in Down's syndrome

retreat **Xádagdè'** /xä'-thä-gthä'/ *v.*, retreat, lit., going back, 1. an act of withdrawing from a situation that could be dangerous 2. refers to tributary creek water going back because of flooding from a larger river

retrieve **Agí'kigdè** /ä-gē'-kē-gthä'/ *v. phr.*, retrieve, to go get his own (something)

return **Íp'ašedà̧** /ē'-p'ä-shä-thoⁿ'/ *v.*, return quickly, usu refers to somebody going to a specific destination to conduct business and returning immediately

return **Xáda dè** /xä-thä thä'/ *v.*, return, connotes returning and going again

return **Xáda gì** /xä'-thä gē'/ *v.*, return, connotes going somewhere and returning or coming back; *gí'*, return

returned **Aki'** /ä-kē'/ *v.*, *3rd pers. sing.*, returned, he/she/it returned

returned **Gdí'ha** /gthē'-hä/ *v.*, *masc.*, returned, connotes somebody has ~ suddenly

returned **Wé'i'** /wä-ē'/ *v.*, *3rd pers. sing.*, returned, giving back, to send back or restore something (~ *ahì*, he/she/it gave it back to us)

returned with **Agdádį'akì** /ä-gthä-thēⁿ-ä-kē'/ *v.*, returned with, brought back his own

returning **Agí** /ä-gē'/ *v.*, returning, to come back to a place after leaving it, usu. refers to someone who went away and is returning

reveal **Giwádišnà** /gē-wä-thē-shnä/ *v.*, reveal, something revealed to a person in a culturally spiritual manner

revealed **Điwádíšna** /thē-wä-thē'-shnä/ *v.*, revealed, exposed, something laid open to view; *gíwadišnà*, to reveal something specifically to somebody

revealed **Wádat'à̧ì** /wä'-thä-t'oⁿ'-ēⁿ/ *v.*, revealed, 1. bringing something to light by someone (*ebéte*, ~, it was ~ to them by somebody.) 2. caused to be revealed by speaking of something often

revealed **Wawét'à̧ì** /wä-wä-t'oⁿ'-ēⁿ/ *v.*, revealed, ~ to us specifically; *į̃wat'à̧i*, ~ to me; *đíwat'à̧i*, ~ to you; *gíwat'à̧i*, ~ to him/her/them; *wéwat'à̧i*, it is clear to us or we understand the revelation of something shown

revenge **Í'mądà** /ē'-moⁿ-thä'/ *n.*, revenge, seeking to administer punishment in return for something that was done in the past

reverberation **Udázaè** /ü-thä'-zä-ä'/ *n.*, reverberation, echo, noise in a large auditorium

reverberation **Udázaì** /ü-thä'-zäē'/ *n.*, reverberation, noise, echo, loud sound, the continuance of a sound after the initial sound is made

reverse **Xáda** /xä'-thä/ *v.*, reverse, back, go in the opposite direction

revert **Điákiwahà** /thē-ä'-kē-wä-hä/ *v.*, revert, to change back, as in going back to the original pattern or style

revolve **Nágè** /noⁿ'-gä/ *v.*, 1. revolve, as in an automobile motor running 2. a wheel spinning 3. *archaic*, a galloping horse

revolving door **T'i'žé'be'ganàge** /t'ē-zhä'-bä-gä-noⁿ'-gä/ *n.*, revolving door

ribbon **Wábatè** /wä'-bä-tä'/ *n.*, ribbon, trimming, a strip of fabric used to decorate another piece of fabric

ribs **Đít'ì'** /thē'-t'ē'/ *n.*, ribs, in human anatomy, the ribs, costae, are long, curved bones that form the rib cage

rice **Síwanidè** /sē'-wä-nē-dä'/ *n.*, rice, *Oryza*

sativa (Asian rice) or *Oryza glaberrima* (African rice)

ridge **Baxú** /bä-xü'/ *n.*, ridge, a long, narrow, elevated piece of land that runs continuously over a distance

ridge **T'ęnä́ka baxú** /t'āⁿ-non'-kä bä-xü'/ *n.*, in carpentry, the ridge of the roof

ridged **Sáda** /sä'-dä/ *adj.*, ridged, stiff, usu. 1. refers to something extended, such as one's legs 2. flattened, as with a stiff collar

ridicule **Wawé'xaxà** /wä-wā'-xä-xä'/ *v.*, ridicule, to deride, mock, or taunt somebody with laughter in their absence — (This is considered to be bad behavior by the Ponca people.)

ridiculous **Ä́dinà** /oⁿ-thē-noⁿ'/ *adj./interj.*, ridiculous, an expression that connotes something done ridiculously or even in a silly manner; *archaic*, nearly acted, nearly said something, nearly did something that did not end appropriately

right away **Šä́šą** /shoⁿ'-shoⁿ/ *adv.*, right away, without ado (When a task is completed or a crisis arises and further immediate action is required and a person or group leaves right away to follow up; *wadítą đišt'ą́itedì ~ adái*, They finished the job and left ~)

right fit **É'nąskà** /ā'-noⁿ-skä'/ *adj.*, right fit, as in clothing

rigid **Dį́dį** /dēⁿ'-dēⁿ/ *adj.*, rigid, something that is stiff or inflexible

ring **Nąbeúdixdà** /noⁿ-bäü'-thē-xthä'/ *n.*, ring, a circular piece of jewelry worn around a finger, usu. made of some precious metal, such as silver or gold

ring finger **Nąbé'wé'dubà** /noⁿ-bā'-wā'-dü-bä'/ *n.*, ring finger

rinse **Ígađužà** /ē'-gä-thü-zhä'/ *v.*, rinse, lit., to stir, as in swirling clothing around in water to remove the detergent

rip **Đisną́** /thē-snoⁿ'/ *v.*, rip, to tear apart, to open a piece of cloth by the seams

ripe **Ní'de** /nē'-dä/ *adj.*, ripe, mature, ready to eat, usu. refers to fruits on plants; *ná̧židè*, sun ripened

ripple **Babáxu'** /bä-bä'-xü/ *v.*, to make a ripple in water, as in a fish swimming upstream

rising **Gamä́ši** /gä-moⁿ'-shē/ *v.*, rising, a cause that forces a thing to rise into the air or ascend upward; *đimä́ši*, to lift something upward; *bamä́ši*, to use the body to push something upward; *bimä́ši*, to press something upward

roach **T'ahį́'wágdą̀** /t'ä-hēⁿ'-wä'-gthoⁿ/ *n.*, roach, a headpiece made of deer tail and porcupine guard hair (some in an earlier period were composed of horsehair) worn by the Heđúškà dancers

road **Užä́ge** /ü-zhoⁿ'-gä/ *n.*, road, a known roadway

roam **K'ú'wixè** /k'ü'-wē-xä'/ *v.*, roam, ramble, wander, etc.

roam **Mąná'dihà** /moⁿ-noⁿ'-thē-hä'/ *v.*, roam, to roam about aimlessly

roar **Xué'** /xü-ā'/ *v.*, roar, to emit a loud sound

roast **Wabásna** /wä-bä'-snä/ *v.*, roast, cutting a piece of meat and placing it over an open fire with a green stick

roast **Žégdą̀** /zhä'-gthoⁿ/ *v.*, roast, to roast something on embers; now to cook or bake in the oven

robe **Waį́'** /wä-ēⁿ'/ *n.*, robe, usu. refers to tanned animal skins

robe **Wa'į́' xúdè** /wä-ēⁿ' xü'-dä/ *n.*, robe, lit., gray robe, made of furs taken from animals with gray fur

robin **Mä́ge'židè** /moⁿ'-gä-zhē-dä/ *n.*, robin, lit., robin redbreast, 1. American robin 2. a migratory bird of the thrush family named for its red breast

rock **Bap'ä́de** /bä-p'oⁿ'-dä/ *v.*, rock, to move back and forth or cause something to move back and forth rock **Bap'ą́p'ą́de** /bä-p'oⁿ'-p'oⁿ'-dä/ *v.*, rock, to continuously move back and forth, as with a table or chair with uneven legs

rock **Biáza** /bē-ä'-zä/ *v.*, rock, to rock something like a baby's cradle

rock **Į́'ę'** /ēⁿ'-äⁿ/ *n.*, rock, stone, solid mineral aggregate

rocket **Mą́ ugánaxdį** /moⁿ' ü-gä'-nä-xthēⁿ'/ *n.*, rocket, sky rocket, space rocket

rocking **Biázazà** /bē-ä'-zä-zä'/ *v.*, rocking, to sway to and fro, backward and forward, or from side to side, usu. caused by pushing with the feet (she sat ~ the chair)

rocking chair **Ágdį baiázazà** /ä'-gthēⁿ bä-ē-ä'-zä-zä'/ *v.*, rocking chair, a chair mounted on two curved pieces of wood made for rocking oneself to and fro

roll **Baną́ge** /bä-noⁿ'-gä/ *v.*, roll, to roll something on wheels or to roll a ball

roll **Ubát'ądà** /ü-bä-t'oⁿ-thä'/ *v.*, roll, rolling something over with a tool, such as a lever; *ubít'ądà*, roll something over by pressing

roll call **Ižáže wádadè** /ē-zhä'-zhä wä'-thä-dä'/ *n.*, roll call, refers to calling out a list of names to determine who is present

rooster **Wažį́ga nugà** /wä-zhēⁿ'-gä nü-gä'/ *n.*, rooster, usu. refers to chickens but may refer to other male birds

root **Žą́ką́** /zhoⁿ-koⁿ'/ *n.*, root, the part of a plant that spreads underground, absorbing water and nutrients from the earth for growth

rope **Hážįgà** /hä-zhēⁿ-gä'/ *n.*, rope, cord, twine

rope **T'énážįhà gazą́de wék'ąt'ą̀** /t'ä'-noⁿ'-zhēⁿ-hä' gä-zoⁿ-dä wä-k'oⁿ-t'oⁿ'/ *n.*, rope, braided rope made of hair from the head of a bison

rotten **T'í'a** /t'ē'-ä/ *adj.*, rotten, decaying hides, cured leather, or cloth of various grades

rotten **Xé'gà** /xä'-gä/ *adj./n.*, rotten, decaying substances such as wood or bones

rotten wood **Žą́' xegà** /zhoⁿ' xä-gä'/ *n.*, rotten wood (This type of wood was so named because of its uselessness for construction or burning, but it is useful for finding bait for fishing, as well as morels and other mushrooms, which grow near decaying wood and leaves.)

rough **Šášakà** /shä'-shä-kä'/ *adj.*, rough, marked by ridges, uneven or bumpy, mostly refers to handiwork made with beads, quills, and other craft materials

round **Bibút'a** /bē-bü'-t'ä/ *v.*, round, to make something round

round **Bút'a** /bü-t'ä/ *adj.*, round, circular, ring-shaped, spherical

rounded **Babú't'à** /bä-bü'-t'ä/ *v.*, rounded, to make round by use of force or pushing

rounded **Búbut'ą̀** /bü'-bü-t'oⁿ'/ *adj.*, rounded, refers to a number of things that are rounded; usu. refers to things that are made, such as balls of various sizes, certain foods being prepared to be cooked

roundhouse **T'i'bút'a** /t'ē-bü'-t'ä/ *n.*, roundhouse—traditionally, a large, circular frame building that was used for tribal ceremonies and other gatherings, ca. 1910

rub **Bižú'** /bē-zhü/ *v.*, rub, 1. to remove grain by rubbing 2. to rub parts of the body, as in a massage

rub **Bižú'žu** /bē-zhü'-zhü/ *v.*, rub, 1. to continuously remove grain by rubbing 2. to continuously rub parts of the body, as in a massage

rubber **Hazízigè** /hä-zē'-zē-gä'/ *n.*, rubber, lit., stretchy hide, a stretchy and flexible material that is waterproof, derived from the *Hevea* tree from South America (prehistoric [ca. 1600 BC] use by the Mayans)

ruin **Ðip'íáži** /thē-p'ē'-ä'-zhē/ *v.t.*, ruin,

to ruin or spoil a thing with the hands; *nąp'íáži*, to ruin or spoil a thing, such as machinery, an auto, a lawn mower; *gap'iáži*, to ruin a thing by force or wind; *bip'íáži*, to ruin by pressing

ruins **T'iúdixdigè** /t'ēü-thē-xthē-gā'/ *n.*, ruins, the remains of a once-inhabited dwelling or house, usu. evidenced by piles of dirt and wood or a foundation

rule **Udádekè** /ü-thä'-dä-kā'/ *n.*, rule, the written rule or law

ruler **Wégązè** /wā'-goⁿ-zā'/ *n.*, ruler, 1. a measuring device, tape measure, measuring stick 2. the distance from one point to another

rummaging **Wadíedą̀** /wä-thē'-ā-thoⁿ'/ *v.*, rummaging, to rummage through one's personal property, looking at one's personal property that has not been seen or touched over a long period of time

rumor **Íyeudà** /ē'-yā-ü-thä'/ *n.*, rumor, 1. story, buzz, chitchat, something people are repeating without confirming its truth 2. storytelling. See *Híga*, story.

run **Ną́ge** /noⁿ'-gā/ *v.*, run, something that is running, such as machinery, horses

run **Ną́gedè** /noⁿ'-gā-thä'/ *v.*, run, 1. to operate, to run or control some sort of machinery 2. to control religious or secular meetings

run **T'ą́di** /t'oⁿ'-thē/ *v.*, run, to go faster (in speed) than a walk in such a manner that both feet leave the ground for each springing step

run away **K'imúgdą̀** /k'ē-mü'-gthoⁿ'/ *v.*, run away, break out, or run off, as when a student leaves boarding school without permission

run fast **Nąwáseką̀** /noⁿ-wä'-sā-koⁿ'/ *adj.*, run fast, making machinery run fast, pedaling fast on a bicycle, or engaging the accelerator in an automobile or other conveyance by use of the feet

run out **Nądíge** /noⁿ-theⁿ'-gā/ *v.*, run out, to exhaust supplies, as in "~ of gas"

run over **Ánągè** /ä'-noⁿ-gā/ *v.*, run over, squash, flatten out (she ~ the bicycle)

Russian **Wadá'gè'púkì** /wä-thä'-gā'-pü'-kē'/ *n.*, Russian, lit., big soft hat, Russian people, a native or inhabitant of Russia

rust **U'zí'** /ü-zē'/ *n.*, rust, corrosion, oxidation

rut **Uną́xdùxda** /ü-noⁿ'-xthü'-xthä'/ *n.*, rut, making a rut or groove on a dirt road after rain

rutting season **T'áxt'ì k'ídixè** /t'ä'-xt'ē' k'ē'-thē-xä'/ *n.*, rutting season, that time of the year when deer are in a state of sexual excitement

S

sack **Úžihà** /ü'-zhē-hä'/ *n.*, sack, bag

sacred **Waxúbe** /wä-xü'-bā/ *adj.*, sacred, 1. *n.*, something sacred or holy 2. *n.*, refers to religious relics and certain practices in religious activities

Sacred Pipe **Niní'ba waxúbe** /nē-nē'-bä wä-xü'-bā/ *n.*, Sacred Pipe, the Sacred Pipe of the Ponca people

Sacred Pole **Žą́waxúbe** /zhoⁿ'-wä-xü'-bā/ *n.*, Sacred Pole, the Sacred Pole of the Omaha people

saddened **Ną́dè'gídažì** /noⁿ'-dä-gē'-thä-zhē'/ *v.*, saddened; feeling emotionally sorrowful, unhappy, sad, etc.

saddle **Šą́ąk'ágde** /shoⁿ'-noⁿ-k'ä'-gthā/ *n.*, saddle, a seat used by a person riding on the back of a horse; *šánąk'ágde uži*, saddlebag; *šánąk'ágde ágašt'ągà*, saddle blanket

safe **Edážegà** /ā-thä'-zhä-goⁿ/ *adj.*, safe, secure, in safe hands, safe and sound, free of hardships

safeguard **T'égidè** /t'ā'-gē-thä'/ *n.*, safeguard, save and keep, look after; *čégidè*, safeguard something special

sage **P'é'ži'xút'à** /p'ā'-zhē-xü-t'ä'/ *n.*, sage, Native American cleansing sage, usu. used in prayers by burning the flat leaves, genus *Artemisia*

salamander **S'ihídubà** /s-ē-hē'-dü-bä'/ *n.*, salamander, any of the species of amphibians within the order Caudata

sale **Wadî̧wị úmąk'à** /wä-thę̄ⁿ'-wēⁿ ü-moⁿ-k'ä'/ *n.*, sale, an auction, a garage sale

sallow **Xp'éga** /xp'ā'-gä/ *adj.*, sallow, sickly, pale, ashen, pallid

salmon **Hužíde** /hü-zhē'-dä/ *n.*, salmon, one of the species of fish in the family Salmonidae known by the Ponca

saloon **Úwadát'ą t'í** /ü-wä-thä'-t'oⁿ t'ē'/ *n.*, saloon, bar, beer joint

salt **Niskí'de** /nē-skē'-thä/ *n.*, salt, table salt, sodium chloride

Salt Fork River **Ni'ží'dè** /nē-zhē'-dä/ *n.*, Salt Fork River, Oklahoma, lit., river that is red

saltine crackers **Wamą́skè'násagè** /wä-moⁿ'-skä' nä'-sä-gä'/ *n.*, *s./pl.*, saltine crackers, crackers, a thin, crisp cracker sprinkled with salt

salt shaker **Niskí'deuží'** /nē-skē'-thä-ü-zhē'/ *n.*, saltshaker, a condiment holder for salt

salty **S'á'de** /s-ä'-thä/ *adj.*, salty, having a slightly tart or bitter edge to a flavor

salve **Nié'ísnadè** /nē-ā'-ē'-snä-thä'/ *n.*, salve, a medicinal ointment to soothe and help heal sores or wounds

same **É'gà̧'xt'ì** /ā'-goⁿ-xt'ē'/ *adv.*, same, exactly the same — refers to something that was duplicated, made, or done in the same manner

same **É'kigà̧** /ā'-kē-goⁿ'/ *adj.*, same, refers to two or more things that are identical, matching, or alike; *égą̧xt'iáži*, not quite the same

same height **Ékitą̧hà** /ā'-kē-toⁿ-hä'/ *adj./n.*, 1. same height, of equal height 2. same time (~ *ahí*, they arrived at the ~)

sand **P'izá** /p'ē-zä'/ *n.*, sand, granular material composed of rock and other mineral particles

sandbur **Waxága žį̧gà** /wä-xä'-gä zhēⁿ-gä'/ *n.*, sandbur, stickered weeds that grow in sandy soil, genus *Cenchrus*

sand dunes **P'izá b'ahà̧** /p'ē-zä' b-ä-hoⁿ'/ *n.*, sand dunes, refers to a hill in a desert formed by wind or the flow of water

sandhill crane **P'é't'à̧** /p'ā'-t'oⁿ'/ *n.*, sandhill crane, *Grus canadensis*

sand plum **P'izák'ą́de'** /p'ē-zä'-k'oⁿ'-dä/ *n.*, sand plum, a small, round, edible fruit that grows abundantly in Oklahoma

sang **Wamą́'** /wä-moⁿ'/ *v.*, *1st pers.*, *past t.*, sang, to chant, croon, hum (I ~ at the powwow)

Santee Dakota **Isą́.ąt'ì** /ē-soⁿ'--oⁿ-t'ē'/ *n.*, the Santee Tribe of Native Americans

satellite **Mą́xe'át'atą̧ wadábe** /moⁿ'-xā-ä'-t'ä-toⁿ' wä-doⁿ'-bä/ *n.*, satellite, a man-made object circling the earth or other celestial body for purposes of gathering data or providing services for TV, radio, GPS, personal locators, and other devices

satisfied **Gíšą̧** /gē'-shoⁿ'/ *adj.*, satisfied, content, pleased, made happy and contented; *đíšą̧*, you are ~; *gíšą̧*, he/she/it/they are ~; *wéšą̧*, we are ~

satisfied **Giúdą** /gē-ü'-doⁿ'/ *v.*, satisfied, being, 1. satisfied or contented after a period of sickness 2. to be ~ with something one ate or drank 3. to receive physical pleasure; *i̧udą̀*, I am satisfied; *đíudą̀*, you are satisfied; *gíudą̀*, he/she/it is satisfied; *wéudą̀i*, we are satisfied

Saturday **Ą́ba wé'šap'è** /oⁿm'-bä wā-shä-p'ā'/ *n.*, Saturday, lit., day number six

Sauk and Fox **Zá'ge** /zä'-gä/ *n.*, Sac (or Sauk) and Fox Tribes of Native Americans (Originally two separate tribes, who merged into a single tribe called the Sac and Fox.)

save **Gisí'** /gē-sē'/ *v.*, save, saving something for oneself

save **Sí'** /sē'/ *v.*, save, saving some or holding some back

save **T'éde** /t'ā'-thā/ *v.*, save, put away, conserve

Savior **Waníde** /wä-nē'-thā/ *n.*, Savior, redeemer, the Son of God who saves or rescues one from unethical, unruly, corrupted living when one embraces the biblical truths of righteousness and establishes a standard of decency and honesty

savory **Azé'** /ä-zā'/ *adj.*, savory, tasty, palatable, usu. refers to baked or fried meats

saw **Wébasè** /wā'-bä-sā'/ *n.*, saw, a tool to cut various materials, such as metal, plastics, wood

saw **Žą́'íbasè** /zhoⁿ'-ē'-bä-sā'/ *n.*, saw, lit., wood cutter, a hand or power saw to cut wood or boards

sawhorse **Žą́' ábasè** /zhoⁿ' ä-bä-sā'/ *n.*, sawhorse, orig. a wooden, upright device used to support a log to be sawn

say **Ága** /ä'-gä/ *v.*, say, utter, state, verbalize, say this

say **É'** /ā'/ *v.*, say, to express oneself with words; *edé'a?* what was said?, *e'akà*, somebody said; *ábi*, he said; *ái*, was said; *áme*, they said; *ehé*, I said

scale **Wédihą̀'** /wā'-thē-hoⁿ'/ *n.*, scale, a device to measure the weight of something

scalp dance **Nudą́ wačígaxè** /nü-doⁿ' wä-chē'-gä-xā'/ *n.*, scalp dance, a woman's victory dance for men returning from battle

scapula **Ábak'ù** /ä'-bä-k'ü'/ *n.*, scapula, shoulder blades, the two flat bones at the upper part of the back

scar **Sná'** /snä'/ *n.*, scar, a mark on the flesh caused by a healed wound or burn

scarce **Uwánądè** /ü-wä'-noⁿ-thā/ *adj.*, scarce, rarely found

scare **Wábazè** /wä-bä-zā'/ *n./v.*, scare, to scare somebody; *wábazéát'ašą̀*, to scare somebody extremely and suddenly

scarecrow **K'áxe wádihì** /k'ä'-xä wä'-thē-hē'/ *n.*, scarecrow, a figure of a man made of straw to scare crows and other birds away from crops

scared **K'ú'he** /k'ü'-hā/ *v.*, scared, to be emotionally fearful, usu. refers to being scared of ghosts

scarf **Wadáge štągà** /wä-thä'-gä shtoⁿ-gä'/ *n.*, scarf, a headcovering or neck wrap, usu. used by women and girls

scary **K'ú'he'wadè** /k'ü'-hā-wä-thä'/ *n.*, scary, 1. a place that is scary; something that makes a place scary 2. one of the three ancient Ponca village sites near the confluence of the Niobrara and Missouri Rivers

scatter **Udíaì** /ü-thē'-ä-ē'/ *v.*, scatter, made into small pieces and scattered

scattered **Udí'edą̀** /ü-thē'-ä-thoⁿ'/ *v.*, scattered, scattered in no order

scattered **Uwéda** /ü-wä'-thä/ *adj.*, scattered, any group of things that is sparsely or thinly distributed

scent **Bdą́xt'i** /bthoⁿ'-xt'ē/ *n.*, scent, an odor in the air that is left by a person or animal and can be traced

school **Wagáze t'í'** /wä-goⁿ'-zä t'ē'/ *n.*, school, lit., house of teaching, a place to teach, train, educate

scintillate **Ðíą́babà** /thē'-oⁿ'-bä-bä'/ *v.*, scintillate, to emit sparks, sparkling

scissors **Idábašnà** /ē-thä'-bä-shnä'/ *n.*, scissors, a cutting instrument for cloth, hair, etc.

scissortail **Íbe'žąk'à** /ēⁿ'-bä-zhoⁿ-k'ä'/ *n.*, scissortail, 1. flycatcher, a bird with long forked tail feathers 2. personal male name in the Ðíxidà clan of the Ponca people

sclera **Įštúskà** /ēⁿ-shtü-skä'/ *n.*, sclera, the white part of the eye

scold **Idáhusà** /ē-thä'-hü-sä'/ *v., 1st pers. sing.*, scold, lit., I scold

scold **Íhusà** /ē'-hü-sä'/ *v.*, scold, to scold him/her/it

scold **Wéhusà** /wä'-hü-sä'/ *v.*, scold, to scold him/her/it/them

scorch **Náxudè** /nä'-xü-dä'/ *v.*, scorch, char, burn, usu. refers to preparing food

scrape **Ábaáxe** /ä'-bä-ä'-xä/ *v.*, scrape, to remove by scraping a hard substance against another thing

scrape **Bixábe** /bē-xä'-bä/ *v.*, scrape, scrape the skin; to take off, as in husks from corn or hulls from nuts

scrape **Bixá'xabè** /bē-xä'-xä-bä'/ *v.*, scrape, to take off continuously or repeatedly

scrape **Ðis'ú** /thēs-ü'/ *v.*, scrape, as in "to scrape the wood clean" with the hands

scrape **Gaiáxe** /gä-ēä'-xä/ *v.*, scrape, scraping the bottom of a pail with a dipper for water (*néxe ké* ~aì, he ~d the pail)

scrape **Wádidaxè** /wä'-thē-dä-xä'/ *v.*, scrape, 1. a bear making scratch or claw marks on a tree 2. a male name in the Wažážè clan of the Ponca people

scraper **Wébaù'** /wä'-bä-ü'/ *n.*, scraper, an ancient Ponca tool for removing hair from the skin of bison, elk, deer, and other large mammals; a tool composed of an elkhorn handle and flint adz

scratch **Ði·ú'** /thē-·ü'/ *v.*, scratch (an itch); *diú'u'*, 1. to scratch itches continually 2. to scratch around on the ground to find something, as in finding nuts fallen from a tree

scratch **G'i'é'** /g-ē-ä'/ *v.*, scratch, to scratch oneself

scratchy **Xáxagà** /xä'-xä-gä'/ *adj.*, scratchy, coarse, e.g., a blanket that is scratchy

scream **Xdažé** /xthä-zhä'/ *v.*, to scream, to give a loud, high-pitched cry, yell, or scream, to shriek, usu. refers to someone who is in pain or is excited, as at a ball game

screech owl **Né·dažibè** /nä'-·thä-zhē-bä'/ *n.*, screech owl, of the genus *Megascops*

screen **Mázè xáxadè** /moⁿ'-zä xä'-xä-dä'/ *n.*, screen, a frame with a fine wire mesh designed to prevent entry of insects, usu. on doors and windows

scrotum **Šądési** /shoⁿ-dä'-sē/ *n.*, scrotum, pouch that contains the testes in mammals

scrub **Ábaškì** /ä'-bä-shkē'/ *v.*, scrub, to scrub, to rub hard to make something clean, such as clothing

scrub oak **T'áškahì'nušíá'hà** /t'ä'-shkä-hē'-nü-shē'-ä'-hä'/ *n.*, scrub oak, *Quercus alba L.*

scrutinize **Ðiwágazù** /thē-wä'-gä-zü'/ *v.*, scrutinize, scan, inspect, examine

scythe **Mąhį́ ígasè** /moⁿ-hēⁿ' ē'-gä-sä'/ *n.*, scythe, lit., cut heavy brush, a manual implement for cutting heavy grass, grain, etc., having a long handle held with both hands and a long, sharp curved blade

scythe **Žá ígasè** /zhä' ē'-gä-sä'/ *n.*, scythe, a manually operated, long single-edged blade for cutting deep weeds, grass, or crops

seal **Sagí gáxe** /sä-gē' gä'-xä/ *n.*, seal, something that makes a thing tight or airtight

seam **Úbatè** /ü'-bä-tä'/ *n.*, seam, the stitching of thread joining two pieces of cloth or other material at their edges

search **Uné'** /ü-nä'/ *v.*, search, look for, seek out, to search for somebody or something that is missing; *uwáne*, I searched; *udáne*, you searched; *unái*, he/she/it searched; *uwíne*, I searched for you; *udíne*, he/she/it searched for you; *udínaì*, they searched for you; *unána*, searching, attempting to find something in different places

seashell **Níkidè** /nē'-kē-dä/ *n.*, seashell, the shell or outer layer made by snails and other crustaceans

seat **Ugdį́'** /ü-gthēⁿ'/ *n.*, seat, a place to sit, e.g., a place to sit on the ground, a bench, a chair, etc.

seatbelt **Ugdį́'íp'idagè** /ü-gthēⁿ'-ē'-p'ē-thä-gä/ *n.*, seatbelt, in automobiles, a device that is used to restrain passengers

second **Wé'nąbà** /wä'-noⁿ-bä/ *adj.*, second, a second thing in a row of items or the second person or group of people coming in succession

second toe **Sip'aút'ągà uduátą** /sē-p'äü'-t'oⁿ-gä' ü-thüä'-toⁿ/ *n.*, second toe (the toe next to the big toe)

see **Dą́'be** /doⁿ-bä/ *v.*, see, visualize, view, behold, to see or observe

seed **Sí'** /sē'/ *n.*, seed, an embryonic plant or the grain of plants

seeds **Wamíde** /wä-mē'-dä/ *n.*, seeds, seeds stored for planting later

seek **Wé'de** /wä'-thä/ *n./v.*, seeking, look for, usu. used in reference to finding appropriate wood or kindling for cooking or warming a dwelling

seem **Į́'štè** /ēⁿ'-shtä/ *v.t.*, seem, kind of an impression that something is a certain way, or appears to be

seemingly **Į́'štegà** /ēⁿ'-shtä-goⁿ/ *adv.*, seemingly, apparent to the senses but not necessarily real

segment **Hébe** /hä'-bä/ *n.*, segment, part, piece, bit

seize **Gínąšè** /gē'-noⁿ-shä/ *v.*, seize, take away from, take control of

seizures **T'ę́'štą** /t'äⁿ'-sht'oⁿ/ *n.*, seizures, usu. epilepsy

select **Bahí** /bä-hē'/ *v.*, select, to choose from or decide on which one of a group

self-caused **Éwakìą** /ä'-wä-kē-oⁿ'/ *n.*, an unfortunate situation or something that a person brought upon themselves; *dífwadakìą*, you brought it upon yourself

self-deception **Úšįkidè** /ü'-shēⁿ-kē-thä/ *n.*, self-deception, a condition of an individual not being able to rationalize what is there in a logical way

self-respect **K'igdíežubà** /k'ē-gthē'-ä-zhü-bä/ *n.*, self-respect, self-esteem, pride, dignity

sell **Wédiwį** /wä'-thē-wēⁿ'/ *v.*, sell, the transfer of money for something, as in disposing of clothing, food, and other products for money

semblance **Égąįgà** /ä'-goⁿ-ēⁿ-goⁿ'/ *n.*, semblance, something that is similar, likeness of another thing

semitruck **K'ip'ínągè wat'ú'gdą t'ągà** /k'ē-p'ē'-noⁿ-gä' wä-t'ü'-gthoⁿ t'oⁿ-gä/ *n.*, semitruck, eighteen-wheeler

send **Đéde** /thä'-thä/ *v.t.*, send, to make something move from one place to another (he will ~ a letter to his friend); *gdéde*, to send back

sent **Đédaì** /thä'-thäē'/ *v.*, *past part.*, sent, 1. to have ~ something (or mail something) away 2. to cause somebody to be moved from one place to another (refers to a person imprisoned or institutionalized)

sent here **Tí'de** /tē'-thä/ *v.*, sent here, something sent to this place, such as a letter

sentry **Ákidà** /ä'-kē-dä/ *n.*, sentry, sentinel, guard, 1. a person who is on duty to provide security for an establishment or prison 2. caretaker or caregiver, somebody who looks after somebody, or somebody physically ill or emotionally disabled

separate **Gašíbəát'a** /gä-shē'-bəä'-t'ä/ *adj.*, separate, outside of or separated from an inner group, tribe, or organization; *gašíbe k'igđíze*, to get oneself out of an organization, group, etc.

separate **Gaxát'a** /gä-xä'-t'ä/ *adv.*, separate, separated or apart from others

separate **Uk'áde** /ü-k'ä'-dä/ *v.*, separate, not connected or attached to anything

separately **Ak'ídahà** /ä-k'ē'-thä-hä/ *adv.*, separately, refers to two, both (*máze-skàte ~ awá'i*, I gave money ~ to both of them; *ak'íwahà*, refers to more than two, all (*wágidèxtì, ~ waí xđíxđí waí*, every one present was given a Pendleton blanket)

September **Ápą hútą mí'** /oⁿ'-poⁿ hü'-toⁿ mē'/ *n.*, September, lit., moon when the elk bellow, the ninth month in the year

seriously **Į́'štegažì** /ēⁿ'-shtä-goⁿ-zhē'/ *adv.*, seriously, not a triviality, significantly, of value

servant **Wašį́'** /wä-shē'/ *n.*, servant, a helper not by force but by social standards, namely, among the Ponca people, to place oneself in a position of servitude in somebody's household where one is given shelter as a temporary guest; *archaic*, in an ancient period, an older child without parents might have been taken in by a household to live as one of their own children and might have served by hunting, planting, cutting wood, and carrying water

set **Ágdą'** /ä'-gthoⁿ/ *v.*, set, to set something upon something

settle **Gasp'é** /gä-sp'ä'/ *v.*, settle, lit., go to the bottom, sink, as in certain kinds of debris going to the bottom in a container of water

seven **P'é'nąbà** /p'ä'-noⁿ-bä/ (**P'é'dąbà** /p'ä'-thoⁿ-bä/) *n.*, seven, the number seven (7), lit., five and two (The Ponca count by fives and do not use the decimal system or tens.)

seventh **Wé'p'é'nąbà** /wä-p'ä'-noⁿ-bä/ (**Wé'p'é'dąbà** /wä-p'ä'-thoⁿ-bä/) *adj.*, seventh, the seventh thing in a row of items or the seventh person or group of people coming in succession

several **Ánąxt'iegà** /ä'-noⁿ-xt'ē-ä-goⁿ'/ *adj.*, several, more than a few but not too much of something

sew **Wabáte** /wä-bä'-tä/ *v.*, sew, stitch, seam; *baté*, sew; *įđébatè*, you sewed it for me

sewing machine **Mą́ze wébate** /moⁿ'-zä wä-bä-tä'/ *n.*, sewing machine, a machine used to sew various materials together with thread

sew on **Á'batè** /ä-bä-tä'/ *v. phr.*, sew on, to ~ something, as in a patch on a child's blue jeans or a ribbon on a shawl

shade **Ázè** /oⁿ'-zä/ *n.*, shade, the blocking of sunlight by an object

shadow **G'énąxdè** /g-ä'-noⁿ-xthä/ *n.*, shadow, a dark area standing between something and rays of light

shadowy **Zébe** /zä'-bä/ *adj.*, shadowy, clouded, dark, dim

shake **Đip'áde** /thē-p'oⁿ'-dä/ *v.*, shake, rock, or sway by use of the hands, as in leaning on a table; *đip'ąp'ądè*, shaking, continuously rocking, or swaying movement caused by the use of the hands

shake **Gašką́** /gä-shkoⁿ'/ *v.*, shake, to be shaken by the wind or other forceful medium

shake **K'igđíšk'ą́šk'ą́** /k'ē-gthē'-shk'oⁿ'-shk'oⁿ'/ *v.*, shake, to shake oneself, as a dog exiting from the river stands and shakes the water off

shake **Šk'ą́šk'ą** /shk'oⁿ'-shk'oⁿ'/ *v.*, shake, tremble, shiver, to move with short and quick, jerky body movements, as in trembling in fear

shaking **Đižą́žą** /thē-zhoⁿ'-zhoⁿ'/ *v.*, shaking, shaking something with hands; *gažą́žą,* shaking by use of wind or other forceful means; *bážą́žą*, shake by pushing with the body; *bižą́žą*, shake by pressing down, *ną-žą́žą*, shake with the feet

shaking **Gap'ą́de** /gä-p'on'-dä/ *v.*, shaking, being caused to move from side to side by the force of something

shaky **Šąšą́da** /shon-shon-thä/ *adj.*, shaky, wobbly, something not sturdy

shallow **X·ébe** /x·ä'-bä/ *adj.*, shallow, not deep, as in a river or stream

shame **Íšte** /ē'-shtä/ *v.*, shame, as in embarrassment about something personal, to be made uncomfortable

shameful **Íštewade** /ē'-shtä-wä-thä'/ *adj.*, shameful, disgraceful, as in an act that brings embarrassment or dishonor to oneself or others

shampoo **Nąžíha ídižà** /non-zhē'-hä ē'-thē-zhä'/ *n.*, shampoo, a product to wash hair

share **Wégdàè** /wä-gthä-ē'/ *v.*, share, share out, one individual giving something to a specific group of people

shared **Í'k'igdaè** /ē'-k'ē-gthä-ä'/ *v., pres./ past t.*, share, shared, giving each person in the group the same amount (*mázeskàte* ~ they ~ the money among themselves)

sharp **B'aí** /b-ä-ē'/ *adj.*, sharp, razor sharp; *dib'ái*, sharpen

sharpen **Gap'ái** /gä-p'ä'-ē/ *adj.*, sharpen, to make sharp with an instrument, such as a revolving sharpening stone; *dip'ái*, sharpening with the hands using a whetstone

sharpshooter **Wamúp'i** /wä-mü-p'ē/ *n.*, sharpshooter, a person who is skilled at shooting bullets from a rifle to hit a target

shave **Íkihį́ ígaskébe** /ēn'-kē-hēn' ē'-gä-skä'-bä/ *v.*, shave, to remove hair from the chin with a sharp instrument

shawl **Waí'gabdà** /wä-ēn'-gä-bthä'/ *n.*, shawl, any open shawl

shed **Há'baxdúde** /hä-bä-xthü'-dä/ *v.*, shed, 1. refers to snake shedding its skin 2. proper male name in the Wažážè clan of the Ponca people

sheep **Haxúde** /hä-xü'-dä/ *n.*, sheep, livestock known and raised throughout the world, of the family Bovidae, *Ovis aries*

sheet **Umížexáxáde** /ü-mē'-zhä-xä-xä'-dä/ *n.*, sheet, a bedsheet, usu. two pairs of thin linen cloth, one used to cover a mattress and the other to cover up the sleeper

shelter **Uwą́he** /ü-won'-hä/ *n.*, shelter, refuge, sanctuary, safe haven

sheltered **Ábdagè** /ä-bthä-gä/ *v.*, sheltered, usu. on the side sheltered from the wind

sheltered place **Udú'ábdaget'à** /ü-thü'-ä'-bthä-gä-t'ä'/ *prep. phr.*, sheltered place, refers to a sheltered place where there is no wind

shepherd **Haxúde wákidà** /hä-xü'-dä wä'-kē-dä'/ *n.*, shepherd, a person or persons who tends to and guards a flock of sheep

shield **T'ahá'wagdè** /t'ä-hä'-wä-gthä'/ *n.*, shield, a piece of armor carried on the arm and used for protection against arrows and in hand-to-hand battles with war clubs

shimmering **Sąsą́** /son'-son'/ *adj.*, shimmering, glittering, iridescent

shin **Ną́xp'ehì** /non'-xp'ä-hē'/ *n.*, shin, the front part of the two bones (the tibia and fibula) in the leg below the knee

shine **Bidíąba** /bē-thē'-on'-bä/ *v.*, shine, to polish, to restore a luster on something that was dull

shinny **T'abégasì** /t'ä-bä'-gä-sē'/ *n.*, shinny, a Ponca men's game played four times every seven days during the springtime (The game is similar to hockey but is played on a field.)

shinny **Wabášnadè** /wä-bä'-shnä-dä/ *n.*, shinny, a woman's shinny game played during the spring that is similar to the men's shinny game

shiny **Są́** /soⁿ/ *adj.*, shiny, gleaming, glistening

shirt **Unážį** /ü-noⁿ-zhēⁿ/ *n.*, shirt, usu. refers to a man's garment for the upper part of the body

shiver **Sąsą́** /soⁿ-soⁿ/ *v.*, shiver, usu. involuntary trembling caused by cold or cold wind hitting the body or caused by fear

shoelaces **Hįbéką** /hēⁿ-bā'-koⁿ/ *n.*, shoelaces, shoestrings

shoes **Hįbé** /hēⁿ-bā'/ *n.*, shoes, foot covering, usu. made of leather, now made of many synthetic materials

shoes **Žą́'hįbè** /zhoⁿ'-hēⁿ-bā'/ *n.*, shoes, lit., wooden shoes

shoot **Kí'de** /kē'-dā/ *v.*, shoot, to discharge a projectile at a target by bow or firearm; *k'ídagà*, shoot it; *dákíkíde*, you shot yourself (The term was derived from a scalp dance song speaking of an enemy warrior.)

shopping **Wadį́wį** /wä-thēⁿ-wēⁿ/ *v.*, shopping, 1. to purchase something or some things 2. *n.*, purchases, things that have been bought

shopping mall **Údįwįt'ì ážidądà** /ü-thēⁿ-wēⁿ-t'ē ä'-zhe-thoⁿ-thoⁿ/ *n.*, shopping mall, a large enclosed building complex containing many stores and businesses

shore **Ník'ąhà** /nē'-k'oⁿ-hä/ *n.*, shore, bank, land along the edge of a river, lake, sea, or ocean

short **Č'éškà** /ch-ä'-shkä/ *adj.*, short, not long

short **Gdą́p'a** /gthoⁿ'-p'ä/ *adj.*, short, something that has been made short or worn away

short **Nušíáha** /nü-shē'-ä'-hä/ *pron.*, short, lit., small or short person, usu. relates to stature, i.e., size

short **Xé'a** /xā'-ä/ *adj.*, short, usu. refers to clothing, e.g., ~ skirt (The word is sometimes pronounced *xį́'a*.)

short distance **Uhí'aškà** /ü-hē'-ä-shkä/ *adj.*, short distance, not far, nearby, adjacent

short dog **Hí'nušiáha** /hē'-nü-shēä'-hä/ *n.*, short dog, smaller than a Ponca aborginal dog, called *įšt'á dubà*, four eyes

short-sleeved **Hánit'à č'éškà** /hä'-nē-t'ä' ch-ä'-shkä'/ *n.*, short-sleeved, refers to any garment with short sleeves

short-sleeved shirt **Unážį xé'a** /ü-noⁿ-zhēⁿ xā-ä/ *n.*, short-sleeved shirt

shoulder blade **Ábak'ù** /ä'-bä-k'ü/ *n.*, shoulder blade, anatomy, the bone that connects the upper arm bone with the collarbone

should have **Edé'gą** /ā-dā'-goⁿ/ *aux. v.*, should have, refers to something that somebody ~ done because it was the correct or right thing to do when it availed itself

shove **Bahé** /bä-hä'/ *v.*, shove, push, shoving or pushing something or someone away from oneself; *bahé dédé*, pushing something or somebody completely away

shovel **T'ą́deínąšpè** /t'oⁿ'-dä-ē'-noⁿ-shpä/ *n.*, shovel, a tool for digging into the soil or other materials

show **Bahá** /bä-hä'/ *v.*, to show, illustrate, present, display; *n.*, *wábahà*, showing, a presentation or performance, the act of showing or displaying something

shower **Ni'ugabí'xą̀ uhída** /nē-ü-gä-bē'-xoⁿ ü-hē'-thä/ *n.*, shower, in a bath or bath stall; a shower house

show-off **K'ip'áhahà** /k'ē-p'ä'-hä-hä'/ *n.*, show-off, one who always stands out in front of others to be seen

show off **Wawédąbè** /wä-wä'-doⁿ-bä/ *v.*, show off, flaunt, to display something somebody thinks is worthy of showing in a flagrant way, such as a piece of jewelry, clothing, a car

shows itself **Giwádišnà** /gē-wä'-thē-shnä'/ *n.*, something that shows itself or is made clear by some spiritual entity

shred **Đibdá'bđazè** /thē-bthä'-bthä-zā'/ *v.*, shred, to shred to pieces, to tear to pieces

shuck **Đixábe** /thē-xä'-bä/ *v.*, shuck, to skin, as to remove the husk or pod from something with tools or the hands; *đixá'xabè*, to continuously skin, to continuously shuck in order to remove the husk or pod from something with the hands

shuffle **Í'nasnúsnu** /ē'-noⁿ-snü'-snü/ *v.*, shuffle, to walk without lifting the feet, dragging the feet or taking sliding steps

shut **Égià** /ā'-gē-oⁿ'/ *v.*, shut, close, as in closing a door

shut off **Ánasè** /ä'-noⁿ-sā'/ *v.*, shut off, turn off, switch off something, as in turning the water off

sick **Wakéga** /wä-kā'-gä/ *adj.*, sick or ill

sicken **Íwakegà** /ē'-wä-kä-gä'/ *v.*, sicken, usu. refers to becoming sickened by something consumed; to become sickened by exposure to extreme cold weather conditions

sickly **Waxáxą** /wä-xoⁿ'-xoⁿ/ *adj.*, sickly, always ailing, always sickly or hurting somewhere

sickness **Ú'nièt'ą** /ü'-nē-ā'-t'oⁿ/ *n.*, sickness, ill health; a disease

sideburns **Nądádehà hį** /noⁿ-thä'-dä-hä' hēⁿ'/ *n.*, sideburns, hair in front of the ears

side glance **Đédehà wadábe** /thä'-dä-hä' wä-doⁿ'-bä/ *adj. phr.*, side glance, looking to the side without turning the head

sides **Agdákahà** /ä-gthoⁿ'-kä-hä'/ *n.*, sides, both the left and right side of an object

sides above hips **Št'ašt'áde** /sht'ä-sht'ä'-dä/ *n.*, sides above hips

sidewalk **Í'e átą** /ēⁿ'-ä ä'-toⁿ/ *n.*, sidewalk, a concrete walkway along the side of a street

sift **Đibdípe** /thē-bthē'-pä/ *v.*, sift, to separate particles, as in sifting flour; *ide'bđìpe*, 2nd *pers.*, you sifted it for me

sign **Wébaxù udá** /wä'-bä-xü' ü-thoⁿ'/ *v.*, sign, lit., to hold a writing instrument, to write one's signature, to make a "mark" on a document

sign language **Wagáxe** /wä-gä'-xä/ *n.*, sign language, a system of communication by use of hand gestures

silence **Sáka** /sä'-kä/ *n.*, silence, be silent, the absence of noise, an archaic expression used to tell children at bedtime to be silent (say *sáka*, you may not talk until morning)

silver fox **T'í'k'a'xúdè** /t'ē'-k'ä-xü'-dā/ *n.*, silver fox, a variant of the red fox, *Vulpes vulpes*

similar **-égą** /ä'-goⁿ/ *suffix*, denotes something that has a general likeness or resemblance, as in *žíde~*, reddish, *hú'te é'xt'i~*, his voice is really similar to ——

similar **Égaigà** /ä'-goⁿ-ē-goⁿ'/ *adj.*, similar, comparable; generally, a likeness or resemblance

simultaneous **Ék'itąhà** /ä'-k'ē-toⁿ-hä/ *adj.*, simultaneous, concurrent, at the same time

since **Atáditą** /ä-toⁿ'-dē-toⁿ'/ *conj.*, since, since that time

since darkness **Hádi'tà** /hoⁿ'-dē-toⁿ'/ *conj.*, since darkness, or since night

sincere **Điéžubà** /thē-ä'-zhü-bä'/ *n.*, sincere, person who is truthful, honest, straight, and frank

sinew **T'aką hà** /t'ä-koⁿ' hä'/ *n.*, sinew, fibers of animal tendon, esp. of the American bison, used for thread and cordage for sewing or binding

sing **Tidéde** /tē-thä'-thä/ *v.*, *sing.*, to start a song, usu. refers to somebody starting a tribal song

sing **Waá** /wä-oⁿ'/ *v.*, sing, chant, hum

singe **Ná'zudè** /nä'-zü-thä/ *v.*, singe, char (The process of cooking certain animals included singeing the hair off the animal.)

singer **Waá niášigà** /wä-oⁿ' nē-ä'-shē-gä/ *n.*,

singer, lit., one who sings, usu. refers to a male person who sings or leads tribal songs at tribal ceremonies and church functions

Sioux **Šaá** /shä-o^n/ *n.*, the Sioux Tribe of Native Americans

sister **Wihé** /wē-hä'/ *n.*, *masc./fem.*, sister, used to address a younger female sibling (this is my ~) (same as *winá'*)

sister **Wináži̧gà** /wē-no^n-zhē^n-gä/ *n.*, *masc.*, sister, refers to younger or "little" sister

sister **Wit'á̧ge** /wē-t'o^n-gä/ *n.*, *masc.*, sister, used to address an elder female sibling (this is my ~)

sister **Wižáde** /wē-zho^n-thä/ *n.*, *fem.*, sister, used to address an elder female sibling (*duádikè* ~, this is my ~)

sister-in-law **Wihá̧ga** /wē-ho^n-gä/ *n.*, *masc.*, sister-in-law (*duádikè* ~, this is my ~)

sister-in-law **Wišíką** /wē-shē'-ko^n/ *n.*, *fem.*, sister-in-law (*duádikè* ~, this is my ~); *šiká*, sister-in-law, used when addressing her

sit **A'gdí̧'** /ä-gthē^n'/ *v.*, *1st pers. sing.*, sit, I sit; *ágdi̧*, to sit on something

sit **Gdí̧'** /gthē^n'/ *v.*, sit, to sit; *gdí'idą̀*, to sit down at once

sitting **Đizá̧de** /thē-zo^n-dä/ *adj.*, sitting, ~ motionless or unmoving; *đizádext'ì*, sitting pompously

situation **Ú'šk'ą** /ü'-shk'o^n/ *n.*, situation, state of affairs

six **Šá'p'ȩ̀** /shä-p'ä^n/ *n.*, six, the number six (6)

sixth **Wé'šap'è** /wä-shä-p'ä'/ *adj.*, sixth, the sixth thing in a row of items or the sixth person or group of people coming in succession

size **Ánąskà** /ä'-no^n-skä/ *n.*, size, dimension, sizing to fit (~ *à?*, what ~?)

sizzle **Nážuè** /nä-zhü-ä'/ *adj.*, sizzle, sizzling, the sound of food frying in a pan, namely, bacon, meats, potatoes

skewer **Wébasnà̧** /wä'-bä-sno^n/ *n.*, skewer, a stick or piece of metal used to roast meat or vegetables over a fire

skilled **Đip'iát'ašà̧** /thē-p'ēä'-t'ä-sho^n/ *adj.*, skilled, accomplished, 2. *n.*, expert, a skilled person in some field, a specialist

skillet **Wíúdisà̧** /wē'-ü'-thē-so^n/ *n.*, skillet, a pan for frying or braising foods

skin **Đixábe** /thē-xä-bä/ *v.*, skin, 1. to skin, to scrape one's knee, elbow, etc. 2. to remove the peel from a banana, to shuck corn

skinny **Xdá'** /xthä'/ *adj.*, skinny, thin, lean, emaciated

skirt **Waté'čéškà** /wä-tä-chä-shkä'/ *n.*, skirt, a ladies' outergarment, a skirt of any length or a half skirt

skittish horse **Šáge ná̧xexidà** /sho^n-gä no^n-xä-xē-thä'/ *n.*, skittish horse, a horse that is nervous, jumpy, and edgy

skull **Nąšk'í'wahí** /no^n-shk'ē'-wä-hē'/ *n.*, skull, the part of the human skeleton that is part of the structure of the face and has a cavity that houses the brain

skunk **Má'ga** /mo^n'-gä/ *n.*, skunk, a mammal of the order Carnivora, family Mephitidae

sky **Má̧xèat'a** /mo^n-xä-ä'-t'ä/ *n.*, sky, the sky, heavens, everything above the earth

slanted **Ádikà** /ä'-thē-ko^n/ *v.*, to be slanted, imbalanced, something that is not level or even

slap **Gačáki** /gä-chä'-kē/ *v.*, slap, usu. to strike with the flat of the hand

slay **Gaxdí'** /gä-xthē'/ *v.*, slay, 1. usu. refers to slaughter of animals 2. to beat up or whip a person

sledding **Gasnú'gidè** /gä-snü'-gē-thä'/ *v./n.*, sledding, child play involving sliding downhill on a sled or sliding on ice

sleep **Žá̧** /zho^n/ *n.*, sleep, a period of time when consciousness is suspended

sleep paralysis **Šką·điá** /shko^n·-thē-ä'/ *n.*,

sleep paralysis, a temporary inability to move and speak; a state between being awake and asleep

sleepy **Žą́təidįgè** /zhoⁿ'-təē-thēⁿ-gā'/ *adj.*, sleepy, drowsy

sleet **Mási'žįgà** /mä'-sē-zhēⁿ-gä/ *n.*, sleet, 1. small ice pellets formed by freezing raindrops 2. a proper male name in the Hísadà clan among the Ponca people

sleeve **Há'nit'à** /hä'-nē-t'ä'/ *n.*, sleeve, that part of clothing that covers the arms

slender **Bdą́ze** /bthoⁿ-zā/ *adj.*, slender, having small proportions in width and height, long and thin

slice **Á'ma'è** /ä'-mä-ä'/ *v.*, slice, as in slicing potatoes

slide **Gasnú** /gä-snü'/ *v.*, slide, to slide by force, usu. on the snow or ice; to slide on a smooth surface; *basnú*, slide by pushing; *đisnú*, slide by pulling with hands; *bisnú*, slide by pressing on with use of the hands on an instrument; *nąsnú*, slide by using feet

slight **Ujábe** /ü-jä'-bā/ *adj.*, slight, 1. a small opening, such as a door left ajar, a window slightly opened 2. listening but hearing only a small part of the information passed on, usu. refers to gossip

slingshot **Wažį́ga íkidè** /wä-zhēⁿ'-gä ē'-kē-dä'/ *n.*, slingshot, lit., bird shooter, also called bean shooter, a homemade object used to shoot small projectiles, usu. rocks

slip **Nąšnáha** /noⁿ-shnä'-hä/ *v.*, slip, to lose footing, as in slipping on ice

slippery **Šnahá'** /shnä-hä'/ *adj.*, slippery, slick, as in ice on a sidewalk or highway

slippery **Šníšnidè** /shnē'-shnē-dä/ *adj.*, slippery, something being oily or greasy

slit **Uđísne** /ü-thē'-snä/ *v.*, slit, 1. to cut apart, may refer to cloth or deerskin, e.g., that may be cut into strips 2. *n.*, a straight, narrow cut

sliver **Žą́'ubáxą** /zhoⁿ'-ü-bä'-xoⁿ/ *n.*, sliver, splinter, a small, slender, sharp piece of wood

slouch **Čák'ì** /chä-k'ē'/ *v.*, slouch, 1. to walk or sit lazily or in a lazy way; an extremely casual way of walking 2. a lazy way of keeping house

slow **Ídap'idį** /ē'-thä-p'ē-thēⁿ'/ *adj.*, slow, something that is sluggish or dawdling, usu. refers to speed, as in walking or the movement of an automobile

slow **Wasní'de** /wä-snē'-dä/ *v.*, slow, lit., slow, late, to be late or overdue

slowly **Ídap'idįxt'ì** /ē'-thä-p'ē-thēⁿ'-xt'ē'/ *adv.*, very slowly, gradually, bit by bit or little by little

slurp **Đaxúbe** /thä-xü'-bä/ *v.*, slurp, to drink something noisily; to sip, gulp, swig

smacking sound **Gasá'p'ì** /gä-sä'-p'ē'/ *v.*, smacking sound, to strike something with a strap, making a smacking sound, as with a bullwhip; *đisáp'i*, make a snapping sound with the use of something in the hands, such as a rubber band stretched to snap; *nąsáp'i*, make a snapping sound by stepping on or rolling something over something

small **T'ą́gáxt'iáži** /t'oⁿ-gä-xt'ē-ä'-zhē/ *adj.*, small, lit. not very large

small **Žįgá'** /zhēⁿ-gä'/ *adj.*, small, 1. small, little, etc. 2. *n.*, little ones, children (your ~ ones are growing up)

small amount **Júba** /jü'-bä/ *n.*, small amount, a little bit

smaller **Đižíga** /thē-zhēⁿ'-gä/ *adj.*, smaller, lesser, making something smaller; *điží'ga*, you are young, usu. refers to an elder addressing a young man concerning history or some matter that he may think the younger man doesn't know; *đi·žį́ga*, you are younger, refers to age

small hill **P'ahé žįgà** /p'ä-hä' zhēⁿ-gä/ *n.*,

1. small hill 2. proper name in the Mąk'ą́ clan of the Ponca people

small intestine **Šíbe'užíga** /shē'-bā-ü-zhē'-gä/ *n.*, small intestine

small opening **Ugdé'** /ü-gthä'/ *n.*, small opening, as in a small opening to an animal's den or one that allows cold wind to come into a dwelling or house

short people **Niášigà nušiáha** /nē-ä'-shē-gä' nü-shēä'-hä/ *n.*, lit., short people, Native Americans who live in the Southwest

smallpox **Dí'xe** /dē'-xā/ *n.*, smallpox, an infectious disease caused by two virus variants, variola major and variola minor; orignally known as the pox in England

smartweed **Hánugahì** /hä'-nü-gä-hē'/ *n.*, smartweed, genus *Polygonum* of the Polygonaceae family, causes skin to itch on contact

smear **Ádahà** /ä'-thä-hä'/ *n.*, smear, a dirty spot made by touching or rubbing something on something else

smeared **Đigdé'gdéžè** /thē-gthä'-gthä'-zhä'/ *v.*, smeared, applied unevenly

smell **Bdą́'** /bthonⁿ/ *n./v.*, smell, an odor or smell that can be either agreeable or disagreeable (the perfume has a good ~, the garbage can has a bad ~)

smell **Ná'bdą̀** /nä'-bthonⁿ/ *v.*, smell, usu. 1. a good smell that is derived from something delightfully cooked 2. a bad smell that comes from anything that is burnt

smelly **Xuhį́'** /xü-hēnⁿ/ *adj.*, smelly, something that has an undesirable smell, usu. refers to a person

Smithsonian Institution **I't'í'gąde'àt'à edéštaštà ité'daikè t'ì** /ē-t'ē'-gonⁿ-thä-ä'-t'ä ä-dä'-shtä-shtä' ē-tä'-thäē-kä' t'ē'/ *n.*, Smithsonian Institution, Washington DC, lit., the building where all kinds of things are stored

smoke **Šúde** /shü'-dä/ *n.*, smoke, unburnt fuel, tiny particles that rise in the air from something burning

smoke ritual **Ášudè** /ä'-shü-dä'/ *n./v.*, smoke ritual, usu. refers to ritual use of smoke from the needle-like leaves of the cedar tree; *ášudekidè*, to fan oneself with the cedar smoke (The Hísadà clan of the Ponca people was designated as the clan to handle the cedar-burning ritual that is considered a sacred rite of the people.)

smoke self **Ášudek'idè** /ä'-shü-dä-k'ē-thä'/ *v.*, smoke self, refers to ritual use of smoke from the needle-like leaves of the cedar tree as directed by the one conducting the rite

smoking **Đašúde** /thä-shü'-dä/ *n.*, smoking, exhaling smoke (The term apparently became used after cigarettes and cigars were introduced.)

smoking **Niní'į'** /nē-nē'-ēnⁿ/ *n.*, smoking, the inhaling of tobacco smoke or fumes into the lungs

smoky **Šúde đip'áze** /shü'-dä thē-p'ä'-zā/ *adj.*, smoky, usu. refers to something very smoky or making a lot of smoke from some source

smooth **Bišná'hà** /bē-snä'-hä/ *v.*, smooth, to smooth a surface, polishing, applying furniture polish to treat wood

smooth out **Đišnáha** /thē-snä'-hä/ *v.*, smooth out, to smooth out something that is rough and bumpy by use of the hands and hand tools

smooth running **Nąsúi** /nonⁿ-sü'-ē/ *adj.*, smooth running, a quiet, smooth-running automobile, bus, or train

snag **Uk'íądè** /ü-k'ē'-onⁿ-thä'/ *v.*, snag, to be caught or to be held by getting caught on something sharp

snake **Wés'à** /wā's-ä'/ *n.*, snake, 1. a reptile that

is long and legless, such as a black snake, bull snake, or rattlesnake 2. a male name in the Wažážè clan among the Ponca people

snapping turtle Gʼéʼ tʼągà /g-āʼ tʼoⁿ-gä/ *n.,* snapping turtle, a turtle with a smooth, hard shell with a ridge from front to rear; *gʼéʼ tʼatʼaxì,* a large turtle with large projections or bumps on its hard shell

snatch Đikápi /thē-kä'-pē/ *v.,* snatch, to grasp hastily, to grab suddenly

sneak Gdáde /gthä'-dā/ *v.,* sneak, sneak up on, to approach stealthily, usu. upon large animals or men; *gdáje,* sneak, sneak up on with delight (~ up on small game)

sneeze Héčį /hä'-chēⁿ/ *v.,* sneeze, an involuntary expulsion of air through the nose and mouth caused by some irritation in the nasal passage

sniff Udíbdą̀ /ü-thē'-bthoⁿ'/ *v.,* sniff, to draw air through the nose to smell or detect an odor that belongs to something desirable or undesirable, such as certain foods being prepared or animals being tracked as prey

sniffling Pʼáxdí daxù /p'ä-xthē' thä-xü'/ *v.,* sniffling, to sniffle continuously because of a bad head cold in order to prevent mucus from flowing out of the nose

snore Žą̀xdudè /zhoⁿ'-xthü-dā'/ *v.,* snore, the making of harsh or coarse sounds while sleeping, caused by vibration of the upper mouth

snow Máʼ /mä'/ *n.,* snow, precipitation consisting of snowflakes that fall from the clouds during the winter

snowbird Máde wažį́ʼgà /mä'-thä wä-zhēⁿ'-gä'/ *n.,* snowbird, generic term for birds that come during snowy winters

snow blindness Išt'ákiadà /ē-sht'ä'-kē-ä-dä'/ *n.,* snow blindness, inflammation of the eyes caused by exposure to rays reflected from snow or ice

snowing Máʼdè /mä-thā'/ *v.,* snowing, precipitation falling from the clouds as snow

snow on Áʼmadè /ä'-mä-thā'/ *v.,* snow on, usu. refers to being snowed on while doing something

snowshoe hare Mąščí'geʼsí'snedè /moⁿsh'-chē'-gä-sē'-snä-dä/ *n.,* snowshoe hare, *Lepus americanus,* so named because of its large hind legs and feet; also called snowshoe rabbit; its fur turns white during the winter and brown during the summer

snow storm Máʼdè gašúde /mä-thā' gä-shü'-dä/ *v.,* snowstorm, refers to a cold blast of air driving snow over the land, blizzard conditions

snuff out Điná'ži /thē-nä'-zhē/ *n./v.,* snuff out, to turn off a household oil lamp, to ~ a fire (now, to turn off electric lights)

so Éʼde /ā'-dä/ *adv.,* so, consequently, hence

soak Niúgašpą̀ /nēü'-gä-shpoⁿ'/ *v.,* soak, absorbed with water

soap Wédit'egà /wä-thē-t'ä-gä/ *n.,* soap, a cleansing agent that comes in varied forms, such as bars, flakes, liquid, and granules

sob Niúwagduzè /nēü'-wä-gthü-zā'/ *v.,* sob, sobbed, sobbing, to catch the breath spasmodically, caused by contractions in the throat that follow weeping or crying

soda Nigá't'ušì /nē-gä'-t'ü-shē'/ *n.,* soda, lit., water that pops, a sweet soft drink also called pop, coke, any carbonated beverage; *gá't'ušì,* abbr. form

soft Št'ągá /sht'oⁿ-gä'/ *adj.,* soft, supple, malleable

soften Đištą́ga /thē-shtoⁿ'-gä/ *v., archaic,* soften, to make softer or to become softer by use of the hands and hand tools (Deerskin was drawn over a blunt pole continuously until it became soft and supple; the term applies to modern uses of chemicals to soften skins.)

soft-shelled turtle **G'ehábedą̀** /g-ā-hä'-bā-doⁿ'/ *n.*, soft-shelled turtle, genus *Apalone*, family Trionychidae, the species known by the Ponca were referred to as sand turtles

soldier dance **Waną́še wačígaxè** /wä-noⁿ'-shä wä-chē'-gä-xä'/ *n.*, soldier dance, a man's dance, a form of the Heⁿúškà dance

sole **Sihátą** /sē-hä'-toⁿ/ *n.*, sole, in anatomy, the bottom of the foot

some **Ánąxt'ì** /ä'-noⁿ-xt'ē'/ *adj.*, some, a suggestion of more in number rather than fewer

some **Dúba** /dü'-bä/ *adj.*, some, a few, several, as in number of people or things

some **Júba** /jü'-bä/ *adj.*, some, a few, several, as in number of people or things, sometimes used to characterize less than few or several; *n.*, a thing left in small amounts

somebody **E'bé'** /ā-bā'/ *n.*, somebody, an unspecified person; *ebéšt'iwą̀*, anybody

somebody **E'bé'** /ā-bā'/ *n.*, somebody, a person of significance or a person of position in the community (*niášigà ~ te éí· akè*, he is *the ~*)

somebody else **Ážiámà** /ä'-zhē-ä'-mä/ *pron.*, somebody else, somebody not from here

someday **Ą́batąštì** /oⁿ'-bä-toⁿ-shtē'/ *adv.*, someday, one of these days

somehow **Áwategąštì** /ä'-wä-tä-goⁿ-shtē'/ *adv.*, somehow, by some means or way, in one way or another

someone **Ebéšt'i** /ā-bā'-sht'ē'/ *pron.*, someone, a person not named who has to or is called upon to do something

somersault **Basį́mągdè** /bäs-ēⁿ'-moⁿ-gthä'/ *n.*, somersault, a movement usu. done by children in which the body is rolled over forward, head on the ground, before returning to an upright position

something **Įdádą** /ēⁿ-dä'-doⁿ/ *pron.*, something, more of an inquiry, as in "What is it?"

something **Įdádąšt'ì** /ēⁿ-dä'-doⁿ-sht'ē'/ *pron.*, something, an unspecified thing

something **Įdádąšt'iwą̀** /ēⁿ-dä'-doⁿ-sht'ē-woⁿ'/ *pron.*, something, a suggestion for getting or selecting any of several things

sometimes **Atą́šti** /ä-toⁿ'-shtē/ *adv.*, sometimes, at times, now and then

somewhere **Áwadi'štì** /ä'-wä-dē-shtē'/ *adv.*, somewhere, wherever

somniloquy **Žą'dádįgè** /zhoⁿ-dä'-thēⁿ-gä'/ *n.*, somniloquy, 1. *žą'dádįgè íye*, talking in one's sleep 2. sleepwalking or noctambulism

son **Ižį́ge** /ē-zheⁿ'-gä/ *n.*, son, lit., his/her son; in the Ponca kinship system, the relationship of child to parent

son **Wižį́ge** /wē-zheⁿ'-gä/ *n.*, *1st pers. sing.*, son, (man or woman saying, my ~) in the Ponca kinship system, the relationship of child to parent

song **Waą́** /wä-oⁿ'/ *n.*, song, a musical composition

song maker **Waą́ gáxe** /wä-oⁿ' gä'-xä/ *n.*, song maker, composer of songs, usu. refers to a person who composes a song concerning a significant deed or accomplishment of another

son-in-law **Wit'ą́de** /wē-t'oⁿ'-dä/ *n.*, son-in-law (man or woman saying, my ~); in the Ponca kinship system, the relationship of father- and mother-in-law to son-in-law

Son of God **Wak'ą́da Ižį́gè** /wä-k'oⁿ'-dä ē-zheⁿ'-gä/ *n.*, Son of God, Jesus Christ or the Anointed One, the Messiah

soon **Uxdé'** /ü-xthä'/ *adv.*, soon, shortly, in a little while, before long, as in ~ *t'í'ga*, come here

sorcery **Gdą́xe** /gthoⁿ'-xä/ *n.*, sorcery, the practice of someone who is supposedly able to cast some evil upon another

sore **Ni'é** /nē-ä'/ *n.*, sore, blister, boil, carbuncle, or any skin complaint sore eyes **Įšt'á'snì** /ēⁿ-sht'ä'-snē/ *n.*, sore eyes, usu. referring to a stye

sore throat **Núde'ni'é** /nü'-dā-nē-ā'/ *n.*, sore throat, a pain or irritation in the throat often caused by acute pharyngitis, an inflammation of the throat

sorrowful **Nąde gídažì** /noⁿ-dā gē'-thä-zhē'/ *adj.*, sorrowful, heartbroken, an expression of sadness, as when hearing of the death of a friend

sorry **Udúmą** /ü-thü'-moⁿ/ *adj.*, sorry, a feeling of sorrow combined with anguish and torment over something said or done, or something not said or done

soul **Nąxe** /noⁿ'-xā/ *n.*, soul, spirit of man, the essence of man

soup **T'aní'** /t'ä-nē'/ *n.*, soup, a liquid food usu. made with meat or vegetable stock

sour **X'á'de** /x'ä'-thā/ *adj.*, sour, bitter, tart; *us'áde*, refers to canned foods or drinks that become bitter, tart, or sour by standing too long; may also be caused by overuse of spices

soured **Uskíde** /ü-skē'-thā/ *v.*, soured, to become spoiled or soured by fermentation, usu. refers to canned fruit or preserves in a jar

south **Mąštéát'a** /moⁿ-shtā'-ä'-t'ä/ *n.*, south, compass point

southeast **Hidéát'a** /hē-dā'-ä'-t'ä/ *n.*, southeast, lit., at the bottom, one of the forty-five-degree nautical points on the compass

southeasterly **Hidéá't'adišą** /hē-dā'-ä'-t'ä-thē-shoⁿ/ *adj.*, southeasterly, in a southeasterly direction

southerly **Mąštéá't'adišą** /moⁿ-shtā'-ä'-t'ä-thē-shoⁿ/ *adj.*, southerly, in a southerly direction

southwest **Í'šnugat'à** /ē'-shnü-gä-t'ä/ *n.*, southwest, one of the forty-five-degree nautical points on the compass

southwesterly **Í'šnuga't'adišą** /ē'-shnü-gä-t'ä-thē-shoⁿ/ *adj.*, southwesterly, in a southwesterly direction

sow **Úži** /ü'-zhē/ *v.*, sow, to plant seeds in the ground to grow crops

spaceship **Mą́xe'át'a mądé'gi'ą** /moⁿ-xā-ä'-t'ä moⁿ-dā-gē-oⁿ/ *n.*, spaceship, space shuttle

Spaniard **Š'p'áíúni** /sh-p'ä-ē'-ü'-nē/ *n.*, Spaniard, corruption of *Spaniard*, a native or inhabitant of Spain

spark **Đidáze** /thē-dä'-zā/ *n.*, spark, flash; *đidádazè*, sparkle

sparkling **Đią́babà** /thē-oⁿ'-bä-bä'/ *adj.*, sparkling, dazzling, shining

sparrow **Wazí'zi'jè** /wä-zē'-zē-jä'/ *n.*, sparrow, a common small bird of the family Passeridae

sparse **Wí'dądą̀** /wē'-thoⁿ-thoⁿ'/ *adj.*, sparse, 1. scanty, scarce, skimpy 2. refers to individuals entering a place one at a time

spasm **Músisi'** /mü-sē-sē/ *n.*, spasm, usu. refers to an involuntary contraction somewhere in the body

spatula **Wé'basądà** /wā-bä-soⁿ-thä'/ *n.*, spatula, a flat kitchen utensil; *wét'a íbisądà*, egg turner

speak **Í'yè'** /ē'-yā'/ *v.*, speak, to speak, to talk, to verbalize

speak conceitedly **Íye'mąsà** /ē'-yā-moⁿ-sä'/ *v.*, speak conceitedly, 1. to speak boastfully 2. to speak with high and lofty words as though one is better or smarter than others

speaking voices **Įgdéze** /ēⁿ-gthā'-zā/ *n.*, speaking voices, esp. the sound of many people speaking at once

speckle **Gdežé** /gthā-zhā'/ *v.*, speckle, to spot with a mottled, blotchy, messy pattern of color

speak of **Íde** /ē'-thā/ *v.*, speak of, to speak of a person, place, or thing; *íwiđè*, *1st pers. sing./pl. pres./past t.*, speak of, I speak/

spoke of you; *í'ɖaɖè, 2nd pers. sing./pl. pres. /past t.*, speak of, you speak/spoke of it/these/those/them/this; *íɖaì'*, *3rd pers. sing./pl. pres./past t.*, speak of, he/she/it speaks/spoke of it/these/those/them/this

speech **Íyegàxe** /ē'-yā-gä'-xā/ *n.*, speech, lit. making talk, a verbal communication to an audience

speed **Waséką** /wä-sā'-koⁿ/ *v.*, speed, to move faster with the use of the feet, as in driving some sort of vehicle or conveyance

speed up **Nąwáseką** /noⁿ-wä-sā'-koⁿ/ *v.*, speed up, to speed up by depressing the accelerator in an automobile or other conveyance with the feet

speeding **Gišką** /gē-shkoⁿ/ *adj.*, speeding, causing any vehicle to move fast or to speed

speeding **K'ué'** /k'ü-ā'/ *n., adj.*, speeding, moving quickly toward, refers to a person in a vehicle that comes quickly toward a person or thing

spicy **Waséką** /wä-sā'-koⁿ/ *adj.*, spicy, peppery, refers to food or drink

spider **Údiskè** /ü'-thē-skä'/ *n.*, spider, arachnid, an eight-legged insect that spins webs to catch its prey

spill **Ðišáɖa** /thē-shoⁿ'-thä/ *v.*, spill, to spill; *ɖišá'șaɖà*, spill or sprinkle out continuously any substance, liquid or solid, from a container

spill out **Bašášáɖà** /bä-shoⁿ'-shoⁿ'-thä/ *v.*, to spill out continuously, to empty something continously from a container

spin **Ganágè** /gä-noⁿ'-gä'/ *v.*, spin, the revolving motion of something caused by some force, such as wind, water, or mechanical means; *ganánągè*, spin, the continuous revolving motion of something; *ɖinágè*, spin, the revolving motion of something caused by use of the hands; *ɖinánągè*, spin, the con-

tinuous revolving motion of something caused by use of the hands

spiral **Ugáwįxè** /ü-gä'-wēⁿ-xā'/ *v.*, spiral, something moving downward through the air in circles

spirit **Ną́'xe** /noⁿ'-xā/ *n.*, spirit, 1. phantom, apparition 2. transparent

spit **Čú'** /chü'/ *v.*, spit, to spit out or expel saliva from the mouth

spittle **T'áxe'čú'** /t'ä'-xā-chü'/ *n.*, spittle, saliva, a fluid coming from salivary glands in the mouth

splash **Gabíxe** /gä-bēⁿ'-xā/ *v.*, splash, to cause liquid to splash or small solid substances to blow into the air; *ágabixà*, to be splashed upon, as when a pot boils over

split **Ubásnè** /ü-bä'-snä/ *v.*, split, divide something lengthwise into parts; crack, as in to ~ an automobile window or glass tumbler

split **Ugásnè** /ü-gä'-snä/ *v.*, split, to split into two separate pieces by cutting, chopping, sawing

split wood **Žą́' gasnésne** /zhoⁿ' gä-snä'-snä/ *n.*, split wood, usu. refers to blocks split with the grain of the wood

spoon **T'ehé** /t'ā-hä'/ *n.*, spoon, lit., buffalo horn; *t'ehé žįgà*, teaspoon; *t'ehé t'ągà*, tablespoon

spotted **Gɖežé** /gthā-zhā'/ *adj.*, spotted, marked with spots; more than spots, a mottled, blotchy, messy pattern of color; *gɖéška*, spotted, refers to a specific thing that is spotted

Spotted Tail **Sįdé gɖéškà** /seⁿ-dā' gthā'-shkä'/ *n.*, Spotted Tail, a Sioux war leader

spray **Mú'bixà** /mü'-bē-xoⁿ/ *v.*, spray, water spraying from a sprinkler

spread **Bɖá'adihà** /bthā'-ä-thē-hä'/ *v.*, spread, the range over which things extend (when a group of things are arranged some distance apart)

spread out **Ágabđà** /ä'-gä-bthä'/ *v.*, spread out, an opening up caused by something, such as wind

spread out **Đibđá** /thē-bthä'/ *v.*, spread out, as in to spread a quilt out, to open a package and spread out the contents

spread out **Múxa** /mü-xä/ *adj.*, spread out, unfold or open out, as when flowering or blooming

spring **Mé'** /mä'/ *n.*, spring, the season that precedes summertime; *me'ádi*, last spring; *mé'dą*, in the spring

spring snow **Mé máde** /mä' mä'-thä/ *v.*, archaic, spring snow (The term probably has its origins in the North Country, as it rarely snows in the spring in Oklahoma; however, when it does snow, the term applies.)

sprinkle **Á'đi'ą** /ä'-thē-on/ *v.*, sprinkle, to sprinkle something upon something, e.g., salt on food

sprinkle **Ubí'xą** /ü-bē'-xon/ *n./v.*, sprinkle, a sprinkling of rain before a rainstorm

sprinkled on **Ganáxe** /gä-nä-xä/ *v.* sprinkled on, usu. refers more to being sprinkled upon in the rain or by a water hose; *ugánaxèxt'ì, past t.*, to have been sprinkled on resulting in being drenched

sprinkling **Nąžíúbixą** /non-zhē'-ü'-bē-xon/ *n.*, sprinkling, sprinkling rain, drizzle

sprouting **Ugí'i** /ü-gē'-ē/ *v.*, sprouting, the germination of a seed, esp. a perennial plant, one that comes forth year after year

squash **Bidúže** /gä-dü-zhä/ *v.*, squash, to squash by pressing down on; *badúže*, to squash by using force; *đidúže*, squash with the use of the hands; *gadúže*, squash by hitting; *nądúže*, crush or mash with the feet

squash **Watą́ hášugà** /wä-ton' hä'-shü-gä'/ *n.*, squash, an edible, round, thick-skinned squash, genus *Cucurbita*

squash **Watą́ múxa** /wä-ton' mü-xä/ *n.*, squash, straight-necked yellow squash, *Cucurbita pepo* var. *recticollis*

squash **Watą́ níde'bazù** /wä-ton' nē'-dä-bä-zü'/ *n.*, squash, an edible striped squash with a long neck, genus *cucurbita*

squat **Žémusnadè** /zhä'-mü-snä-dä'/ *v.*, squat, to sit on one's heels

squeak **Bagíze** /bä-gē'-zä/ *v.*, squeak, to make a sharp, high-pitched sound usu. caused by two things rubbing against each other; *bagígíze*, squeaky (the prefix *ba* indicates the pushing of something against something else repeatedly, as in using a bow and violin to make high- and low-pitched sounds); *bigíze*, squeak by pressing down; *bigígíze*, squeaking continuously; *nągíze*, squeaky (the prefix *ną* indicates the use of the feet to make a squeaking sound, e.g., squeaky shoes or a squeaky floor); *nągígíze*, the making of a continuous squeaking, as in walking on a squeaky floor

squeeze **Ánąsądè** /ä'-non-son-dä'/ *v.*, squeeze, usu. done with the feet; to be pressed down by a person or thing

squirrel **Síga** /sēn'-gä/ *n.*, squirrel, a small animal with a bushy tail that lives in the trees, a rodent of the genus *Sciurus*

stab **Wé'žahè** /wä'-zhä-hä'/ *n.*, stab, something to ~ with, something to thrust forward with

stab **Žáhe** /zhä'-hä/ *v.*, stab, pierce, gore, stick; to pierce or wound with a pointed weapon

stable **Šą́ge unáži** /shon'-gä ü-non'-zhēn/ *n.*, stable, a building where horses are kept

stack **Á'k'iá'stà** /ä'-k'ēä'-stä/ *v.*, to stack, making a large pile of things heaped up high or piled up staff **Í'mągdè** /ē'-moⁿ-gthā'/ *n.*, staff, walking stick

staff **Waxdéxde** /wä-xthā'-xthā/ *n.*, staff, an ornamented, feathered staff carried by a man of honor bestowing honors upon worthy recipients

stagger **T'ákikį** /t'ä'-kē-kēⁿ'/ *v.*, stagger, to walk unsteadily

stand **Anáži** /ä-noⁿ'-zhēⁿ'/ *v.*, *1st pers. sing.*, stand, I stand; *á'nążì, n.*, the act of standing upon something

stand **Nązį́** /noⁿ-zēⁿ'/ *v.*, stand, to stand; *nążíga, masc. command form*, stand up; *nążįá, fem. command form*, stand up

stand in **Unáži** /ü-noⁿ'-zhēⁿ'/ *v.*, stand in, as in a child playing and standing in a puddle

Standing Bear **Mącú Nążį̀** /moⁿ-chü' noⁿ-zhēⁿ'/ *n.*, Standing Bear, a chief of the Ponca people (The chief filed a writ of habeus corpus against the U.S. government in 1879, resulting in the landmark declaration that Indians are persons and entitled to all rights under the Constitution of the United States of America.)

star **Miká'e** /mē-kä'-ā/ *n.*, star, a luminous sphere of plasma (The nearest star to the earth is the sun.)

stare **Wadą́besnedè** /wä-doⁿ'-bä-snä-dā'/ *n./v.*, stare, 1. to look extendedly at somebody without moving the eyes 2. to constantly look at different people or things in a public place

start a fire **Bináxdį** /bē-nä'-xthēⁿ'/ *v.*, to start a fire by blowing on embers

start a fire **Néde** /nā'-thā/ *v.*, start a fire, start a fire with kindling

starve **Nąp'éhi t'è** /noⁿ-p'ä'-hē t'āⁿ'/ *v.*, starve, go hungry, to not have anything to eat

station **Unáštą** /ü-noⁿ'-shtoⁿ'/ *n.*, station, a place where a public conveyance stops for passengers

statue **Níkašigè wasésą** /nē'-kä-shē-gä' wä-sā'-soⁿ/ *n.*, statue, e.g., a figure of a man, large or small

stayed **Adá'ži** /ä-thā'-zhē/ *v.*, stayed, to stay or remain in place

steal **Wamą́dą** /wä-moⁿ'-thoⁿ/ *v.*, steal, to steal, to take property or something belonging to someone without permission, usu. done in secret

stem **Hí'** /hē'/ *n.* stem, what woody and herbaceous plants can be identified by; *éžąhì'*, elm tree; *wamą́skihì'*, wheat plant

step **Á'tą** /ä'-toⁿ/ *n.* step, stair, rung, staircase, stairway, flight of steps

step **Sidíze** /sē-thē'-zā/ *n.*, step, footstep, stride, to take steps

stick **Ábaxą** /ä'-bä-xoⁿ/ *v.*, stick, to stick something in the hair, clothing, anything

stick **Ádaskabè** /ä'-thä-skä-bā/ *v.*, stick, adhere, to stick on the surface of something

stick **Ákigdaskabè** /ä'-kē-gthä-skä-bā/ *v.*, to stick, two things sticking or glued together

sticks **Žą́' žįgà** /zhoⁿ' zhēⁿ-gä'/ *n.*, sticks, twigs, a slender tree limb

sticky **Skáskabè** /skä'-skä-bā/ *v.*, sticky, something that is gummy or gluey

stiff **Udídį** /ü-dēⁿ'-dēⁿ/ *adj.*, stiff, rigid, unbendable, usu. refers to the body, as in "his legs were ~"

still **Šetą́ną** /shä-toⁿ'-noⁿ/ *adv.*, still, refers to something that is always there or a condition that remains the same

sting **Žáhe** /zhä'-hä/ *v.*, sting, refers to an insect sting

stingy **Waníte** /wä-nē'-tä/ *adj.*, stingy, refers to somebody who doesn't give or spend and is not generous

stink **X'wį́'** /x'wēⁿ'/ *n./v.*, stink, horrible smell, unpleasant smell

stir **Í'gadužè** /ē'-gä-thü-zhä'/ *v.*, stir, to stir with a ladle something cooking in a pot

stir **Udúgahì** /ü-thü'-gä-hē'/ *v.*, stir, to stir in or blend in cooking ingredients; *ígahì*, mix in

stirrup **Šánạk'agdè sí unážị** /shonⁿ-nonⁿ-k'ä-gthāⁿ' sē' ü-nonⁿ-zhēⁿ/ *n.*, stirrup, foot support on a saddle

stir up **Wádihì** /wä'-thē-hē'/ *v.*, stir up, disturb, usu. refers to scaring up game

stockings **Hịbégawịxe** /hēⁿ-bā'-gä-wēⁿ'-xä/ *n.*, stockings, hose, nylons, socks, a soft knitted covering worn on the feet

stoke **Žá uwá** /zhonⁿ ü-woⁿ/ *v.*, stoke, add fuel, refers to putting firewood into a wood stove

stomach **Níxa** /nē'-xä/ *n.*, stomach (The stomach's function is to digest food.)

stomachache **Níxa'ni'é** /nē'-xä-nē-ā'/ *n.*, stomachache

stone brick **Ị́ẹ ná'židè** /ēⁿ'-āⁿ nä'-zhē-dā'/ *n.*, stone brick, used for construction of houses and buildings; *ị́ẹ nážidedè*, to make bricks

stoop **Bamáxe** /bä-moⁿ'-xä/ *v.*, stoop, bend forward, to bend over with head down, stoop down

stop **Nạštá'** /noⁿ-shtoⁿ'/ *v.*, stop, end, discontinue, bring to a standstill

stopped **Đišt'á** /thē-sht'oⁿ'/ *v.*, stopped, finished, wrapped up, that's the end of it

stopped burning **Náži** /nä'-zhē/ *v., past t.*, stopped burning, went out (*p'éde ke* ~, the fire ~)

store **Inạ́de** /ē-noⁿ'-thā/ *v.*, store, to put a thing away in a particular place

store **Itéde** /ē-tā'-thā/ *v.*, store, putting away some things; *itạáde*, I put some things away; *itédadè*, you put some things away; *itédaì*, he/she/they put some things away; *ihéde*, to put something away; *ihạádè*, I put it away; *ihédadè*, you put it away; *ihédaì*, he/she/they put it away

store **Údịwit'ì** /ü'-thēⁿ-wē-t'ē'/ *n.*, store, a place where merchandise is offered for retail sale

storekeeper **Údịwit'ì adị̀** /ü'-thēⁿ-wē-t'ē' ä-thēⁿ'/ *n.*, storekeeper, 1. one who sells merchandise 2. Ponca name for a white storekeeper named John Hron Sr. who lived on the reservation ca. 1910

storm **Ába p'íáži** /onⁿ-bä p'ē'-ä'-zhē/ *n.*, storm, lit., bad weather, rainstorm, snowstorm, thunderstorm

story **Híga** /hē'-gä/ *n.*, story, legend, fable, saga, a true historical or mythological narrative

storyteller **Íye'udà** /ē'-yä-ü-thä'/ *n./v.*, storyteller, 1. to tell a story 2. a proper male name among the Ponca people

stove **P'édeunéde** /p'ā'-dä-ü-nä'-thä/ *n.*, stove, wood-burning stove

straight **Đút'ạ** /thü'-t'oⁿ/ *adj.*, straight, without an angle, bend, or curve, exactly vertical or horizontal; *bidú'tạ̀*, to straighten by pressing down on with or without tools; *didú't'ạ̀*, to straighten out by use of the hands; *gadú't'ạ̀*, to straighten by force with a tool

straightaway **Í'wadanạžì** /ē'-wä-thä-noⁿ-zhē'/ *adv.*, straightaway, immediately, without delay

straw **Sáhị** /sä'-hēⁿ/ *n.*, straw, stalks of threshed wheat, barley, or such used for weaving hats, baskets, etc.

strawberry **Baxt'é** /bäx-t'ā'/ *n.*, strawberry, a small, edible sweet red berry, *Fragaria x ananassa*

straw hat **Sáhị wadáge** /sä'-hēⁿ wä-thä'-gä/ *n.*, straw hat, a brimmed head covering woven out of straw and worn during the summer for protection against the sun

streaming **Ásnu'è** /ä'-snü-ā'/ *v.*, streaming, issuing or flowing, as in tears (*ịdédạ ịštabdì*

~ *gd̠í'akà*, she was sitting with tears ~ down her face)

street **T'í'utáną** /t'ē̠-ü-t'ä̠-noⁿ/ *n.*, street, lit., space between buildings, avenue, boulevard, alleyway, a public thoroughfare in a city or town

stretch **Đizí'** /thē̠-zē̠'/ *v.*, stretch, to stretch something out, such as a rubber band

stretch **Đizí'zi** /thē̠-zē̠'-zē̠/ *v.*, stretch, to stretch something over and over again

stretch **Đisáda** /thē̠-sä̠'-dä̠/ *v.*, stretch, extending one's limbs or body out full length; *k'iną̠sadà*, stretch self by walking; *ak'íną̠sadà*, I stretched or stretched by walking; *đak'íną̠sadà*, you stretched or stretched by walking; *ą̠k'íną̠sadài*, we stretched or stretched by walking

stretchable **Zízigè** /zē̠'-zē̠-gä̠'/ *adj./n.*, stretchable, something that can be stretched

string **Wék'ą̠t'ą̠** /wä̠-k'oⁿ-t'oⁿ/ *n.*, string, refers to a strip of material (cord, rope, strap) used for tying up a package or for something like hobbling or tethering a horse

strip **K'igđísiduà'** /k'ē̠-gthē̠'-sē̠-dü-ä̠'/ *n.*, a person who is undressed, nude; has sexual implications

striped **Gđezá'zà** /gthä̠-zä̠'-zä̠'/ *adj.*, striped, something painted or made in stripes, refers to something having bands or lines of varied colors

strive **K'iwášką̠** /k'ē̠-wä̠-shkoⁿ'/ *v.*, strive, making a personal, exceptional effort, trying hard

strive **Wašką́** /wä̠-shkoⁿ'/ *v.*, strive, to try very hard to do or achieve something; *awášką̠*, I tried hard; *wađášką̠*, you tried hard; *waškái*, he/she/they tried hard

strong **Wašką́t'ą̠gà** /wä̠-shkoⁿ'-t'oⁿ-gä̠'/ *adj.*, strong, physically strong and powerful, muscular

strong bow **Haxúde hé't'ą̠gà mą́de** /hä̠-xü̠'-dä̠ hä̠'-t'oⁿ-gä̠' moⁿ'-dä̠/ *n.*, strong bow, lit., bighorn sheep bow (The elders tell a story of a strong bow made of the horns of the bighorn sheep and wood.)

struggle **Ą̠'wą́šką̠'ì** /oⁿ-woⁿ'-shkoⁿ-ē̠'/ *v.*, *1st pers. pl.*, struggle, we tried hard

stubborn **Edége udį́šį̠** /ā̠-dä̠'-gä̠ ü-thē̠ⁿ'-shē̠ⁿ/ *adj.*, stubborn, a person or animal that is inflexible or pigheaded

stuffed **Bajáška** /bä̠-jä̠'-shkä̠/ *adj.*, stuffed, overstuffed, overfed (*níxa etáikè*, ~, his stomach was overstuffed)

stuffed **Ubískì** /ü-bē̠'-skē̠'/ *v.*, stuffed, filled to the brim, packed, crammed, jammed

stumble **K'ináąsa** /k'ē̠-noⁿ'-sä̠/ *v.*, stumble, trip, trip up, lose footing

stump **Žą́' hidè** /zhoⁿ' hē̠-dä̠/ *n.*, stump, the base part of a tree left in the ground after the tree is cut down

suave **Udúk'ąp'ì** /ü-thü̠'-k'oⁿ-p'ē̠'/ *adj.*, suave, handsome, good or fine looking, being appropriately neat, as in "the suit fits perfectly and looks good on him"

submerge **Ugđáge** /ü-gthoⁿ'-gä̠/ *v.*, submerge, go underwater, swim underwater

subsequently **Edí udáţą̠** /ā̠-dē̠' ü-thä̠'-toⁿ/ *adv.*, subsequently, next, the next one

success **Šą́'xt'i k'igáxe** /shoⁿ'-xt'ē̠ k'ē̠-gä̠-xä̠/ *n.*, success, favorable outcome of some task or undertaking

suck **Đaxú** /thä̠-xü̠'/ *v.*, suck, to draw liquid out of something, 1. with the mouth, as in using a straw in a soft drink 2. with machinery, as in a dairy's automized milking machines

sudden **Sabáži** /sä̠-bä̠-zhē̠/ *adj.*, sudden, abrupt and unexpected

suddenly **Í'waną̠žį̠xt'i** /ē̠'-wä̠-noⁿ-zhē̠ⁿ'-xt'ē̠/ *conj.*, suddenly, without hesitation, responding to something said or done

sudden move **K'u'é** /k'ü-ā'/ *v.*, sudden move, usu. a vehicle unexpectedly moving rapidly toward or away from a person or place

suffer **Ísabè** /ē'-sä-bä/ *v.*, suffer, to suffer 1. being ill, having a medical condition, affliction 2. distress or concern, worry

sufficient **Šénąxt'ì** /shä'-noⁿ-xt'ē'/ *adj.*, sufficient, a sufficient amount of things

suffocate **Niú't'adì** /nēü'-t'ä-thē'/ *v.*, suffocate, to have no respiration or to be deprived of oxygen, then die

sugar **Žąní'** /zhoⁿ-nē'/ *n.*, sugar, lit., wood water (The term probably derived from the word for maple syrup.)

sugar bowl **Žąní'uží'** /zhoⁿ-nē'-ü-zhē'/ *n.*, sugar bowl, a condiment holder for sugar

sugarcane **Žąní'hì** /zhoⁿ-nē'-hē'/ *n.*, sugarcane, a plant native to South Asia and Melanesia of the genus *Saccharum*, grass family Poaceae (Evidently the plant was grown in various parts of the United States, as the Ponca knew about it.)

suicide **T'ę́'k'idè** /t'āⁿ'-k'ē-thä/ *n.*, suicide, to take one's own life

suitable **É'gidą̀** /ā'-gē-doⁿ/ *n.*, suitable, something that a person is especially suited for, as in a place, employment, or their condition, situation, and/or state of affairs (The Ponca would include clothing, family composition, and property, including things that are just right for him/her/ them.)

sumac **Mí'bidehì** /mē'-bē-dä-hē'/ *n.*, sumac, one of the shrubs or trees belonging to the genus *Rhus*

summer **Nugé** /nü-gā'/ *n.*, summer, that period of the year that encompasses the months of May, June, July, and August; *nugeádi*, last summer; *nugeádą*, in the summer

sun **Mí'** /mē'/ *n.*, sun, in our solar system, a star that is a hot ball of fire

Sun dance **Nidą́bewačì** /nē-doⁿ'-bä-wä-chē'/ *n.*, Sun dance, the Ponca Sun dance ceremony

Sunday **Ą́ba'waxúbe** /oⁿm'-bä-wä-xü'-bä/ *n.*, Sunday, the day set aside for worship

sundown **Mí'idé** /mē'-ē-thä'/ *n.*, sundown

sunflower **Žaxdá** /zhä-xthä'/ *n.*, sunflower, *Helianthus* x *annuus*

sunny day **Mąšt'é** /moⁿ-sht'ä'/ *n.*, sunny day, a beautiful sunshiny day

sun perch **Hubdáska žįgà** /hü-bthä'-skä zhēⁿ-gä'/ *n.*, sun perch, genus *Perca* of the family Percidae

sunup **Mí édąbè** /mē' ä'-thoⁿ-bä/ *n.*, sunup, sunrise, daybreak, break of day

supernatural powers **Xubé** /xü-bä'/ *n.*, supernatural powers, things that occur according to a set of principles apart from the laws of nature

supper **P'áze wadáte** /p'ä'-zā wä-thä'-tä/ *n.*, supper, lit., evening meal, considered by some to be the main meal of the day, but could be a snack

support **Úwašką̀** /ü'-wä-shkoⁿ/ *n./v.*, support, a source of encouragement and aid

surgery **Wap'áde** /wä-p'ä'-dä/ *n.*, surgery, a medical procedure for operating or making an incision into the body for treating an injury or removing a disease

surrender **Nabé bahá** /nä-bä' bä-hä'/ *v.*, lit., show of hands, surrender, a hand gesture to declare one is defeated (The word originated during World Wars I and II, when enemy soldiers were captured. In ancient times, the Ponca took no captives except women and children.)

surround **Égaxè** /ä'-gä-xä'/ *v.*, surround, encircle, to enclose on all sides, besiege

swallow **Đahúni** /thä-hü'-nē/ *v.*, swallow, gulp down, to cause food to pass through the mouth and throat into the stomach without much chewing (A colloquial expression or slang suggesting taking food into one's system without chewing.)

swan **Míxa skà** /mē'-xä skä'/ *n.*, swan, one of the family of geese and ducks — genus *Cygnus*

sweater **Unáž̧į'zizigè** /ü-non'-zhēn-zē-zē-gä'/ *n.*, sweater, usu. a knitted outergarment covering the upper body

sweep **Ábašudè** /ä'-bä-shü-dä'/ *v.*, sweep, to sweep dust upon somebody or something

sweep **Babé'x̧į** /bä-bä'-xēn'/ *v.*, sweep, to sweep, to make a sweeping motion by pushing with an instrument such as a wide broom or an automated sweeper of some sort

sweep **Đibéx̧į** /thē-bä'-xēn'/ *v.*, sweep, to sweep with a common broom by use of the hands

sweet **Skíde** /skē'-thä/ *adj.*, sweet, sugary; *skídeáži*, not sweet

sweetbread **T'enáxdadè** /t'ä-non'-xthä-dä'/ *n.*, sweetbread, a culinary name for part of an animal stomach or belly

sweet corn **Watą́zi skídè** /wä-ton'-zē skē'-thä'/ *n.*, sweet corn

sweet potato **Núskidè** /nü'-skē'-thä'/ *n.*, sweet potato, an edible, orange-colored root

sweets **Waskíde** /wä-skē'-thä/ *n.*, sweets, something that is sugary or that contains sugar, as in candies, cookies, pastries

swell **Í'ba** /ē'-bä/ *adj.*, swell, a temporary increase in size of an area of the body due to an injury or illness

swept **Bđí'bex̧į** /bthē'-bä-xēn'/ *v.*, swept, *past t. sing.* of sweep — I swept

swift **Waséką** /wä-sä'-kon/ *adj.*, swift, fast, rapid

swift hawk **Gđedą́** /gthä-don'/ *n.*, swift hawk, probably pigeon hawk, *Falco columbarius*

swim **Hidá** /hē-thä'/ *v.*, swim, go swimming

swing **Hedú'baž̧à** /hā-thü'-bä-zhon'/ *n.*, swing, a child's swing

swinging **Gaiyázazà** /gä-ē-yä'-zä-zä'/ *v.*, swinging, to swing between two points as an open door swings to and fro by the force of the wind

sword **Mą́hi t'ągà** /mon'-hē t'on-gä'/ *n.*, sword, lit., big knife, a weapon with a long steel blade

sycamore tree **Ž̧ąsą́'** /zhon-son'/ *n.*, sycamore tree, *Platanus occidentalis*, a tall, white-barked tree with yellow foliage in the fall

sympathetic **Wadáede** /wä-thä'-ä-thä/ *adj.*, sympathetic, having an understanding, compassionate, benevolent feeling or attitude toward someone in need

synchronized **Nąp'í'** /non'-p'ē'/ *v.*, to be synchronized or work together in unison, usu. refers to foot movement in dancing

syrup **Ž̧ąní'snu'snù** /zhon-nē'-snü-snü'/ *n.*, syrup, lit., slippery sugar, refers to all varieties, including corn syrup, maple syrup, glucose syrup, etc.

syrupy **Á'snusnu'ì** /ä'-snü-snü-ē'/ *adj.*, syrupy, slithery and gooey

T

table **Wá'datè** /wä'-thä-tä'/ *n.*, table, something to place food upon and eat; *wíádatè*, foodstuff; *wadáte*, eat, consume food

tablecloth **Wádate'ádibdà** /wä'-thä-tä-ä'-thē-bthä'/ *n.*, tablecloth, usu. a cloth covering for the dining room table

tablespoon **T'ehé t'ągà** /t'ä-hä' t'on-gä'/ *n.*, tablespoon, used for serving food; a culinary measure, abbr. tbs. or tbsp., three teaspoons to one ~

tableware **Idádáte** /ē-thä'-thä'-tä/ *n.*, tableware, refers to items used to set a table for eating, such as bowls, dishes, knives, forks, and spoons

tackle **Á'nąxiádaidą** /ä-noⁿ-xē-ä'-thä-ē-thoⁿ'/ *v.*, tackle, as in the game of football, to chase and bring down an opponent

tactless **Niášigà wasé'žįgà** /nē-ä'-shē-gä' wä-sä'-zhēⁿ-gä'/ *adj./n.*, tactless, a person without tact and inconsiderate of others

tail **Sįde** /sēⁿ-dā/ *n.*, tail, the extended part of the rear end of the body of an animal, such as a monkey's tail, the tail feathers of a bird

tail **Sįde đihą** /sēⁿ-dā thē-hoⁿ'/ *n.*, tail, lifted tail, refers to the flash of the tail of the whitetail deer, *Odocoileus virginianus*, as it disappears into the bush

tailbone **Sįdéhi'** /sēⁿ-dā-hē/ *n.*, tailbone, the last bone at the bottom of the vertebral column, coccyx

tail feathers **Įbe** /ēⁿ'-bä/ *n.*, tail feathers, ~ of any bird

tails **Sįde'ádį** /sēⁿ'-dā-ä'-thēⁿ'/ *n.*, tails, lit., those who have tails, those with ~ (Refers to the warriors of the Đíxidą clan of the Ponca people, whose hairstyle included the shaving of both sides of the head. The hair from the crown of the head was left long and was braided.)

take **Đizé** /thē-zā'/ *v.*, take, get, obtain

take away **Gínąšè** /gē-noⁿ-shä'/ *v.*, take away, as in to take away from him/her/it, carry away from them/him/her/it

take away **Įnąšè** /ēⁿ-noⁿ-shä'/ *v.*, take away, as in to take away from me, carry away from me

take away **Wénąšè** /wä'-noⁿ-shä'/ *v.*, take away, take possession of, 1. take from them, carry away from them 2. take or carry away from us

take home **Adį gdè** /ä-theⁿ' gthä'/ *v.*, take home, a gift or earnings being taken home

take off **Bašnúde** /bä-shnü'-dā/ *v.*, take off, as in taking a nail from a board by the action of pushing with the hands and the use of a tool (e.g., a claw hammer or crowbar); *baš-núšnúde*, take off continuously, as in taking a nail from a board by the action of pushing with the hands and the use of a tool (e.g., claw hammer or crowbar)

take off **Đišnúde** /thē-shnü'-dā/ *v.*, take off, as in taking a screw off a device or removing one's coat by use of the hands; remove, to remove by use of hands and hand tools; *đišnú'šnudè*, take off continuously, as in taking bolts off some machinery or removing one's clothing

talcum powder **Bđípe** /bthē'-pä/ *n.*, talcum powder, derived from a clay mineral, *hydrated magnesium silicate* (The products of talcum include fragrant cosmetic powder that women use for keeping skin dry and that is used on babies to prevent rashes.)

talent **Wadíp'į'** /wä-thē'-p'ē'/ *n.*, talent, lit., one who knows how to do or make a thing, 1. talent, knack, aptitude 2. something done by a conjurer or magician

talk **Íye** /ē'-yā/ *v.*, talk, speak

talking **Íyečàčà** /ē'-yā-chä-chä'/ *v.*, talking, making "small talk" about no particular subject

talking in sleep **Žądá'đįgè íye** /zhoⁿ-dä'-thēⁿ-gä' ē'-yā/ *n.*, talking in one's sleep, somniloquy

tall **Snedé't'ągà** /snā-dā-t'oⁿ-gä'/ *n.*, tall, refers to the height of somebody

tallgrass **Mąhí'** /moⁿ-hē'/ *n.*, tallgrass, prairie grasses such as indiangrass (*Sorghastrum nutans*), big bluestem (*Andropogon gerardii*), and little bluestem (*Schizachyrium scoparium*) (The Ponca lands in Nebraska included these tall grasses. In modern times any tall grass is referred to as *mąhí'*.)

tallow **Wégdisagì** /wā'-gthē-sä-gē'/ *n.*, tallow, solid rendered fat of cattle

tame **Wašt'áge** /wä-sht'ä'-gä/ *adj.*, tame, domesticated, docile, meek

tan **Ná'zi** /nä'-zē/ *v.*, tan, burn to yellow, e.g., toasted bread

tangle **Į'k'idì** /ēⁿ'-k'ē-thē'/ *v.*, tangle, knot, snarl, kink, something that is tangled and twisted, such as hair

tanned **Nášabè** /nä'-shä-bā'/ *past t.*, tanned, refers to making hides of animals' skins, producing varied tanned colors

tanning **T'ą́dai** /t'oⁿ'-thä-ē/ *v.*, *archaic*, tanning, the process of softening animal skins for making clothing and other personal items, such as footwear and bags

tarantula **Údisket'ąga** /ü-thē-skä-t'oⁿ-gä'/ *n.*, tarantula, a very large, hairy spider, an arachnid belonging to the Theraphosidae family

taste **Ígaskądè** /ē'-gä-skoⁿ-thä'/ *v.*, taste, to test or discern the flavor of something— (To ~ something to determine if the food is too sweet, bitter, bland, sour, tart, etc.)

tasteless **Azá'żì** /ä-zä'-zhē'/ *adj.*, tasteless, not tasty, not delicious, not yummy, bland

tattletale **Waíye udádá** /wä-ē'-yä ü-thä'-thä'/ *n.*, tattletale, tattler, gossiper

tattoo **Xdexdé** /xthä-xthä'/ *n.*, tattoo, 1. *archaic*, refers to a tattoo ceremony or ritual for women 2. now refers to any tattoo

T-bone steak **T'é'žéga** /t'ä'-zhä'-gä/ *n.*, T-bone steak, a cut of beef from the loin region

tea **Xáde mąk'ą́** /xä-dä moⁿ-k'oⁿ/ *n.*, tea, lit., grass medicine

teach **Wegą́ze** /wä-goⁿ'-zä/ *v.*, teach, to teach, show, or demonstrate

teacher **Wagą́ze wádį** /wä-goⁿ'-zä wä'-thēⁿ/ *n.*, teacher, the instructor, the tutor or educator

tear **Bdazáde** /bthä-zä'-thä/ *v.*, tear, slit, rip, rend; *bdábdázadè*, continuous tearing, ripping

tear **Đibdáze** /thē-bthä'-zä/ *v.*, tear, to tear, as in tearing a piece of cloth by use of the hands; *đibdábdazè*, to continuously tear to pieces, as by use of the hands; *bibdáze*, tearing a piece of cloth by pressing down; *gabdáze*, tearing a piece of cloth by use of force, such as by the wind

tear **Įšt'ábdì** /ēⁿ-sht'ä'-bthē'/ *n.*, a tear, clear saline fluid secreted by the lacrimal gland

tear off **Đišpé** /thē-shpä'/ *v.*, tear off, to tear off a piece of something by the use of the hands

tease **Đahí'de** /thä-hē'-dä/ *v.*, tease, to taunt or kid somebody

tease **K'igdáhidè** /k'ē-gthä-hē-dä/ *v.*, tease, two persons who habitually tease each other

tease **Wádahidè** /wä'-thä-hē-dä/ *v.*, tease, saying or doing something comical in an annoying way to cause laughter

teasingly **Wegáxe** /wä-gä'-xä/ *adv.*, teasingly, teasing good-naturedly, teasing mischievously

teaspoon **T'ehé żįgà** /t'ä-hä' zhēⁿ-gä'/ *n.*, teaspoon, abbr. tsp., a utensil usu. used for drinking tea or coffee and consuming desserts

teeth **Hí** /hē'/ *n.*, teeth (The purpose of teeth is to cut or break down food or crush it to small pieces in the digestive system.)

telegraph **Mą́ze'utį́** /moⁿ'-zā-ü-tēⁿ'/ *n.*, *archaic*, telegraph, lit., hit the metal (The telegraph was the first electric device used to send messages through wire using the invention by Samuel Morse called Morse code. Messages were coded by using dots and dashes embossed on a strip of paper.)

telephone **Mą́ze'í'udà** /moⁿ'-zā-ē-ü-thä'/ *n.*,

telephone, a telecommunications device that permits two or more persons to speak to one another when they are far apart

television **Máze įdé'wábaxù'škášką** /moⁿ-zā ēⁿ-dā-wä'-bä-xü'-shkoⁿ'-shkoⁿ/ *n.*, television

tell **Udá** /ü-thä'/ *v.*, tell, inform, divulge something that happened; *uwíbđà*, I told you; *uwída*, tell him/her; *úwagiđà*, tell them

tell of **Đadé** /thä-dä'/ *v.*, tell of, telling the name of a person or thing

tell of **Ugđá'** /ü-gthä'/ *v.*, tell of, to tell of or to give an account of something that happened; *ukígđà*, to tell of something about oneself

temple **Nądádehà** /noⁿ-thä'-dā-hä/ *n.*, temple, the side of the head between the eyes and ears

tempt **Wégašt'ąká'** /wā'-gä-sht'oⁿ-kä/ *v.*, tempt, using something to entice or appeal to somebody or a group of people to act or to say something

ten **Gđébą** /gthā'-boⁿ/ *n.*, ten, the number ten (10)

tend **Á'ki'hidè'** /ä'-kē-hē-dā/ *v.*, tend, watch over, look after, to take care of

tender **Í'čegąđà** /ē'-chä-goⁿ-thä/ *adj.*, tender, physically painful when touched or slightly bumped

tender **Wačéga** /wä-chä'-gä/ *adj.*, tender, associated with food, such as meat easily chewed

tenderloin **T'eá'** /t'ā-ä'/ *n.*, tenderloin, any beef cut in the loin region

ten-dollar bill **Gdébą'í'dawà** /gthā'-boⁿ-ē'-thä-wä'/ *n.*, ten-dollar bill, U.S. currency

tension **Wadíse** /wä-thē'-sä/ *v.*, tension, usu. refers to a toddler flexing all his/her muscles

tent **T'í'sné'de** /t'ē'-snā-dā/ *n.*, tent, lit., long house

tenth **Wé'gđebà** /wā'-gthā-boⁿ/ *adj.*, tenth, the tenth thing in a row of items or the tenth person or group of people coming in succession

termite **Žądáte wagđíška** /zhoⁿ-thä'-tā wä-gthē'-shkä/ *n.*, termite, any of the many of the order Isoptera that feed on wood and are very destructive to buildings

terrapin **G'egdéze** /g-ā-gthä'-zä/ *n.*, terrapin, family Emydidae

tether **Ugáški inące** /ü-gä'sh-kē ē-noⁿ'-thä/ *v.*, tether, tie, as in fastening a rope or chain to an animal to restrict its movement to a certain area

Teton **Sičáxu** /sē-chä'-xü/ *n.*, the Teton Dakota people

thank **Ąk'íwahąì** /oⁿ'-k'ē'-wä-hoⁿ'-ē'/ *v.*, thank, to thank others for oneself and others; *ák'iwahąì*, to thank others for oneself

thank **Wahące** /wä-hoⁿ'-ā/ *v.*, thank, express thanks, express gratitude, be grateful; *wíbđahà*, 1st pers. sing., I ~ you

thankful **Wék'išnà** /wā'-k'ē-shnoⁿ/ *adj.*, thankful, to be thankful; *i'k'išnà*, to be personally thankful; *wąák'išnà*, we are personally thankful

thankfulness **Đistúbe** /thē-stü'-bä/ *n.*, thankfulness, a hand gesture of thankfulness, gratitude, appreciation, etc. to somebody for something (Draw down the right arm and raise the open hand toward an individual as a signal of respect and acknowledgement. It is also a gesture of thanking a person or persons.)

thankless **Wažé'dįgè** /wä-zhä'-thēⁿ-gä'/ *adj.*, thankless, ungrateful, refers to somebody who shows no gratitude

thank you **Wíbdahà** /wē'-bthä-hoⁿ/ *interj.*, thank you, thanks, expression of gratitude for something; acknowledgement in gratitude for something

that **Šé'** /shā'/ *pron.*, that; *šé'áka*, that one, usu. refers to one particular person; *šé'ma*, refers to a group of people or animals; *šę́'dą̀*, that round one, usu. refers to some specific place on the land; *šę́'kè*, that one, usu. refers to one specific thing; *šé'te*, that one, usu. refers to a group of things; *šét'a*, refers to something standing away from the speaker

that side **Gúədišą̀** /güə'-thē-shoⁿ'/ *prep.*, on that side, around on that side

that's it **É'akà** /ā'-ä-kä'/ *interj.*, that's it, that was it, that was them, that was him/her

the **Áka** /ä'-kä/ *art.*, the, definite article (originally used with singular animate subjects, now used with inanimate subjects)

the **Áma** /ä'-mä/ *art.*, the, definite article (with animate subjects, can be either singular or plural showing action or movement; however, in certain usage the term may show no action or movement)

the **Đą́** /thoⁿ'/ *art.*, the (used with nouns that describe parts of the human body; also used with circular objects; can be either singular or plural)

the **Đą́kà** /thoⁿ'-kä/ *art.*, the, definite article (describes animate subjects and is in the plural form; like the article *đíkè*, it is a descriptive word that is used in connection with the position a person or object is in, i.e., at rest, reclining, or sitting—connotes a place such as home, office, or a familiar place)

the **Đíke** /thēⁿ'-kä/ *art.*, the, definite article (designates a particular or specific animate subject; this article has also been described as a word that is used in connection with the position a person or object is in, i.e., at rest, reclining, or sitting, and connotes a place such as a home, office, or familiar place)

the **Gé** /gä'/ *art.*, the, plural article (desig-

nates things that are in groups, a collection of things, or things that are naturally scattered)

the **Ké** /kä'/ *art.*, the, singular article (used with words that describe an inanimate thing or idea); *máze wédixđì ~ úđą̀*, ~ computer is good

the **Má** /mä'/ *art.*, the, plural article (designates animate subjects; can be confused with *áma*, which can be either plural or singular); *šą́t'ągà ~ wat'é'đè đip'i-*, ~ wolves know how to kill

the **Tą́'** /toⁿ'/ *art.*, the, singular article (designates singular, standing, animate subjects); *núžįgà ~ snęđé t'ągà*, ~ boy is tall

the **Té** /tä'/ *art.*, the, plural article (used with words that describe an inanimate thing or idea); *t'í' ~ é'gazizì'xtì gáxà bíkè*, they have built ~ houses in a row

the **Wí'** /wē'/ *art.*, the, indefinite article (used to designate indefinite singular animate or inanimate objects; similar to the English *a* and *an*)

their **Et'ái** /ā-t'ä'-ē/ *pron.*, their, something belonging to them, as in "that is ~ father"

them **Šé'amà** /shā'-ä-mä/ *pron.*, them, usu. refers to those things or that group of people standing away from the speaker; *đéámà*, those standing closest to the speaker; *duáma*, those standing slightly farther away from the speaker; *gááma*, those standing, running, speaking, sitting, eating, etc., out of sight of the speaker

then **Edí'teđąđì** /ā-dē'-tā-thoⁿ-dē'/ *adv.*, then, at that time, at that point in time

then **Edíhi** /ā-dē'-hē/ *adv.*, then, reaching that point and time

then **Gátedì** /gä'-tä-dē'/ *adv.*, then, at that time

the one **Amé** /ä-mä'/ *n.*, the one, as in "he's the one."

there **Edí·** /ā-thē'·/ *n.*, there, refers to a location or place (*núžįgà tą ~ akà*, the boy was ~)

there **Et'á** /ā-t'ä'/ *n.*, there, refers to a place mentioned at an earlier time (*~ ǫgáhì umą́dįkà ą́mątedądì*, we went ~ last year)

there **Gáhidéát'a** /gä-hē-thā'-ä'-t'ä/ *adv.*, there, "over there" (The speaker is giving the general direction of a place, including the distance from where he/she stands.)

there **Gáwadì** /gä'-wä-dē'/ *adv.*, there, refers, 1. to a specific physical place away from the speaker or out of sight of the speaker and hearer 2. a specific word or statement where an interjected idea should have or could have been said

there **Šédudì** /shā'-thü-dē'/ *adv.*, 1. there, right there—pointing to something physical 2. in a speech, bringing attention to something

there **Šégedì** /shā'-gā-dē'/ *adv.*, there, to put, place, observe, remain at some physical location close by

there **Šéwadì** /shā'-wä-dē'/ *adv.*, there, indicates a place or position of a thing away from the speaker, usu. refers to distance from the speaker, as in an object across the room as opposed to an object close at hand, far away, out of sight

therefore **Á'dą̀** /ä'-doⁿ'/ *adv.*, therefore, so, and so, for that reason

these **Ðédąkà** /thā'-thoⁿ-kä'/ *pron.*, these, refers to people or animals (plural of *ðéke*, this)

these **Duádąkà** /dü-ä'-thoⁿ-kä'/ *pl. pron.*, these, refers to people or animals here

these **Duáte** /düä-tā/ *pl. pron.*, these, refers to things (plural of *duáke*, this)

thick **Ákišugà** /ä'-kē-shü-gä'/ *adj.*, thick, dense, 1. usu. refers to crowded things, people close together 2. may refer to torrential rain (*nąží ~*, torrential rain)

thick **Šugá** /shü-gä'/ *adj.*, thick, bulky

thief **Wamą́dąšt'ą̀** /wä-moⁿ'-thoⁿ-sht'oⁿ'/ *n.*, thief, somebody who habitually steals things

thigh **Sižú'** /sē-zhü'/ *n.*, thigh, usu. refers to the upper part of the human leg, that area between the pelvis and knee

thin **Bdé'ka** /bthā'-kä/ *adj.*, thin, sheer

thin **Xáxadè** /xä'-xä-dä/ *adj.*, thin, thin garment or fabric, a material woven loosely; *unáži' xáxadè*, a woman's thin blouse; *máze xáxadè*, screen, a metal mesh frame

thing **Ą̀ska** /oⁿ'-skä/ *n.*, thing, an unspecified item, whachacallit

things **Edéšt'ą̀** /ā-dā'-sht'ä-sht'ä'/ *n.*, things, objects, bits and pieces of things, lots of different things

think **Edégą** /ā-thā'-goⁿ/ *v.*, to think, imagine, reflect, reason; *ebdégą*, I think; *enégą*, you think; *edégąì*, he/she/it/they think

think **Síde** /sē'-thā/ *v.*, think, to think of something that happened or think of somebody (*~ nąmá*, I ~ of you)

third **Wé'dabdì** /wā'-thä-bthē'/ *adj.*, third, the third thing in a row of items or the third person or group of people coming in succession

thirsty **Ní'íbizè** /nē'-ē'-bē-zā'/ *adj.*, thirsty, lit., dry from lack of water, the want of drink; *ǫdą́bizè*, desirous of doing something

thirteen **Agdídabdį̀** /ä-gthē'-thä-bthēⁿ'/ *n.*, thirteen, the number thirteen (13); something consisting of ~ units; *agdídabdįhà*, a group of ~; *agdídabdįą̀*, ~ times; *agdídabdįą̀žà*, ~ times again, or always; *agdídabdįxčì*, only ~; *agdídabdįegà*, just about ~; *agdídabdįdą*, the ~th one; *agdídabdįdądą̀*, ~ apiece or ~ each

this **Ðé** /thā'/ *adj./pron.*, this, indicates somebody or something distinct from somebody else or another thing this **Ðéke** /thä'-kä/ *adj./pron.*, this, some person or something that is close by the speaker

this **Ðuádįkè** /düä-thēⁿ-kä'/ *adj./pron.*, this, this person or animal standing, sitting, or lying close to the speaker

this **Duáke** /düä-kä/ *adj./pron.*, this, a thing that is in hand or closer to the speaker

this **Gádįkè** /gä-thēⁿ-kä'/ *adj./pron.*, this, someone or something away from the speaker that is out of sight; someone or something kept in mind

this **Gáke** /gä-kä/ *adj./pron.*, this, something that is away from the speaker, something that is out of sight, or something that is kept in mind or is part of a plan

this far **Ðétą** /thä-toⁿ/ *adv.*, this far, 1. in measurement, in length 2. in making or doing something as in completing a task in part 3. in time as it relates to the time of day

this far **Gátą'hì'** /gä-toⁿ-hē'/ *adv.*, this far, refers to something that was done or a period of time being passed when another thing was finally begun, as in dinner served an hour late

this much **Ðéną** /thä-noⁿ/ *adv.*, this much (measurement), as in showing with hands; *dénądądà*, giving of some things to each of a group of people (~ *waí' dédaì*, he gave away ~) or accounting for something that remains (~ *ušté*, ~ is left)

this one **Ðédįkè** /thä-thēⁿ-kä'/ *adv./n.*, this one, refers to somebody standing close by or somebody spoken of; *déke*, this one, refers to something close by

this side **Dúədišą** /dü'-ə-thē-shoⁿ'/ *prep.*, this side, around ~

this size **Ðénąskà** /thä'-noⁿ-skä'/ *adv./adj.*, this size, the accounting of things of the same size; *dénąskaskà*, these sizes

this way **Ðégą** /thä-goⁿ/ *adv.*, this way, like this, like so, instructions on how to do something (~ *gáxagà*, do it ~)

thorn tree **Ną́'t'i't'ahì** /noⁿ-t'ē-t'ä-hē'/ *n.*, thorn tree, one of the species known to the Ponca in Oklahoma that has long pods with large black seeds

thorny **P'aí'dadà** /p'ä-ē'-thä-thä'/ *n.*, thorny, usu. refers to plants that have thorns, including sandbur, cocklebur, and "goat heads" or "stickers"

thorny tree **Žą́'p'aí'dadàhì** /zhoⁿ'-p'ä-ē'-thä-thä'-hē'/ *n.*, thorny tree, any of the many species of thorny trees and bushes

those **Šédąkà** /shä'-thoⁿ-kä'/ *pl. pron.*, those, usu. refers to people, animals, or things within a short distance from the speaker; *gádąkà*, refers to people, animals, or things out of sight or in the mind

those **Šé'gè** /shä'-gä'/ *pl. pron.* of *that*, those, refers to things placed close by; *šé'gešt'ì*, even ~ over there

those over there **Gáhideamà** /gä-hē-thä-ä-mä'/ *pron.*, those over there, refers to any group of people within a short distance from the speaker or those who are not in sight

thought **Edéga** /ā-thä'-goⁿ/ *n.*, thought, contemplation, ideas, or plans that come from thinking

thoughtless **Wadí'gdą digè** /wä-thē'-gthoⁿ' thē-gä'/ *adj.*, foolish, thoughtless, unable to think

thousand **K'ú'gè** /k'ü'-gä'/ *n.*, one thousand, the highest number in Ponca (The number one thousand was called *gdébą'hiwì' t'ągà*, big one hundred. According to some historians, the U.S. government issued one thousand dollars in cash to the Ponca in the early 1800s in exchange for passage through their territory and use of the Missouri River. The money was delivered in a case, *k'úgè*. Thereafter the Ponca used the term to mean one thousand.)

thousand-dollar bill **K'ú'ge'hįwį'ídawà** /k'ü'-gä-hēⁿ-wēⁿ'-ē'-thä-wä/ *n.*, thousand dollar bill, U.S. currency

thrash **Wanáȥudè** /wä-noⁿ'-zhü-thä'/ *v.*, thrash (thresh), to separate seeds from husks and straw

thread **Wahą́'** /wä-hoⁿ'/ *n.*, thread, 1. string, cord 2. *v.*, to move and camp out somewhere

threadbare **Díáda** /dē'-ä'-thä/ *adj.*, threadbare, said of a piece of old cloth that tears easily

three **Ðábdì** /thä'-bthē'/ *n.*, three, the number three (3)

threes **Ðábdį'dą̀dą̀** /thä'-btheⁿ-thoⁿ'-thoⁿ'/ *n.*, threes, by threes, as in they came in three at a time

threshing machine **Wé'nąȥudè** /wä'-noⁿ-zhü-thä'/ *n.*, *archaic*, threshing machine (Now the term refers to the modern combine, a machine that separates seeds from husks and straw.)

thrice **Ðábdį'ą̀** /thä'-btheⁿ-oⁿ'/ *n.*, thrice, three times

throat **Nú'de** /nü'-dä/ *n.*, throat, the digestive and breathing passage in the neck

throbbing **Múdadà** /mü'-dä-dä/ *adj.*, throbbing, usu. associated with pain, hurting, agonizing, aching

through **Íhe** /ē'-hä/ *prep.*, through, by way of, 1. a person performed an action through something 2. a person traveled by a particular route

throughout **Idáugdè** /ē-thä'-ü-gthä'/ *prep.*, throughout, through the whole of something or all parts of; *há'dą̀'idáugdè*, throughout the night, right through the night, during all the night; *ą́ba'idáugdè*, throughout the day

throw **Ą́dadéde** /oⁿ'-thä-thä'-thä'/ *v.*, throw, toss or throw something, such as a ball, a discus, or a frisbee in games

throw away **Ą́da** /oⁿ'-thä/ *v.*, throw away, to discard, toss something or throw something away

throw out **Ą́ši'ądà** /ä'-shē-oⁿ-thä'/ *v.*, throw out, evict, force a person out of, 1. dismissing or ousting somebody from an office or a place 2. banish from an organization or tribe

thrust **Baxą́'** /bä-xoⁿ'/ *v.*, thrust, to stab or ~ a knife into a wild animal or a person

thud **Gapúki** /gä-pü'-kē/ *n.*, thud, a dull, heavy sound made by a heavy object impacting a surface

thumb **Nąbéhi ut'ága** /noⁿ-bä'-hē ü-t'oⁿ'-gä/ (*masc./fem.*) (**Nąbóhot'ągà** /noⁿ-bō'-hō-t'oⁿ'-gä'/ [*masc.*]) *n.*, thumb

thunder **Įgdą́'hút'ą̀** /ēⁿ-gthoⁿ'-hü'-t'oⁿ'/ *n.*, thunder, the sound of the mythological creature called *Į́gdą̀*

Thursday **Ą́ba'wé'dubà** /oⁿm'-bä-wä'-dü-bä'/ *n.*, Thursday, lit., day number four

tick **T'ádazap'à** /t'ä'-thä-zä-p'ä'/ *n.*, tick, a bloodsucking parasite of the superfamily Ixodoidea that attaches itself to warmblooded animals

tidy up **Ðišúp'a** /thē-shü'-p'ä/ *v.*, tidy up, to put things in order, to neaten or clean up

tie **Idádisądè** /ē-thä'-thē-soⁿ-dä'/ *v.*, tie, wrapping something around a thing to stabilize or secure it

tie **K'ą́t'ą** /k'oⁿ'-t'oⁿ/ *v.*, tie, to bind, secure, to tie or tether an animal up so that it cannot get away; *ak'ą́t'ą̀, 1st pers. sing.*, I tied; *idágik'ąt'ą̀, 3rd pers.*, he tied his own; *idák'ąt'ą̀, 1st pers.*, I tied with (something)

tie **Ugáški** /ü-gä'-shkē/ *v.*, tie, tie to, fasten onto or strap on, as in to tie an animal up temporarily tight **Điskí'** /thē-skē'/ *v.*, to be tight, taut, to fix something that is unyielding

tighten **Ubádą** /ü-bä'-doⁿ/ *v.*, tighten, to make tight, locking up something very tight; *ušp'ádą*, you tightened or locked; *ubádąì*, he/she tightened or locked; *ągú'ąbádąì*, we tightened or locked

tighten **Ubískì** /ü-bē'-skē/ *v.*, tighten, to tighten by pressing down on, as in pressing down on clothing in a suitcase, fill to the brim, pack, cram, jam

tighten **Udíski** /ü-thē'-skē/ *v.*, tighten, to make tighter, as in tightening a nut on a bolt using a wrench

tight fitting **Ádasądè** /ä'-thä-soⁿ-dā'/ *adj.*, tight fitting, as in tight-fitting clothes or a tight-fitting cover

till **Đibđí** /thē-bthē'/ *v.*, till, plow, as in plowing up a field to sow grain

timid **Unízi** /ü-nē'-zhē/ *adj.*, timid, without self-confidence and courage to do something

tiny **Žįáx'čì** /zheⁿ-ä'x-chē'/ *adj.*, tiny, miniature, teeny

tipi **T'íúkeđì** /t'ē'-ü'-kā-thēⁿ'/ *n.*, tipi, lit., common dwelling, a conical dwelling once covered with bison hides, now canvas

tipi door flap **T'ižébeudà** /t'ē-zhā'-bā-ü-thoⁿ'/ *n.*, tipi door flap, doorknob

tipi poles **T'í'šì'** /t'ē'-shē'/ *n.*, tipi poles, wooden poles that provide a frame for the structure to be covered with canvas (In their earlier history, the Ponca used bison hides to cover their tipis.)

tip of fingers **Nąbép'asì** /noⁿ-bā'-p'ä-sē'/ *n.*, tip of fingers

tip of nose **P'á'šižé** /p'ä'-shē-zhā'/ *n.*, tip of the nose

tiptoe **Nąstáp'i** /noⁿ-stä-p'ē/ *n.*, 1. tiptoe song 2. dance step made quietly on the toes

tiptoeing dance **Nąst'áp'i wačígaxè** /noⁿ-st'ä'-p'ē wä-chē'-gä-xä/ *n.*, a tiptoeing dance, a man's dance, a ceremonial dance similar to the trot dance, a part of the *He-đúškà wačígaxè*

tiptop **P'asiát'à** /p'ä-sēä'-t'ä/ *adj.*, tiptop, the highest point of something, such as a pinnacle or the top of a tree, house, or structure (he was working at the ~ part of the tower)

tired **Užéda** /ü-zhā'-thä/ *adj./n.*, tired or tiredness, weary, worn out, etc.

tired of **Ámąk'ažì** /ä'-moⁿ-k'ä-zhē'/ *adj./v.*, to be tired of, to grow disgusted with something or somebody, to be sick of it or him, annoy, to irritate, aggravate, or get on one's nerves; *ámąk'ažiwađè*, something that a person can get tired of

tired out **Uwák'igđižedà** /ü-wä'-k'ē-gthē-zhä-thä/ *n./v.*, tired out, causing oneself to become mentally or physically fatigued, worn down, usu. caused by doing some activity

toad **Ik'ą́'git'è** /ē-k'oⁿ'-gē-t'ä/ *n./v.*, toad, lit., death of his/her/its grandmother; a small amphibian similar to a frog

toast **Wamą́ske náxudedè** /wä-moⁿ'-skā nä'-xü-dā-thä/ *n.*, toast, a toasted slice of bread

tobacco **Niní'** /nē-nē'/ *n.*, tobacco, orig. a mixture of certain plant leaves (of unknown species) used for smoking in tribal ceremonials and rituals (Now a word for present-day tobacco products, esp. those tobacco plants grown in the Southeast in the genus *Nicotiana* of the Solanaceae family.)

tobacco pouch **Niníú'žihà** /nē-nē'-ü'-zhē-hä'/ *n.*, tobacco pouch, a decorated, fringed tobacco pouch

today **Àba adáikeđì** /oⁿ'-bä ä-thä'-ē-kā-dē'/ *adv.*, today, on this day as they go forth in their lives today **Ą̀badè** /oⁿ-bä-thä'/ *adv.*, today, in the present day

today **Ą̀ba duákedì** /oⁿ-bä dü-ä'-kä-dē'/ *adv.*, today, on this day

toenails **Si'uša̧ge'wahì** /sē-ü-shä'-gä-wä-hē'/ *n.*, toenails

toes **Sip'á'** /sē-p'ä'/ *n.*, *pl.*, toes; *sipáhi*, toe

together **Gaxdą̀** /gä-xthoⁿ'/ *adv.*, *archaic*, together, something done jointly by a group of people, such as a bison hunt (The families of hunters were part of the entourage.)

together **Zą́zą̀dè** /zoⁿ-zoⁿ-dä'/ *adv.*, together, collectively, groups of people or things in a scattered position in a large area; may also refer to individuals sitting in a row apart from each other

together **Žúk'igdè** /zhü-k'ē-gthä'/ *adv.*, together, 1. jointly (the pipes fit ~) 2. mutually (the crowd agreed ~) 3. as partners (the man and the woman were ~, the boys were ~)

toilet **T'í'žįgà** /t'ē'-zheⁿ-gä'/ *n.*, toilet, restroom, bathroom, the outhouse

toilet paper **Í'gadì** /ē'-gä-dē'/ *n.*, toilet paper

token **Wéši** /wä'-shē/ *n.*, token, usu. an item or items used in a gambling game, 1. the Ponca used carved seeds or bone for counting scores in the "bowl dice game" 2. in the Ponca handgame, the handheld *wéši* are hidden from the guesser

tomahawk **Mą́zep'è žįgà** /moⁿ'-zä-p'ä' zhēⁿ-gä'/ *n.*, tomahawk, a term of Algonquian origin, a tool brought by the Europeans and later used by Native Americans and European people as a weapon

tomato **Waží'de** /wä-zhē'-dä/ *n.*, tomato, a round, red vegetable that can be eaten raw or cooked

tomorrow **Gasą́di** /gä-soⁿ'-thē/ *n.*, tomorrow, the day after today

tongue **Đéze** /thä'-zä/ *n.*, tongue, the organ inside the mouth of humans and most animals that is used for tasting, swallowing, licking, and in humans, speech; *déze p'asì*, tip of the tongue

tonight **Há̧de** /hoⁿ'-thä/ *n.*, tonight, this present night

tools **Wédihidè** /wä-thē-hē-dä'/ *n.*, tools, orig. something made to be used for some specific manual work, such as a hoe (*wé'e*) for gardening; now metal tools, motorized equipment such as a forklift, earth mover, etc.

toothache **Hí'ni'é** /hē'-nē-ä'/ *n.*, toothache, a sharp, throbbing pain around a tooth that is caused by dental problems such as a cavity, a cracked tooth, an abscessed tooth, or gum disease

toothbrush **Hí'ídižà** /hē'-ē'-thē-zhä'/ *n.*, toothbrush, a device that consists of bristles on a handle used to clean the teeth and gums

toothpick **Hiúbagudè** /hēü'-bä-gü-dä'/ *n.*, toothpick, lit. dig into the teeth; a small stick made of wood or plastic and used to remove food particles from the teeth after a meal

toothpick **Hiúgašáde íbagudè** /hēü'-gä-shä'-dä ē'-bä-gü-dä'/ *n.*, toothpick, lit. something to use to dig between the teeth; a small stick made of wood or plastic and used to remove food particles from the teeth after a meal

top of head **T'axp'í** /t'ä-xp'ē'/ *n.*, top of head, the crown of the human head

tore **Bdazáde** /bthä-zä'-thä/ *v.*, tore, *past. t.* of tear, slit, rip, rend

tornado **T'adé'sagì't'ą̀gà** /t'ä-dä'-sä-gē'-t'oⁿ-gä'/ *n.*, tornado, a strong rotating column of air formed between the surface of the ground and a cumulonimbus cloud

torso **Điʃ'** /thē-ʃ/ *n.*, torso, upper body, chest

totter **T'ákįkį** /t'ä'-kēⁿ-kēⁿ/ *v.*, totter, to walk unsteadily, to stagger, to have a wobbly gait

touch **Á'bit'à** /ä'-bē-t'ä'/ *v.*, touch, 1. pressing with fingers, as in pressing a lever on a water fountain 2. *2nd pers. sing.*, you touch

touch **Íbist'à** /ē'-bē-st'ä'/ *v.*, touch, touching with tips of fingers, as in touching a sacred relic

touch **Í't'a** /ē'-t'ä/ *v.*, touch, usu. reaching with the tips of the fingers to touch something, as in the act of touching ceremonial sacred items

tow **Ðidą́** /thē-doⁿ/ *v.*, tow, to draw or pull along behind

toward **Et'ádišą̀** /ā-t'ä'-thē-shoⁿ/ *prep.*, toward, in the direction of something

toward the evening **P'ázet'adišą̀** /p'ä'-zā-t'ä-thē-shoⁿ/ *prep.*, toward the evening

toward the night **Hą́dą't'adišà** /hoⁿ'-doⁿ-t'ä-thē-shoⁿ/ *prep.*, toward the night

towel **Nąbé'ibík'à** /noⁿ-bä-ē-bē'-k'ä'/ *n.*, towel, hand towel; *idéibik'à*, face towel (Both terms refer to an absorbent cloth used to dry hands, face, and body.)

town **T'ą́wągdà** /t'oⁿ-woⁿ-gthoⁿ/ *n.*, town, metropolis, city, clan; *t'ą́wągdəàdi*, at or in the town; *t'ą́wągdəadítą*, from the town; *t'ą́wągdəát'a*, to the town; *t'ą́wągdəát'áha*, toward town; *t'ą́wągdəát'adišà*, toward or in the direction of town

town crier **Iyé bahá** / ē-yä' bä-hä'/ *n.*, *archaic*, town crier or herald, a person in the Ponca Nation designated as one who makes public announcements in the camp and proclamations during ceremonies

town crier **Wajép'a** /wä-jä'-p'ä/ *n.*, town crier or herald, a person in the Osage Nation designated as one who makes public announcements in the camp and proclamations during ceremonies

toy **Wádixà** /wä'-thē-xoⁿ/ *n.*, toy, a thing that children play with, such as games, models, dolls, a teddy bear

track **Sigdé** /sē-gthä'/ *n.*, track, a mark left by an animate or inanimate moving thing, such as a footprint or a rut left by a wheel

track **Sigdé udúhe** /sē-gthä' ü-thü-hä/ *n./v.*, track, to track, to track a person or animal

train **E'wáš'nągè** /ā-wä'sh-noⁿ-gä'/ *n.*, train, locomotive; *e'wáš'nągè niášigà wé'ì*, passenger train; *e'wáš'nągè wat'úgdà*, freight train

train depot **E'wáš'nągè unášt'à** /ā-wä'sh-noⁿ-gä' ü-noⁿ'-sht'oⁿ'/ *n.*, train depot, a station where people embark on or disembark from a passenger train

traits **Á'bitądè** /ä'-bē-toⁿ-thä'/ *adj.*, having traits in common, bearing resemblance, as in a person having the traits and mannerisms of another by virtue of their behavior

transfusion **Wamídizè** /wä-mē'-thē-zä'/ *n.*, transfusion, transferring whole blood from a healthy donor to somebody who has lost blood or who has a blood disorder

trap **Mą́ze uk'íądè** /moⁿ'-zä ü-k'ē'-oⁿ-thä'/ *n.*, trap, a metal device to catch animals

travel **Ugášą** /ü-gä'-shoⁿ/ *v.*, travel, 1. journey, trek, tour 2. *archaic*, travel, to take a trek into enemy territory to take something

travois **Wahé'ą** /wä-hä'-oⁿ/ *n.*, travois, sled made of two poles connected to the sides of an animal, usu. a horse or dog, to transport material goods; *wábahè*, travois

treatment **Zé'de** /zä'-thä'/ *v.*, treatment, medical treatment, to use medicines or therapy to cure sickness

tree **Xdabé'** /xthä-bä'/ *n.*, tree, 1.generally, a large woody plant having few branches on its lower part with many smaller branches on its upper parts 2. timber or forest

tree branch **Žą́'gaxà** /zhoⁿ'-gä-xä'/ *n.*, tree branch, usu. refers to large branches reaching out

tree fork **Žą́žát'a** /zhoⁿ'-zhä-t'ä/ *n.*, tree fork, where other limbs fork out from the main body of the tree

tree frog **P'éniškà** /p'ä'-nē-shkä'/ *n.*, tree frog, 1. a little green frog, *Hyla cinerea*, family Hylidae 2. a common male name among the Ponca people

tree leaves **Žą́'ábe** /zhoⁿ-ä'-bā/ *n.* tree leaves; *ábe*, leaves

treetop **Xdabé'p'asi** /xthä-bā'-p'ä-sē/ *n.*, treetop

tree trunk **Žą́'hidè** /zhoⁿ'-hē-dä'/ *n.*, tree trunk, the main or large base of a tree

tremble **Žúgadišʲągi** /zhü'-gä-thē-shēⁿ'-ə-gē/ *v.*, tremble, twitch, usu. refers to a medical condition that involves an involuntary contraction of muscles in the upper part of the body, esp. the shoulder area

trembling **Sąsą́** /soⁿ-soⁿ'/ *adj.*, trembling, 1. somebody who is quivering or shaking, as in fear 2. *v.*, deliberate shaking of one's dance paraphernalia (bells or other clicking sound makers such as deer hooves) while dancing 3. *v.*, shiver, usu. caused by cold or cold wind hitting the body

Tribal Affairs Building **Gahí'e út'í** /gä-hē'-ä ü'-t'ē'/ *n.*, (new word, ca. 2005) Ponca Tribal Affairs Building, a building in White Eagle Community where some tribal offices are located

tribal hunt **Gaxdą́** /gä-xthoⁿ'/ *n.*, tribal bison hunt, when a group of hunters, with their families and belongings, pursued the bison until they were successful in making the kill

trip **K'inąse** /k'ē-noⁿ'-sä/ *v.*, trip, to fall down by slipping or by one's feet catching something; *ak'ínąsè*, I tripped; *đak'ínąsè*, you tripped; *k'inąsaì*, he/she/they tripped; *ąk'ínąsaì*, we tripped

tripe **T'é'níxà** /t'ä'-nē'-xä'/ *n.*, tripe, the rubbery lining of the stomach of cattle, used as food

tripod **Wiúhą udúgaškè** /wē-ü'-hoⁿ ü-thü'-gä-shkä'/ *n.*, tripod, a stand or support usu. made of metal with three legs and used to support pots and pans

trot **Sésasà** /sä'-sä-sä'/ *v.*, trot, 1. the gait between a walk and run in humans 2. the slow gait of a four-legged animal

trot dance **Sésasà wačígaxè** /sä'-sä-sä' wä-chē'-gä-xä'/ *n.*, trot dance, a man's dance, a form of the Heđúškà dance

trouble **Účižè** /ü'-chē-zhä'/ *n.*, trouble, a state of distress or difficulty

trouble **Ú'p'ežì** /ü'-p'ä-zhē'/ *n.*, trouble, dilemma, strife, disruption; somebody or something that agitates mentally, physically, or spiritually

troubled **Gí't'exì** /gē'-t'ä-xē'/ *v.*, troubled, 1. being emotionally disturbed, as in ~ over something that has happened 2. suggests being troubled over some physical problem, as in having a stomachache, headache or any physical illness

troubled **Ną́de ąpí'mąžì** /noⁿ'-dä oⁿ-pē'-moⁿ-zhēⁿ'/ *adj./n.*, troubled, lit., heart, love, distressed, 1. emotional distress 2. suppressed anger, disturbed feelings over an incident or action by another that may lead to a confrontation

troublemaker **Wép'iáži** /wä'-p'ē-ä'-zhē/ *n.*, troublemaker, connotes someone or something coming alongside causing unnecessary problems

trough **Wanágde úđatè** /wä-nä'-gthä ü'-thä-tä'/ *n.*, trough, a feeding box, usu. to hold food or water for domestic animals

trousers **Níde'uđíši** /nē'-dä-ü-thē'-shē/ *n.*, 1. trousers, pants, slacks 2. panty

truck **K'ip'ínągè wat'úgdą** /k'ē-p'ē'-noⁿ-gä' wä-t'ü'-gthoⁿ/ *n.*, truck, refers to light, medium, or heavy trucks that carry vending foods, pickup trucks, fire trucks, dump trucks, etc., but not semitrucks. See also *K'ip'ínągè wat'ú'gdè t'ągà*, semitruck.

true **Wíke** /wē'-kā/ *adj.*, true, truth, truism

truly **Wíkext'ì** /wē'-kā-xt'ē'/ *adv.*, truly, beyond doubt, factually

truthful **Gíwikè** /gē'-wē-kā/ *adj.*, truthful, truthful to him/her, being honest or straightforward; *wéwikè*, I am truthful to you/them; *wéwikài*, he/she/they was/were truthful to us

try **Ígaskądè** /ē'-gä-skoⁿ-thā/ *v.*, try, attempt, sample, 1. to try or attempt to do something or accomplish something 2. to test the effect of something, as in tasting food or drink

try on **Édąskadè** /ā'-thoⁿ-skä-thā/ *v.*, try on, as in trying on clothing

tub **Údižà** /ü'-thē-zhä/ *n.*, tub, a broad, round, and open metal container, usu. used to wash clothing

tuberculosis **Máge'ni'é** /moⁿ'-gā-nē-ā'/ *n.*, tuberculosis, also called TB (A disease of the lungs, TB may spread to any part of the body, such as the brain, kidney, or spine. It is caused by a bacterium called *Mycobacterium tuberculosis*.)

Tuesday **Ába'wé'nąbà** /oⁿm'-bä-wā-noⁿ-bä'/ *n.*, Tuesday, lit., day number two

tug **Í'didądą̀** /ē'-thē-doⁿ'-doⁿ'/ *v.*, tug, to tug or jerk and yank repeatedly

Tulsa OK **Wé'gdì't'ąwągdą̀** /wā'-gthē'-t'oⁿ-woⁿ-gthoⁿ'/ *n.*, Tulsa, Oklahoma, lit., "oil town"

tumble **Ugát'ąt'ądà** /ü-gä'-t'oⁿ-t'oⁿ-thä/ *n./v.*, tumble, an athletic movement; *ugát'ąt'ądì*, something tumbling, as a tumbling weed

tumbling **Bas'ímągdè** /bä-s'-ēⁿ'-moⁿ-gthä/ *v.*, tumbling, a movement usu. done by children in which the body is rolled forward,

over the head on the ground, returning to an upright position

turbid **U'gášudè** /ü-gä'-shü-dä/ *adj.*, turbid, usu. refers to water that is stirred up with other matter, causing a clouded effect

turkey **Zizík'à** /zē-zē'-k'ä/ *n.*, turkey, a large game bird, *Meleagris gallopavo*

turmoil **Úp'ežì** /ü'-p'ā-zhē'/ *n.*, turmoil, something disrupting an event, chaos, mayhem

turn **Đibéni** /thē-bā'-nē/ *v.*, turn, to turn any vehicle by use of the hands, e.g., a horse-drawn wagon, an automobile with a steering device; *nąbéni*, to turn a vehicle (horse-drawn wagon, automobile, train) with a steering mechanism that turns at some point, whether on a track or a road; *đibébéni*, turning, making more turns as one travels

turnip **Núgdè** /nü'-gthä/ *n.*, turnip, a hard, round root that can be eaten raw or cooked, genus *Brassica*

turn over **Biákigdašą̀** /bē-ä'-kē-gthä-shoⁿ'/ *v.*, turn over, refers to a vehicle turning over

turn over **Ídisądè** /ē'-thē-soⁿ'-thā/ *v.*, turn over, turn something over, food being cooked; *ídisáda*, *fem.*, command to turn something over; *ídisądagà*, *masc.*, command to turn something over

turtle **G'é'** /g-ā'/ *n.*, turtle, any of various types of reptiles of the order Testudines or Chelonia

turtledove **Đít'i't'ągà** /thē'-t'ē-t'oⁿ-gä/ *n.*, turtledove, refers to the mourning dove, *Zanaida macroura*

tweezers **P'ehį́ ídišnà** /p'ā-hēⁿ' ē'-thē-shnä/ *n.*, tweezers, a small tool used to pick up small things or to remove small splinters; refers to a woman's tool for removing human hair from the eyebrows

twenty-dollar bill **Gdébą'nąbà'ídawà** /gthā-boⁿ-noⁿ-bä-ē'-thä-wä/ *n.*, twenty-dollar bill, U.S. currency

twice **Nąbá'ą̀** /noⁿ-bä-oⁿ/ *adv.*, twice, two times

twins **Nąbá' ída** /noⁿ-bä' ē'-dä/ *n.*, twins, two children conceived in the same pregnancy (Twins may be monozygotic [identical], looking alike, or dizygotic [fraternal], not looking alike.)

twist **Đibés'į̀** /thē-bä's-ēⁿ/ *v.*, twist, to twist up; *bibés'į̀*, twist by pressing down on; *gabés'į̀*, twist by force; *nąbés'į̀*, twist by stepping on or driving over

twisted **Á'gabdįdà** /ä'-gä-bthēⁿ-thä/ *v.*, twisted, something causing a thing to become twisted or uneven

two **Nąbá** /noⁿ-bä/ *n.*, two, the number two (2)

twos **Nąbádądà** /noⁿ-bä-thoⁿ-thoⁿ'/ *n.*, twos, "by twos," as in they came in by twos or two at a time; *dábdįdądà*, by threes; *dúbadądà*, by fours, etc.

U

ugly **Đaégą** /thä-ä'-goⁿ/ *adj./n.*, ugly, unattractive, a person or thing that is not good to look at

umami **Ną́'be** /noⁿ'-bä/ *adj.*, umami, Japanese origin, describes tastes in cheeses, vegetables, soy sauce

umbrella **Ą̀'zegaxè** /oⁿ'-zä-gä-xä/ *n.*, umbrella, a handheld, collapsible canopy to provide shade from the sun or protection from rain

unable **Điá'wadè** /thē-ä'-wä-thä/ *adj./n.*, unable, a task or situation that is not possible to do or overcome

unadorned **Đigdą́'p'à** /thē-gthoⁿ'-p'ä'/ *v.*, to be unadorned, plain, bare, bald, as with a haircut

unagreeable **Gišą́·bazì** /gē-shoⁿ'·-bä-zhē'/ *adj.*, unagreeable, not coming to an agreeable end with another person or persons; dissatisfied, not pleased or happy with something

unallotted lands **Gaé mą̀zą̀** /gä-ä' moⁿ-zhoⁿ'/ *n.*, unallotted lands, public lands on the Ponca reservation (Under the Dawes Act of 1887, these lands were part of the trust lands on the reservation but still held in trust for the tribe. They are restricted by the U.S. government.)

unashamed **Wawéštažì** /wä-wä'-shtä-zhē'/ *adj.*, unashamed, unembarrassed, blatant, ~ for it/them/anyone

unattainable **Udúhi điáwadè** /ü-thü'-hē thē-ä'-wä-thä'/ *adj.*, unattainable, not reachable, cannot be done, inaccessible

unaware **Šą́' éską edégabažì** /shoⁿ' ä'-skoⁿ ä-thä'-goⁿ-bä-zhē'/ *adj.*, unaware, being unprepared or naïve about some possible impending danger

uncertain **K'ixída** /k'ē-xē'-thä/ *adj.*, uncertain, unsure, doubtful, that which causes doubt about accomplishing a task

uncertainty **Wažį́'xídadì** /wä-zhēⁿ'-xē'-dä-thē'/ *n.*, uncertainty, feeling of uncertainty, having reservations

unchewable **Đaį'** /thä-ēⁿ/ *adj.*, unchewable, 1. meat that is sinewy, stringy, fibrous, or just tough to chew 2. *v.*, to spit up, vomit

uncle **Negí** /nä-gē'/ *n.*, *masc./fem.*, uncle, my mother's brother, also my mother's brother's son; *đinégi*, your uncle; *inégi*, his/her uncle, *winégi*, my uncle

uncompromising **Udíáge** /ü-thē'-ä'-gä/ *adj.*, uncompromising, unbending, doesn't want to

unconcerned **Šédešt'iąžì** /shä'-thä-sht'ē-oⁿ-zhē'/ *adj.*, unconcerned, indifferent, undaunted, nonchalant

unconfident **Gíxek'à** /gē'-xä-k'ä'/ *adj.*, uncon-

fident, self doubting, not being sure something can be done

unconsumed **Đaá'** /thä-ä'/ *adj./v.*, unconsumed, uneaten, could not consume all the
food, usu. refers to food that is left in the
dish

undaunted **Šédažì** /shä'-thä-zhē'/ *adj.*, undaunted, fearless, showing no concern
to him/her, usu. refers to a person whom
somebody has something against

undaunted **Šéwaɖažì** /shä'-wä-thä-zhē'/ *adj.*,
undaunted, fearless, showing no concern
about them, usu. refers to a person whom
some people may have something against

undemonstrative **Ą'ɖàwąɖišp'egà** /oⁿ-thoⁿ'-
woⁿ-thē-shp'ä-gä'/ *adj.*, undemonstrative,
in control of yourself, calm, as in "I am kept
back or restrained on account of it"

undependable **Udúnążįwaɖažì** /ü-thü'-noⁿ-
zhēⁿ-wä-thä-zhē'/ *adj.*, undependable,
being unreliable or unpredictable, usu.
refers to a person, weather conditions, old
machinery

under **Égihà** /ä'-gē-hä'/ *prep.*, under, something or somebody goes ~ a thing, entering
willingly or unwillingly, as in slipping into a
pool of water; *v.*, refers to entering or going
into something

undergrowth **Učí'žè** /ü-chē'-zhä'/ *n.*, undergrowth, thick undergrowth and bushes

underneath **K'igɖá't'à** /k'ē-gthä'-t'ä'/ *prep.*,
underneath, under something (*wáɖatè keɖì
~ itéɖagà*, place it ~ the table)

undershirt **Unążį' màte** /ü-noⁿ'-zhēⁿ moⁿ'-tä/
n., undershirt, T-shirt

underskirt **Waté'mątè** /wä-tä'-moⁿ-tä'/ *n.*,
underskirt, a ladies' undergarment, slip

understanding **Íɖaeɖè** /ē'-thä-ä-thä'/ *n.*, an
understanding, having knowledge and
interpretation of something where modern science is unable to explain certain

phenomena; phenomena, that process of
human experiences that may or may not be
observable, sometimes seem physically impossible, and may be termed paranormal in
the modern world

undertone **Zizí'je'íyè** /zē-zē'-jä-ē'-yä'/ *v.*,
undertone, whisper, to speak in a low voice

underwear **Nídeuɖíšį mątè** /nē'-dä-ü-thēⁿ'-
shēⁿ moⁿ-tä'/ *n.*, underwear, men's undershorts, boxer shorts or briefs

undesirable **Gáɖažiwaɖè** /goⁿ'-thä-zhē-wä-
dä'/ *adj.*, undesirable, somebody or something that is not wanted

unerring **Nąɖibažì** /noⁿ'-thē-bä-zhē'/ *adj.*,
unerring, faultless, no mistakes (The term
more often is used sarcastically toward one
who has a "know it all" attitude.)

unethical **Úškąp'iáži** /ü'-shkoⁿ-p'ē-ä'-zhē/
adj., unethical, unprincipled, wrong, bad,
corrupt

uneven **Š'į'k'a** /sh-ēⁿ'-k'ä/ *adj.*, uneven,
something that has furrows or ridges, such
as an uneven wooden board or a wrinkle in
the nose

uneven **Ukíbašnà** /ü-kē'-bä-shnoⁿ'/ *adj.*, uneven, as in carpentry where two boards do
not meet evenly

unevenly **Šášáka** /shä'-shä'-kä/ *adv.*, unevenly,
not level, not smooth, irregular, usu. refers
to crafts or things made with the hands
that are marked by ridges, uneven, bumpy,
mostly in reference to handiwork made
with beads, quills, and other craft materials
(*hįbé ukéɖi te hiská áɖiaye te ~ xt'i gáxaì*, the
beads are ~ placed on the moccasins)

unfold **Đibɖá'** /thē-bthä'/ *v.*, unfold, unfolding, unfurling, spreading out something
with the hands; *gabɖá*, unfold, unfolding
or unfurling by force of wind

unforgettable **Gisíɖewaɖažixt'ì** /gē-sē'-
thä-wä-thä-zhē-xt'ē'/ *adv.*, unforgettable,

memorable, treasured or cherished, something that stays in one's mind

ungrateful **Waẓéd̨įgè** /wä-zhä'-thēⁿ-gä'/ *adj.*, ungrateful, a person being unappreciative or thankless

unhappy **Gídaẓì** /gē'-thä-zhē'/ *adj.*, unhappy, lit., not happy

unimportant **Đixt'áẓi** /thē-xt'ä'-zhē/ *n./v.*, to see something as unimportant, something that is of no consequence (Note the pronounciation and spelling with *díxt'aẓì, v., 2nd pers. sing.*, you don't like.)

unintelligent **Há'xd̨ú'à** /hä'-xthü'-ä'/ *n.*, unintelligent, a person who lacks the mental capacity to solve problems and is regarded as one lacking in intelligence

unintentional **Mąnád̨ì** /moⁿ-noⁿ'-thē'/ *adj.*, unintentional, accidental, inadvertent, not on purpose

uninteresting **Đaxt'áẓi** /thä-xt'ä'-zhē'/ *adj.*, uninteresting, boring, someone who says that something was uninteresting

uninteresting **Úxt'aẓì** /ü'-xt'ä-zhē'/ *adj.*, uninteresting, boring, dull, unexciting

uninvolved **Uką́habaẓì** /ü-k'oⁿ'-hä-bä-zhē'/ *v.*, uninvolved, being nearby but impassive, close by but not with or in (*niášigà d̨įkè* ~, the person was ~)

unkempt **Čáza** /chä'-zä/ unkempt, not orderly or neat

unkind **Mąd̨ą́ xd̨ít'ù** /moⁿ-thoⁿ' xthē'-t'ü'/ *adj.*, unkind, being underhandedly offensive, sneaky, mean

unlikeable **Í't'adè'wadè** /ē'-t'ä-thä'-wä-thä'/ *v.*, to be unlikeable, to make or do something undesirable; *n.*, something unlikeable

unlikely **Áxt'ą̀** /ä'x-t'oⁿ'/ *adj.*, unlikely, not likely to happen

unlikely **-ud̨íšį** /ü-thē'-shēⁿ/ *adj., suffix*, unlikely, improbable, something not likely to occur

unlock **Đišíbe** /thē-shē'-bä/ *v.*, unlock, unbolt

unlucky **Gí'ẓuaẓì** /gē'-zhü-ä-zhē'/ *adj.*, unlucky, unsuccessful, ill omened

unravel **Gdadá** /gthä-thä'/ *v.*, unravel, come unbraided, when a thing that has been woven comes apart

unravel **Snądá** /snoⁿ-thä'/ *v.*, unravel, come loose, as in threads of seams in clothing

unsettled **Éšte'ą̀'à** /ä'-shtä-oⁿ-oⁿ'/ *adj.*, unsettled, lacking in stability, order, and certainty

unsightly **Ną́degda'wadè** /noⁿ'-dä-gthä-wä-thä'/ *adj.*, unsightly, unpleasant, unlikeable, repulsive, disgusting, nauseating, gross, abhorrent

unskilled **Gą́ẓįgà** /goⁿ'-zhēⁿ-gä'/ *adj.*, unskilled, inexpert, doesn't know how

unspeakable **Ídewadaẓì** /ē'-thä-wä-thä-zhē'/ *adj.*, unspeakable, not to speak of extremely bad things, things that are foul or revolting

unsurpassable **Gaxáud̨íšį** /gä-xä'-ü-thēⁿ'-shēⁿ/ *adj.*, unsurpassable, cannot be exceeded, incomparable

untalented **Edí'úk'íhibaẓì** /ä-dē'-ü'-k'ē'-hē-bä-zhē'/ *adj.*, untalented, inept, incompetent, unskilled

untaught **Gązé'd̨įgè** /goⁿ-zä'-thēⁿ-gä'/ *adj.*, untaught, more directed toward children and teenagers who behave badly (The period for usage of the term preceded the concept of the influence of peer pressure notwithstanding parental teachings.)

unthinkable **Sídewadaẓì** /sē'-thä-wä-thä-zhē'/ *adj.*, unthinkable, something undesirable to think about

unthinking **Edégąwadaẓì** /ä-thä'-goⁿ-wä-thä-zhē'/ *adj.*, unthinking, not reasoning, did not take any consideration of the situation at hand but acted upon it

untied **Đišké** /thē-shkä'/ *adj.*, untied, unhooked, undone

untrue **Égǫ̀zì** /ä'-goⁿ-zhē'/ *adj.*, untrue, false, not factual

untruthful **Wíkažì** /wē'-kä-zhē'/ *adj.*, untruthful, dishonest, or deceptive

unwanted **Į́'įgè** /ēⁿ'-ēⁿ-gä'/ *adj.*, unwanted, not needed, something left over that was not wanted

unwilling **Udíagè** /ü-thē'-ä-gä'/ *adj.*, unwilling, adverse, don't want to

unwrap **Đigđá'** /thē-gthä'/ *v.*, unwrap, undo, open something up that was tied together, such as a bundle

uphill **Uwíđabè** /ü-wē'-thoⁿ-bä'/ *adj.*, uphill, going up to higher ground from a lower level

upon **Ágahà** /ä'-gä-hä'/ *prep.*, upon, on the surface

upper arm **A'ut'ǭga** /ä-ü-t'oⁿ'-gä/ *n.*, upper arm, humerus, the armbone that extends from the shoulder to the elbow

upper back **Ábak'ù** /ä'-bä-k'ü'/ *n.*, upper back, in human anatomy that part between the shoulders

uppity person **Níkašigà mása** /nē'-kä-shē-gä' moⁿ'-sä/ *n.*, uppity person, a person who puts on airs of superiority or arrogance

upright **Mǫ́gđè** /moⁿ'-gthä'/ *adj.*, upright, something or somebody that is standing upright, vertical; *đimǫ́gđè*, to erect something

upside down **Ákigđašǫ̀** /ä'-kē-gthä-shoⁿ'/ *adj. phr.*, upside down, as in the position of an automobile that overturns in an accident

upside down **P'as'į́** /p'ä-s-ēⁿ'/ *adj. phr.*, upside down, going or rolling over head first

upstairs **T'í' p'ahášì** /t'ē' p'ä-hä'-shē'/ *n.*, upstairs, the second floor of a house or building

upward **Mǫ́xeà't'adišǫ̀** /moⁿ'-xä-ä'-t'ä-thē-shoⁿ'/ *adv.*, upward, in the direction of the sky; *mǫ́xeá't'a*, up

urgency **Ú'sǫgà** /ü'-soⁿ-gä'/ *n.*, urgency, expectancy, the feeling that something is about to happen

urinal **Unéže** /ü-nä'-zhä/ *n.*, urinal, a sanitary receptacle in which to urinate

urine **Néže** /nä'-zhä/ *n.*, urine, a liquid secreted by the kidneys and expelled from the body through a process called urination

us **Ǫguágadį̀** /oⁿ-gü-ä'-gä-thēⁿ'/ *pron.*, us, a group that includes me; *ǫgù, ~ ǫguádi*, "it is or was ~"; *ǫgúáwawǫ̀*, it was caused by ~; *ǫguášt'ì, ~ too*; *ǫgúágǫdit'adišǫ̀*, toward ~

used **Á'wǫ** /ä'-woⁿ/ *adj.*, used, worn out, usu. refers to old clothing; *áwǫžixt'ì*, not too worn or old

used to **-nǫmǫ́** /noⁿ-moⁿ'/ *adj.*, *suffix*, used to, something that was done before, as in *égǫ̀ páxe~*, I ~ do that

useful **Wiúšį̀** /wēü'-shēⁿ'/ *adj.*, useful, helpful, refers to something or someone that is helpful for certain things

usually **Skéwǫ** /skä'-woⁿ/ *adv.*, usually, customarily, habitually, ordinarily

utility poles **Mǫ́ze'i'udà** /moⁿ'-zä-ē'-ü-thä'/ *n.*, telephone, a telecommunications device that permits two or more persons to speak to one another when they are far apart

utilize **Í'đihidè** /ē'-thē-hē-dä'/ *v.*, utilize, to make use of something such as a tool

V

vacant **Úkizà** /ü-kē-zä'/ *adj.*, vacant, unoccupied, a place where no one is

vacuum cleaner **T'í'umíže wé'basihì** /t'ē'-ü-mē'-zhä wä'-bä-sē-hē'/ *n.*, vacuum cleaner, lit., carpet cleaner

vagina **Į́že** /ēⁿ'-zhä/ *n.*, vagina, the female organ for copulation; part of the birth canal that leads from the uterus to the external orifice

valley **Uspé** /ü-spā'/ *n.*, valley, dale, gully

vanish **Đigétigdè** /thēⁿ-gā'-tē-gthā'/ *v.*, vanish, to disappear suddenly, to be here and then gone (The usage entails ancient stories of men possessing powers to disappear from the presence of others only to appear elsewhere. The term is also used in modern times for people who clear a building or any gathering immediately after an event.)

vase **Waxt'á uxp'é** /wäx-t'ä' ü-xp'ā'/ *n.*, vase, an open container used to hold flowers, usu. made of decorated glass or ceramics

vengeance **Égǫxt'i wé'ǫ** /ā'-goⁿ-xt'ē wā'-oⁿ/ *n.*, vengeance, to punish another or another group in retaliation for injury

vengeful **Í'mǫdà** /ē'-moⁿ-thä/ *adj.*, vengeful, retaliatory, somebody who wants revenge, ready to take counteraction

vent **T'íhukǫ̀** /t'ē'-hü-koⁿ/ *n.*, vent, smoke hole, opening at the top of the tipi

Venus **Miká'e t'ǫgà** /mē-kä-ā t'oⁿ-gä/ *n.*, Venus (The planet, seen sometimes in the evening and other times in the morning, appears large because of its luminosity.)

verbose **Đébahì t'ǫgà** /thä-bä-hē' t'oⁿ-gä'/ *adj.*, verbose, refers to somebody who uses an excessive number of words and keeps talking

verifiable **Égǫxt'ì** /ā'-goⁿ'-xt'ē'/ *adj.*, verifiable, factual, not questionable

vertebrae **Nǫ́kawahì** /noⁿ'-kä-wä-hē'/ *n.*, vertebrae, also pronounced *nǫ́xahì*, the vertebrate spine or spinal column; *nǫ́ka uk'íte*, the joints of the vertebrae

vertical **Mǫ́gde** /moⁿ'-gthä/ *adj.*, vertical, standing, upright

very **-čábe** /chä'-bä/ *adv. suffix*, very, exceedingly, intensely, as in *usníčábe*, very cold (The suffix *-čábe* is a derivative of the word *át'ašǫ̀*, which means very, exceedingly, and intensely.)

very small **Žįáx'čì** /zhēⁿ-ä'x-chē'/ *adj.*, very small, miniature, very little in size

vest **Đíʃ'idádisǫdè** /thē'-ʃ-ē-thä'-thē-soⁿ-dä/ *n.*, vest, a man's garment for the upper body

veteran **Nudǫ́ ahǝá'ma** /nü-doⁿ ä-hǝä'-mä/ *n.*, veteran, those who were engaged in warfare for their country

veteran's songs **Nudǫ́ ahǝá'ma waǫ́'** /nü-doⁿ' ä-hǝä'-mä wäoⁿ'/ *n.*, veteran's songs, songs that were specifically composed for returning veterans of war

vibrate **P'ǫp'ǫde** /p'oⁿ-p'oⁿ'-dä/ *v.*, vibrate, something inanimate that causes something to make small, rapid movements, as in the wind making an outdoor table with uneven legs rock

vice president **Í't'ígǫdè žįgà** /ē'-t'ē'-goⁿ-thä' zhēⁿ-gä'/ *n.*, vice president, namely, the vice president of the United States of America

violin **Žǫ́'í'bagizè** /zhoⁿ'-ē'-bä-gē-zä'/ *n.*, violin or fiddle, lit., making a wood squeak, a stringed musical instrument used to play classical music (violin) or country music (fiddle)

visit **T'iúp'è** /t'ē-ü'-p'ä'/ *v.*, visit, to visit; *t'ápè*, *n.*, *archaic*, visit

voice **Hú** /hü'/ *n.*, voice, sounds made by a human with the mouth in talking, laughing, singing, crying; *húsagì*, strong or loud voice; *hú'údǫ*, good voice; *hú žíga*, little voice (personal Wažáźè clan name); *hú đit'íze*, speaking through the noise

voice loudly **Đadídį** /thä-dēⁿ'-dēⁿ/ *v.*, voice loudly, make an extreme pronouncement with the vocal cords

volunteer **K'igdáde** /k'ē-gthä'-thä/ *v.*, volunteer, to offer oneself for service without receiving anything in return; *gigdáde*, to offer or present a very personal gift to somebody

vomit **Gdé'be** /gthā'-bä/ *n./v.*, vomit, heave, throw up; *í'gđebè*, vomitus, usu. refers to something specifically expelled from the stomach or ejected beyond the mouth from the stomach

W

wade **Žúhè** /zhü'-hä'/ *v.*, wade, to wade; to walk in water

wag **Gabíže** /gä-bē'-zhä/ *v.*, wag, to move something to and fro, such as a dog wagging its tail; *gabíbíže*, wagging

wager **Wak'á** /wä-k'oⁿ'/ *v.*, wager, bet, gamble, to take a chance in order to win something

wagon **Žádí'nągè** /zhoⁿ-thē'-noⁿ-gä'/ *n.*, wagon, 1. horse-drawn wagon 2. child's wagon

wail **Xagéda'é** /xä-gä'-thä-ä'/ *v.*, wail, intensified crying, sad or mournful expression of sorrow

waist **T'éze** /t'ä'-zä/ *n.*, waist, that part of the abdomen between the ribcage and hips

wait **Nąhé'be** /noⁿ-hä'-bä/ *v./n.*, wait, pause, hang on or hold on, usu. refers to somebody who is anxiously ready to leave while the job or conditions are not complete

waiting **Ábaè** /ä'-bä-ä'/ *v.*, waiting, waiting on prey or the enemy to come by

waiting **Wép'è** /wä'-p'ä'/ *n.*, waiting, waiting on someone or others; *idágip'è*, waited for his

walk **Mądí'** /moⁿ-thē'/ *v.*, walk, 1. to walk, stride, move on foot 2. "in the walk of life," as in *údą ~ tenà údą*, to ~ a good life is good

walk close by **Íną'ù** /ē'-noⁿ-ü'/ *v. phr.*, walk close by, to walk or go close by something; *ądáną'ù, v., past t.*, passed by me, went close by me

walk further **Nądáha** /noⁿ-dä'-hä/ *adv.*, walk further, refers to a person's condition in life, to live long in continuing good health

walking **Nąmą́mądà** /noⁿ-moⁿ'-moⁿ-thä'/ *v.*,

walking, 1. refers to the way a person or animal walks, usu. with a upper-body swaying motion 2. *n.*, a name for nonclan members among the Ponca people

walk strong **Sagí'gi'à** /sä-gē'-gē-ä'/ (*fem.*) (**Sagí'gi'àgá** /sä-gē'-gē-ä'-gä/ [*masc.*]) *v.*, walk strong, lit., come walking strongly, commonly said to children in times when people had to walk great distances

walk through **Uwáha** /ü-wä'-hä/ *v.*, walk through, refers to walking through a certain passageway, such as walking through the woods, forest, or a stream of water or along a lake or river

walk upon **Á'he** /ä'-hä/ *v.*, walk upon, 1. walking on steps going up 2. climbing

walk upon **Ámądì** /ä'-moⁿ-thē'/ *v.*, walk upon, to walk upon (*žigá dįkè mí'xe kè', ~ kidaì*, they caused the child to ~ the grave of his father)

wallet **Mázeskà užì** /moⁿ'-zä-skä' ü-zhē'/ *n.*, wallet, a small folded leather case for money

wallow **Ušnáha gáxe** /ü-shnä'-hä gä'-xä/ *n.*, wallow, buffalo wallow, usu. refers to bison rolling on the ground and eventually leaving a large dusty depression on the ground

Walmart **Údįwį̀t'ì't'àgà** /ü'-thēⁿ-wēⁿ-t'ē'-t'oⁿ-gä/ *n.*, Walmart, lit., a large building to buy, a corporation that has a chain of stores offering discount department store products, electronics, etc.

walnut **T'áge't'ągà** /t'ä'-gä-t'oⁿ-gä/ *n.*, walnut, genus *Juglans* of the family Juglandaceae

walnut tree **T'áge't'ągàhì'** /t'ä'-gä-t'oⁿ-gä-hē'/ *n.*, walnut tree, black walnut, *Juglans nigra*

wander **K'inák'uwįxè** /k'ē-noⁿ'-k'ü-wēⁿ-xä'/ *v.*, wander, to go and do something in a haphazard manner; *ak'íṇk'uwįxè*, I wandered around in a haphazardly manner

wander **K'úwįxè** /k'ü'-wēⁿ-xā'/ *v.*, wander, to go or travel from place to place without a plan or itinerary

wander **Mąṇą́dihahà** /moⁿ-noⁿ'-thē-hä-hä'/ *v.*, wander, to drift, to stray from the pathway by mistake or error — suggests searching

wander **Niáda** /nē-ä'-thä/ *v.*, wander, not knowing exactly which way to go to find or return to a familiar place, to wander aimlessly

want **Gą́da** /goⁿ'-thä/ *v.*, want, wanting some material needs, such as food, clothing, an automobile, or enough money to take a trip; *ągą́daì*, we want; *gą́daì*, they want; *ągą́dagatà*, we, who were wanting

want **Idá'dą'wagądà** /ē-dä'-doⁿ-wä-goⁿ'-thä/ *v.*, want, usu. refers to a person who yearns for, wishes for, desires material goods; a greedy person

war club **Wét'į** /wā'-t'ēⁿ/ *n.*, war club, 1. a club composed of a hard stone tied tightly at the end of a strong piece of wood with sinew 2. *Wétįwį*, Club Woman, proper female name in the Ðíxidą̀ clan of the Ponca people

warfare **Nagé** /nä-gā'/ *n.*, warfare, armed conflict between nations; fight

war leader **Nudą́hągà** /nü-doⁿ'-hoⁿ-gä'/ *n.*, war leader, lit., war leader, 1. now, one in charge, boss, the headman, etc. 2. male name in the Ðíxidą̀ clan of the Ponca people

warm **Nášta** /nä'-shtä/ *adj.*, warm, refers to water, usu. heated water, hot water cooled down to warm water

warm **Št'íde** /sht'ē'-dä/ *adj.*, warm, refers to warmth in a dwelling

warming **Ná'šti'dè** /nä'-shtē-dä/ *v.*, warming, to increase the temperature to a desirable level, as in a dwelling (house) or water being warmed over the fire

warn **P'ahą́ga uwída** /p'ä-hoⁿ'-gä ü-wē'-thä/ *v.*, warn, tell something to somebody in advance

warpath **Nudą́ adái** /nü-doⁿ' ä-thä'-ē/ *n.*, warpath, *archaic*, a war expedition

warped **Bdibdį́da** /bthē-bthēⁿ'-thä/ *adj.*, warped, something that is misshapen, bent, twisted; something that is out of shape from a straight form

warring **Nudą́** /nü-doⁿ'/ *v.*, warring, the act of going to battle with another nation

warrior **Nudą́ mądį̀** /nü-doⁿ' moⁿ-thēⁿ'/ *n.*, warrior, 1. one or more persons going to battle with another person or nation 2. proper name in the Ðíxidą̀ clan of the Ponca people

warrior fraternity **Tukáda** /tü-kä'-thä/ *n.*, warrior fraternity, an ancient war society of young Ponca men; *P'adánik'ì*, seasoned warriors of the Ponca tribe; *T'ę́ ną́p'ažì*, not afraid to die Ponca warriors; *T'ę́ gáxe*, Ponca warriors who pretend to be killed; *Wasná t'ągà*, big belly, elderly Ponca warriors' organization (The elders of the Ponca people provided the names of these ancient warrior fraternities when the Ponca lived in the North Country.)

war upon **Á'nudà** /ä'-nü-doⁿ'/ *v.*, war upon, to go and make war upon someone

wash **Ðižá'** /thē-zhä'/ *v.*, wash, cleanse, rinse; *wadíža*, wash, the act of washing clothes, linens; *k'igdíža*, to wash up

washbasin **Nąbéudíža** /noⁿ-bā'-ü-thē'-zhä/ *n.*, washbasin, 1. a bowl-shaped plumbing fixture used to wash one's hands 2. a sink (*įdéudíža*, to wash one's face in)

washboard **Wébiškì** /wā'-bē-shkē'/ *n.*, washboard, a flat board with a metal corrugated surface used to clean and remove soil from clothing and other cloth products

Washington DC **I't'ígạde'át'à** /ē-t'ē'-goⁿ-thā-ä'-t'ä'/ *n.*, Washington DC, lit., where the president of the United States of America is

washtub **Ú'dižà** /ü'-thē-zhä/ *n.*, washtub, a tub for washing clothing, linens

wasp **K'igdą́xe** /k'ē-gthoⁿ'-xā/ *n.*, 1. wasp, a stinging insect with a slender body 2. bee, wasp, yellow jacket

watch **Ð̶édehawadą́be** /thä'-dā-hä-wä-doⁿ'-bā/ *v.t./ v.i.*, watch, looking, using the eyes to search without moving the head, to watch somebody or something with peripheral vision

watch **Wábanà** /wä'-bä-noⁿ'/ *v.*, watch, to watch some activity, such as a movie, theatrical play, or pow-wow

watch **Wagít'ạbagà** /wä-gē'-t'oⁿ-bä-gä'/ *v.*, watch, keep vigil looking after us, usu. refers to a devout petition to Wak'ạda to keep watch over one who prays

watchful **Dą́dạbè** /doⁿ'-doⁿ-bā'/ *adj.*, watchful, observant, vigilant

water **Ní'** /nē'/ *n.*, water, a colorless liquid on which all living things depend for survival, a liquid composed of oxide of hydrogen, H_2O

watered down **Nigdúze** /nē-gthü'-zā/ *adj.*, watered down, weak, watery, usu. refers to drinks such as coffee, tea, juices

waterfall **Ní'uxp'áde** /nē-üx-p'ä'-thä/ *n.*, waterfall, the falling of water from a stream at a higher level

water lily **T'édawị̀** /t'ä'-thä-wēⁿ'/ *n.*, water lily, an edible aquatic plant with floating leaves and flowers

watermelon **Sákadidè** /sä'-kä-thē-dä'/ *n.*, watermelon, a large, round, sometimes elongated fruit with a hard green skin and sweet, juicy red or yellow flesh, *Citrullus*

lanatus var. *lanatus*, of the family Curcurbitaceae

water moccasin **Nidá'xup'à** /nē-thä'-xü-p'ä'/ *n.*, water moccasin, cottonmouth water moccasin, *Agkistrodon piscivorus*, a venomous snake

water pump **Nisní** /nē-snē'/ *n.*, water pump, lit., cold water, a pump to draw water for drinking (also *ní' íbixt'ạ̀*, to cause water to come out)

water stand **Ni'ágdè** /nē-ä'-gthä'/ *n.*, *archaic*, water stand, a framework or structure that was designed to hold a washpan and a pail of water

water trough **Ní' udát'ạ** /nē' ü-thä'-t'oⁿ/ *n.*, water trough, a trough for animals to drink from

water turkey **Núze** /nü'-zā/ *n.*, water turkey; the anhinga (*Anhinga anhinga*), snake bird, darter, American darter (some cultural practices refer to it as "water bird")

water well **Ní'snì** /nē'-snē'/ *n.*, water well, where cool water comes from, a water pump

wayside **Uhé sakíbadì** /ü-hä' sä-kē'-bä-dē'/ *n.*, wayside, to be situated beside the road, street, or highway

we **Ạgú'** /oⁿ-gü'/ *pron.*, we, refers to the self and one or more persons (~ *edí ạgáhi*, us, we went there)

we **Ạguą́gadì** /oⁿ-güoⁿ'-gä-thēⁿ'/ *pron.*, we, used more as a reference to ~ as a group who planned, accomplished, etc.

weak **Wahéhe** /wä-hä'-hā/ *adj.*, weak, refers to something that can break easily, as in an old rotten step

weak **Wašką́ dị̀gè** /wä-shkoⁿ' thēⁿ-gä'/ *adj.*, weak, physically weak, a person who is physically weak or does not have the muscle power to accomplish a task

weak **Žuáži** /zhü-ä'-zhē/ *adj.*, weak, physically weak, being ill or deathly ill weak man **Niášigà wašádįgè** /nēä'-shē-gä' wä-shä'-thēⁿ-gä'/ *n.*, *archaic*, ca. 1800s, weak man

wealth **Wadį́** /wä-thēⁿ'/ *n.*, wealth, to own much, usu. refers to material goods

wealthy **Mázeskà t'á'** /moⁿ-zā-skä' t'oⁿ'/ *adj.*, wealthy, rich, very prosperous

wear **Ádahà** /ä'-thä-hä'/ *v.*, wear, 1. putting on a piece of clothing 2. to smear something on the surface of something, as in smearing food on one's clothing

wear **Ną́p'į̀** /noⁿ'-p'ēⁿ'/ *v.*, wear, displaying or showing something on clothing (This may include rings, bracelets, necklaces, brooches, pins, etc.)

wear **Utą́** /ü-toⁿ'/ *v.*, wear, put on, have on, be dressed in; *mą́'*, wore, *sing. past t.* of *wear*, I wore, to adorn oneself with clothing, shoes, etc.; *á'*, to wear or put on

wear **Wádahà** /wä-thä-hä'/ *v.*, wear, 1. putting on certain kinds of dancing paraphernalia (In the Ponca Heḋúškà organization men, in addition to their deerskin shirt and leggings, wore symbols of war honors that included eagle feathers, skins of certain animals, bandoliers, hairpipe beads, or a roach, as well as other symbolic items.) 2. refers also to any uniformed clothing identifying persons, such as soldiers

weather **Ą́batè** /oⁿ'-bä-t'ä'/ *n.*, weather, usu. this weather, as in the current conditions of the weather (*ą́bätè eą́'a?*, how's the weather?)

wedge **Žą́'udúgasnè** /zhoⁿ'-ü-thü'-gä-snä'/ *n.*, wedge, a metal tool, usu. thick on one end and tapering to a thin edge, used for splitting wood

wedged **Ut'á'** /ü-t'ä'/ *adj.*, wedged, lodged, stuck in between (his arm got ~ between two limbs on the tree)

Wednesday **Ą́ba'wé'dabdį̀** /oⁿm'-bä-wä'-thä-bthēⁿ'/ *n.*, Wednesday, lit., day number three

weed cutter **Xáde ígasè** /xä'-dā ē'-gä-sä'/ *n.*, weed cutter, a serrated double-edged cutting blade about fourteen by two inches long attached to an approximately thirty-six-inch wooden handle for cutting moderately tall grass or weeds

weed eater **Xádeídatè** /xä'-dā-ē'-thä-tä'/ *n.*, weed eater, an electric- or gasoline-powered tool to trim grass along a walk or near a house or other structure

weeds **Žá'** /zhä'/ *n.*, weeds, plants that grow in their natural environment

weeds **Žá'škúbe** /zhä'-shkü'-bä/ *n.*, weeds, refers to deep, thick weeds

weedy **Mąhį́'** /moⁿ-hēⁿ'/ *adj.*, weedy, a piece of land full of or consisting of weeds

week **Údizè** /ü'-thē-zä'/ *n.*, week, seven days

weep **Xagé'** /xä-gä'/ *v.*, weep, to cry

weep **Xé'de** /xä-thä'/ *v.*, weep, to cause someone to weep (*isága etái ḋįkè xé'ḋaì*, he made his little brother cry)

weigh **Wédihà** /wä'-thē-hoⁿ'/ *adj.*, 1. weigh or weight (~ *te ánąnià?*, how much do you weigh?) 2. a scale

well **Úḋądehà** /ü'-doⁿ-thä-hä'/ *adj.*, well, refers to somebody recovering; *úḋątehà*, refers to something being completed in a skillful manner; *úḋąxt'ìą*, very well, refers to anything from recovering to doing something skillfully

wellness **Nié ḋįgè** /nē-ā' thēⁿ-gä'/ *n.*, wellness, refers to good physical health and well-being, esp. through proper diet and excercise

went **Idé'** /ē-thä'/ *v.*, *past t.* of *go*, went

west **Mí'idé't'à** /mē-ē-thä'-t'ä'/ *n.*, west, lit., where the sun goes away, one of the cardinal points on the compass

westerly **Mí'idé't'adišą̀** /mē'-ē-thä'-t'ä-thē-shoⁿ/ *adj./adv.*, in a westerly direction, toward the west

wet **Núka** /nü'-kä/ *adj.*, wet, damp, soaked, moist, watery

wetlands **Ništ'ášt'à** /nē-sht'ä'-sht'ä/ *n.*, wetlands, an area of land that characteristically has a high moisture content, such as bogs or swamps

we too **Ągúšt'ì** /oⁿ-gü'-sht'ē'/ *pron. phr.*, we too, us too

we were there **Edí'ą́dì** /ā-dē'-oⁿ-thē'/ *v.*, 1st *pers. pl.*, *past t.*, we were there, usu. refers to a specific or a particular location where something occurred

what **Á'ąà** /ä'-oⁿ-ä'/ *adj.*, what, a word used in direct or indirect questions concerning the outcome of a situation; a related term is *eą́'a?*, what do you think?

what **Há'** /hä'/ *adj./pron.*, *fem.* what?

what **Ịdáda'ą̀** /ēⁿ-dä'-dä-oⁿ/ *pron.*, what, connotes a thing or something (*šé'te ~à ?*, ~ is that?)

what **P'ú'** /p'ü'/ *interj.*, male exclamation: what the . . . , huh? . . .

whatever **Ịdádąšt'ì** /ēⁿ-dä'-doⁿ-sht'ē'/ *pron.*, whatever, something, an unspecified thing (~ *égidą̀ gą́dái k'í égidą ną́i*, he says ~ he likes to say)

whatsoever **Ịdádąšt'ìšt'ì** /ēⁿ-dä'-doⁿ-sht'ē'-sht'ē'/ *pron.*, whatsoever

wheat **Wamą́ske'sì'** /wä-moⁿ'-skä-sē'/ *n.*, wheat, seed wheat; *wamą́ske'hì*, wheat plant

wheel **Nąnáge** /noⁿ-noⁿ'-gä/ *n.*, wheel, 1. tire 2. bicycle (Probably a description of the early bicycle with one large front wheel and one small rear wheel, now refers to all types of bicycles.)

when ** Atą́dià** /ä-toⁿ'-dē-ä/ *adv.*, when, introduces a question regarding at what time a thing happened; *atą́xtiádi*, in the remote past

when **Edítedą̀dì** /ā-dē'-tä-thoⁿ-dē'/ *adv.*, when, what point something happened at the time something else happened

where **Áwa** /ä'-wä/ *adv.*, where (Prefix *áwa* is also "where"; however, singular usage of the word is rare; used to ask about the whereabouts of somebody or something.) (*áwadià?*, ~ is he, she, it?; *áwakeà?*, ~ is it?)

where **Áwa** /ä'-wä/ *prefix.*, where; *áwat'aneà*, where are you going?

where **Áwadià** /ä'-wä-thē-ä'/ *adv.*, where (~ is he/she/it?)

where **Áwaket'à** /ä'-wä-kä-t'ä'/ *adv.*, where, used to ask about a direction that somebody or something is coming from or going to

wherever **Águdištiwą̀** /ä'-gü-dē-shtē-woⁿ'/ *n.*, wherever, anyplace, no matter where

whetstone **Wédimą̀** /wä'-thē-moⁿ'/ *n.*, whetstone, usu. a stone used to sharpen a thing; now a grinder, electric knife sharpener

which **Áwa** /ä'-wä/ *pron.*, which, a thing out of a group (*Áwa* can serve as a prefix or suffix in words asking a question.)

which **Áwake** /ä'-wä-kä/ *adv.*, which, asking which one of several items or things; *áwatè*, group or selected items from many things

which **Awíʃwadą̀** /ä-wē'-ʃ'-wä-thoⁿ'/ *pron.*, which, a question asking (refers to things); *awíʃwaą̀*, which one of them (persons)

which direction **Áwaket'adišą̀** /ä'-wä-kä-t'ä-thē-shoⁿ'/ *adv. phr.*, which direction, a question asking for a direction

which **Wíʃwaą́št'i** /wēʃ'-wä-oⁿ'-sht'ē/ *pron.*, whichever, usu. refers to a question asking for the selection of a thing among many things

which one **Wíʃwaą̀** /wēʃ'-wä-oⁿ'/ *pron.*, which one, inquiry as to which of several things or people

which side **Áwat'adišą̀** /ä'-wä-t'ä-thē-shoⁿ'/ *adv.*, which side, question asking which side of something

which way **Áwawat'à** /ä'-wä-woⁿ-t'ä/ *adv.*, which way, refers to a question asking in which direction a thing or a person is located

whimper **Bį'bį'že** /bēⁿ-bēⁿ'-zhä/ *v.*, whimper, weep, snivel

whimpering **Bi'bį'bįžè** /bē-bēⁿ'-bēⁿ-zhä/ *v.*, whimpering, continuously whimpering, weeping, sniveling

whine **Edéšt'e'à** /ā-dā'-sht'ā-ä/ *v.*, whine, bellyache, to continue to complain in an annoying way; *n.*, someone who grumbles and complains, usu. because of discontent

whip **Gasáp'i** /gä-sä'-p'ē/ *n./v.*, whip, to make a whip (bullwhip) snap or to make a cracking sound; to use any flexible material, such as a piece of leather, to hit any surface, making a snapping sound

whip **Gaxɖí** /gä-xthē'/ *v.*, whip, flog, to beat someone up

Whip **Wégasap'ì** /wā'-gä-sä-p'ē'/ *n.*, Whip, principal chief of the Ponca people before their removal to Indian Territory, from the early nineteenth century through ca. 1868

whip **Wégasap'ì** /wā'-gä-sä-p'ē'/ *n.*, whip, 1. a device to lash at animals to keep them under control 2. proper male name in the Ðíxidà clan of the Ponca people

whip **Wétį** /wā'-tēⁿ/ *n.*, whip, a flexible branch or stick or thin strips of leather attached to a handle and used to strike people or animals. Also see *Wé'tį*, club.

whip-poor-will **Há'k'ugdè** /hä'-k'ü-gthä/ *n.*, whip-poor-will, of the family Caprimulgidae, *Astrostomus vociferus*

whirl **Gaúdį** /gä-ü'-thēⁿ/ *v.*, whirl, twirl, spin

whirlwind **T'adą́he** /t'ä-doⁿ'-hä/ *n.*, whirlwind, a vertical, fast-spinning column of air, a dust devil

whirly wind **T'ádé'gaúbɖì** /t'ä-dā'-gä-ü'-bthēⁿ/ *n.*, whirly wind, wind blowing in circles at an inner corner outside a building

whiskers **Ík'ihį** /ēⁿ'-k'ē-hēⁿ/ *n.*, whiskers, beard, the hair on a man's chin, cheeks, and above the upper lip

whiskey **Péde ní'** /pā'-dā nē'/ *n.*, whiskey, lit., fire water, *p'éde*, fire, *ní'* water, an alcoholic liquor

whisper **Žįžį́'íye** /zhēⁿ-zhēⁿ'-ē'-yä/ *v.*, whisper, speak softly

whistle **Nisúde** /nē-sü-dä/ *n.*, whistle, flute, any wind instrument

whistle **Zudé'** /zü-dä'/ *v.*, whistle, to produce a high-pitched sound by blowing through the teeth and lips

white **Ská'** /skä'/ *adj./n.*, white, the color white

white blanket **Waxíha skà waį** /wä-xēⁿ'-hä skä' wä-ēⁿ'/ *n.*, white blanket (The Ponca Sun dancers wore a white buckskin robe or wraparound from the waist to the ankles. Following contact with whites and trade goods, a white cloth sheet was worn, as shown in photographs from the late nineteenth to early twentieth centuries.)

White Eagle **Xidá Skà** /xē-thä' skä'/ *n.*, White Eagle, 1. principal chief of the Ponca people at the time of forced removal to Indian Territory, ca. 1876 2. White Eagle Community, formerly Ponca Agency, in Kay County, Oklahoma

white elm tree **É'žą̀'skà** /ā'-zhoⁿ'-skä/ *n.*, white elm tree

white faces **Įdé skámà** /ēⁿ-dä' skä-mä/ *n.*, white faces, refers to warrior enemies of the Ponca people

White House **It'ígądài t'í et'áidą̀** /ē-t'ē'-goⁿ-thä'ē t'ē' ä-t'ä'ē-thoⁿ/ *n.*, White House, ca. 1870, the house of the president of the United States

white swan **Míxa skà** /mē'-xä skä'/ *n.*, white swan, 1. a large waterfowl of the family Anatidae, genus *Cygnus* 2. a proper male

name for nonclansmen among the Ponca
people

White Tail **Síde Skà** /sēⁿ-dā skä'/ *n.*, White
Tail (He was the principal chief of the
Ponca, succeeding White Star, and a
member of the Mą́k'ą́ clan, who was subsequently succeeded by Wégasap'ì, Whip,
member of the Đíxidą̀ clan.)

white-tailed deer **T'áxt'ì síde skà** /t'ä'-xt'ē'
sēⁿ-dā skä'/ *n.*, white-tailed deer, *Odocoileus
virginianus*, a medium-sized deer native to
most of the North American continent

white-tailed hawk **Gdedą́ xidáégą** /gthā-
doⁿ' xē-thä'-ä'-goⁿ/ *n.*, white-tailed hawk,
the rough-legged hawk (*Buteo lagopus*, a
hawk that flaps its wings and glides in upwinds, sometimes appearing stationary in
the air.)

white wolf **Šą́t'ągà skà** /shoⁿ'-t'oⁿ-gä' skä'/
n., white wolf, 1. *Canis lupus arctos*, species
known by the Ponca in ancient times
2. male name in the Wašábe clan of the
Ponca people

who **Ebé'** /ā-bā'/ *pron.*, who, introduces a
question about a person or persons; *ebéwa-
đakè*, who are you speaking of?

whoever **Ebé'št'ì** /ā-bā'-sht'ē'/ *pron.*, whoever

whomever **Ebé'št'iwą̀** /ā-bā'-sht'ē-woⁿ'/ *pron.*,
whomever

whomsoever **Ebé'št'ìšt'ewą̀** /ā-bā'-sht'ē'-
sht'ā-woⁿ'/ *pron.*, whomsoever

whose **Ebé'et'a** /ā-bā'-ā-t'ä'/ *poss. pron.*, whose,
something that belongs to somebody

whosoever **Ebé'št'ìšt'è** /ā-bā'-sht'ē'-sht'ä'/
pron., whosoever

why **Eát'ą** /ā-ä'-t'oⁿ/ *adv.*, why, for what purpose, cause, or reason (~ *né'a?*, ~ are you
going?)

Wichita **Wiət'šíta** /wēə-t'shē'-tä/ *n.*, the
Wichita Tribe of Native Americans

wick **Weánakągdè ugdè** /wā-ä'-nä-koⁿ-gthā'
ü-gthā'/ *n.*, wick, the spun or braided cotton fibers that draw up oil to burn in an oil
lamp or candle

widow **Nudį́ge** /nü-thēⁿ'-gā/ *n.*, widow, a
woman who has lost her husband by death
and who has not remarried 2. bachelorette,
an unmarried woman

wife **Ąt'íbadì** /oⁿ-t'ē'-bä-dē'/ *n.*, *slang*, wife,
"the one who lives in my house"

wife **Wigá'xdą̀** /wē-gä'-xthoⁿ'/ *n.*, wife, my
wife; *igáxdą̀*, his wife; *đigáxdą̀*, your wife

wiggle **K'igđíškąškà** /k'ē-gthē'-shkoⁿ-shkoⁿ'/
v., wiggle, to move with quick, jerky motions

wild **Mąt'ánąhà** /moⁿ-t'ä'-noⁿ-hä/ *adj.*, wild,
usu. refers to certain nondomesticated animals, such as horses or cats

wild onion **Mąžáxe** /moⁿ-zhoⁿ'-xā/ *n.*, wild
onion, genus *Allium*

wild potatoes **T'ą́dehanù** /t'oⁿ'-dā-hä-nü'/ *n.*,
wild potatoes, American groundnut, a root
with knots that resemble a potato

wild rice **Síwanidè** /sē'-wä-nē-dä'/ *n.*, wild
rice, of the genus *Zizania*

wild sweet peas **Hįbđį́ge** /hēⁿ-bthēⁿ'-gā/ *n.*,
wild sweet peas, *Lathyrus japonicus*

wild turnip **Núgdè** /nü-gthā'/ *n.*, wild turnip,
Psoralea esculenta

willow tree **Đíxu'sagì'hì** /thē'-xü-sä-gē'-hē'/
n., willow tree, a tall willow used for tipi
poles

willow tree **Đíxu'šp'ą̀ hì** /thē'-xü-shp'oⁿ' hē'/
n., willow tree, one of the three willows
known and used by the Ponca in northern
Nebraska and Oklahoma

win **Úhi** /ü'-hē/ *v.*, win, usu. to triumph or win
in a competitive game; may refer to winning in other gambling games, such as dice,
cards, or Indian dice; *uwáhi*, I won; *úđahì*,

you won; *éúhi*, they won; *é'ąwą́hi*, he/she/
they won from me

wind **T'a'dé** /t'ä-dā/ *n.*, wind, current of air
or airstream

winding **Bawíwíze** /bä-wē-wē'-zā/ *adj.*,
winding, zigzagging, as of a roadway that
has lots of curves

window **Wiúgąbà** /wēü'-goⁿ-bä/ *n.*, window,
lit., to brighten, a glass-covered opening,
usu. on a building, house, or automobile

windowpane **Wiúgąbà nąxé** /wēü'-goⁿ-bä'
noⁿ-xā'/ *n.*, windowpane, a sheet of glass in
a wooden or metal frame that is part of a
window

windy **T'adé'sagì** /t'ä-dā'-sä-gē'/ *n.*, windy,
strong wind, blustery weather

wine **Házi ní'** /hä'-zē nē'/ *n.*, wine, the fermented juice of grapes

wing **Áhi** /ä'-hēⁿ/ *n.*, wing, the wings of birds

wink **Į'štá ígabiže** /ēⁿ-shtä' ē'-gä-bē-zhä/ *n.*,
wink, a way of communicating by closing
or blinking one eye; flirting by blinking one
eye at the opposite sex

Winnebago **Hútągà** /hü'-toⁿ-gä/ *n.*, the Winnebago Tribe of Native Americans

winter **Má'de** /mä'-thā/ *n.*, winter, lit., snowing, one of the four seasons in the year;
mádeádi, in the past winter; *mádedà*, in the
wintertime

wipe **Biká** /bē-kä'/ *v.*, wipe, to wipe up, to
clean; *biká*, *2nd pers. sing.*, you wipe or
clean it

wish **Ú'ži** /ü'-zhē/ *v.*, wish, want or desire for
something, often refers to something to eat

with **Žúgde** /zhü'-gthä/ *prep.*, with, in the
company of, together with

withhold **Udísp'e** /ü-thē'-sp'ä/ *v.*, withhold,
to hold back something

witness **Wawé'bahà** /wä-wä'-bä-hoⁿ/ *n.*, witness, somebody who gives information

about seeing or hearing something, usu.
refers to legal matters

wolf **Šą́t'ągà** /shoⁿ-t'oⁿ-gä/ *n.*, wolf, *Canis
lupus*, more often known as the gray wolf,
a carnivore found mostly in the wilderness

wolf hide **Šą́t'ągà hà'** /shoⁿ-t'oⁿ-gä' hä'/ *n.*,
wolf hide, an ancient piece of the Ponca
Hedúškà dance paraphernalia (This symbolic piece, the head and entire hide of the
wolf, was worn over the right shoulder of
the dancer.)

woman **Waú'** /wä-ü'/ *n.*, 1. woman, female
2. girlfriend (In modern times, the term
is used to denote some man's girlfriend.)

women singers **Udázaì** /ü-thä'-zä-ē'/ *n.*,
women singers, lit., make loud sound,
refers to women who sit and sing behind
men singing at tribal dances (Orig. the
women singers sang only the chorus of
the song.)

wonder **Edégaxt'ì** /ā-thä'-gä-xt'ē'/ *v.*, wonder,
to think curiously about something

won't **Udiáge** /ü-thēä'-gä/ *v.*, won't, will not,
unbending, doesn't want to

wood **Žą́'** /zhoⁿ'/ *n.*, wood, 1. a fibrous tissue found in trees and other plants, out of
which boards and planks are made 2. wood
used for fire to heat and cook

wood chips **Žą́'gášpe** /zhoⁿ-gä'-shpä/ *n.*,
wood chips, small chips that come from
cutting firewood and are used to start a fire

wood cutting **Žą́' gáse** /zhoⁿ' gä'-sä/ *n.*, wood
cutting, the act of cutting wood

wooden bowl **Žą́'uxp'é** /zhoⁿ'-ü-xp'ä'/ *n.*,
wooden bowl

woodpecker **Tų́skà** /tüⁿ'-skä/ *n.*, woodpecker,
large redheaded woodpecker (family Picidae), a bird with a beak that hammers into
wood to find insects

woodpecker, pileated **Wažígap'à** /wä-zhē'-

gä-p'ä'/ *n.*, pileated woodpecker, 1. a large North American woodpecker, *Dryocopus pileatus* 2. the name (Birdhead) of one of the last Northern Ponca Indian doctors

wool **Ha'xúde hį** /hä-xü'-dä hēⁿ'/ *n.*, wool, the fibers or fleece taken from sheep and other animals to make textiles

work **Wadít'ą** /wä-thē'-t'oⁿ/ *v.*, work, to work, labor; *ú'dit'ą, n.*, job, to have a particular job

worm **Mądíka šíbe** /moⁿ-thē'-kä shē'-bä/ *n.*, worm, lit., earth intestines, an elongated, soft-bodied nonvertebrate, usu. called fishing worms

worm **Šágešibè** /shoⁿ'-gä-shē-bä'/ *n.*, worm, lit., horse intestine, usu. refers to a type of worm that appears above ground after a rain

worn **Diáda** /dēä'-thä/ *v.*, to be worn, a fabric that is old and easily torn

worn out **Đixdíge** /thē-xthē'-gä/ *v.*, to be worn out, something that is old, shabby, dilapidated

worried **Nąde ąp'ímąžį** /noⁿ-dä oⁿ-p'ē'-moⁿ-zhēⁿ'/ *aux. v., 1st pers. sing.*, worried, I am worried

worship **Wak'ąda wadahą** /wä-k'oⁿ'-dä wä-thä-hoⁿ'/ *n.*, worship, a show of reverence, adoration, and devotion to Wak'ąda, the Creator, that may include prayers, songs, readings, and other acts of worship

wounded **K'í'u** /k'ē'-ü/ *v.*, wounded (in war)

wrap **Đibébetą** /thē-bä'-bä-toⁿ'/ *v.*, wrap, wrapping something carelessly around a thing

wrap **Udíšį** /ü-thē'-shēⁿ/ *v.*, wrap, to ~ a thing (cloth or other substance) around something, as in covering or wrapping a gift

wrap around **Ubétą** /ü-bä'-toⁿ/ *v.*, wrap around or swaddle, to place a baby on a cradle board wrapped with appropriate blankets and woven belts to hold the infant in place; *idábetą*, to wrap something around a thing, as with a package

wrapped around **Udíp'up'ù** /ü-thē'-p'ü-p'ü'/ *v.*, wrapped around, wrapping oneself tightly with a blanket or robe

wretched **Đaégą** /thä-ä'-goⁿ/ *adj.*, wretched, pitiable, dejected, deplorably bad in body, dismal, awful

wring **Điškí** /thē-shkē'/ *v.*, wring, wringing out; *udíškì*, the process of twisting and squeezing out water from washed clothing; *udíškiškì*, to continuously wring

wrinkle **Š'įˀk'a** /sh-ēⁿ'-k'ä/ *adj.*, wrinkle, something that has furrows or ridges (a wooden board, a wrinkle in the nose)

wrinkle **Xįxįdà** /xēⁿ'-xēⁿ-thä'/ *n.*, wrinkle, usu. refers to the skin

wrist **Nąbé'ušášą** /noⁿ-bä'-ü-shoⁿ'-shoⁿ/ *n.*, wrist

write **Baxú** /bä-xü'/ *v.*, write, to write, as in writing a letter

write **Wabágdezè** /wä-bä'-gthä-zä'/ *v., archaic*, ca. nineteenth century, write, to write, writing

write on **Ábaxù** /ä'-bä-xü'/ *v.*, write on, to write on the surface of something, such as paper or stone; to write over something or to copy something

writing **Wabáxu** /wä-bä'-xü/ *n.*, writing, something that has been written, as in a letter, newspaper, or any kind of document

written rule **Udáde** /ü-thä'-dä/ *n.*, written rule, a written law, sayings, moral teachings, mores

wrongdoing **Wadíp'iáži** /wä-thē'-p'ēä'-zhē/ *n.*, wrongdoing, illegal acts of behavior, a criminal act

Y

Yankton Sioux **Iháṭąwį** /ē-hoⁿ-toⁿ-wēⁿ/ *n.*, the Yankton Tribe of Native Americans

yarn belt **T'éhįžidè** /t'ä-hēⁿ-zhē-dā/ *n.*, yarn belt, 1. an ornament of the Heɖúškà dance paraphernalia 2. an ornament used on an infant's cradle

yawn **Yəáda** /yəä-thä/ *v.*, yawn, to open the mouth and breath deeply, usu. associated with sleepiness

year **Umáɖikà** /ü-moⁿ-thē-kä/ *n.*, year, the period of 365 or 366 days

yearn **É'skąnà** /ä'-skoⁿ-noⁿ/ *v.*, yearn, having a strong desire for something that is possible to receive or reach

yell **Xdažé** /xthä-zhä/ *n.*, yell, scream, shriek

yellow **Zí'** /zē'/ *n.*, yellow, the color yellow

yes **Á**·/ä'·/ *interj.*, yes, affirmative, yeah, uh-huh

yesterday **Sidádi** /sē-dä'-dē/ *n.*, yesterday, the day before today

yesterday **Sidádi guádišà** /sē-dä'-dē güä'-thē-shoⁿ/ *n.*, yesterday, the day before yesterday

yesteryear **Umáɖikà'ámą** /ü-moⁿ-thē-kä'-oⁿ-moⁿ/ *n.*, yesteryear, last year, the year before this year

yet **Šą́ną** /shoⁿ-noⁿ/ *adv.*, yet, even more, notwithstanding

yolk **Wét'a uzì** /wä'-t'ä ü-zē'/ *n.*, yolk, the edible yellow internal part of an egg that is rich in protein and fat; the part that nourishes a developing embryo

yonder **Gát'a** /gä'-t'ä/ *adv.*, yonder, something not within sight and a longer distance away

yonder **Guáhiɖat'à** /gü-ä'-hē-thä-t'ä'/ *adv.*, yonder, something not within sight over there, to that place over there a shorter distance away

yonder **Šéhiɖəát'a** /shä-hē-thəä'-t'ä/ *adv.*, yonder, a place within sight over there

yonder **Šét'adišà** /shä'-t'ä-thē-shoⁿ/ *adv.*, yonder, designation of a place or thing closer to the speaker; over there within sight

you **Ðí'** /thē'/ *pron.*, you; *ɖiəni*, you're the one; *ɖínąnì*, you only; *ɖínąket'adišà*, toward you

you, over there **Šę́háí'mà** /shäⁿ-hä-ē'-mä'/ *pl. pron.*, you, over there, usu. shouted out to get the attention of someone

you are, you have **-daɖį́še** /thä-thēⁿ-shä/ *pron./v.*, *suffix*, you are, you have (The suffix usu. refers to Wak'áɖa or somebody who outstandingly has special abilities or talent, as in *Wak'áɖa bɖúga íšp'ahą~*, God ~ knowledgeable of all things.)

you know **Í'šp'ahą** /ē'-shp'ä-hoⁿ/ *v.*, *2nd pers. sing.*, you know

you know **Í'šp'ahą'ì** /ē'-shp'ä-hoⁿ-ē'/ *v.*, *2nd pers. pl.*, you all know

younger brother **Wisą́'ga** /wē-soⁿ'-gä/ *n.*, younger brother (man or woman saying, my ~)

younger sister **Wihé'** /wē-hä'/ *n.*, younger sister (man or woman saying, my ~)

young men **Šénužįgà** /shä-nü-zhēⁿ-gä'/ *n.*, young men, usu. refers to young men who have come of age or are old enough to be married, provide for their family, and defend the camp (The Ponca use this term often in their Heɖúškà dance songs, namely, going to meet the enemy.)

young woman **Šémižįgà** /shä-mē-zhēⁿ-gä'/ *n.*, young woman, a female in the first years of womanhood, having the appearance of a woman

your **Ðít'à** /thē'-t'ä'/ *adj.*, your, refers to something that belongs or relates to you (*wadáge ~ ké údą, ~* hat is a good one)

yours **Ðidít'a** /thē-thē'-t'ä/ *pl. pron.*, yours, refers to things that belong to you

yours **Ðidít'aì** /thē-thē'-t'äē'/ *pl. pron.*, yours, refers to something that belongs to a group of people being spoken to

you were there **Edí'ni** /ā-dē'-nē/ *v., 2nd pers. sing., past t.*, you were there

Z

zany **Gdą́di** /gtho^n-thē/ *n.*, zany, crazy, wacky

zealous **Waną́dehidè** /wä-no^n'-dā-hē-dā'/ *adj./n.*, zealous, enthusiastic, 1. a passionate interest, usu. in a personal project one is pursuing 2. concern to aid another person in their human situation

zigzag **Ðigúgúže** /thē-gü'-gü'-zhā/ *n.*, zigzag, a series of short turns and angles

BIBLIOGRAPHY

Boas, Franz. 1907. "Notes on the Ponka Grammar." In *Congrès International des Américanistes*, fifteenth session, Québec, 1906, 2:317–37.

Dorsey, James Owen. 1890. *The Degiha Language*. Washington DC: Smithsonian, Bureau of American Ethnology.

Dorsey, James Owen. 1891. *Omaha and Ponka Letters*. Washington DC: Smithsonian, Bureau of American Ethnology.

Fletcher, Alice, and Francis LeFlesche. (1911). 1972. *The Omaha Tribe*. Bureau of American Ethnology. Repr., Lincoln: University of Nebraska Press.

Howard, J. H. 1965. *The Ponca Tribe*. Washington DC: U.S. GPO.

———. 1970, May. "Known Sites of the Ponca." *Plains Anthropologist* 15 (48): 109–34.

Pike, Kenneth. 1947. *Phonemics: A Technique for Reducing Languages to Writing*. Ann Arbor: University of Michigan Press.